Negotiation

sixth edition

Roy J. Lewicki
The Ohio State University

Bruce Barry
Vanderbilt University

David M. Saunders
Queen's University

McGraw-Hill Irwin

Boston   Burr Ridge, IL   Dubuque, IA   New York   San Francisco   St. Louis
Bangkok   Bogotá   Caracas   Kuala Lumpur   Lisbon   London   Madrid   Mexico City
Milan   Montreal   New Delhi   Santiago   Seoul   Singapore   Sydney   Taipei   Toronto

The McGraw-Hill Companies

McGraw-Hill
Irwin

NEGOTIATION

Published by McGraw-Hill/Irwin, a business unit of The McGraw-Hill Companies, Inc., 1221 Avenue of the Americas, New York, NY, 10020. Copyright © 2010, 2006, 2003, 1999, 1994, 1985 by The McGraw-Hill Companies, Inc. All rights reserved. No part of this publication may be reproduced or distributed in any form or by any means, or stored in a database or retrieval system, without the prior written consent of The McGraw-Hill Companies, Inc., including, but not limited to, in any network or other electronic storage or transmission, or broadcast for distance learning.

Some ancillaries, including electronic and print components, may not be available to customers outside the United States.

This book is printed on acid-free paper.

3 4 5 6 7 8 9 0 DOC/DOC 1 0 9 8 7 6 5 4 3 2 1

ISBN   978-0-07-338120-6
MHID   0-07-338120-9

Vice president and editor-in-chief: *Brent Gordon*
Publisher: *Paul Ducham*
Managing developmental editor: *Laura Hurst Spell*
Editorial assistant: *Jane Beck*
Associate marketing manager: *Jaime Halteman*
Project manager: *Dana M. Pauley*
Full service project manager: *Jodi Dowling, Aptara®, Inc.*
Production supervisor: *Gina Hangos*
Design coordinator: *Joanne Mennemeier*
Media project manager: *Suresh Babu, Hurix Systems Pvt. Ltd.*
Cover design: *JoAnne Schopler*
Typeface: *10/12 Times Roman*
Compositor: *Aptara®, Inc.*
Printer: *R. R. Donnelley*

Credit text: ©Artville (Photodisc)/PunchStock

Library of Congress Cataloging-in-Publication Data

Lewicki, Roy J.
    Negotiation / Roy J. Lewicki, Bruce Barry, David M. Saunders. — 6th ed.
       p. cm.
    Includes index.
    ISBN-13: 978-0-07-338120-6 (alk. paper)
    ISBN-10: 0-07-338120-9 (alk. paper)
    1. Negotiation in business. I. Barry, Bruce, 1958- II. Saunders, David M. III. Title.
HD58.6.L49 2010
658.4'052—dc22

                                                    2009000717

www.mhhe.com

We dedicate this book to all negotiation, mediation, and dispute resolution professionals who try to make the world a more peaceful and prosperous place.

And to John W. Minton (1946–2007): friend, colleague, and co-author.

Roy J. Lewicki   is the Irving Abramowitz Memorial Professor of Business Ethics and Professor of Management and Human Resources at the Max. M. Fisher College of Business, The Ohio State University. He has authored or edited 32 books, as well as numerous research articles. Professor Lewicki has served as the president of the International Association for Conflict Management. He received the Academy of Management's Distinguished Educator Award in 2005 and the David Bradford Outstanding Educator award from the Organizational Behavior Teaching Society for his contributions to the field of teaching in negotiation and dispute resolution.

Bruce Barry   is a professor of Management and Sociology at Vanderbilt University. His research on negotiation, influence, ethics, power, and justice has appeared in numerous scholarly journals and volumes. Professor Barry is a past-president of the International Association for Conflict Management and a past chair of the Academy of Management Conflict Management Division.

David M. Saunders   is the dean of Queen's School of Business. Since joining Queen's in 2003 he has led the development of a new strategic plan for the School, launched two unique MBA programs, and strengthened Queen's international network with the addition of top business school partners in Europe, Asia and South America. Outside of Queen's, David is the co-author of several articles on negotiation, conflict resolution, employee voice, and organizational justice. He is on the Board of the two major international business school associations: U.S.-based AACSB International and EFMD, the European Foundation for Management Development. He is also Past Chair of the Canadian Federation of Business School Deans.

Preface

Welcome to the sixth edition of *Negotiation!*

Those familiar with the fifth edition will note that there has been no substantial change in the fundamental organization of this book. As you are aware, we made substantial changes in the fifth edition, increasing the number of chapters in the book from 13 in the fourth edition to 20 in the fifth edition. This was accomplished by breaking many of the larger chapters, some of which often covered two or three separate major topics, into smaller chapters that focus on a narrower domain. This reorganization was done for two major reasons: first, the research literature in many of these areas continues to increase, requiring a more extensive treatment of that work; second, feedback from instructors indicated that many would use only parts of chapters (e.g., using the section on teams but not on coalitions, or using them in separate weeks of a course). A review of the organization of the chapters can be found at the end of Chapter 1.

While this reorganization was the most visible change, faculty familiar with previous editions will also note the following other changes:

1. All of this book has been revised and updated. The authors reviewed every chapter, utilizing extensive feedback from faculty who have used the book in previous editions. The content in some of the chapters has been reorganized to present the material more effectively.

2. In our continued effort to enhance the book's readability, we have also updated many of the features and cartoons that offer lively perspectives on negotiation dynamics.

3. We have further improved the graphics format and page layout of the book to make it visually more interesting and readable.

4. We have added learning objectives to the beginning of each chapter.

5. The new structure of this book will be paralleled by a significant revision to our readings and classroom activities book, *Negotiation: Readings, Exercises and Cases,* sixth edition, edited by Roy Lewicki, Bruce Barry, and David Saunders, to appear in 2010. This text and reader can be used together or separately. A shorter version of this text, *Essentials of Negotiation* (sixth edition), by Roy Lewicki, Bruce Barry, and David Saunders, will be released in 2010 and can also be used in conjunction with the readings book. We encourage instructors to contact their local McGraw-Hill/ Irwin representative for an examination copy (or call 800-634-3963, or visit the Web site at www.mhhe.com).

6. Instructional resources—including a test bank, chapter outlines, PowerPoint slides, and extensive resource materials on teaching negotiation skills for new instructors— are available to accompany this volume. Instructors should contact their McGraw-Hill/ Irwin representative.

Once again, this book could not have been completed without the assistance of numerous people. We especially thank

- Many of our colleagues in the negotiation and dispute resolution field, whose research efforts have made the growth of this field possible and who have given us helpful feedback about earlier editions to improve the content of this edition.

- The work of John Minton, who helped shape the second, third, and fourth editions of this book and passed away in the fall of 2007.

- The excellent editorial assistance of Steve Stenner, specifically for his help on copy-editing, permissions, and the bibliography and for refining the test bank and Power-Point slides. In addition, Roy Lewicki would like to acknowledge the contributions of Curtis Gutter for his research assistance with locating resource materials, and Bruce Barry thanks his research assistant, Amanda Carrico, whose help on this revision has been invaluable.

- The staff of McGraw-Hill/Irwin, especially our current editor, Laura Spell, and our previous editors, Ryan Blankenship, John Weimeister, John Biernat, Kurt Strand, and Karen Johnson; Jane Beck, Allison Cleland, and Trina Hauger, editorial assistants who can solve almost any problem; and Jodi Dowling, our tireless project manager who turns our confusing instructions and tedious prose into eminently readable and usable volumes!

- Our families, who continue to provide us with the time, inspiration, and opportunities for continued learning about effective negotiation and the personal support required to sustain this project.

Roy J. Lewicki
Bruce Barry
David M. Saunders

Contents in Brief

Part 6: Resolving Differences

Part 7: Summary

Contents

Chapter 4

Negotiation: Strategy and Planning   107

Part 5: Negotiation across Cultures

Chapter 16
International and Cross-Cultural Negotiation   441

Part 6: Resolving Differences

Chapter 17
Managing Negotiation Impasses   474

CHAPTER 1

The Nature of Negotiation

Objectives

1. Understand the definition of *negotiation,* the key elements of a negotiation process, and the distinct types of negotiation.

2. Explore how people use negotiation to manage situations of interdependence—that is, that they depend on each other for achieving their goals.

3. Consider how negotiation fits within the broader perspective of processes for managing conflict.

4. Gain an overview of the organization of this book and the content of its chapters.

"That's it! I've had it! This car is dead!" screamed Chang Yang, pounding on the steering wheel and kicking the door shut on his 10-year-old Toysun sedan. The car had refused to start again, and Chang was going to be late for class (again)! Chang wasn't doing well in that management class, and he couldn't afford to miss any more classes. Recognizing that it was finally time to do something about the car, which had been having numerous mechanical problems for the last three months, Chang decided he would trade the Toysun in for another used car, one that would hopefully get him through graduation. After classes that day, he got a ride to the nearby shopping area, where there were several repair garages and used car lots. He knew almost nothing about cars, and didn't think he needed to—all he needed was reliable transportation to get him through the next 18 months.

A major international airline company is close to bankruptcy. The fear of terrorism, a number of new "budget-fare" airlines, and rising costs for fuel have all put the airline under massive economic pressure. The company seeks $800 million in wage and benefit cuts from the pilots' union, the third round of cuts in two years, in order to head off the bankruptcy. Rebuffed by the chief union negotiator for the pilots, the company seeks to go directly to the officers of the Air Line Pilots Association—the international union—to discuss the cuts. If the pilots do not agree to concessions, it is unlikely that other unions—flight attendants, mechanics, and so on—will agree, and bankruptcy will be inevitable.

Janet and Jocelyn are roommates. They share a one-bedroom apartment in a big city where they are both working. Janet, an accountant, has a solid job with a good company, but she has decided that it is time to go back to school to get her MBA. She has enrolled in Big City University's evening MBA program and is now taking classes. Jocelyn works for an advertising company and is on the fast track. Her job not only requires a lot of travel, but also requires a lot of time socializing with clients. The problem is that when Janet is not in evening class, she needs the apartment to read and study and has to have quiet to get her work done. However, when Jocelyn is at the apartment, she talks a lot on the phone, brings friends home for dinner, and is either getting ready to go out for the evening or coming back in very late (and noisily!). Janet has had enough of this disruption and is about to confront Jocelyn.

Thousands of demonstrators opposed to the policies of a nation's government seek to protest a national political convention that will nominate the government's leader to run for reelection. City police forbid protesters from demonstrating near the convention site and authorize a protest location under a crumbling urban expressway, half a mile away from the convention. In response, demonstration organizers request permission to hold a rally in one of the city's major metropolitan parks. The city attempts to ban the demonstration because that park was recently landscaped at a major expense to the city, and it fears the mass of demonstrators will ruin the work. Each side attempts negotiation but also pursues complex legal maneuvers to get the courts on their side.

Ashley Johnson is one of the most qualified recruits this year from a top 25 business school. She is delighted to have secured a second interview with a major consumer goods company, which has invited her to its headquarters city and put her up in a four-star hotel that is world-renowned for its quality facilities and service. After getting in late the night before due to flight delays, she wakes at 7:30 a.m. to get ready for an 8 a.m. breakfast meeting with the senior company recruiter. She steps in the shower, grabs the water control knob to turn it, and the knob falls off in her hand! There is no water in the shower at all; apparently, repairmen started a repair job on it, turned the water off somewhere, and left the job unfinished. Ashley panics at the thought of how she is going to deal with this crisis and look good for her breakfast meeting in 30 minutes.

Do these incidents look and sound familiar? These are all examples of negotiation—negotiations that are about to happen, are in the process of happening, or have happened in the past and created consequences for the present. And they all serve as examples of the problems, issues, and dynamics that we will address throughout this book.

People negotiate all the time. Friends negotiate to decide where to have dinner. Children negotiate to decide which television program to watch. Businesses negotiate to purchase materials and sell their products. Lawyers negotiate to settle legal claims before they go to court. The police negotiate with terrorists to free hostages. Nations negotiate to open their borders to free trade. Negotiation is not a process reserved only for the skilled diplomat, top salesperson, or ardent advocate for an organized lobby; it is something that everyone does, almost daily. Although the stakes are not usually as dramatic as peace accords or large corporate mergers, everyone negotiates; sometimes people negotiate for major things like a new job, other times for relatively minor things like who will wash the dishes.

Negotiations occur for several reasons: (1) to agree on how to share or divide a limited resource, such as land, or property, or time; (2) to create something new that neither party could do on his or her own, or (3) to resolve a problem or dispute between the parties. Sometimes people fail to negotiate because they do not recognize that they are in a negotiation situation. By choosing options other than negotiation, they may fail to achieve their goals, get what they need, or manage their problems as smoothly as they might like to. People may also recognize the need for negotiation but do poorly because they misunderstand the process and do not have good negotiating skills. After reading this book, we hope you will be thoroughly prepared to recognize negotiation situations; understand how negotiation works; know how to plan, implement, and complete successful negotiations; and, most importantly, be able to maximize your results.

A Few Words about Our Style and Approach

Before we begin to dissect the complex social process known as negotiation, we need to say several things about how we will approach this subject. First we will briefly define negotiation. Negotiation is "a form of decision making in which two or more parties talk with one another in an effort to resolve their opposing interests" (Pruitt, 1981, p. xi). Moreover, we will be careful about how we use terminology in this book. For most people, *bargaining* and *negotiation* mean the same thing; however, we will be quite distinctive in the way we use the two words. We will use the term *bargaining* to describe the competitive, win–lose situations such as haggling over price that happens at a yard sale, flea market, or used car lot; we will use the term *negotiation* to refer to win–win situations such as those that occur when parties are trying to find a mutually acceptable solution to a complex conflict.

Second, many people assume that the "heart of negotiation" is the give-and-take process used to reach an agreement. While that give-and-take process is extremely important, negotiation is a very complex social process; many of the most important factors that shape a negotiation result do not occur during the negotiation; they occur *before* the parties start to negotiate, or shape the context *around* the negotiation. In the first few chapters of the book, we will examine why people negotiate, the nature of negotiation as a tool for managing conflict, and the primary give-and-take processes by which people try to reach agreement. In the remaining chapters, we examine the many ways that the differences in substantive issues, the people involved, the processes they follow, and the context in which negotiation occurs enrich the complexity of the dynamics of negotiation. We will return to a more complete overview of the book at the end of this chapter.

Third, our insights into negotiation are drawn from three sources. The first is our experience as negotiators ourselves and the rich number of negotiations that occur every day in our own lives and in the lives of people around the world. The second source is the media—television, radio, newspaper, magazine, and Internet—that report on actual negotiations every day. We will use quotes and examples from the media to highlight key points, insights, and applications throughout the book. Finally, the third source is the wealth of social science research that has been conducted on numerous aspects of negotiation. This research has been conducted for more than 50 years in the fields of economics, psychology, political science, communication, labor relations, law, sociology, and anthropology. Each discipline approaches negotiation differently. Like the parable of the blind men who are attempting to describe the elephant by touching and feeling different parts of the animal, each social science discipline has its own theory and methods for studying elements of negotiation, and each tends to emphasize some parts and ignore others. Thus, the same negotiation events and outcome may be examined simultaneously from several different perspectives.[1] When standing alone, each perspective is limited; combined, we begin to understand the rich and complex dynamics of this amazing animal. We draw from all these research traditions in our approach to negotiation. When we need to acknowledge the authors of a major theory or set of research findings, we will use the standard social science research process of citing their work in the text by the author's name and the date of publication of their work; complete references for that work can be found in the bibliography at the end of the book. When we have multiple sources to cite, or anecdotal side comments to make, that information will appear in an endnote at the end of each chapter.

We began this chapter with several examples of negotiations—future, present, and past. To further develop the reader's understanding of the foundations of negotiation, we will develop a story about a husband and wife—Joe and Sue Carter—and a not-so-atypical day in their lives. In this day, they face the challenges of many major and minor negotiations. We will then use that story to highlight three important themes:

1. The definition of negotiation and the basic characteristics of negotiation situations.
2. An understanding of *interdependence,* the relationship between people and groups that most often leads them to need to negotiate.
3. The definition and exploration of the dynamics of conflict and conflict management processes, which will serve as a backdrop for different ways that people approach and manage negotiations.

Joe and Sue Carter

The day started early, as usual. Over breakfast, Sue Carter raised the question of where she and her husband, Joe, would go for their summer vacation. She wanted to sign up for a tour of the Far East being sponsored by her college's alumni association. However, two weeks on a guided tour with a lot of other people he barely knew was not what Joe had in mind. He needed to get away from people, crowds, and schedules, and he wanted to charter a sailboat and cruise the New England coast. The Carters had not argued (yet), but it was clear they had a real problem here. Some of their friends handled problems like this by taking separate vacations. With both of them working full-time, though, Joe and Sue did agree that they would take their vacation together.

Moreover, they were still not sure whether their teenage children—Tracy and Ted—would go with them. Tracy really wanted to go to a gymnastics camp, and Ted wanted to stay home and do yard work in the neighborhood so he could get in shape for the football team and buy a motor scooter with his earnings. Joe and Sue couldn't afford summer camp and a major vacation, let alone deal with the problem of who would keep an eye on the children while they were away.

As Joe drove to work, he thought about the vacation problem. What bothered Joe most was that there did not seem to be a good way to manage the conflict productively. With some family conflicts, they could compromise but, given what each wanted this time, a simple compromise didn't seem obvious. At other times they would flip a coin or take turns—that might work for choosing a restaurant (Joe and Ted like steak houses, Sue and Tracy prefer Chinese), but it seemed unwise in this case because of how much money was involved and how important vacation time was to them. In addition, flipping a coin might make someone feel like a loser, an argument could start, and in the end nobody would really feel satisfied.

Walking through the parking lot, Joe met his company's purchasing manager, Ed Laine. Joe was the head of the engineering design group for MicroWatt, a manufacturer of small electric motors. Ed reminded Joe that they had to settle a problem created by the engineers in Joe's department: the engineers were contacting vendors directly rather than going through MicroWatt's purchasing department. Joe knew that purchasing wanted all contacts with a vendor to go through them, but he also knew that his engineers badly needed technical information for design purposes and that waiting for the information to come through the purchasing department slowed things considerably. Ed Laine was aware of Joe's views about this problem, and Joe thought the two of them could probably find some way to resolve it if they really sat down to work on it. Joe and Ed were also both aware that upper management expected middle managers to settle differences among themselves; if this problem "went upstairs" to senior management, it would make both of them look bad.

Shortly after reaching his desk, Joe received a telephone call from an automobile salesman with whom he had been talking about a new car. The salesman asked whether Sue wanted to test-drive it. Joe wasn't quite sure that Sue would go along with his choice; Joe had picked out a sporty luxury import, and he expected Sue to say it was too expensive and not very fuel efficient. Joe was pleased with the latest offer the salesman had made on the price but thought he might still get a few more concessions out of him, so he introduced Sue's likely reluctance about the purchase, hoping that the resistance would put pressure on the salesman to lower the price and make the deal "unbeatable."

As soon as Joe hung up the phone, it rang again. It was Sue, calling to vent her frustration to Joe over some of the procedures at the local bank where she worked as a senior loan officer. Sue was frustrated working for an old "family-run" bank that was not very automated, heavily bureaucratic, and slow to respond to customer needs. Competitor banks were approving certain types of loans within three hours while Sue's bank still took a week. Sue had just lost landing two big new loans because of the bank's slowness and bureaucratic procedures, and this was becoming a regular occurrence. But whenever she tried to discuss the situation with the bank's senior management, she was met with resistance and a lecture on the importance of the bank's "traditional values."

Most of Joe's afternoon was taken up by the annual MicroWatt budget planning meeting. Joe hated these meetings. The people from the finance department came in and arbitrarily cut everyone's figures by 30 percent, and then all the managers had to argue endlessly to try to get some of their new-project money reinstated. Joe had learned to work with a lot of people, some of whom he did not like very much, but these people from finance were the most arrogant and arbitrary number crunchers imaginable. He could not understand why the top brass did not see how much harm these people were doing to the engineering group's research and development efforts. Joe considered himself a reasonable guy, but the way these people acted made him feel like he had to draw the line and fight it out for as long as it took.

In the evening, Sue and Joe attended a meeting of their town's Conservation Commission, which, among other things, was charged with protecting the town's streams, wetlands, and nature preserves. Sue is a member of the Conservation Commission, and Sue and Joe both strongly believe in sound environmental protection and management. This evening's case involved a request by a real estate development firm to drain a swampy area and move a small creek to build a new regional shopping mall. All projections showed that the new shopping mall would attract jobs and revenue to the area and considerably increase the town's treasury. The new mall would keep more business in the community and discourage people from driving 15 miles to the current mall, but opponents—a coalition of local conservationists and businessmen—were concerned that it would significantly hurt the downtown business district and do major harm to the natural wetland and its wildlife. The debate raged for three hours, and the commission agreed to continue hearings the following week.

As Joe and Sue drove home from the council meeting, they discussed the things they had been involved in that day. Each privately reflected that life is kind of strange—sometimes things go very smoothly and other times things seem much too complicated. As they went to sleep later, they each thought about how they might have approached certain situations differently during the day and were thankful they had a relationship where they could discuss things openly with each other. But they still didn't know what they were going to do about that vacation. . . .

Characteristics of a Negotiation Situation

The Joe and Sue Carter story highlights the variety of situations that can be handled by negotiation. Any of us might encounter one or more of these situations over the course of a few days or weeks. As we defined earlier, *negotiation* is a process by which two or more parties attempt to resolve their opposing interests. Thus, as we will point out later on this chapter, negotiation is one of several mechanisms by which people can resolve conflicts. Negotiation situations have fundamentally the same characteristics, whether they are peace negotiations between countries at war, business negotiations between buyer and seller or labor and management, or an angry guest trying to figure out how to get a hot shower before a critical interview. Those who have written extensively about negotiation argue that there are several characteristics common to all negotiation situations (see Lewicki, 1992; Rubin and Brown, 1975):

1.   There are two or more parties—that is, two or more individuals, groups, or organizations. Although people can "negotiate" with themselves—as when someone debates whether to spend a Saturday afternoon studying, playing tennis, or going to the football game—we consider negotiation as a process *between* individuals, within groups, and between groups.[2] In the Carter story, Joe negotiates with his wife, the purchasing manager, and the auto salesman, and Sue negotiates with her husband, the senior management at the bank, and the Conservation Commission, among others. Both still face an upcoming negotiation with the children about the vacation.

2.   There is a conflict of needs and desires between two or more parties—that is, what one wants is not necessarily what the other one wants—and the parties must search for a way to resolve the conflict. Joe and Sue face negotiations over vacations, management of their children, budgets, automobiles, company procedures, and community practices for issuing building permits and preserving natural resources, among others.

3.   The parties negotiate by *choice!* That is, they negotiate because they think they can get a better deal by negotiating than by simply accepting what the other side will voluntarily give them or let them have. Negotiation is largely a voluntary process. We negotiate because we think we can improve our outcome or result, compared with not negotiating or simply accepting what the other side offers. It is a strategy pursued by choice; seldom are we required to negotiate. There are times to negotiate and times not to negotiate

There are times when you should avoid negotiating. In these situations, stand your ground and you'll come out ahead.

When you'd lose the farm:

If you're in a situation where you could lose everything, choose other options rather than negotiate.

When you're sold out:

When you're running at capacity, don't deal. Raise your prices instead.

When the demands are unethical:

Don't negotiate if your counterpart asks for something you cannot support because it's illegal, unethical, or morally inappropriate—for example, either paying or accepting a bribe. When your character or your reputation is compromised, you lose in the long run.

When you don't care:

If you have no stake in the outcome, don't negotiate. You have everything to lose and nothing to gain.

When you don't have time:

When you're pressed for time, you may choose not to negotiate. If the time pressure works against you, you'll make mistakes, you give in too quickly, and you may fail to consider the implications of your concessions. When under the gun, you'll settle for less than you could otherwise get.

When they act in bad faith:

Stop the negotiation when your counterpart shows signs of acting in bad faith. If you can't trust their negotiating, you can't trust their agreement. In this case, negotiation is of little or no value. Stick to your guns and cover your position, or discredit them.

When waiting would improve your position:

Perhaps you'll have a new technology available soon. Maybe your financial situation will improve. Another opportunity may present itself. If the odds are good that you'll gain ground with a delay, wait.

When you're not prepared:

If you don't prepare, you'll think of all your best questions, responses, and concessions on the way home. Gathering your reconnaissance and rehearsing the negotiation will pay off handsomely. If you're not ready, just say "no."

Source: J. C. Levinson, M. S. A. Smith, and O. R. Wilson, *Guerrilla Negotiating: Unconventional Weapons and Tactics to Get What You Want* (New York: John Wiley, 1999), pp. 22–23. This material is used by permission of John Wiley & Sons, Inc.

(see Box 1.1 for examples of when we should not negotiate). Our experience is that most individuals in Western culture do not negotiate enough—that is, we assume a price or situation is nonnegotiable and don't even bother to ask or to make a counteroffer!

4. When we negotiate we expect a "give-and-take" process that is fundamental to the definition of negotiation itself. We expect that both sides will modify or move away from their opening statements, requests, or demands. Although both parties may at first argue strenuously for what they want—each pushing the other side to move first—ultimately both sides will modify their opening position in order to reach an agreement. This

BOX 1.2   Sign in a New York Deli

"For those of you who need to haggle over the price of your sandwich, we will gladly raise the price so we can give you a discount!"

movement may be toward the "middle" of their positions, called a compromise. Truly creative negotiations may not require compromise, however; instead the parties may invent a solution that meets the objectives of *all* parties. Of course, if the parties do NOT consider it a negotiation, then they don't necessarily expect to modify their position and engage in this give and take (see Box 1.2).

5. The parties prefer to negotiate and search for agreement rather than to fight openly, have one side dominate and the other capitulate, permanently break off contact, or take their dispute to a higher authority to resolve it. Negotiation occurs when the parties prefer to invent their own solution for resolving the conflict, when there is no fixed or established set of rules or procedures for how to resolve the conflict, or when they choose to bypass those rules. Organizations and systems invent policies and procedures for addressing and managing those procedures. Video rental stores have a policy for what they should charge if a rental is kept too long. Normally, people just pay the fine. They might be able to negotiate a fee reduction, however, if they have a good excuse for why the video is being returned late. Similarly, attorneys negotiate or plea-bargain for their clients who would rather be assured of a negotiated settlement than take their chances with a judge and jury in the courtroom. Similarly, the courts may prefer to negotiate as well to clear the case off the docket and assure some punishment. In the Carter story, Joe pursues negotiation rather than letting his wife decide where to spend the vacation; pressures the salesman to reduce the price of the car, rather than paying the quoted price; and argues with the finance group about the impact of the budget cuts, rather than simply accepting them without question. Sue uses negotiation to try to change the bank's loan review procedures, rather than accepting the status quo, and she works to change the shopping mall site plan to make both conservationists and businesses happy, rather than letting others decide it or watch it go to court.

6. Successful negotiation involves the management of *tangibles* (e.g., the price or the terms of agreement) and also the resolution of *intangibles*. Intangible factors are the underlying psychological motivations that may directly or indirectly influence the parties during a negotiation. Some examples of intangibles are (a) the need to "win," beat the other party, or avoid losing to the other party; (b) the need to look "good," "competent," or "tough" to the people you represent; (c) the need to defend an important principle or precedent in a negotiation; and (d) the need to appear "fair," or "honorable" or to protect one's reputation, or (e) the need to maintain a good relationship with the other party after the negotiation is over, primarily by maintaining trust and reducing uncertainty (Saorin-Iborra, 2006). Intangibles are often rooted in personal values and emotions. Intangible factors can have an enormous influence on negotiation processes and outcomes; it is almost impossible to ignore intangibles because they affect our judgment about what is fair, or right, or appropriate in the resolution of the tangibles. For example, Joe may not want to make Ed Laine angry about the purchasing problem because he needs Ed's support in the upcoming budget negotiations,

There are times when the urge to win overwhelms logic. Authors Malhotra, Ku, and Murnighan offer the example of a takeover battle between Johnson & Johnson and Boston Scientific to buy Guidant, a medical device maker. Even though Guidant was in the middle of recalling 23,000 pacemakers and telling another 27,000 patients who had pacemakers already implanted to "consult their doctors," the bidding war between the two buyers lead to a final price of $27.2 billion, $1.8 billion more than J&J's initial bid. After the recall, Guidant shares went from $23 to $17 a share. *Fortune* magazine later called the acquisition "arguably the second worst ever," only surpassed by AOL's infamous purchase of Time Warner.

What fuels these competitive dynamics that lead to bad decisions. The authors identify several key factors:

- *Rivalry.* When parties are intensely competitive with one another, they are willing to suspend rational decision making.
- *Time pressure.* An artificial deadline, or time pressures such as those in an auction, can push people into quick (and often erroneous) decision making.
- *The spotlight.* If audiences are watching and evaluating the actor, he is more likely to stick to his guns and escalate his investment just to look strong and tough to the audience (see Chapter 11).
- *The presence of attorneys.* The authors indicate that attorneys, who are more oriented toward "winning" and "losing" in legal battles, may pressure their clients toward winning when options for settlement may clearly be present.

The authors offer several important suggestions to reduce or eliminate the negative impact of these competitive pressures, in order to make more sound and reasoned decisions.

Source: D. H. Malhotra, G. Ku, and J. K. Murnighan, "When Winning is Everything," *Harvard Business Review,* May 2008, pp. 78–86.

but Joe also doesn't want to lose face to his engineers, who expect him to support them. Thus, for Joe, the important intangibles are preserving his relationship with Ed Laine and looking strong and "tough" to his engineers.

Intangibles become a major problem in negotiation when negotiators fail to understand how they are affecting decision making or when they dominate negotiations on the tangibles. For example, see Box 1.3 about the problems that the urge to win can create for negotiators.

Interdependence

One of the key characteristics of a negotiation situation is that the parties need each other in order to achieve their preferred objectives or outcomes. That is, either they *must* coordinate with each other to achieve their own objectives, or they *choose* to work together because the possible outcome is better than they can achieve by working on their own. When the parties depend on each other to achieve their own preferred outcome they are *interdependent*.

Most relationships between parties may be characterized in one of three ways: independent, dependent, or interdependent. *Independent* parties are able to meet their own needs without the help and assistance of others; they can be relatively detached, indifferent, and uninvolved with others. *Dependent* parties must rely on others for what they need;

because they need the help, benevolence, or cooperation of the other, the dependent party must accept and accommodate to that provider's whims and idiosyncrasies. For example, if an employee is totally dependent on an employer for a job and salary, the employee will have to either do the job as instructed and accept the pay offered, or go without a job. *Interdependent* parties, however, are characterized by interlocking goals—the parties need each other in order to accomplish their objectives. For instance, in a project management team, no single person could complete a complex project alone; the time limit is usually too short, and no individual has all the skills or knowledge to complete it. For the group to accomplish its goals, each person needs to rely on the other project team members to contribute their time, knowledge, and resources and to synchronize their efforts. Note that having interdependent goals does not mean that everyone wants or needs exactly the same thing. Different project team members may need different things, but they must work together for each to accomplish their goals. This mix of convergent and conflicting goals characterizes many interdependent relationships. (See Box 1.4 for a perspective on interdependence and the importance of intangibles from a famous agent who represents professional athletes.)

Types of Interdependence Affect Outcomes

The interdependence of people's goals, and the *structure* of the situation in which they are going to negotiate, strongly shapes negotiation processes and outcomes. When the goals of two or more people are interconnected so that only one can achieve the goal—such as running a race in which there will be only one winner—this is a competitive situation, also known as a *zero-sum* or *distributive* situation, in which "individuals are so linked together that there is a negative correlation between their goal attainments" (Deutsch, 1962, p. 276). Zero-sum or distributive situations are also present when parties are attempting to divide a limited or scarce resource, such as a pot of money, a fixed block of time, and the like. To the degree that one person achieves his or her goal, the other's goal attainment is blocked. In contrast, when parties' goals are linked so that one person's goal achievement helps others to achieve their goals, it is a *mutual-gains* situation, also known as a *non-zero-sum* or *integrative* situation, where there is a positive correlation between the goal attainments of both parties. If one person is a great music composer and the other is a great writer of lyrics, they can create a wonderful Broadway musical hit together. The music and words may be good separately, but fantastic together. To the degree that one person achieves his or her goal, the other's goals are not necessarily blocked, and may in fact be significantly enhanced. The strategy and tactics that accompany each type of situation are discussed further in the upcoming section, Value Claiming and Value Creation, and in Chapters 2 and 3.

Alternatives Shape Interdependence

We noted at the beginning of this section that parties choose to work together because the possible outcome is better than what may occur if they do not work together. Evaluating interdependence therefore also depends heavily on the desirability of *alternatives* to working together. Roger Fisher, William Ury, and Bruce Patton (1991), in their popular book *Getting to Yes: Negotiating Agreement without Giving In,* stress that "whether you should or should

I have been representing athletes for almost a quarter century, longer than some of them have been alive. During the course of that time, I have developed deep relationships—friendships and partnerships—with many of the executives with whom I do business. We have done dozens of deals with one another over the years. There has been contention and struggle. There have been misunderstandings at times. But in the end, not unlike a marriage, we have stayed together, moved forward, and grown. That kind of shared relationship over time results in a foundation of trust and respect that is immeasurably valuable.

But that kind of trust must be earned. I understood this when I did my first deal 23 years ago. A basic premise of my entire career has been the knowledge that I will be working with the same people again and again. That means that I am always thinking about the deal I am making right now but also about a given player's future deals. It means I see the other party as a potential partner, not as a foe to be vanquished.

If it were not for the team owners, I would not have a profession. If they did not feel that they could operate at a profit, we would not have an industry. I may believe that a player deserves every penny he is paid, but that is only half the equation. The other half depends upon whether the owner believes he can profit by making that payment.

These are not showdowns. In the end they are collaborations. We each have an interest in the success and health of the other. I need and want professional sports to survive and thrive. The various leagues need a steady supply of quality players who are quality people. Each side has something to offer the other. Each side depends on the other.

In any industry in which repeat business is done with the same parties, there is always a balance between pushing the limit on any particular negotiation and making sure the other party—and your relationship with him—survives intact. This is not to suggest that you subordinate your interests to his. But sometimes it is in your best long-term interest to leave something on the table, especially if the other party has made an error that works to your advantage.

No one likes being taken advantage of. We are all human beings. We all have the potential to make a mistake. No matter how much each side stresses preparation, there is no way to consider every factor in a negotiation. There may be times during the process where one party realizes he has made an error in calculation or in interpretation and may ask that that point be revised. There may be times where terms have been agreed to but the other party then sees a mistake and asks you to let him off the hook. You don't have to do it. You could stick him on that point. But you need to ask yourself, Is it worth it? Is what I have to gain here worth what I will lose in terms of this person's willingness to work with me in the future? In most cases, the long-term relationship is much more valuable than the short-term gain. Sometimes the other party may make a mistake and not know it. There are times when the GM or owner I am dealing with makes a major error in his calculations or commits a major oversight, and I can easily take advantage of that and just nail him.

But I don't. He shows me his jugular, and instead of slashing it, I pull back. I might even point out his error. Because if I do crush him, he will eventually realize it. And although I might make a killing on that particular deal, I will also have killed our relationship and, very likely, any possibility of future agreements. Or it might be that the person's mistake costs him his job, in which case someone else might take his place—who is much rougher to deal with and is intent on paying me back for taking his predecessor to the cleaners.

Source: Leigh Steinberg, *Winning with Integrity* (New York: Random House, 1998), pp. 217–18. Used with permission.

not agree on something in a negotiation depends entirely upon the attractiveness to you of the best available alternative" (p. 105). They call this alternative a BATNA (an acronym for best alternative to a negotiated agreement) and suggest that negotiators need to understand their own BATNA and the other party's BATNA. The value of a person's BATNA is always relative to the possible settlements available in the current negotiation. A BATNA may offer independence, dependence, or interdependence with someone else. A student who is a month away from graduation and has only one job offer at a salary far lower than he hoped has the choice of accepting that job offer or unemployment; there is little chance that he is going to influence the company to pay him much more than their starting offer. A student who has two offers has a choice between two future interdependent relationships; not only does he have a choice, but he can probably use each job offer to attempt to improve the agreement by playing the employers off against each other (asking employer A to improve his offer over B, etc.). Remember that every possible interdependency has an alternative; negotiators can always say "no" and walk away, although the alternative might not be a very good one. We will further discuss the role and use of BATNAs in Chapters 2, 3, 4, and 7.

Mutual Adjustment

When parties are interdependent, they have to find a way to resolve their differences. Both parties can influence the other's outcomes and decisions, and their own outcomes and decisions can be influenced by the other.[3] This mutual adjustment continues throughout the negotiation as both parties act to influence the other.[4] It is important to recognize that negotiation is a process that transforms over time, and mutual adjustment is one of the key causes of the changes that occur during a negotiation.[5]

Let us return to Sue Carter's job in the small community bank. Rather than continuing to have her loans be approved late, which means she loses the loan and doesn't qualify for bonus pay, Sue is thinking about leaving the small bank and taking a job with Intergalactic Bank in the next city. Her prospective manager, Max, thinks Sue is a desirable candidate for the position and is ready to offer her the job. Max and Sue are now attempting to establish Sue's salary. The job advertisement announced the salary as "competitive." After talking with her husband Joe and looking at statistics on bank loan officers' pay in the state, Sue identified a salary below which she will not work ($50,000) and hopes she might get considerably more. But because Intergalactic Bank has lots of job applicants and is a very desirable employer in the area, Sue has decided not to state her minimally acceptable salary; she suspects that the bank will pay no more than necessary and that her minimum would be accepted quickly. Moreover, she knows that it would be difficult to raise the level if it should turn out that $50,000 was considerably below what Max would pay. Sue has thought of stating her ideal salary ($65,000), but she suspects that Max will view her as either presumptuous or rude for requesting that much. Max might refuse to hire her, or even if they agreed on salary, Max would have formed an impression of Sue as a person with an inflated sense of her own worth and capabilities.

Let's take a closer look at what is happening here. Sue is making her decision about an opening salary request based in part on what bank loan officers are paid in the area, but also very much on how she anticipates Max will react to her actions. Sue recognizes that her actions will affect Max. Sue also recognizes that the way Max acts toward her in the future will be influenced by the way her actions affect him now. As a result, Sue is assessing the indirect impact of her behavior on herself. Further, she also knows that Max is probably alert to this and will look upon any statement by Sue as reflecting a preliminary position on salary rather than a final one. To counter this expected view, Sue will try to find some way to state a proposed salary that is higher than her minimum, but lower than her "dream" salary offer. Sue is choosing among opening requests with a thought not only to how they will affect Max but also to how they will lead Max to act toward Sue. Further, Sue knows that Max believes she will act in this way and makes her decision on the basis of this belief.

The reader may wonder if people really pay attention to all these layers of nuance and complexity or plot in such detail about their negotiation with others. Certainly people don't do this most of the time, or they would likely be frozen into inactivity while they tried to puzzle through all the possibilities. However, this level of thinking can help anticipate the possible ways negotiations might move as the parties move, in some form of mutual adjustment, toward agreement. The effective negotiator needs to understand how people will adjust and readjust, and how the negotiations might twist and turn, based on one's own moves and the others' responses.

It might seem that the best strategy for successful mutual adjustment to the other is grounded in the assumption that the more information one has about the other person, the better. There is the possibility, however, that too much knowledge only confuses (Beisecker, Walker, and Bart, 1989; Raven and Rubin, 1973). For example, suppose Sue knows the average salary ranges for clerical, supervisory, and managerial positions for banks in her state and region. Does all this information help Sue determine her actions, or does it only confuse things? In fact, even with all of this additional information, Sue may still not have reached a decision about what salary she should be paid, other than a minimum figure below which she will not go. This state of affairs is typical to many negotiations. Both parties have defined their outer limits for an acceptable settlement (how high or low they are willing to go), but within that range, neither has determined what the preferred number should be. The parties need to exchange information, attempt to influence each other, and problem solve. They must work toward a solution that takes into account each person's requirements and, hopefully, optimize the outcomes for both.[6]

Mutual Adjustment and Concession Making

Negotiations often begin with statements of opening positions. Each party states its most preferred settlement proposal, hoping that the other side will simply accept it, but not really believing that a simple "yes" will be forthcoming from the other side (remember our key definitional element of negotiation as the expectation of give-and-take). If the proposal isn't readily accepted by the other, negotiators begin to defend their own initial proposals and critique the others' proposals. Each party's rejoinder usually suggests alterations to the other party's proposal and perhaps also contains changes to his or her own position. When one party agrees to make a change in his or her position, a concession has been made (Pruitt, 1981). Concessions restrict the range of options within which a solution or agreement will be reached; when a party makes a concession, the *bargaining range* (the difference between the preferred acceptable settlements) is further constrained. For instance, Sue would like to get a starting salary of $65,000, but she scales her request down to $60,000, thereby eliminating all possible salary options above $60,000. Before making any concessions to a salary below $60,000, Sue probably will want to see some willingness on the part of the bank to improve their salary offer.

Two Dilemmas in Mutual Adjustment

Deciding how to use concessions as signals to the other side and attempting to read the signals in the other's concessions are not easy tasks, especially when there is little trust between negotiators. Two of the dilemmas that all negotiators face, identified by Harold Kelley (1966), help explain why this is the case. The first dilemma, the *dilemma of honesty,* concerns how much of the truth to tell the other party. (The ethical considerations of these dilemmas are discussed in Chapter 9.) On the one hand, telling the other party everything about your situation may give that person the opportunity to take advantage of you. On the other hand, not telling the other person anything about your needs and desires may lead to a stalemate. Just how much of the truth should you tell the other party? If Sue told Max that she would work for as little as $50,000 but would like to start at $60,000, it is quite possible that Max would hire her for $50,000 and allocate the extra money that he might have paid her elsewhere in the budget.[7] If, however, Sue did not tell Max any information about her salary aspirations, then Max would have a difficult time knowing Sue's aspirations and what she would consider an attractive offer. He might make an offer based on the salary of the last person he hired, and wait for her reaction to determine what to say next.

Kelley's second dilemma is the *dilemma of trust:* how much should negotiators believe what the other party tells them? If you believe everything the other party says, then he or she could take advantage of you. If you believe nothing that the other party says, then you will have a great deal of difficulty in reaching an agreement. How much you should trust the other party depends on many factors, including the reputation of the other party, how he or she treated you in the past, and a clear understanding of the pressures on the other in the present circumstances. If Max told Sue that $52,000 was the maximum he was allowed to pay her for the job without seeking approval "from the corporate office," should Sue believe him or not? As you can see, sharing and clarifying information is not as easy as it first appears.

The search for an optimal solution through the processes of giving information and making concessions is greatly aided by trust and a belief that you're being treated honestly and fairly. Two efforts in negotiation help to create such trust and beliefs—one is based on perceptions of outcomes and the other on perceptions of the process. Outcome perceptions can be shaped by managing how the receiver views the proposed result. If Max convinces Sue that a lower salary for the job is relatively unimportant given the high potential for promotion associated with the position, then Sue may feel more comfortable accepting a lower salary. Perceptions of the trustworthiness and credibility of the process can be enhanced by conveying images that signal fairness and reciprocity in proposals and concessions (see Box 1.5). When one party makes several proposals that are rejected by the other party and the other party offers no proposal, the first party may feel improperly treated and may break off negotiations. When people make a concession, they trust the other party and the process far more if a concession is returned. In fact, the belief that concessions will occur in negotiations appears to be almost universal. During training seminars, we have asked negotiators from more than 50 countries if they expect give-and-take to occur during negotiations in their culture; all have said they do. This pattern of give-and-take is not just a characteristic of negotiation; it is also essential to joint problem solving in most interdependent

Having information about your negotiation partner's perceptions is an important element of negotiation success. When your expectations of a negotiated outcome are based on faulty information, it is likely that the other party will not take you seriously. Take, for example, the following story told to one of the authors:

> At the end of a job interview, the recruiter asked the enthusiastic MBA student, "And what starting salary were you looking for?"
>
> The MBA candidate replied, "I would like to start in the neighborhood of $150,000 per year, depending on your benefits package."

The recruiter said, "Well, what would you say to a package of five weeks' vacation, 14 paid holidays, full medical and dental coverage, company matching retirement fund up to 50 percent of your salary, and a new company car leased for your use every two years . . . say, a red Porsche?"

The MBA sat up straight and said, "Wow! Are you kidding?"

"Of course," said the recruiter. "But you started it."

relationships.[8] *Satisfaction with negotiation is as much determined by the process through which an agreement is reached as with the actual outcome obtained.* To eliminate or even deliberately attempt to reduce this give-and-take—as some legal and labor–management negotiating strategies have attempted[9]—is to short-circuit the process, and it may destroy both the basis for trust and any possibility of achieving a mutually satisfactory result.

Value Claiming and Value Creation

Earlier, we identified two types of interdependent situations—zero-sum and non-zero-sum. Zero-sum or *distributive situations* are ones in which there can be only one winner or where the parties are attempting to get the larger share or piece of a fixed resource, such as an amount of raw material, money, time, and the like. In contrast, non-zero-sum or *integrative or mutual gains situations* are ones in which many people can achieve their goals and objectives.

The structure of the interdependence shapes the strategies and tactics that negotiators employ. In distributive situations negotiators are motivated to win the competition and beat the other party or to gain the largest piece of the fixed resource that they can. To achieve these objectives, negotiators usually employ win–lose strategies and tactics. This approach to negotiation—called *distributive bargaining*—accepts the fact that there can only be one winner given the situation and pursues a course of action to be that winner. The purpose of the negotiation is to *claim value*—that is, to do whatever is necessary to claim the reward, gain the lion's share, or gain the largest piece possible (Lax and Sebenius, 1986). An example of this type of negotiation is purchasing a used car or buying a used refrigerator at a yard sale. We fully explore the strategy and tactics of distributive bargaining, or processes of claiming value, in Chapter 2, and some of the less ethical tactics that can accompany this process in Chapter 9.

In contrast, in integrative situations the negotiators should employ win–win strategies and tactics. This approach to negotiation—called *integrative negotiation*—attempts to find solutions so both parties can do well and achieve their goals. The purpose of the negotiation is to create value—that is, to find a way for all parties to meet their objectives, either by identifying more resources or finding unique ways to share and coordinate the use of existing resources.

An example of this type of negotiation might be planning a wedding so that the bride, groom, and both families are happy and satisfied, and the guests have a wonderful time. We fully explore the strategy and tactics of integrative, value-creating negotiations in Chapter 3.

It would be simple and elegant if we could classify all negotiation problems into one of these two types and indicate which strategy and tactics are appropriate for each problem. Unfortunately, *most actual negotiations are a combination of claiming and creating value processes*. The implications for this are significant:

1. *Negotiators must be able to recognize situations that require more of one approach than the other:* those that require predominantly distributive strategy and tactics, and those that require integrative strategy and tactics. Generally, distributive bargaining is most appropriate when time and resources are limited, when the other is likely to be competitive, and when there is no likelihood of future interaction with the other party. Every other situation should be approached with an integrative strategy.

2. *Negotiators must be versatile in their comfort and use of both major strategic approaches.* Not only must negotiators be able to recognize which strategy is most appropriate, but they must be able to use both approaches with equal versatility. There is no single "best," "preferred," or "right" way to negotiate; the choice of negotiation strategy requires adaptation to the situation, as we will explain more fully in the next section on conflict. Moreover, if most negotiation issues or problems have components of both claiming and creating values, then negotiators must be able to use both approaches in the same deliberation.

3. *Negotiator perceptions of situations tend to be biased toward seeing problems as more distributive/competitive than they really are.* Accurately perceiving the nature of the interdependence between the parties is critical for successful negotiation. Unfortunately, most negotiators do not accurately perceive these situations. People bring baggage with them to a negotiation: past experience, personality, moods, habits, and beliefs about how to negotiate. These elements dramatically shape how people perceive an interdependent situation, and these perceptions have a strong effect on the subsequent negotiation. Moreover, research has shown that people are prone to several systematic biases in the way they perceive and judge interdependent situations.[10] While we discuss these biases extensively in Chapter 5, the important point here is that the predominant bias is to see interdependent situations as more distributive or competitive than they really are. As a result, there is a tendency to assume a negotiation problem is more zero-sum than it may be and to overuse distributive strategies for solving the problem. As a consequence, negotiators often leave unclaimed value at the end of their negotiations because they failed to recognize opportunities for creating value.

The tendency for negotiators to see the world as more competitive and distributive than it is, and to underuse integrative, creating-value processes, suggests that many negotiations yield suboptimal outcomes. At the most fundamental level, successful coordination of interdependence has the potential to lead to synergy, which is the notion that "the whole is greater than the sum of its parts." There are numerous examples of synergy. In the business world, many research and development joint ventures are designed to bring together experts from different industries, disciplines, or problem orientations to maximize their innovative potential beyond what each company can do individually. Examples abound of new technologies in the areas of medicine, communication, computing, and the like. The fiber-optic cable industry was pioneered by research specialists from the glass industry and specialists in the manufacturing of electrical wire and cable, industry groups that had little previous conversation or contact. A vast amount of new medical instrumentation and technology has been pioneered in partnerships between biologists and engineers. In these situations, interdependence was created between two or more of the parties, and the creators of these enterprises, who successfully applied the negotiation skills discussed throughout this book, enhanced the potential for successful value creation.

Value may be created in numerous ways, and the heart of the process lies in exploiting the differences that exist between the negotiators (Lax and Sebenius, 1986). The key differences among negotiators include these:

1. *Differences in interests.* Negotiators seldom value all items in a negotiation equally. For instance, in discussing a compensation package, a company may be more willing to concede on a signing bonus than on salary because the bonus occurs only in the first year, while salary is a permanent expense. An advertising company may be quite willing to bend on creative control of a project, but very protective of control over advertising placement. Finding compatibility in different interests is often the key to unlocking the puzzle of value creation.

2. *Differences in judgments about the future.* People differ in their evaluation of what something is worth or the future value of an item. For instance, is that piece of swamp land a good or bad investment of your hard-earned income? Some people can imagine the future house site and swimming pool, whereas others will see it as a bug-infested flood control problem. Real estate developers work hard to identify properties where they see future potential that current owners fail to recognize.

3. *Differences in risk tolerance.* People differ in the amount of risk they are comfortable assuming. A young, single-income family with three children can sustain less risk than a mature, dual-income couple without children. A company with a cash flow problem can assume less risk of expanding its operations than one that is cash rich.

4. *Differences in time preference.* Negotiators frequently differ in how time affects them. One negotiator may want to realize gains now while the other may be happy to defer gains into the future; one needs a quick settlement while the other has no need for any change in the status quo. Differences in time preferences have the potential to create value in a negotiation. For instance, a car salesman may want to close a deal by the end of the week in order to be eligible for a special company bonus, while the potential buyer intends to trade his car in "sometime in the next six months."

In summary, while value is often created by exploiting common interests, differences can also serve as the basis for creating value. The heart of negotiation is exploring both common and different interests to create this value and employing such interests as the foundation for a strong and lasting agreement. Differences can be seen as insurmountable, however, and in that case serve as barriers to reaching agreement. As a result, negotiators must also learn to manage conflict effectively in order to manage their differences while searching for ways to maximize their joint value. Managing conflict is the focus of the next section.

Conflict

A potential consequence of interdependent relationships is conflict. Conflict can result from the strongly divergent needs of the two parties or from misperceptions and misunderstandings. Conflict can occur when the two parties are working toward the same goal and generally want the same outcome or when both parties want very different outcomes. Regardless of the cause of the conflict, negotiation can play an important role in resolving it effectively. In this section, we will define conflict, discuss the different levels of conflict that can occur, review the functions and dysfunctions of conflict, and discuss strategies for managing conflict effectively.

Definitions

Conflict may be defined as a "sharp disagreement or opposition, as of interests, ideas, etc." and includes "the perceived divergence of interest, or a belief that the parties' current aspirations cannot be achieved simultaneously" (both from Pruitt and Rubin, 1986, p. 4). Conflict results from "the interaction of interdependent people who perceived incompatible goals and interference from each other in achieving those goals" (Hocker and Wilmot, 1985).

Levels of Conflict

One way to understand conflict is to distinguish it by level. Four levels of conflict are commonly identified:

1. *Intrapersonal or intrapsychic conflict.* These conflicts occur within an individual. Sources of conflict can include ideas, thoughts, emotions, values, predispositions, or drives that are in conflict with each other. We want an ice cream cone badly, but we know that ice cream is very fattening. We are angry at our boss, but we're afraid to express that anger because the boss might fire us for being insubordinate. The dynamics of intrapsychic conflict are traditionally studied by various subfields of psychology: cognitive psychologists, personality theorists, clinical psychologists, and psychiatrists (c.f. Bazerman, Tenbrunsel, and Wade-Benzoni, 1998). Although we will occasionally delve into the internal psychological dynamics of negotiators (e.g., in Chapters 5 and 15), this book generally doesn't address intrapersonal conflict.

2. *Interpersonal conflict.* A second major level of conflict is between individuals. Interpersonal conflict occurs between co-workers, spouses, siblings, roommates, or neighbors. Most of the negotiation theory in this book is drawn from studies of interpersonal negotiation and directly addresses the management and resolution of interpersonal conflict.

3. *Intragroup conflict.* A third major level of conflict is within a group—among team and work group members and within families, classes, living units, and tribes. At the intragroup level, we analyze conflict as it affects the ability of the group to make decisions, work productively, resolve its differences, and continue to achieve its goals effectively. Within-group negotiations, in various forms, are discussed in Chapters 11, 12, and 13.

4. *Intergroup conflict.* The final level of conflict is intergroup—between organizations, ethnic groups, warring nations, or feuding families or within splintered, fragmented communities. At this level, conflict is quite intricate because of the large number of people involved and the multitudinous ways they can interact with each other. Negotiations at this level are also the most complex. We will discuss the nature of intergroup negotiations throughout the book, particularly in Chapters 11 and 13.

Functions and Dysfunctions of Conflict

Most people initially believe that conflict is bad or dysfunctional. This belief has two aspects: first, that conflict is an indication that something is wrong, broken or dysfunctional, and, second, that conflict creates largely destructive consequences. Deutsch (1973) and others[11] have elaborated on many of the elements that contribute to conflict's destructive image:

1. *Competitive, win–lose goals.* Parties compete against each other because they believe that their interdependence is such that goals are in opposition and both cannot simultaneously achieve their objectives.[12] Competitive goals lead to competitive processes to obtain those goals.

2. *Misperception and bias.* As conflict intensifies, perceptions become distorted. People come to view things consistently with their own perspective of the conflict. Hence, they tend to interpret people and events as being either with them or against them. In addition, thinking tends to become stereotypical and biased—parties endorse people and events that support their position and reject outright those who oppose them.

3. *Emotionality.* Conflicts tend to become emotionally charged as the parties become anxious, irritated, annoyed, angry, or frustrated. Emotions overwhelm clear thinking, and the parties may become increasingly irrational as the conflict escalates.

4. *Decreased communication.* Productive communication declines with conflict. Parties communicate less with those who disagree with them and more with those who agree. The communication that does occur is often an attempt to defeat, demean, or debunk the other's view or to strengthen one's own prior arguments.

5. *Blurred issues.* The central issues in the dispute become blurred and less well defined. Generalizations abound. The conflict becomes a vortex that sucks in unrelated issues and innocent bystanders. The parties become less clear about how the dispute started, what it is "really about," or what it will take to solve it.

6. *Rigid commitments.* The parties become locked into positions. As the other side challenges them, parties become more committed to their points of view and less willing to back down from them for fear of losing face and looking foolish. Thinking processes become rigid, and the parties tend to see issues as simple and "either/or" rather than as complex and multidimensional.

7. *Magnified differences, minimized similarities.* As parties lock into commitments and issues become blurred, they tend to see each other—and each other's positions—as polar opposites. Factors that distinguish and separate them from each other become highlighted and emphasized, while similarities that they share become oversimplified and minimized. This distortion leads the parties to believe they are further apart from each other than they really may be, and hence they may work less hard to find common ground.

8. *Escalation of the conflict.* As the conflict progresses, each side becomes more entrenched in its own view, less tolerant and accepting of the other, more defensive and less communicative, and more emotional. The net result is that both parties attempt to win by increasing their commitment to their position, increasing the resources they are willing to spend to win, and increasing their tenacity in holding their ground under pressure. Both sides believe that by adding more pressure (resources, commitment,

enthusiasm, energy, etc.), they can force the other to capitulate and admit defeat. As most destructive conflicts reveal, however, nothing could be further from the truth! Escalation of the conflict level and commitment to winning can increase so high that the parties will destroy their ability to resolve the conflict or ever be able to deal with each other again.

These are the processes that are commonly associated with escalating, polarized, "intractable" conflict (see also Chapter 17). However, conflict also has many *productive* aspects (Coser, 1956; Deutsch, 1973). Figure 1.1 outlines some of these productive aspects. From this perspective, conflict is not simply destructive or productive; it is both. The objective is not to eliminate conflict but to learn how to manage it to control the destructive elements while enjoying the productive aspects. Negotiation is a strategy for productively managing conflict.

Factors That Make Conflict Easy or Difficult to Manage

Figure 1.2 presents a conflict diagnostic model. This model offers some useful dimensions for analyzing any dispute and determining how easy or difficult it will be to resolve. Conflicts with more of the characteristics in the "difficult to resolve" column will be harder to

FIGURE 1.1 | Functions and Benefits of Conflict

- Discussing conflict makes organizational members more aware and able to cope with problems. Knowing that others are frustrated and want change creates incentives to try to solve the underlying problem.
- Conflict promises organizational change and adaptation. Procedures, assignments, budget allocations, and other organizational practices are challenged. Conflict draws attention to those issues that may interfere with and frustrate employees.
- Conflict strengthens relationships and heightens morale. Employees realize that their relationships are strong enough to withstand the test of conflict; they need not avoid frustrations and problems. They can release their tensions through discussion and problem solving.
- Conflict promotes awareness of self and others. Through conflict, people learn what makes them angry, frustrated, and frightened and also what is important to them. Knowing what we are willing to fight for tells us a lot about ourselves. Knowing what makes our colleagues unhappy helps us to understand them.
- Conflict enhances personal development. Managers find out how their style affects their subordinates through conflict. Workers learn what technical and interpersonal skills they need to upgrade themselves.
- Conflict encourages psychological development—it helps people become more accurate and realistic in their self-appraisals. Through conflict, people take others' perspectives and become less egocentric. Conflict helps people believe they are powerful and capable of controlling their own lives. They do not simply need to endure hostility and frustration but can act to improve their lives.
- Conflict can be stimulating and fun. People feel aroused, involved, and alive in conflict, and it can be a welcome break from an easygoing pace. It invites employees to take another look and to appreciate the intricacies of their relationships.

Source: Reprinted with the permission of Lexington Books, an imprint of The Rowman and Littlefield Publishing Group from *Working Together to Get Things Done: Managing for Organizational Productivity* by Dean Tjosvold. Copyright © 1986 by Lexington Books.

FIGURE 1.2 | Conflict Diagnostic Model

Dimension	Viewpoint Continuum	
	Difficult to Resolve	Easy to Resolve
Issue in question	Matter of "principle"—values, ethics, or precedent a key part of the issue	Divisible issue—issue can be easily divided into small parts, pieces, units
Size of stakes—magnitude of what can be won or lost	Large—big consequences	Small—little, insignificant consequences
Interdependence of the parties—degree to which one's outcomes determine the other's outcomes	Zero sum—what one wins, the other loses	Positive sum—both believe that *both* can do better than simply distributing current outcomes
Continuity of interaction—will they be working together in the future?	Single transaction—no past or future	Long-term relationship—expected interaction in the future
Structure of the parties—how cohesive, organized they are as a group	Disorganized—uncohesive, weak leadership	Organized—cohesive, strong leadership
Involvement of third parties—can others get involved to help resolve the dispute?	No neutral third party available	Trusted, powerful, prestigious third party available
Perceived progress of the conflict—balanced (equal gains and equal harm) or unbalanced (unequal gain, unequal harm)	Unbalanced—one party feels more harm and will want revenge and retribution whereas stronger party wants to maintain control	Balanced—both parties suffer equal harm and equal gain; both may be more willing to call it a "draw"

Source: Reprinted from "Managing Conflict" by L. Greenhalgh, *Sloan Management Review*, Summer 1986, pp. 45–51, by permission of the publisher. Copyright © 1986 by the Sloan Management Review Association. All rights reserved.

settle, while those that have more characteristics in the "easy to resolve" column will be settled quicker.

Effective Conflict Management

Many frameworks for managing conflict have been suggested, and inventories have been constructed to measure negotiator tendencies to use these approaches.[13] Each approach begins with a similar two-dimensional framework and then applies different labels and descriptions to five key points. We will describe these points using the framework proposed by Dean Pruitt, Jeffrey Rubin, and S. H. Kim (1994).

The two-dimensional framework presented in Figure 1.3 is called the *dual concerns model*. The model postulates that people in conflict have two independent types of concern: concern about their own outcomes (shown on the horizontal dimension of the figure) and concern about the other's outcomes (shown on the vertical dimension of the figure). These concerns can be represented at any point from none (representing very low concern) to high (representing very high concern). The vertical dimension is often referred to as the cooperativeness dimension, and the horizontal dimension as the assertiveness dimension. The stronger their concern for their own outcomes, the more likely people will be to pursue strategies located on the right side of the figure, whereas the weaker their concern for their own outcomes, the more likely they will be to pursue strategies located on the left side of the figure. Similarly, the stronger their concern for permitting, encouraging, or even helping the other party achieve his or her outcomes, the more likely people will be to pursue strategies located at the top of the figure. The weaker their concern for the other party's outcomes, the more likely they will be to pursue strategies located at the bottom of the figure.

FIGURE 1.3 | The Dual Concerns Model

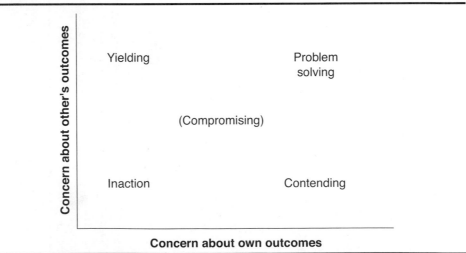

Source: Reprinted from *Social Conflict: Escalation, Stalemate and Settlement* (2nd ed.) by J. Rubin, D. Pruitt and S. H. Kim by permission of the publisher. Copyright © 1994 by The McGraw-Hill Companies.

    Although we can theoretically identify an almost infinite number of points within the two-dimensional space based on the level of concern for pursuing one's own and the other's outcomes, five major strategies for conflict management have been commonly identified in the dual concerns model:

1.   *Contending* (also called competing or dominating) is the strategy in the lower right-hand corner. Actors pursuing the contending strategy pursue their own outcomes strongly and show little concern for whether the other party obtains his or her desired outcomes. As Pruitt and Rubin (1986) state, "[P]arties who employ this strategy maintain their own aspirations and try to persuade the other party to yield" (p. 25). Threats, punishment, intimidation, and unilateral action are consistent with a contending approach.

2.   *Yielding* (also called accommodating or obliging) is the strategy in the upper left-hand corner. Actors pursuing the yielding strategy show little interest or concern in whether they attain their own outcomes, but they are quite interested in whether the other party attains his or her outcomes. Yielding involves lowering one's own aspirations to "let the other win" and gain what he or she wants. Yielding may seem like a strange strategy to some, but it has its definite advantages in some situations.

3.   *Inaction* (also called avoiding) is the strategy in the lower left-hand corner. Actors pursuing the inaction strategy show little interest in whether they attain their own outcomes, as well as little concern about whether the other party obtains his or her outcomes. Inaction is often synonymous with withdrawal or passivity; the party prefers to retreat, be silent, or do nothing.

"My concession speech will be brief. You win."

4. *Problem solving* (also called collaborating or integrating) is the strategy in the upper right-hand corner. Actors pursuing the problem-solving strategy show high concern for attaining their own outcomes and high concern for whether the other party attains his or her outcomes. In problem solving, the two parties actively pursue approaches to maximize their joint outcome from the conflict.

5. *Compromising* is the strategy located in the middle of Figure 1.3. As a conflict management strategy, it represents a moderate effort to pursue one's own outcomes and a moderate effort to help the other party achieve his or her outcomes. Pruitt and Rubin (1986) do not identify compromising as a viable strategy; they see it "as arising from one of two sources—either lazy problem solving involving a half-hearted attempt to satisfy the two parties' interests, or simple yielding by both parties" (p. 29). However, because other scholars who use versions of this model (see footnote 12) believe that compromising represents a valid strategic approach to conflict, we have inserted it in Pruitt, Rubin, and Kim's framework in Figure 1.3.

Much of the early writing about conflict management strategies—particularly the work in the 1960s and 1970s—had a strong normative value bias against conflict and toward co-operation (Lewicki, Weiss, and Lewin, 1992). Although the models suggested the viability of all five strategic approaches to managing conflict, problem solving was identified as the distinctly preferred approach. These writings stressed the virtues of problem solving, advocated using it, and described how it could be pursued in almost any conflict. However, more recent writing, although still strongly committed to problem solving, has been careful to stress that each conflict management strategy has its advantages and disadvantages and can be more or less appropriate to use given the type of interdependence and conflict context (see Figure 1.4).

Overview of the Chapters in This Book

The book is organized into seven sections with 20 chapters, which can be viewed schematically in Figure 1.5. Section 1, Negotiation Fundamentals, contains three chapters in addition to this introductory chapter and examines the basic processes of negotiation. In Section 2, Negotiation Subprocesses, five chapters examine the key subprocesses of negotiation that explain why negotiations unfold as they do. Section 3, Negotiation Contexts, contains four chapters that place negotiations in a broader social context of multiple parties playing many different roles. Section 4 contains two chapters that address the many ways individuals differ in their approach to negotiation as a result of their gender and personality. Section 5 contains a single chapter, addressing the interesting questions of how negotiation processes change as we move from a Western view to other national or cultural backgrounds. In the three chapters of Section 6, we explore ways that negotiators can move past impasse, deadlock, and mismatches in their negotiation styles—either on their own initiative or with the help of a third party. Finally, the book concludes with Section 7, in which we offer 10 summary comments and observations about the wealth of material contained herein.

In the next two chapters (2 and 3), we describe the two fundamental strategies of negotiation: distributive and integrative. Chapter 2 describes and evaluates the strategies and

FIGURE 1.4 | Styles of Handling Interpersonal Conflict and Situations Where They Are Appropriate or Inappropriate

Conflict Style	Situations Where Appropriate	Situations Where Inappropriate
Integrating	1. Issues are complex. 2. Synthesis of ideas is needed to come up with better solutions. 3. Commitment is needed from other parties for successful implementation. 4. Time is available for problem solving. 5. One party alone cannot solve the problem. 6. Resources possessed by different parties are needed to solve their common problems.	1. Task or problem is simple. 2. Immediate decision is required. 3. Other parties are unconcerned about outcome. 4. Other parties do not have problem-solving skills.
Obliging	1. You believe you may be wrong. 2. Issue is more important to the other party. 3. You are willing to give up something in exchange for something from the other party in the future. 4. You are dealing from a position of weakness. 5. Preserving relationship is important.	1. Issue is important to you. 2. You believe you are right. 3. The other party is wrong or unethical.
Dominating	1. Issue is trivial. 2. Speedy decision is needed. 3. Unpopular course of action is implemented. 4. Necessary to overcome assertive subordinates. 5. Unfavorable decision by the other party may be costly to you. 6. Subordinates lack expertise to make technical decisions. 7. Issue is important to you.	1. Issue is complex. 2. Issue is not important to you. 3. Both parties are equally powerful. 4. Decision does not have to be made quickly. 5. Subordinates possess high degree of competence.
Avoiding	1. Issue is trivial. 2. Potential dysfunctional effect of confronting the other party outweighs benefits of resolution. 3. Cooling off period is needed.	1. Issue is important to you. 2. It is your responsibility to make decision. 3. Parties are unwilling to defer; issue must be resolved. 4. Prompt attention is needed.
Compromising	1. Goals of parties are mutually exclusive. 2. Parties are equally powerful. 3. Consensus cannot be reached. 4. Integrating or dominating style is not successful. 5. Temporary solution to a complex problem is needed.	1. One party is more powerful. 2. Problem is complex enough to need a problem-solving approach.

Source: Modified and reproduced by special permission of the publisher, Consulting Psychologists Press, Inc., Palo Alto, CA 94303 from *Rahim Organizational Conflict Inventories: Professional Manual* by M. A. Rahim, Copyright © 1990 by Consulting Psychologists Press, Inc. All rights reserved. Further reproduction is prohibited without the publisher's written consent.

FIGURE 1.5 | Schematic Overview of Chapters in This Book

Section 1: Negotiation Fundamentals
1. The Nature of Negotiation
2. Strategy and Tactics of Distributive Bargaining
3. Strategy and Tactics of Integrative Negotiation
4. Negotiation: Strategy and Planning

Section 2: Negotiation Subprocesses
5. Perception, Cognition, and Emotion
6. Communication
7. Finding and Using Negotiation Power
8. Influence
9. Ethics in Negotiation

Section 3: Negotiation Contexts
10. Relationships in Negotiation
11. Agents, Constituencies, Audiences
12. Coalitions
13. Multiple Parties and Teams

Section 4: Individual Differences
14. Individual Differences I: Gender and Negotiation
15. Individual Differences II: Personality and Abilities

Section 5: Negotiation across Cultures
16. International and Cross-Cultural Negotiation

Section 6: Resolving Differences
17. Managing Negotiation Impasses
18. Managing Negotiation Mismatches
19. Third-Party Approaches to Managing Difficult Negotiations

Section 7: Concluding Comments
20. Best Practices in Negotiations

tactics that characterize the competitive (win–lose) distributive bargaining process. This chapter reviews the tactics most commonly associated with distributive bargaining and evaluates the consequences of using them. The chapter concludes with a section on how to close negotiations, an aspect that many negotiators neglect in their preparation process.

Chapter 3 describes and evaluates the basic strategies and tactics common to the co-operative (win–win) integrative bargaining process. Integrative negotiation is significantly different from distributive bargaining. Whereas distributive bargaining is often character-ized by mistrust and suspicion and by strategies designed to beat the other party, integrative negotiation is characterized by trust and openness and by tactics designed to achieve the best possible solution for all parties involved. Integrative negotiation often resembles the process of problem solving.

The Negotiation Fundamentals section continues with Chapter 4, in which we discuss how negotiators should create strategies and plans to achieve their desired outcomes. This chapter first examines the broad nature and role of strategy. We present a general model of strategic choice and identify the key factors that affect how a strategy is designed. We then move to the more specific elements of effective planning for negotiation. Planning and preparation are the most important steps in negotiation, yet many negotiators neglect or even completely ignore them. Effective planning requires (1) a thorough understanding of the negotiation process so the negotiator has a general idea of what will happen and how things will evolve; (2) a clear formulation of goals and aspirations; (3) research—gathering information and arguments to support and defend desired goals; and (4) knowledge of the other party, his or her goals, and the ability to use that knowledge to design a strategy to reach an effective resolution. The chapter includes a series of diagnostic questions negotiators may use in planning for any negotiation.

Section 2, Negotiation Subprocesses, has five chapters. Chapter 5 addresses how perception, cognition, and emotion shape the data we receive and process about the issues, other parties, and negotiation dynamics. Perception, cognition, and emotion are the basic building blocks of all social encounters in the sense that our social actions are guided by how we perceive and analyze the other party, the situation, and our own interests and positions. A working knowledge of how humans perceive and process information is important to understanding why people behave the way they do during negotiations. Moreover, we experience and express emotion when we interact with others, and negotiating is certainly no exception. The chapter explores the role of emotion and moods in shaping negotiation dynamics.

Reduced to its essence, negotiation is a form of interpersonal communication. Communication processes, both verbal and nonverbal, are critical to achieving negotiation goals and to resolving conflicts. Chapter 6 examines the process by which negotiators communicate their own interests, positions, and goals—and in turn make sense of those of the other party and of the negotiation as a whole. This chapter opens with a discussion of the basic mechanisms through which messages are encoded, sent, received, and decoded. It then considers in some depth *what* is communicated in a negotiation, followed by an exploration of *how* people communicate in negotiation; the chapter concludes with discussions of how to improve communication in negotiation.

Chapter 7 focuses on power in negotiation. By *power*, we mean the capabilities negotiators can assemble to give themselves an advantage or increase the probability of achieving their objectives. All negotiators want power; they want to know what they can do to put pressure on the other party, persuade the other to see things their way, get the other to give them what they want, get one up on the other, or change the other's mind. The chapter begins by defining the nature of power and discussing some of the dynamics of its use in negotiation. It focuses on the power sources that give negotiators the capacity to exert influence.

Chapter 8 examines the way negotiators actually exert influence—the actual strategies and messages that individuals deploy to bring about desired attitudinal or behavioral change. During negotiations, actors frequently need to convince the other party they have offered something of value, that their offer is reasonable, and that they cannot offer more. Negotiators may also want to alter the other party's beliefs about the importance of his own objectives and convince him that his concessions are not as valuable as he first believed. Negotiators may portray themselves as likable people who should be treated decently. All these efforts are designed to use information, as well as the qualities of the sender and receiver of that information, to adjust the other party's positions, perceptions, and opinions.

Finally, in Chapter 9, we explore the question of whether there are, or should be, accepted ethical standards for behavior in negotiations. It is our view that fundamental questions of ethical conduct arise in every negotiation. The effective negotiator must recognize when the questions are relevant and what factors must be considered to answer them. We will identify the major ethical dimensions raised in negotiations, describe how people tend to think about these ethical choices, and provide a framework for making informed ethical decisions. Along the way, we will highlight research that has yielded worthwhile findings in this area.

The chapters in Section 3, Negotiation Contexts, examine ways the broader social environment shapes negotiation processes. One major way that context affects negotiation is that people are in relationships that have a past, present, and future. In Chapter 10, we focus on the ways these past and future relationships impact present negotiations. Our treatment of relationships will come in two major sections. First, we examine how a past, ongoing, or future relationship between negotiators affects the negotiation process. Second, we look at three major themes—reputations, trust, and justice—that are particularly critical to effective negotiations within a relationship.

In Chapter 11, we explore how negotiation changes when (1) we move beyond simple 1:1 negotiations and add other parties to the process, and (2) when negotiators act as agents in the process—that is, they are not necessarily presenting their own issues and interests, but are also representing the views of others who may or may not be at the table. This situation is called an *agency relationship*. We examine the ways negotiations change when negotiators are representing the interests of others rather than arguing for their own interests. Within this larger context, individuals and groups attempt to exert both direct and indirect pressures on negotiators to advocate their interests. We examine the type of influence strategies negotiators use and the different types of influence attempts that occur as the number of parties increases. We conclude with a section on how constituencies can manage agents, and how agents can manage constituencies.

In Chapter 12, our focus is on situations in which multiple (more than two) parties are negotiating with one another—in essence, how parties ally into *coalitions* to achieve these objectives. We present an overview of what a coalition is and describe the different forms that coalitions take. We then analyze how and why coalitions form and develop, the nature of coalition decision making, and the role of power and leverage in coalitions. The chapter concludes with some practical advice for building and maintaining coalitions.

Finally, in Chapter 13, we extend the analysis to two situations that involve multiple parties. In one situation, multiple parties are negotiating with one another and attempting to achieve a collective or group consensus. We discuss this kind of team or group decision making as a process of multiparty negotiation. In the second situation, multiple individuals are present on each "side" of the negotiation—in other words, the parties to a negotiation are teams against teams, rather than individuals.

The two chapters in Section 4, Individual Differences, examine the way individual differences shape the approaches people take in negotiation. Some people are better negotiators than others. What characteristics of individuals make a difference in negotiation? In Chapter 14, we focus exclusively on the individual difference that has received more attention from negotiation researchers than any other: gender differences. Our examination of gender differences, which some might prefer to call sex differences, will begin by distinguishing between the terms *sex* and *gender.* We then examine research on gender differences in negotiation. We look at both the rationale for why there should be gender differences and the empirical research evidence for them. Some exciting new research developments in this area have occurred in the last few years, giving us a clearer picture of the underlying psychology of gender in negotiation.

In Chapter 15 we examine a range of other individual difference factors, including personality traits and abilities. We begin with a brief review of early research on individual differences. We then focus on more recent research on individual differences and negotiation, segmenting our discussion into two major categories: (1) dimensions of *personality* that appear to have an influence on negotiation and (2) the role of native *abilities* in negotiation, including cognitive ability and the relatively new domain of emotional intelligence. The chapter then concludes with a discussion of the behavioral approach to studying individual differences in negotiations, which explores how superior negotiators behave differently from average negotiators.

Section 5, Negotiation across Cultures, contains only a single chapter, but it is an important one: International and Cross-Cultural Negotiation. People today travel more frequently and farther, and business is more international in scope and extent than ever before. For many people and organizations, international negotiation has become the norm rather than an exotic activity that only occasionally occurs. Negotiation increases significantly in complexity as parties move across national and cultural boundaries. This chapter discusses some of the factors that make international negotiation different, including both the environmental context (macropolitical factors) and the immediate context (microstrategic factors). We then turn to a discussion of the most frequently studied aspect of international negotiation: the effect of *culture,* be it national, regional, or organizational. Next we examine the influence of culture on negotiations, discussing this from managerial and research perspectives. The chapter concludes with a discussion of culturally responsive strategies available to the international negotiator.

Section 6 of the text examines ways that parties can deal with failures to complete negotiation successfully. Negotiations break down and stall for many reasons. In Chapter 17, we address situations in which negotiations become especially difficult, often to the point of impasse, stalemate, or breakdown. Parties can become angry or entrenched in their positions. Perceptions become distorted, and judgments are biased. The parties stop communicating effectively and instead accuse and blame each other. The chapter examines the nature of those negotiations that are difficult to resolve. We examine the nature of impasses and what makes negotiations intractable. We then explore the fundamental mistakes that negotiators make that cause negotiation impasses, and we discuss strategies that negotiators can use to resolve impasses and get negotiations back on track.

In Chapter 18, we turn to situations in which parties are using *different* models to guide their negotiation, either because they have diagnosed the situation differently or they possess different levels of negotiation sophistication, or simply from habit. We direct our discussion and advice to negotiators who wish to be collaborative but find they must deal with others who are reluctant to do so—who wish, intend, or are actively trying to be distributive. We call them "difficult" people. There are several challenges to negotiators who want to convert a distributive bargainer toward a more collaborative approach. We begin by discussing ways to manage the social contract and the shadow negotiation. Next, we turn to a discussion of how to respond to the other party's hard distributive tactics, which is followed by a discussion of the options available to negotiators who are faced with another party who is more powerful. We then discuss possible tactics to use with generally difficult negotiators, examine how to respond to ultimatums, and conclude the chapter with a discussion of how to manage difficult conversations.

Finally, in Chapter 19, we discuss the many ways that third parties can help negotiators resolve their differences. There is a long history of third-party involvement in helping parties resolve disputes or reaching a decision for them when they cannot. Third parties tend to become involved when negotiators have tried all other options and are not making progress, when mistrust and suspicion are high, or when the parties cannot take actions toward defusing conflict without those actions being misinterpreted and mistrusted by others. In this chapter, we describe the typical roles that third parties play and how they can contribute to resolving conflict. This is followed by an examination of the types of third-party interventions, with special attention paid to three formal third-party roles: arbitration, mediation, and process consultation. We then discuss informal third parties, and we conclude the chapter with an examination of the institutionalization of third-party processes through the establishment and maintenance of alternative dispute resolution (ADR) systems.

Section 7 contains the last chapter in the book. In this final chapter (20), we reflect on negotiation at a broad level. Negotiation is an integral part of daily life and the opportunities to negotiate surround us. While some people may look like born negotiators, negotiation is fundamentally a skill involving analysis and communication that everyone can learn. In this final chapter, we look back at the broad perspective we have provided and provide 10 "best practices" for negotiators who wish to continue to improve their negotiation skills.

Chapter Summary

In this chapter, we have set the groundwork for a thorough and detailed examination of the negotiation process. We began with examples—examples from the news of events around the world and examples from our everyday experience. We used these examples to introduce the variety of negotiations that occur daily and to discuss how we will present material in this book. We then turned to the extended example of a day in the life of Joe and Sue Carter and showed how negotiations permeate daily experience. We also used this example to help define the key parameters of a negotiation situation.

Our definition and these examples lead us to explore four key elements of the negotiation process: managing interdependence, engaging in mutual adjustment, creating or claiming value, and managing conflict. Each of these elements is foundational to understanding how negotiation works. Managing interdependence is about

the parties understanding the ways they are dependent on each other for attaining their goals and objectives. Mutual adjustment introduces the ways parties begin to set goals for themselves in a negotiation and adjust to goals stated by the other party in order to emerge with an agreement that is satisfactory to both. Claiming or creating value are the processes by which parties handle negotiation opportunities to share or "win" a scarce resource or to enhance the resource so both sides can gain. Finally, managing conflict helps negotiators understand how conflict is functional and dysfunctional. It involves some basic strategies to maximize the benefits of conflict and limit its costs.

These four processes are central to any negotiation, and they serve as the foundation for our expanded treatment of this subject. In the remainder of this chapter, we provided an overview of our broader approach by introducing the overall organization and chapters in the book.

Endnotes

[1] E.g., Hochberg and Kressel, 1996; Oliver, Balakrishnan, and Barry, 1994; Olekalns, Smith, and Walsh, 1996; Weiss, 1997.

[2] See Bazerman, Tenbrunsel, and Wade-Benzoni on the challenge of negotiating with yourself.

[3] Goffman, 1969; Pruitt and Rubin, 1986; Raven and Rubin, 1973; Ritov, 1996.

[4] Alexander, Schul, and Babakus, 1991; Donohue and Roberto, 1996; Eyuboglu and Buja, 1993; Pinkley and Northcraft, 1994.

[5] Gray, 1994; Kolb, 1985; Kolb and Putnam, 1997.

[6] Fisher, Ury, and Patton, 1991; Follett, 1940; Nash, 1950; Sebenius, 1992; Sen, 1970; Walton and McKersie, 1965.

[7] We are not suggesting that Max should do this; rather, because the long-term relationship is important in this situation, Max should ensure that both parties' needs are met (see Chapter 3 for an expanded discussion of this point).

[8] Kimmel, Pruitt, Magenau, Konar-Goldband, and Carnevale, 1980; Putnam and Jones, 1982; Weingart, Thompson, Bazerman, and Carroll, 1990.

[9] Raiffa, 1982; Selekman, Fuller, Kennedy, and Baitsel, 1964.

[10] Bazerman, Magliozzi, and Neale, 1985; Neale and Bazerman, 1985; Neale and Northcraft, 1991; Pinkley, 1992; Thompson, 1990b.

[11] Folger, Poole, and Stutman, 1993; Hocker and Wilmot, 1985.

[12] As mentioned earlier, however, the goals may not actually be in opposition, and the parties need not compete. Perception is more determinant than reality.

[13] Filley, 1975; Hall, 1969; Rahim, 1983, 1992; Thomas, 1992; Thomas and Kilmann, 1974.

Strategy and Tactics of Distributive Bargaining

Objectives

1. Understand the basic elements of a distributive bargaining situation as well as the strategy and tactics of distributive bargaining.
2. Explore options for closing the deal in a distributive situation.
3. Consider the strategic impact of position taken during a negotiation and the role of concessions.
4. Gain an appeciation for commitment as a communication tactic.

Eighteen months ago Jackson decided to move closer to where he works. Following this decision to move, he put his condo on the market and started to look for a new one—but with no results. Fourteen months later, Jackson finally received an offer to buy his condo and, after a brief negotiation, settled on the selling price. Because he had not yet found a condo to buy, he postponed closing the sale for six months to give himself additional time to look. The buyer, Barbara, was not happy about having to wait that long because of the inconvenience and the difficulty of getting a bank to guarantee an interest rate for a loan so far in advance. Jackson adjusted the price so Barbara would accept this postponement, but it was clear that she would be much happier if he could move the closing date earlier.

There were relatively few condos on the market in the area where Jackson wanted to live, and none of them was satisfactory. He jokingly said that unless something new came on the market, he would be sleeping in a tent on the town common when the leaves turned in the fall. Two months later a condo came on the market that met his requirements. The seller, Sofia, set the asking price at $145,000, which was $10,000 above what Jackson hoped to pay but $5,000 below the most he would be willing to pay. Jackson knew that the more he paid for the condo, the less he would have to make some very desirable alterations, buy draperies and some new furniture, and hire a moving company.

This illustration provides the basic elements of a *distributive bargaining situation*. It is also called competitive, or win–lose, bargaining. In a distributive bargaining situation, the goals of one party are usually in fundamental and direct conflict with the goals of the other party. Resources are fixed and limited, and both parties want to maximize their share. As a result, each party will use a set of strategies to maximize his or her share of the outcomes to be obtained. One important strategy is to guard information carefully—negotiators should only give information to the other party when it provides a strategic advantage. Meanwhile, it is highly desirable to get information from the other party to improve negotiation power. Distributive bargaining is basically a competition over who is going to get the most of a limited resource, which is often money. Whether or not one or both parties achieve their objectives will depend on the strategies and tactics they employ (Walton and McKersie, 1965).

For many, the strategies and tactics of distributive bargaining are what negotiation is all about. Images come to mind of smoke-filled rooms packed with men arguing for their points of view. Many people are attracted to this view of negotiation and look forward to learning and sharpening an array of hard-bargaining skills; others are repelled by distributive bargaining and would rather walk away than negotiate this way. They argue that distributive bargaining is old-fashioned, needlessly confrontational, and destructive.

There are three reasons every negotiator should be familiar with distributive bargaining. First, negotiators face some interdependent situations that are distributive, and to do well in them they need to understand how they work. Second, because many people use distributive bargaining strategies and tactics almost exclusively, all negotiators need to understand how to counter their effects. Third, every negotiation situation has the potential to require distributive bargaining skills when at the "claiming-value" stage (Lax and Sebenius, 1986). Integrative negotiation focuses on ways to create value but also includes a claiming stage, where the value created is distributed. (Integrative negotiation is discussed extensively in Chapter 3.) Understanding distributive strategies and tactics is important and useful, but negotiators need to recognize that these tactics can also be counterproductive, costly, and may not work. Often they cause the negotiating parties to focus so much on their differences that they ignore what they have in common (Thompson and Hrebec, 1996). These negative effects notwithstanding, distributive bargaining strategies and tactics are quite useful when a negotiators want to maximize the value obtained in a single deal, when the relationship with the other party is not important, and when they are at the claiming-value stage of negotiations.

Some of the tactics discussed in this chapter will also generate ethical concerns. The topic of ethics and negotiation is discussed in detail in Chapter 9. Do not assume that the other party shares your ethical values when negotiating. While you may not believe that it is ethical to use some of the tactics discussed in this chapter, other negotiators will be quite comfortable using them. Alternatively, you may be comfortable using some tactics that make other negotiators uneasy. Some of the tactics discussed are commonly accepted as ethical when bargaining distributively (portraying your best alternative deal as more positive than it really is, for instance), whereas other tactics are generally considered unacceptable (see the discussion of typical hardball tactics later in this chapter).

The discussion of strategies and tactics in this chapter is intended to help negotiators understand the dynamics of distributive bargaining and thereby obtain a better deal. A thorough understanding of these concepts will also allow negotiators who are by nature not comfortable with distributive bargaining to manage distributive situations proactively.

Finally, an understanding of these strategies and tactics will help negotiators at the claiming-value stage of any negotiation.

The Distributive Bargaining Situation

To describe how the distributive bargaining process works, we return to our opening example of Jackson's condo purchase. Several prices were mentioned: (1) Sofia's asking price, (2) the price Jackson would like to pay for a condo, and (3) the price above which Jackson would not buy Sofia's condo. These prices represent key points in the analysis of any distributive bargaining situation. Jackson's preferred price is the *target point,* the point at which a negotiator would like to conclude negotiations—his optimal goal. The target is also sometimes referred to as a negotiator's *aspiration.* The price beyond which Jackson will not go is the *resistance point,* a negotiator's bottom line—the most he will pay as a buyer (for a seller, it's the smallest amount she will settle for). It is also sometimes referred to as a reservation price. Finally, the *asking price* is the initial price set by the seller; Jackson might decide to counter Sofia's asking price with his *initial offer*—the first number he will quote to the seller. Using the condo purchase as an example, we can treat the range of possible prices as a continuum (see Figure 2.1).

How does Jackson decide on his initial offer? There are many ways to answer this question. Fundamentally, however, to make a good initial offer Jackson must understand something about the process of negotiation. In Chapter 1, we discussed how people expect give-and-take when they negotiate, and Jackson needs to factor this into his initial offer. If Jackson opened the negotiation at his target point ($135,000) and then had to make a concession, this first concession would have him moving away from his target point to a price closer to his resistance point. If he really wants to achieve his target, he should make an initial offer that is lower than his target point to create some room for making concessions. At the same time, the starting point cannot be too far from the target point. If Jackson made the first offer too low (e.g., $100,000), Sofia might break off negotiations, believing him to be unreasonable or foolish. Although judgments about how to determine first offers can often be quite complex and can have a dramatic influence on the course of negotiation, let us stay with the simple case for the moment and assume that Jackson decided to offer $133,000 as a reasonable first offer—less than his target point and well below his resistance point. In the meantime, remember that although this illustration concerns only price, all other issues or agenda items for the negotiation have starting, target, and resistance points.

Both parties to a negotiation should establish their starting, target, and resistance points before beginning negotiation. Starting points are often in the opening statements each party makes (i.e., the seller's listing price and the buyer's first offer). The target point is usually

FIGURE 2.1 | The Buyer's View of the Condo Negotiation

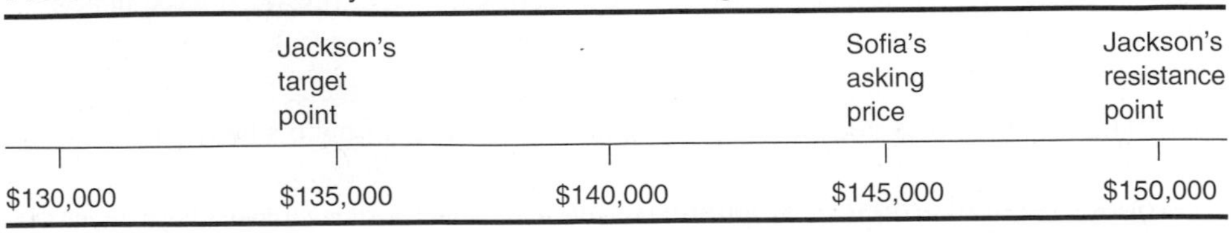

	Jackson's target point		Sofia's asking price	Jackson's resistance point
$130,000	$135,000	$140,000	$145,000	$150,000

DILBERT ©UFS. Reprinted by permission.

learned or inferred as negotiations get under way. People typically give up the margin between their starting points and target points as they make concessions. The resistance point, the point beyond which a person will not go and would rather break off negotiations, is not known to the other party and should be kept secret (Raiffa, 1982). One party may not learn the other's resistance point even after the end of a successful negotiation, and frequently may underestimate how much the other party would have paid or accepted (Larrick and Wu, 2007). After an unsuccessful negotiation, one party may infer that the other's resistance point was near the last offer the other was willing to consider before the negotiation ended.

Negotiators' starting and resistance points are usually arranged in reverse order, with the resistance point being a high price for the buyer and a low price for the seller. Thus, continuing the illustration, Jackson would have been willing to pay up to $150,000 for the condo Sofia listed at $145,000. Jackson can speculate that Sofia may be willing to accept something less than $145,000 and might well regard $140,000 as a desirable figure. What Jackson does not know (but would dearly like to) is the lowest figure that Sofia would accept. Is it $140,000? $135,000? Jackson assumes it is $130,000. Sofia, for her part, initially knows nothing about Jackson's position but soon learns his starting point when he offers $133,000. Sofia may suspect that Jackson's target point is not too far away (in fact it is $135,000, but Sofia doesn't know this) but has no idea of his resistance point ($150,000). This information—what Jackson knows or infers about Sofia's positions—is represented in Figure 2.2.

The spread between the resistance points, called the *bargaining range, settlement range,* or *zone of potential agreement,* is particularly important. In this area the actual bargaining takes place, because anything outside these points will be summarily rejected by one of the two negotiators. When the buyer's resistance point is above the seller's—he is minimally willing

FIGURE 2.2 | The Buyer's View of the Condo Negotiation (Extended)

Sofia's resistance point (inferred)	Jackson's initial offer (public)	Jackson's target point (private)	Sofia's target point (inferred)	Sofia's asking price (public)	Jackson's resistance point (private)
$130,000	$133,000	$135,000	$140,000	$145,000	$150,000

to pay more than she is minimally willing to sell for, as is true in the condo example—there is a *positive bargaining range*. When the reverse is true—the seller's resistance point is above the buyer's, and the buyer won't pay more than the seller will minimally accept—there is a *negative bargaining range*. In the condo example, if Sofia would minimally accept $145,000 and Jackson would maximally pay $140,000, then a negative bargaining range would exist. Negotiations that begin with a negative bargaining range are likely to stalemate. They can be resolved only if one or both parties are persuaded to change their resistance points or if someone else forces a solution upon them that one or both parties dislike. However, because negotiators don't begin their deliberations by talking about their resistance points (they're discussing initial offers and demands instead), it is often difficult to know whether a positive settlement range exists until the negotiators get deep into the process. Both parties may realize that there is no overlap in their resistance points only after protracted negotiations have been exhausted; at that point, they will have to decide whether to end negotiations or reevaluate their resistance points, a process described in more detail later on.

Target points, resistance points, and initial offers all play an important role in distributive bargaining. Target points influence both negotiator outcomes and negotiator satisfaction with their outcomes (Galinsky, Mussweiter, and Medvec, 2002); opening offers play an important role in influencing negotiation outcomes (see below); resistance points play a very important role as a warning for the possible presence of hardball tactics (see below); and a positive bargaining range increases the likelihood of settlements (Krause, Terpend and Petersen, 2006).

The Role of Alternatives to a Negotiated Agreement

In addition to opening bids, target points, and resistance points, a fourth factor may enter the negotiations: an alternative outcome that can be obtained by completing a deal with someone else. In some negotiations, the parties have only two fundamental choices: (1) reach a deal with the other party or (2) reach no settlement at all. In other negotiations, however, one or both parties may have the possibility of an alternative deal with another party. Thus, in the case of Jackson and Sofia, another condo may come on the market in the neighborhood where Jackson wishes to buy. Similarly, if Sofia waits long enough (or drops the price of the condo far enough), she will presumably find another interested buyer. If Jackson picks a different condo to buy and negotiates the best price that he can with the owner, that price represents his alternative. For the sake of argument, let's assume that Jackson's alternative condo costs $142,000 and that Sofia's alternative buyer will pay $134,000.

An alternative point can be identical to the resistance point, although the two do not have to be the same. If Jackson's alternative is $142,000, then (taking no other factors into account) he should reject any price Sofia asks above that amount. But Jackson's alternative may not be as desirable for reasons other than price—perhaps he likes the neighborhood less, the condo is 10 minutes farther away from where he works, or he likes the way Sofia has upgraded her condo. In any of these situations, Jackson may maintain his resistance point at $150,000; he is therefore willing to pay Sofia up to $8,000 more than his alternative (see Figure 2.3).

Alternatives are important because they give negotiators the power to walk away from any negotiation when the emerging deal is not very good. The number of realistic alternatives that negotiators have will vary considerably from one situation to another. For negotiations in

FIGURE 2.3 | The Buyer's View of the Condo Negotiation (Extended with Alternatives)

Sofia's resistance point (inferred)	Jackson's initial offer (public)	Sofia's alternative buyer (private)	Jackson's target point (private)	Sofia's target point (inferred)	Jackson's alternative house (private)	Sofia's asking price (public)	Jackson's resistance point (private)
$130,000	$133,000	$134,000	$135,000	$140,000	$142,000	$145,000	$150,000

which they have many attractive alternatives, they can set their goals higher and make fewer concessions. For negotiations in which they have no attractive alternative, such as when dealing with a sole supplier, they have much less bargaining power. Good distributive bargainers identify their realistic alternatives before starting discussions with the other party so that they can properly gauge how firm to be in the negotiation (Fisher and Ertel, 1995). Good bargainers also try to improve their alternatives while the negotiation is underway. If Jackson's negotiations with Sofia extend over a period of time, he should keep his eye on the market for other alternatives. He may also continue to negotiate with the owner of the other condo for a better deal. Both courses of action involve efforts by Jackson to maintain and expand his bargaining power by improving the quality of his alternatives. We discuss power and leverage in bargaining in detail in Chapter 7.

Strong BATNAs can also influence how a negotiation unfolds. Negotiators with stronger BATNAs are more likely to make the first offer in a negotiation and appear to negotiate better outcomes (Magee, Galinsky, and Gruenfeld, 2007). The positive benefits of a good BATNA appear particularly strong when we bargaining range is small because negotiations with smaller bargaining ranges are more competitive and less likely to yield agreements (Kim and Fragale, 2005).

Finally, negotiators need to ensure that they have a clear understanding of their *best alternative to a negotiated agreement,* or BATNA (Fisher, Ury, and Patton, 1991). Having a number of alternatives can be useful, but it is really one's *best* alternative that will influence the decision to close a deal or walk away. Understanding the BATNA and making it as strong as possible provides a negotiator with more power in the current negotiation because the BATNA clarifies what he or she will do if an agreement cannot be reached. Negotiators who have a strong BATNA, that is a very positive alternative to a negotiated agreement, will have more power throughout the negotiation and accordingly should be able to achieve more of their goals (the power of BATNAs is discussed further in Chapter 7).

Settlement Point

The fundamental process of distributive bargaining is to reach a settlement within a positive bargaining range. The objective of both parties is to obtain as much of the bargaining range as possible—that is, to reach an agreement as close to the other party's resistance point as possible.

Both parties in distributive bargaining know that they might have to settle for less than what they would prefer (their target point), but they hope that the agreement will be better than their own resistance point. For agreement to occur, both parties must believe that the settlement, although perhaps less desirable than they would prefer, is the best that they can get. This belief is important, both for reaching agreement and for ensuring support for the agreement after the negotiation concludes. Negotiators who do not think they got the best agreement possible, or who believe that they lost something in the deal, may try to get out of the agreement later or find other ways to recoup their losses. If Jackson thinks he got the short end of the deal, he could make life miserable and expensive for Sofia by making extraneous claims later—claiming that the condo had hidden damages, that the fixtures that were supposed to come with the condo were defective, and so on. Another factor that will affect satisfaction with the agreement is whether the parties will see each other again. If Sofia is moving out of the region, then Jackson may be unable to contact her later for any adjustments and should therefore ensure that he evaluates the current deal very carefully (good advice in any situation, but especially the case here).

Bargaining Mix

In the condo-purchase illustration, as in almost all negotiations, agreement is necessary on several issues: the price, the closing date of the sale, renovations to the condo, and the price of items that could remain in the condo (such as drapes and appliances). The package of issues for negotiation is the *bargaining mix*. Each item in the mix has its own starting, target, and resistance points. Some items are of obvious importance to both parties; others are important only to one party. Negotiators need to understand what is important to them and to the other party, and they need to take these priorities into account during the planning process. See Chapter 4 for a detailed discussion of planning.

For example, in the condo negotiation, a secondary issue important to both parties is the closing date of the sale—the date when the ownership will actually be transferred. The date of sale is part of the bargaining mix. Jackson learned when Sofia's new condo was going to be completed and anticipated that she would want to transfer ownership of her old condo to Jackson shortly after that point. Jackson asked for a closing date very close to when Sofia would probably want to close; thus, the deal looked very attractive to her. As it turned out, Jackson's closing date on his old condo was close to this date as well, thus making the deal attractive for both Jackson and Sofia. If Jackson and Sofia had wanted different closing dates, then that issue would have been a more contentious issue in the bargaining mix (although if Jackson could have moved his closing date earlier, he might have been able to strike a better deal with Barbara, the buyer of his condo). As the bargaining mix gets larger there is more opportunity for trade-offs across issues where negotiator preferences are not identical on each issue. When this occurs, integrative negotiation strategies and tactics may be appropriate; they are discussed in Chapter 3.

Fundamental Strategies

The prime objective in distributive bargaining is to maximize the value of the current deal. In the condo example, the buyer has four fundamental strategies available:

1.   To push for a settlement close to the seller's (unknown) resistance point, thereby yielding the largest part of the settlement range for the buyer. The buyer may attempt to influence the seller's view of what settlements are possible by making extreme offers and small concessions.

2. To convince the seller to change her resistance point by influencing the seller's beliefs about the value of the condo (e.g., by telling her that the condo is overpriced), and thereby increasing the bargaining range.

3. If a negative settlement range exists, to convince the seller to reduce her resistance point or to change his own resistance point, to create a positive settlement range. Thus, Sofia could be persuaded to accept a lower price, or Jackson could decide he has to pay more than he wanted to.

4. To convince the seller to believe that this settlement is the best that is possible— rather than having her think that it is all she can get, or that she is incapable of getting more, or that the buyer is winning the negotiation. The distinction between a party believing that an agreement is the best possible (and not the other interpretations) may appear subtle and semantic. However, in getting people to agree it is important that they feel as though they got the best possible deal. Ego satisfaction is often as important as achieving tangible objectives (recall the discussion of tangibles and intangibles in Chapter 1).

In all these strategies, the buyer is attempting to influence the seller's perceptions of what is possible through the exchange of information and persuasion. Regardless of the general strategy taken, two tasks are important in all distributive bargaining situations: (1) discovering the other party's resistance point and (2) influencing the other party's resistance point.

Discovering the Other Party's Resistance Point

Information is the life force of negotiation. The more you can learn about the other party's target, resistance point, motives, feelings of confidence, and so on, the more able you will be to strike a favorable agreement (see Box 2.1). At the same time, you do not want the other party to have certain information about you. Your resistance point, some of your targets, and confidential information about a weak strategic position or an emotional vulnerability are best concealed (Stein, 1996). Alternatively, you may want the other party to have certain information—some of it factual and correct, some of it contrived to lead the other party to believe things that are favorable to you. Each side wants to obtain some information and to conceal other information. Each side also knows that the other party wants to obtain and conceal information. As a result of this communication can become complex. Information is often conveyed in a code that evolves during negotiation. People answer questions with other questions or with incomplete statements to influence the other's perceptions, however, they must establish some points effectively and convincingly.

Influencing the Other Party's Resistance Point

Central to planning the strategy and tactics for distributive bargaining is locating the other party's resistance point and the relationship of that resistance point to your own. The resistance point is established by the value expected from a particular outcome, which in turn is the product of the worth and costs of an outcome. Jackson sets his resistance point based on the amount of money he can afford to pay (in total or in monthly

BOX 2.1 The Piano

When shopping for a used piano, Orvel Ray answered a newspaper ad. The piano was a beautiful upright in a massive walnut cabinet. The seller was asking $1,000, and it would have been a bargain at that price, but Orvel had received a $700 tax refund and had set this windfall as the limit that he could afford to invest. He searched for a negotiating advantage.

He was able to deduce several facts from the surroundings. The piano was in a furnished basement, which also contained a set of drums and an upright acoustic bass. Obviously the seller was a serious musician, who probably played jazz. There had to be a compelling reason for selling such a beautiful instrument.

Orvel asked the first, obvious question, "Are you buying a new piano?"

The seller hesitated. "Well, I don't know yet. See, we're moving to North Carolina, and it would be very expensive to ship this piano clear across the country."

"Did they say how much extra it would cost?" Orvel queried.

"They said an extra $300 or so."

"When do you have to decide?"

"The packers are coming this afternoon."

Now Orvel knew where the seller was vulnerable. He could ship the piano cross-country, or sell it for $700 and still break even. Or he could hold out for his asking price and take his chances. "Here's what I can do: I can give you $700 in cash, right now," Orvel said as he took seven $100 bills out of his pocket and spread them on the keyboard. "And I can have a truck and three of my friends here to move it out of your way by noon today."

The seller hesitated, then picked up the money. "Well, I suppose that would work. I can always buy a new piano when we get settled."

Orvel left before the seller could reconsider. By the time the group returned with the truck, the seller had received three other offers at his asking price, but because he had accepted the cash, he had to tell them that the piano had already been sold.

If the seller had not volunteered the information about the packers coming that afternoon, Orvel might not have been able to negotiate the price.

Source: From J. C. Levinson, M. S. A. Smith, and O. R. Wilson, *Guerrilla Negotiating* (New York: John Wiley, 1999), pp. 15–16.

mortgage payments), the estimated market value or worth of the condo, and other factors in his bargaining mix (e.g., closing date). A resistance point will also be influenced by the cost an individual attaches to delay or difficulty in negotiation (an intangible) or in having the negotiations aborted. If Jackson, who had set his resistance point at $150,000, were faced with the choice of paying $151,000 or living on the town common for a month, he might well reevaluate his resistance point. Resistance points should not be changed without considerable thought, however. They play an important role in setting negotiators' limits and unless there is an objective reason to change them they should not be changed.

A significant factor in shaping the other person's understanding of what is possible—and therefore the value he or she places on particular outcomes—is the other's understanding of your own situation. Therefore, when influencing the other's viewpoint, you must also deal with the other party's understanding of your value for a particular outcome, the costs you attach to delay or difficulty in negotiation, and your cost of having the negotiations aborted.

To explain how these factors can affect the process of distributive bargaining, we will make four major propositions:[1]

1. *The higher the other party's estimate of your cost of delay or impasse, the stronger the other party's resistance point will be.* If the other party sees that you need a settlement quickly and cannot defer it, he or she can seize this advantage and press for a better outcome. Expectations will rise and the other party will set a more demanding resistance point. The more you can convince the other party that your costs of delay or aborting negotiations are low (that you are in no hurry and can wait forever), the more modest the other's resistance point will be. For instance, Sofia could act as if she was not in a great rush to sell her condo to signal her price is firm.

2. *The higher the other party's estimate of his or her own cost of delay or impasse, the weaker the other party's resistance point will be.* The more a person needs a settlement, the more modest he or she will be in setting a resistance point. Therefore, the more you can do to convince the other party that delay or aborting negotiations will be costly, the more likely he or she will be to establish a modest resistance point. In contrast, the more attractive the other party's alternatives, the more likely he or she will be to set a high resistance point. If negotiations are unsuccessful, the other party can move to an attractive alternative. In the earlier example, we mentioned that both Jackson and Sofia have satisfactory alternatives. Sofia can portray her alternatives as more positive by mentioning several people have asked to see the condo.

3. *The less the other party values an issue, the lower their resistance point will be.* The resistance point may soften as the person reduces how valuable he or she considers that issue. If you can convince the other party that a current negotiating position will not have the desired outcome or that the present position is not as attractive as the other believes, then he or she will adjust their resistance point. For instance, Jackson could suggest that while the fixtures in the condo are nice, they are not exactly to his taste.

4. *The more the other party believes that you value an issue, the lower their resistance point may be.* The more you can convince the other that you value a particular issue the more pressure you put on the other party to set a more modest resistance point with regard to that issue. Knowing that a position is important to the other party, however, you will expect the other to resist giving up on that issue; thus, there may be less possibility of a favorable settlement in that area. As a result, you may need to lower your expectations to a more modest resistance point. For instance, Jackson could insist he loves the appliances and wants them included in the deal without raising his offer.

Tactical Tasks

Within the fundamental strategies of distributive bargaining there are four important tactical tasks concerned with targets, resistance points, and the costs of terminating negotiations for a negotiator in a distributive bargaining situation to consider: (1) assess the other party's target, resistance point, and cost of terminating negotiations; (2) manage the other party's impression of the negotiator's target, resistance point, and cost of terminating negotiation, (3) modify the other party's perception of his or her own target, resistance point, and cost of terminating negotiation, and (4) manipulate the actual costs of delaying or terminating negotiations. Each of these tasks is discussed in more detail below.

Assessing the Other Party's Target, Resistance Point, and Costs of Terminating Negotiations

An important first step for a negotiator is to obtain information about the other party's target and resistance points. The negotiator can pursue two general routes to achieve this task: obtain information indirectly about the background factors behind an issue *(indirect assessment)* or obtain information directly from the other party about their target and resistance points *(direct assessment)*. (See Box 2.2 for some advice on gathering information for negotiation.)

Indirect Assessment   An individual sets a resistance point based on many potential factors. For example, how do you decide how much rent or mortgage payment you can afford each month? How do you decide what a condo or used car is really worth? There are lots of ways to go about doing this. Indirect assessment means determining what information an individual likely used to set target and resistance points and how he or she interpreted this information. For example, in labor negotiations, management may infer whether or not a union is willing to strike by how hard the union bargains or by the size of its strike fund. The union decides whether or not the company can afford a strike based on the size of inventories, market conditions for the company's product, and the percentage of workers who are members of the union. In a real estate negotiation, how long a piece of property has been on the market, how many other potential buyers actually exist, how soon a buyer needs the property for business or living, and the financial health of the seller will be important factors. An automobile buyer might view the number of new cars in inventory on the dealer's lot, refer to newspaper articles about automobile sales, read about a particular car's popularity in consumer buying guides (i.e., the more popular the car, the less willing the dealer may be open to bargaining on price), or consult reference guides to find out what a dealer pays wholesale for different cars.

A variety of information sources can be used to assess the other party's resistance point. One can make observations, consult readily available documents and publications, and speak to knowledgeable experts. It is important to note, however, that these are indirect indicators. One person may interpret a given set of data very differently from another person. Having a large inventory of automobiles may make a dealer willing to reduce the price of a car. However, the dealer may expect the market to change soon, may have just started a big promotional campaign of which the buyer is unaware, or may see no real need to reduce prices and instead intends to wait for a market upturn. Indirect measures provide valuable information that *may* reflect a reality the other person will eventually have to face. It is important to remember, however, that the same piece of information may mean different things to different people and therefore may not tell you exactly what you think it does.

Direct Assessment   In bargaining, the other party does not usually reveal accurate and precise information about his or her targets, resistance points, and expectations. Sometimes, however, the other party will provide accurate information. When pushed to the absolute limit and in need of a quick settlement, the other party may explain the facts quite

Sources of Negotiation Information BOX 2.2

Gathering information before you go to the negotiating table is one of the most critical factors for success in negotiation. Many expert negotiators stress that effective information gathering is absolutely essential to being prepared and that the "lead time" between knowing that a negotiation will take place and actually beginning the negotiation should be filled with information collection activities. Negotiators who wait until the last minute risk undercutting themselves because they haven't done enough "homework."

Some of the most important information should be gathered on the *substantive issues* under negotiation. For instance, if you are planning to buy a new car, you should find information about the makes and models that interest you: list prices and selling prices, ratings of the automobiles' quality, how well they have been selling, etc. Sources for this kind of information include:

- Internet Web sites that evaluate brands and models of new cars, and provide up-to-date information on manufacturer pricing and dealer incentives.

- Magazines that test and rate automobiles (found in most book stores and libraries).

- Web sites that evaluate the reputation of car dealerships.

- Friends who may have owned this make and model of car.

A second critical topic for information search is to find out as much as you can about the people with whom you'll be interacting, and the company or organization that they represent. Knowing the other party—even if you have never met him or her before—can help you shape your strategy. Master negotiator Herb Cohen suggests the following questions that would help you negotiate with this individual:

- Why are they negotiating with me?
- What are their time constraints and deadlines?
- By whom and how will their decisions be made?
- How do they react to conflict?
- What is their negotiating style?
- What are the limits to their authority?
- Who do they report to?
- Does he or she have a budget or quota?
- How are they compensated?
- What is their negotiating experience and background?
- Do they have a realistic alternative to making this deal?
- What incentives do they have to make this deal?
- What are their underlying interests and concerns?
- What is their track record for honesty and integrity?
- What are their expectations with respect to the outcome?

Author John Patrick Dolan recommends that once face-to-face interaction is under way, you should listen more than you talk. Asking open-ended questions—which usually begin with what, why, where, when, or how—can encourage the other party to volunteer potentially valuable information. The more you know about the other party's agenda, the better you will be able to use that information to enhance your ability to achieve your desired outcome.

Sources: Adapted from Herb Cohen, *Negotiate This!* (New York: Warner Books, 2003); and John Patrick Dolan, *Negotiate Like the Pros* (New York: Putnam, 1992).

clearly. If company executives believe that a wage settlement above a certain point will drive the company out of business, they may choose to state that absolute limit very clearly and go to considerable lengths to explain how it was determined. Similarly, a condo buyer may tell the seller his absolute maximum price and support it with an explanation of income and other expenses. In these instances, the party revealing the information believes that the proposed agreement is within the settlement range—and that the other party will accept the offered information as true rather than see it as a bargaining ploy. An industrial salesperson may tell the purchaser about product quality and service, alternative customers who want to buy the product, and the time required to manufacture special orders.

Most of the time, however, the other party is not so forthcoming, and the methods of getting direct information are more complex. In international espionage, government agencies may cultivate sources, intercept messages, and break codes. In labor negotiations, companies have been known to recruit informers or bug union meeting rooms, and unions have had their members collect papers from executives' wastebaskets. In real estate negotiations, a seller may entertain a prospective buyer with abundant alcoholic beverages to loosen the buyer's tongue with the hope that he will reveal information (see Schweitzer and Kerr, 2000). Additional approaches include provoking the other party into an angry outburst or putting the other party under pressure designed to cause him or her to make a slip and reveal valuable information. Negotiators will also simulate exasperation and angrily stalk out of negotiations in the hope that the other, in an effort to avoid a deadlock, will reveal what they really want.

Manage the Other Party's Impressions

An important tactical task for negotiators is to control the information sent to the other party about your target and resistance points, while simultaneously guiding him or her to form a preferred impression of them. Negotiators need to screen information about their positions and to represent them as they would like the other to believe. Generally speaking, screening activities are more important at the beginning of negotiation, and direct action is more useful later on. This sequence also allows time to concentrate on gathering information from the other party, which will be useful in evaluating resistance points, and on determining the best way to provide information to the other party about one's own position.

Screening Activities The simplest way to screen a position is to say and do as little as possible. Silence is golden when answering questions; words should be invested in asking the other negotiator questions. Reticence reduces the likelihood of making verbal slips or presenting any clues that the other party could use to draw conclusions. A look of disappointment or boredom, fidgeting and restlessness, or probing with interest all can give clues about the importance of the points under discussion. Concealment is the most general screening activity.

Another approach, available when group negotiations are conducted through a representative, is calculated incompetence. With this approach, constituents do not give the negotiating agent all the necessary information, making it impossible for him or her to leak information. Instead, the negotiator is sent with the task of simply gathering facts and bringing them back to the group. This strategy can make negotiations complex and tedious, and it often causes the other party to protest vigorously at the negotiator's inability to divulge important data or to make agreements. Lawyers, real estate agents, and investigators frequently perform this role. Representatives may also be limited, or limit themselves, in their authority to make decisions. For example, a man buying a car may claim that he must consult his wife before making a final decision.

When negotiation is carried out by a team—as is common in diplomacy, labor–management relations, and many business negotiations—channeling all communication through a team spokesperson reduces the chance of inadvertently revealing information. Team negotiations are discussed more extensively in Chapter 13. In addition to reducing the number of people who can actively reveal information, this allows members of the negotiating team to observe and listen carefully to what the other party is saying so they can detect clues and pieces of information about their position. Still another screening activity is to present a great many items for negotiation, only a few of which are truly important to the presenter. In this way, the other party has to gather information about so many different items that it becomes difficult to detect which items are really important. This tactic, called the snow job or kitchen sink, may be considered a hardball tactic (discussed later in this chapter) if carried to an extreme (Karrass, 1974).

Direct Action to Alter Impressions   Negotiators can take many actions to present facts that will directly enhance their position or make it appear stronger to the other party. One of the most obvious methods is *selective presentation,* in which negotiators reveal only the facts necessary to support their case. Negotiators can also use selective presentation to lead the other party to form the desired impression of their resistance point or to create new possibilities for agreement that are more favorable than those that currently exist. Another approach is to explain or interpret known facts to present a logical argument that shows the costs or risks to oneself if the other party's proposals are implemented. An alternative is to say, "If you were in my shoes, here is the way these facts would look in light of the proposal you have presented."

Negotiators should justify their positions and desired outcomes in order to influence the other party's impressions. Power and influence tactics are discussed in more detail in Chapter 7 and 8. Negotiators can use industry standards, benchmarks, appeals to fairness, and arguments for the good of the company to draw a compelling picture for the other party to agree to what they want. These arguments are most convincing when the facts have been gathered from a neutral source because then the other party will not see them as biased by your preferred outcome. However, even with facts that you provide, selectivity can be helpful in managing the other party's impression of your preferences and priorities. It is not necessary for the other to agree that this is the way things would look if he or she were you. Nor must the other agree that the facts lead only to the conclusion you have presented. As long as the other party understands how you see things, then his or her thinking is likely to be influenced.

Displaying *emotional reaction* to facts, proposals, and possible outcomes is another form of direct action negotiators can take to provide information about what is important to them. Disappointment or enthusiasm usually suggests that an issue is important, whereas boredom or indifference suggests it is trivial or unimportant. A loud, angry outburst or an eager response suggests the topic is very important and may give it a prominence that will shape what is discussed. Clearly, however, emotional reactions can be real or feigned. We discuss emotions in more detail in Chapter 5. The length of time and amount of detail used in presenting a point or position can also convey importance. Carefully checking through the details the other side has presented about an item, or insisting on clarification and verification, can convey the impression of importance. Casually accepting the other party's arguments as true can convey the impression of disinterest in the topic being discussed.

Taking direct action to alter another's impression raises several potential hazards. It is one thing to select certain facts to present and to emphasize or de-emphasize their importance accurately, but it is a different matter to fabricate and lie. The former is expected and understood in distributive bargaining; the latter, even in hardball negotiations, is resented and often angrily attacked if discovered. Between the two extremes, however, what is said and done as skillful puffery by one may be perceived as dishonest distortion by the other. Ethical considerations are explored in detail in Chapter 9. Other problems can arise when trivial items are introduced as distractions or minor issues are magnified in importance. The purpose is to conceal the truly important and to direct the other's attention away from the significant, but there is a danger: the other person may become aware of this maneuver and, with great fanfare, concede on the minor points, thereby gaining the right to demand equally generous concessions on the central points. In this way the other party can defeat the maneuverer at his or her own game.

Modify the Other Party's Perceptions

A negotiator can alter the other party's impressions of his or her own objectives by making outcomes appear less attractive or by making the cost of obtaining them appear higher. The negotiator may also try to make demands and positions appear more attractive or less unattractive to the other party.

There are several approaches to modifying the other party's perceptions. One approach is to interpret for the other party what the outcomes of his or her proposal will really be. A negotiator can explain logically how an undesirable outcome would result if the other party really did get what he or she requested. This may mean highlighting something that has been overlooked. For example, in union–management negotiations, management may demonstrate that a union request for a six-hour workday would, on the one hand, not increase the number of employees because it would not be worthwhile to hire people for two hours a day to make up for the hours taken from the standard eight-hour day. On the other hand, if the company were to keep production at the present level, it would be necessary to use the present employees on overtime, thereby increasing the total labor cost and, subsequently, the price of the product. This rise in cost would reduce demand for the product and, ultimately, the number of hours worked or the number of workers.

Another approach to modifying the other's perceptions is to conceal information. An industrial seller may not reveal to a purchaser that certain technological changes are going to reduce significantly the cost of producing the products. A seller of real estate may not tell a prospective buyer that in three years a proposed highway will isolate the property being sold from key areas of the city. Concealment strategies may carry with them the ethical hazards mentioned earlier.

"Mr. Mosbacher, are you expecting anything via U.P.S.?"

Manipulate the Actual Costs of Delay or Termination

Negotiators have deadlines. A contract will expire. Agreement has to be reached before an important meeting occurs. Someone has to catch a plane. Extending negotiations beyond a deadline can be costly, particularly to the person who has the deadline, because that person has to either extend the deadline or go home empty-handed. At the same time, research and practical experience suggest that a large majority of agreements in distributive bargaining are reached when the deadline is near.[2] In addition, time pressure in negotiation appears to reduce negotiatior demands (de Dreu, 2003), and when a negotiator represents a constituency, time pressure appears to reduce the likelihood of reaching an agreement (Mosterd and Rutte, 2000). The effects of representing a constituency are discussed in more detail in Chapter 11. Manipulating a deadline or failing to agree by a particular deadline can be a powerful tool in the hands of the person who does not face deadline pressure. In some ways, the ultimate weapon in negotiation is to threaten to terminate negotiations, denying both parties the possibility of a settlement. One side then will usually feel this pressure more acutely than the other, and so the threat is a potent weapon. There are three ways to manipulate the costs of delay in negotiation: (1) plan disruptive action, (2) form an alliance with outsiders, and (3) manipulate the scheduling of negotiations.

Disruptive Action   One way to encourage settlement is to increase the costs of not reaching a negotiated agreement through disruptive action. In one instance, a group of unionized food-service workers negotiating with a restaurant rounded up supporters, had them enter the restaurant just prior to lunch, and had each person order a cup of coffee and drink it leisurely. When regular customers came to lunch, they found every seat occupied (Jacobs, 1951). In another case, people dissatisfied with automobiles they purchased from a certain dealer had their cars painted with large, bright yellow lemons and signs bearing the dealer's name, then drove them around town in an effort to embarrass the dealer into making a settlement. Public picketing of a business, boycotting a product or company, and locking negotiators in a room until they reach agreement are all forms of disruptive action that increase the costs to negotiators for not settling and thereby bring them back to the bargaining table. Such tactics can work, but they may also produce anger and escalate the conflict.

Alliance with Outsiders   Another way to increase the costs of delay or terminate negotiations is to involve other parties who can somehow influence the outcome in the process. In many business transactions, a private party may suggest that if negotiations with a merchant are unsuccessful, he or she will go to the Better Business Bureau and protest the merchant's actions. Individuals who are dissatisfied with the practices and policies of businesses or government agencies form task forces, political action groups, and protest organizations to bring greater collective pressure on the target. For example, individual utility consumers often enhance their negotiation with public service providers on consumer rates and service by citing compliance with public utility commissions' guidelines to substantiate their requests.

Schedule Manipulation   The negotiation scheduling process can often put one party at a considerable disadvantage, and the negotiation schedule can be used to increase time pressure on negotiators. Businesspeople going overseas to negotiate with customers or suppliers often find that negotiations are scheduled to begin immediately after their arrival, when they are still suffering from the fatigue of travel and jet lag. Alternatively, a host party can use delay tactics to squeeze negotiations into the last remaining minutes of a session in order to extract concessions from the visiting party (Cohen, 1980). Automobile dealers likely negotiate differently with a customer half an hour before quitting time on Saturday than at the beginning of the workday on Monday. Industrial buyers have a much more difficult negotiation when they have a short lead time because their plants may have to sit idle if they cannot secure a new contract for raw materials in time.

The opportunities to increase or alter the timing of negotiation vary widely across negotiation domains. In some industries it is possible to stockpile raw materials at relatively low cost or to buy in large bulk lots; in other industries, however, it is essential that materials arrive at regular intervals because they have a short shelf life (as many manufacturing firms move to just-in-time inventory procedures, this becomes increasingly true). There are far fewer opportunities for an individual to create costly delays when negotiating a home purchase than when negotiating a bulk order of raw materials. Nonetheless, the tactic of increasing costs by manipulating deadlines and time pressures is an option that can both enhance your own position and protect you from the other party's actions (Camerer and Loewenstein, 1993; Stuhlmacher, Gillespie, and Champagne, 1998).

Positions Taken during Negotiation

Effective distributive bargainers need to understand the process of taking positions during bargaining, including the importance of the opening offer and the opening stance, and the role of making concessions throughout the negotiation process (see Tutzauer, 1992). At the beginning of negotiations, each party takes a position. Typically, one party will then change his or her position in response to information from the other party or in response to the other party's behavior. The other party's position will also typically change during bargaining. Changes in position are usually accompanied by new information concerning the other's intentions, the value of outcomes, and likely zones for settlement. Negotiation is iterative. It provides an opportunity for both sides to communicate information about their positions that may lead to changes in those positions.

Opening Offers

When negotiations begin, the negotiator is faced with a perplexing problem. What should the opening offer be? Will the offer be seen as too low or too high by the other negotiator and be contemptuously rejected? An offer seen as modest by the other party could perhaps have been higher, either to leave more room to maneuver or to achieve a higher eventual settlement. Should the opening offer be somewhat closer to the resistance point, suggesting a more cooperative stance? These questions become less perplexing as the negotiator learns more about the other party's limits and planned strategy. While knowledge about the other party helps negotiators set their opening offers, it does not tell them exactly what to do.

Research by Adam Galinsky and Thomas Mussweiler (2001) suggests that making the first offer in a negotiation is advantageous to the negotiator making the offer. It appears that first offers can anchor a negotiation, especially when information about alternative negotiation outcomes is not considered. Negotiators can dampen the "first-offer effect" by the other negotiator, however, by concentrating on their own target and focusing on the other negotiator's resistance point. In general, negotiators with better BATNAs are more likely to make the first offer (Magee et al., 2007). Negotiators need to be cautious when they know the other party's BATNA, however, because there is a tendency to make a more conservative first offer when the other party's BATNA is known (Buelens and Van Poucke, 2004).

The fundamental question is whether the opening offer should be exaggerated or modest. Studies indicate that negotiators who make exaggerated opening offers get higher settlements than do those who make low or modest opening offers.[3] There are at least two reasons that an exaggerated opening offer is advantageous.[4] First, it gives the negotiator room for movement and therefore allows him or her time to learn about the other party's priorities. Second, an exaggerated opening offer acts as a meta-message and may create, in the other party's mind, the impression that (1) there is a long way to go before a reasonable settlement will be achieved, (2) more concessions than originally intended may have to be made to bridge the difference between the two opening positions, and (3) the other may have incorrectly estimated his or her own resistance point (Putnam and Jones, 1982; Yukl, 1974). Two disadvantages of an exaggerated opening offer are that (1) it may be summarily rejected by the other party and halt negotiations prematurely, and (2) it communicates an attitude of toughness that may be harmful to long-term relationships. The more exaggerated the offer, the greater is the likelihood that it will be summarily rejected by the other side.

Therefore, negotiators who make exaggerated opening offers should also have viable alternatives they can employ if the opposing negotiator refuses to deal with them.

Opening Stance

A second decision negotiators should make at the outset of distributive bargaining concerns the stance or attitude to adopt during the negotiation. Will you be competitive (fighting to get the best on every point) or moderate (willing to make concessions and compromises)? Some negotiators take a belligerent stance, attacking the positions, offers, and even the character of the other party. In response, the other party may mirror the initial stance, meeting belligerence with belligerence. Even if the other party does not directly mimic a belligerent stance, he or she is unlikely to respond in a warm and open manner. Some negotiators adopt a position of moderation and understanding, seeming to say, "Let's be reasonable people who can solve this problem to our mutual satisfaction." Even if the attitude is not mirrored, the other's response is likely to be constrained by such a moderate opening stance.

It is important for negotiators to think carefully about the message that they wish to signal with their opening stance and subsequent concessions because there is a tendency for negotiators to respond "in kind" to distributive tactics in negotiation (Weingart, Prietula, Hyder, and Genovese, 1999). That is, negotiators tend to match distributive tactics from the other party with their own distributive tactics.

To communicate effectively, a negotiator should try to send a consistent message through both the opening offer and stance (Eyuboglu and Buja, 1993). A reasonable bargaining position is usually coupled with a friendly stance, and an exaggerated bargaining position is usually coupled with a tougher, more competitive stance. When the messages sent by the opening offer and stance are in conflict, the other party will find them confusing to interpret and answer. Timing also plays a part, as is shown in Box 2.3. Ethical considerations are explored in detail in Chapter 9.

Initial Concessions

An opening offer is usually met with a counteroffer, and these two offers define the initial bargaining range. Sometimes the other party will not counteroffer but will simply state that the first offer (or set of demands) is unacceptable and ask the opener to come back with a more reasonable set of proposals. In any event, after the first round of offers, the next question is, what movement or concessions are to be made? Negotiators can choose to make none, to hold firm and insist on the original position, or to make some concessions. Note that it is not an option to escalate one's opening offer, that is, to set an offer further away from the other party's target point than one's first offer. This would be uniformly met with disapproval from the other negotiator. If concessions are to be made, the next question is, how large should they be? Note that the first concession conveys a message, frequently a symbolic one, to the other party about how you will proceed.

Opening offers, opening stances, and initial concessions are elements at the beginning of a negotiation that parties can use to communicate how they intend to negotiate. An exaggerated opening offer, a determined opening stance, and a very small initial concession

In 1997, Mississippi was one of 40 states that initiated legal action against tobacco companies to recover money they spent on health care problems associated with smoking. In July of that year, Mississippi announced that it had reached a settlement with the four largest tobacco companies, guaranteeing that the state would receive $3.6 billion over 25 years and $136 million per year thereafter.

The settlement was a personal battle for Mississippi attorney general Michael Moore, who single-handedly began an effort in 1994 to recoup his state's losses from tobacco-related illness. Over the next three years, he convinced 39 other states and Puerto Rico to join Mississippi in the suit. Their efforts led to a national-level settlement that banned billboard advertising and also forced tobacco companies to include stronger warning labels on cigarettes.

Moore parlayed his efforts into the first successful settlement with the tobacco companies, guaranteeing payment even before federal action was taken. By acting first, he ensured that Mississippi would receive adequate compensation for its losses.

Source: Adapted from M. Geyelin, "Mississippi Becomes First State to Settle Suit against Big Tobacco Companies," *The Wall Street Journal,* July 7, 1997.

signal a position of firmness; a moderate opening offer, a reasonable, cooperative opening stance, and a reasonable initial concession communicate a basic stance of flexibility. By taking a firm position, negotiators attempt to capture most of the bargaining range for themselves so that they maximize their final outcome or preserve maximum maneuvering room for later in the negotiation. Firmness can also create a climate in which the other party may decide that concessions are so meager that he or she might as well capitulate and settle quickly rather than drag things out. Paradoxically, firmness may actually shorten negotiations (see Ghosh, 1996). There is also the very real possibility, however, that firmness will be reciprocated by the other. One or both parties may become either intransigent or disgusted and withdraw completely.

There are several good reasons for adopting a flexible position (Olekalns, Smith, and Walsh, 1996). First, when taking different stances throughout a negotiation, one can learn about the other party's targets and perceived possibilities by observing how he or she responds to different proposals. Negotiators may want to establish a cooperative rather than a combative relationship, hoping to get a better agreement. In addition, flexibility keeps the negotiations proceeding; the more flexible one seems, the more the other party will believe that a settlement is possible.

Role of Concessions

Concessions are central to negotiation. Without them, in fact, negotiations would not exist. If one side is not prepared to make concessions, the other side must capitulate or the negotiations will deadlock. People enter negotiations expecting concessions. Negotiators are less satisfied when negotiations conclude with the acceptance of their first offer, likely because they feel they could have done better (Galinsky, Seiden, Kim, and Medvec, 2002). Immediate concessions are perceived less valuable than gradual, delayed concessions, which appear to increase the perceived value of the concession (Kwon and Weingart, 2004). Good distributive bargainers will not begin negotiations with an opening offer too close to their own resistance point, but rather will ensure that there is enough room in the bargaining

BOX | 2.4 | 12 Guidelines for Making Concessions

Donald Hendon, Matthew Roy, and Zafar Ahmed (2003) provide the following 12 guidelines for making concessions in negotiation:

1. Give yourself enough room to make concessions.

2. Try to get the other party to start revealing their needs and objectives first.

3. Be the first to concede on a minor issue but not the first to concede on a major issue.

4. Make unimportant concessions and portray them as more valuable than they are.

5. Make the other party work hard for every concession you make.

6. Use trade-offs to obtain something for every concession you make.

7. Generally, concede slowly and give a little with each concession.

8. Do not reveal your deadline to the other party.

9. Occasionally say "no" to the other negotiator.

10. Be careful trying to take back concessions even in "tentative" negotiations.

11. Keep a record of concessions made in the negotiation to try to identify a pattern.

12. Do not concede "too often, too soon, or too much."

Source: D. W. Hendon, M. H. Roy, and Z. U. Ahmed, "Negotiation concession patterns: A multicountry, multiperiod study." *American Business Review, 21* (2003), pp. 75–83.

range to make some concessions. Research suggests that people will generally accept the first or second offer that is better than their target point (see Rapoport, Erev, and Zwick, 1995), so negotiators should try to identify the other party's target point accurately and avoid conceding too quickly to that point. (See Box 2.4 for guidelines on how to make concessions.)

Negotiators also generally resent a take-it-or-leave-it approach; an offer that may have been accepted had it emerged as a result of concession making may be rejected when it is thrown on the table and presented as a *fait accompli*. This latter approach, called Boulwarism,[5] has been illustrated many times in labor relations. In the past, some management leaders objectively analyzed what they could afford to give in their upcoming contract talks and made their initial offer at the point they intended for the agreement (i.e., they set the same opening offer, target point, and resistance point). They then insisted there were no concessions to be made because the initial offer was fair and reasonable based on their own analysis. Unions bitterly fought these positions and continued to resent them years after the companies abandoned this bargaining strategy.

There is ample data to show that parties feel better about a settlement when the negotiation involved a progression of concessions than when it didn't.[6] Rubin and Brown (1975) suggest that bargainers want to believe they are capable of shaping the other's behavior, of causing the other to choose as he or she does. Because concession making indicates an acknowledgment of the other party and a movement toward the other's position, it implies recognition of that position and its legitimacy. The intangible factors of status and recognition may be as important as the tangible issues themselves. Concession making also exposes the concession maker to some risk. If the other party does not reciprocate, the concession maker may appear to be weak. Thus, not reciprocating a concession may send a powerful message about firmness and leaves the concession maker open to feeling that his or her esteem has been damaged or reputation diminished.

A reciprocal concession cannot be haphazard. If one party has made a major concession on a significant point, it is expected that the return offer will be on the same item or one of similar weight and somewhat comparable magnitude. To make an additional concession when none has been received (or when the other party's concession was inadequate) can imply weakness and can squander valuable maneuvering room. After receiving an inadequate concession, negotiators may explicitly state what they expect before offering further concessions: "That is not sufficient; you will have to concede X before I consider offering any further concessions."

To encourage further concessions from the other side, negotiators sometimes link their concessions to a prior concession made by the other. They may say, "Because you have reduced your demand on X, I am willing to concede on Y." A powerful form of concession making involves wrapping a concession in a package. For example, "If you will move on A and B, I will move on C and D." Packaging concessions can lead to better outcomes for negotiators than making concessions singly on individual issues.[7] A particularly effective package is to concede more on lower priority items to gain more on higher priority items. This is an integrative negotiation tactic known as logrolling and is discussed in Chapter 3.

Pattern of Concession Making

The pattern of concessions a negotiator makes contains valuable information, but it is not always easy to interpret. When successive concessions get smaller, the obvious message is that the concession maker's position is getting firmer and that the resistance point is being approached. This generalization needs to be tempered, however, by noting that a concession late in negotiations may also indicate that there is little room left to move. When the opening offer is exaggerated, the negotiator has considerable room available for packaging new offers, making it relatively easy to give fairly substantial concessions. When the offer or counteroffer has moved closer to a negotiator's target point, giving a concession the same size as the initial one may take a negotiator past the resistance point. Suppose a negotiator makes a first offer $100 below the other's target price; an initial concession of $10 would reduce the maneuvering room by 10 percent. When negotiations get to within $10 of the other's target price, a concession of $1 gives up 10 percent of the remaining maneuvering room. A negotiator cannot always communicate such mechanical ratios in giving or interpreting concessions, but this example illustrates how the receiver might construe the meaning of concession size, depending on where it occurs in the negotiating process.

The pattern of concession making is also important. Consider the pattern of concessions made by two negotiators, George and Mario, shown in Figure 2.4. Assume that the negotiators are discussing the unit price of a shipment of computer parts, and that each is dealing with a different client. Mario makes three concessions, each worth $4 per unit, for a total of $12. In contrast, George makes four concessions, worth $4, $3, $2, and $1 per unit, for a total of $10. Both Mario and George tell their counterparts that they have conceded about all that they can. George is more likely to be believed when he makes this assertion because he has signaled through the pattern of his concession making that there is not much left to concede. When Mario claims to have little left to concede, his counterpart is less likely to believe him because the pattern of Mario's concessions (three concessions

FIGURE 2.4 | Pattern of Concession Making for Two Negotiators

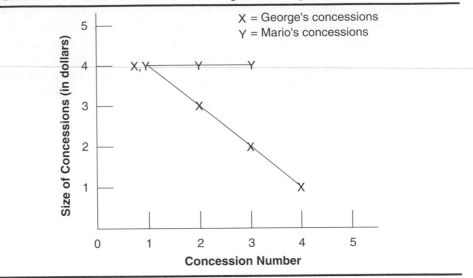

worth the same amount) suggests that there is plenty left to concede, even though Mario has actually conceded more than George (see Yukl, 1974). Note that we have not considered the words spoken by Mario and George as these concessions were made. It is also important to justify concessions to the other party, especially those involving price reductions (Yama, 2004). Behaviors and words are interpreted by the other party when we negotiate; it is important to signal to the other party with both our actions and our words that the concessions are almost over.

In multi-issue negotiations, skilled negotiators will also suggest different forms of a potential settlement that are worth about the same to them. They recognize that not all issues are worth the same amount to both parties. For example, a negotiator in a purchasing agreement may be interested solely in the total revenue of a package and not care whether it is paid in full within one month without interest or over six months with a financing fee at current interest rates. The length of the repayment period may, however, be critical to the other party who has a cash flow problem; that party may be willing to pay the financing fee for the right to spread the payments over six months. In fact, different combinations of principal, interest rate, and payback period may have the same value for one party but quite a different value for the other.

Final Offers

Eventually a negotiator wants to convey the message that there is no further room for movement—that the present offer is the final one. A good negotiator will say, "This is all I can do" or "This is as far as I can go." Sometimes, however, it is clear that a simple statement will not suffice; an alternative is to use concessions to convey the point. A negotiator might simply let the absence of any further concessions convey the message in spite of urging from the other party. The other party may not recognize at first that the last offer was the final one and might volunteer a further concession to get the other to respond. Finding that no further concession occurs, the other party may feel betrayed and perceive that the pattern of concession–counterconcession was violated. The resulting bitterness may further complicate negotiations.

One way negotiators may convey the message that an offer is the last one is to make the last concession more substantial. This implies that the negotiator is throwing in the remainder of the negotiating range. The final offer has to be large enough to be dramatic yet not so large that it creates the suspicion that the negotiator has been holding back and that there is more available on other issues in the bargaining mix (Walton and McKersie, 1965). A concession may also be personalized to the other party ("I went to my boss and got a special deal just for you"), which signals that this is the last concession the negotiator will make.

Commitment

A key concept in creating a bargaining position is that of commitment. One definition of commitment is the taking of a bargaining position with some explicit or implicit pledge regarding the future course of action (Walton and McKersie, 1965, p. 82). An example is a sports agent who says to the general manager of a professional sports team, "If we do not get the salary we want, my player will sit out next year." This act identifies the negotiator's bargaining position and pledges future action if that position is not reached. The purpose of a commitment is to remove ambiguity about the negotiator's intended course of action. By making a commitment, a negotiator signals his or her intention to take this course of action, make this decision, or pursue this objective—the negotiator says, "If you pursue your goals as well, we are likely to come into direct conflict; either one of us will win or neither of us will achieve our goals." Commitments also reduce the other party's options; they are designed to constrain the other party to a reduced portfolio of choices.

A commitment is often interpreted by the other party as a threat—if the other doesn't comply or give in, some set of negative consequences will occur. Some commitments can be threats, but others are simply statements of intended action that leave the responsibility for avoiding mutual disaster in the hands of the other party. A nation that publicly states that it is going to invade another country and that war can be averted only if no other nation tries to stop the action is making a bold and dramatic commitment. Commitments can also involve future promises, such as, "If we get this salary increase, we'll agree to have all other points arbitrated as you request."

Because of their nature, commitments are statements that usually require a follow-through in action. A negotiator who states consequences (e.g., the player will sit out next year), and subsequently fails to get what he or she wanted in the negotiation, is not going to be believed in the future unless he or she acts on the consequences (e.g., the player does not report to training camp). In addition, a person would likely suffer a loss to self-image after not following through on a publicly made commitment. Once a negotiator makes a commitment, therefore, there is strong motivation to hold to it. Because the other party probably will understand this, a commitment, once accepted, will often have a powerful effect on what the other party believes is possible (Pruitt, 1981).

Tactical Considerations in Using Commitments

Like many tools, commitments are two-edged. They may be used to gain the advantages described earlier, but they may also fix a negotiator to a particular position or point. Commitments exchange flexibility for certainty of action, but they create difficulties if one wants to move to a new position. For example, suppose that after committing yourself to a course of action, you find additional information indicating that a different position is desirable, such as information showing that your earlier estimate of the other party's resistance point was wrong and that there is actually a negative bargaining range. It may be desirable or even necessary to shift positions after making a commitment. For these reasons, when one makes commitments one should also make contingency plans for a graceful exit should it be needed. For the original commitment to be effective, the contingency plans must be secret. For example, the player's agent might have planned to retire shortly after the expected completion of negotiations. By advancing retirement, the agent can thereby cancel the commitment and leave a new negotiator unencumbered. The purchaser of a condo may be able to back away from a commitment to buy by discovering the hitherto unnoticed cracks in the plaster in the living room or being unable to obtain financing from the bank. (In Box 2.5, see examples of how to avoid premature commitments in salary negotiations.)

Commitments may be useful to you as a negotiator, but you will find it advantageous to prevent the other party from becoming committed. Further, if the other party should take a committed position, it is to your advantage to keep open one or more ways for him or her to get out of the commitment. The following sections examine these tactical issues in more detail.

Establishing a Commitment

Given that strong, passionate statements—some of which are pure bluff—are made during negotiation, how does a negotiator establish that a statement is to be understood as a commitment? A commitment statement has three properties: a high degree of *finality,* a high degree of *specificity,* and a clear statement of *consequences* (Walton and McKersie, 1965). A buyer could say, "We need a volume discount, or there will be trouble." This statement is far less powerful than "We must have a 10 percent volume discount in the next contract, or we will sign with an alternative supplier next month." The latter statement communicates finality (how and when the volume discount must be granted), specificity (how much of a volume discount is expected), and a clear statement of consequences (exactly what will happen if the discount is not given). It is far stronger than the first statement and much more difficult to get released from. Several ways to create a commitment are discussed next.

Public Pronouncement   A commitment statement increases in potency when more people know about it. The sports agent's statement about sitting out the season would have a different impact if made during a television sportscast than if made only at the bargaining table. Some parties in negotiations have called press conferences or placed ads in newspapers or other publications stating what they want and what will or will not happen if they don't get it. In each of these situations, the wider the audience, the less likely the commitment will be changed. The effect of the broader social context on negotiations will be discussed in Chapters 10 and 11.

Myron Liebschutz, writing in *The Wall Street Journal,* offers these tips for success when job applicants must negotiate a salary package with a prospective employer:

- Delay discussion of compensation until after you have been offered the job.

- After the employer presents the offer and quotes the salary range, remain silent for about 30 seconds. By remaining quiet, you invite the other person to mention a higher figure or talk about flexibility. Then negotiations can begin.

- Don't comment on the salary offer immediately. Instead, clarify some other aspect of the job's responsibilities, and reaffirm where and how you believe you can benefit the organization.

- Then say that the offer is a bit on the conservative side, although the position is still very attractive. Say you would like to think it over and talk again the next day.

- Don't discuss benefits before salary. Get agreement on salary first, then negotiate the fringe benefits.

- Be aware of overnegotiating. Asking for too much, even if you get it, may cause you to be viewed with resentment and can hinder you in future salary reviews.

- Whatever the offer, do not accept it on the spot. Express interest, but again ask for a day to think it over. The job won't go away, and the employer may be able to come up with a better offer given some additional time to get approval.

- If the company cannot meet your annual salary requirements, look for other options such as a one-time, up-front bonus, extended vacation, or specific monetary rewards for performance goals. Typically, there is little room for negotiation when you are applying for a low-level job, when the company is highly bureaucratic, or when the labor supply exceeds demand. There are more opportunities to negotiate when you are applying for a new or high-level, high-profile position and when you possess multiple or unique skills.

Source: Adapted from Myron Liebschutz, "Negotiating the Best Deal Requires a Poker Strategy," *The Wall Street Journal,* June 8, 1997, p. B1.

Linking with an Outside Base   Another way to strengthen a commitment is to link with one or more allies. (Negotiation coalitions are discussed in Chapter 12.) Employees who are dissatisfied with management can form a committee to express their concerns. Industry associations may coalesce to set standards for a product. A variation of this process occurs when negotiators create conditions that make it more difficult for them to break a commitment they have made. For example, by encouraging dedicated colonists to settle on the West Bank near Jerusalem, the Israeli government made it more difficult for Israel to concede this land to the Palestinians, a point the Israelis initially wanted to reinforce.

Increase the Prominence of Demands   Many things can be done to increase the prominence of commitment statements. If most offers and concessions have been made orally, then writing out a statement may draw attention to the commitment. If prior statements have been written, then using a different size typeface or different colored paper will draw attention to the new one. Repetition is one of the most powerful vehicles for making a statement prominent. Using different communication channels to convey a commitment makes the point strongly—for example, telling the other party of a commitment; then handing over a written statement; then reading aloud the statement; then circulating the commitment to others.

Reinforce the Threat or Promise   When making a threat, there is the danger of going too far—stating a point so strongly that you look weak or foolish rather than threatening. Statements like "If I don't get a concession on this point, I'll see that you don't stay in business another day!" are more likely to be greeted with annoyance or dismissal than with concern or compliance. Long, detailed statements that are highly exaggerated undermine credibility. In contrast, simple, direct statements of demands, conditions, and consequences are more effective.

Several things can be done to reinforce the implicit or explicit threat in a commitment. One is to review similar circumstances and their consequences; another is to make obvious preparations to carry out the threat. Facing the prospect of a strike, companies build up their inventories and move cots and food into their factories; unions build strike funds and give advice to their members about how to get by with less income should there be a strike. Another route is to create and carry out minor threats in advance, thereby leading the other party to believe that major threats will be fulfilled. For example, a negotiator could say, "If the progress of these negotiations does not speed up, I am not going to return to the negotiation table after lunch," and then do just that.

Finally, research on threats in negotiation suggests that negotiators who make threats are perceived as more powerful than negotiators who do not (see de Dreu, 1995; Shapiro and Bies, 1994). This perception of greater power does not appear to translate into higher negotiation outcomes for threat users, however. In fact, threat users are also perceived as less cooperative, and their outcomes in integrative situations seem to be lower than those of negotiators who do not use threats (Shapiro and Bies, 1994). Integrative negotiations are discussed in greater detail in Chapter 3.

Preventing the Other Party from Committing Prematurely

All the advantages of a committed position work against a negotiator when the other party becomes committed, so it is important to try to prevent the other negotiator from becoming committed. People often take committed positions when they become angry or feel pushed to the limit; these commitments are often unplanned and can work to the disadvantage of both parties. Consequently, negotiators should pay careful attention to the other party's level of irritation, anger, and impatience.

Good, sound, deliberate commitments take time to establish, for the reasons already discussed. One way to prevent the other party from establishing a committed position is to deny him or her the necessary time. In a real estate deal with an option about to run out, a seller may use up the time by being unavailable or requiring extensive checking of deeds and boundaries, thereby denying time to a potential buyer to make an offer by the deadline and ultimately allowing another buyer who would pay more to enter into negotiation. Another approach to keep the other party from taking a committed position is to ignore or downplay a threat by not acknowledging the other's commitment, or even by making a joke about it. A negotiator might lightheartedly say, "You don't really mean that," or "I know you can't be serious about really going through with that," or simply move negotiations along as though the commitment statement was not heard or understood. If the negotiator can pretend not to hear the other party's statement or not to consider it significant, the statement can be ignored at a later point without incurring the consequences that would have ensued had it been taken seriously. Although the other negotiator can still carry out the threat, the belief that it must be carried out may be reduced.

There are times, however, when it is to a negotiator's advantage for the other party to become committed. When the other party takes a position on an issue relatively early in a negotiation, it may be very much to a negotiator's advantage to solidify that position so it will not be changed as the negotiation on other issues progresses. A negotiator may handle this situation in one of two ways: by identifying the significance of a commitment when it is made or by taking notes and keeping track of the other's statements. An employee might be very upset about the way a particular problem was handled but might also say that she will never get upset enough about it to resign. The manager might focus on this point at the time it is made or refer to it later if the employee has not calmed down. Both actions are designed to keep the employee from making a rash decision out of anger, and may allow a cooling off period before resuming discussions.

Finding Ways to Abandon a Committed Position

Frequently negotiators want to get the other party out of a committed position, and many times that party will also want a way out. How can this be done? We suggest four avenues for escaping commitments.

Plan a Way Out   One method has already been noted: when establishing a commitment, a negotiator should simultaneously plan a private way out. The negotiator may also reword a commitment to indicate that the conditions under which it applied have changed. Sometimes information provided by the other party during negotiations can permit a negotiator to say, "Given what I've learned from you during this discussion, I see I am going to have to rethink my earlier position." The same could be done for the other party. A negotiator, wanting to make it possible for the other to abandon a committed position and yet not lose credibility, might say, "Given what I've told you about the situation [or given this new information], I believe you will see that your earlier position no longer holds." Needless to say, the last thing a negotiator wants to do is to embarrass the other party or make judgmental statements about the shift in position; rather, the other party should be given every opportunity to retreat with dignity and without losing face.

Let It Die Silently   A second way to abandon a commitment is to let the matter die silently. After a lapse of time, a negotiator can make a new proposal in the area of the commitment without mentioning the earlier one. A variation on this process is to make a tentative step in a direction previously excluded by the other's commitment. For example, an employee who has said that he would never accept a certain job assignment may be asked to consider the benefits to his career of a "temporary" placement in that job. In bureaucratic institutions, changes can be introduced as "innovative experiments" to see if they work before they are formally adopted. If the other party, in response to either of these variations, indicates through silence or verbal comment a willingness to let things move in that direction, the negotiation should simply be allowed to progress.

Restate the Commitment   A third route is to restate the commitment in more general terms. The party that wants to abandon a commitment will make a new proposal, changing some of the details to be more in line with his or her current needs, while ostensibly still living with the general principles of the earlier wording. For example, the purchasing agent who demanded a 10 percent volume discount may rephrase this statement later to say simply that a significant volume discount is needed. The other party can then explore what level this "significant" discount could be.

Minimize the Damage   Finally, if the other party backs off from a committed position, it is important to help him or her save face, which means helping minimize any possible damage to the other party's self-esteem or to constituent relationships. One strategy to use in this instance is to make a public attribution about the other party's move to some noble or higher outside cause. Diplomats can withdraw from a committed position because of their deep concern for peace and humankind. A buyer or seller can back off from a point during a real estate transaction to support the economic well-being of the community. Managers can leave a committed position for the good of the company.

A committed position is a powerful tool in negotiation; it is also a rigid tool and must therefore be used with care. As with any other tool, we must be as alert to ways of denying it to the other party as we are to ways we can use it for ourselves. Unfortunately, many commitments are made impulsively out of anger or a desire to stop making concessions, rather than as a result of clearly thought-out tactical planning. In either case, the essential effect of a committed position is to remove an issue from further discussion—to make it no longer negotiable except at serious risk to one or both parties. The committed position has to be believable, and it must appear inevitable—if X happens, Y is inevitable. Convincing the other party that fate is sealed on the matter at hand is a demanding task and requires preparation, time, and skill. Consequently, getting out of a committed position is not easy, but the process is made simpler by planning a means of escape at the time the commitment is being established. Many of the steps a negotiator can use to get out of a commitment can also be used to help the other party get out of a committed position or, even better, to keep him or her from establishing one in the first place.

Closing the Deal

After negotiating for a period of time, and learning about the other party's needs, positions, and perhaps resistance point, the next challenge for a negotiator is to close the agreement. Negotiators can call on several tactics when closing a deal (see Cellich, 1997; Girard, 1989); choosing the best tactic for a given negotiation is as much a matter of art as science.

Provide Alternatives   Rather than making a single final offer, negotiators can provide two or three alternative packages for the other party that are more or less equivalent in value. People like to have choices, and providing a counterpart with alternative packages can be a very effective technique for closing a negotiation. This technique can also be used when a task force cannot decide on which recommendation to make to upper management. If in fact there are two distinct, defensible possible solutions, then the task force can forward both with a description of the costs and benefits of each.

Assume the Close   Salespeople use an assume-the-close technique frequently. After having a general discussion about the needs and positions of the buyer, often the seller will take out a large order form and start to complete it. The seller usually begins by asking for the buyer's name and address before moving on to more serious points (e.g., price, model). When using this technique, negotiators do not ask the other party if he or she would like to make a purchase. Rather, they may say something like "Shall I get the paperwork started?" and act as if the decision to purchase something has already been made (see Girard, 1989).

Split the Difference   Splitting the difference is perhaps the most popular closing tactic. The negotiator using this tactic will typically give a brief summary of the negotiation ("We've both spent a lot of time, made many concessions, etc.") and then suggest that, because things are so close, "why don't we just split the difference?" While this can be an effective closing tactic, it does presume that the parties started with fair opening offers. A negotiator who uses an exaggerated opening offer and then suggests a split-the-difference close is using a hardball tactic (see below).

Exploding Offers   An exploding offer contains an extremely tight deadline in order to pressure the other party to agree quickly and is an extreme version of manipulating negotiating schedules. For example, a person who has interviewed for a job may be offered a very attractive salary and benefits package, but also be told that the offer will expire in 24 hours. The purpose of the exploding offer is to convince the other party to accept the settlement and to stop considering alternatives. This is particularly effective in situations where the party receiving the exploding offer is still in the process of developing alternatives that may or may not turn out to be viable (such as the job candidate who is still interviewing with other firms). People can feel quite uncomfortable about receiving exploding offers, however, because they feel as if they're under unfair pressure. Exploding offers appear to work best for organizations that have the resources to make an exceptionally attractive offer early in a negotiation in order to prevent the other party from continuing to search for a potentially superior offer.

Sweeteners   Another closing tactic is to save a special concession for the close. The other negotiator is told, "I'll give you X if you agree to the deal." For instance, when selling a condo the owner could agree to include the previously excluded curtains, appliances, or light fixtures to close the deal. To use this tactic effectively, however, negotiators need to include the sweetener in their negotiation plans or they may concede too much during the close.

Hardball Tactics

We now turn to a discussion of hardball tactics in negotiation. Many popular books of negotiation discuss using hardball negotiation tactics to beat the other party.[8] Such tactics are designed to pressure negotiators to do things they would not otherwise do, and their presence usually disguises the user's adherence to a decidedly distributive bargaining approach. It is not clear exactly how often or how well these tactics work, but they work best against poorly prepared negotiators. They also can backfire, and there is evidence that very adversarial negotiators are not effective negotiators (Schneider, 2002). Many people find hardball tactics offensive and are motivated for revenge when such tactics are used against them. Many negotiators consider these tactics out-of-bounds for any negotiation situation.

(Negotiation ethics are discussed in Chapter 9). We do not recommend the use of any of the following techniques. In fact, it has been our experience that these tactics do more harm than good in negotiations. They are much more difficult to enact than they are to read, and each tactic involves risk for the person using it, including harm to reputation, lost deals, negative publicity, and consequences of the other party's revenge. It is important that negotiators understand hardball tactics and how they work, however, so they can recognize and understand them if hardball tactics are used against them.

Dealing with Typical Hardball Tactics

The negotiator dealing with a party who uses hardball tactics has several choices about how to respond. A good strategic response to these tactics requires that the negotiator identify the tactic quickly and understand what it is and how it works. Most of the tactics are designed either to enhance the appearance of the bargaining position of the person using the tactic or to detract from the appearance of the options available to the other party. How best to respond to a tactic depends on your goals and the broader context of the negotiation (With whom are you negotiating? What are your alternatives?). No one response will work in all situations. We now discuss four main options that negotiators have for responding to typical hardball tactics.[9]

Ignore Them   Although ignoring a hardball tactic may appear to be a weak response, it can in fact be very powerful. It takes a lot of energy to use some of the hardball tactics described here, and while the other side is using energy to play these games, you can be using your energy to work on satisfying your needs. Not responding to a threat is often the best way of dealing with it. Pretend you didn't hear it. Change the subject and get the other party involved in a new topic. Call a break and, upon returning, switch topics. All these options can deflate the effects of a threat and allow you to press on with your agenda while the other party is trying to decide what trick to use next.

Discuss Them   Fisher, Ury, and Patton suggest that a good way to deal with hardball tactics is to discuss them—that is, label the tactic and indicate to the other party that you know what she is doing (Fisher, Ury, and Patton, 1991; Ury, 1991; Weeks, 2001). Then offer to negotiate the negotiation process itself, such as behavioral expectations of the parties, before continuing on to the substance of the talks. Propose a shift to less aggressive methods of negotiating. Explicitly acknowledge that the other party is a tough negotiator but that you can be tough too. Then suggest that you both change to more productive methods that can allow you both to gain. Fisher, Ury, and Patton suggest that negotiators separate the people from the problem and then be hard on the problem, soft on the people. It doesn't hurt to remind the other negotiator of this from time to time during the negotiation.

Respond in Kind   It is always possible to respond to a hardball tactic with one of your own. Although this response can result in chaos, produce hard feelings, and be counterproductive, it is not an option that should be dismissed. Once the smoke clears, both parties will realize that they are skilled in the use of hardball tactics and may recognize that it is time to try something different. Responding in kind may be most useful when dealing with another party who is testing your resolve or as a response to exaggerated positions taken in negotiations. A participant in a negotiation seminar told one of the authors the following story about bargaining for a carpet in a northern African country:

> I knew that the value of the carpet was about $2,000 because I had been looking at carpets throughout my trip. I found the carpet that I wanted and made sure not to appear too interested. I discussed some other carpets with the vendor before moving on to the carpet that I really wanted. When I asked him the price of this carpet, he replied $9,000. I replied that I would give him *negative* $5,000. We bargained for a while and I bought the carpet for $2,000.

The purchaser in this negotiation clearly responded to a hardball tactic with one of his own. When asked if he felt comfortable with his opening bid, he responded:

> Sure. Why not? The seller knew the value of the carpet was about $2,000. If anything, he seemed to respect me when I bargained this way. If I had opened with a positive number I would have ended up having to pay more than the carpet was worth. And I really wanted the carpet.

Co-Opt the Other Party   Another way to deal with negotiators who are known to use aggressive hardball tactics is to try to befriend them before they use the tactics on you. This approach is built on the theory that it is much more difficult to attack a friend than an enemy. If you can stress what you have in common with the other party and find another element upon which to place the blame (the system, foreign competition), you may then be able to sidetrack the other party and thereby prevent the use of any hardball tactics.

Typical Hardball Tactics

We now discuss some of the more frequently described hardball tactics and their weaknesses.

Good Cop/Bad Cop   The good cop/bad cop tactic is named after a police interrogation technique in which two officers (one kind, the other tough) take turns questioning a suspect; it can frequently be seen in episodes of popular television series such as *Law and Order* and *CSI*. The use of this tactic in negotiations typically goes as follows: the first interrogator (bad cop) presents a tough opening position, punctuated with threats, obnoxious behavior, and intransigence. The interrogator then leaves the room to make an important telephone call or to cool off—frequently at the partner's suggestion. While out of the room, the other interrogator (good cop) tries to reach a quick agreement before the bad cop returns and makes life difficult for everyone. A more subtle form of this tactic is to assign the bad cop the role of speaking only when the negotiations are headed in a direction that the team does not want; as long as things are going well, the good cop does the talking. Although the good cop/bad cop tactic can be somewhat transparent, it often leads to concessions and negotiated agreements (Brodt and Tuchinsky, 2000; Hilty and Carnevale, 1993).

This tactic has many weaknesses. As mentioned earlier, it is relatively transparent, especially with repeated use. It can be countered by openly stating what the negotiators are doing. A humorously delivered statement like "You two aren't playing the old good cop/bad cop game with me, are you?" will go a long way to deflating this tactic even if both of the

other parties deny it self-righteously. The good cop/bad cop tactic is also much more difficult to enact than it is to read; it typically alienates the targeted party and frequently requires negotiators to direct much more energy toward making the tactic work smoothly than toward accomplishing the negotiation goals. Negotiators using this tactic can become so involved with their game playing and acting that they fail to concentrate on obtaining their negotiation goals.

Lowball/Highball Negotiators using the lowball/highball tactic start with a ridiculously low (or high) opening offer that they know they will never achieve. The theory is that the extreme offer will cause the other party to reevaluate his or her own opening offer and move closer to or beyond their resistance point. For example, one of the authors of this book was in a labor–management negotiation where the union's first offer was to request a 45 percent salary increase over three years. Given that recent settlements in neighboring universities had been 3 to 4 percent, this qualified as a highball offer!

The risk of using this tactic is that the other party will think negotiating is a waste of time and will stop the process. Even if the other party continues to negotiate after receiving a lowball (or highball) offer, however, it takes a very skilled negotiator to be able to justify the extreme opening offer and to finesse the negotiation back to a point where the other side will be willing to make a major concession toward the outrageous bid.

The best way to deal with a lowball/highball tactic is not to make a counteroffer, but to ask for a more reasonable opening offer from the other party (the union in the preceding example responded to this request by tabling an offer for a 6 percent increase, above the industry average but not qualifying as a highball offer). The reason that requesting a reasonable opening offer is important is because this tactic works in the split second between hearing the other party's opening offer and the delivery of your first offer. If you give in to the natural tendency to change your opening offer because it would be embarrassing to start negotiations so far apart, or because the other party's extreme opening makes you rethink where the bargaining zone may lie, then you have fallen victim to this tactic. When this happens, you have been "anchored" by the other party's extreme first offer.

Good preparation for the negotiation is a critical defense against this tactic (see Chapter 4). Proper planning will help you know the general range for the value of the item under discussion and allow you to respond verbally with one of several different strategies: (1) insisting that the other party start with a reasonable opening offer and refusing to negotiate further until he or she does; (2) stating your understanding of the general market value of the item being discussed, supporting it with facts and figures, and, by doing so, demonstrating to the other party that you won't be tricked; (3) threatening to leave the negotiation, either briefly or for good, to demonstrate dissatisfaction with the other party for using this tactic; and (4) responding with an extreme counteroffer to send a clear message you won't be anchored by an extreme offer from the other party.

Bogey   Negotiators using the bogey tactic pretend that an issue of little or no importance to them is quite important. Later in the negotiation, this issue can then be traded for major concessions on issues that are actually important to them. This tactic is most effective when negotiators identify an issue that is quite important to the other side but of little value to themselves. For example, a seller may have a product in the warehouse ready for delivery. When negotiating with a purchasing agent, however, the seller may ask for large concessions to process a rush order for the client. The seller can reduce the size of the concession demanded for the rush order in exchange for concessions on other issues, such as the price or the size of the order. Another example of a bogey is to argue as if you want a particular work assignment or project (when in fact you don't prefer it) and then, in exchange for large concessions from the other party, accept the assignment you actually prefer (but had pretended not to).

This tactic is fundamentally deceptive, and as such it can be a difficult tactic to enact. Typically, the other party will negotiate in good faith and take you seriously when you are trying to make a case for the issue that you want to bogey. This can lead to the very unusual situation of both negotiators arguing against their true wishes—the other party asks for large concessions on other issues to give you the bogey issue (that you really don't want), and you spend time evaluating offers and making arguments for an issue you know you do not want. It can also be very difficult to change gracefully and accept an offer in completely the opposite direction. If this maneuver cannot be done, however, then you may end up accepting a suboptimal deal—the bogey may be something you do not really want, and perhaps the other party doesn't either.

Research by O'Connor and Carnevale (1997) suggests that bogeys occur more often by omission than commission. They suggest that negotiators who wish to use the bogey should "get the other person to state his or her preferences on all the issues first and look for common value" (p. 513). This presumes that the other person will state their preferences accurately, which is not always true—negotiators may deliberately misstate their true preferences to try to set up a bogey. O'Connor and Carnevale do suggest that the tactic may be harmful to relationships, however, if the other party reacts strongly to being misled. We explore ethical issues involved in the use of this and other deceptive tactics in Chapter 9.

Although the bogey is a difficult tactic to defend against, being well prepared for the negotiation will make you less susceptible to it. When the other party takes a position completely counter to what you expected, you may suspect that a bogey tactic is being used. Probing with questions about why the other party wants a particular outcome may help you reduce the effectiveness of a bogey. Finally, you should be very cautious about sudden reversals in positions taken by the other party, especially late in a negotiation. This may be a sign that the bogey tactic has been in use. Again, questioning the other party carefully about why the reverse position is suddenly acceptable and not conceding too much after the other party completely reverses a position may significantly reduce the effectiveness of the bogey.

The Nibble   Negotiators using the nibble tactic ask for a proportionally small concession (e.g., 1 to 2 percent of the total profit of the deal) on an item that hasn't been discussed previously in order to close the deal. Herb Cohen (1980) describes the nibble as follows: after trying many different suits in a clothing store, tell the clerk that you will take a given suit if a tie is included for free. The tie is the nibble. Cohen claims that he usually gets the tie. In a business context, the tactic occurs like this: after a considerable amount of time has been spent in negotiation, when an agreement is close, one party asks to include a clause that hasn't been discussed previously and that will cost the other party a proportionally small amount. This amount is too small to lose the deal over, but large enough to upset the other party. This is the major weakness with the nibble tactic—many people feel that the party using the nibble did not bargain in good faith (as part of a fair negotiation process, all items to be discussed during the negotiation should be placed on the agenda early). Even if the party claims to be very embarrassed about forgetting this item until now, the party who has been nibbled will not feel good about the process and will be motivated to seek revenge in future negotiations.

According to Landon (1997), there are two good ways to combat the nibble. First, respond to each nibble with the question "What else do you want?" This should continue until the other party indicates that all issues are in the open; then both parties can discuss all the issues simultaneously. Second, have your own nibbles prepared to offer in exchange. When the other party suggests a nibble on one issue, you can respond with your own nibble on another.

Chicken   The chicken tactic is named after the 1950s challenge, portrayed in the James Dean movie *Rebel without a Cause,* of two people driving cars at each other or toward a cliff until one person swerves to avoid disaster. The person who swerves is labeled a chicken, and the other person is treated like a hero. Negotiators who use this tactic combine a large bluff with a threatened action to force the other party to "chicken out" and give them what they want. In labor–management negotiations, management may tell the union representatives that if they do not agree to the current contract offer the company will close the factory and go out of business (or move to another state or country). Clearly this is a high-stakes gamble. On the one hand, management must be willing to follow through on the threat—if the union calls their bluff and they do not follow through, they will not be believed in the future. On the other hand, how can the union take the risk and call the bluff? If management is telling the truth, the company may actually close the factory and move elsewhere.

The weakness of the chicken tactic is that it turns negotiation into a serious game in which one or both parties find it difficult to distinguish reality from postured negotiation positions. Will the other party really follow through on his or her threats? We frequently cannot know for sure because the circumstances must be grave in order for this tactic to be believable; but it is precisely when circumstances are grave that a negotiator may be most tempted to use this tactic. Compare, for instance, the responses of Presidents Bill Clinton and George W. Bush to Iraq's defiance of the United Nations weapons inspection program. It appears that Iraq felt it could "stare down" President Bush because it had successfully avoided outright conflict during President Clinton's term. The subsequent war in Iraq demonstrated the error of this assessment.

The chicken tactic is very difficult for a negotiator to defend against. To the extent that the commitment can be downplayed, reworded, or ignored, however, it can lose its power. Perhaps the riskiest response is to introduce one's own chicken tactic. At that point neither party may be willing to back down in order not to lose face. Preparation and a thorough understanding of the situations of both parties are absolutely essential for trying to identify where reality ends and the chicken tactic begins. Use of external experts to verify information or to help to reframe the situation is another option.

Intimidation   Many tactics can be gathered under the general label of intimidation. What they have in common is that they all attempt to force the other party to agree by means of an emotional ploy, usually anger or fear. For example, the other party may deliberately use *anger* to indicate the seriousness of a position. One of the authors of this book had the following experience:

> Once while I was negotiating with a car salesman he lost his temper, destroyed his written notes, told me to sit down and listen to him, and went on to explain in a loud voice that this was the best deal in the city and if I did not accept it that evening I should not bother returning to that dealership and wasting his time. I didn't buy the car and I haven't been back, nor I suspect have any of the students in my negotiation classes, to whom I relate this story every year! I suspect that the salesman was trying to intimidate me into agreeing to the deal and realized that if I went elsewhere his deal would not look as good. What he didn't realize was that I had asked the accountant at the dealership for further information about the deal and had found that he had lied about the value of a trade-in; he really lost his cool when I exposed the lie.

Another form of intimidation includes increasing the appearance of *legitimacy*. When legitimacy is high, set policies or procedures are in place for resolving disputes. Negotiators who do not have such policies or procedures available may try to invent them and then impose them on the other negotiator while making the process appear legitimate. For example, policies that are written in manuals or preprinted official forms and agreements are less likely to be questioned than those that are delivered verbally (Cohen, 1980); long and detailed loan contracts that banks use for consumer loans are seldom read completely (Hendon and Hendon, 1990). The greater the appearance of legitimacy, the less likely the other party will be to question the process being followed or the contract terms being proposed.

Finally, *guilt* can also be used as a form of intimidation. Negotiators can question the other party's integrity or the other's lack of trust in them. The purpose of this tactic is to place the other party on the defensive so that they are dealing with the issues of guilt or trust rather than discussing the substance of the negotiation.

To deal with intimidation tactics, negotiators have several options. Intimidation tactics are designed to make the intimidator feel more powerful than the other party and to lead people to make concessions for emotional rather than objective reasons (e.g., a new fact). When making any concession, it is important for negotiators to understand why they are doing so. If one starts to feel threatened, assumes that the other party is more powerful (when objectively he or she is not), or simply accepts the legitimacy of the other negotiator's "company policy," then it is likely that intimidation is having an effect on the negotiations.

If the other negotiator is intimidating, then discussing the negotiation process with him or her is a good option. You can explain that your policy is to bargain in a fair and respectful manner, and that you expect to be treated the same way in return. Another good option is to ignore the other party's attempts to intimidate you, because intimidation can only influence you if you let it. While this may sound too simplistic, think for a moment about why some people you know are intimidated by authority figures and others are not—the reason often lies in the perceiver, not the authority figure.

Another effective strategy for dealing with intimidation is to use a team to negotiate with the other party. Teams have at least two advantages over individuals in acting against intimidation. First, people are not always intimidated by the same things; while you may be intimidated by one particular negotiator, it is quite possible that other members on your team won't be. In an ongoing negotiation in China when he was younger, one of the authors of this book found that his Chinese counterparts were frequently changing their team members so that older and older members appeared in each subsequent negotiation session. He decided to bring a senior colleague of his own to subsequent meetings in order not to be intimidated by the age and experience of the counterparts on the other negotiating team. The second advantage of using a team is that the team members can discuss the tactics of the other negotiators and provide mutual support if the intimidation starts to become increasingly uncomfortable.

Aggressive Behavior   Similar to tactics described under intimidation, aggressive behavior tactics include various ways of being aggressive to push your position or attack the other person's position. Aggressive tactics include a relentless push for further concessions ("You can do better than that"), asking for the best offer early in negotiations ("Let's not waste any time. What is the most that you will pay?"), and asking the other party to explain and justify his or her proposals item by item or line by line ("What is your cost breakdown for each item?"). The negotiator using these techniques is signaling a hard-nosed, intransigent position and trying to force the other side to make many concessions to reach an agreement.

When faced with another party's aggressive behavior tactics, an excellent response is to halt the negotiations in order to discuss the negotiation process itself. Negotiators can explain that they will reach a decision based on needs and interests, not aggressive behavior. Again, having a team to counter aggressive tactics from the other party can be helpful for the same reasons discussed under intimidation tactics. Good preparation and understanding both one's own and the other party's needs and interests together make responding to aggressive tactics easier because negotiators can highlight the merits to both parties of reaching an agreement.

Snow Job   The snow job tactic occurs when negotiators overwhelm the other party with so much information that he or she has trouble determining which facts are real or important and which are included merely as distractions. Governments use this tactic frequently when releasing information publicly. Rather than answering a question briefly, they release thousands of pages of documents from hearings and transcripts that may or may not contain the information that the other party is seeking. Another example of the snow job is the use of highly technical language to hide a simple answer to a question asked by a nonexpert. Any group of professionals—such as engineers, lawyers, or computer network administrators—can use this tactic to overwhelm ("snow") the other party with information and technical language so that the nonexperts cannot make sense of the answer. Frequently, in order not to be embarrassed by asking "obvious" questions, the recipient of the snow job will simply nod his or her head and passively agree with the other party's analysis or statements.

Negotiators trying to counter a snow job tactic can choose one of several alternative responses. First, they should not be afraid to ask questions until they receive an answer they understand. Second, if the matter under discussion is in fact highly technical, then negotiators may suggest that technical experts get together to discuss the technical issues. Finally, negotiators should listen carefully to the other party and identify consistent and inconsistent information. Probing for further information after identifying a piece of inconsistent information can work to undermine the effectiveness of the snow job. For example, if one piece of incorrect or inconsistent information is discovered in the complete snow job package, the negotiator can question the accuracy of the whole presentation (e.g., "Because point X was incorrect, how can I be sure that the rest is accurate?"). Again, strong preparation is very important for defending effectively against the snow job tactic.

Distributive Bargaining Skills Applicable to Integrative Negotiations

This chapter has provided an overview of distributive bargaining situations and discussed the classic strategies and tactics that are used in distributive bargaining. Negotiators in a distributive bargaining situation need to execute these strategies and tactics well in order to increase their chances of obtaining a positive agreement. For instance, negotiators need to set clear target and resistance points, understand and work to improve their BATNA, start with a good opening offer, make appropriate concessions, and manage the commitment process. Many of these skills are also applicable to the latter stages of integrative negotiation when negotiators need to *claim value,* that is to decide how to divide their joint gains. Negotiators need to be careful, however, not to seriously change the tone of those negotiations by adopting an overtly aggressive stance at this stage. Integrative negotiation is discussed in detail in Chapter 3.

Chapter Summary

In this chapter we examined the basic structure of competitive or distributive bargaining situations and some of the strategies and tactics used in distributive bargaining. Distributive bargaining begins with setting opening, target, and resistance points. One soon learns the other party's starting points and his or her target points directly or through inference. Usually one won't know the other party's resistance points (the points beyond which she or he will not go) until late in negotiation—they are often carefully concealed. All points are important, but the resistance points are the most critical. The spread between the parties' resistance points defines the bargaining range. If positive, it defines the area of negotiation within which a settlement is likely to occur, with each party working to obtain as much of the bargaining range as possible. If negative, successful negotiation may be impossible.

It is rare that a negotiation includes only one item; more typically, a set of items, referred to as a bargaining mix, is negotiated. Each item in a bargaining mix can have opening, target, and resistance points. The bargaining mix may provide opportunities for bundling issues together, trading off across issues, or displaying mutually concessionary behavior.

Under the structure of distributive bargaining, a negotiator has many options to achieve a successful resolution, most of which fall within two broad efforts: to influence the other party's belief about what is possible and to learn as much as possible about the other party's position, particularly about their resistance points. The negotiator's basic goal is to reach a final settlement as close to the other party's resistance point as possible. To achieve this goal, negotiators work to gather information about the opposition and its positions; to convince members of the other party to change their minds about their ability to achieve their own goals; and to justify their own objectives as desirable, necessary, or even inevitable.

Distributive bargaining is basically a conflict situation, wherein parties seek their own advantage—sometimes through concealing information, attempting to mislead, or using manipulative actions. All these tactics can easily escalate interaction from calm discussion to bitter hostility. Yet negotiation is the attempt to resolve a conflict without force, without fighting. Further, to be successful, both parties to the negotiation must feel at the end that the outcome was the best they could achieve and that it is worth accepting and supporting. Hence, effective distributive bargaining is a process that requires careful planning, strong execution, and constant monitoring of the other party's reactions. Finally, distributive bargaining skills are important when at the value claiming stage of any negotiation. This is discussed in more detail in the next chapter on integrative negotiation.

Endnotes

[1] Refer to Walton and McKersie (1965, pp. 59–82) for a more extensive treatment of this subject.

[2] See Lim and Murnighan (1994); Roth, Murnighan, and Schoumaker (1988); and Walton and McKersie (1965).

[3] See Brodt (1994); Chertkoff and Conley (1967); Cohen (2003); Donohue (1981); Hinton, Hamner, and Pohlan (1974); Komorita and Brenner (1968); Liebert, Smith, and Hill (1968); Pruitt and Syna (1985); Ritov (1996); Van Pouke and Buelens (2002); and Weingart, Thompson, Bazerman, and Carroll (1990).

[4] See Pruitt (1981) and Tutzauer (1991) for further discussion of these points.

[5] The term *Boulwarism* is named after the chief labor negotiator for the General Electric Company in the 1950s. Rather than let the union present its contract demands first, the company placed a single "fair" offer on the table and refused to negotiate further. The National Labor Relations Board eventually ruled against GE by stating that this practice was unfair because management did not engage in "good faith bargaining." See Northrup (1964) and Selekman, Selekman, and Fuller (1958) for further discussion of this point.

[6] See Baranowski and Summers (1972); Crumbaugh and Evans (1967); Deutsch (1958); and Gruder and Duslak (1973).

[7] See Froman and Cohen (1970); Neale and Bazerman (1991); and Pruitt (1981).

[8] For instance, see Aaronson (1989); Brooks and Odiorne (1984); Cohen (1980); Levinson, Smith, and Wilson (1999); and Schatzski (1981).

[9] See Fisher, Ury, and Patton (1991); Ury (1991); and Adler, Rosen, and Silverstein (1996) for an extended discussion of these points.

CHAPTER 3

Strategy and Tactics of Integrative Negotiation

Objectives

1. Understand the basic elements of an integrative negotiation situation.
2. Explore the strategy and tactics of integrative negotiation.
3. Consider the key factors that facilitate successful integrative negotiation.
4. Gain an understanding of why successful integrative negotiations are often difficult to achieve.

Introduction

Even well-intentioned negotiators can make the following three mistakes: failing to negotiate when they should, negotiating when they should not, or negotiating when they should but choosing an inappropriate strategy. As suggested by the dual concerns model described in Chapter 1, being committed to the other party's interests as well as to one's own makes problem solving the strategy of choice. In many negotiations there does not need to be winners and losers—all parties can gain. Rather than assume that negotiations are win–lose situations, negotiators can look for win–win solutions—and often they will find them. Integrative negotiation—variously known as cooperative, collaborative, win–win, mutual gains, or problem solving—is the focus of this chapter.

In distributive bargaining, the goals of the parties are initially at odds—or at least appear that way to some or all of the parties. Central to such conflict is the belief that there is a limited, controlled amount of key resources to be distributed—a fixed-pie situation. Both parties may want to be the winner; both may want more than half of what is available. For example, both management (on behalf of the shareholders) and labor (on behalf of the rank and file) may believe they deserve the larger share of the company's profits. Both may want to win on the same dimension, such as the financial package or control of certain policy decisions. In these situations, their goals are mutually exclusive and lead to conflict.

In contrast, the goals of the parties in integrative negotiation are not mutually exclusive. If one side achieves its goals, the other is not precluded from achieving its goals as well. One party's gain is not at the other party's expense. The fundamental structure of an

BOX 3.1 Characteristics of the Interest-Based Negotiator

A successful interest-based negotiator models the following traits:

Honesty and integrity. Interest-based negotiating requires a certain level of trust between the parties. Actions that demonstrate interest in all players' concerns will help establish a trusting environment.

Abundance mentality. Those with an abundance mentality do not perceive a concession of monies, prestige, control, and so on as something that makes their slice of the pie smaller, but merely as a way to enlarge the pie. A scarcity or zero-sum mentality says, "anything I give to you takes away from me." A negotiator with an abundance mentality knows that making concessions helps build stronger long-term relationships.

Maturity. In his book *Seven Habits of Highly Effective Leaders,* Stephen Covey refers to maturity as having the courage to stand up for your issues and values while being able to recognize that others' issues and values are just as valid.

Systems orientation. Systems thinkers will look at ways in which the entire system can be optimized, rather than focusing on suboptimizing components of the system.

Superior listening skills. Ninety percent of communication is not in one's words but in the whole context of the communication, including mode of expression, body language, and many other cues. Effective listening also requires that one avoid listening only from his or her frame of reference.

Source: Chris Laubach, "Negotiating a Gain-Gain Agreement," *Healthcare Executive,* January/February 1997, p. 14.

integrative negotiation situation is such that it allows both sides to achieve their objectives.[1] Although the situation may initially appear to the parties to be win–lose, discussion and mutual exploration will often suggest alternatives where both parties can gain. A description of the efforts and tactics that negotiators use to discover these alternatives is the major part of this chapter.

What Makes Integrative Negotiation Different?

In Chapter 1 we listed elements common to all negotiations. For a negotiation to be characterized as integrative, negotiators must also:

- Focus on commonalties rather than differences.
- Attempt to address needs and interests, not positions.
- Commit to meeting the needs of all involved parties.
- Exchange information and ideas.
- Invent options for mutual gain.
- Use objective criteria for standards of performance.

These requisite behaviors and perspectives are the main components of the integrative process (see Box 3.1).

An Overview of the Integrative Negotiation Process ⸱

Past experience, biased perceptions, and the truly distributive aspects of bargaining make it remarkable that integrative agreements occur at all. But they do, largely because negotiators work hard to overcome inhibiting factors and search assertively for common ground. Those wishing to achieve integrative results find that they must manage both the *context* and the *process* of the negotiation in order to gain the cooperation and commitment of all parties. Key contextual factors include creating a free flow of information, attempting to understand the other negotiator's real needs and objectives, emphasizing commonalities between parties, and searching for solutions that meet the goals and objectives of both parties. Managing integrative negotiations involves creating a process of problem identification, understanding the needs and interests of both parties, generating alternative solutions, and selecting among alternative solutions.

Creating a Free Flow of Information

Effective information exchange promotes the development of good integrative solutions (Butler, 1999; Pruitt, 1981; Thompson, 1991). Research shows that the failure to reach integrative agreements is often linked to the failure to exchange enough information to allow the parties to identify integrative options (Butler, 1999; Kemp and Smith, 1994). For the necessary exchange to occur, negotiators must be willing to reveal their true objectives and to listen to each other carefully. In short, negotiators must create the conditions for a free and open discussion of all related issues and concerns. In contrast, a willingness to share information is not a characteristic of distributive bargaining situations, in which the parties may distrust one another, conceal and manipulate information, and attempt to learn about the other purely for their own competitive advantage.

Creating a free flow of information includes having both parties know and share their alternatives. Pinkley (1995) discovered that negotiators who are aware of each other's alternatives to a negotiated agreement were more likely to make their resistance points less extreme, improve negotiating trade-offs, and increase the size of the resource pie compared with situations in which one or both negotiators were not aware of the alternatives. Pinkley concluded that "it is the negotiator with the alternative who is responsible for expanding the pie, but both members of the dyad determine its distribution" (p. 409). Negotiators who did not reveal the availability of a good alternative received some benefits to themselves, but those who did share information about their alternatives received additional benefits.

Attempting to Understand the Other Negotiator's Real Needs and Objectives

Negotiators differ in their values and preferences, as well as their thoughts and behaviors (Barki and Hartwick, 2004). What one side needs and wants may or may not be the same as what the other party needs and wants. One must understand the other's needs before helping to satisfy them. When negotiators are aware of the possibility that the other's priorities are not the same as their own, this can stimulate the parties to exchange more information, understand the nature of the negotiation better, and achieve higher joint gains (Kemp and Smith, 1994). Similarly, integrative agreements are facilitated when parties exchange information about their priorities for particular issues, but not necessarily about their positions on those issues (Olekalns, Smith, and Walsh, 1996). Throughout the process of sharing information about preferences and priorities, negotiators must make a true effort to understand what the other side really wants to achieve. This is in contrast to distributive bargaining, where negotiators either make no effort to understand the other side's needs and objectives or do so only to challenge, undermine, or even deny the other party the opportunity to have those needs and objectives met. The communicative aspects of information flow and understanding, while critical to integrative negotiation, also require that Kelley's (1966) dilemmas of trust and honesty be managed (see Chapter 1). In addition, negotiators may differ in their ability to differentiate needs and interests from positions, such as when one party knows and applies a truly integrative process while the other party is unskilled or naive about negotiations. In such situations, the more experienced party may need to assist the less experienced party in discovering his or her underlying needs and interests.

Emphasizing the Commonalities between the Parties and Minimizing the Differences

To sustain a free flow of information and the effort to understand the other's needs and objectives, negotiators may need a different outlook or frame of reference (see Chapter 4 for a discussion of framing). Individual goals may need to be redefined as best achieved through collaborative efforts directed toward a collective goal. Sometimes the collective goal is clear and obvious. For example, politicians in the same party may recognize that their petty squabbles must be put aside to ensure the party's victory at the polls. Managers who are quarreling over cutbacks in their individual departmental budgets may need to recognize that unless all departments sustain appropriate budget cuts, they will be unable to change an unprofitable firm into a profitable one. At other times, the collective goal is neither so clear nor so easy to keep in sight. For example, one of the authors worked as a consultant to a company that was closing a major manufacturing plant while simultaneously opening several other plants in different parts of the country. The company was perfectly willing to transfer employees to new plants and let them take their seniority up to the time of their move with them; the union agreed to this arrangement. However, conflict developed over the transfer issue. Some employees were able to transfer immediately, whereas others—those who were needed to close and dismantle the old plant—could not. Because workers acquired seniority in the new plants based on the date they arrived, those who stayed to close the old plant would have comparatively less seniority once they arrived at the new plants. The union wanted everyone to go at the same time to avoid this inequity. This was unworkable for management. In the argument that resulted, both parties lost sight of the larger goal—to transfer all willing employees to the new plants with their seniority intact. Only by constantly stressing this larger goal were the parties able to maintain a focus on commonalities that eventually led to a solution; management allowed the workers to select their new jobs in advance and transferred their seniority to those jobs when the choice was made, not when the physical move actually occurred.

Searching for Solutions That Meet the Needs and Objectives of Both Sides

The success of integrative negotiation depends on the search for solutions that meet the needs and objectives of both sides. In this process, negotiators must be firm but flexible—firm about their primary interests and needs, but flexible about how these needs and interests are met (Fisher, Ury, and Patton, 1991; Pruitt and Rubin, 1986). When the parties are used to taking a combative, competitive orientation toward each other, they are generally concerned only with their own objectives. In such a competitive interaction, a low level of concern for the other's objectives may cause two forms of behavior. First, negotiators may work to ensure that what the other obtains does not take away from one's own accomplishments. Second, negotiators may attempt to block the other from obtaining his or her objectives because of a strong desire to win or to defeat the opponent. In contrast, successful integrative negotiation requires both negotiators not only to define and pursue their own goals, but also to be mindful of the other's goals and to search for solutions that satisfy both sides. Outcomes are measured by the degree to which they meet both negotiators' goals. They are not measured by determining whether one party is doing better than the other. If the objective of one party is simply to get more than the other, successful integrative negotiation is very difficult; if both strive to get more than the other, integrative negotiation may be impossible.

In summary, integrative negotiation requires a process fundamentally different than distributive bargaining. Negotiators must attempt to probe below the surface of the other party's position to discover his or her underlying needs. They must create a free and open flow of information and use their desire to satisfy both sides as a guide to structure their dialogue. If negotiators do not have this perspective—if they approach the problem and their "opponent" in win–lose terms—integrative negotiation cannot occur.

Key Steps in the Integrative Negotiation Process

There are four major steps in the integrative negotiation process: (1) identify and define the problem, (2) understand the problem and bring interests and needs to the surface, (3) generate alternative solutions to the problem, and (4) evaluate those alternatives and select among them. The first three steps of the integrative negotiation process are important for *creating value*. To work together to create value, negotiators need to understand the problem, identify the interests and needs of both parties, and generate alternative solutions. The fourth step of the integrative negotiation process, the evaluation and selection of alternatives, involves *claiming value*. Claiming value involves many of the distributive bargaining skills that were discussed in Chapter 2.

The relationship between creating and claiming value is shown graphically in Figure 3.1. The goal of creating value is to push the potential negotiation solutions toward the upper-right-hand side of Figure 3.1. When this is done to the fullest extent possible, the line is called the *Pareto efficient frontier,* and it contains a point where "there is no agreement that would make any party better off without decreasing the outcomes to any other party" (Neale and Bazerman, 1991, p. 23). One way to conceptualize integrative negotiation is that it is the process of identifying Pareto efficient solutions.

The graph shows that there are several possible solutions in a negotiation, in this case between a buyer and a seller. The first three steps to integrative negotiation aim to ensure that negotiators do not agree to solutions that are below the Pareto efficient frontier because these solutions are suboptimal for both negotiators. The fourth step, choosing a solution or claiming value, uses some of the same skills as distributive bargaining. The transition from creating to claiming value in an integrative negotiation must be managed carefully and is discussed in more detail later in this chapter.

FIGURE 3.1 | Creating and Claiming Value and the Pareto Efficient Frontier

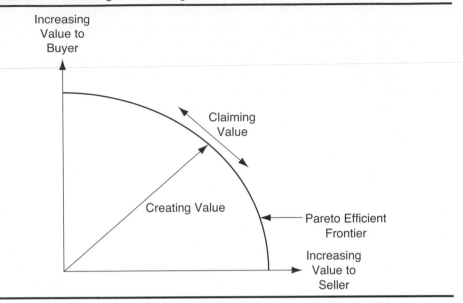

It is important that processes to create value precede those to claim value for two reasons: (1) the creating-value process is more effective when it is done collaboratively and without a focus on who gets what and (2) because claiming value involves distributive bargaining processes, it may derail the focus on creating value and may even harm the relationship unless it is introduced effectively.

Identify and Define the Problem

The problem identification step is often the most difficult one, and it is even more challenging when several parties are involved. Consider the following example: a large electronics plant experienced serious difficulty with a product as it moved from the subassembly department to the final assembly department. Various pins and fittings that held part of the product in place were getting bent and distorted. When this happened, the unit would be laid aside as a reject. At the end of the month, the rejects would be returned to the subassembly department to be reworked, often arriving just when workers were under pressure to meet end-of-the-month schedules and were also low on parts. As a result, the reworking effort had to be done in a rush and on overtime. The extra cost of overtime did not fit into the standard cost allocation system. The manager of the subassembly department did not want the costs allocated to his department. The manager of the final assembly department insisted that she should not pay the additional cost; she argued that the subassembly department should bear the cost because its poor work caused the problem. The subassembly department manager countered that the parts were in good condition when they left his area and that it was the poor workmanship in the final assembly area that created the damage. The immediate costs were relatively small. What really concerned both managers was setting a long-term precedent for handling rejects and for paying the costs.

Eventually an integrative solution was reached. During any given month, the subassembly department had some short slack-time periods. The managers arranged for the final assembly department to return damaged products in small batches during those slack periods. It also became clear that many people in the final assembly department did not fully understand the parts they were handling, which may have contributed to some of the damage. These workers were temporarily transferred to the subassembly department during assembly department slack periods to learn more about subassembly and to process some of the rush orders in that department.

This example captures several key aspects of the problem definition process (see Filley, 1975, and Shea, 1983, for fuller treatments of these points). The problem definition process is critical for integrative negotiation because it sets broad parameters regarding what the negotiation is about and provides an initial framework for approaching the discussion. It is important that this framework is comprehensive enough to capture the complexities inherent in the situation, while not making the situation appear more complex than it actually is.

Define the Problem in a Way That Is Mutually Acceptable to Both Sides   Ideally, parties should enter the integrative negotiation process with few preconceptions about the solution and with open minds about each other's needs. As a problem is defined jointly, it should accurately reflect both parties' needs and priorities. Unfortunately, this often does not occur. An understandable and widely held concern about integrative negotiation is that during the problem definition process, the other party will manipulate information to state the problem to his or her own advantage. For positive problem solving to occur, both parties must be committed to stating the problem in neutral terms. The problem statement must be acceptable to both sides and not worded so that it lays blame or favors the preferences or priorities of one side over the other. The parties may be required to revise the problem statement several times until they agree on its wording. It is critical to note that problem definition is, and should be, separate from any effort to generate or choose alternatives. Problems must be defined clearly at this stage, if only to accomplish an initial structure within which parties agree to disagree, albeit on a common, distinct issue.

State the Problem with an Eye toward Practicality and Comprehensiveness   The major focus of an integrative agreement is to solve the core problem(s). Anything that distracts from this focus should be removed or streamlined to ensure that this objective is achieved. As a result, one might argue that problem statements should be as clear as possible. Yet if the problem is complex and multifaceted, and the statement of the problem does not reflect that complexity, then efforts at problem solving will be incomplete. In fact, if the problem is complex, the parties may not even be able to agree on a statement of the problem. The objective should be to state the problem as succinctly as possible while at the same time ensuring that the most important dimensions and elements are included in the definition. This approach is in stark contrast to the distributive bargaining process (see Chapter 2), in which parties may enhance their positions by bringing in a large number of secondary issues and concerns in order to trade these items off during the hard-bargaining phase. If there are several issues in an integrative negotiation, the parties may want to clearly identify the link among them and decide whether they will be approached as separate problems that may be packaged together later, or as one larger problem.

State the Problem as a Goal and Identify the Obstacles to Attaining This Goal   The parties should define the problem as a specific goal to be attained rather than as a solution process. That is, they should concentrate on what they want to achieve rather than how they are going to achieve it. They should then proceed to specify what obstacles must be overcome for the goal to be attained. In the previous example, the goal might have been "to minimize the number of rejects." A clearer and more explicit definition would be "to cut the number of rejects in half." After defining the goal, the parties should specify what they need to know about how the product is made, how defects occur, what must be done to repair the defects, and so on. One key issue is whether the obstacles specified can be changed or corrected by negotiating parties. If the parties cannot address the obstacles effectively, given limited time or other resources, the obstacles then become boundary markers for the overall negotiation. A clear understanding of which obstacles are addressable and which are not can be just as critical to realistic integrative negotiation as an explicit awareness of what is negotiable and what is not.

Depersonalize the Problem   When parties are engaged in conflict, they tend to become evaluative and judgmental. They view their own actions, strategies, and preferences in a positive light and the other party's actions, strategies, and preferences in a negative light. Such evaluative judgments can interfere with clear and dispassionate thinking. (See Chapters 17 and 18 for a discussion of depersonalizing the issues.) Telling the other party that "Your point of view is wrong and mine is right" inhibits integrative negotiating because you cannot attack the problem without attacking the other negotiator. In contrast, depersonalizing the definition of the problem—stating, for example, "We have different viewpoints on this problem"—allows both sides to approach the issue as a problem external to the individuals rather than as a problem that belongs to one party only. Another way to say this is "I respect that you have constraints and a way of looking at this problem that may be different than mine. I ask that you recognize that I do as well."

Separate the Problem Definition from the Search for Solutions   Finally, it is important not to jump to solutions until the problem is fully defined. In distributive bargaining, negotiators are encouraged to state the problem in terms of their preferred solution and to make concessions based on this statement. In contrast, parties engaged in integrative negotiation should avoid stating solutions that favor one side or the other until they have fully defined the problem and examined as many alternative solutions as possible.

Instead of premature solutions, negotiators should develop standards by which potential solutions will be judged for how well they fit. These standards can be created by asking interested parties questions such as the following:

- How will we know the problem has been solved?
- How will we know that our goal has been attained?
- How would a neutral third party know that our dispute has been settled?
- Is there any legitimate interest or position that remains unaddressed by our outcome?
- Is there any legitimate interest or position that has been disenfranchised by our outcome?

Developing standards in this way and using them as measures for evaluating alternatives will help negotiators avoid a single-minded, tunnel-vision approach and allow them to differentiate a particular favorite alternative from one that may be less favorable individually but that will accomplish a collaborative, integrative resolution.

Understand the Problem Fully—Identify Interests and Needs

Many writers on negotiation—most particularly, Roger Fisher, William Ury, and Bruce Patton in their popular book, *Getting to Yes* (1991)—have stressed that a key to achieving an integrative agreement is the ability of the parties to understand and satisfy each other's *interests*. Identifying interests is a critical step in the integrative negotiation process. Interests are the underlying concerns, needs, desires, or fears that motivate a negotiator to take a particular position. Fisher, Ury, and Patton explain that while negotiators may have difficulty satisfying each other's specific positions, an understanding of the underlying interests may permit them to invent solutions that meet each other's interests. In this section, we will first define interests more completely and then discuss how understanding them is critical to effective integrative negotiation.

This example reveals the essence of the difference between interests and positions:

> Consider the story of two men quarreling in a library. One wants the window open and the other wants it closed. They bicker back and forth about how much to leave it open: a crack, halfway, three-quarters of the way. No solution satisfied them both. Enter the librarian. She asks one why he wants the window open. "To get some fresh air." She asks the other why he wants it closed. "To avoid the draft." After thinking a minute, she opens wide a window in the next room, bringing in fresh air without a draft. (Fisher, Ury, and Patton, 1991, p. 40; originally told by Follett, 1940)

This is a classic example of negotiating over positions and failing to understand underlying interests. The positions are "window open" and "window closed." If they continue to pursue positional bargaining, the set of possible outcomes can include only a victory for the one who wants the window open, a victory for the one who wants it shut, or some compromise in which neither gets what he wants. Note that a compromise here is more a form of lose–lose than win–win for these bargainers because one party believes he won't get enough fresh air with the window partially open and the other believes that any opening is unsatisfactory. The librarian's questions transform the dispute by focusing on *why* each man wants the window open or closed: to get fresh air, to avoid a draft. Understanding these interests enables the librarian to invent a solution that meets the interests of both sides—a solution that was not at all apparent when the two men were arguing over their positions.

In this description, the key word is *why*—why they want what they want. When two parties begin negotiation, they usually expose their position or demands. In distributive bargaining, negotiators trade positions back and forth, attempting to achieve a settlement as close to their targets as possible. However, in integrative negotiation, both negotiators need to pursue the other's thinking and logic to determine the factors that motivated them to arrive at their goals. The presumption is that if both parties understand the motivating factors for the other, they may recognize possible compatibilities in interests that permit them to invent new options that both will endorse. Consider the following dialogue between a company recruiter and a job applicant over starting salary:

RECRUITER: What were you thinking about as a starting salary?

APPLICANT: I would like $40,000.

RECRUITER: We can only offer $35,000.

APPLICANT: That's not acceptable.

Thus far, the parties have only exposed their positions. They are $5,000 apart. Moreover, the applicant may be afraid to bargain positionally with the recruiter, whereas the recruiter may be afraid that the applicant—whom she very much wants to hire—will walk out. Now let us extend their dialogue to help them focus on interests.

RECRUITER: $40,000 is a problem for our company. Can you tell me why you decided you wanted $40,000?

APPLICANT: Well, I have lots of education loans to pay off, and I will need to pay for a few more courses to finish my degree. I can't really afford to pay these bills and live comfortably for less than $40,000.

RECRUITER: Our company has a program to help new employees refinance their education loans. In addition, we also have a program to provide tuition assistance for new courses if the courses you need to take are related to your job. Would these programs help you with your problem?

APPLICANT: Yes!

Bringing the applicant's interests—paying off education loans and future education costs—to the surface allows the recruiter to offer a financial package that meets the needs of both the company and the applicant. Similarly, the applicant might have asked why the company could pay only $35,000 and discovered that it was company policy not to offer more than this to any applicant with the same qualifications. However, the question might also have revealed that the company can pay performance bonuses and would be willing to review the salary after six months. Thus, the applicant may well make $40,000 by the end of the first year and so have her financial goal met.

Types of Interests   Lax and Sebenius (1986) have suggested that several types of interests may be at stake in a negotiation and that each type may be intrinsic (the parties value it in and of itself) or instrumental (the parties value it because it helps them derive other outcomes in the future).

Substantive interests are related to focal issues that are under negotiation—economic and financial issues such as price or rate, or the substance of a negotiation such as the division of resources (like the tangible issues discussed in Chapter 1). These interests may be intrinsic or instrumental or both; we may want something because it is intrinsically satisfying to us and/or we may want something because it helps us achieve a long-range goal. Thus, the job applicant may want $40,000 both because the salary affirms her intrinsic sense of personal worth in the marketplace and because it instrumentally contributes toward paying off her education loans.

Process interests are related to *how* the negotiation unfolds. One party may pursue distributive bargaining because he enjoys the competitive game of wits that comes from nose-to-nose, hard-line bargaining. Another party may enjoy negotiating because she believes she has not been consulted in the past and wants to have some say in how a key problem is resolved. In the latter case, the negotiator may find the issues under discussion less important than the opportunity to voice her opinions.[2] Process interests can also be both intrinsic and instrumental. Having a voice may be intrinsically important to a group—it allows them to affirm their legitimacy and worth and highlights the key role they play in the organization; it can also be instrumentally important, in that if they are successful in gaining voice in this negotiation, they may be able to demonstrate that they should be invited back to negotiate other related issues in the future.

Relationship interests indicate that one or both parties value their relationship with each other and do not want to take actions that will damage it. Intrinsic relationship interests exist when the parties value the relationship both for its existence and for the pleasure or fulfillment that sustaining it creates. Instrumental relationship interests exist when the parties derive substantive benefits from the relationship and do not wish to endanger future benefits by souring it.

Finally, Lax and Sebenius (1986) point out that the parties may have *interests in principle*. Certain principles—concerning what is fair, what is right, what is acceptable, what is ethical, or what has been done in the past and should be done in the future—may be deeply held by the parties and serve as the dominant guides to their action. These principles often involve intangible factors (see Chapter 1). Interests in principles can also be intrinsic (valued because of their inherent worth) or instrumental (valued because they can be applied to a variety of future situations and scenarios).

Bringing interests in principles to the surface will lead negotiators to discuss explicitly the principles at stake and invent solutions consistent with them. For example, suppose three students who are also good friends collaborate on an essay, enter it in a competition, and win a prize of $300. The issue is how to split the prize money. One obvious way to split the prize is for each to take $100. But two of the students contributed equally, and together they did 90 percent of the work, so if they split it based on what they each contributed, the two hardworking students would get $135 each and the third student would get $30. The students may also decide, however, that it is not worth fighting over the workload, that they don't want to alienate their third friend, or that the difference in money is trivial—and so simply decide to split the prize into $100 shares after all. Only by discussing the interests at stake—principles about what is fair in this situation and about their relationship—can they arrive at a solution that divides the prize, minimizes animosity, and maintains their relationship.

Some Observations on Interests   We have several observations about interests and types of interests in negotiation:

1. *There is almost always more than one type of interest underlying a negotiation.* Parties will often have more than substantive interests about the issues (Clyman and Tripp, 2000). They can also care deeply about the process, the relationship, or the principles at stake. Note that interests in principles effectively cut across substantive, procedural, and relationship interests as well, so the categories are not exclusive.

2. *Parties can have different types of interests at stake.* One party may care deeply about the specific issues under discussion while the other cares about how the issues are resolved—questions of principle or process. Bringing these different interests to the surface may enable the parties to see that they care about very different things and that there is a need to invent solutions that address the interests of both negotiators.

3. *Interests often stem from deeply rooted human needs or values.* Several authors have suggested that frameworks for understanding basic human needs and values are helpful for understanding interests (Holaday, 2002; Nierenberg, 1976). According to these frameworks, needs are hierarchical, and satisfaction of the basic or lower order needs will be more important in negotiation than that of higher order needs. For example, Nierenberg (1976) proposed a need theory of negotiation based on Maslow's well-known hierarchy of needs. In this hierarchy, basic physiological and safety (security) needs will take precedence over higher order needs such as recognition, respect, affirmation, and self-actualization. Similarly, Burton (1984) has suggested that the intensity of many international disputes reflects deep underlying needs for security, protection of ethnic and national identity, and other such fundamental needs.

4. *Interests can change.* Like positions on issues, interests can change over time. What was important to the parties last week—or even 20 minutes ago—may not be important now. Interaction between the parties can put some interests to rest, but it may raise others. Negotiators must constantly be attentive to changes in their own interests and the interests of the other side. When one party begins speaking about things in a different way—when the language or emphasis changes—the other party should look for a change in interests.

5. *Surfacing interests.* There are numerous ways to surface interests. Sometimes people are not even sure about their own interests. Negotiators should not only ask themselves "What do I want from this negotiation?" but also "Why do I want that?" "Why is that important to me?" "What will achieving that help me do?" and "What will happen if I don't achieve my objective?" Listening to your own inner voices—fears, aspirations, hopes, desires—is important in order to bring your own interests to the surface.

The same dialogue is essential in clarifying the other party's interests. Asking probing questions and paying careful attention to the other party's language, emotions, and nonverbal behavior are essential keys to the process (see Chapters 5 and 6). You might also want to distinguish between intrinsic interests—which need to be satisfied as ends in themselves—and instrumental interests—which help one get other outcomes. In both cases, once these interests are understood, it may be possible to invent a variety of ways to address them. The result is a mutually satisfactory solution.

6. *Surfacing interests is not always easy or to one's best advantage.* Critics of the "interests approach" to negotiation have identified the difficulty of defining interests and taking them into consideration. Provis (1996) suggests that it is often difficult to define interests and that trying to focus on interests alone often oversimplifies or conceals the real dynamics of a conflict. In some cases parties do not pursue their own best objective interests but instead focus on one or more subjective interest(s), which may mislead the other party (Provis, 1996). Thus, a car buyer may prefer a fast, flashy car (his subjective interest) even though his objective interest is to buy a safe, conservative one.

Most people see negotiation as a game in which the gains of one come at the expense of another. Winning means getting 6 pieces from a 10-piece pie. But negotiation has the potential to be a win–win process by which both parties cooperate to create a bigger, better-tasting pie. The basic principle of win–win negotiating is that there is always a bigger, better deal. Only after searching and finding that deal do they worry about how to share it. These avenues might be explored in a typical purchasing contract negotiation:

Taxes. It's safe to assume that the parties to a negotiation have different tax needs. Accountants might be able to point out some unseen opportunities (particularly in foreign transactions).

Payment terms. Some sellers need quick payment; others might prefer a deferred payment (for tax or other reasons). There are many win–win variations.

Specifications. A better deal may be possible if changes can be made to balance the buyer's end-use requirements against the seller's specific production capabilities.

Transportation. Transportation costs can often be reduced at no expense to either party. Perhaps the buyer's empty trucks will pass the seller's facility.

Or maybe the seller has access to low bulk rates.

Delivery date or performance specifications. The reality is this: a buyer's delivery requirements never represent the seller's optimum production economics.

Quantity. One of the best win–win strategies I know is to close a price gap by changing quantity.

Processes. In my experience, the surest path to finding a better way to do anything is to study the detailed production and paperwork processes.

Risk and contract type. All business involves risk. Incentives might be used to balance the seller's risk with potential for earning greater profit.

Like successful entrepreneurs everywhere, win–win negotiators find hidden opportunities in what each could do for the other. Win–win raises the stakes in a negotiation. It raises the level and content of the relationship between the bargainers. It also reduces the tensions inherent in bargaining. There are few phrases that more quickly capture the attention of the other party than, "Let's find a better deal for both of us."

Source: Chester L. Karrass, "The Art of Win–Win Negotiations," *Purchasing,* May 6, 1999, p. 28.

Generate Alternative Solutions

The search for alternatives is the creative phase of integrative negotiation. Once the parties have agreed on a common definition of the problem and understood each other's interests, they need to generate a variety of alternative solutions. The objective is to create a list of options or possible solutions to the problem; evaluating and selecting from among those options will be their task in the final phase.

Several techniques have been suggested to help negotiators generate alternative solutions. These techniques fall into two general categories. The first requires the negotiators to redefine, recast, or reframe the problem (or problem set) to create win–win alternatives out of what earlier appeared to be a win–lose problem (see Box 3.2). The second takes the problem as given and creates a long list of options from which the parties can choose. In integrative negotiation over a complex problem, both types of techniques may be used and even intertwined.

Inventing Options: Generating Alternative Solutions by Redefining the Problem or Problem Set The techniques in this category call for the parties to define their underlying needs and to develop alternatives to meet them.

Peter Carnevale has recently created an Agreement Circumplex that classifies potential agreements into four main types, each with two subtypes (see Figure 3.2). There are four important dimensions underlying this model. Each of these dimensions is discussed here, and the strategies consistent with them are identified. A more complex discussion of the strategies and an extended example to highlight each is in the next section.

1. **Position Accommodation vs. Position Achievement**
   Positions are achieved when each party gets exactly what they wanted in their initial demand. Strategies that achieve positions include expanding the pie and modifying the resource pie. This is in contrast to position accommodation when the parties receive a portion of their initial demand.

FIGURE 3.2 | The Agreement Circumplex

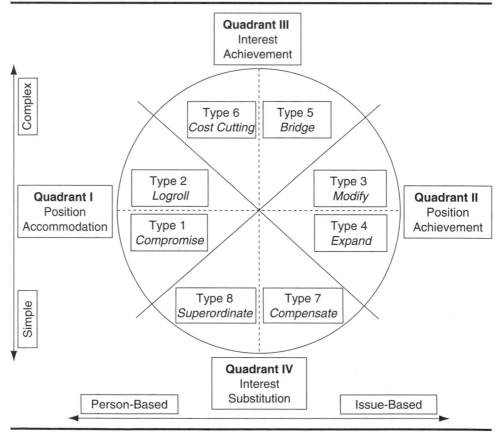

Source: P. J. D. Carnevale, 2006.

2. **Achieve Underlying Interests vs. Substitute Underlying Interests**
   When underlying interests are achieved, the negotiators' interests are completely met. Strategies to meet underlying interests include bridging and cost cutting. Underlying interests may also be substituted, modified, or changed. Nonspecific compensation and superordination are two strategies that change whether or not a negotiator's interests are met or modified in some way.

3. **Simple vs. Complex**
   Some negotiation situations are quite simple in nature, such as a two- or three-item agreement to purchase items from a manufacturer. Other situations can be extremely complex, such as comprehensive lease agreements that cover multiple locations, sizes, and types of property. The strategies at the bottom of the Agreement Circumplex are more suited to simple situations, while the strategies at the top are more appropriate for more complex situations.

4. **Person-based vs. Issue-based**
   Person-based strategies involve having negotiators making concessions and changing positions such that an agreement is reached through modifying positions on the issues under discussion. Issue-based strategies modify the issues under discussion to fit them to the negotiators needs and desires. Person-based strategies are on the left side of the Agreement Circumplex, while issue-based strategies are on the right side.

Carnevale presents eight different methods for achieving integrative agreements in the Circumplex, which we discuss next.[3] Each method refocuses the issues under discussion and requires progressively more information about the other side's true needs. Solutions move from simpler, distributive agreements to more complex and comprehensive, integrative ones, and there are several paths to finding joint gain (Olekalns, 2002).

Each approach will be illustrated by the example of Samantha and Emma, two partners in a successful enterprise called Advanced Management Consulting, that employs eight other nonpartner consultants. The partners are deciding where to locate their new office; half their clients are downtown and half are in the suburbs. There are two possible locations that they are considering leasing. Samantha prefers the downtown location. It has less floor space but is a more prestigious address. While its offices are smaller, its location is equidistant from where both partners live. Emma prefers the location in the suburbs. It has more floor space and larger offices, and it is newer. It is also located closer to Emma's house, but farther from Samantha's.

Compromise (Position Accommodation)   A compromise solution that would not further the interests of either Samantha or Emma would be to stay in their current location and to maintain the status quo. Compromises are not considered to be a good integration strategy except for circumstances where parties are very entrenched and it is unlikely that a more comprehensive agreement is possible.

Logroll (Position Accommodation)   Successful logrolling requires the parties to find more than one issue in conflict and to have different priorities for those issues (Tajima and Fraser, 2001). The parties then agree to trade off among these issues so that one party achieves a highly preferred outcome on the first issue and the other person achieves a highly preferred outcome on the second issue. If the parties do in fact have different preferences on different issues and each party gets his or her most preferred outcome on a high-priority issue, then each should receive more and the joint outcomes should be higher (Moran and Ritov, 2002). For instance, the Advanced Management Consulting could lease the downtown location and give Emma the bigger office. Samantha would get her preferred location, which is more important to her, and Emma would receive better working space, which is more important to her.

Logrolling is frequently done by trial and error—as part of the process of experimenting with various packages of offers that will satisfy everyone involved. The parties must first establish which issues are at stake and then decide their individual priorities on these issues. If there are already at least two issues on the table, then any combination of two or more issues may be suitable for logrolling. Research suggests that negotiators reach better agreements as the number of issues being negotiated increases (Naquin, 2002). Negotiator satisfaction may be less when more issues are negotiated, however, because negotiators believe that they could have done better on one or more issues. (Negotiator cognition and satisfaction is discussed in more detail in Chapter 5.) If it appears initially that only one issue is at stake, the parties may need to engage in "unbundling" or "unlinking," which is the process of separating a single issue into two or more issues so that the logrolling may begin (Lax and Sebenius, 1986; Pruitt, 1981). Additional issues of concern may also be generated through the brainstorming processes described later.

Finally, research by Mannix, Tinsley and Bazerman (1995) suggests that logrolling is less likely in a series of negotiations when the negotiator believes that there is a higher probability that the negotiator representing the other firm will be changed in someone else.

Modifying the Resource Pie (Position Achievement)   While expanding the resource pie may be attractive, it does not always work because the environment may not be plentiful enough. For instance, the Advanced Management Consulting may not have enough demand for its services to have two offices. A related approach is to modify the resource pie. For instance, Advanced Management Consulting could start a new service and offer information technology (IT) consulting or Web-based marketing consulting in addition to its traditional business consulting. In this case the resource pie is modified in a way to support opening offices both downtown and in the suburbs.

Expand the Pie (Position Achievement)   Many negotiations begin with a shortage of resources, and it is not possible for both sides to satisfy their interests or obtain their objectives under the current conditions. A simple solution is to add resources—expand the pie—in such a way that both sides can achieve their objectives. For instance, the Advanced Management Consulting could lease offices both downtown and in the suburbs to serve both sets of its clients. A projected expansion of the business could pay for both leases. In expanding the pie, one party requires no information about the other party except her interests; it is a simple way to solve resource shortage problems. In addition, the approach assumes that simply enlarging the resources will solve the problem. Thus, leasing both locations would be a very satisfactory solution if Samantha and Emma liked both locations and wanted to expand their business. However, expanding the pie would not be a satisfactory solution if their disagreement was based on other grounds—if, for example, they had different visions about the future of the firm—or if the whole firm had to gather for meetings frequently. In addition, to the extent that the negotiation increases the costs of a person or organization not directly involved in the negotiation (e.g., the employees in this example), the solution may be integrative for the negotiators but problematic for other stakeholders (Gillespie and Bazerman, 1997).

Find a Bridge Solution (Interest Achievement)   When the parties are able to invent new options that meet all their respective needs they have created a bridge solution. For instance, the Advanced Management Consulting could decide to expand the number of partners in the firm and lease a larger space downtown, with new office furniture for everyone and a prestigious street address.

Successful bridging requires a fundamental reformulation of the problem so that the parties are not discussing positions but, rather, they are disclosing sufficient information to discover their interests and needs and then inventing options that will satisfy those needs (Butler, 1996). Bridging solutions do not always remedy all concerns. Emma may not enjoy the commute and Samantha may not be convinced about growing the firm, but both have agreed that working together is important to them, and they have worked to invent a solution that meets their most important needs. If negotiators fundamentally commit themselves to a win–win negotiation, bridging solutions are likely to be highly satisfactory to both sides.

Cut the Costs for Compliance (Interest Achievement)   Through cost cutting, one party achieves her objectives and the other's costs are minimized if she agrees to go along. For instance, the Advanced Management Consulting could decide to lease in the suburbs and provide Samantha with a travel subsidy, a new company car, and a reserved parking space. In this case Emma gets her preferred location, while Samantha's costs for agreeing to the new office location are reduced.

Unlike nonspecific compensation, where the compensated party simply receives something for agreeing, cost cutting is designed to minimize the other party's costs for agreeing to a specific solution. The technique is more sophisticated than logrolling or nonspecific compensation because it requires a more intimate knowledge of the other party's real needs and preferences (the party's interests, what really matters to him, how his needs can be specifically met).

Nonspecific Compensation (Interest Substitution)   Another way to generate alternatives is to allow one person to obtain his objectives and compensate the other person for accommodating his interests. The compensation may be unrelated to the substantive negotiation, but the party who receives it nevertheless views it as adequate for agreeing to the other party's preferences. Such compensation is nonspecific because it is not directly related to the substantive issues being discussed. For instance, the Advanced Management Consulting could decide to lease in the suburbs and give Samantha all new office furniture. In this case, Emma gets her preferred location, while Samantha receives new office furniture as nonspecific compensation for agreeing to the new office location.

For nonspecific compensation to work, the person doing the compensating needs to know what is valuable to the other person and how seriously she is inconvenienced (i.e., how much compensation is needed to make her feel satisfied). Emma might need to test several different offers (types and amounts of compensation) to find out how much it will take to satisfy Samantha. This discovery process can turn into a distributive bargaining situation, as Samantha may choose to set very high demands as the price for locating in the suburbs while Emma tries to minimize the compensation she will pay.

Superordination (Interest Substitution)   Superordination solutions occur when "the differences in interest that gave rise to the conflict are superseded or replaced by other interests" (Carnevale, 2006, p. 426). For instance, after extensive discussion about the office location Samantha may discover that she would prefer to follow her dream of becoming an artist and become a silent partner in the business. At this point, the office location negotiation stops and Emma chooses how she would like to proceed in the new business model.

The successful pursuit of these eight strategies requires a meaningful exchange of information between the parties. The parties must either volunteer information or ask each other questions that will generate sufficient information to reveal win–win options. We present a series of refocusing questions that may reveal these possibilities in Table 3.1 (Pruitt and Carnevale, 1993; Pruitt and Rubin, 1986).

TABLE 3.1 | Refocusing Questions to Reveal Win–Win Options

Expanding or Modifying the Pie
1.   How can both parties get what they want?
2.   Is there a resource shortage?
3.   How can resources be expanded to meet the demands of both sides?

Logrolling
1.   What issues are of higher and lower priority to me?
2.   What issues are of higher and lower priority to the other negotiator?
3.   Are there any issues of high priority to me that are of low priority for the other negotiator, and vice versa?
4.   Can I "unbundle" an issue—that is, make one larger issue into two or more smaller ones that can then be logrolled?
5.   What are things that would be inexpensive for me to give and valuable for the other negotiator to get that might be used in logrolling?

Nonspecific Compensation
1.   What are the other negotiator's goals and values?
2.   What could I do that would make the other negotiator happy and simultaneously allow me to get my way on the key issue?
3.   What are things that would be inexpensive for me to give and valuable for the other negotiator to get that might be used as nonspecific compensation?

Cost Cutting
1.   What risks and costs does my proposal create for the other negotiator?
2.   What can I do to minimize the other negotiator's risks and costs so that he or she would be more willing to agree?

Bridging and Superordination
1.   What are the other negotiator's real underlying interests and needs?
2.   What are my own real underlying interests and needs?
3.   What are the higher and lower priorities for each of us in our underlying interests and needs?
4.   Can we invent a solution that meets the relative priorities, underlying interests, and needs of both negotiators?

NB: Compromise is not considered a win–win option.

Generating Alternative Solutions to the Problem as Given   In addition to the techniques mentioned earlier, there are several other approaches to generating alternative solutions. These approaches can be used by the negotiators themselves or by a number of other parties (constituencies, audiences, bystanders, etc.). Several of these approaches are commonly used in small groups. Groups are frequently better problem solvers than individuals, particularly because groups provide more perspectives and can invent a greater variety of ways to solve a problem. Groups should also adopt procedures for defining the problem, defining interests, and generating options, however, to prevent the group process from degenerating into a win–lose competition or a debating event.

Brainstorming   In brainstorming, small groups of people work to generate as many possible solutions to the problem as they can. Someone records the solutions, without comment, as they are identified. Participants are urged to be spontaneous, even impractical, and not to censor anyone's ideas (including their own). Moreover, participants are required not to discuss or evaluate any solution when it is proposed so they do not stop the free flow of new ideas. The success of brainstorming depends on the amount of intellectual stimulation that occurs as different ideas are generated. The following rules should be observed:

1.   *Avoid judging or evaluating solutions.* Creative solutions often come from ideas that initially seem wild and impractical, and criticism inhibits creative thinking. It is important to avoid judging solutions early, therefore, and no idea should be evaluated or eliminated until the group is finished generating options.

2.   *Separate the people from the problem.* Group discussion and brainstorming processes are often constrained because the parties take ownership of preferred solutions and alternatives (Filley, 1975; Fisher, Ury, and Patton, 1991; Walton and McKersie, 1965). Because competitive negotiators assume an offensive posture toward the other party, they are unlikely to see the merits of a suggested alternative that comes from that party or appears to favor that party's position. It is often not possible to attack the problem without attacking the person who owns it. For effective problem solving to occur, therefore, negotiators must concentrate on depersonalizing the problem and treating all possible solutions as equally viable, regardless of who initiated them. For example, collectively listing suggestions on a blackboard or flip chart will help parties depersonalize any particular idea and will allow participants to choose the solution that best solves the problem without regard to who originated it. Techniques for generating options that ensure anonymity may minimize the likelihood that interpersonal conflict will escalate.

3.   *Be exhaustive in the brainstorming process.* Often the best ideas come after a meeting is over or the problem is solved. Sometimes this happens because the parties were not persistent enough. Research has shown that when brainstormers work at the process for a long time, the best ideas are most likely to surface during the latter part of the activity. As Shea (1983) notes, "Generating a large number of ideas apparently increases the probability of developing superior ideas. Ideas, when expressed, tend to trigger other ideas. And since ideas can be built one upon the other, those that develop later in a session are often superior to those without refinement or elaboration. What difference does it make if a lot of impractical ideas are recorded? They can be evaluated and dismissed rapidly in the next step of the win–win process. The important thing is to ensure that few, if any, usable ideas are lost" (p. 57).

4. *Ask outsiders*. Often people who know nothing about the history of the negotiation, or even about the issues, can suggest options and possibilities that have not been considered. Outsiders can provide additional input to the list of alternatives, or they can help orchestrate the process and keep the parties on track.

Surveys   The disadvantage of brainstorming is that it does not solicit the ideas of those who are not present at the negotiation. A different approach is to distribute a written questionnaire to a large number of people, stating the problem and asking them to list all the possible solutions they can imagine. This process can be conducted in a short time. The liability, however, is that the parties cannot benefit from seeing and hearing each other's ideas, a key advantage of brainstorming.

Electronic Brainstorming   An innovative method for gathering ideas is to engage a professional facilitator and use electronic brainstorming (Gallupe and Cooper, 1993; Dennis and Reinicke, 2004). The facilitator uses a series of questions to guide input from participants who type their responses anonymously into a computer that displays them to the group in aggregate. The facilitator may then ask additional probing questions. Electronic brainstorming may be especially useful for integrative negotiations that involve multiple parties (see Chapter 13) or during preparation for integrative negotiations when there are disparate views within one's team (see Chapter 4 on preparation).

Section Summary

Our discussion of the two basic approaches to generating alternative solutions—generating options to the problem as given and generating options by redefining the problem—may give the impression that if negotiators simply invent enough different options, they will find a solution to solve their problem rather easily. Although identifying options sometimes leads to a solution, solutions are usually attained through hard work and pursuit of several related processes: information exchange, focusing on interests rather than positions, and firm flexibility (Fisher, Ury, and Patton, 1991; Pruitt, 1983). Information exchange allows parties to maximize the amount of information available. Focusing on interests allows parties to move beyond opening positions and demands to determine what the parties really want—what needs truly must be satisfied. Finally, firm flexibility allows parties to be firm with regard to what they want to achieve (i.e., interests) while remaining flexible on the means by which they achieve it. Firm flexibility recognizes that negotiators have one or two fundamental interests or principles, although a wide variety of positions, possible solutions, or secondary issues may get drawn into the negotiations. Thus, among the many viable alternatives that will satisfy a negotiator, the important ones directly address the top priorities. Negotiators need to be able to signal to the other side the positions on which they are firm and the positions on which they are willing to be flexible. Pruitt (1983) and Fisher, Ury, and Patton (1991) suggest several tactics to communicate firm flexibility to the other negotiator shown in Box 3.3.

1. Use competitive tactics to establish and defend basic interests rather than to demand a particular position or solution to the dispute. State what you want clearly.

2. Send signals of flexibility and concern about your willingness to address the other party's interests. Openly express concern for the other's welfare and "acknowledge their interests as part of the problem" (Fisher, Ury, and Patton, 1991, p. 55). In doing so, you communicate that you have your own interests at stake but are willing to try to address the other's as well.

3. Indicate a willingness to change your proposals if a way can be found to bridge both negotiators' interests.

4. Demonstrate problem-solving capacity. For example, use experts on a negotiating team or bring them in as consultants based on their expertise at generating new ideas.

5. Maintain open communication channels. Do not eliminate opportunities to communicate and work together, if only to demonstrate continually that you are willing to work with the other party.

6. Reaffirm what is most important to you through the use of clear statements—for example, "I need to attain this; this is a must; this cannot be touched or changed." These statements communicate to the other party that a particular interest is fundamental to you, but it does not necessarily mean that the other's interests can't be satisfied as well.

7. Reexamine any aspect of your interests that are clearly unacceptable to the other party and determine if they are still essential to you. It is rare that negotiators will find that they truly disagree on basic interests.

8. Separate and isolate contentious tactics from problem-solving behavior to manage the contentious behavior. This may be accomplished by clearly specifying a change in the negotiation process, by separating the two processes with a break or recess, or, in team negotiations, by having one party act contentiously and then having a second negotiator offer to engage in problem solving.[a]

---

[a] This last approach, called "good cop/bad cop" or "black hat/white hat," is also frequently used as a purely distributive bargaining tactic, as we discussed in Chapter 2. In this situation, however, separate the competitive from the collaborative elements of the process by changing the individuals who represent those tasks.

Evaluate and Select Alternatives

The fourth stage in the integrative negotiation process is to evaluate the alternatives generated during the previous phase and to select the best ones to implement. When the challenge is a reasonably simple one, the evaluation and selection steps may be effectively combined into a single step. For those uncomfortable with the integrative process, though, we suggest a close adherence to a series of distinct steps: definitions and standards, alternatives, evaluation, and selection. Following these distinct steps is also a good idea for those managing complex problems or a large number of alternative options. Negotiators will need to weigh or rank-order each option against clear criteria. If no option or set of options appears suitable and acceptable, this is a strong indication that the problem was not clearly defined *(return to definitions),* or that the standards developed earlier are not reasonable, relevant, and/or realistic *(return to standards).* Finally, the parties will need to engage in some form of decision-making process in which they debate the relative merits of each negotiator's preferred options and come to agreement on the best options. The following guidelines should be used in evaluating options and reaching a consensus.[4]

Narrow the Range of Solution Options   Examine the list of options generated and focus on those that one or more negotiators strongly support. This approach is more positive than allowing people to focus on negative, unacceptable criteria and options. Solutions that are not strongly advocated by at least one negotiator should be eliminated at this time.

Evaluate Solutions on the Basis of Quality, Standards, and Acceptability   Solutions should be judged on two major criteria: how good they are and how acceptable they will be to those who have to implement them. To the degree that parties can support their arguments with statements of hard fact, logical deduction, and appeals to rational criteria, their arguments will be more compelling in obtaining the support of others. Fisher, Ury, and Patton (1991) suggest that the parties appeal to *objective standards* for making decisions. Thus, the parties should search for precedents, industry standards, arbitration decisions, or other objectively fair outcomes and processes that can be used as benchmarks for legitimizing the fairness of the current settlement. These criteria may be different from what the negotiators judge to be most rational or the best solution. Negotiators have to be prepared to make trade-offs to ensure that the criteria of both quality and acceptability are met.

Agree to the Criteria in Advance of Evaluating Options   Negotiators should agree to the criteria for evaluating potential integrative solutions early in the process (Fisher, Ury, and Patton, 1991). Negotiators can use these criteria when they have to narrow the choice of options to a single alternative—for example, one candidate for a new job—or to select the option most likely to succeed. If the parties first debate criteria and determine which ones are most important, they will be able to decide on criteria independent of the consideration of any particular candidate or option. Then, when they consider the individual candidates or options, they will pick the best one based on these criteria, not on the individual preferences of one side or the other. If the parties agree, they may revise their criteria later to improve their choice, but they should do so only with the agreement of all negotiators. It is a good idea to check criteria periodically and determine whether each negotiator places the same priority on them as before.

Be Willing to Justify Personal Preferences   People often find it hard to explain why they like what they like or dislike what they dislike. When asked "Why do you like that?" the reply is often, "I don't know, I just do." Moreover, negotiators gain little by pressing opponents to justify themselves—doing so usually just makes them angry and defensive; they may feel that a simple statement of preference is not viewed as sufficient. For example, if the topic under negotiation is what to have for dinner, and one party states that she hates clam chowder, no amount of persuasive effort is likely to induce her to eat clam chowder. Yet personal preferences often have a deep-seated rationale—recall our discussion of how interests, values, and needs underlie positions. Inquiries about the other party's preferences may be an effort to probe behind a position and identify underlying interests and needs. If the other party responds defensively to a why question, the negotiator should explain that the intent is to probe for possible underlying interests that might facilitate a collaborative settlement rather than to challenge one's perspective.

Be Alert to the Influence of Intangibles in Selecting Options   One party may favor an option because it helps satisfy an intangible—gaining recognition, looking strong or tough to a constituency, feeling like a winner, and so on. Intangibles or principles can serve as strong interests for a negotiator. Intangibles can lead the negotiator to fight harder to attain a particular solution if that option satisfies both tangible and intangible needs. Some parties may be uncomfortable with discussing intangibles, or even be unaware of their nature and power in the negotiation process. It is useful to help the other party identify those intangibles and make them an open part of the evaluation process. The other party is likely to prefer options that satisfy those intangibles, and to the degree that you can accept them, agreeing to those options may be important concessions.

Use Subgroups to Evaluate Complex Options   Small groups may be particularly helpful when several complex options must be considered or when many people will be affected by the solution. For example, in a recent university collective agreement negotiation a team of management and faculty members formed a subgroup to examine numerous issues around benefits to be included in the next contract. Groups of six to eight people, composed of representatives from each faction, side, or subgroup, are able to work more effectively than large groups. Group processes in negotiation are discussed in more detail in Chapter 13.

Take Time Out to Cool Off   Even though the parties may have completed the hardest part of the process—generating a list of viable options—they may become upset if communication breaks down, they feel their preferences are not being acknowledged, or the other side pushes too hard for a particular option. If the parties become angry, they should take a break. They should make their dissatisfaction known and openly discuss the reasons for it. The parties should feel that they are back on an even emotional keel before continuing to evaluate options. Finally, they should work as hard as possible to keep discussions on the specifics of the proposals, not on the people advocating them. The parties should depersonalize the discussion as much as possible so that the options for settlement are not associated with the people who advocated them.

Explore Different Ways to Logroll   Earlier we discussed a variety of ways to invent options. The strategy of logrolling is effective not only in inventing options but also as a mechanism to combine options into negotiated packages. Neale and Bazerman (1991) identify a variety of approaches in addition to simply combining several issues into a package. Three of these relate to the matters of outcome, probabilities, and timing—in other words, *what* is to happen, the *likelihood* of it happening, and *when* it happens.

1. Explore Differences in Risk Preference   People have different tolerances for risk, and it may be possible to create a package that recognizes differences in risk preferences (Lax and Sebenius, 2002). For instance, suppose two entrepreneurs are discussing a future business venture. One has little to risk at the moment and everything to gain in the future; the other has a lot on the line now that he does not want to risk losing if the future is bad. If the entrepreneurs simply agree to split profits in the future, the one with a large amount of current risk may feel vulnerable. Logrolling around these interests can create a solution that protects one entrepreneur's current investment first while providing long-term profits for the other entrepreneur as well.

2. Explore Differences in Expectations   As with differences in risk, differences in expectations about the likelihood of future events can permit the parties to invent a solution that addresses the needs of both. For example, the entrepreneur with a lot to lose now may also have pessimistic expectations about the future of the joint venture, whereas the entrepreneur with little to lose may be more optimistic about it. The optimist may thus be willing to gamble more on the future profitability and payout, whereas the pessimist may be willing to settle for a smaller but more assured payment. It is also possible to use contingent contracts to manage different expectations about the future (Lax and Sebenius, 2002; Bazerman and Gillespie, 1999). Contingent contracts adjust as circumstances unfold. For instance, one can include changing oil prices into a contract and adjust delivery fees based on quarterly oil prices.

3. Explore Differences in Time Preferences   Negotiators may have different time preferences—one may be concerned about meeting short-term needs while the other may be interested in the long-term rewards of their relationship (Lax and Sebenius, 2002). Parties with short-term interests will need immediate gratification, whereas parties who look for long-term rewards may be willing to make immediate sacrifices to ensure a future payoff. Parties with different time preferences can invent solutions that address both their interests.

Keep Decisions Tentative and Conditional Until All Aspects of the Final Proposal Are Complete   Even though a clear consensus may emerge about the solution option(s) that will be selected, the parties should talk about the solution in conditional terms—a sort of *soft bundling.* Maintaining a tentative tone allows negotiators to suggest changes or revise the final package throughout this stage. Ideally, the integrative negotiation process should be open and flexible. Points agreed upon in earlier discussions are not firm until the entire package is determined. Parties should feel they are able to reopen an earlier option if circumstances in the discussion have changed; nothing should be considered final until everything is final. For instance, when buying a house recently, one of the authors of this text returned to an earlier discarded option and chose to renovate an older home rather than to pay more for an already renovated house.

Minimize Formality and Record Keeping until Final Agreements Are Closed   Strong integrative negotiators do not want to lock themselves into specific language or written agreements until they are close to an agreement. They want to make sure they will not be firmly held to any comments recorded in notes or transcripts. In general, the fewer the written records during the solution-generating phase, the better. In contrast, when the parties are close to agreement, one side should write down the terms of the agreement. This document may then be used as a single text, to be passed from party to party as often as necessary until all sides agree to the phrasing and wording of their agreement (Fisher, Ury, and Patton, 1991).

We strongly urge groups to avoid the apparent expediency of voting on final agreements, and encourage negotiations to continue until a consensus is reached. While voting closes the discussion, it can also create disenfranchisement of the losing party and make it more likely that "losers" will be less committed than "winners" to the implementation of the negotiated outcome.

Factors That Facilitate Successful Integrative Negotiation

We have stressed that successful integrative negotiation can occur if the parties are predisposed to finding a mutually acceptable joint solution. Many other factors contribute to a predisposition toward problem solving and a willingness to work together to find the best solution. These factors are also the preconditions necessary for more successful integrative negotiations. In this section, we will review in greater detail seven factors: (1) the presence of a common goal, (2) faith in one's own problem-solving ability, (3) a belief in the validity of the other party's position, (4) the motivation and commitment to work together, (5) trust, (6) clear and accurate communication, and (7) an understanding of the dynamics of integrative negotiation.

Some Common Objective or Goal

When the parties believe they are likely to benefit more from working together than from competing or working separately, the situation offers greater potential for successful integrative negotiation. Three types of goals—common, shared, and joint—may facilitate the development of integrative agreements.

A *common goal* is one that all parties share equally, each one benefiting in a way that would not be possible if they did not work together. A town government and an industrial manufacturing plant may debate the amount of taxes the plant owes, but they are more likely to work together if the common goal is to keep the plant open and employ half the town's workforce.

A *shared goal* is one that both parties work toward but that benefits each party differently. For example, partners can work together in a business but not divide the profits equally. One may receive a larger share of the profit because he or she contributed more experience or capital investment. Inherent in the idea of a shared goal is that parties will work together to achieve some output that will be divided among them. The same result can also come from cost cutting, by which the parties can earn the same outcome as before by working together, but with less effort, expense, or risk. This is often described as an "expandable pie" in contrast to a "fixed pie" (see Chapter 5).

A *joint goal* is one that involves individuals with different personal goals agreeing to combine them in a collective effort. For example, people joining a political campaign can have different goals: one wants to satisfy personal ambition to hold public office, another wants to serve the community, and yet another wants to benefit from policies that will be implemented under the new administration. All will unite around the joint goal of helping the new administration get elected.

The key element of an integrative negotiation situation is the belief that all sides can benefit. Whether the sides attain the same outcome or different outcomes, all sides must believe that they will be better off by working in cooperation than by working independently or competing.

Faith in One's Problem-Solving Ability

Parties who believe they can work together are more likely to be able to do so. Those who do not share this belief in themselves and others are less willing to invest the time and energy in the potential payoffs of a collaborative relationship, and they are more likely to assume a contending or accommodating approach to negotiation. If a negotiator has expertise in the focal problem area this strengthens her understanding of the problem's complexity, nuances, and possible solutions. Neale and Northcraft (1986) demonstrated in a real estate problem that expert negotiators—corporate real estate executives—achieved significantly better integrative agreements than amateurs did. Expertise increases both the negotiator's knowledge base and his or her self-confidence, both of which are necessary to approach the problem at hand with an open mind. Similarly, direct experience in negotiation increases the negotiator's sophistication in understanding the bargaining process and approaching it more creatively (Thompson, 1990a). Finally, there is also evidence that knowledge of integrative tactics leads to an increase in integrative behavior (Weingart, Prietula, Hyder, and Genovese, 1999). Taken together, these results suggest that a faith in one's ability to negotiate integratively is positively related to successful integrative negotiations.

A Belief in the Validity of One's Own Position and the Other's Perspective

In distributive bargaining, negotiators invest time and energy inflating and justifying the value of their own point of view and debunking the value and importance of the other's perspective. In contrast, integrative negotiation requires negotiators to accept both their own and the other's attitudes, interests, and desires as valid (Fisher, Ury, and Patton, 1991). First, one must believe in the validity of your own perspective—that what you believe is worth fighting for and should not be compromised. Kemp and Smith (1994) found that negotiators who were firmer about insisting that their own point of view become incorporated into the group solution achieved more integrative agreements than those who were less firm. But one must also accept the validity of the other party's perspective. If one challenges the other party's views, he or she may become angry, defensive, and unproductive in the problem-solving process. The purpose of integrative negotiation is not to question or challenge the other's viewpoint, but to incorporate it into the definition of the problem and to attend to it as the parties search for mutually acceptable alternatives. In addition, the other party's views should be valued no less or more than the negotiator's own position and viewpoint. Kemp and Smith also found that parties who were able to take the perspective of the other appeared to make better agreements than those who were less able to do so. Believing in the validity of the other negotiator's perspective does not mean empathizing with the other party. In fact, there is evidence that negotiators with high empathy for the other party may increase the size of the joint outcomes but receive less of the larger pie than less empathic negotiators (Foo, Elfenbein, Tan, and Aik, 2004; Nelson and Wheeler, 2004).

The Motivation and Commitment to Work Together

For integrative negotiation to succeed, the parties must be motivated to collaborate rather than to compete. They need to be committed to reaching a goal that benefits both of them rather than to pursuing only their own ends. They should adopt interpersonal styles that are more congenial than combative, more open and trusting than evasive and defensive, more flexible (but firm) than stubborn (but yielding). Specifically, they must be willing to make their own needs explicit, to identify similarities, and to recognize and accept differences. They must also tolerate uncertainties and unravel inconsistencies.

It might appear that for successful integrative negotiation to occur, each party should be just as interested in the objectives and problems of the other as he is in his own—that each must assume responsibility for the other's needs and outcomes as well as for his own. This is an *incorrect* interpretation; in fact, such behavior is more likely to be dysfunctional than successful. Parties who are deeply committed to each other and each other's welfare often do not achieve the best solution (Fry, Firestone, and Williams, 1979; Kelley and Schenitzki, 1972). As close as the parties may feel to each other, it is unlikely that they will completely understand each other's needs, objectives, and concerns, and thus they can fall into the trap of not meeting each other's objectives while thinking they are (Rubin and Brown, 1975). While parties strongly committed to each other are likely to yield more than they would otherwise, the result is that they may arrive at a joint outcome that is less satisfactory than one they would have reached had they remained firm in pursuing their own objectives.

Parties in negotiation maximize their outcomes when they assume a healthy, active self-interest in achieving their own goals while also recognizing that they are in a collaborative, problem-solving relationship (Kelley and Schenitzki, 1972). Maximizing outcomes may also be negatively correlated with one party's ability to punish the other party. Even cooperatively motivated negotiators have less trust, exchange less information about preferences and priorities, and achieve agreements of lower joint profit when they can punish the other party than when they do not have this capability (de Dreu, Giebels, and van de Vliert, 1998).

Motivation and commitment to problem solving can be enhanced in several ways:

1. Negotiators can learn that they share a common fate. To quote Ben Franklin, "If we do not hang together, we will surely hang separately."

2. Negotiators can demonstrate to each other that there is more to be gained by working together (to increase the payoffs or reduce the costs) than by working separately. The parties can emphasize that they may have to work together after the negotiations are over and will continue to benefit from the relationship they have created. In spite of these efforts, competitive and contentious behavior may persist. In Chapter 18, we will elaborate on approaches that may be used to encourage parties to negotiate cooperatively.

3. Negotiators can engage in commitments to each other before the negotiations begin; such commitments have been called *presettlement settlements* (Gillespie and Bazerman, 1998) and are distinguished by three major characteristics:

   a. The settlement results in a firm, legally binding written agreement between the parties (it is more than a gentlemen's agreement).

   b. The settlement occurs in advance of the parties undertaking full-scale negotiations, but the parties intend that the agreement will be replaced by a more clearly delineated long-term agreement that is to be negotiated.

   c. The settlement resolves only a subset of the issues on which the parties disagree and may simply establish a framework within which the more comprehensive agreement can be defined and delineated.

4. Negotiators could create an umbrella agreement that provides a framework for future discussions. Stefanos Mouzas (2006) suggests that umbrella agreements manage three negotiation challenges:

    a. Umbrella agreements allow flexibility when the negotiating relationship between the parties is evolving.

    b. Umbrella agreements provide flexibility for claiming value when the actual future gains are not known at the time of the negotiation.

    c. Umbrella agreements can be used when all the issues and contingencies have yet to be identified but the parties know they wish to work together.

An example of an umbrella agreement is in Box. 3.4.

Trust

Although there is no guarantee that trust will lead to collaboration, there is plenty of evidence to suggest that mistrust inhibits collaboration. People who are interdependent but do not trust each other will act tentatively or defensively. Defensiveness means that they will not accept information at face value but instead will look for hidden, deceptive meanings. When people are defensive, they withdraw and withhold information. Defensive people also attack the other party's statements and position, seeking to defeat their position rather than to work together. Either of these responses is likely to make the negotiator hesitant, cautious, and distrustful of the other, undermining the negotiation process (Gibb, 1961).

Deepak Malhotra and Mac Bazerman (2007) suggest three tactics to elicit information from the other negotiator when he or she mistrusts *you:*

1. *Share information and encourage reciprocity.* One approach is to suggest to the other negotiator that you are willing to describe your needs and interests if he agrees to share his as well. Malhotra and Bazerman caution to ensure there is agreement about the explicit ground rules before proceeding, and to proceed incrementally to be sure.

2. *Negotiate multiple issues simultaneously.* Negotiating several offers simultaneously allows negotiators to identify relative priorities of the other negotiator, as well as obtain some information about his interests. Malhotra and Bazerman suggest watching for issues where the other party is very engaged, emotional and attempting to control the discussion in order to infer high priority issues.

3. *Make multiple offers at the same time.* A third approach to obtaining information when the other party is distrusting is to make two or three offers at the same time. These offers should be the same value to you. The way that the other negotiator responds to these offers should provide you with information about his relative interests.

In summary, integrative negotiation is easier when the parties trust each other. When there is distrust, negotiating will be more challenging but the three tactics we presented here will help manage this challenge.

Generating trust is a complex, uncertain process; it depends in part on how the parties behave and in part on the parties' personal characteristics. When people trust each other, they are more likely to share information and to communicate accurately their needs, positions, and the facts of the situation (Butler, 1999; Tenbrunsel, 1999). In contrast, when people do not trust

Framework of Focal Points	Umbrella Clauses
Product range/services	Laundry and cleaning products.
Exolucivity	Both parties have the right to obtain competitive offers at any time.
Information	Parties defined three performance indicators. Mutual notification regarding all future capital investment and research and development.
Notification	Notification regarding product damages needs to be made within two weeks.
Subcontracting	Subcontracting is only possible upon consent.
Assignment	All requests need to be made in writing. Verbal requests need to be confirmed in writing.
Volume/price	To be agreed/continuous stock replenishment.
	Unilateral price determination.
Invoicing	Unless otherwise agreed, on a monthly basis.
	Payment in 60 days; delivery cost is paid by the supplier. (Delivered duty paid.)
Renegotiation	Annual renegotiation/business reviews quarterly.
	Any controversy shall be finally settled by arbitration. (International Chapter of Commerce.)
Force majeure	Parties bear no liability for damages occurred as a result of war, political unrest, strikes, lockouts, and governmental interventions.
Guarantee	The retailer reserves the right to demand the elimination of deficiencies or to allow the return of products within twenty days at suppliers' cost.
Liability	The obligation to remedy deficiencies applies also to services obtained from subcontractors.
Secrecy	All information exchanged is confidential and shall not be made available to third parties without written consent of the other party.
Property rights	No transfer of property rights. Supplier ensures that no third person has obtained property rights.
Saving clause	Unless it is of major importance, invalidity of one or more clauses will not have any effect on the umbrella agreement as a whole.
Legal venue	London/U.K.
Amendments	The supplier has the obligation to revoke in writing any orders that she does not wish to accept.
Addition	Need to be made in writing.
Duration	Indefinite agreement/annual renegotiation.
Termination	Each party has the right to terminate the agreement immediately with regard to a particular type of services.

Source: Stefanos Mouzas, "Negotiating Umbrella Agreements," *Negotiation Journal,* July 2006, pp. 292–93.

each other, they are more likely to engage in positional bargaining, use threats, and commit themselves to tough positions (Kimmel, Pruitt, Magenau, Konar-Goldband, and Carnevale, 1980). As with defensiveness, mistrust is likely to be reciprocated and to lead to unproductive negotiations. To develop trust effectively, each negotiator must believe that both she and the other party choose to behave in a cooperative manner; moreover, each must believe that this behavior is a signal of the other's honesty, openness, and a similar mutual commitment to a joint solution (see Chapter 10 for an extensive discussion of trust in negotiation).

Clear and Accurate Communication

Another precondition for high-quality integrative negotiation is clear and accurate communication. First, negotiators must be willing to share information about themselves (Neale and Bazerman, 1991). They must be willing to reveal what they want and, more important, must be willing to state why they want it in specific, concrete terms, avoiding generalities and ambiguities. Second, the other negotiators must understand the communication. At a minimum, they must understand the meaning they each attach to their statements; hopefully, the parties each interpret the basic facts in the same way, but if they don't then they should reconcile them. Other members of the negotiating team can frequently identify ambiguities and breakdowns in communication. If someone on a bargaining team makes a confusing statement, others can address it and try to clarify it. When one person on the other side does not grasp a difficult point, someone else from the same side will often be able to find the words or illustrations to bring out the meaning. Mutual understanding is the responsibility of both sides. The communicator must be willing to test whether the other side has received the message that was intended. Similarly, the listener must engage in active listening, testing to make sure that what he or she received and understood is the message that the sender intended.

Multiple communication channels, such as opportunities for the two sides to communicate outside formal negotiations, will help negotiators clarify the formal communication or exchange information if the formal channels break down. Conversations over coffee breaks, separate meetings between chief negotiators outside the formal sessions, and off-the-record contacts between key subordinates are all alternatives to the formal channel. The negotiators must exercise care, however, to make sure that the multiple messages and contacts are consistent. Sending conflicting messages during integrative negotiation can confuse the other party at best, and threaten or anger at worst.

Metaphors may also play an important role in communicating during negotiation. Metaphors may be defined as "talking about one thing in terms of another" (Smith, 2005, p. 346) and are useful when direct communication is difficult or threatening. Thomas Smith (2005) suggests that metaphors may play two important roles in negotiation: (1) metaphors help negotiators understand *why* the other party is saying what they said, and (2) metaphors may help identify areas for mutual gain because they provide insight into the other party's needs and motives (see Box 3.5).

When there are strong negative feelings or when one or more parties are inclined to dominate, negotiators may create formal, structured procedures for communication. Under these circumstances, negotiators should follow a procedure that gives everyone a chance to speak. For example, most rules for debates limit statements to five minutes, and similar rules are often adopted in contentious open meetings or public hearings. In addition, the parties may agree to follow a previously agreed-on agenda so that everyone can be heard

Statement	Message
Nothing ventured, nothing gained.	Risk
Only the fit survive.	Renewal
It's a dog eat dog world.	Hyper competition
Adapt or die.	Change
We're all in this together.	Interdependence family

and their contributions noted. Effective communication processes in negotiation are covered extensively in Chapters 5 and 17. In Chapter 19 we describe how third parties can help facilitate disabled communication processes.

An Understanding of the Dynamics of Integrative Negotiation

Negotiators frequently assume that the distributive bargaining process is the only way to approach negotiations. Several studies indicate that training in integrative negotiation enhances the ability of the parties to negotiate integratively. For example, Weingart, Hyder, and Prietula (1996) demonstrated that training negotiators in integrative tactics—particularly in how to exchange information about priorities across issues and preferences within issues, and how to set high goals—significantly enhanced the frequency of integrative behaviors and led the parties to achieve higher joint outcomes. This study also found that using distributive tactics, such as strongly trying to persuade the other of the validity of one's own views, was negatively related to joint outcomes. In addition, Lowenstein, Thompson, Gentner, and their colleagues have found that analogical training appears to be an especially powerful way to learn about integrative negotiation.[5] Analogical learning involves the direct comparison of different negotiation examples to identify and understand the underlying principles and structure of the negotiation.

Section Summary

We identified seven fundamental preconditions for successful integrative negotiation: some form of shared or common goals, faith in one's ability to solve problems, a belief in the validity and importance of the other's position, the motivation and commitment to work together, trust in the opposing negotiator, the ability to accurately exchange information in spite of conflict conditions, and an understanding of the dynamics of integrative negotiation. If the parties are not able to meet these preconditions successfully, they will need to resolve challenges in these areas as the integrative negotiation evolves.

Why Integrative Negotiation Is Difficult to Achieve

Integrative negotiation is a collaborative process in which the parties define their common problem and pursue strategies to solve it. Negotiators do not always perceive integrative potential when it exists or cannot always sustain a productive integrative discussion. People frequently view conflict-laden situations with a fundamentally more distrustful, win–lose attitude than is necessary. The approach that individuals take toward conflict and negotiation is essential to understanding the differences between distributive bargaining and integrative negotiation. The primary reason negotiators do not pursue integrative agreements is that they fail to perceive a situation as having integrative potential and are primarily motivated to achieve outcomes that satisfy only their own needs. Four additional factors contribute to this difficulty: (1) the history of the relationship between the parties, (2) the belief that an issue can only be resolved distributively, (3) the mixed-motive nature of most bargaining situations, and (4) short time perspectives.

The History of the Relationship between the Parties

The more competitive and conflict-laden their past relationship, the more likely negotiators are to approach the current negotiation with a defensive, win–lose attitude. Long-term opponents are not likely to trust each other or to believe that a cooperative gesture is not a ruse or setup for future exploitation. Because the other party has never shown any genuine interest in cooperation in the past, why should the present be any different? Laboratory research shows that negotiations who had an impasse in a previous negotiation were more likely to reach impasses on subsequent negotiations on different topics, even if the other party was a different negotiator (O'Connor, Arnold, and Burris, 2005).

Even if the parties have no history with each other, the expectation of a competitive opponent is sufficient to create defensiveness. Research suggests that the majority of people enter negotiations expecting them to be win–lose, not win–win (Thompson and Hastie, 1990a). In addition, perceptions are often loaded with self-serving rationalizations—for instance, see the other party as more unreasonable and difficult to work with than a neutral third party would—and these perceptions in turn deter them form initiating an integrative negotiation process. Negotiators can proceed past a negative history, but it takes effort. For instance, Post and Bennett (1994) report a successful transformation of union–management relations by using a five-step process (see Box 3.6).

A Belief That an Issue Can Only Be Resolved Distributively

Conflict dynamics tend to lead negotiators to polarize issues or see them only in win–lose terms. In addition, negotiators may be prone to several cognitive biases or heuristic decision rules that systematically bias their perception of the situation, the range of possible outcomes, and the likelihood of achieving possible outcomes, all of which tend to preclude negotiators from engaging in the behaviors necessary for integrative negotiation (Neale and Bazerman, 1985, 1991; we discuss these biases in detail in Chapter 5). For example, unions and management have historically clashed over the introduction of new procedures or technology that "de-skills" labor or replaces workers with machines. Labor usually pursues job security, believing that the new machines will eliminate workers, whereas management takes the position that the new machines will increase efficiency, quality, and profit and that it is management's right to make decisions regarding these issues. On the surface, the two positions seem irreconcilable: either the workers pressure the company to keep employees at the expense of machines, or management makes the decisions about how to introduce new technology. However, recent experience shows that labor and management have devised solutions to the problem that satisfy both sides—such as retraining and reallocating employees or reducing the number of employees through attrition rather than layoff.

BOX 3.6

Using Integrative Negotiation to Enhance Collective Bargaining

Union–management collective bargaining has often been used as a classic example of the distributive bargaining process. Often, the tendency for the parties to use collective bargaining rests on a long history of perceived abuse and mistrust on both sides of the table. But recent work shows that integrative negotiation can be successful even in this context, although unions may need to use some conflict tactics to ensure their share of mutual gains (Bacon and Blyton, 2007).

Post and Bennett (1994) report the results of a five-step integrative process that successfully reduced grievances from 40 per year under the previous contract to 2 in 18 months under the new contract, significantly reduced anger and hostility between the parties, and significantly enhanced the spirit of cooperation in the plant. The five steps were as follows:

1. A *commitment phase,* occurring 12 and 6 months before the expiration of the current contract, during which the parties commit to participate in a collaborative process, including commitments to harmonize negotiation philosophy, harmonize the negotiation process, and articulate the respective interests of the parties.

2. An *explanation phase,* occurring one month before contract expiration, during which the parties hold their first meeting, present their respective proposals to each other, introduce supporting documentation, and set a timetable for remaining meetings.

3. A *validation phase,* occurring two to four weeks prior to contract expiration, in which the parties gather information from employees and employers about the validity of the interests expressed in the opening statements. This information is used to generate a collective consensus about the relative importance and priority of the interests to the constituencies of both groups.

4. A *prioritization phase,* occurring two weeks prior to contract expiration, in which the parties work together to develop a joint list of priorities based on the data. This process is often facilitated by a mediator, who uses the commitments generated in the commitment phase to help the parties represent their priorities genuinely and candidly.

5. A *negotiation phase,* occurring one week prior to the contract expiration, in which the parties meet in a series of frequent and intensive gatherings to negotiate a resolution to the prioritized list of interests. Once again, this process is often facilitated by a mediator, whose role is to vigorously ask questions of the parties, hold them to their agenda, and ensure that the negotiations proceed in an open and trusting atmosphere.

Note that this process requires the ongoing participation of a mediator, who acts as a referee and as a monitor of the parties' commitment to stay with an integrative process. Whether the parties could learn to trust each other to sustain such a process without an active third-party role is still a matter of debate.

Source: Adapted from F. R. Post and R. J. Bennett, "Use of Collaborative Collective Bargaining Processes in Labor Negotiations," *International Journal of Conflict Management,* 5 (1994), pp. 34–61.

The Mixed-Motive Nature of Most Negotiating Situations

Purely integrative or purely distributive negotiation situations are rare. Most situations are mixed-motive, containing some elements that require distributive bargaining processes and others that require integrative negotiation. For example, when people become partners in a business, the common goal of making a profit provides a basis for their collaboration. How to allocate the profits becomes a different matter, however, and is much more likely to create conflict. In this example, the parties must recognize that the integrative element is more important; that is, there must be a successful business before there can be profits to divide. Nevertheless, their competitiveness over profit distribution may make it difficult for them to stay in business at all. As a general rule, because people are more likely to perceive negotiations as win–lose than win–win, conflict and competitiveness drive out cooperation and trust, making it more difficult for the parties to find common ground.

One of the most fundamental challenges in integrative negotiation is that parties fail to recognize or search for the integrative potential in a negotiation situation. The primary cause of this failure is the desire to satisfy one's own concerns without regard to the other's concerns. Negotiators too often assume that the other party has the same objectives and goals as they do, and accordingly they fail to search for information about the other party's preferences and priorities (Kemp and Smith, 1994). Negotiators may also be led to this assumption when they are highly accountable to someone else for their performance, when the parties have had a history of conflict, and when the issues are too complex to disentangle and are easily interpreted in simple win–lose terms. As a result, negotiators fail to invest the time and energy necessary to search for and find integrative options.

Short Time Perspectives

Effective integrative negotiation requires sufficient time to process information, reach true understanding of one's own and the other party's needs, and to manage the transition from creating value to claiming value.

Recent research suggests that a shorter length of time between the negotiation and implementation of an agreement may contribute to suboptimal integration outcomes. A series of studies by Marlone Henderson, Yaacov Trope, and Peter Carnevale (2006) suggest that negotiations to be implemented sooner tend to be more piecemeal and fragmented than those which were to be implemented later. While temporally near negotiations were better than straight compromises, negotiations that were not to be implemented until later had significantly more integrative outcomes. The pace and time pressures of modern business negotiations appear to be an important factor interfering with effective integrative negotiations. When practical, negotiators should leave enough time before the implementation of a deal so that effective integrative negotiation can occur.

Distributive Bargaining versus Integrative Negotiation

Research and practice in negotiation has seen many changes to the way people negotiate over the past 20 years. Since the publication of the first edition of *Getting to Yes* in 1981, there has been a steady growth in integrative negotiating, and it is a concept that has permeated the research and practice of negotiation (see Menkel-Meadow, 2006). Many would argue that the world would be a better place if all negotiations were integrative and suggest that distributive bargaining is an outdated approach to creating value and resolving differences.

Chapters 2 and 3 have discussed various aspects of both approaches, and our view is a strong understanding of both is important for two reasons. First, some negotiators use a purely distributive approach and there is no evidence that integrative negotiating will be effective against a strong, consistent distributive bargainer. This does not mean the distributive bargainer will do better than the integrative negotiator. In fact, there is good evidence that bargaining distributively in an integrative situation will be suboptimal. The more troubling question when faced with a distributive bargainer is whether responding distributively or integratively is more effective. Research has not addressed this point explicitly, but we believe that negotiators who understand the dynamics and processes of both distributive bargaining and integrative negotiation will be better prepared to respond strategically to whatever situation or challenge they face.

The second reason to understand both processes is that integrative situations involve a claiming-value portion and this may involve the use of distributive tactics. Some negotiators portray themselves as win–win while in fact are solely out for themselves. These wolves-in-sheeps-clothing negotiators can be very challenging to negotiate with because they speak like integrative negotiators while acting like distributive bargainers. It can be very difficult to identify such negotiators because they appear to be negotiating integratively when they are not. The best way to manage this is to watch what they do and understand the positions that they take. A sound understanding of distributive bargaining makes it more likely that these negotiators will be identified.

Chapter Summary

In this chapter, we have reviewed the strategy and tactics of integrative negotiation. The fundamental structure of integrative negotiation is one within which the parties are able to define goals that allow both sides to achieve their objectives. Integrative negotiation is the process of defining these goals and engaging in a process that permits both parties to maximize their objectives.

The chapter began with an overview of the integrative negotiation process. A high level of concern for both sides achieving their own objectives propels a collaborative, problem-solving approach. Negotiators frequently fail at integrative negotiation because they fail to perceive the integrative potential of the negotiating situation. However, breakdowns also occur due to distributive assumptions about negotiating, the mixed-motive nature of the issues, the negotiators' previous relationship with each other, and short time perspectives. Successful integrative negotiation requires several processes. First, the parties must understand each other's true needs and objectives. Second, they must create a free flow of information and an open exchange of ideas. Third, they must focus on their similarities, emphasizing their commonalities rather than their differences. Finally, they must engage in a search for solutions that meet the goals of both sides. This is a very different set of processes from those in distributive bargaining, described in Chapter 2. The four key steps in the integrative negotiation process are identifying and defining the problem, identifying interests and needs, generating alternative solutions, and evaluating and selecting alternatives. For each of these steps, we discussed techniques and tactics to make the process successful.

We then discussed various factors that facilitate successful integrative negotiation. First, the process will be greatly facilitated by some form of common goal or objective. This goal may be one that the parties both want to achieve, one they want to share, or one they could not possibly attain unless they worked together. Second, they must have faith in their problem-solving ability. Third, the parties must be willing to believe that the other's needs are valid. Fourth, they must share a motivation and commitment to work together, to make their relationship a productive one. Fifth, they must be able to trust each other and to work hard to establish and maintain that trust. Sixth, there must be clear and accurate communication about what each one wants and an effort to understand the other's needs. Instead of talking the other out of his or her needs or failing to acknowledge them as important, negotiators must be willing to work for both their own needs and the other's needs to find the best joint arrangement. Finally, there must be an understanding of the dynamics of integrative negotiations.

In spite of all of these suggestions, integrative negotiation is not easy—especially for parties who are locked in conflict, defensiveness, and a hard-line position. Only by working to create the necessary conditions for integrative negotiation can the process unfold successfully. In Chapters 17 and 18, we discuss several ways that parties can defuse hostility, defensiveness, and the disposition toward hard-line negotiating to create the conditions for successful integrative negotiation.

Endnotes

[1] Our descriptions draw heavily on the writings of several experts who have studied the integrative process in great detail, and we will note recent research findings that have affirmed the validity of particular strategies and tactics. See Follett (1940), formalized by Walton and McKersie (1965); Fisher, Ury and Patton (1991); Lax and Sebenius (1986); Carnevale and Pruitt (1992); Filley (1975); and Pruitt (1981, 1983), among numerous others. We also draw extensively on Pruitt and Carnevale (1993).

[2] See Chapter 5 of Sheppard, Lewicki, and Minton (1992) for a more complete discussion of the role of "voice" in organizations.

[3] For example, see Neale and Bazerman (1991), Pruitt (1981, 1983), Pruitt and Carnevale (1993), and Pruitt and Lewis (1975).

[4] For more detailed discussion of this step see Filley (1975); Pruitt and Carnevale (1993); Shea (1983); and Walton and McKersie (1965).

[5] See Gentner, Loewenstein, and Thompson (2003); Loewenstein and Thompson (2000), Loewenstein, Thompson, and Gentner (1999, 2003); Nadler, Thompson, and Van Boven (2003); and Thompson, Gentner, and Loewenstein (2000).

CHAPTER 4

Negotiation: Strategy and Planning

Objectives

1. Understand the importance of setting goals for an upcoming negotiation.
2. Explore the major elements of a negotiation strategy and a process for selecting a strategy.
3. Consider how most negotiations evolve through understandable stages and phases.
4. Gain a comprehensive set of tools for effectively planning for an upcoming negotiation.

In this chapter, we discuss what negotiators should do before opening negotiations. Effective strategy and planning are the most critical precursors for achieving negotiation objectives. With effective planning and target setting, most negotiators can achieve their objectives; without them, results occur more by chance than by negotiator effort.

Regrettably, systematic planning is not something that most negotiators do willingly. Although time constraints and work pressures make it difficult to find the time to plan adequately, for many, planning is simply boring and tedious, easily put off in favor of getting into the action quickly. It is clear, however, that *devoting insufficient time to planning is one weakness that may cause negotiators to fail.* These are some consequences of failed planning:

- Negotiators fail to set clear objectives or targets that serve as benchmarks for evaluating offers and packages. Negotiators who do not have clear objectives are not in a position to evaluate proposals quickly and accurately. As a result, negotiators may agree to deals that they later regret. Alternatively, negotiators may become confused or defensive and delay the process, causing the other party to lose patience.

- If negotiators have not done their homework, they may not understand the strengths and weaknesses of their own positions or recognize comparable strengths and weaknesses in the other party's arguments. As a result, they may not be able to formulate convincing arguments to support their own position or rebut the other party's arguments.

- Negotiators need to consider their alternatives to doing this deal. If negotiators understand what alternatives are available to them if the current deal does not succeed, they will have more confidence and power to walk away from a bad deal.

- Negotiators cannot simply depend on being quick and clever during the give-and-take of negotiation. Should the other party plan to win by stalling and delaying, or holding on to a position just to wear the negotiator down, the approach may have to be revised. Negotiators often find that being "a great salesman" in presenting their position is not helpful when the other party assails that position as illegal, inefficient, or ineffective.

Almost every popular book on negotiation devotes at least one or two chapters to planning (e.g., Cohen, 2003; Latz, 2004; Lax and Sebenius, 2006; Lewicki and Hiam, 2006); indeed, there are books that are wholly devoted to how to plan and prepare effectively (e.g., Fisher and Ertel, 1995). Yet there is scant empirical evidence on the impact of carefully planning one's negotiation process. One study of successful negotiators by Rackham (1980) suggested that in the planning process, skilled negotiators (compared with "average" negotiators) (1) explored a wider range of options for action; (2) worked harder to find common ground with the other party; (3) spent more time considering the long-term implications of the issues; and (4) were significantly more likely to set upper and lower limits, or a "range" of acceptable settlements. While these findings appear reasonable and logical, the profession needs more hard research evidence to confirm the effectiveness of the strategy and planning process described in this chapter.

Our discussion of strategy and planning begins by exploring the broad process of strategy development, starting with defining the negotiator's goals and objectives. We then move to developing a strategy to address the issues and achieve one's goals. Finally, we address the typical stages and phases of an evolving negotiation and how different issues and goals will affect the planning process. Figure 4.1 shows how these elements are related. Although this model suggests that the relationships between these elements are linear—that is, goals lead to strategy leads to planning—in fact, parties often begin at any point in this sequence and work their way "backward/forward" until the three steps of the preparation process are aligned.

Goals—The Focus That Drives a Negotiation Strategy

The first step in developing and executing a negotiation strategy is to determine one's goals. Negotiators must anticipate what goals they want to achieve in a negotiation and focus on how to achieve those goals. As noted in Chapter 1, negotiators must consider substantive goals (e.g., money or a specific outcome), intangible goals (e.g., winning, beating the other party, or getting a settlement at any cost), and procedural goals (e.g., shaping the agenda or simply having a voice at the table). Effective preparation requires a thorough, thoughtful approach to these goals; negotiators should specify their goals and objectives clearly. This includes listing all goals they wish to achieve in the negotiation, determining the priority

FIGURE 4.1 | Relationship between Key Steps in the Planning Process (Overview of Chapter 4)

among these goals, identifying potential multigoal packages, and evaluating possible trade-offs among multiple goals.

Direct Effects of Goals on Choice of Strategy

Four aspects of how goals affect negotiation are important to understand:

1. Wishes are not goals, especially in negotiation. Wishes may be related to interests or needs that motivate goals (see Chapter 3), but they are not goals themselves. A wish is a fantasy, a hope that something might happen; a goal is a specific, focused target that one can realistically plan to achieve.

2. Goals are often linked to the other party's goals. The linkage between the two parties' goals defines an issue to be settled (see the discussion of issues later in this chapter) and is often the source of conflict. My goal is to get a car cheaply, and the dealer's goal is to sell it at the highest possible price (and profit); thus, the "issue" is the price I will pay for the car. If I could achieve my goal by myself, without the other party, I probably wouldn't need to negotiate.

3. There are boundaries or limits to what goals can be (see the discussion of walkaways and alternatives later in this chapter). If what we want exceeds these limits (i.e., what the other party is capable of or willing to give), we must either change our goals or end the negotiation. Goals must be attainable. If my goal—"to buy this car at a cheap price"—isn't possible because the dealer won't sell the car "cheaply" (notice that "cheaply" is an ambiguous goal at this point), I'm going to either have to change my goal or find another car to buy (perhaps from a different dealer).

4. Effective goals must be concrete, specific, and measurable. The less concrete and measurable our goals are, the harder it is to *(a)* communicate to the other party what we want, *(b)* understand what the other party wants, and *(c)* determine whether an offer on the table satisfies our goals. "To get a car cheaply" or "to agree on a price so that the loan payment does not use all of my paycheck" is not a very clear goal. What do I mean by "use up my paycheck"? Is this every week's paycheck or only one check a month? Do I want the payment to be just under 100 percent of the paycheck, or about 50 percent, or perhaps even 25 percent? Today's paycheck only, or the paychecks expected over the life of the loan? Is this payment the largest amount I think I can possibly pay? Is it the payment that could be paid with little or no inconvenience? Or is it the payment calculated after reading that one shouldn't pay more than 15 percent of one's monthly salary for a car payment? The negotiator has to determine exactly how big a payment can comfortably come out of his or her paycheck at present interest rates and add to that what is available for a down payment in order to be able to negotiate exactly what he or she is willing to pay a month. But as you can see, even this figure is not totally clear.

Goals can also be intangible or procedural. In the car purchase example, intangible goals might include enhancing reputation among one's friends by owning and driving a slick sports car; maintaining an image as a shrewd, pennywise negotiator; or paying any price to ensure convenient, reliable transportation. In other negotiations, intangible goals might include maintaining a reputation as a tough but principled negotiator, establishing a precedent for future negotiations, or conducting the negotiations in a manner that is fair to all sides and assures each party fair treatment. (Refer back to Chapter 1 for further discussion of intangible goals.)

Which of these many criteria should we use? The answer depends on *you:* your specific objectives and your priorities among multiple objectives. Trade-offs will be inevitable and can cloud your perspective while negotiating, so you have to clearly remember what you wanted to achieve when the negotiation started.

Indirect Effects of Goals on Choice of Strategy

Simple and direct goals can often be attained in a single negotiation session and with a simple negotiating strategy. As a result, we often limit our view on the impact of pursuing short-term goals, particularly when the impact is long term. This short-term thinking affects our choice of strategy; in developing and framing our goals, we may ignore the present or future relationship with the other party in favor of a simplistic concern for achieving only the substantive outcome. As only one example, suppose your beloved aging grandmother decides she is too old to drive and asks you whether you want to buy her car. She says she knows nothing about cars and simply wants to sell it to you because she trusts you to take care of it. You may be able to offer her a very small amount of money, far less than what it is really worth, and strike a very favorable deal on the price. But if she or other family members discover that you took advantage of her age and ignorance about car prices, the long-term consequences for you may be very severe! You'd be likely to lose their trust, gain a negative reputation, and have a very difficult time in any future dealings within the family.

Other negotiation goals—particularly ones that are more difficult or require a substantial change in the other party's attitude—may require you to develop a long-range plan for goal attainment. In these cases, progress will be made incrementally, and it may depend on establishing a strong relationship with the other party. Examples here include a substantial increase in one's line of credit with a financial institution or the establishment of a privileged status with an important trading partner. Such relationship-oriented goals should motivate the negotiator toward a strategy choice in which the relationship with the other party is valued as much as (or even more than) the substantive outcome. Thus, relational goals tend to support the choice of a collaborative or integrative strategy (refer back to the dual concerns model described in Chapter 1).

Strategy—The Overall Plan to Achieve One's Goals

After negotiators articulate goals, they move to the second element in the sequence: selecting and developing a strategy. Experts on business strategy define *strategy* as "the pattern or plan that integrates an organization's major targets, policies, and action sequences into a cohesive whole" (Mintzberg and Quinn, 1991). Applied to negotiations, strategy refers to the overall plan to accomplish one's goals in a negotiation and the action sequences that will lead to the accomplishment of those goals.

Strategy versus Tactics

How are strategy and tactics related? Although the line between strategy and tactics may seem fuzzy, one major difference is that of scale, perspective, or immediacy (Quinn, 1991). Tactics are short-term, adaptive moves designed to enact or pursue broad (or higher-level)

In 1999, I began construction on the tallest residential tower in the world, Trump World Tower and the United Nations Plaza.

The location was terrific—the East Side of Manhattan, close to the United Nations, with both river views and city views. It was hot stuff, but not everyone was happy about it, especially some diplomats at the United Nations, who didn't want their 38-story building to be outclassed by our 90-story tower. According to CNN, UN secretary general Kofi Annan acknowledged talking with New York City mayor Rudy Giuliani about the project and how to stop it.

"It will not fit here," the Ukranian ambassador, Volodymyr Yel'chenko told CNN, "because it overshadows the United Nations complex."

When the protests became vocal, I used my own brand of diplomacy and refused to say anything critical of the United Nations. I predicted that many ambassadors and UN officials would end up buying apartments in the building. Sure enough, they have.

But as soon as we were in business, the city hit us with an enormous tax assessment, costing us over $100 million more than we thought we should pay. We decided to take the only action possible.

For four years, we fought this case. The city lawyers held their ground, and we held ours. We could have given up. It's not easy to take on the government and win, especially when the issue is taxes, but I knew we had a case.

Finally, after many conversations, we reached a settlement. The city agreed to cut our taxes 17 percent and give us the ten year tax abatement that we sought if we would agree to withdraw our lawsuit and subsidize 200 units of affordable housing in the Bronx.

The lawsuit saved us approximately $97 million. We never would have gotten any of it if we hadn't taken dramatic action.

Source: Donald J. Trump with Meredith McIver, *Trump: How to Get Rich* (New York: Random House, 2004), pp. 136–37.

strategies, which in turn provide stability, continuity, and direction for tactical behaviors. For example, your negotiation strategy might be integrative, designed to build and maintain a productive relationship with the other party while using a joint problem-solving approach to the issues. In pursuing this strategy, appropriate tactics include describing your interests, using open-ended questions and active listening to understand the others' interests, and inventing options for mutual gain. Tactics are subordinate to strategy; they are structured, directed, and driven by strategic considerations. In Chapters 2 and 3, we outlined the strategies of distributive bargaining and integrative negotiation, along with the associated tactics that are likely to accompany each strategy.

Unilateral versus Bilateral Approaches to Strategy

A unilateral choice is one that is made without the active involvement of the other party. Unilaterally pursued strategies are almost completely one-sided and intentionally ignorant of any information about the other negotiator. However, unilateral strategies can be problematic for exactly this reason. Any reasonable strategy should also include processes for gaining information about the other party, and incorporating that information into the choice of a negotiation strategy is always useful. Therefore, while we are going to initially describe strategies as unilateral in nature, they should clearly evolve into ones that fully consider the impact of the other's strategy on one's own. For an example of a unilateral strategy, see Box 4.1.

FIGURE 4.2 | The Dual Concerns Model

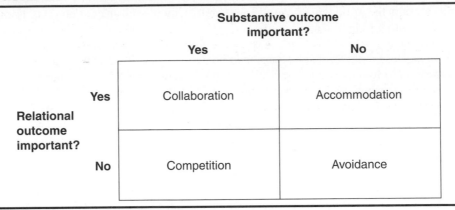

Source: ACADEMY OF MANAGEMENT EXECUTIVE by NEWSOM, WALTER B. Copyright 1989 by ACAD OF MGMT. Reproduced with permission of ACAD OF MGMT in the format Textbook via Copyright Clearance Center.

The Dual Concerns Model as a Vehicle for Describing Negotiation Strategies

In Chapter 1, we used the dual concerns model to describe the basic orientation that people take toward conflict (Pruitt and Rubin, 1986). This model proposes that individuals in conflict have two levels of related concerns: a level of concern for their own outcomes, and a level of concern for the other's outcomes (refer back to Figure 1.3). Savage, Blair, and Sorenson (1989) propose a similar model for the choice of a negotiation strategy. According to this model, a negotiator's unilateral choice of strategy is reflected in the answers to two simple questions: (1) How much concern does the actor have for achieving the substantive outcomes at stake in this negotiation (substantive goals)? (2) How much concern does the negotiator have for the current and future quality of the relationship with the other party (relationship goals)? The answers to these questions result in the mix of alternative strategies presented in Figure 4.2.

Alternative Situational Strategies   The power of this model lies in requiring the negotiator to determine the relative importance and priority of the two dimensions in the desired settlement. As Figure 4.2 shows, answers to these two questions suggest at least four types of initial strategies for negotiators: avoidance, accommodation, competition, and collaboration. A strong interest in achieving only substantive outcomes—getting this deal, winning this negotiation, with little or no regard for the effect on the relationship or on subsequent exchanges with the other party—tends to support a competitive (distributive) strategy. A strong interest in achieving only the relationship goals—building, preserving, or enhancing a good relationship with the other party—suggests an accommodation strategy. If both substance and relationship are important, the negotiator should pursue a collaborative (integrative) strategy. Finally, if achieving neither substantive outcomes nor an enhanced relationship is important, the party might be best served by avoiding negotiation. Each of these different strategic approaches also has different implications for negotiation planning and preparation (see also Johnston, 1982). We discuss both nonengagement and engagement strategies next.

It's been a long night. Bill Gates, the founder of Microsoft, is sitting around with a group of friends. They're famished. Someone gets the idea to call Domino's Pizza for a late-night delivery. The owner–manager of Domino's answers the phone, but unfortunately the store has just closed. Disappointed, the caller is ready to hang up when someone in the group says, "Tell them you're Bill Gates and pay them a lot of money to deliver a pizza." Bill

Gates hesitates. "Bill," someone prods, "what's it worth to you to have a pizza?" "Two hundred forty dollars," Gates responds. He gets on the phone and says, "OK, I'm Bill Gates and I'll pay you $240 to bring this pizza." They got the pizza.

Source: Roger J. Volkema, *The Negotiation Tool Kit* (New York: AMACOM, 1999), p. 6.

The Nonengagement Strategy: Avoidance   Avoidance may serve a number of strategic negotiation purposes. In fact, there are many reasons negotiators might choose not to negotiate (similar to the reasons for conflict avoidance discussed in Chapter 1):

• If one is able to meet one's needs without negotiating at all, it may make sense to use an avoidance strategy.

• It simply may not be worth the time and effort to negotiate (although there are sometimes reasons to negotiate in such situations; see the section on accommodation below).

• The decision to negotiate is closely related to the desirability of available alternatives— the outcomes that can be achieved if negotiations don't work out. In Chapter 2, we discussed the role that resistance points play in defining a strategy and the possibility that alternative deals are available; in Chapters 2 and 3, we explored the key role of a BATNA in evaluating the value of a particular agreement. A negotiator with very strong alternatives has considerable power because he or she doesn't need this negotiation to succeed in order to achieve a satisfactory outcome. Having weak alternatives puts negotiators at a disadvantage. The presence of an alternative can influence the decision about whether to avoid negotiation in two ways. First, the negotiator with a strong alternative may wish to avoid negotiation strictly on efficiency grounds—it is simply quicker and easier to take the alternative than to get involved in a negotiation. But having a weak alternative may also suggest avoiding negotiation—once negotiations begin, the pressure of the negotiation process may lead to a poor outcome, which the negotiator may feel obligated to accept because the alternative is also very poor. Alternatively, she or he might gain the desired outcome, but perhaps at a significant cost (see Box 4.2).

Active-Engagement Strategies: Accommodation, Competition and Collaboration
Competition and collaboration were described extensively in the last two chapters. Competition is described throughout this book as distributive or win–lose bargaining, and collaboration as integrative or win–win negotiation.

Accommodation is as much a win–lose strategy as competition, although it has a decidedly different image—it involves an imbalance of outcomes, but in the opposite direction ("I lose, you win" as opposed to "I win, you lose"). As Figure 4.2 shows, an accommodative strategy may be appropriate when the negotiator considers the relationship outcome more important than the substantive outcome. In other words, the negotiator wants to let the other win, keep the other happy, or not endanger the relationship by pushing hard to achieve some goal on the substantive issues. This strategy is often used when the primary goal of the exchange is to build or strengthen the relationship (or the other party) and the negotiator is willing to sacrifice the outcome. An accommodative strategy may also be necessary if the negotiator expects the relationship to extend past a single negotiation episode. The idea is that if "I lose and you win" this time, over multiple negotiations in the relationship the win–lose accounts will balance. In any long-term social relationship, it is probably healthy for one negotiator or the other to accept a suboptimal outcome in a given negotiation while expecting reciprocal accommodation (tit for tat) from the other negotiator in the future (Homans, 1961). Such reciprocity has been called the glue that holds social groups together (e.g., Cialdini, 2001).

How do these three strategies—competition, collaboration, and accommodation—differ? Table 4.1 (adapted from Johnston, 1982) summarizes the three types of strategies (distributive, integrative, and accommodative) and compares and contrasts them across a number of different dimensions.

In addition to their positive characteristics, as described in the table, each of these three negotiation strategies also has certain predictable drawbacks if the strategy is applied blindly, thoughtlessly, or inflexibly:

• Distributive strategies tend to create "we–they" or "superiority–inferiority" patterns and may lead to distortions in judgment regarding the other side's contributions and efforts, as well as to distortions in perceptions of the other side's values, needs, and positions (see the discussion of framing biases in Chapter 5).

• If a negotiator pursues an integrative strategy without regard to the other's strategy, then the other may manipulate and exploit the collaborator and take advantage of the good faith and goodwill being demonstrated. Blind pursuit of an integrative process can also lead negotiators to cease being accountable to their constituencies in favor of pursuit of the negotiation process for its own sake (see Chapter 11 for a discussion of negotiator–constituency dynamics). For example, negotiators who approach the process with an aggressive "we can solve any problem" attitude may produce an agreement that is unacceptable to their constituency (e.g., their companies), which will then be rejected and force the negotiator to resume discussions that others thought were settled.

• Accommodative strategies may generate a pattern of constantly giving in to keep the other happy or to avoid a fight. This pattern establishes a precedent that is hard to break. It could also lead the other to a false sense of well-being due to the satisfaction that comes with the "harmony" of a good relationship, which may completely ignore all the giveaways on substance. Over time, this imbalance is unlikely to perpetuate, but efforts to stop the giving or restore the balance may be met with surprise and resentment.

It is also useful to remember that in presenting these strategies we are describing pure forms that do not capture the mixture of issues and motivations that actually characterize the evolution of most actual negotiation strategies (Lax and Sebenius, 1986). Just as most conflicts are neither purely competitive nor purely cooperative, most negotiation strategies reflect a variety of goals, intentions, and situational constraints that tend to make any "pure" strategy difficult to follow.

TABLE 4.1 | Characteristics of Different Engagement Strategies

Aspect	Competition (Distributive Bargaining)	Collaboration (Integrative Negotiation)	Accommodative Negotiation
Payoff structure	Usually a fixed amount of resources to be divided	Usually a variable amount of resources to be divided	Usually a fixed amount of resources to be divided
Goal pursuit	Pursuit of own goals at the expense of those of others	Pursuit of goals held jointly with others	Subordination of own goals in favor of those of others
Relationships	Short-term focus; parties do not expect to work together in the future	Long-term focus; parties expect to work together in the future	May be short term (let the other win to keep the peace) or long term (let the other win to encourage reciprocity in the future)
Primary motivation	Maximize own outcome	Maximize joint outcome	Maximize others' outcome or let them gain to enhance relationship
Trust and openness	Secrecy and defensiveness; high trust in self, low trust in others	Trust and openness, active listening, joint exploration of alternatives	One party relatively open, exposing own vulnerabilities to the other
Knowledge of needs	Parties know own needs but conceal or misrepresent them; neither party lets the other know real needs	Parties know and convey real needs while seeking and responding to needs of the other	One party is overresponsive to other's needs so as to repress own needs
Predictability	Parties use unpredictability and surprise to confuse other side	Parties are predictable and flexible when appropriate, trying not to surprise	One party's actions totally predictable, always catering to other side
Aggressiveness	Parties use threats and bluffs, trying to keep the upper hand	Parties share information honestly, treat each other with understanding and respect	One party gives up on own position to mollify the other
Solution search behavior	Parties make effort to appear committed to position, using argumentation and manipulation of the other	Parties make effort to find mutually satisfying solutions, using logic, creativity, and constructiveness	One party makes effort to find ways to accommodate the other
Success measures	Success enhanced by creating bad image of the other; increased levels of hostility and strong in-group loyalty	Success demands abandonment of bad images and consideration of ideas on their merit	Success determined by minimizing or avoiding conflict and soothing all hostility; own feelings ignored in favor of harmony
Evidence of unhealthy extreme	Unhealthy extreme reached when one party assumes total zero-sum game; defeating the other becomes a goal in itself	Unhealthy extreme reached when one subsumes all self-interest in the common good, losing self-identity and self-responsibility	Unhealthy extreme reached when one abdication to other is complete, at expense of personal and/or constituent goals
Key attitude	Key attitude is "I win, you lose"	Key attitude is "What's the best way to address the needs of all parties?"	Key attitude is "You win, I lose"
Remedy for breakdown	If impasse occurs, mediator or arbitrator may be needed	If difficulties occur, a group dynamics facilitator may be needed	If behavior becomes chronic, party becomes negotiationally bankrupt

Source: Adapted and expanded from Robert W. Johnston, "Negotiation Strategies: Different Strokes for Different Folks," *Personnel 59* (March–April 1982), pp. 38–39. Used with permission of the author.

115

Understanding the Flow of Negotiations: Stages and Phases

Before we explore the specific planning processes for negotiation, it is important to understand the typical steps or flow in a negotiation in order to understand how negotiations are likely to evolve and why planning is so important.

Several researchers have studied the flow of negotiations over time—often by classifying the type of communication parties use at various points in the process. This work has confirmed that negotiation, like communication in problem-solving groups and in other forms of ritualistic social interaction, proceeds through distinct phases or stages (Douglas, 1962; Greenhalgh, 2001; Morley and Stephenson, 1977).

Holmes (1992) states that "phase models provide a narrative explanation of negotiation process; that is, they identify sequences of events that constitute the story of a negotiation . . . [A] phase is a coherent period of interaction characterized by a dominant constellation of communicative acts" that "serves a set of related functions in the movement from initiation to resolution of a dispute" (p. 83). Phase research typically addresses three types of questions (Holmes and Poole, 1991):

- How does the interaction between parties change over time?
- How do the interaction processes relate to inputs and outcomes over time?
- How do the tactics used by the parties affect the development of the negotiation?

Recent years have seen a marked increase in work on negotiation phase modeling. This work has been both descriptive and prescriptive—some authors describe what they have observed in natural settings, whereas others advise or prescribe certain activity sequences they feel should lead to more effective negotiation (refer to our discussion of the Zartman and Berman formula-detail model in Chapter 5). Much of this work is summarized in Table 4.2.

As the table shows, the various models fit into a general structure of three phases or stages: a beginning (or initiation) phase, a middle (bargaining or problem-solving) phase, and a closing (or resolution) phase. However, as Holmes (1992) points out, these stages are likely to be descriptive of *successful* negotiations. As Holmes notes, "*unsuccessful* negotiations do not proceed through the orderly stages of phase models, but tend to stall interminably in the intermediate phase or cycle within or between the beginning and middle stages, without achieving successful closure" (p. 92, emphasis added). Although phase modeling of negotiation offers much potential value in enhancing our understanding of negotiation, further research is necessary before it becomes a proactive tool for improving negotiation practice. Simple descriptions of the order of events in a negotiation are insufficient to improve negotiation practice.

More recently, Greenhalgh (2001) has articulated a stage model of negotiation that is particularly relevant for integrative negotiation. Greenhalgh suggests that there are seven key steps to an ideal negotiation process (see Figure 4.3):

Preparation: deciding what is important, defining goals, thinking ahead how to work together with the other party.

Relationship building: getting to know the other party, understanding how you and the other are similar and different, and building commitment toward achieving a mutually beneficial set of outcomes. Greenhalgh argues that this stage is extremely critical to satisfactorily moving the other stages forward.

TABLE 4.2 | Phase Models of Negotiation: Labels and Descriptions

Phases	Prescriptive Models	Descriptive Models
Initiation	Exploration[1] Preliminaries[2] Diagnostic[3] Introduction and relationship development[4]	Establishing the range[5] Search for arena, agenda, and issue identification[6] Agenda definition and problem formulation[7]
Problem solving	Expectation structuring, movement, and solution development[1] Positioning, bargaining, exploration[2] Formulation[3] Problem clarification and relationship development, problem solving[4]	Reconnoitering the range[5] Exploring the range, narrowing the range, preliminaries to final bargaining[6] Narrowing differences[7]
Resolution	Conclusion[1] Settlement[2] Details[3] Resolution structuring[4]	Precipitating the decision-making crisis[5] Final bargaining, ritualization, execution[6] Testing, agreement, and implementation[7]

1. Atkinson (1980)
2. Carlisle and Leary (1981)
3. Zartman and Berman (1982)
4. Donohue, Kaufman, Smith, and Ramesh (1990)
5. Douglas (1962)
6. Gulliver (1979)
7. Putnam, Wilson, and Turner (1990).

Source: Adapted from M. Holmes, "Phase Structures in Negotiation," in L. Putnam and M. Roloff (eds.), *Communication and Negotiation* (Newbury Park, CA: Sage, 1992). Tables 4.1 and 4.2, pp. 87–88. Reprinted by permission of Sage Publications, Inc.

FIGURE 4.3 | Phases of Negotiation

Phase 1	Phase 2	Phase 3	Phase 4	Phase 5	Phase 6	Phase 7
Preparation →	Relationship building →	Information gathering →	Information using →	Bidding →	Closing the deal →	Implementing the agreement

Source: Reprinted with the permission of The Free Press, an imprint of Simon & Schuster Adult Publishing Group, from *Managing Strategic Relationships: The Key to Business Success* by Leonard Greenhalgh. Copyright © 2001 by Leonard Greenhalgh.

Information gathering: learning what you need to know about the issues, about the other party and their needs, about the feasibility of possible settlements, and about what might happen if you fail to reach agreement with the other side.

Information using: at this stage, negotiators assemble the case they want to make for their preferred outcomes and settlement, one that will maximize the negotiator's own needs. This presentation is often used to "sell" the negotiator's preferred outcome to the other.

Bidding: the process of making moves from one's initial, ideal position to the actual outcome. Bidding is the process by which each party states their "opening offer" and then makes moves in that offer toward a middle ground. We describe this process extensively in Chapter 2.

Closing the deal: the objective of this stage is to build commitment to the agreement achieved in the previous phase. Both the negotiator and the other party have to assure themselves that they reached a deal they can be happy with, or at least accept.

Implementing the agreement: determining who needs to do what once the agreement is reached. Not uncommonly parties discover that the agreement is flawed, key points were missed, or the situation has changed and new questions exist. Flaws in moving through the earlier phases arise here, and the deal may have to be reopened or issues settled by mediators, arbitrators, or the courts.

Greenhalgh (2001) argues that this model is largely prescriptive—that is, this is the way people ought to negotiate—and he creates a strong case for why this is so. However, examination of the actual practice of negotiators shows that they frequently deviate from this model and that one can track differences in their practice according to his or her national culture (see Chapter 16). For example, American negotiators typically view the process more in "win–lose" or distributive terms; they don't do much relationship building or planning, and they move directly to bidding, closing, and implementation. In contrast, Asian negotiators spend a great deal of time on relationship building and truncate the steps toward the end of the negotiation process.

Getting Ready to Implement the Strategy: The Planning Process

The foundation for success in negotiation is not in the game playing or the dramatics. The dominant force for success in negotiation is in the planning that takes place prior to the dialogue. Effective planning also requires hard work on the following points:

- Defining the issues.
- Assembling issues and defining the bargaining mix.
- Defining interests.
- Defining resistance points.
- Defining alternatives (BATNA).
- Defining one's own objectives (targets) and opening bids (where to start).
- Assessing constituents and the social context in which the negotiation will occur.
- Analyzing the other party.
- Planning the issue presentation and defense.
- Defining protocol—where and when the negotiation will occur, who will be there, what the agenda will be, and so on.

The remainder of this chapter discusses each of these steps in detail (see also a summary of the planning guide in Table 4.3 that may be used to plan one's own negotiation). The list represents the collective wisdom of several sources,[1] each of which has its own list of key steps, which often vary in order.

Before commencing this discussion, we want to note four things:

• First, we assume that a single planning process can be followed for both a distributive and an integrative process. Although we have highlighted the differences between the two in the last two chapters, we believe that with the exception of the specific tactics negotiators intend to use, one comprehensive planning process can be used for either form of negotiation.

• Second, at this point in the book, we have concentrated on distributive and integrative processes and the differences between them. However, as we note in Chapter 1, there are several structural and contextual factors "beyond" the bargaining table that may also affect the strategizing and planning processes. These factors include which parties are actually at the table or will have an influence on negotiation, whether there are multiple negotiations that need to be "sequenced," what issues or interests will be represented, how the time limits are managed, and the broader network of relationships among parties at the table and decision makers away from the table (cf. Lax and Sebenius, 2006; Watkins, 2002, 2006). Lax and Sebenius describe this as "setting the table," while Watkins talks about it as "shaping the game." They both point out that while less experienced negotiators primarily focus on strategic and tactical planning for what will take place at the table, but that more experienced negotiators are more likely to attempt to orchestrate the deal they want by attending to these questions as well. The broad impact and implications of these structural or contextual elements will be discussed in later chapters.

• Third, we assume that negotiations will be conducted primarily one to one—that is, you and another individual negotiator. This is the simplest model to understand and plan for. However, it is not uncommon for negotiations to have two sides and multiple parties on each side, or agents representing negotiators, or multiple parties represented at the table. The dynamics created by extending negotiations to agents and multiple negotiators will be considered further in Chapters 11, 12, and 13.

• Finally, while we describe these steps in a relatively linear fashion, complete and up-to-date planning will require a certain degree of shuttling back and forth between steps to ensure alignment of strategy and plan. For example, information often cannot be obtained and accumulated simply and straightforwardly, and information discovered in some of the later steps may force a negotiator to reconsider and reevaluate earlier steps. As a result, the first iteration through the planning process should be tentative, and the negotiator should be flexible enough to modify and adjust previous steps as new information becomes available.

1. Defining the Issues

This step itself usually begins with an analysis of what is to be discussed in the negotiation. Some negotiations may only consist of a single issue—for example, the price of an item, such as the price of a coffee table being purchased at a yard sale or the price of a used car. Other negotiations are more complex. Thus, the purchase of one company by

TABLE 4.3 | Negotiation Planning Guide

1. What are the issues in the upcoming negotiation?

2. Based on a review of *all* the issues, what is the "bargaining mix"? (Which issues do we have to cover? Which issues are connected to other issues?)

3. What are my interests?

4. What is my resistance point—what is my walkaway?

5. What is my alternative?

6. Defining targets and asking prices—where will I start, what is my goal?

7. Who are my constituents and what do they want me to do?

8. Who are the opposing negotiators and what do they want?

9. What overall strategy do I want to select?

10. What protocol needs to be followed in conducting this negotiation?

another may include a large number of questions such as price; transfer of inventory; executives and workers who will be retained, transferred, or laid off; new headquarters location; and the like.

The number of issues in a negotiation, together with the relationship between the negotiator and the other party, are often the primary determinant of whether one uses a distributive or integrative strategy. Single-issue negotiations tend to dictate distributive negotiations because the only real negotiation issue is the price or "distribution" of that issue. In contrast, multiple-issue negotiations lend themselves more to integrative negotiations because parties can use processes such as logrolling to create issue "packages" that are mutually beneficial. A simple representation of this is presented in Figure 4.4. The vertical axis represents increasingly valuable outcomes for the buyer, and the horizontal axis represents increasingly valuable payoffs to the seller. In a one-issue negotiation, each party is striving to realize as much value for herself or himself as possible. If the buyer dominates, she or he will receive an outcome high on the buyer's axis, which will not be advantageous to the seller (e.g., point A); if the seller dominates, she or he will receive an outcome high on the seller's axis, but not advantageous to the buyer (e.g., point B). If they are equally strong, the best they can possibly do is some point along a line between points A and B (e.g., point C). Any point along the A–C–B line represents a possible solution to the single-issue negotiation. However, multiple issues may allow the parties to "create value" by finding solutions that improve the outcomes for *both* parties. The choice of whether to pursue a claiming value or creating value strategy is described as the "negotiator's

FIGURE 4.4 | How Issues Affect the Choice between Distributive and Integrative Strategy

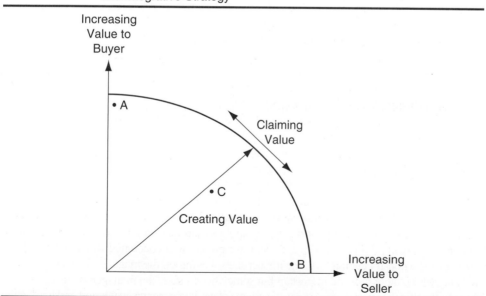

Sources: After Lax and Sebenius, 1986; Raiffa, 1996; Watkins, 2002.

dilemma" (Lax and Sebenius, 1986). Single-issue negotiations and the absence of a long-term relationship with the other party are the strongest drivers of claiming-value strategies; multiple-issue negotiations and the importance of a long-term relationship with the other party are the strongest drivers of creating-value strategies.

While the number of issues affects strategy, it does not preclude the possibility that single-issue negotiations can be made integrative or that multiple-issue negotiations will remain distributive. Single-issue negotiations can often be made integrative by working to *increase* the number of issues. For instance, in buying a house, both parties may begin by believing that price is the only issue but may quickly realize that other issues are equally central: how the purchase will be financed, date of sale, or date of occupancy. They might also identify other issues, such as appliances or patio furniture to be included, repair of a broken fence, or payment for the fuel oil left in the storage tank. During the purchase process, the buyer's lawyer, mortgage financer, or real estate agent might draw up a list of other things to consider: taxes to pay, escrow amounts for undiscovered problems, or a written statement that the seller must leave the house in "broom-clean" condition (as well as the fees to be paid to all these professionals!). Note that it does not take long to generate a fairly detailed list. In any negotiation, a complete list of the issues at stake is best derived from the following sources:

1. An analysis of all the possible issues that need to be decided.

2. Previous experience in similar negotiations.

3. Research conducted to gather information (e.g., study the neighborhood, have the house inspected, or read up on how to buy a house).

4. Consultation with experts in that industry (real estate agents, mortgage lenders, attorneys, accountants, or friends who have bought a house recently).

Similarly, even in multiple-issue negotiations, the opportunity to create value may be lost in competitive dynamics that minimize trust and information sharing and that treats each issue in a distributive manner. This is discussed further in the next section.

Before considering ways to manage the list of issues, a word of caution is necessary. Note that we have used a simple, traditional example here—the purchase of a house. Many negotiations will differ markedly from this example because a traditional agreement or contract is not the issue. In addition, many negotiations are not based on quantitatively defined issues like the price of a house. In these situations, defining the key issues may be much more complex and elusive. For example, suppose a manager gets signals from his boss that his performance is not up to par, yet whenever he tries to confront the boss to obtain a realistic performance appraisal, the boss won't talk directly about the problem (which raises the manager's anxiety even further). Although the conflict in this situation is evident, the "issues" are elusive. The central issue for the employee is the performance appraisal and why the boss won't give it. Maybe the boss is uncomfortable with the performance appraisal process or has a problem confronting other people about poor performance. Perhaps the boss is so preoccupied with her own job security that she doesn't even realize the impact she is having on the manager. In a situation like this one, where the issues are important but somewhat elusive, the manager needs to be clear about both what the issue is (in this case, getting a clear performance evaluation and getting the boss to talk about it) and how to initiate a productive discussion.

2. Assembling the Issues and Defining the Bargaining Mix

The next step in planning is to assemble all the issues that have been defined into a comprehensive list. The combination of lists from each side in the negotiation determines the bargaining mix (see Chapter 2). In generating a list of issues, negotiators may feel that they put too much on the table at once or raise too many issues. This may happen if the parties do not talk frequently or if they have lots of business to transact. As we noted in step 1, however, introducing a long list of issues into a negotiation often makes success more, rather than less, likely—provided that all the issues are real. Large bargaining mixes allow many possible components and arrangements for settlement, thus increasing the likelihood that a particular package will meet both parties' needs and therefore lead to a successful settlement (Rubin and Brown, 1975). At the same time, large bargaining mixes can lengthen negotiations because they present so many possible combinations of issues to consider, and combining and evaluating all these mixes makes valuing the deal very complex.

After assembling issues on an agenda, the negotiator next must prioritize them. Prioritization includes two steps:

1. *Determine which issues are most important and which are less important.* Once negotiation begins, parties can easily be swept up in the rush of information, arguments, offers, counteroffers, trade-offs, and concessions. For those who are not clear in advance about what they want and what they can do without, it is easy to lose perspective and agree to suboptimal settlements or to get distracted by long debates over points that are relatively unimportant. When negotiators do not have priorities, they may be more likely to yield on those points aggressively argued by the other side rather than to yield based on their own priorities.

Priorities can be set in a number of ways. One simple way is for the negotiator to rank-order the issues by asking "What is most important?" "What is second most important?" and "What is least important?" An even simpler process is to group issues into categories of high, medium, or low importance. When the negotiator represents a constituency, it is important to involve that group in setting priorities. Priorities can be set for both interests and more specific issues. A third, more precise method is to award a total of 100 points to the total package of issues, and then to divide the points among the issues in proportion to each issue's relative importance. If the negotiator has confidence in the relative weighting of points across the issues, then trading off and "packaging" possible settlements together becomes more systematic (see Simons and Tripp, 2002, 2006, for one example).

It is also important to set priorities (and possibly assign points) for both tangible and intangible issues. Intangible issues are often difficult to discuss and rank-order, yet if they remain subjective and not quantified, negotiators may overemphasize or underemphasize them. It is easy to push such issues aside in favor of concrete, specific, numerical issues—and negotiators must be careful not to let the "hard bargaining" over numbers drive out more ephemeral discussion of intangible issues and interests. More than one negotiator has received a rude shock when his or her constituency has rejected a settlement because it ignored the intangibles or dealt with them suboptimally in the final agreement.

Finally, negotiators may also wish to specify a bargaining range for each issue in the mix. Thus, not only would a "best possible" and "minimally acceptable" package be specified, but also a target and minimally acceptable level would be specified for each issue in the mix.

2.   *Determine whether the issues are linked together or separate.* If the issues are separate, they can be easily added or subtracted; if connected, then settlement on one will be linked to settlement on the others and making concessions on one issue will inevitably be tied to some other issue. The negotiator must decide whether the issues are truly connected— for instance, whether the price he will pay for the house is dependent on what the bank will loan him—as opposed to simply being connected in his own mind for the sake of achieving a good settlement.

3. Defining Interests

After defining the issues, the negotiator must proceed to define the underlying interests and needs. As we extensively discussed in Chapters 2 and 3, *positions*—an opening bid or a target point—are what a negotiator wants. *Interests* are why she wants them. A target point of $200,000 for a condo would be a position; this is what the negotiator hopes to pay. The interest would be "to pay a fair market price, and one I can afford, for that two-bedroom condominium." Although defining interests is more important to integrative negotiation than to distributive bargaining, even distributive discussions can benefit from one or both parties identifying the key interests. If issues help us define *what* we want, then understanding interests requires us to ask *why* we want it. Asking "why" questions usually helps critical values, needs, or principles surface that we want to achieve in the negotiation (Ury, 1991) (see Chapter 6). Interests may be

- Substantive, that is, directly related to the focal issues under negotiation.
- Process-based, that is, related to how the negotiators behave as they negotiate.
- Relationship-based, that is, tied to the current or desired future relationship between the parties.

Interests may also be based on the intangibles of negotiation—including principles or standards to which the parties wish to adhere, the informal norms by which they will negotiate, and the benchmarks they will use to guide them toward a settlement—to achieve a fair or reasonable deal or to get the negotiation concluded quickly.

Wallihan (2003) offers several excellent examples that help highlight why getting at interests may be essential to understanding another side's position. In one case, a union negotiated for a lower wage than management was actually willing to offer; in that case, the union was actually trying to hold wages down so management would not be tempted to contract with nonunion crews. In a second case, a buyer asked a building contractor to quote a higher bid, just so the builder would have an incentive to complete the job well and on time. From the point of view of "positions," having buyers ask for a higher bid or unions ask for a lower wage would be seen as irrational; however, from an interests perspective, the requests make eminently good sense.

4. Knowing Limits

What will happen if the other party refuses to accept some proposed items for the agenda or states issues in such a way that they are unacceptable? Good preparation requires that you establish two clear points: your *resistance point* and your *alternatives.*

A *resistance point* is the place where you decide that you should absolutely stop the negotiation rather than continue, because any settlement beyond this point is not minimally acceptable. If you are the seller, your resistance point is the least you will take for the item you have for sale; if you are the buyer, your resistance point is the most you will pay for the item.

Setting resistance points as a part of planning is critical. Most of us have been involved in buying situations in which the item we wanted wasn't available, but we allowed ourselves to be talked into a more expensive model. Moreover, some competitive situations generate intense pressures to escalate the price. For example, in an auction, if there is a bidding war with another person, one may pay more than was planned. Gamblers, analogously, may encounter a losing streak and end up losing more money than they had planned. Clear resistance points help keep people from agreeing to deals that they later realize weren't very smart.

5. Knowing Alternatives

On the other hand, *alternatives* are other agreements negotiators could achieve and still meet their needs. Alternatives are very important in both distributive and integrative processes because they define whether the current outcome is better than another possibility. In any situation, the better the alternatives, the more power you have because you can walk away from the current negotiation and still know that your needs and interests can be met (see also Chapters 2 and 7). In the house-purchase example, the more a buyer has researched the real estate market and understands what other comparable houses are available, the more she knows that she can walk away from this negotiation and still have acceptable housing choices.

6. Setting Targets and Asking Prices

After negotiators have defined the issues, assembled a tentative agenda, and consulted others as appropriate and necessary, the next step is to define two other key points: the specific *target point* where one realistically expects to achieve a settlement and the *asking price,* representing the best deal one can hope to achieve.

There are numerous ways to set a target. One can ask, "What is an outcome that I would be pleased with?" "At what point would I be very satisfied?" "What have other people achieved in this situation?" "What would be a fair and reasonable settlement?" Targets may not be as firm and rigid as resistance points or alternatives; one might be able to set a general range or a class of several outcomes that would be equally acceptable.

Similarly, there are numerous ways to set an initial asking price. An opening bid may be the best possible outcome, an ideal solution, something even better than was achieved last time. It is easy to get overly confident, however, and to set an opening that is so unrealistic that the other party immediately laughs, gets angry, or walks away before responding. While openings are usually formulated around a "best possible" settlement, it is also easy to inflate them to the point where they become self-defeating because they are too unrealistic in the eyes of the other negotiator or observers with a more realistic perspective.

There are several principles to keep in mind when setting a *target point:*

1. *Targets should be specific, difficult but achievable, and verifiable.* A lot can be learned about setting a target point from researchers who have studied goal setting as a motivation and performance management tool (e.g., Locke and Latham, 1984). First, goals need to be specific. If negotiating a salary, one should set a specific number (e.g., $75,000) rather than a more general goal (e.g., anything better than $60,000 a year). Second, goals should be difficult but achievable. A goal should be set so that it is an improvement over the current situation or circumstances, but not so difficult that it can't be achieved. Finally, it should be possible to define a goal so that it is clear when it is or is not achieved. This is not a problem if one has set a quantifiable goal like a payment amount or a dollar salary, but it can be a problem if one is setting a more diffuse goal (e.g., get a decent salary that will pay me what I am worth. "Decent" and "what I am worth" are highly subjective targets, and it will be most difficult for the negotiator—and others—to judge when that goal has been truly achieved).

2. *Target setting requires positive thinking about one's* own *objectives.* When approaching a negotiation, it is possible to pay too much attention to the other party—how they behave, what they will probably demand, and what it is like to deal with them. If negotiators focus attention on the other party to the exclusion of themselves, they may set their goals strictly as a reaction to the other's anticipated goals and targets. Reactive strategies are likely to make negotiators feel threatened and defensive and lessen their flexibility and creativity (and perhaps limit the goals they think are achievable). In contrast, being proactive about target setting permits negotiators to be flexible in what they will accept and improves the likelihood of arriving at a mutually satisfactory outcome.

3. *Target setting often requires considering how to package several issues and objectives.* Most negotiators have a mixture of bargaining objectives, so they must consider the best way to achieve satisfaction across multiple issues. To package issues effectively, negotiators need to understand the issues, the relative priorities across the issues, and the bargaining mix. It is possible to define and evaluate some of these packages as "opening bids" and others as "targets" in the same ways as evaluating individual issues. When packages involve intangible issues, or issues for which it is difficult to specify definite targets, it is harder to evaluate and compare the packages explicitly, but efforts should be made to do so.

4. *Target setting requires an understanding of trade-offs and throwaways.* The discussion of packaging raises another possible challenge: What if the other party proposes a package that puts issues A, B, and C as major issues in their opening bid, but only mentions issue D. In the next offer, they never mention issue D—but issue D happens to be something you can easily give them. If you can give easily on issue D, would they be willing to take less on A, B, or C? Negotiators may want to consider giving away "something for nothing" if such an item can be part of the transaction. Even if an issue is unimportant or inconsequential to you, it may be valuable or attractive to the other party. Awareness of the actual or likely value of such concessions in a package can considerably enrich the value of what one offers to the

other party at little or no cost to oneself. Using the house example again, the seller may have eight months left on a local parking-lot pass or access to a community recreation facility. Because the money the seller paid for the pass is nonrefundable, the pass will be worthless to the seller once she leaves the area, but the buyer could see the pass as a valuable item.

To evaluate these packages, negotiators need to have some idea of what each item in the bargaining mix is worth in terms that can be compared or traded-off across issues. As mentioned earlier, it may be desirable to find a common dimension such as dollar value or a scale of utility points to compare issues in the bargaining mix, or to compare tangibles with intangibles, so that one can evaluate all items in the mix on a common dimension. For example, in labor negotiations, each side often tries to value an issue in dollar cost/benefit terms. Even if the fit is not perfect, any guide is better than none. Moreover, if intangibles are a key part of the bargaining mix, negotiators must know the point at which they are willing to abandon the pursuit of an intangible in favor of substantial gains on tangibles.

7. Assessing Constituents and the Social Context of the Negotiation

When people are negotiating for themselves—for example, buying a used racing bicycle or exercise machine—they can determine the bargaining mix on their own. But when people negotiate in a professional context, there may be more than two parties. First, there may be more than two negotiators at the table. Multiple parties at the table often lead to coalitions of negotiators who align with each other in order to win the negotiation (cf. Wheeler, 2002, and our discussion of coalition dynamics in Chapter 12). Second, negotiators also have "constituents"—bosses, superiors who make the final decision, or other parties who will evaluate and critique the solution achieved. Moreover, there may be observers of the negotiation who also watch and critique the negotiation. When one has a constituent or observer, other issues arise, such as who conducts the negotiation, who can participate in the negotiation, and who has the ultimate power to ratify negotiated agreements; these issues are addressed in Chapter 11. Finally, negotiation occurs in a context of rules—a social system of laws, customs, common business practices, cultural norms, and political cross-pressures.

One way to assess all the key parties in a negotiation is to complete a "field analysis." Imagine that you are the captain of a soccer team, about to play a game on the field (see Figure 4.5). Assessing constituents is the same as assessing all the parties who are in the soccer stadium:

1. Who is, or should be, on the team on my side of the field? Perhaps it is just the negotiator (a one-on-one game). But perhaps we want other help: an attorney, accountant, or an expert to assist us; someone to coach us, give us moral support, or listen closely to what the other side says; a recorder or note-taker.

2. Who is on the other side of the field? This is discussed in more detail in the next section.

3. Who is on the sidelines and can affect the play of the game? Who are the negotiation equivalents of owners, managers, and strategists? This includes one's direct superior or the person who must approve or authorize the agreement reached. Most importantly, these considerations directly affect how decisions will be made about what is acceptable or unacceptable to those on each side.

FIGURE 4.5 | A Field Analysis of Negotiation

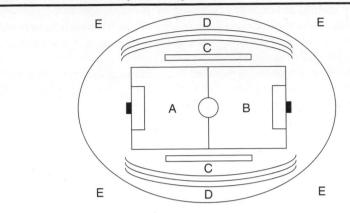

A. The direct actors (who is on the field on our side?)

B. The opposition actors (who is on the field on their side?)

C. Indirect actors (who is on the sidelines?)

D. Interested observers (who is in the stands?)

E. Environmental factors (what is going on in the broad environment of the game—outside the stadium, but shaping and defining what happens in the stadium?)

4. Who is in the stands? Who is watching the game, is interested in it, but can only indirectly affect what happens? This might include senior managers, shareholders, competitors, financial analysts, the media, or others. When multiple parties enter the negotiation—whether they are parties on the sidelines who are active in the negotiation or "interested parties" who may be affected by the settlement—negotiations will become more complex. The nature of these complexities is explored in Chapters 11, 12, and 13.

5. What is going on in the broader environment in which the negotiation takes place? A number of "context" issues can affect negotiation:

   - What is the history of the relationship with the other party, and how does it affect the overall expectations they bring to this negotiation (see Chapter 10)?

   - What kind of a relationship with the other party is expected or desired for the future, and how do these expectations affect the current negotiation (see Chapter 10)?

   - How often do we expect to negotiate in the future—that is, how many rounds of negotiation will there be? Multiround negotiations create issues of managing precedents, planning future agendas, and ensuring that current agreements are enacted and monitored (Wheeler, 2002).

   - What are the deadlines or time limits? To extend the game metaphor, games have a finite time period that is broken down into periods or segments. Are there similar constraints that bound this negotiation?

   - What are the "rules of the game" by which this agreement will be managed? Is there a set of fixed rules, such as a legal structure that will bind and enforce contracts? What are the common and acceptable practices in the legal system in which the deal is being done? Is the rule structure itself negotiable so that we can make up our own rules about how certain problems and situations will be handled? Will one party try to impose rules unilaterally, and what can the other side do? Are negotiations occurring across cultures, and what "cultural rules" or practices may apply (Chapter 16)? Finally, is there a forum in which certain negotiations should take place—a public space, a private office, a lawyer's office, a courthouse—and are there dispute resolution mechanisms in place to guide how we should behave if we cannot agree? Are referees or "third parties" available to officiate the game and intervene when there has been a breach of the rules (see Chapter 19) (Watkins, 2002)?

   - What is common and acceptable practice in the ethical system in which the deal is being done (see Chapter 9)? How will we decide if one party "cheats"; are there clear rules about what is and is not fair?

Considering these questions is important to the progress of the negotiation process. A negotiator bargaining on behalf of others (a company, union, department, club, family, etc.) must consult with them so that their concerns and priorities are included in the mix. In the house-buying illustration used earlier, let's assume that one member of a couple is doing the negotiating, and the other can't attend the meeting. If that person fails to consider his partner's concerns about the condition in which the house is left, or their children's wish that the move not occur during the school year, then the negotiated resolution may be rejected by the constituents. A negotiator who is representing a constituency is accountable to that constituency and must include their wishes in proposals—subsequently either fulfilling those wishes for them through negotiation or explaining why their desires were not met. When negotiating for a large constituency, such as an entire company or a union or a community, the process of consulting with the constituency can be elaborate and exhaustive. The negotiator may recognize that the constituency's wish list is unrealistic and unobtainable, requiring the negotiator to negotiate with the constituency over what should be included on the agenda and what is realistic to expect. It is also critical to understand what happens when the two parties get close to an agreement. Does the negotiator have authority to reach agreement, or does the approval of the constituents have to be obtained? Constituents control negotiators by limiting how much they can decide on their own, and understanding these limits will keep negotiators in alignment with their constituents. (We explore this further in detail in Chapter 11.)

8. Analyzing the Other Party

Earlier in this section, we discussed the importance of assigning priorities to one's own goals and objectives. Gathering information about the other party is also a critical step in preparing for negotiation. Learning the other's issues, preferences, priorities, interests, alternatives and constraints is almost as important as determining one's own. If negotiators have not had the opportunity to meet with people from the other side, then they should find a way to start to see the negotiation from the other party's perspective or to gather information to learn about their issues, interests, and priorities. Negotiators might call the other party and speak to them prior to the formal meeting or try to take their perspective and anticipate what they might want. It may also be possible to speak to others who know the other party or to people who have been in their situation before. The goal is to understand how they are approaching the negotiation and what they are likely to want. By comparing this assessment against your own, one can begin to define areas where there may be strong conflict (both parties have a high priority for the same thing), simple trade-offs (both parties want the same group of things but in differing priorities), or no conflict at all (both parties want very different things and both can easily have their objectives and interests met).

What information does one party need about the other party in order to prepare effectively? Several key pieces of background information will be of great importance, including their

- Resources, issues, and bargaining mix.
- Interests and needs.
- Walkaway point and alternative(s).
- Targets and opening bids.
- Constituents, social structure, and authority to make an agreement.
- Reputation and negotiation style.
- Likely strategy and tactics.

In theory, it would be extremely useful to have as much of this information as possible before negotiations occur. In reality, it may not be possible to obtain this information before the negotiation starts. If this is the case, the negotiator should plan to collect as much of this information as possible during the opening stages of the actual deliberations.

The Other Party's Resources, Issues, and Bargaining Mix   The more information one can gather about the other through initial research the better. Which data are most relevant will depend on the issues and likely elements in the bargaining mix. An analysis of the other party's business history or previous negotiations, successful and otherwise, might provide useful clues. Financial data about the other party might be obtained through channels such as Internet searches, financial statements, company records, stock reports, interviews and court documents, or legal judgments. One might investigate the other party's inventories. Sometimes one can learn a great deal simply by visiting the other party or speaking to his or her friends and peers. Another way to learn is to ask questions of people who have done business with the other party. The more the negotiator can get even a general sense of how much the other is capable of addressing and meeting the party's issues or needs, and of what issues they will bring to the bargaining table, the better one can predict how the process is likely to unfold.

The Other Party's Interests and Needs   In addition to learning about the party's major issues and resources, one also needs to get information about his or her current interests and needs (see Chapter 3). This information may be obtained through a variety of routes:

- Conducting a preliminary interview, including a broad discussion of what the other party would like to achieve in the upcoming negotiations (focus on broad interests, not just issues).
- Anticipating the other party's interests (as if you were "in their shoes").
- Asking others who know or have negotiated with the other party.
- Reading how the other party portrays himself or herself in the media.

The importance of the issues or interests, along with the nature of the past relationship with the other party, will influence the depth to which one probes to get information. Although it does take time and effort to get information, the results are usually more than worth the investment because valuable information can often be gathered through a phone call or a visit.

The Other Party's Walkaway Point and Alternatives   We also need to get a sense of the other party's walkaway point and alternatives. How far can they go? What is the maximum they can give us? And what will they do if this negotiation does not succeed? Understanding the other party's limits and alternatives is important because it will give us some information about how far we can "push" them. How good are their alternatives? If the other party has a strong and viable alternative, he or she will probably be confident in negotiation, set high objectives, and be willing to push hard for those objectives. In contrast, if the other party has a weak alternative, then she or he will be more dependent on achieving a satisfactory agreement with you and be less likely to push as hard.

Bear in mind that in a distributive negotiation, the other party may be less likely to disclose this information and/or may misrepresent their limits and alternatives so as to pressure us into a deal that is better for them. In an integrative negotiation, there should be more openness between the parties, which should lead to more accurate disclosure of limits and alternatives.

The Other Party's Targets and Openings   After negotiators have obtained information about the other side's issues, bargaining mix, and interests, they also need to understand his or her goals. People often think stereotypically about the other party's interests and targets; they use their own targets and values as a benchmark and assume (often inappropriately) that others are like themselves and want similar things. A manager who is always after a bigger paycheck may be surprised to learn that some of his subordinates are more interested in having a challenging job, schedule flexibility, or increased leisure time than they are in maximizing their salary.

How can one understand and appraise the other party's targets? Although speculation about another's objectives is seldom sufficient, most people do *not* gather information systematically—but they should. One of the best ways to get this information is directly from the other party. Because information about the other party's targets is so important to the strategy formulation of both parties, professional negotiators will often exchange information about targets or opening proposals days or even weeks before negotiations begin. If this does not occur, then the negotiator should plan to collect as much of this information as possible at the first meeting with the other party.

The Other Party's Constituents, Social Structure, and Authority   As in planning step 7, it is important to understand the broader social context in which the negotiation will occur for the other party. Who will they bring to the table? Who are they accountable to? What rules or procedures are they likely to follow? This analysis can be quite simple for purchasing a used computer but quite complex in a large multinational negotiation.

The most direct impact of the broader social context is on the other negotiator's ability to make binding agreements. When negotiators represent others, their power to make agreements may be restricted in many ways. Sometimes a constituency stipulates that negotiators cannot make any binding agreements; often negotiators can only present proposals from the constituency or collect information and take it back to their superiors.

There are many reasons for limiting a negotiator's authority. Negotiators without decision authority cannot be won over by a persuasive presentation to commit their constituency to something they do not want. They cannot give out sensitive information carelessly. Although these limitations may be helpful to a negotiator, they can also be frustrating. The other party might ask, "Why should I speak with this person, if she cannot make a commitment and may not even be well informed about what I want?" Negotiation under these circumstances can seem like an exercise in futility. When a negotiator always has to check things out with those he represents, the other party may refuse to continue until someone who has the power to answer questions and make decisions is brought to the table. Negotiating teams should think seriously about sending in a negotiator with limited authority. Although that person will not be able to make unauthorized (and perhaps problematic) agreements, the limited authority may frustrate the other party and create an unproductive tension in the negotiating relationship (see Chapter 11).

More broadly, the negotiator needs to know how the other party's organization makes decisions to support or ratify an agreement. Is there a senior executive who will dictate the decision? Will people vote? Or is the decision by committee? How decisions are made can have dramatic implications for who needs to be directly influenced on the other side.

The Other Party's Reputation and Negotiation Style   As noted earlier, the other party's past negotiating behavior is a good indication of how he or she will behave in the future. Even if a bargainer has had no previous experience with the other person, speaking to those who have dealt with that person in the past can be very valuable. Has the other party acted distributively or integratively?

This kind of information is an important determinant of how to approach the other party in the negotiation. Whether or not they have a reputation for being cooperative or competitive may affect the strategy pursued in the next negotiation. On the other hand, there is a potential danger in drawing conclusions from this information. Assuming that the other party will act in the future as he or she has been described as acting in the past is just that—an assumption. People can act differently in different circumstances at different times. Although gathering information about the other party's past behavior is a reasonable starting point for making assumptions, keep in mind that people do change over time. One author on negotiation notes:

> Assumptions are potential hurdles that can move us in the wrong direction . . . The reality of negotiation is that we must and should make assumptions about the opposing party . . . The important thing to remember is that your assumptions are just that. They are no better than poorly educated guesses at best. Don't fall in love with your assumptions. Check them out; they are neither right nor wrong until proven so. (Karrass, 1974, p. 11)

One's impression of the other party's reputation may be based on several factors:

1. How the other party's predecessors have negotiated with you in the past.
2. How the other party has negotiated with you in the past, either in the same or in different contexts.
3. How the other party has negotiated with others in the past.

These different bases for one's assumptions have different degrees of relevance and usefulness for predicting future behavior. One can use the information to prepare and to alert oneself to what might happen; but one should also act with caution and actively look for new information that confirms or denies the validity of the assumptions. There is always the danger, however, that invalid assumptions will lead a negotiator into incorrect self-fulfilling prophecies (see Chapter 5 for our extensive discussion of perception and decision biases). That is, there is a tendency to seek and recognize information that confirms one's desires and assumptions while failing to seek or recognize information that disconfirms or counters them. Thus, a negotiator who assumes the other party is going to be demanding and aggressive may decide that the best defense is a good offense and therefore open with aggressive demands and belligerent behavior. The other party may take this behavior in stride or may decide to reply in kind, even though he or she initially intended to be cooperative. Of course, when the other party does fight back, the first negotiator's assumptions seem to be confirmed. If this initial misunderstanding is all that occurs, the problem may be recognized and corrected before it escalates. However, certain expectations can trigger an escalating cycle of competitive mistrust and hostility, particularly when negotiations occur in longstanding relationships. These cycles are common in relationships between nations and between labor and management groups (see Lewicki and Alderfer, 1973; Pruitt and Rubin, 1986).

The Other Party's Strategy and Tactics   Finally, it is also helpful to gain information about the other party's intended strategy and tactics. Although it is unlikely the other party will reveal his or her strategy outright—particularly if he or she is intending to use distributive tactics—one can infer this information from data collected during preparation. Information collected about issues, objectives, reputation, style, alternatives, and authority may indicate a great deal about what strategy the other party intends to pursue. As we have noted before, negotiators will have to gather this information on an emergent basis as the negotiation unfolds; if their expectations have been incorrect, it will be necessary to recalibrate their strategic response.

9. Presenting Issues to the Other Party

One important aspect of negotiations is to present a case clearly and to provide ample supporting facts and arguments; another is to refute the other party's arguments with counterarguments.

Because of the breadth and diversity of issues that can be included in negotiations, it is not possible to specify all the procedures that can be used to assemble information. There are, however, some good general guides that can be used. A negotiator can ask these questions:

1.   What facts support my point of view? How can I validate this information as credible?

2.   Whom may I consult or talk with to help me elaborate or clarify the facts? What records, files, or data sources exist that support my arguments? Can I enlist experts to support my arguments?

3.   Have these issues been negotiated before by others under similar circumstances? Can I consult those negotiators to determine what major arguments they used, which ones were successful, and which were not?

4.   What is the other party's point of view likely to be? What are her or his interests? What arguments is she or he likely to make? How can I respond to those arguments and seek more creative positions that go further in addressing both sides' issues and interests?

5.   How can I develop and present the facts so they are most convincing? What visual aids, pictures, charts, graphs, expert testimony, and the like can be helpful or make the best case?

In Chapters 7 and 8, we offer extensive advice to the negotiator on how to use power and how to structure the presentation of information to be maximally influential.

10. What Protocol Needs to Be Followed in This Negotiation?

A negotiator should consider a number of elements of protocol or process:

- *What agenda should we follow?* We briefly mentioned this issue in step 7, in assessing the social structure. A negotiator may unilaterally draw up a firm list of issues well before the initial negotiation meeting. This process is valuable because it forces negotiators to think through their positions and decide on objectives. The unilateral list of issues constitutes a preliminary agenda for negotiation. It is what the negotiator wants to discuss, and the *order* or *priority* in which he wants to discuss them (e.g., least versus most important issue first, etc.). Pendergast (1990) suggests five major concerns to be considered in developing a negotiation agenda:

1. *Scope:* what issue should be considered?

2. *Sequence:* in what order should those issues be addressed?

3. *Framing:* how should the issues be presented (see Chapter 5)?

4. *Packaging:* whether to take the issues one at a time, or in various groupings/packages?

5. *Formula:* should we strive to first get an agreement on general principles, or should we immediately begin to discuss each of the issues?

While the negotiator may propose agendas unilaterally, this approach has a potential risk. If the negotiator's list differs from a preset agenda or the other side's preferred list, the negotiator may bring issues to the table that the other party is unprepared to discuss or may define priorities that cannot be achieved realistically. Negotiators do not welcome surprises or the embarrassment that may come when the other side raises an issue they are completely unprepared to discuss. In this situation, experienced negotiators will ask for a recess to get information and prepare themselves on the new issue, thus creating unanticipated delays. They may even refuse to include the new item on the agenda because they haven't had time to prepare for it. If the other party is also accountable to a constituency, he or she may not want to reopen earlier decisions or take the time to evaluate the new issue. For this reason, many professional negotiators such as labor negotiators and diplomats often exchange and negotiate the agenda in advance. They want to agree on what issues will be discussed on the agenda before engaging in the substantive discussion of those issues.

- *Where should we negotiate?* Negotiators are more comfortable on their home turf—their own office, building, or city. They know the space, they feel comfortable and relaxed, they have direct access to all the amenities—secretaries, research information, expert advice, computers, and so on. In cross-cultural negotiations (see Chapter 16), language and cultural differences may come into play, and the parties may have to travel across many time zones, stay in unfamiliar locations, eat unfamiliar food, and deal with similar potential problems. If negotiators want to minimize the advantage that comes with home turf, then they need to select neutral territory in which neither party will have an advantage. In addition, negotiators can choose the degree of formality of the environment. Formal deliberations are often held in board or conference rooms or hotel meeting rooms; informal deliberations can be held in restaurants, cocktail lounges, or private airline clubs.

- *What is the time period of the negotiation?* If negotiators expect long, protracted deliberations, they might want to negotiate the time and duration of sessions. When do we start? How long do we meet? When do we need to end? When can we call for coffee breaks or time to caucus with our team?

BOX 4.3   Redoing the Deal

Negotiation advisor Jeswald Salacuse suggests that renegotiations generally occur for one of two reasons: the agreement was imperfect when it was designed or the circumstances surrounding the agreement have changed. Salacuse offers two sets of advice: what to do before the deal breaks down, and what to do after the deal breaks down.

Before the deal breaks down:

1. Build a relationship with the other side that can be used in case the deal falters.
2. Take the time to build the relationship.
3. Provide for mechanisms to renegotiate if the deal breaks down.
4. Consider how to involve a third party if the deal breaks down (Chapter 19).

After the deal breaks down:

1. Avoid negativity and anger.
2. Decide whether what you want to renegotiate could ruin the relationship, and whether it is worth it.
3. Create new value through the renegotiation.
4. Fully evaluate the costs of failure.
5. Involve all the critical parties.
6. Design the right environment and process to do the renegotiation.
7. Consider how to involve a mediator or other third party to help out.

Source: From J. Salacuse, "Redoing the Deal," *Negotiation Newsletter,* Harvard Business School Publishing, August 2005.

- *What might be done if negotiation fails?* What will happen if we deadlock? Can we "redo" the deal? Will we go to a third-party neutral (see Chapter 19)? Might we try some other techniques? (See Chapters 17 and 18 for suggestions on getting negotiations back on track.)

- *How will we keep track of what is agreed to?* Many negotiators don't consider the importance of recording exactly what was discussed and agreed to. Being a recording secretary may be perceived as a tedious and uninteresting job. Experienced negotiators know that this role is critical, however. First, the person with the best notes often becomes the "memory" of the session, as her or his notes are later consulted to determine what was said and discussed. Second, the person with the best notes may also volunteer to draft the initial agreement; this person may have some latitude in how the agreement is stated and what points are emphasized or deemphasized. Finally, if the agreement is highly technical or complex, one certainly wants to have the agreement reviewed by experts and specialists— attorneys, financial analysts, accountants, engineers, and so on.

  In new bargaining relationships, discussions about these procedural issues should occur *before* the major substantive issues are raised. The ease or difficulty of resolving these procedural issues can be used as litmus tests to determine how the negotiation on the larger substantive issues will proceed. If the negotiator enjoys success in these procedural negotiations, it may be easier to reach agreement later on the substantive issues.

- *How do we know whether we have a good agreement?* Finally, do we have a process in place for ensuring that once the negotiation has concluded, we can systematically evaluate how the deal compares with (1) our initial plan and (2) our sense of the best we can do given the other party and all of the structural and procedural constraints? (see Box 4.3).

Chapter Summary

Planning is a critically important activity in negotiation. As we noted at the outset, however, negotiators frequently fail to plan for a variety of reasons. Effective planning allows negotiators to design a road map that will guide them to agreement. While this map may frequently need to be modified and updated as discussions with the other side proceed, and as the world around the negotiation changes, working from the map is far more effective than attempting to work without it.

We began this chapter with a basic understanding of the concepts of strategy, and we presented a model of negotiation strategy choice, returning to the familiar framework of the dual concerns model. Having described the model, we then discussed the importance of setting clear goals, based on the key issues at stake. A negotiator who carefully plans will make an effort to do the following:

1. Understand the key issues that must be resolved in the upcoming negotiation.

2. Assemble all the issues together and understand the complexity of the bargaining mix.

3. Understand and define the key interests at stake that underlie the issues.

4. Define the limits—the point where we will walk away or stop negotiating.

5. Define the alternatives—other deals we could do if this deal does not work out.

6. Clarify the target points to be achieved and the opening points—where we will begin the discussion.

7. Understand my constituents and what they expect of me.

8. Understand the other party in the negotiation—their goals, issues, strategies, interests, limits, alternatives, targets, openings, and authority.

9. Plan the process by which I will present and "sell" my ideas to the other party (and perhaps to my own constituency).

10. Define the important points of protocol in the process—the agenda, who will be at the table or observing the negotiation, where and when we will negotiate, and so on.

When negotiators are able to consider and evaluate each of these factors, they will know what they want and will have a clear sense of direction on how to proceed. This sense of direction, and the confidence derived from it, is a very important factor in affecting negotiating outcomes.

Endnotes

[1] See Richardson (1977); Asherman and Asherman (1990); Burnstein (1995); Fisher and Ertel (1995); Lewicki, Hiam, and Olander (1996); Lewicki and Hiam (1999); Greenhalgh (2001); and Watkins (2002).

CHAPTER

Perception, Cognition, and Emotion

Objectives

1. Understand the important role played by perceptions, cognitions, and emotions in negotiation.

2. Explore how perceptions can become distorted and lead to biases in negotiation and judgment.

3. Consider the ways that cognitions (information processing) in negotiation can also be affected by biases and framing processes, and how emotions and mood can shape a negotiation.

4. Gain advice on how to manage perception, cognition, and emotions in negotiation situations.

Perception, cognition, and emotion are the basic building blocks of all social encounters, including negotiation, in the sense that our social actions are guided by how we perceive, analyze, and feel about the other party, the situation, and our own interests and positions. A working knowledge of how humans perceive the world around them, process information, and experience emotions is important to understanding why people behave the way they do during negotiations.

We begin the chapter by examining how psychological **perception** is related to the process of negotiation, with particular attention to forms of perceptual distortion that can cause problems of understanding and meaning making for negotiators. We then look at how negotiators use information to make decisions about tactics and strategy—the process of **cognition.** Our discussion here pursues two angles. First, we focus on *framing*—the strategic use of information to define and articulate a negotiating issue or situation. Second, we discuss the various kinds of systematic errors, or *cognitive biases,* in information processing that negotiators are prone to make and that may compromise negotiator performance. This section will also consider how negotiators can manage misperceptions and cognitive biases in order to maximize strategic advantage and minimize their adverse effects.

Social encounters are, however, more than just occasions for perception and cognition. We experience and express **emotion** when we interact with others, and negotiating is certainly no exception. In the final major section of this chapter, we discuss the role of moods and emotions in negotiation—both as causes of behavior and as consequences of negotiated outcomes.

Perception

Perception Defined

In this section, we examine some of the psychological principles of perception and communication, and draw examples to the negotiation domain. Negotiators approach each situation guided by their perceptions of past situations and current attitudes and behaviors. Their expectations of the future behaviors of other parties and subsequent outcomes are based in large part on information gained through direct experience or observations.

Perception is the process by which individuals connect to their environment. We are interested here in perceptions that connect a person with a social environment such as a negotiation encounter. Many things influence how a person understands and assigns meaning to messages and events, including the perceiver's current state of mind, role, and comprehension of earlier communications.[1] In negotiation the goal is to perceive and interpret with accuracy what the other party is saying and meaning. Doing so also depends on other parties' perceptions of the situation as well as on the perceiver's own behavioral dispositions. We now examine in more detail how perceptions are created and how they affect what happens in negotiation.

Perception is a complex physical and psychological enterprise. It has been defined as "the process of screening, selecting, and interpreting stimuli so that they have meaning to the individual" (Steers, 1984, p. 98). Perception is a "sense-making" process; people interpret their environment so that they can respond appropriately (see Figure 5.1). Environments are typically complex—they present a large number and variety of stimuli, each having different properties such as magnitude, color, shape, texture, and relative novelty. This complexity makes it impossible to process all the available information, so as perceivers we become selective, tuning in on some stimuli while tuning out others. This selective perception occurs through a number of perceptual "shortcuts" that allow us to process information more readily. Unfortunately, the perceptual efficiencies that result may come at the expense of accuracy. We turn next to forms of perceptual distortion that are particularly relevant for negotiation.

Perceptual Distortion

In any given negotiation, the perceiver's own needs, desires, motivations, and personal experiences may create a predisposition about the other party. This is cause for concern when it leads to biases and errors in perception and subsequent communication. Research on perception and

FIGURE 5.1 | The Perceptual Process

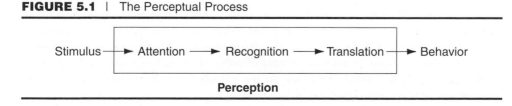

communication goes back several decades (e.g., Bruner and Tagiuri, 1954), with attention to this topic in the negotiation domain coming much later (e.g., Thompson, 1995). We discuss four major perceptual errors: stereotyping, halo effects, selective perception, and projection. Stereotyping and halo effects are examples of perceptual distortion by generalization: small amounts of information are used to draw large conclusions about individuals. Selective perception and projection are, in contrast, forms of distortion that involve anticipating certain attributes and qualities in another person. The perceiver filters and distorts information to arrive at a predictable and consistent view of the other person.

Stereotyping is a very common distortion of the perceptual process. It occurs when one individual assigns attributes to another solely on the basis of the other's membership in a particular social or demographic category. Stereotypes are formed about a wide variety of different groups; examples include the younger generation, males or females, Italians or Germans, or people of different races, religions, or sexual orientations. In each case, stereotypes tend to be formed in the same way. People assign an individual to a group based on one piece of perceptual information (e.g., the individual is young or old); then they assign a broad range of other characteristics of the group to this individual (e.g., "Old people are conservative; this person is old and therefore is conservative" or "Young people are disrespectful; this person is young and therefore is disrespectful"). There may be no factual basis for the conclusion that this particular older individual is conservative; the conclusion is based on the generalization of qualities that have been attributed—accurately or not—to the larger group. Applying other traits associated with the category to this particular individual may further compound the error.

Once formed, stereotypes can be highly resistant to change. The simple process of using a single criterion—even an arbitrary one—to divide people into groups encourages group members to begin to define themselves as "we" and the other group as "they" and then to make evaluative comparisons between them. Individuals are more likely to resort to stereotyping under certain conditions. Examples include time pressure, cognitive stress, and mood, which have all been linked to greater reliance on stereotypes (de Dreu, 2003; Forgas and Fiedler, 1996; Devine, 1989). In addition, conflicts involving values, ideologies, and direct competition for resources among groups increase the likelihood that stereotyping will occur (Sherif, Harvey, White, Hood, and Sherif, 1988).

Halo effects in perception are similar to stereotypes. Rather than using a person's group membership as a basis for classification, however, halo effects occur when people generalize about a variety of attributes based on the knowledge of one attribute of an individual (Cooper, 1981). A smiling person is judged to be more honest than a frowning or scowling person, for example, even though there is no consistent relationship between smiling and honesty. Halo effects may be positive or negative. A good attribute may be generalized so that people are seen in a very positive light, whereas a negative attribute has the reverse effect. The more prominent the attribute is in influencing the overall judgment about an individual, the more likely that it will be used to cast further information into a perspective consistent with the initial judgment. Research shows that halo effects are most likely to occur in perception (1) when there is very little experience with a person along some dimension (and so the perceiver generalizes about that person from knowledge acquired in other contexts), (2) when the person is well known, and (3) when the qualities have strong moral implications (Bruner and Tagiuri, 1954).

Halo effects and stereotypes are common hazards in negotiation. Negotiators are apt to (and may well be under pressure to) form rapid impressions of each other based on very limited initial information, such as appearance, group membership, or initial statements. Negotiators tend to maintain these judgments as they get to know each other better, fitting each piece of new information into some consistent pattern. Finally, as Bruner and Tagiuri suggest, the mere suggestion that the other party can be viewed in moral terms—for example, honest or dishonest, ethical or unethical—is likely to affect the perception of a wide variety of their other attributes.

Selective perception occurs when the perceiver singles out certain information that supports or reinforces a prior belief and filters out information that does not confirm to that belief. Selective perception has the effect of perpetuating stereotypes or halo effects: after forming quick judgments about someone on the basis of limited information, people may then filter out further evidence that might disconfirm the judgment. An initial smile from the other party, which leads the negotiator to believe that he or she is honest or cooperative, might also lead the negotiator to downplay any of that party's statements that demonstrate an intention to be crafty or competitive. If the negotiator perceives the same initial smile as a smirk, then the negotiator may downplay the other party's offers to establish an honest and cooperative relationship. In both cases, the negotiator's own biases—the predisposition to view the smile as honest or dishonest—may affect how the other party's behavior is perceived and interpreted.

Projection occurs when people assign to others the characteristics or feelings that they possess themselves. Projection usually arises out of a need to protect one's own self-concept—to see oneself as consistent and good. Negotiators may assume that the other party would respond in the same manner they would if positions were reversed. For instance, if a negotiator feels that he or she would be frustrated if he or she were in the other party's position, then he or she is likely to perceive that the other party is frustrated. People respond differently to similar situations, however, and projecting one's own feelings and beliefs onto the other negotiator may be incorrect. For instance, if a negotiator is very bothered by delays in negotiations but needs to tell the other party that there will be an unavoidable delay, the negotiator may expect the other party to exhibit frustration at the announcement. While it is possible that the other party will be frustrated, it is also possible that he or she will welcome the delay as an opportunity to complete work on a different project and that any frustration was only a projection from the negotiator's mind. The tendency to project also may lead a negotiator to overestimate how much the other party knows about his or her preferences or desires. In other words, negotiators tend to think their preferences are more obvious to the other party than they actually are (Van Boven, Gilovic, and Medvec, 2003).

Perceptual distortions can influence many aspects of the negotiation process and can be quite persistent once they are formed. These shortcuts help individuals make sense of complex environments and situations, but they come with significant costs—perceptual errors, which typically occur without people being aware that they are happening and which can have unfortunate consequences. For example, distortions affect expectations about the other party and lead to assumptions about his or her position, willingness to cooperate or make concessions, and so on. These assumptions, in turn, may lead negotiators to assume a competitive, defensive stance early in a negotiation. The problem with this chain of events is that if the initial assumptions are incorrect, then negotiators may not be able to reverse their effects; by the time negotiators are in a position to judge the predisposition of the other party accurately, the other party may have interpreted the initial competitive mood and defensive posture of the negotiator as aggressive and antagonistic. This problem may be most acute between groups that have longstanding hostile relationships: unions and management that have been plagued by bitter strikes, ethnic groups with ongoing disagreements, or marital partners in divorce proceedings.

Framing

A key issue in perception and negotiation is framing. A frame is the subjective mechanism through which people evaluate and make sense out of situations, leading them to pursue or avoid subsequent actions (Bateson, 1972; Goffman, 1974). Framing helps explain "how bargainers conceive of ongoing sets of events in light of past experiences"; framing and reframing, along with reevaluation of information and positions, "are tied to information processing, message patterns, linguistic cues, and socially constructed meanings" (Putnam and Holmer, 1992, p. 129). Framing is about focusing, shaping, and organizing the world around us. It is about making sense of a complex reality and defining it in terms that are meaningful to us. Frames, in short, define a person, event, or process and separate it from the complex world around it (Buechler, 2000).

Framing is a popular concept among social scientists who study cognitive processes, decision making, persuasion, and communication. The importance of framing stems from the fact that two or more people who are involved in the same situation or in a complex problem often see it or define it in different ways (Thompson, 1998). For example, two individuals walk into a room full of people and see different things: one (the extrovert) sees a great party; the other (the introvert) sees a scary and intimidating unfriendly crowd. Because people have different backgrounds, experiences, expectations, and needs, they frame people, events, and processes differently. Moreover, these frames can change depending on perspective, or they can change over time. What starts out as a game of tag between two boys may turn into a fistfight. A football quarterback is a "hero" when he throws a touchdown, but a "loser" when he throws an interception.

Frames are important in negotiation because disputes are often nebulous and open to different interpretations as a result of differences in people's backgrounds, personal histories, prior experiences (Roth and Sheppard, 1995). A frame is a way of labeling these different individual interpretations of the situation. Early management theorist Mary Parker Follett (1942; Kolb, 1995), who was one of the first to write about integrative negotiation, observed that parties who arrive at a joint agreement achieve unity "not from giving in [compromise] but from 'getting the desires of each side into one field of vision'" (Follett, 1942, quoted in Putnam and Holmer, 1992). Although she didn't use the term, Follett is describing how frames emerge and converge as the parties talk about their preferences and priorities; they allow the parties to begin to develop a shared or common definition of the issues related to a situation and a process for resolving them.

Frames are critical in negotiation because how parties frame and define a negotiating issue or problem is a clear and strong reflection of what they define as central and critical to negotiating objectives, what their expectations and preferences are for certain possible outcomes, what information they seek and use to argue their case, the procedures they use to try to present their case, and the manner in which they evaluate the outcomes actually achieved.[2] Frames are inevitable; one cannot "avoid" framing. By choosing to define and articulate an aspect of a complex social situation, one has already implicitly "chosen" to use certain frames and to ignore others. This process often occurs without any real intention by the negotiator; one can frame a situation based on deeply buried past experiences, deep-seated attitudes and values, or strong emotions. Frames can also be shaped by the type of information chosen, or the setting and context in which the information is presented.

Understanding framing dynamics helps negotiators consciously elevate the framing process, thereby better controlling it; negotiators who understand how they are framing a problem may understand more completely what they are doing, what the other party is doing, and how to have more control over the negotiation process. Finally, both current theory and a stream of supportive empirical research show that frames may be malleable and, if so, can be shaped or reshaped as a function of information and communication during negotiation. In the next few pages, we will discuss several aspects of frames:

- Different types of frames.
- How frames work in negotiation situations.
- The interests/rights/power approach to negotiation framing.
- How frames change as a negotiation encounter evolves.

Types of Frames

Several researchers have studied different types of frames in different contexts. Drawing on extensive work on framing in the area of environmental disputes (Gray, 1997; Gray and Donnellon, 1989; Lewicki, Gray, and Elliott, 2003), we offer the following examples of frames that parties use in disputes:

1. *Substantive*—what the conflict is about. Parties taking a substantive frame have a particular disposition about the key issue or concern in the conflict.

2. *Outcome*—a party's predisposition to achieving a specific result or outcome from the negotiation. To the degree that a negotiator has a specific, preferred outcome he or she wants to achieve, the dominant frame may be to focus all strategy, tactics, and communication toward getting that outcome. Parties with a strong outcome frame that emphasizes self-interest and downplays concern for the other party are more likely to engage primarily in distributive (win–lose or lose–lose) negotiations than in other types of negotiations.

3. *Aspiration*—a predisposition toward satisfying a broader set of interests or needs in negotiation. Rather than focusing on a specific outcome, the negotiator tries to ensure that his or her basic interests, needs, and concerns are met. Parties who have a strong aspiration frame are more likely to be primarily engaged in integrative (win–win) negotiation than in other types.

4. *Process*—how the parties will go about resolving their dispute. Negotiators who have a strong process frame are less concerned about the specific negotiation issues but more concerned about how the deliberations will proceed, or how the dispute should be managed. When the major concerns are largely procedural rather than substantive, process frames will be strong.

5. *Identity*—how the parties define "who they are." Parties are members of a number of different social groups—gender (male), religion (Roman Catholic), ethnic origin (Italian), place of birth (Brooklyn), current place of residence (London), and the like. These are only a few of the many categories people can use to construct an identity frame that defines themselves and distinguishes themselves from others.

6. *Characterization*—how the parties define the other parties. A characterization frame can clearly be shaped by experience with the other party, by information about the other party's history or reputation, or by the way the other party comes across early in the negotiation experience. In conflict, identity frames (of self) tend to be positive; characterization frames (of others) tend to be negative.

7. *Loss–gain*—how the parties define the risk or reward associated with particular outcomes. For example, a buyer in a sales negotiation can view the transaction in loss terms (the monetary cost of the purchase) or in gain terms (the value of the item). This form of frame is discussed in more detail later in this chapter when we address cognitive biases.

How Frames Work in Negotiation

Although the concept of frames and their role in negotiation is compelling, research in this area is difficult to conduct. It is difficult to know what frame a party is using unless that party tells you (you might listen to or read his or her exact words) or unless you make inferences from the party's behavior. Even then, such inferences and interpretations may be difficult and prone to error. Also, the frames of those who hear or interpret communication may create biases of their own. For example, researchers who are coding the messages of parties in a dispute may have their own frames, which may bias their judgment about the negotiators' frames. Nevertheless, research exploring frames is important as a window on how parties define what a negotiation is about, how they use communication to argue for their own frames and try to shape the other's orientation, and how they resolve differences when the two parties are clearly operating from different frames. Here are some insights drawn from linguistic analyses of negotiation transcripts (Gray, 1991, 1997; Lewicki, Gray, and Elliott, 2003) and other studies of framing effects:

1. *Negotiators can use more than one frame.* A land developer discussing a conflict over a proposed golf course that will fill in a wetland can speak about the golf course (the substantive issue), his preferences for how the land should be filled in (an outcome frame), and how much input neighborhood and environmental groups should be able to have in determining what happens to that wetland on his private property (a procedural frame), as well as whether he views these groups favorably or unfavorably (a characterization frame).

2. *Mismatches in frames between parties are sources of conflict.* Two negotiators may be speaking to each other from different frames (e.g., one has an outcome frame and the other has a procedural frame), using different content in the same frame (e.g., they both have a procedural frame but have strong preferences for different procedures), or using different levels of abstraction (e.g., a broad aspiration frame versus a specific outcome frame). Such mismatches cause conflict and ambiguity, which may create misunderstanding,

lead to conflict escalation and even stalemate, or lead one or both parties to "reframe" the conflict into frames that are more compatible and that may lead to resolution. For highly polarized disputes, mutual reframing may not occur without the help of a third party.

3. *Parties negotiate differently depending on the frame.* Frames may evoke certain strategies or cognitive and emotional responses from negotiators. For example, when parties are prompted to frame a negotiation in emotional terms, they tend to be more highly involved and behave competitively, leading to higher impasse rates (Conlon and Hunt, 2002; Hunt and Kernan, 2005). Likewise, those using an identity frame tend to employ strategies that protect that identity while negotiating; they resist information or proposals perceived as threatening or compromising their personal or social identity (Cohen et al., 2007).

4. *Specific frames may be likely to be used with certain types of issues.* In a negotiation over a job offer, for instance, parties discussing salary may be likely to use outcome frames, while parties discussing relationship issues may be likely to use characterization frames.

5. *Particular types of frames may lead to particular types of agreements.* For example, parties who achieve integrative agreements may be likely to use aspiration frames and to discuss a large number of issues during their deliberations. In contrast, parties who use outcome or negative characterization frames may be likely to hold negative views of the other party and a strong preference for specific outcomes, which may in turn lead to intensified conflict and distributive outcomes (or no agreement at all).

6. *Parties are likely to assume a particular frame because of various factors.* Value differences between the parties, differences in personality, power differences, and differences in the background and social context of the negotiators may lead the parties to adopt different frames. As an example, see Box 5.1. Many of these factors will receive further attention in later chapters, including Chapter 7 (leverage), Chapter 15 (individual differences), and Chapter 16 (international negotiation).

Another Approach to Frames: Interests, Rights, and Power

Ury, Brett, and Goldberg (1988) proposed an approach to framing disputes that view parties in conflict as using one of three frames:

Interests. People are often concerned about what they need, desire, or want. People talk about their "positions," but often what is at stake is their underlying interests. A person says he "needs" a new text messaging cell phone, but what he really wants is a new electronic toy because all his friends have one. Parties who focus on interests in a dispute are often able to find ways to resolve that dispute.

Rights. People may also be concerned about who is "right"—that is, who has legitimacy, who is correct, or what is fair. Disputes about rights are often resolved by helping the parties find a fair way to determine who is "right," or that they can both be "right." This resolution often requires the use of some standard or rule such as "taking turns," "split it down the middle," or "age before beauty" to settle the dispute. Disputes over rights are sometimes referred to formal or informal arbitrators to decide whose standards or rights are more appropriate (see Chapter 19).

approach the negotiation with initial frames that resemble the categories described earlier, the ongoing interaction between them shapes the discussion as each side attempts to argue from his or her own perspective or counterargue against the other's perspective. Several factors can affect how conversations and frames are shaped:

1.   Negotiators tend to argue for stock issues, or concerns that are raised every time the parties negotiate. For example, wage issues or working conditions may always be discussed in a labor negotiation; the union always raises them, and management always expects them to be raised and is ready to respond. Jensen (1995) reports that negotiations over stock issues can be restructured to include more or fewer issues, increasing the likelihood that a resolution can be found. Discussing international negotiations, Spector (1995) suggests that conflicts framed as "nationalist, ethnic, or ideological" may be quite difficult to resolve, and a major task for mediators in these types of disputes is to provide creative new frames (see Chapter 19).

2.   Seeking to make the best possible case for his or her preferred perspective, one party may assemble facts, numbers, testimony, or other evidence to persuade the other party of the validity of his or her argument or perspective. Early in a negotiation, it is not uncommon for the parties to "talk past each other," with each trying to control the conversation with a certain frame or perspective rather than listening to and engaging with the other's case. Eventually, arguments and frames begin to shift as the parties focus on either refuting the other's case or modifying their own arguments on the basis of the other's (Putnam and Wilson, 1989; Putnam, Wilson, and Turner, 1990).

3.   Frames may define major shifts and transitions in a complex overall negotiation. Ikle (1964), discussing diplomatic negotiations, suggested that successful bargaining results from a two-stage process he called "formula/detail." In this process, parties start by developing a broad framework of principles and objectives upon which they can agree. Only after that is accomplished do they work toward detailed points of agreement. As Lewicki, Weiss, and Lewin (1992, p. 225) put it, "The framework defines the subset of points that is debatable, while the detail phase permits the debate and packaging of specific issues to construct a settlement acceptable to both sides." William Zartman and his colleagues

"Now, when we explain this to Mom and Dad, let's make sure we give it the right spin."

© 1998; Reprinted courtesy of Bunny Hoest and *Parade Magazine*.

lead to conflict escalation and even stalemate, or lead one or both parties to "reframe" the conflict into frames that are more compatible and that may lead to resolution. For highly polarized disputes, mutual reframing may not occur without the help of a third party.

3. *Parties negotiate differently depending on the frame.* Frames may evoke certain strategies or cognitive and emotional responses from negotiators. For example, when parties are prompted to frame a negotiation in emotional terms, they tend to be more highly involved and behave competitively, leading to higher impasse rates (Conlon and Hunt, 2002; Hunt and Kernan, 2005). Likewise, those using an identity frame tend to employ strategies that protect that identity while negotiating; they resist information or proposals perceived as threatening or compromising their personal or social identity (Cohen et al., 2007).

4. *Specific frames may be likely to be used with certain types of issues.* In a negotiation over a job offer, for instance, parties discussing salary may be likely to use outcome frames, while parties discussing relationship issues may be likely to use characterization frames.

5. *Particular types of frames may lead to particular types of agreements.* For example, parties who achieve integrative agreements may be likely to use aspiration frames and to discuss a large number of issues during their deliberations. In contrast, parties who use outcome or negative characterization frames may be likely to hold negative views of the other party and a strong preference for specific outcomes, which may in turn lead to intensified conflict and distributive outcomes (or no agreement at all).

6. *Parties are likely to assume a particular frame because of various factors.* Value differences between the parties, differences in personality, power differences, and differences in the background and social context of the negotiators may lead the parties to adopt different frames. As an example, see Box 5.1. Many of these factors will receive further attention in later chapters, including Chapter 7 (leverage), Chapter 15 (individual differences), and Chapter 16 (international negotiation).

Another Approach to Frames: Interests, Rights, and Power

Ury, Brett, and Goldberg (1988) proposed an approach to framing disputes that view parties in conflict as using one of three frames:

Interests. People are often concerned about what they need, desire, or want. People talk about their "positions," but often what is at stake is their underlying interests. A person says he "needs" a new text messaging cell phone, but what he really wants is a new electronic toy because all his friends have one. Parties who focus on interests in a dispute are often able to find ways to resolve that dispute.

Rights. People may also be concerned about who is "right"—that is, who has legitimacy, who is correct, or what is fair. Disputes about rights are often resolved by helping the parties find a fair way to determine who is "right," or that they can both be "right." This resolution often requires the use of some standard or rule such as "taking turns," "split it down the middle," or "age before beauty" to settle the dispute. Disputes over rights are sometimes referred to formal or informal arbitrators to decide whose standards or rights are more appropriate (see Chapter 19).

BOX 5.1   **Chinese Negotiation Frames**

Although skilled negotiators know that their and their opponents' negotiation frames are shaped through experience and culture, few stop to critically examine the cultural elements that shape others' perceptions about conflict. For example, Catherine Tinsley of Georgetown University has identified the five concepts from Chinese culture that those attempting to negotiate in China should recognize:

- *Social linkage.* The Chinese believe that people should be viewed in the context of their larger social groups rather than as isolated individuals.

- *Harmony.* Because people are inherently imbedded in their social network, peaceful coexistence is highly valued.

- *Roles.* To maintain social harmony, people must understand and abide by the requirements of their role in the relationship network. Roles specify duties, power, and privileges while specifying where in the relational hierarchy an individual falls.

- *Reciprocal obligations.* Each role specifies the obligations that people expect to fulfill and receive within the social network. These obligations persist over time, solidifying the relational network across generations.

- *Face.* The value the Chinese place on saving "face" is central to their perception of social interaction. Face is lost if an individual acts in a manner that is inconsistent with his or her role or fails to fulfill reciprocal obligations. Face is so valued that the threat of losing it is the primary force that ensures fulfillment of obligations and, consequently, continuance of the relational hierarchy.

Negotiators approaching discussions with the Chinese would do well to consider the perspective on conflict that these cultural realities have created. For example, individual negotiators often rely on the power of their personal network to achieve desired ends. This perspective, which Tinsley called the "relational bargaining frame," encourages parties to augment their power by both soliciting the support of powerful people and arguing for the social legitimacy of their position. While those from a more individualistic culture might reject out of hand the argument that a proposed settlement would be unpopular, such an argument would have great power in the more collectivist Chinese culture. Similarly, parties in the relational frame would be more likely to solicit outside opinions. A powerful strategy might be to encourage parties to align their positions to be compatible with the goals of a greater social collective.

Source: C. H. Tinsley, "Understanding Conflict in a Chinese Cultural Context," in R. Bies, R. Lewicki, and B. Sheppard (Eds.), *Research on Negotiation in Organizations,* vol. 6 (Stamford, CT: JAI, 1997), pp. 209–25.

Power. People may elect to frame a negotiation on the basis of power. Negotiations resolved by power are sometimes based on who is physically stronger or is able to coerce the other, but more often, it is about imposing other types of costs— economic pressures, expertise, legitimate authority, and so on. Disputes settled by power usually create clear winners and losers, with all the consequences that come from polarizing the dispute and resolving it in this manner.

Parties have a choice about how they approach a negotiation in terms of interests, rights, and power; the same negotiation can be framed in different ways and will likely lead to different consequences. For example, consider the situation of a student who has a dispute with a local car repair shop near campus over the cost of fixing an automobile. The student thinks she was dramatically overcharged for the work—the garage did more work than requested, used the most expensive replacement parts, and didn't give her the chance to review the bill before the work was done. The student might "frame" the dispute in one of these three ways:

Interests. The student might argue, "Well, small businesses have a right to charge a fair price for good quality work. I will go in and try to understand the shop owner's system for pricing repair work; we will talk about what is a fair price for the work and I will pay it, and I will probably go back to the shop again."

Rights. The student worked in a garage herself one summer and knows that car repairs are priced on what standard manuals state it will generally cost for the labor (Hours of work $\times$ Payment per hour), plus the cost of the parts. "I will ask to see the manual and the invoice for the parts. I will also go to the garage where I worked myself and ask the owner of that garage if he thinks this bill is inflated. I'll propose to pay for the parts at cost and the labor based on the mechanic's hourly pay rate."

Power. "I'll go in and start yelling at the owner about gouging, and I'll also threaten to tell all my friends not to use this garage. I'll write letters to the student newspaper about how bad this repair shop is. My mom is a lawyer and I'll have her call the owner. I'll teach them a thing or two!"

Note that the different frames are likely to lead to very different discussions between the student and the garage owner. Moreover, the way the student approaches the problem with the garage owner will probably influence how the garage owner responds. The more the student uses power, the more likely the garage owner is to respond with power of his own (e.g., keep the car until the student pays and not reduce the price at all, and call his own lawyer); the confrontation could become angry and lead the parties into small claims court. In contrast, the more the student uses interests, the more the garage owner may be likely to use interests. The parties will have a discussion about what is fair given the services rendered; while the student may wind up paying more (than if she "won" the power argument), the tone of the discussion is likely to be far different, and the student may be in a much better position to get discounts or consideration in the future.

The Frame of an Issue Changes as the Negotiation Evolves

The definition of issues at stake in a negotiation may change as the discussion evolves. Rather than focus only on the dominant frames that parties hold at the beginning of a negotiation, it is also important to consider patterns of change (transformation) that occur as parties communicate with each other. For example, in a classic study of legal disputes and grievances, Felstiner, Abel, and Sarat (1980–81) suggested that these disputes tend to be transformed through a process of "naming, blaming, and claiming." *Naming* occurs when parties in a dispute label or identify a problem and characterize what it is about. *Blaming* occurs next, as the parties try to determine who or what caused the problem. Finally, *claiming* occurs when the individual who has the problem decides to confront, file charges, or take some other action against the individual or organization that caused the problem.

Frames are shaped by conversations that the parties have with each other about the issues in the bargaining mix. As Putnam and Holmer (1992, p. 138) put it, frames "are not simply features of individual cognition, they are constructed in the ways that bargainers define problems and courses of action jointly through their talk." Although both parties may approach the negotiation with initial frames that resemble the categories described earlier, the ongoing interaction between them shapes the discussion as each side attempts to argue from his or her own perspective or counterargue against the other's perspective. Several factors can affect how conversations and frames are shaped:

1.   Negotiators tend to argue for stock issues, or concerns that are raised every time the parties negotiate. For example, wage issues or working conditions may always be discussed in a labor negotiation; the union always raises them, and management always expects them to be raised and is ready to respond. Jensen (1995) reports that negotiations over stock issues can be restructured to include more or fewer issues, increasing the likelihood that a resolution can be found. Discussing international negotiations, Spector (1995) suggests that conflicts framed as "nationalist, ethnic, or ideological" may be quite difficult to resolve, and a major task for mediators in these types of disputes is to provide creative new frames (see Chapter 19).

2.   Seeking to make the best possible case for his or her preferred perspective, one party may assemble facts, numbers, testimony, or other evidence to persuade the other party of the validity of his or her argument or perspective. Early in a negotiation, it is not uncommon for the parties to "talk past each other," with each trying to control the conversation with a certain frame or perspective rather than listening to and engaging with the other's case. Eventually, arguments and frames begin to shift as the parties focus on either refuting the other's case or modifying their own arguments on the basis of the other's (Putnam and Wilson, 1989; Putnam, Wilson, and Turner, 1990).

3.   Frames may define major shifts and transitions in a complex overall negotiation. Ikle (1964), discussing diplomatic negotiations, suggested that successful bargaining results from a two-stage process he called "formula/detail." In this process, parties start by developing a broad framework of principles and objectives upon which they can agree. Only after that is accomplished do they work toward detailed points of agreement. As Lewicki, Weiss, and Lewin (1992, p. 225) put it, "The framework defines the subset of points that is debatable, while the detail phase permits the debate and packaging of specific issues to construct a settlement acceptable to both sides." William Zartman and his colleagues

**"Now, when we explain this to Mom and Dad,
let's make sure we give it the right spin."**

(Zartman, 1977; Zartman and Berman, 1982) elaborated on the formula-detail model to propose three stages: *(a) diagnosis,* in which the parties recognize the need for change or improvement, review relevant history, and prepare positions; *(b) formula,* in which the parties attempt to develop a shared perception of the conflict, including common terms, referents, and fairness criteria; and *(c) detail,* in which the parties work out operational details consistent with the basic formula.

4.   Finally, multiple agenda items operate to shape issue development. Although parties usually have one or two major objectives, priorities, or core issues, there are often a number of lesser or secondary items. When brought into the conversation, these secondary concerns often transform the conversation about the primary issues (Putnam and Geist, 1985). Analyzing teacher negotiations in two school districts, Putnam (1994) showed how issues became transformed throughout a negotiation. For instance, an issue of scheduling was reframed as an issue of teacher preparation time, and a concern about the cost of personal insurance shifted to an issue about the extent of insurance benefits (Putnam, 1994).

Critical to issue development is the process of *reframing*—changes to the thrust, tone, and focus of a conversation as the parties engage in it. Issues are shaped and reframed by several things, including (1) arguments attacking the significance or stability of problems or the feasibility of solutions, (2) the ways parties "make a case" to others concerning the logic of needs or positions, and (3) the management and interaction (e.g., addition, deletion, packaging) of multiple issues on the negotiation agenda (Putnam and Holmer, 1992). Reframing is a dynamic process that may occur many times in a conversation as parties challenge each other or search for ways to reconcile seemingly incompatible perspectives. Reframing can also occur as one party uses metaphors, analogies, or specific cases to illustrate a point, leading the other to use the metaphor or case as a new way to define the situation. Reframing may be done intentionally by one side or the other, or it may emerge from the conversation as one person's challenges fuel the other's creativity and imagination. In either case, the parties often propose a new way to approach the problem. Research by Mara Olekalns and her colleagues shows that negotiators alter their own message strategies (e.g., away from a competitive orientation) as they come to understand that an opponent's frame has shifted (Olekalns, Robert, Probst, Smith, and Carnevale, 2005).

Section Summary

Framing is about focusing, shaping, and organizing the world around us—making sense of complex realities and defining them in ways that are meaningful to us. We discussed the different type of frames that exist and their importance for understanding strategic choices in negotiation. The way a negotiation problem is defined, and the manner in which a conversation between negotiators leads to a reframing of the issues, are critical elements to consider as negotiators develop and implement their strategy. We can offer the following prescriptive advice about problem framing for the negotiator:

•   *Frames shape what the parties define as the key issues and how they talk about them.* To the extent that the parties have preferences about the issues to be covered, outcomes to be achieved, or processes to be addressed, they should strive to ensure that their own preferred frames are accepted and acknowledged by the others.

- *Both parties have frames.* When the frames match, the parties are more likely to focus on common issues and a common definition of the situation; when they do not match, communication between the parties is likely to be difficult and incomplete. Negotiators who are communicating from different frames should first recognize that they may be talking "past each other," raise the issue with each other, and work to reframe their dialogue so that they are communicating on a more compatible "wavelength."

- *Frames are controllable, at least to some degree.* If negotiators understand what frame they are using and the frame the other party is using, they may be able to shift the conversation toward the frame they would like the other to adopt.

- *Conversations transform frames in ways negotiators may not be able to predict but may be able to manage.* As parties discuss an issue, introduce arguments and evidence, and advocate a course of action, the conversation changes, and the frame may change as well. It is critical for negotiators to track this shift and understand where it might lead.

- *Certain frames are more likely than others to lead to certain types of processes and outcomes.* For example, parties who are competitive are likely to have positive identity frames of themselves, negative characterization frames of each other, and a preference for win–lose approaches to resolving their dispute. Recognizing these tendencies empowers negotiators to reframe their views of themselves, the other, or the dispute resolution mechanism in play in order to pursue a process that will resolve the conflict more productively.

Cognitive Biases in Negotiation

So far in this chapter we have examined how information is perceived, filtered, distorted, and framed. In this section, we examine how negotiators use information to make decisions during the negotiation. Rather than being perfect processors of information, it is quite clear that negotiators (like all decision makers) have a tendency to make systematic errors when they process information.[3] These errors, collectively labeled cognitive biases, tend to impede negotiator performance; they include (1) the irrational escalation of commitment, (2) the mythical belief that the issues under negotiation are all fixed-pie, (3) the process of anchoring and adjustment in decision making, (4) issue and problem framing, (5) the availability of information, (6) the winner's curse, (7) negotiator overconfidence, (8) the law of small numbers, (9) self-serving biases, (10) the endowment effect, (11) the tendency to ignore others' cognitions, and (12) the process of reactive devaluation. Next, we discuss each of these in more detail.

1. Irrational Escalation of Commitment

Negotiators sometimes maintain commitment to a course of action even when that commitment constitutes irrational behavior on their part. This is an example of a broader psychological phenomenon known as "escalation of commitment," which is the tendency for an individual to make decisions that stick with a failing course of action (Brockner, 1992; Staw, 1981; Teger, 1980). Classic examples include a country that continues to pour military resources into an unwinnable armed conflict or an investor who continues to put more money into a declining stock in hopes its fortunes will turn ("throwing good money after bad," as escalation of commitment is sometimes colloquially described). Escalation of commitment situations are defined by "repeated (rather than one-shot) decision making in the face of negative feedback about prior resource allocations, uncertainty surrounding the likelihood of goal attainment, and choice about whether to continue" (Brockner, 1992, p. 40).

Escalation of commitment is due in part to biases in individual perception and judgment. Once a course of action is decided, negotiators often seek supportive (confirming) evidence for that choice, while ignoring or failing to seek disconfirming evidence. Initial commitments become set in stone (see the later section on anchoring and adjustment), and a desire for consistency prevents negotiators from changing them. This desire for consistency is often exacerbated by a desire to save face and to maintain an impression of expertise or control in front of others (see Chapter 11). No one likes to admit error or failure, especially when the other party may perceive doing so as a weakness. Escalation of commitment is common when a union goes on strike and expects management to capitulate eventually, in competitive bidding or auction situations, or when negotiators make a threat in anger and then find that they have to follow through on it.

One way to combat these tendencies is to have an advisor serve as a reality checkpoint—someone who is not consumed by the "heat of the moment" and who can warn negotiators when they inadvertently begin to behave irrationally. Also, a study by Ku (2008) found that decision makers are less likely to escalate if they experienced regret following a previous escalation situation. Unfortunately, many negotiators and decision makers may not have previously experienced such a situation to learn from, so it is important to highlight Ku's finding in a follow-up experiment: even just having people *imagine* escalation-related regret before making a crucial decision induces them to de-escalate.

2. Mythical Fixed-Pie Beliefs

Many negotiators assume that all negotiations involve a fixed pie (Thompson, 1990b). Negotiators often approach integrative negotiation opportunities as zero-sum situations or win–lose exchanges. Those who believe in the mythical fixed pie assume there is no possibility for integrative settlements and mutually beneficial trade-offs, and they suppress efforts to search for them (see Pinkley, Griffith, and Northcraft, 1995; Thompson and Hastie, 1990a, 1990b). In a salary negotiation, the job applicant who assumes that salary is the only issue may insist on $55,000 when the employer is offering $52,000. Only when the two parties discuss the possibilities further do they discover that moving expenses and starting date can also be negotiated, which may facilitate resolution of the salary issue.

The tendency to see negotiation in fixed-pie terms varies depending on how people view the nature of a given conflict situation. This was shown in a clever experiment by Harinck, de Dreu, and Van Vianen (2000) involving a simulated negotiation between prosecutors and defense lawyers over jail sentences. Some participants were told to view their goals in terms of personal interests (e.g., arranging a particular jail sentence will help your career), others were told to view their goals in terms of effectiveness (a particular sentence is most likely to prevent recidivism), and still others were told to focus on values (a particular jail sentence is fair and just). Negotiators focusing on personal interests were most likely to come under the influence of fixed-pie beliefs and approach the situation competitively. Negotiators

BOX 5.2 Cultural Effects on Fixed-Pie Perceptions

Michele Gelfand and Sophia Christakopoulou (1999) investigated whether the tendency to view negotiations in fixed-pie terms might vary according to cultural values held by negotiators. They argued that fixed-pie judgments are probably commonly experienced across cultures at the start of negotiations but are stronger in some cultures than others by the end of a negotiation encounter. Gelfand and Christakopoulou compared negotiators in an individualistic culture, where cultural norms emphasize individual rights, accomplishments, and competition, with negotiators in a collectivistic culture, where the emphasis is on group accomplishment, interdependence, and harmony. They predicted that negotiators from individualistic cultures would focus more on their own interests and priorities, which may diminish the negotiator's ability to accurately gauge the other party's interests, leading to persistent assumptions that the pie is fixed.

Gelfand and Christakopoulou tested this prediction in a simulated business negotiation involving students from an American university (a highly individualistic culture) and students from a university in Greece (a highly collectivistic culture). Participants were asked both before and after the negotiation, which took place via e-mail, to record their judgments of the other party's interests and desires. With this method, fixed-pie perceptions are present to the extent that an individual regards the other party's interests as directly opposed to his or her own interests. (Such perceptions were inaccurate in this study because the negotiation task did incorporate some integrative potential.)

As expected, the researchers found that there was no difference in the level of fixed-pie error between U.S. and Greek negotiators at the start of the negotiations. After the negotiation, however, Americans were significantly more likely than Greeks to make errors in judging the other party's interests, indicating a bias toward assuming a fixed pie. Transcripts of the negotiations revealed that Greek negotiators made more statements about insight into and awareness of the other party's interests. Curiously, although American negotiators made more judgment errors, they expressed more confidence after the negotiation than Greek negotiators that their understanding of the other party's interests was accurate!

Source: Adapted from M. J. Gelfand and S. Christakopoulou, "Culture and Negotiator Cognition: Judgment Accuracy and Negotiation Processes in Individualistic and Collectivistic Cultures," *Organizational Behavior and Human Decision Processes* 79 (1999), pp. 248–69.

focusing on values were least likely to see the problem in fixed-pie terms and more inclined to approach the situation cooperatively. Stressful conditions such as time constraints contribute to this common misperception, which in turn may lead to less integrative agreements (de Dreu, 2003). Fixed-pie beliefs may also vary with cultural values that negotiators bring to the exchange (see Box 5.2).

In Chapter 3 we provided advice on minimizing this fixed-pie belief through procedures for inventing options. A study by de Dreu, Koole, and Steinel (2000) showed that fixed-pie perceptions can also be diminished by holding negotiators accountable for the way they negotiate. In their experiment, some negotiators were told that they would be interviewed afterward by experts to discuss what happened. Fixed-pie perceptions were weaker for these negotiators compared with negotiators who were not expecting an "accountability interview." Negotiators operating under accountability also reached agreements having higher joint value for the two parties. It appears that introducing accountability into the negotiation context is one way to increase the chances that individuals will overcome fixed-pie beliefs and strive for more integrative agreements.

3. Anchoring and Adjustment

Cognitive biases in anchoring and adjustment are related to the effect of the standard (or anchor) against which subsequent adjustments are made during negotiation. A classic example of an anchor in negotiation is hearing the other side's first offer and then thinking, "Gee, that offer was much lower than I expected; perhaps I've misconstrued the value here and should reconsider my goals and tactics." Anchors like this set a potentially hazardous trap for the negotiator on the receiving end because the choice of an anchor (e.g., an initial offer or an intended goal) might well be based on faulty or incomplete information and thus be misleading in and of itself. However, once the anchor is defined, parties tend to treat it as a real, valid benchmark by which to adjust other judgments, such as the value of the thing being negotiated, or the size of one's counteroffer (Kristensen and Garling, 1997, 2000).[4] A study of real estate agents, for example, showed that agents appraising the value of a house were very strongly affected by its asking price (Northcraft and Neale, 1987). The asking price served as a convenient anchor to use in appraising the value of the house. Goals in negotiation—whether set realistically or carelessly—can also serve as anchors. These anchors may be visible or invisible to the other party (a published market price versus an uncommunicated expectation), and, similarly, the person who holds them may do so consciously or unconsciously (a specific expectation versus an unexamined, unquestioned expectation or norm). There is also evidence that anchors operate differently in different cultural settings; in one recent study, opening offers induced anchoring and hindered joint gains among American negotiators but facilitated mutually beneficial outcomes among Japanese negotiators (Adair, Weingart, and Brett, 2007). Thorough preparation, along with the use of a devil's advocate or reality check, can help prevent errors of anchoring and adjustment.

4. Issue Framing and Risk

As we discussed earlier in this chapter, a frame is a perspective or point of view that people use when they gather information and solve problems. The framing process can cause people to exhibit certain types of behavior while avoiding others. Frames can lead people to seek, avoid, or be neutral about risk in negotiation. The way a negotiation is framed can make negotiators more or less risk averse or risk seeking. For instance, people respond quite differently when they are negotiating to "gain" something rather than to "not lose" something (Schurr, 1987).[5] Simply focusing on the target price during negotiations rather than the lower boundary can lead to higher outcomes (Galinsky, Mussweiler, and Medvec, 2002), although the exact nature of how framing and risk propensity influence negotiation outcomes seems to be influenced by the negotiation task (Bottom, 1998; Bottom and Studt, 1993).

The way an issue is framed influences how negotiators perceive risk and behave in relation to it. A basic finding from research that led to the development of what is known as "prospect theory" (Kahneman and Tversky, 1979) is that people are more risk-*averse* when a decision problem is framed as a possible *gain,* and risk-*seeking* when it is framed as a *loss.* To illustrate, consider this typical salary negotiation (adapted from Bazerman and Neale, 1992):

1. Your current salary ($47,000).
2. Your potential employer's initial offer to you ($52,000).

3. The least amount you are willing to accept ($55,000).

4. Your estimate of the most the company is willing to offer to you ($57,000).

5. Your initial salary request ($52,000).

The tendency to either seek or avoid risk may be based on the *reference point* against which offers and concessions are judged. The reference point is important because it is the number against which you may evaluate negotiation progress and success. In this salary example, there are various possible reference points. If you adopt your current salary ($47,000) as your reference point, then you would view (frame) a settlement offer of $52,000 as a gain in relation to your current salary. But as your standard of comparison moves down the list, that same offer of $52,000 becomes progressively framed as a loss (e.g., if your reference point is your reservation price of $55,000). This distinction is important because if you frame the employer's offer as a gain, you are more apt to settle (be risk-averse) rather than take a chance (be risk-seeking) that a better outcome can be obtained. But if the offer is framed as a loss, you are more likely to take risks for a better deal. In a recent experiment illustrating this effect, Ghosh and Boldt (2006) asked corporate managers to focus either on the profit that would be earned or the profit that would be forgone in a prospective transaction. They found that managers primed with a negative frame (profit forgone) were less flexible, held higher expectations, and claimed a larger share of the profit available compared with those primed with a positive frame.

Two things to keep in mind about the effect of frames on risk in negotiation are (1) negotiators are not usually indifferent to risk, but (2) they should not necessarily trust their intuitions regarding it (Neale and Bazerman, 1992a). In other words, negotiators may overreact to a perceived loss when they might react more positively to the same situation if it is framed as a perceived gain. Hence, as a negotiator you must "avoid the pitfalls of being framed while, simultaneously, understanding positively and negatively framing your opponent" (Neale and Bazerman, 1992a, p. 50). When negotiators are risk-averse, they are more likely to accept any viable offer simply because they are afraid of losing. In contrast, when negotiators are risk-seeking, they are apt to wait for a better offer or for future concessions.

This positive/negative framing process is important because, as we saw in the preceding salary negotiation example, the same offer can elicit markedly different courses of action depending on how it is framed in gain–loss terms. Negotiations in which the outcomes are negatively framed tend to produce fewer concessions and reach fewer agreements, and negotiators perceive outcomes as less fair than negotiations in which the outcomes are positively framed (Bazerman and Neale, 1992). Remedies for the potentially pernicious effects of framing are similar to those we have mentioned for other cognitive biases (e.g., awareness of the bias, sufficient information, thorough analysis, and reality checks) but can be difficult to achieve because frames are often tied to deeply held values and beliefs or to other anchors that are hard to detect.

5. Availability of Information

Negotiators must also be concerned with the potential bias caused by the availability of information or how easy information is to retrieve—that is, how easily it can be recalled and used to inform or evaluate a process or a decision (Tversky and Kahneman, 1982). One way the availability bias operates in negotiation is through presentation of information in vivid, colorful, or attention-getting ways, making it easy to recall, and making it central and critical in evaluating events and options. Information presented through a particularly clear message, diagram, or formula (even one that is oversimplified) will likely be believed more readily than information presented in a confusing or detailed format—regardless of the accuracy of each.

The availability of information also affects negotiation through the use of established search patterns. If negotiators have a favorite way of collecting information or looking for key signals, they will use these patterns repeatedly and may overvalue the information that comes from them. In Chapter 4, we noted that many negotiators fail to plan and that the planning they do tends to focus on a limited subset of information that is easily available. Negotiators who do not plan properly run the risk of being overwhelmed by the availability bias and thus losing the benefits of thorough analysis.

6. The Winner's Curse

The winner's curse refers to the tendency of negotiators, particularly in an auction setting, to settle quickly on an item and then subsequently feel discomfort about a negotiation win that comes too easily (Bazerman and Samuelson, 1983).[6] If the other party capitulates too quickly, the negotiator is often left wondering, "Could I have gotten this for less?" or asking "What's wrong with the item/product/option?" The negotiator may suspect that the other party knows too much or has insight into an unseen advantage; thus, either "I could have done better" or "This must be a bad deal."

For example, in an antique store several years ago one of the authors of this book saw a clock that he and his wife fell in love with. After spending the afternoon in the neighborhood deciding on a negotiation strategy (opening offer, bottom line, timing, feigned disinterest, the good guy/bad guy tactic), the author and his wife returned to the store to enact their strategy. The store owner accepted their first offer. Upon arriving home, suffering from the winner's curse, they left the clock in the garage, where it remains collecting dust.

Recent research suggests that the winner's curse stems, in part, from counterfactual thought processes. Counterfactual thoughts involve entertaining the possibility of "what might have been" if that offer hadn't been accepted (Kahneman and Miller, 1986). The easier it is to imagine a better alternative to an agreement, the less satisfied the negotiator will be (Naquin, 2002). Thinking counterfactually about "what might have been" doesn't just create dissatisfaction in the wake of a bad outcome; it also affects future behavior. One study showed that negotiators who were dissatisfied after having their first offer accepted reported that they would be less likely to make the first offer in future negotiations (Galinsky, Seiden, Kim, and Medvec, 2002). Another study found that negotiators encouraged to engage in counterfactual thinking were less likely to reach integrative agreements that satisfy mutual interests (Kray, Galinsky, and Markman, 2007). This decline in collaboration may depend, however, on the kind of counterfactual thinking that occurs: Kray and colleagues found in a follow-up experiment that negotiators who dwelled on mistakes made (things I shouldn't have done) were less likely to reach integrative agreements that those who thought about forgone opportunities (things I could have done).

The best remedy for the winner's curse is to prevent it from occurring in the first place by doing the advance work needed to avoid making on offer that is unexpectedly accepted. Thorough investigation and preparation can provide negotiators with independent verification of appropriate settlement values. Negotiators can also try to secure performance or quality guarantees from the other party to make sure the outcome is not faulty or defective.

7. Overconfidence

Overconfidence is the tendency of negotiators to believe that their ability to be correct or accurate is greater than is actually true. Overconfidence has a double-edged effect: (1) it can solidify the degree to which negotiators support positions or options that are incorrect or inappropriate, and (2) it can lead negotiators to discount the worth or validity of the judgments of others, in effect shutting down other parties as sources of information, interests, and options necessary for a successful integrative negotiation. For instance, Neale and Bazerman (1983) found that negotiators who were not trained to be aware of the overconfidence heuristic tended to overestimate their probability of being successful, and they were significantly less likely to compromise or reach agreements than trained negotiators.

Lim (1997) also studied overconfident negotiators. Before negotiations began, those negotiators who had been identified as overconfident estimated that agreements would be more likely and that they would have higher profits than did realistically confident negotiators. Lim also reported that the overconfident individuals were more persistent and were more concerned about their own outcomes than were the realistically confident negotiators.

Thus, it appears that negotiators have a tendency to be overconfident about their own abilities and that this overconfidence affects a wide variety of perceptions and behavior during negotiations. In particular, overconfidence can undermine the prospects for finding and exploiting integrative potential. This does not mean, however, that negotiators should always seek to suppress confidence or optimism. Bottom and Paese (1999), in a study of distributive bargaining, found that negotiators biased toward optimism achieved more profitable settlements compared with negotiators with accurate perceptions or with a bias toward pessimism. Clearly, more research is needed on the interplay of optimism, overconfidence, and negotiation outcomes.

8. The Law of Small Numbers

In decision theory, the law of small numbers refers to the tendency of people to draw conclusions from small sample sizes. In negotiation, the law of small numbers applies to the way negotiators learn and extrapolate from their own experience. If that experience is limited in time or in scope (e.g., if all of one's prior negotiations have been hard-fought and distributive), the tendency is to extrapolate prior experience onto future negotiations (e.g., all negotiations are distributive). This tendency will often lead to a self-fulfilling prophecy, as follows: people who expect to be treated in a distributive manner will (1) be more likely to perceive the other party's behavior as distributive and (2) treat the other party in a more distributive manner. The other party will then likely interpret the negotiator's behavior as evidence of a distributive tendency and will therefore respond in kind. The smaller the prior

How are negotiations affected by time delays between a negotiation encounter and the later occasion when the negotiated agreement will be implemented? The classic negotiation problem of a couple planning a vacation illustrates the issue:

> A couple might have opposing preferences for the vacation and they might set a date in the near or distant future to sit down and try to resolve their differences for the vacation. Moreover, a couple might try settling their differences for a vacation that is set to occur in the near or distant future. In both cases, when temporal distance is increased, the realization of whatever agreement that is reached is also pushed farther into the future. (Henderson, Trope, and Carnevale, 2006, p. 714)

Researchers in recent years have focused attention on this question of "temporal distance." A series of experiments by Okhuysen, Galinsky, and Uptigrove (2003) looked at how delays between agreements and their implementation affect the efficiency and quality of those agreements. These researchers found clear evidence that when negotiators believe that there is more time (one year vs. two weeks in their experiments) between the negotiation and the onset of its outcome, agreements yield better results for both parties, and negotiators regard the experience afterward as less contentious and their opponent as less aggressive. Why would this happen? Okhuysen and colleagues suggest

that with more time to implementation, the pressure to maximize self-interest is lessened, making it easier for negotiators to make the kinds of concessions and compromises that lead to better agreements.

If this is true, then we would expect that negotiators with lots of time between encounter and implementation to exhibit the kinds of behaviors during the negotiation that foster mutual gain. Henderson, Trope, and Carnevale (2006) ran three experiments seeking evidence on this point. They found that with more time between settlement and implementation, negotiators are more likely to (1) hold firm on high priority issues, but make concessions on low-priority issues; (2) make multi-issue offers rather than adopt a single-issue focus; and (3) be willing to logroll (trade off priorities with the other party). These are precisely the sorts of negotiation behaviors that we know (see Chapter 2) contribute to integrative settlements.

Time, it appears, is indeed on your side when mutual gains and integrative outcomes are desired.

Sources: G. A. Okhuysen, A. D. Galinsky, and T. A. Uptigrove, "Saving the Worst for Last: The Effect of Time Horizon on the Efficiency of Negotiating Benefits and Burdens," *Organizational Behavior and Human Decision Processes* 91 (2003), pp. 269–79; M. D. Henderson, Y. Trope, and P. J. Carnevale, "Negotiation from a Near and Distant Time Perspective," *Journal of Personality and Social Psychology* 91 (2006), pp. 712–29.

sample (i.e., the more limited the negotiation experience), the greater the possibility that past lessons will be erroneously used to infer what will happen in the future. Styles and strategies that worked in the past may not work in the future, and they certainly will not work if future negotiations differ significantly from past experiences. (Box 5.3 summarizes some intriguing research insights on how time influences negotiation behavior.)

An interesting example of the law of small numbers in action is the "hot hand" fallacy—the incorrect belief that a streak of events is due to momentum and will continue. This fallacy results in a tendency to believe that a small sequence of events is representative, while ignoring base rate data from a larger universe of events (Tversky and Kahneman, 1971). Research examining the presence of "hot hand" streaks in sports such as baseball, basketball, and hockey shows no statistical evidence for the presence of this phenomenon (e.g., Gilovich, Vallone, and Tversky, 1985; Koehler and Conley, 2003). A study by Vergin (2000) looked at winning and losing streaks during an entire season for all 28 professional

Major League Baseball teams and all 29 National Basketball Association teams. Analyses showed that winning and losing streaks were no longer than would be expected under random conditions, and no evidence was found that a win or loss was correlated with the outcome of a preceding game.

9. Self-Serving Biases

People often explain another person's behavior by making attributions, either to the person (i.e., the behaviors were caused by internal factors such as ability, mood, or effort) or to the situation (i.e., the behaviors were caused by external factors such as the task, other people, or fate) (Heider, 1958). In "explaining" another person's behavior, the tendency is to overestimate the causal role of personal or internal factors and underestimate the causal role of situational or external factors. This tendency is known as the *fundamental attribution error* (Ross, 1977). For example, consider the student who arrives late for a morning class. Perhaps she is lazy (an internal, dispositional explanation), or perhaps she had a flat tire driving to campus (an external, situational explanation). The fundamental attribution error suggests a tendency for the professor, absent other information, to be biased toward the internal explanation (she's lazy). Perceptual biases are often exacerbated by the actor–observer effect, in which people tend to attribute their own behavior to situational factors, but attribute others' behaviors to personal factors (Jones and Nisbett, 1976), saying in effect, "If I mess up, it's bad luck (the situation, someone else's fault, etc.); if you mess up, it's your fault!"

Research has documented the effects of self-serving biases on the negotiation process. For instance, Babcock, Wang, and Loewenstein (1996) found that negotiators in different school districts chose comparison school districts in a self-serving way; that is, the districts they chose as comparison standards for their own district's activities were those that made their districts look most favorable. In another example, de Dreu, Nauta, and van de Vliert (1995) found that negotiators believed that they used more constructive tactics than their counterparts and that the strength of this self-serving bias increased with the strength of the conflict between the parties. Finally, Thompson (1995) found that participants in a negotiation were less accurate in estimating the other party's preferred outcomes than were nonpartisan observers watching the negotiation. Thompson also found that for partisan observers, involvement in the negotiation reduced the accuracy of their perceptions of the other party's preferences, while it increased the perceptual accuracy of nonpartisan observers. Thompson's sobering finding reveals that when people "know" they are right, confidence is not related to perceptual accuracy.

Self-serving biases have been shown to influence perceptions of fairness in a negotiation context. Michele Gelfand and colleagues (Gelfand et al., 2002), investigating cultural differences in self-serving biases, found that relative to Japanese subjects, Americans tend to hold egocentrically distorted perceptions of fairness. Participants in the study believed that their own actions were more fair than the actions of others, and they predicted that their own actions would be deemed more fair by a third party than the actions of their counterparts. Findings revealed a link between these self-serving fairness biases and negotiation outcomes: those with more egocentric perceptions achieved lower profits and reached fewer agreements.

Perceptual error may also be expressed in the form of biases or distortions in the evaluation of information. For instance, the false-consensus effect is a tendency to overestimate the degree of support and consensus that exists for one's own position, opinions, or behaviors (Ross, Greene, and House, 1977). If consensus information is available, but expressed in numerical probabilities (e.g., one chance in a hundred), many observers neglect to use the information, falling subject to a bias called the base rate fallacy (Bar-Hillel, 1980). We also have a tendency to assume that our personal beliefs or opinions are based on credible information, while opposing beliefs are based on misinformation (Fragale and Heath, 2004). This tendency suggests that although individuals may desire judgment accuracy, this desire can often result in perceived accuracy rather than objective accuracy. Any of these biases can seriously damage a negotiation effort—negotiators subject to them would make faulty judgments regarding tactics or outcome probabilities.

10. Endowment Effect

The endowment effect is the tendency to overvalue something you own or believe you possess. Kahneman, Knetsch, and Thaler (1990) demonstrated the existence of the endowment effect rather dramatically in a series of experiments involving coffee mugs. In one experiment, some participants were asked whether they would prefer a sum of money or the mug at various possible dollar levels. Based on their responses, it could be determined that they assigned an average value of just over $3.00 to the mug. Other participants were asked to value the mug as a potential buyer; the average value they assigned to the mug was just under $3.00. Members of a third group were actually given the mug and then asked if they would sell the mug for various amounts. Their answers indicated that they placed a value of more than $7.00 on the mug![7] Thus, the simple act of possessing something seems to induce people to elevate its perceived value, even when its actual value is known.

In negotiation, the endowment effect can lead to inflated estimations of value that interfere with reaching a good deal. Bazerman, Moore, and Gillespie (1999) discussed endowment effects in the context of negotiations over environmental issues. Viewing the endowment effect as an inflated personal attachment to the status quo, Bazerman and colleagues argued that the status quo serves as a "potentially dysfunctional anchor point, making mutually beneficial trades more difficult" (p. 1288). They illustrate with a hypothetical environmentalist who places excessive value on preserving existing wilderness at the expense of pursuing opportunities to protect or restore other lands. "The result," say Bazerman et al., "is likely to be a steep, sticky slope in which environmentalists will fight to preserve natural areas they perceive as being pristine but in which, once lost, wilderness is unlikely to be restored" (p. 1288).

A similar process occurs upon accepting an offer in a negotiation. Curhan, Neale, and Ross (2004) demonstrated that once accepted, a proposal was liked more by negotiators than other proposals that they themselves had offered during the negotiation process. This finding can be interpreted in light of cognitive dissonance theory (Festinger, 1957), which holds (in general terms) that inconsistencies between cognitions, attitudes, beliefs or behaviors within a person generate feelings of psychological discomfort. In this case, dissonance results from inconsistency between a negotiator's desired outcomes and the outcomes actually received. To reduce this discomfort, individuals add more subjective value to the outcomes just received.

11. Ignoring Others' Cognitions

Negotiators often don't ask about the other party's perceptions and thoughts, which leaves them to work with incomplete information, and thus produces faulty results. Failure to consider others' cognitions allows negotiators to simplify their thinking about otherwise complex processes; this usually leads to a more distributive strategy and causes a failure to recognize the contingent nature of both sides' behaviors and responses. Although this "failure to consider" might be attributed to some basic, underlying bias against the other party, research suggests that it is more often a way to make the complex task of decision making under conditions of risk and uncertainty more manageable (Carroll, Bazerman, and Maury, 1988). Research also suggests that training and awareness of this trap reduces its effects only modestly (Carroll, Delquie, Halpern, and Bazerman, 1990). The drive to ignore others' cognitions is very deep-seated, and it can be avoided only if negotiators explicitly focus on putting in the effort needed to form an accurate understanding of the other party's interests, goals, and perspectives.

12. Reactive Devaluation

Reactive devaluation is the process of devaluing the other party's concessions simply because the other party made them (Stillenger, Epelbaum, Keltner, and Ross, 1990). Such devaluation may be based in emotionality ("I just don't like him") or on distrust fostered by past experience. Reactive devaluation leads negotiators to minimize the magnitude of a concession made by a disliked other, to reduce their willingness to respond with a concession of equal size, or to seek even more from the other party once a concession has been made (Neale and Bazerman, 1992b). One study found this effect even when there were no negative emotions directed toward the other party (Moran and Ritov, 2002). Reactive devaluation may be minimized by maintaining an objective view of the process, by assigning a colleague to do this task, by clarifying each side's preferences on options and concessions before any are made (Stillenger et al., 1990), or by using a third party to mediate or filter concession-making processes (see Chapter 19).

Managing Misperceptions and Cognitive Biases in Negotiation

Misperceptions and cognitive biases typically arise out of conscious awareness as negotiators gather and process information. The more complex the situation, the more opportunities that exist for information bias and distortion to hinder judgment and decision making (Hammond, Keeney, and Raiffa, 1998). Box 5.4 presents a sizable inventory of the variety of decision traps that can occur. The result for negotiators can be overreliance on faulty assumptions and data, ultimately leading to deals that are suboptimal.

The question of how best to manage perceptual and cognitive bias is a difficult one. Certainly the first level of managing such distortions is to be aware that they can occur. However, awareness by itself may not be enough; research evidence shows that simply telling people about misconceptions and cognitive biases does little to counteract their effects (Babcock and Loewenstein, 1997; Thompson and Hastie, 1990a). For example, Foreman and Murnighan (1996) tried to teach students to avoid the winner's curse in a series of auction simulations. They told students about the results of 128 auctions over a four-week period but found that the training had little impact on reducing the winner's curse.

1. *Plunging in* involves reaching a conclusion to a problem before fully identifying the essence or crux of the problem (e.g., forcing negotiations into the end stage prematurely by pushing for a quantitative or substantive resolution to a problem that has been incompletely defined or is basically relational).

2. *Overconfidence in one's own judgment* involves blocking, ignoring, or failing to seek factual information that might contradict one's own assumptions and opinions (e.g., strictly adhering to a unilateral strategy, regardless of other information that emerges during the course of the negotiation).

3. *Frame blindness* involves perceiving, then solving, the wrong problem, accompanied by overlooking options and losing sight of objectives because they do not fit the frame being used (e.g., forcing resolution of a complex, mixed-motive dispute into some simplistic, concrete measure of performance such as money).

4. *Lack of frame control* involves failing to test different frames to determine if they fit the issues being discussed or being unduly influenced by the other party's frame (e.g., agreeing to a suboptimal outcome because the other party has taken advantage of our aversion to not reaching an agreement—see Neale and Bazerman, 1992a).

5. *Shortsighted shortcuts* involve misusing heuristics or rules of thumb, such as convenient (but misleading) referent points (e.g., accepting the other party's commitment to turning over a new leaf when past experience suggests that he or she is really unlikely to do so).

6. *Shooting from the hip* involves managing too much information in one's head rather than adopting and using a systematic process of evaluation and choice (e.g., proceeding on gut feelings or eye contact alone in deciding to accept a resolution, trusting that problems will not occur or that they will be easily worked out if they do).

7. *Group failure* involves not managing the group process effectively and instead assuming that smart and well-intentioned individuals can invariably produce a durable, high-quality group decision (see Janis's 1982 work on "groupthink"; e.g., in order to move stalled decisions, a group might take a vote on accepting a resolution, thereby disenfranchising the minority who do not vote for the resolution and stopping the deliberative process short of achieving its integrative possibilities).

8. *Fooling yourself about feedback* involves failing to use feedback correctly, either to protect one's ego or through the bias of hindsight (e.g., dealing with the embarrassment of being outmaneuvered by the other party because of a lack of good information or a failure to prepare rigorously).

9. *Not keeping track* involves assuming that learning occurs automatically and thus not keeping systematic records of decisions and related outcomes (e.g., losing sight of the gains and deals purchased with concessions and trade-offs made during the negotiation, or not applying the lessons of one negotiation episode to future negotiations).

10. *Failure to audit one's own decision processes* involves failing to establish and use a plan to avoid the traps mentioned here or the inability or unwillingness to fully understand one's own style, warts and all (thus, doggedly adhering to a flawed or inappropriate approach to negotiation, even in the face of frequent failures and suboptimal outcomes).

Source: Adapted from J. E. Russo and P. J. H. Schoemaker, *Decision Traps: The Ten Barriers to Brilliant Decision Making and How to Overcome Them* (New York: Simon & Schuster, 1989).

"Careful—it might be a trap!"

Whyte and Sebenius (1997) took a different approach to trying to reduce the effects of the anchoring and adjustment bias. They had negotiators participate in a group discussion to see if the group process reduced the use of inappropriate anchors to set initial offers, aspiration levels, and bottom lines for an upcoming real estate negotiation. The results showed that both individuals and groups used inappropriate anchors to set their initial offers, aspiration levels, and bottom lines and that groups were as susceptible to the effects of anchoring and adjustment as were individuals. This suggests that merely discussing how to set opening offers, aspiration levels, and bottom lines with team members will not reduce the effects of anchoring and adjustment.

Some of the biases we have discussed pertain to the framing of negotiations, such as the effects of positive (gain) and negative (loss) frames on how negotiators deal with risk. When these frames are mismatched between negotiators, agreement can be difficult to achieve. Reframing is a potentially effective remedy. For instance, rather than treating a particular possible outcome as a loss, the negotiator might reframe it as an opportunity to gain (e.g., Kahneman and Tversky, 1979), that is, as a bright-side alternative to approaching a given situation. Negotiators can also reframe by trying to perceive or understand the situation in a different way or from a different perspective. For instance, they can constructively reframe a problem by defining it in terms that are broader or narrower, bigger or smaller, riskier or less risky, or subject to a longer or shorter time constraint. Because reframing requires negotiators to be flexible during the negotiation itself, they should anticipate—during planning—that multiple contingencies may arise during negotiations and be prepared for shifts in the discussion. Box 5.5 describes one useful way of thinking about how negotiators can be more effective at crafting better outcomes through reframing.

Emotions are inevitable in negotiations, and it isn't realistic to try to avoid them or eradicate them from the encounter. Negotiation scholar Barbara Gray argues that effective negotiators figure out how to handle emotional outbursts from others who may be simply trying to "push our hot buttons." She offers these suggestions for dealing with an opponent who has expressed their feelings in a volatile or even hurtful way:

1. *Separate the emotion from its expression.* Perhaps the emotion is really a way for the other person to signal an important interest. Why is the other person acting this way? What interest is important enough to justify it?

2. *Turn the table.* Put yourself in the other person's position, and ask yourself, "Why would I behave that way?" This may help you identify a circumstance in which this sort of emotional outburst would be legitimate. The idea is not to accept the other person's (unacceptable) behavior, but to view it as a reflection of some identifiable need or interest to be addressed in the negotiation.

3. *Reflect the emotion being expressed back to the other party.* Sometimes strong feelings are an indication that the other party simply wants to be heard. Confirm that you are listening and that the concern that triggered the emotion is understood. This need not signal that you are agreeing with the concern or conceding anything; you are simply acknowledging that the other party is human and has feelings. This may be all the other party needs.

4. *Ask questions to uncover the issue or interest behind the emotion.* Knowing what the underlying concern makes it possible for you to move on from emotion to substance, and to treat that concern (once you know what it is) as an issue on the table for negotiation.

Source: Adapted from B. Gray, "Negotiating with Your Nemesis," *Negotiation Journal* 19 (2003a), pp. 299–310.

Clearly, telling people about a perceptual or cognitive bias, or having them discuss things in a group setting, does not make the bias go away. Unfortunately, there has been little other research done on managing perceptual biases. An exception is a study by Arunachalam and Dilla (1995), who had subjects participate in a simulated negotiation to set transfer prices between two divisions of the same company, in either an unstructured or a structured communication condition. In the unstructured communication condition, participants were given their role-play information and asked to prepare for the negotiation. Before bargaining in the structured communication condition, however, participants were also asked to complete a questionnaire asking them to identify what they thought their counterpart's priorities were in the negotiation. They then received training on how to identify and discuss issues and priorities in negotiation effectively. Finally, participants in both conditions negotiated either face-to-face or via computer terminals. Arunachalam and Dilla found that (1) negotiators in the structured communication condition negotiated higher profit outcomes and made fewer fixed-pie errors than negotiators in the unstructured communication condition, and (2) negotiators in the face-to-face condition negotiated higher profits and had fewer fixed-pie errors than negotiators in the computer terminal condition. These findings suggest that both problem definition and problem evaluation are important components of reducing fixed-pie bias. Careful discussion of the issues and preferences by both negotiators may reduce the effects of perceptual biases.[8]

More research is needed to provide negotiators with advice about how to overcome the negative effects of misperception and cognitive biases in negotiation. Until then, the best advice that negotiators can follow is simply to be aware of the negative aspects of these effects and to discuss them in a structured manner within their team and with their counterparts. Given the strength of the biases, this advice is admittedly somewhat anemic, and we hope that researchers will be able to identify other useful techniques for managing misperceptions and biases.

Mood, Emotion, and Negotiation

Research on negotiation has been dominated by views that have favored rational, cognitive, economic analyses of the negotiation process. These approaches have tended to analyze the rationality of negotiation, examine how negotiators make judgment errors that deviate from rationality, or assess how negotiators can optimize their outcomes. Negotiators are portrayed as rational beings who seem calculating, calm, and in control. But, as noted by Barry (2008), Davidson and Greenhalgh (1999), and others, we have not fully explored the role played by emotions in the negotiation process. While cognitive and emotional processes have a strong relationship to each other (see Fiske and Taylor, 1991; Kumar, 1997), the emotional component and its role have received considerably less attention.

The role of mood and emotion in negotiation has been the subject of an increasing body of recent theory and research during the last decade, and there are several helpful reviews of this literature (most recently, Barry, Fulmer, and Goates, 2006).[9] The distinction between mood and emotion is based on three characteristics: specificity, intensity, and duration. Mood states are more diffuse, less intense, and more enduring than emotion states, which tend to be more intense and directed at more specific targets (Forgas, 1992; Parrott, 2001). It is both theoretically reasonable and intuitively plausible to assume that emotions play important roles at various stages of negotiation interaction (Barry and Oliver, 1996). Like most emerging areas of study, there are many new and exciting developments in the study of mood, emotion, and negotiation, and we can present only a limited overview here. The following are some selected findings.

Negotiations Create Both Positive and Negative Emotions   Negotiation processes and outcomes may create both positive and negative feelings. Positive emotions can result from being attracted to the other party, feeling good about the development of the negotiation process and the progress that the parties are making (Carver and Scheir, 1990), or liking the results that the negotiations have produced. Thus, a cognitive assessment of a "good outcome" leads parties to feel happy and satisfied (Lazarus, 1991). Conversely, negative emotions can result from being turned off by the other party, feeling bad about the development of the negotiation process and the progress being made, or disliking the results. As noted by Kumar (1997), many positive emotions tend to be classified under the single term *happiness,* but we tend to discriminate more precisely among negative emotions. Some negative emotions may tend to be based in dejection while others are based in agitation. Dejection-related emotions result from feeling disappointed, frustrated, or dissatisfied, while agitation-related emotions result from feeling anxious, fearful, or threatened

(Higgins, 1987). Most researchers agree that emotions tend to move the parties toward some form of action in their relationship, such as initiating a relationship, maintaining or fixing the relationship, or terminating the relationship. Dejection-related emotions may lead negotiators to act aggressively (Berkowitz, 1989), while agitation-related emotions may lead negotiators to try to retaliate or to get out of the situation.

Positive Emotions Generally Have Positive Consequences for Negotiations   Positive emotions generally lead to three sets of consequences: improving the negotiating (decision-making) process, creating positive feelings toward the other negotiator(s), and making negotiators more persistent. Let us briefly review each:

- *Positive feelings are more likely to lead the parties toward more integrative processes.* Researchers have shown that negotiators who feel positive emotions toward each other are more likely to try, and feel successful at, shaping integrative agreements (Carnevale and Isen, 1986; Hollingshead and Carnevale, 1990). In addition, negotiators who feel positive emotions are more likely to be flexible in how they arrive at a solution to a problem, and hence may be less likely to get caught up in escalating their commitment to a single course of action (Isen and Baron, 1991).

- *Positive feelings also create a positive attitude toward the other side.* When negotiators like the other party, they tend to be more flexible in the negotiations (Druckman and Broome, 1991). In addition, having a positive attitude toward the other increases concession making (Pruitt and Carnevale, 1993) and lessens hostile behaviors (Baron, 1990). Findings from one study suggest that positive feelings build trust among the parties, although interestingly, the tendency toward positive emotion on the part of the more powerful party mattered more than the emotionality of the less powerful party (Anderson and Thompson, 2004). Another way to built trust is through empathy directed toward the other side, which has been shown to yield better individual negotiation outcomes for the party conveying empathy (Olekalns, Lau, and Smith, 2007).

- *Positive feelings promote persistence.* If negotiators feel positively attracted, they are more likely to feel confident and, as a result, to persist in trying to get their concerns and issues addressed in the negotiation and to achieve better outcomes (Kramer, Pommerenke, and Newton, 1993).

Aspects of the Negotiation Process Can Lead to Positive Emotions   Researchers have only recently begun to explore the emotional consequences of negotiation. Here are two findings regarding how the negotiation process shapes emotion-related outcomes:

- *Positive feelings result from fair procedures during negotiation.* Hegtvedt and Killian (1999) explored how emotional responses are related to the experience of fairness during the negotiation process. Their findings indicated that negotiators who see the process as fair experience more positive feelings and are less inclined to express negative emotions following the encounter.

- *Positive feelings result from favorable social comparisons.* Novemsky and Schweitzer (2004) found that individual satisfaction after a negotiation is higher when the individual negotiator's outcomes compare favorably with others in similar situations. Interestingly, however, this finding for so-called *external* social comparisons (comparing your outcome to others outside the negotiation that just took place) do not hold for *internal* social comparisons (comparing your outcome to the counterpart with whom you just negotiated). This means that negotiators may be more dismayed to know how well their opponent did, even when the opponent did less well! Novemsky and Schweitzer believe that this occurs because comparisons with an opponent—even favorable ones—focus the negotiator's attention on missed opportunities to claim additional value in this negotiation.

Negative Emotions Generally Have Negative Consequences for Negotiations   As positive feelings have been generally shown to have positive consequences for negotiations, so negative emotions tend to have negative consequences. As we noted earlier, negative feelings may be based either in dejection or in agitation, one or both parties may feel the emotions, and the behavior of one may prompt the emotional reaction in the other. Some specific research findings follow. (See Box 5.5 for some advice on how to deal with an opponent who brings negative emotion to the table.)

- *Negative emotions may lead parties to define the situation as competitive or distributive.* Veitch and Griffith (1976) demonstrate that a negative mood increases the likelihood that the actor will increase belligerent behavior toward the other. In a negotiation situation, this negative behavior is most likely to take the shape of a more distributive posture on the issues.

- *Negative emotions may undermine a negotiator's ability to analyze the situation accurately, which adversely affects individual outcomes.* In a series of experiments, Gonzalez, Lerner, Moore, and Babcock (2004) found that angry negotiators were less accurate at judging the other party's interests and at recalling their own interests, compared with negotiators with neutral emotion. The angry negotiators earned lower outcomes for themselves in a simulation with integrative potential, although interestingly they were more satisfied than neutral-emotion negotiators with those outcomes. It is noteworthy that the experimental manipulation of anger in this study was unrelated to the negotiation itself—anger was aroused during what subjects believed was a separate experiment preceding the negotiation experiment. This carryover effect of anger highlights the power of negative emotion to divert one's attention and focus from the negotiation problem at hand.

- *Negative emotions may lead parties to escalate the conflict.* When the mood is negative—more specifically, when both parties are dejected, frustrated, and blame the other—conflict is likely to become personal, the number of issues in the conflict may expand, and other parties may become drawn into the dispute (Kumar, 1997). In a study of online dispute resolution examining the mediation of disputes arising from eBay online auction transactions, Ray Friedman and colleagues (2004) found that expressions of anger by one party triggered anger from the other party, reducing the chances for a successful settlement of the dispute.

- *Negative emotions may lead parties to retaliate and may thwart integrative outcomes.* When the parties are angry with each other, and when their previous interaction has already led one party to seek to punish the other, the other may choose to retaliate (Allred, 1998; Bies and Tripp, 1998). Negative emotions may also lead to less effective outcomes. The more a negotiator holds the other responsible for destructive behavior in a previous interaction, the more anger and less compassion he or she feels for the other party. This in turn leads to less concern for the other's interests and a lower likelihood of discovering mutually beneficial negotiated solutions (Allred, Mallozzi, Matsui, and Raia, 1997).

• *Not all negative emotions have the same effect.* Anger may tend to escalate conflict and foster retaliation, but what about less "hot" negative emotions, such as worry, disappointment, guilt, and regret? Van Kleef, de Dreu, and Manstead (2006) examined how people react to negotiation opponents who are experiencing these kinds of emotions. They found that negotiators made smaller demands of worried or disappointed opponents, presumably feeling sorry for their situation, but made fewer concessions to guilty or regretful opponents. Negotiators did, however, report more favorable impressions of regretful opponents, viewing them as more interpersonally sensitive than opponents experiencing worry or disappointment.

Aspects of the Negotiation Process Can Lead to Negative Emotions   As with positive emotion, research exploring the negative emotional consequences of negotiation is recent and limited. Here are two findings:

• *Negative emotions may result from a competitive mind-set.* Negotiators with a fixed-pie perception of the situation tend to be less satisfied with negotiated outcomes than those with an integrative orientation. This may stem from the perception that when a negotiation is viewed as zero-sum, the other party's gains mean an equivalent loss for self (Thompson and DeHarpport, 1994). In a similar vein, individualistic (egoistic) parties report less satisfaction with their outcomes compared to those with a prosocial (altruistic) value orientation (Gillespie, Brett, and Weingart, 2000).

• *Negative emotions may result from impasse.* When a negotiation ends in impasse, negotiators are more likely to experience negative emotions such as anger and frustration compared with negotiators who successfully reach agreement (O'Connor and Arnold, 2001). These researchers found, however, that people with more confidence in their negotiating ability were less likely to experience negative emotion in the wake of impasse. This is important because impasse is not always a bad thing—the goal is achieving a good outcome, not merely reaching an agreement.

• *Negative emotions may result merely from the prospect of beginning a negotiation.* We might assume that inexperienced negotiators are most prone to be nervous about an upcoming bargaining session, Wheeler (2004) points out that even experienced negotiators may feel anxiety going in to the encounter. He identifies several sources of anxiety at the outset of negotiation: doubts about one's competence, concerns about the opponents' attitudes or likely behaviors, and "the inevitable uncertainty about what path negotiation will take" (p. 153). Anxiety isn't all bad, however; Wheeler argues it may spark creativity that can help produce constructive outcomes.

The Effects of Positive and Negative Emotion in Negotiation   It is possible for positive emotion to generate negative outcomes and for negative feelings to elicit beneficial outcomes, as we explain here:

• *Positive feelings may have negative consequences.* First, negotiators in a positive mood may be less likely to examine closely the other party's arguments. As a result, they may be more susceptible to a competitive opponent's deceptive tactics (Bless, Bohner, Schwartz, and Strack, 1988). In addition, because negotiators with positive feelings are less focused on the arguments of the other party, they may achieve less-than-optimal outcomes (Kumar, 1997). Finally, if positive feelings create strong positive expectations, parties who are not able to find an integrative agreement are likely to experience the defeat more strongly and perhaps treat the other party more harshly (Parrott, 1994).

• *Negative feelings may create positive outcomes.* Just as positive emotions can create negative outcomes, it is clear that negative emotions can create positive consequences for negotiation. First, negative emotion has information value. It alerts the parties that the situation is problematic and needs attention, which may motivate them to either leave the situation or resolve the problem (van de Vliert, 1985). There is also recent evidence that when a negotiator uses words that trigger negative emotions, others become more optimistic that the negotiation will be successfully resolved (Schroth, Bain-Chekal, and Caldwell, 2005). Schroth and her colleagues note that this optimism is justified if the intention of the party triggering emotion is to convey seriousness of purpose and a desire to focus the discussion, but not if the point is merely to wield (or match) power. In short, anger and other negative emotions can serve as a danger signal that motivates both parties to confront the problem directly and search for a resolution (Daly, 1991).

Anger, of course, may also signal that a negotiator is tough or ambitious, and researchers have found negotiation concede more often to an angry opponent than to a happy or unemotional partner (Sinaceur and Tiedens, 2006; Van Kleef, de Dreu, and Manstead, 2004). These findings are somewhat inconsistent with other work finding that anger provokes angry or competitive responses (e.g., Friedman et al., 2004). A possible reconciliation comes from recent work by Van Kleef and Côté (2007), who found that whether the expression of anger provokes conciliatory or competitive behavior depends on the appropriateness of the anger: negotiators in their study made lower demands and more concessions when they perceived their opponent's display of anger to be appropriate for the situation (i.e., when it appears that the angry individual has a legitimate reason to be angry). But even if it sometimes pays to be angry in competitive negotiations (as a signal of toughness or reluctance to compromise), research also tells us when anger can backfire. Anger is less likely to elicit concessions when the party on the receiving end of anger either (1) has the opportunity to respond with deception (e.g., misrepresent his own interests) or (2) has little at stake, meaning little to fear from having the angry opponent say no to an offer (van Dijk, Van Kleef, Steinel, Wolfgang, and van Beest, 2008).

Emotions Can Be Used Strategically as Negotiation Gambits   Finally, we have been discussing emotions as though they were genuine. Given the power that emotions may have in swaying the other side toward one's own point of view, emotions may also be used strategically and manipulatively as influence tactics within negotiation. For example, negotiators may intentionally manipulate emotion in order to get the other side to adopt certain beliefs or take certain actions. Barry (1999) asked negotiators to assess their own ability to manipulate emotions (such as anger, disgust, sympathy, enthusiasm, caring, and liking) and to judge the appropriateness of using such tactics in negotiation as a form of deception. The participants in Barry's study rated emotional manipulation as a highly appropriate tactic—more appropriate than deception about informational aspects of negotiation (such as goals or plans or bottom lines). Negotiators also expressed greater confidence in their ability to use tactics of emotional manipulation effectively compared to other forms of deception. It is important to keep in mind that there are ethical implications to the use of contrived emotion as a vehicle for deception, just as for any other form of deception (Barry, Fulmer, and Long, 2000). (We will discuss ethical issues in negotiation in detail in Chapter 9.)

Kopelman, Rosette, and Thompson (2006) conducted a series of experiments examining how the strategic use of positive and negative emotion affect negotiation outcomes. In their study, negotiators who were coached to implement a positive emotional tone were more likely to reach agreements that incorporated a future business relationship between the parties compared to those implementing a negative or neutral emotional strategy. They also found that negotiators exhibiting positive emotionality were more likely to induce compliance with ultimatum offers.

Recent evidence points to the effects of the emotions of the *other* party on a negotiator's choice of strategy. A study by Van Kleef, de Dreu, and Manstead (2004) found that negotiators track the emotions of the other party and adjust their strategy accordingly. Specifically, when subjects negotiated with an angry party, they tended to make lower demands and smaller concessions when the other party's anger seemed to be threatening to the outcomes of the negotiation. Also, as we noted earlier, there is evidence that negotiators make lower demands of opponents who are worried or disappointed, but more demands of opponents experiencing guilt or regret (Van Kleef, de Dreu, and Manstead, 2006).

Lastly, beyond the strategic expression of one's own (genuine or fabricated) emotions, negotiators may also engage in the regulation or management of the emotions of the other party. As noted by Thompson, Nadler, and Kim (1999), effective negotiators are able to adjust their messages to adapt to what they perceive as the other party's emotional state—a process they label "emotional tuning." Some psychologists regard the ability to perceive and regulate emotions as a stable individual difference that has come to be known as emotional intelligence (e.g., Mayer, Salovey, and Caruso, 2000). We consider the potential role of emotional intelligence in negotiation within our broader treatment of individual differences in Chapter 15.

In summary, emotions are critical features of negotiation encounters that supplement the classical view that negotiation is primarily a rational process of decision making under risk and uncertainty. In the traditional view, we understand negotiation by looking at how negotiators weigh information and make judgments that optimize their outcomes. Negotiators, as we said at the outset of this chapter, are seen as rational actors who are calculating, calm, and in control. But as researchers have come to realize, negotiations involve humans who not only deviate from rational judgments, but who inevitably experience and express emotions in circumstances where much is at stake. The role of emotions in negotiation is complex because, as Box 5.6 highlights, human emotions themselves are dynamic and complicated.

BOX 5.6

The Inescapable Messiness of Human Emotion

Daniel Shapiro, the author of *Beyond Reason: Using Emotions as You Negotiate,* observes that using emotions effectively to promote successful negotiation is inherently difficult because of the complex nature of human emotion. He illustrates this complexity by pointing to six features of emotions that influence how they play out at the negotiation table:

- Emotions are *unavoidable.* People can't avoid them any more than they can avoid thinking.

- Emotions are *numerous.* In a given situation a negotiator can experience and encounter numerous emotional states, such as anger, frustration, enthusiasm, regret, and so forth.

- Emotions are *fluid.* They change from moment to moment, often without warning.

- Emotions are *multilayered.* People sometimes experience multiple emotions simultaneously, even seemingly opposite emotions (e.g., liking and disappointment at the same time).

- Emotions are *varied in their impact.* Different people may react differently to the same emotion expressed in a similar situation. For instance, one person may be more easily angered by something than another.

- Emotions are *triggered by multiple causes.* The source of emotions can be hard to identify—triggered perhaps by a situation, or by the actions of the other party, or even by one's biological state (e.g., neurochemicals present in the brain).

Source: Adapted from D. L. Shapiro, "Teaching Students How to Use Emotions as They Negotiate," *Negotiation Journal* 22 (2006), pp. 105–09.

Chapter Summary

In this chapter we have taken a multifaceted look at the role of perception, cognition, and emotion in negotiation. The first portion of the chapter presented a brief overview of the perceptual process and discussed four types of perceptual distortions: stereotyping, halo effects, selective perception, and projection. We then turned to a discussion of how framing influences perceptions in negotiation and how reframing and issue development both change negotiator perceptions during negotiations.

The chapter then reviewed the research findings from one of the most important recent areas of inquiry in negotiation, that of cognitive biases in negotiation. The effects of 12 different cognitive biases were discussed: irrational escalation of commitment, mythical fixed-pie beliefs, anchoring and adjustment, framing, availability of information, the winner's curse, overconfidence, the law of small numbers, self-serving biases, endowment effects, ignoring others' cognitions, and reactive devaluation. This was followed by consideration of ways to manage misperception and cognitive biases in negotiation, an area that has received relatively little research attention. In a final section of the chapter we considered mood and emotion in negotiation, which provides an important alternative to cognitive and perceptual processes for understanding negotiation behavior.

Endnotes

[1] See Babcock, Wang, and Loewenstein (1996); de Dreu and van Lange (1995); Thompson (1995); and Thompson and Hastie (1990a).

[2] Note that frames themselves cannot be "seen." They are abstractions, perceptions, and thoughts that people use to define a situation, organize information, determine what

is important and what is not important, and so on. We can infer other people's frames by asking them directly about their frames, by listening to their communication, and by watching their behavior. Similarly, we can try to understand our own frames by thinking about what aspects of a situation we should pay attention to, emphasize, focus on, or ignore—and by observing our own words and actions. One cannot see or directly measure a frame, however.

3 For extensive reviews of research on cognitive biases in negotiation, see Bazerman and Carroll (1987), Neale and Bazerman (1992b), and Thompson and Hastie (1990b). Whether negotiators misperceive information or misprocess information remains a technical debate in the communication and negotiation literature that is beyond the scope of this book.

4 See also Diekmann, Tenbrunsel, Shah, Schroth, and Bazerman (1996); and Ritov (1996).

5 See also Bazerman, Magliozzi, and Neale (1985); de Dreu, Carnevale, Emans, and Van de Vliert (1994); and Neale, Huber, and Northcraft (1987).

6 See also Ball, Bazerman, and Carroll (1991); and Foreman and Murnighan, (1996).

7 In a replication, Kahneman and his colleagues left the price tags on the mugs, making the objective value of the mug clearly visible to participants. Nonetheless, results were consistent with those just described.

8 Arunachalam and Dilla did not study the consequences of only one negotiator following this strategy, however, so it is not clear what would happen if both negotiators did not agree to participate in the decision-making process.

9 Other reviews include Allred, Mallozzi, Matsui, and Raia (1997); Barry, Fulmer, and Van Kleef, 2004; Barry and Oliver (1996); and Kumar (1997).

Communication

Objectives

1. Understand the basic components of communication flow in a negotiation.
2. Explore what is communicated in a negotiation and how people communicate.
3. Consider the ways that communication might be improved in negotiation.
4. Gain practical tools for how to improve communication processes in any negotiation.

Reduced to its essence, negotiation is a form of interpersonal communication. Communication processes, both verbal and nonverbal, are critical to achieving negotiation goals and to resolving conflicts. According to Putnam and Poole (1987),

> . . . the activity of having or managing a conflict occurs through communication. More specifically, communication undergirds the setting and reframing of goals; the defining and narrowing of conflict issues; the developing of relationships between disputants and among constituents; the selecting and implementing of strategies and tactics; the generating, attacking, and defending of alternative solutions; and the reaching and confirming of agreements. (p. 550)

In this chapter we examine the process by which negotiators communicate their own interests, positions, and goals—and in turn make sense of those of the other party and of the negotiation as a whole. Clearly, communication pervades the negotiation process; accordingly, research on communication sheds light on negotiation both as a process of interaction and as a context for communication subtleties that may influence processes and outcomes (Chatman, Putnam, and Sondak, 1991). This chapter opens with a discussion of the basic mechanisms through which messages are encoded, sent, received, and decoded. We then consider in some depth *what* is communicated in a negotiation, followed by an exploration of *how* people communicate in negotiation. The chapter concludes with discussions of how to improve communication in negotiation and of special communication considerations at the close of negotiations.

Basic Models of Communication

Most analyses of communication begin with a basic model of the communication process, and we do so here. An early and influential model developed by Shannon and Weaver (1948) conceptualizes communication as an activity that occurs between two people: a *sender* and a *receiver*.[1] A sender has a thought or *meaning* in mind. The sender *encodes* this meaning into a message that is to be transmitted to a receiver. For instance, the thought could be about the sender's preference for a particular outcome in a negotiation. The message may be encoded into verbal language (e.g., words and sentences), nonverbal expression (e.g., facial gestures, hand waving, and finger pointing), or both. Once encoded, the message is then transmitted (e.g., via voice, facial expression, or written statement) through a *channel* or *medium* (e.g., face-to-face interaction, telephone, e-mail, text message, letter) to the receiver. The person to whom the message is directed receives the transmission and then *decodes* and *interprets* it, giving meaning and understanding to the receiver.

In one-way communication, from sender to receiver, this process would constitute a complete transmission. A sender who writes a message, reads it over to check its clarity, and sends it by e-mail to the receiver generally assumes that the message is received and understood. This one-way view is simplistic, however, because most communication, particularly in negotiation, involves give-and-take, dialogue and discussion. Thus, it is more useful to analyze communication by treating the exchange between parties as a two-way process that continuously cycles back and forth between the individuals involved. Foulger (2004) has proposed a "transactional model" (see Figure 6.1) that captures the bidirectional nature of two-party communication in ongoing conversations, such as occurs routinely in negotiation. Foulger's model appropriately treats communicators as both creators and consumers of messages rather than one or the other.

In a two-party exchange like that depicted in Figure 6.1, a communicator is not a passive recipient of messages; the person who receives a message takes an active role in several ways. First, the recipient receives the message (hears it, reads it, feels it) and then seeks to ascribe meaning to it by interpreting both its information content and the other party's motives for transmitting it. The recipient then becomes a sender, encoding a verbal and/or nonverbal response that may try to accomplish a number of things: convey to the other person information about how the original message was received—perhaps a nod of assent, or a quizzical look of confusion, or maybe a grimace signalling dismay (but not always: in a negotiation, like in a poker game, the receiver at times prefers not to react in a way that is detectable by the communicator); respond in some way to the content of the message of the original sender; avoid a substantive response and change the subject; or any number of other possible goals. Importantly, the communicator responding to a message, like the one who sent the previous message, has the opportunity not only to choose how to encode the response, but also to select a channel or medium to use for transmission. People often make a channel selection out of habit or convenience—he sent me an e-mail so I'll reply by e-mail, or she left me a phone message so I'll return the call. Effective communicators and negotiators, however, will often pause to consider the strategic implications of choices about communication channels (which we discuss later in this chapter) rather than simply respond in kind.

Thus, in negotiation the *feedback* provided by the recipient of a message to its sender can take various forms: a nonverbal gesture, an expressed emotion, a question seeking clarification, a response to information presented, an attempt to build upon the first message, or a rebuttal to an argument, to name just a few, or some combination of these. In two-party communication the entire transaction may range from something as simple as a routine question ("Want to go for a cup of coffee?") and an affirmative nod by another, to complex statements of fact and opinion and equally complex responses as negotiators shape a comprehensive agreement that requires acceptance by several contentious parties.

FIGURE 6.1 | A Transactional Model of Communication Involving Two Parties

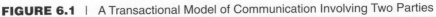

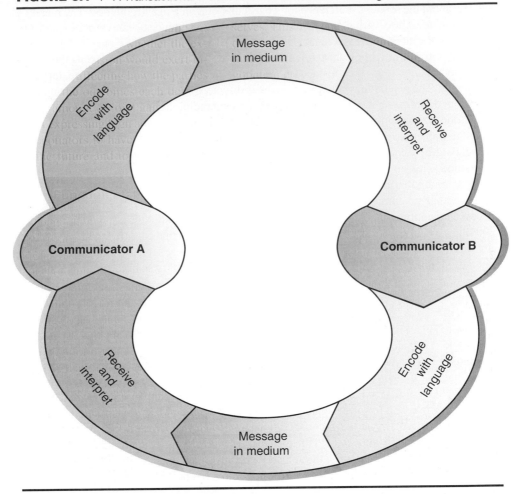

Source: Adapted from D. Foulger, "Models of the Communication Process," February 2004, unpublished paper available at http://foulger.info/davis/research/unifiedModelOfCommunication.htm.

Having sketched this basic, transactional model of the communication process between two parties, we next use the elements of this model as a framework for understanding the distortions that can occur in communication.

Distortion in Communication

Communication "works" to the degree that a wide variety of information—facts, opinions, feelings, preferences, and experiences—is completely and thoroughly shared, and accurately received and decoded, leading to mutual understanding. As most of us know from experience, human communication systems seldom perform optimally. Rather, the elements of the model we have described and the linkages among them are subject to external factors that distort messages and their meaning, which inhibits comprehension and mutual understanding. In the following paragraphs, we explore how distortions occur in communication by looking at some of the individual elements comprising the communication process that we presented earlier (refer again to Figure 6.1).

1. *Individual communicators* (whether sender or receiver at a given point in the exchange) each have goals and objectives, things they want to accomplish. Communicator A may want to change the Communicator B's mind about an issue or secure concessions toward a negotiated agreement. Communicator B may not want to have her mind changed or to make concessions; moreover, she is likely to want the sender to change or make concessions. The more diverse the goals of the two parties, or the more antagonistic they are in their relationship, the greater the likelihood that distortions and errors in communication will occur (de Dreu, Nauta, and Van de Vliert, 1995). Similarly, the two communicators differ in their individual characteristics—each is likely to have different personal values, attitudes toward certain issues and objectives, previous experiences, life history, and personality characteristics (not to mention communication skills). Each of these elements contributes to a different way of viewing the world.

2. *Messages* are the symbolic forms by which information is communicated. Humans are unique in their ability to use symbols—primarily written or spoken language—to transmit information. Some messages are direct expressions of meaning (e.g., I lean over the table and take the pencil I want), whereas others are symbolic representations (e.g., I say to the person seated across the table, "Please pass me the pencil"). The more prone we are to using symbolic communication, the more likely it is that the symbols we choose may not accurately communicate the meaning we intend. In the pencil example, if the other person does not understand English, or if there are several different pencils on the table, the communication will be less effective.

3. *Encoding* is the process by which messages are put into symbolic form. The encoding process will be affected by varying degrees of skill in encoding (e.g., fluency in language, skill at written and oral expression). It will also be affected by earlier communication, including what both parties want to communicate and how they have reacted to earlier communications. One party may encode a message in a form that the other may not prefer (e.g., too complicated or too informal or too cursory). Distortions are likely if the sender encodes the message in a way that impedes understanding or accurate interpretation by the recipient.

4. *Channels* and *media* (we use the terms interchangeably) are the means through which information is sent and received. The choices available to communicators exist at a couple of different levels. First, should the message be transmitted verbally (through spoken or written words), nonverbally (through body posture, hand and facial gestures, tone of voice, and the like) or symbolically (through pictures or graphics of some sort)? Second, having decided whether a message should involve words, symbols, graphics, or gestures, what should be the conduit for its transmission? Spoken words can be transmitted face to face, over the telephone, or online (with or without visual contact). For written words there is paper, e-mail, and texting, with wide variations in formality available to the writer. We tend to think of nonverbal gestures as requiring visual contact, but there are ways to convey reactions and emotions without actual words in a telephone conversation or an online exchange. Symbolic communication is also possible through various conduits, with technology making it possible to convey complex ideas in novel ways. There are numerous opportunities for communication distortion based on the channels used. A complex message may need to be written rather than spoken so that the recipient can consume it at his or her own pace and review if need be. A face-to-face interaction could be unwise if it occurs in a noisy environment that fosters distraction. A communicator who wishes to convey an emotional appeal may risk message distortion in writing when a personal conversation would make it easier to convey emotion. Also, distortion of meaning can result when there is incongruence between multiple channels used at the same time. If a parent says to a child, "Don't do that!" but simultaneously smiles or laughs, the incongruity of the messages can lead to confusion ("Do I stop, or do I keep doing it?").

5. *Reception* is the process of comprehension: receiving messages in their verbal, nonverbal, or symbolic form and decoding them into a form that is understandable to the recipient of the message. If the parties speak the same language or use the same common nonverbal gestures to communicate messages, the process may be reasonably simple, although it is subject to perceptual and cognitive errors (see Chapter 5). When people speak different languages, decoding involves higher degrees of error. Although translators may help decode the other party's messages, full translation may not be possible; that is, it may not be possible to capture fully the other party's meaning or tone along with the words. In fact, translators introduce the possibility of additional error into the communication process.

6. *Interpretation* is the process of ascertaining the meaning and significance of decoded messages for the situation going forward. The facts, ideas, feelings, reactions, or thoughts that exist within individuals act as a set of filters for interpreting decoded messages. If one person has said to the other, "Please pass me that pencil," and the other person has said, "No," the encoded *no* is likely to stimulate a variety of reactions in the first person's search for its exact meaning: Was the *no* a direct refusal of the request? Why did the other person say *no*? Does he need the pencil too? Is he being obstinate and intentionally blocking me? Was it a playful joke? Answers to these questions will vary depending on other aspects of the communication exchange and on the relationship between the parties, all of which lead the person to ascribe particular meanings to the word *no*.

An important way to avoid some of the problems in communication we have mentioned is by giving the other party *feedback:* inform the sender that the message was received, encoded, and ascribed with the meaning the sender intended. The absence of feedback can contribute to significant distortions in communication, especially when a sender does not know whether the message has been received, much less understood. Those addressing a large audience may find themselves either speaking into space or directing comments to people who are nodding their heads to signify agreement, smiling, or otherwise acknowledging that the communication is being received and appreciated. The sender is unlikely to continue directing comments to receivers who are scowling, sleeping, or shaking their heads to signify disagreement, unless the comments are specifically designed to influence them to act otherwise. In negotiation, feedback can distort communication by influencing the offers negotiators make (e.g., Kristensen and Garling, 1997) or by leading them to alter their evaluations of possible outcomes (Larrick and Boles, 1995; Thompson, Valley, and Kramer, 1995). Although feedback is often genuinely intended to improve understanding, negotiators need to keep in mind that feedback can be used strategically to induce concessions, changes in strategy, or altered assessments of process and outcome.

What Is Communicated during Negotiation?

One of the fundamental questions that researchers in communication and negotiation have examined is, What is communicated during negotiation? This work has taken several different forms but generally involves audio taping or videotaping negotiation role-plays and analyzing the patterns of communication that occur in them. For instance, Alexander, Schul, and Babakus (1991) videotaped executives who participated in a 60-minute, three-person negotiation involving two oil companies. The videotapes were classified into 6,432 verbal units, which were then coded into 24 different response categories. The researchers found that more than 70 percent of the verbal tactics that buyers and sellers used during the negotiation were integrative. In addition, buyers and sellers tended to behave reciprocally—when one party used an integrative tactic, the other tended to respond with an integrative tactic.

Most of the communication during negotiation is not about negotiator preferences (Carnevale, Pruitt, and Seilheimer, 1981). Although the blend of integrative versus distributive content varies as a function of the issues being discussed (Weingart, Hyder, and Prietula, 1996), it is also clear that the content of communication is only partly responsible for negotiation outcomes (Olekalns, Smith, and Walsh, 1996). For example, one party may choose not to communicate certain things (e.g., the reason she chose a different supplier), so her counterpart (e.g., the supplier not chosen) may be unaware why some outcomes occur. In the following sections, we discuss five different categories of communication that take place during negotiations and then consider the question of whether more communication is always better than less communication.

1. Offers, Counteroffers, and Motives

According to Tutzauer (1992, p. 67), "Perhaps the most important communications in a bargaining session are those that convey the disputants' offers and counteroffers." Tutzauer assumes that bargainers have definite preferences and exhibit rational behavior by acting in accordance with those preferences, and that the preferences can be expressed according to some numerical scale, that is, that they have different degrees of utility or worth (see also Luce and Raiffa, 1957). A negotiator's preferences reflect in good measure his or her underlying motivations, which are also communicated during a negotiation, and they can have a powerful influence on the actions of the other party and on negotiation outcomes. Evidence for this comes from a study by Langner and Winter (2001) that examined historical examples of political crisis negotiations as well as experimental data. Findings indicate that negotiators with affiliation motives (a concern for friendly relations among people or groups) tend to convey "positive" concessions that de-escalate tensions or facilitate agreement. In contrast, negotiators with power motives (concern for impact, prestige, and reputation) were more likely to reject concessions and escalate conflict.

A communicative framework for negotiation is based on the assumptions that (1) the communication of offers is a dynamic process (the offers change or shift over time), (2) the offer process is interactive (bargainers influence each other), and (3) various internal and external factors (e.g., time limitations, reciprocity norms, alternatives, constituency pressures) drive the interaction and "motivate a bargainer to change his or her offer" (Tutzauer, 1992, p. 73). In other words, the offer–counteroffer process is dynamic and interactive, like the reciprocal influence process described in Chapter 3, and subject to situational and environmental constraints. This process constantly revises the parameters of the negotiation, eventually narrowing the bargaining range and guiding the discussion toward a settlement point.

2. Information about Alternatives

Communication in negotiation is not limited to the exchange of offers and counteroffers, however. Another important aspect that has been studied is how sharing information with the other party influences the negotiation process. For instance, Pinkley and her colleagues (Pinkley, 1995; Pinkley, Neale, and Bennett, 1994) have examined the question of whether simply having a best alternative to a negotiated agreement (BATNA) (Fisher, Ury, and Patton, 1991) is sufficient to give a negotiator an advantage over the other party, or whether the BATNA needs to be communicated to the other person. The existence of a BATNA changed several things in a negotiation: (1) compared to negotiators without attractive BATNAs, negotiators with attractive BATNAs set higher reservation prices for themselves than their counterparts did; (2) negotiators whose counterparts had attractive BATNAs set lower reservation points for themselves; and (3) when both parties were aware of the attractive BATNA that one of the negotiators had, that negotiator received a more positive negotiation outcome. Buelens and Van Poucke (2004) have shown that knowledge of a negotiation partner's BATNA is one of the strongest determinants of a negotiator's initial offer. The results of these studies suggest that negotiators with an attractive BATNA should tell the other party about it if they expect to receive its full benefits. We hasten to add that the style and tone used to convey information about an attractive BATNA matters. Politely (even subtly) making the other party aware of one's good alternative can provide leverage without alienating the other party. On the other hand, waving a good BATNA in the other party's face in an imposing or condescending manner may be construed as aggressive and threatening.

3. Information about Outcomes

In a simulation study of negotiation, Thompson, Valley, and Kramer (1995) examined the effects of sharing different types of information, how the other party evaluated his or her success in the negotiation, and how this influenced negotiators' evaluations of their own success. The study focused on how winners and losers evaluated their negotiation outcomes (winners were defined as negotiators who received more points in the negotiation simulation). Thompson and her colleagues found that winners and losers evaluated their own outcomes equally when they did not know how well the other party had done, but if they found out that the other negotiator had done better, or was simply pleased with his or her outcome, then negotiators felt less positive about their own outcome. A study by Novemsky and Schweitzer (2004) suggests that even when negotiators learn that the other party did relatively poorly, they are less satisfied with the outcome than when they have no comparison information. Taken together, these findings suggest that negotiators should be cautious about sharing their outcomes or even their positive reactions to outcomes with the other party, especially if they are going to negotiate with that party again in the future. In addition, the study suggested that negotiators should evaluate their own success before learning about the other party's evaluations of the outcomes.

4. Social Accounts

Another type of communication that occurs during negotiation consists of the "social accounts" that negotiators use to explain things to the other party (see Bies and Shapiro, 1987; Shapiro, 1991), especially when negotiators need to justify bad news. A review of the relevant literature by Sitkin and Bies (1993) suggests that three types of explanations are important: (1) explanations of mitigating circumstances, where negotiators suggest that they had no choice in taking the positions they did; (2) explanations of exonerating circumstances, where negotiators explain their positions from a broader perspective, suggesting that while their current position may appear negative, it derives from positive motives (e.g., an honest mistake); and (3) reframing explanations, where outcomes can be explained by changing the context (e.g., short-term pain for long-term gain). Sitkin and Bies suggest that negotiators who use multiple explanations are more likely to have better outcomes and that the negative effects of poor outcomes can be alleviated by communicating explanations for them.

5. Communication about Process

Lastly, some communication is about the negotiation process itself—how well it is going or what procedures might be adopted to improve the situation. Some of this communication takes the form of seemingly trivial "small talk" that breaks the ice or builds rapport between negotiators. The effect need not be "small," however; there is evidence that interaction giving rise to shared cognition and shared identity among negotiators before they immerse themselves in the task at hand leads to better integrative outcomes (Swaab, Postmes, van Beest, and Spears, 2007). Clearly, though, some communication about process is not just helpful, but critical, as when conflict intensifies and negotiators run the risk of letting hostilities overtake progress. A study by Brett, Shapiro, and Lytle (1998) examined communication strategies in negotiation that are used to halt conflict spirals that might otherwise lead to impasse or less-than-ideal outcomes. One such strategy involves calling attention to the other party's contentious actions and explicitly labeling the process as counterproductive. More generally, Brett and her colleagues suggest that negotiators seeking to break out of a conflict spiral should resist the natural urge to reciprocate contentious communication from the other party. Negotiators, like other busy humans, may be tempted to forge ahead with offers and counteroffers in pursuit of an outcome rather than pause and "waste" time to discuss a process gone sour. Sometimes that break in the substantive conversation and attention to process is precisely what's needed.

We conclude this section on *what* is communication in negotiation with three key questions.

Are Negotiators Consistent or Adaptive?

A major theme of many guides to negotiation, including this book, is that effective negotiators are able to adapt their strategy and style to particular bargaining situations. But while this may be good advice, research indicates that when it comes to communication patterns, negotiators are more likely to be consistent in their strategies than to vary their approach. Taylor and Donald (2003) analyzed transcripts of divorce and hostage negotiations to examine patterns of behavioral interaction. The results showed that negotiations are clearly a dynamic and interactive process with consistency over time; negotiators' utterances were affected by the ones that preceded it and influenced those that followed. This analysis also showed that negotiators react to only a small proportion of the available cues communicated by their partner and use only a small proportion of possible response. Moreover, this proportion becomes smaller as the negotiation proceeds, meaning there is less variation in forms of communication the longer a negotiation goes on. Taylor and Donald conclude that "negotiators have set responses to different behavioral sequences that they employ consistently irrespective of the context and their negotiation role" (p. 228). It appears that when it comes to making choices about communication, many negotiators prefer sticking with the familiar rather than venturing into improvisation.

Does It Matter What Is Said Early in the Negotiation?

Recently published research shows that a relatively small amount of communication in a negotiation encounter can have large effects on the outcomes that result. Curhan and Pentland (2007) explored the idea that "thin slices" of negotiation—communication patterns during the first five minutes—have a large effect on the negotiated agreements that the parties eventually reach. Using an experimental two-party negotiation simulation, they found that for some negotiators (those in a high-status role), speaking time—the amount of time they were talking and not the other person—during the first five minutes predicted how well that party did in the negotiation. But their study also showed that the tone of the conversation during those first few minutes matters: the more negotiators spoke with emphasis, varying vocal pitch and volume, the worse they did and the better the other party did. In other words, controlling "the floor" early in the negotiation helps, but not dominating it with emotional or hyperbolic communication.

Controlling the conversation early on may help an individual negotiator do better, but does it help the pair achieve integrative outcomes? The negotiation simulation in Curham and Pentland's study did include potential for integrating the parties' interests to achieve mutual gains, but they found that communication during the first five minutes had no effects on the ability of parties to achieve *joint* gains. But there is evidence from other researchers that joint gains are influenced by what happens early on. Adair and Brett (2005) examined communication at various stages of negotiation encounters, focusing specifically on actions that contribute to achieving better joint outcomes. They found greater joint gains when negotiators move beyond posturing to exchanging information about issues and priorities before the negotiation is too far along. "What negotiators do in the first half of a

One of the most difficult aspects of negotiation is the actual give-and-take that occurs at the table. Should I stick with this point, or is it time to fold? Should I open the bidding or wait for the other side to take the lead? It requires good judgment to make these tough decisions. While experience certainly contributes to the development of judgment, other key ingredients are the knack of analyzing situations, the courage to make concessions when they're called for, and the willingness to stick to an unpopular position when necessary. Also important are creativity, persuasiveness, and the ability to see the big picture of the exchange.

James Freund is a lawyer and experienced negotiator. He recommends the following:

- *Stay in balance.* Remember that there is a time to be aggressive and a time to concede, a time to wrap things up and a time to keep options open. It is important to strike some sort of balance in the process, even when you are in the driver's seat, to ensure that your future relationship with this negotiating partner (or your own personal reputation as a negotiator) does not suffer from this single encounter.

- *Manage appearances.* The negotiator who arrives at the meeting with bags packed and a plane ticket obtrusively in the pocket of her coat telegraphs to her counterpart, "Hey, I want to wrap this up and make my plane home." Her opponent will be motivated to slow the tempo of negotiation, expecting that she will be willing to make big concessions as the time for her departure grows closer. Cultivating an appearance that says you will wait patiently for the best deal to be negotiated is a more effective strategy.

- *Be patient.* You can learn a great deal about your counterpart's real level of desire by hanging back and watching. Does he hurry things along? Is she willing to take time to learn the details of a new but complex proposal? Patient adherence to your position provides you with gradually increasing credibility as negotiations wear on.

Freund concluded, "Patience and perseverance are most effective when clothed in a low-key style that emphasizes deliberateness rather than obstinacy. So learn how to insist on your point without being overbearing—and how to say no without seeming too negative" (p. 34).

Source: Adapted from J. C. Freund, "Being a Smart Negotiator," *Directors and Boards* 2, no. 18 (Winter 1994), pp. 33–36.

negotiation," Adair and Brett concluded, "has a significant impact on their ability to generate integrative solutions and with high joint gains" (p. 47).

Is More Information Always Better?

Some research has suggested that receiving too much information during negotiation may actually be detrimental to negotiators; this is sometimes called the information-is-weakness effect.[2] Box 6.1 provides a discussion of ways to manage communication during a negotiation. Negotiators who know the complete preferences of both parties may have more difficulty determining fair outcomes than negotiators who do not have this information. Brodt (1994) conducted a study to examine how a specific type of information—namely, inside information about the other party's deadline—influenced the negotiation process. In a simulation study of a distributive negotiation over an exotic automobile, Brodt found that negotiators with inside information (1) paid less for the car, (2) were less likely to make concessions during negotiation, and (3) made more creative offers during negotiation than did negotiators without inside information. Brodt concluded that having more information enhanced the negotiator's strength, suggesting that the information-is-weakness effect may be limited to very specific circumstances.

An experimental study by O'Connor (1997), however, demonstrates that having more information does not automatically translate into better negotiation outcomes. O'Connor's subjects participated in a simulated union–management negotiation over an employment contract, which included both integrative issues and compatible issues where both parties wanted the same outcome. They negotiated in pairs that were encouraged to be either cooperative (pursue collaborative problem solving) or individualistic (pursue self-interest). O'Connor found that cooperative dyads exchanged more information than individualistic dyads but that the amount of information exchanged did not improve the overall accuracy of the parties' perceptions of each other's preferences. The results of O'Connor's study suggest that the influence of the exchange of accurate information on negotiation outcomes is not as direct as people might expect—that is, simply exchanging information does not automatically lead to better understanding of the other party's preferences or to better negotiation outcomes. Nor does it automatically result in the information-is-weakness effect. Rather, the effect of exchanging information during negotiation depends on the type of issues being discussed and the negotiators' motivation to use the information.

How People Communicate in Negotiation

While it may seem obvious that how negotiators communicate is as important as what they have to say, research has examined different aspects of how people communicate in negotiation. We address three aspects related to the "how" of communication: the characteristics of language that communicators use, the use of nonverbal communication in negotiation, and the selection of a communication channel for sending and receiving messages.

Characteristics of Language

Gibbons, Bradac, and Busch (1992) have proposed that negotiation "represents the exchange of information through language that coordinates and manages meaning" (p. 156). In negotiation, language operates at two levels: the logical level (for proposals or offers) and the pragmatic level (semantics, syntax, and style). The meaning conveyed by a proposition or statement is a combination of one logical surface message and several pragmatic (i.e., hinted or inferred) messages. In other words, it is not only what is said and how it is said that matters but also what additional, veiled, or subsurface information is intended, conveyed, or perceived in reception. By way of illustration, consider threats. We often react not only to the substance of a threatening statement but also (and frequently more strongly) to its unspoken messages that might imply something about the likelihood that the threat will be carried out or about our relationship or our prospects for working together in the future. Box 6.2 illustrates how threats, which on the surface seem straightforward enough as negotiation gambits intended to compel the other party to make a concession, are actually complex and nuanced when analyzed a terms of the specific elements of language used within them.

Whether the intent is to command and compel, sell, persuade, or gain commitment, how parties communicate in negotiation would seem to depend on the ability of the speaker

Is a threat simply a statement about bad things that will happen to the others if they resist? Or is there more to it? Gibbons, Bradac, and Busch (1992) identify five linguistic dimensions of making threats.

1. The use of *polarized language,* in which negotiators use positive words when speaking of their own positions (e.g., generous, reasonable, or even-handed) and negative words when referring to the other party's position (e.g., tight-fisted, unreasonable, or heavy-handed).

2. The conveyance of *verbal immediacy* (a measure of intended immediacy, urgency, or relative psychological distance), either high and intended to engage or compel the other party ("OK, here is the deal" or "I take great care to . . . ") or low and intended to create a sense of distance or aloofness ("Well, there it is" or "One should take great care to . . . ").

3. The degree of *language intensity:* high intensity conveys strong feelings to the recipient (as with statements of affirmation or the frequent use of profanity) and low intensity conveys weak feelings.

4. The degree of *lexical diversity* (i.e., the command of a broad, rich vocabulary), where high levels of lexical diversity denote comfort and competence with language and low levels denote discomfort, anxiety, or inexperience.

5. The extent of a *high-power language style,* with low power denoted by the use of verbal hedges, hesitations, or politeness to the point of deference and subordination and high power denoted by verbal dominance, clarity and firmness of expression, and self-assurance.

According to Gibbons, Bradac, and Busch, threats can be made more credible and more compelling if they carry negatively polarized descriptions of the other party and his or her position, high immediacy, high intensity, high lexical diversity, and a distinctively high-power style.

Source: Adapted from P. Gibbons, J. J. Bradac, and J. D. Busch. "The Role of Language in Negotiations: Threats and Promises," in L. Putnam and M. Roloff (Eds.), *Communication and Negotiation* (Newbury Park, CA: Sage, 1992), pp. 156–75.

to encode thoughts properly, as well as on the ability of the listener to understand and decode the intended message(s). In addition, negotiators' use of idioms or colloquialisms is often problematic, especially in cross-cultural negotiations (see Chapter 16). The meaning conveyed might be clear to the speaker but confusing to the listener (e.g., "I'm willing to stay until the last dog is hung"—a statement of positive commitment on the part of some regional Americans, but confusing at best to those with different cultural backgrounds, even within the United States). Even if the meaning is clear, the choice of a word or metaphor may convey a lack of sensitivity or create a sense of exclusion, as is often done when men relate strategic business concerns by using sports metaphors ("Well, it's fourth down and goal to go; this is no time to drop the ball"). Intentional or not, the message received or inferred by women may be that they're excluded from the club. Deborah Tannen (1990), in her aptly named book *You Just Don't Understand,* states that "male–female miscommunication may be more dangerous [than cross-cultural miscommunication] because it is more pervasive in our lives, and we are less prepared for it" (p. 281). Because people generally aren't aware of the potential for such miscommunication with someone from their own culture, they are less well prepared to deal with such miscommunication than they would be if the person were from a different culture.

Finally, a negotiator's choice of words may not only signal a position but also shape and predict the conversation that ensues. Simons (1993) examined linguistic patterns of communication in negotiation; two of his findings are relevant here:

1. Parties whose statements communicated interests in both the substance of the negotiation (things) and the relationship with the other party achieved better, more integrative solutions than parties whose statements were concerned solely with either substance or relationship.

2. Linguistic patterns early in the negotiation help define issues in ways that may help the parties discover integrative possibilities later on.

Earlier in this chapter we mentioned research showing that the conversations that take place early in the negotiation can affect outcomes, and Simons' work reinforces that point in linguistic terms: "Linguistic patterns from the first half of negotiation were better predictors of agreements than linguistic patterns from the second half of negotiation" (p. 139).

Use of Nonverbal Communication

Much of what people communicate to one another is transmitted with nonverbal communication. Examples include facial expressions, body language, head movements, and tone of voice, to name just a few. Some nonverbal acts, called *attending behaviors,* are particularly important in connecting with another person during a coordinated interaction like negotiation; they let the other know that you are listening and prepare the other party to receive your message. We discuss three important attending behaviors: eye contact, body position, and encouraging.

Make Eye Contact   Dishonest people and cowards are not supposed to be able to look people in the eye. Poets claim that the eye is the lens that permits us to look into a person's soul. These and other bits of conventional wisdom illustrate how important people believe eye contact to be. In general, making eye contact is one way to show others you are paying attention and listening and that you consider them important. If people do not look at you when you are speaking, you may question whether they are listening. Of course, it is possible to listen very well even when not looking at the other person; in fact, it may be easier to look away because you can focus on the spoken words and not be confused by visual information. But the point is that by not making eye contact, you are not providing the other person with an important cue that you are engaged and listening.

In making eye contact, however, people should not keep their eyes continually fixed on the other person. Otherwise they might be accused of staring, which usually leads to suspicion rather than trust. Instead, the eyes should momentarily leave the other person. Generally, breaks in eye contact are fewer and shorter when listening actively than when speaking. When speaking, one may occasionally look away, especially when searching for a word or phrase or trying to remember a detail. Averting the gaze briefly while speaking signals to the other party that the speaker is not finished.

When persuading someone, it is important to make eye contact when delivering the most important part of the message (Beebe, 1980; Burgoon, Coker, and Coker, 1986; Kleinke, 1986). Having the verbal and nonverbal systems in parallel at this point emphasizes the importance of the message that is being sent. Also, one should maintain eye contact not only when speaking but when receiving communication as well (Kellerman, Lewis, and Laird, 1989).

It is important to recognize, however, that the patterns described here are characteristic of Western society. In other parts of the world, different patterns prevail. In some Asian societies, for example, keeping one's eyes down while the other is speaking is a sign of respect (Ivey and Simek-Downing, 1980).

Adjust Body Position   Parents frequently advise their children about how to stand and sit, particularly when they are in formal settings such as school, church, or dinner parties. The command "Sit up!" is often accompanied by "And pay attention!" Here the parent is teaching the child another widely held belief—one's body position indicates whether or not one is paying attention to the other party. To ensure that others know you are attentive to them, hold your body erect, lean slightly forward, and face the other person directly (Ivey and Simek-Downing, 1980). If you accept and endorse the others' message, care needs to be taken not to show disrespect with body position by slouching, turning away, or placing feet on the table (Stacks and Burgoon, 1981). In contrast, crossing arms, bowing the head, furrowing the brow, and squeezing eyebrows together all can signal strong rejection or disapproval of the message (Nierenberg and Calero, 1971).

Nonverbally Encourage or Discourage What the Other Says   One can indicate attention and interest in what another is saying through a variety of simple behaviors. A head nod, a simple hand gesture to go on, or a murmured "unh hunh" to indicate understanding all tell the other person to continue, that you are listening. In fact, you can encourage someone to continue to speak about many subjects by simply nodding your head as he or she is speaking. Brief eye contact or a smile and a nod of the head will both provide encouraging cues. Similarly, a frown, a scowl, a shake of the head, or a grab of one's chest in mock pain will signal disapproval of the other's message.

Nonverbal communication—done well—may help negotiators achieve better outcomes through mutual coordination. Drolet and Morris (2000) compared the development of rapport between negotiators who did or did not have visual access to each other while negotiating. They defined rapport as "a state of mutual positivity and interest that arises through the convergence of nonverbal expressive behavior in an interaction" (p. 27). Findings indicated that face-to-face interaction stimulated rapport through nonverbal communication, which in turn enhanced coordination and led to higher joint gains. Of course, these benefits will presumably arise only to the extent that parties are able to interpret nonverbal communication accurately. This is easier said than done: the ability to judge nonverbal behavior varies with social context and gender, among other factors (Puccinelli, Tickle-Degnan, and Rosenthal, 2003).

Selection of a Communication Channel

Communication is experienced differently when it occurs through different channels. We may think of negotiation as typically occurring face to face—an assumption reinforced by the common metaphor of the "negotiation table." But the reality is that people negotiate through a variety of communication media: over the telephone, in writing, and increasingly through electronic channels such as e-mail, teleconferencing, instant messaging, and even text messaging. The use of network-mediated information technologies in negotiation is sometimes referred to as *virtual negotiation* (also at times "e-negotiation"). The use of a particular channel shapes both perceptions of the communication task at hand and norms regarding appropriate behavior; accordingly, channel variations have potentially important effects on negotiation processes and outcomes (Bazerman, Curhan, Moore, and Valley, 2000; Lewicki and Dineen, 2002).

For our purposes here, the key variation that distinguishes one communication channel from another is *social bandwidth* (Barry and Fulmer, 2004)—the ability of a channel to carry and convey subtle social and relational cues from sender to receiver that go beyond the literal text of the message itself (see also Short, Williams, and Christie, 1976, who used the term "social presence"). Greater social bandwidth means that a channel can convey more cues having social, relational, or symbolic content. For example, as an alternative to face-to-face interaction, the telephone preserves one's ability to transmit social cues through inflection or tone of voice but forfeits the ability to communicate through facial expressions or physical gestures. In written communication, there are only the words and symbols on paper, although one's choice of words and the way they are arranged can certainly convey tone, (in)formality, and emotion.

E-mail, as a ubiquitous mode of personal and organizational communication, can be viewed as simply another form of written communication that happens to involve electronic transmission. There are, however, important distinctions between e-mail and other forms of written communication. Many people, treating e-mail as a highly informal medium, are comfortable sending messages that are stylistically or grammatically unpolished in situations (such as on the job) where they would never send a carelessly written communication on paper. Some people incorporate text-based *emoticons* to convey emotional social cues in their messages (the notorious smiley face [:-)] is the best known emoticon). Early research on interpersonal and small-group communication through computers indicated that the lack of social cues lowers communicator inhibition and leads to more aggressive communication behavior that is unrestrained by social norms, such as *flaming*—a term that refers generally to hostile or insulting communication (Sproull and Kiesler, 1986). However, much of that early research into computer-mediated communication focused on anonymous interaction. It is not clear that reduced social cues have the same effect in a communication context, such as negotiation, where the parties are known to each other, and in fact may know each other quite well (Barry and Fulmer, 2004).

Treating e-mail as just another vehicle for written communication is analytically simplistic because e-mail interactions frequently substitute for communication that would otherwise occur via telephone, face to face, or perhaps not at all. Accordingly, it is not enough to ask how e-mail communication differs from conventional writing; we also need to understand how interaction (such as negotiation) is affected when people choose to use e-mail rather than communicate through channels with higher social bandwidth.

Researchers have been examining the effects of channels in general, and e-mail in particular, on negotiation processes and outcomes during much of the past decade. Unfortunately, there are few consistent findings that point to clear effects. We do know that interacting parties can more easily develop personal rapport in face-to-face communication compared with other channels (Drolet and Morris, 2000) and that face-to-face negotiators are more inclined to disclose information truthfully, increasing their ability to attain mutual gain (Valley, Moag, and Bazerman, 1998). Research has found that negotiation through written channels is more likely to end in impasse than negotiation that occurs face to face or by phone (Valley et al., 1998), although an attempt to extend this to written e-mail did not yield a clear finding (Croson, 1999).

There is also evidence that e-mail negotiators reach agreements that are more equal (a balanced division of resources) than face-to-face negotiators (Croson, 1999). According to Croson, this may occur because electronic communication "'levels the playing field' between stronger and weaker negotiators" (p. 33). By giving the individual a chance to ponder at length the other party's message, and to review and revise one's own communication, e-mail may indeed help less interpersonally skilled parties improve their performance, especially when the alternative is negotiating spontaneously (face to face or by phone) with a more accomplished other party. Analyzing the actions of pairs who negotiated over the Internet, van Es, French, and Stellmaszek (2004) found that online negotiators frequently reread and reviewed previous statements and assumptions. But if this reviewability is an asset, van Es and colleagues point to a couple of drawbacks to negotiating in this kind of written format. First, negotiating in writing online gives parties an excuse to be less prepared, given time lags between conversational turns during which one can reflect on prior statements and contemplate future strategies. Second, negotiating in writing, as one does in e-mail, is inevitably challenging for people who don't like writing or don't write very well. van Es et al. put it this way: "Most people would rather talk than pursue the more arduous task of typing comments. . . . The typing task may motivate negotiators to move too rapidly toward closure" (p. 169). Indeed, many people can express themselves with nuance and subtlety quite well in spoken conversation, but are not accomplished at doing so in writing.

Moore, Kurtzberg, Thompson, and Morris (1999) explored reasons e-mail negotiations sometimes end in impasse. In their experiment, students negotiated over e-mail with other students who were either at the same university (an "in-group" pairing) or at another university ("out-group" pairing). Also, some of the negotiators disclosed personal information about themselves with the other party; others did not. They found that impasse was more likely in e-mail negotiations when people negotiated with out-group parties and when there was no mutual self-disclosure of personal information. Other research shows, perhaps not surprisingly, that reaching agreements with e-mail becomes more difficult as the number of parties involved increases. Kurtzberg, Dunn-Jensen, and Matsibekker (2005) found very high impasse rates in a four-party negotiation simulation via e-mail, with many participants expressing high levels of dissatisfaction afterward.

A growing body of evidence points to the conclusion that negotiators using e-mail need to work harder at building personal rapport with the other party if they are to overcome limitations of the channel that would otherwise inhibit optimal agreements or fuel impasse. What e-mail negotiations lack is *schmoozing*—off-task or relationship-focused conversations that are often present in face-to-face negotiations (Morris, Nadler, Kurtzberg, and Thompson, 2000). Schmoozing is an important avenue for building rapport and establishing trust in the negotiation relationship. In fact, negotiators who schmoozed on the phone prior to e-mail negotiations resulted in more negotiated agreements, better outcomes, increased cooperation, and greater trust and optimism regarding future working relationships with the other party (Morris et al., 2000). In one recent study, researchers tried to overcome the problem of rapport by telling e-mail negotiators about difficulties of using e-mail for negotiation and instructing them to ask questions of their opponent in an effort to create a personal connection (Sheehy and Palanovics, 2006). It worked—there were more agreements following these instructions, and agreements were more integrative, suggesting that some of the pitfalls of e-mail as a channel for negotiation can be overcome if negotiators attend to and adjust to those pitfalls.

With so much attention to e-mail, it is important to keep in mind that other online mechanisms exist for virtual negotiations. One of the few studies to contrast different online channels is an experiment by Loewenstein, Morris, Chakravarti, Thompson, and Kopelman (2005) comparing negotiations over e-mail with those conducted and via instant messaging (IM). Loewenstein et al. argue that the important difference between these two channels is speed of turn-taking: e-mail is a "slow-tempo" medium, while IM is "fast-tempo" medium that more closely approximates oral communication. The study examined how these two channels compare when negotiators have at their disposal complex versus simple arguments. In a simulated buyer–seller negotiation, some sellers were provided with intricate arguments to use in support of their position; others were provided with simple arguments. The researchers predicted and found that sellers did better with complex arguments in the "quick" medium (IM) but not in the "slow" medium (e-mail). This occurred, their results suggest, because sellers armed with intricate arguments were more able to dominate the conversation in the rapid turn-taking environment of IM, and in so doing extract concessions from the other party.

In summary, negotiations via e-mail and other network-mediated technologies create opportunities but also pose crucial challenges that negotiators would do well to understand before selecting a particular medium for an important occasion. In Chapter 5 we discussed various cognitive biases that interfere with rational decision making by negotiators. Analogously, we can think of some of the challenges posed by virtual negotiation as "biases" that put the smoothness, civility, and effectiveness of a negotiation exchange at risk. Thompson and Nadler (2002) identified four specific biases that can hinder success in online negotiations:

1. *Temporal synchrony bias* is the tendency for negotiators to behave as if they are in a synchronous situation when they are not. Face-to-face interactions often involve a "volley" of offers, in which both sides converge in the length of time spent talking as well as the rate of exchange. However, during e-mail negotiations the parties aren't necessarily working on the same time frame and the lack of synchrony can be annoying to one or both parties, therefore negatively affecting both the negotiation relationship and outcomes.

2. *Burned bridge bias* is the tendency for individuals to employ risky behavior during e-mail negotiations that they would not use during a face-to-face encounter. The impoverished social environment of e-mail creates social distance and an illusion of anonymity that can facilitate behavior that would be unacceptable in a face-to-face encounter. For example, negotiators may be more willing to challenge the other party, set ultimatums, or react negatively to an offer when not interacting face to face. Friedman and Currall (2003) argue that e-mail's inherent structural features make it more likely that disputes will escalate compared with face-to-face or telephone interaction.

3.   *Squeaky wheel bias* is the tendency for e-mail negotiators to use a negative emotional style to achieve their goals. If social norms fostering civility are absent or less apparent, then negotiators may become more likely to resort to intimidation, rude behavior, and poor etiquette to achieve outcomes. On the other hand, when e-mail negotiators are part of a cohesive social group, constructive social norms are reinforced, which may moderate any tendency toward incivility. There is also some evidence that emotions that do surface are more muted in e-mail negotiation relative to face-to-face settings (van Es et al., 2004), presumably because the expression of emotion is occurring in writing rather than through the spoken word.

4.   *Sinister attribution bias* occurs when one mistakenly assumes that another's behavior is caused by personality flaws, while overlooking the role of situational factors. This bias is an exaggerated case of the fundamental attribution error, discussed in Chapter 5, "wherein attributions of the other person's behavior are not only dispositional, but also diabolical" (Thompson and Nadler, 2002, p. 119). Thompson and Nadler contend that a lack of trust, dissimilarity between parties, and shortage of rapport that may exist via e-mail lead individuals to project sinister and deceitful motives onto the other party. Sinister attributions, in turn, lead to poorer outcomes (Moore et al., 1999).

Creating a positive rapport with a negotiation partner, either face to face or over the phone, can help to combat these biases. Unfortunately, it may not be possible to extend the negotiation relationship beyond online interactions. In such cases it is important to find ways to create a context of accountability for your actions. Examples include involving a neutral third party in the e-mail exchange or taking the time to schmooze via e-mail to develop a sense of trust and camaraderie prior to negotiating. See Box 6.3 for a list of additional ways to maximize effectiveness when negotiations occur in virtual environments.

How to Improve Communication in Negotiation

Given the many ways that communication can be disrupted and distorted, we can only marvel at the extent to which negotiators can actually understand each other. As we have discussed at length in Chapter 5 and here, failures and distortions in perception, cognition, and communication are the paramount contributors to breakdowns and failures in negotiation. Research cannot confirm this assertion directly because the processes of perception, cognition, and communication are so intertwined with other major factors, including commitment to one's own position and objectives, the nature of the negotiating process, the use of power and power tactics, and the negotiators' personalities. Nevertheless, research has consistently demonstrated that even those parties whose goals are compatible or integrative may fail to reach agreement or reach suboptimal agreements because of the misperceptions of the other party or because of breakdowns in the communication process.

Three main techniques are available for improving communication in negotiation: the use of questions, listening, and role reversal. Each of these is discussed in more detail next.

BOX 6.3   **Top 10 Rules for Virtual Negotiation**

1. Take steps to create a face-to-face relationship before negotiation, or early on, so that there is a face or voice behind the e-mail.

2. Be explicit about the normative process to be followed during the negotiation.

3. If others are present in a virtual negotiation (on either your side or theirs) make sure everyone knows who is there and why.

4. Pick the channel (face to face, videoconference, voice, e-mail, etc.) that is most effective at getting all the information and detail on the table so that it can be fully considered by both sides.

5. Avoid "flaming"; when you must express emotion, label the emotion explicitly so the other knows what it is and what's behind it.

6. Formal turn-taking is not strictly necessary, but try to synchronize offers and counteroffers. Speak up if it is not clear "whose turn it is."

7. Check out assumptions you are making about the other's interests, offers, proposals, or conduct. Less face-to-face contact means less information about the other party and a greater chance that inferences will get you in trouble, so ask questions.

8. In many virtual negotiations (e.g., e-mail) everything is communicated in writing, so be careful not to make unwise commitments that can be used against you. Neither should you take undue advantage of the other party in this way; discuss and clarify until all agree.

9. It may be easier to use unethical tactics in virtual negotiation because facts are harder to verify. But resist the temptation: the consequences are just as severe, and perhaps more so, given the incriminating evidence available when virtual negotiations are automatically archived.

10. Not all styles work equally well in all settings. Work to develop a personal negotiation style (collaboration, competition, etc.) that is a good fit with the communication channel you are using. One of the most difficult aspects of negotiation is the actual give-and-take that occurs at the table. Should I stick with this point, or is it time to fold? Should I open the bidding or wait for the other side to take the lead? It requires good judgment to make these choices.

Source: Adapted from R. J. Lewicki and B. R. Dineen, "Negotiating in Virtual Organizations," in R. Heneman and D. Greenberger (Eds.)., *Human Resource Management in the Virtual Organization* (New York: John Wiley and Sons, 2003).

The Use of Questions

One of the most common techniques for clarifying communication and eliminating noise and distortion is the use of questions. Nierenberg (1976) emphasized that questions are essential elements in negotiations for securing information; asking good questions enables negotiators to secure a great deal of information about the other party's position, supporting arguments, and needs.

Nierenberg proposed that questions could be divided into two basic categories: those that are manageable and those that are unmanageable and cause difficulty (see Table 6.1). Manageable questions cause attention or prepare the other person's thinking for further questions ("May I ask you a question?"), get information ("How much will this cost?"), and generate thoughts ("Do you have any suggestions for improving this?"). Unmanageable questions cause difficulty, give information ("Didn't you know that we couldn't afford this?"), and bring the discussion to a false conclusion ("Don't you think we've talked about

TABLE 6.1 | Questions in Negotiation

Manageable Questions	Examples
Open-ended questions—ones that cannot be answered with a simple yes or no. *Who, what, when, where,* and *why* questions.	"Why do you take that position in these deliberations?"
Open questions—invite the other's thinking.	"What do you think of our proposal?"
Leading questions—point toward an answer.	"Don't you think our proposal is a fair and reasonable offer?"
Cool questions—low emotionality.	"What is the additional rate that we will have to pay if you make the improvements on the property?"
Planned questions—part of an overall logical sequence of questions developed in advance.	"After you make the improvements to the property, when can we expect to take occupancy?"
Treat questions—flatter the opponent at the same time as you ask for information.	"Can you provide us with some of your excellent insight on this problem?"
Window questions—aid in looking into the other person's mind.	"Can you tell us how you came to that conclusion?"
Directive questions—focus on a specific point.	"How much is the rental rate per square foot with these improvements?"
Gauging questions—ascertain how the other person feels.	"How do you feel about our proposal?"

Unmanageable Questions	Examples
Close-out questions—force the other party into seeing things your way.	"You wouldn't try to take advantage of us here, would you?"
Loaded questions—put the other party on the spot regardless of the answer.	"Do you mean to tell me that these are the only terms that you will accept?"
Heated questions—high emotionality, trigger emotional responses.	"Don't you think we've spent enough time discussing this ridiculous proposal of yours?"
Impulse questions—occur "on the spur of the moment," without planning, and tend to get conversation off the track.	"As long as we're discussing this, what do you think we ought to tell other groups who have made similar demands on us?"
Trick questions—appear to require a frank answer, but really are "loaded" in their meaning.	"What are you going to do—give in to our demands, or take this to arbitration?"
Reflective trick questions—reflects the other into agreeing with your point of view.	"Here's how I see the situation—don't you agree?"

Source: From Gerard Nierenberg, *Fundamentals of Negotiating* (New York: Hawthorn Books, 1973), pp. 125–26. Used with permission of the author.

this enough?"). As you can see in Table 6.1, most of the unmanageable questions are likely to produce defensiveness and anger in the other party. Although these questions may yield information, they are likely to make the other party feel uncomfortable and less willing to provide information in the future.

Negotiators can also use questions to manage difficult or stalled negotiations (we discuss difficult situations in depth in Chapters 17 and 18.). Aside from their typical uses for collecting and diagnosing information or assisting the other party in addressing and expressing needs and interests, questions can also be used tactically to pry or lever a negotiation out of a breakdown or an apparent dead end. Deep and Sussman (1993) identify a number of such situations and suggest specific questions for dealing with them (see Table 6.2). The value of such questions seems to be in their power to assist or force the other party to confront the effects or consequences of his or her behavior, intended and anticipated or not. In addition, Ury (1991) suggests that using "why not" questions instead of "why" questions is a good way to unblock negotiations. The other party may be more prepared to discuss what's wrong with a proposal than what's right; using "why not" questions and careful listening skills can thus help negotiators identify the other party's preferences.

Listening

"Active listening" and "reflecting" are terms commonly used in the helping professions such as counseling and therapy (Rogers, 1957, 1961). Counselors recognize that communications are frequently loaded with multiple meanings and that the counselor must try to identify these different meanings without making the communicator angry or defensive. In the decades since Carl Rogers advocated this key communication dynamic, interest in listening skills, and active listening in particular, has continued to grow, both in general communication contexts and in the specific domain of business and organizational settings.[3] There are three major forms of listening:

1. **Passive listening** involves receiving the message while providing no feedback to the sender about the accuracy or completeness of reception. Sometimes passive listening is itself enough to keep a communicator sending information. Some people like to talk and are uncomfortable with long silences. A negotiator whose counterpart is talkative may find that the best strategy is to sit and listen while the other party eventually works into, or out of, a position on his or her own.

2. **Acknowledgment** is the second form of listening, slightly more active than passive listening. When acknowledging, receivers occasionally nod their heads, maintain eye contact, or interject responses like "I see," "mm-hmm," "interesting," "really," "sure," "go on," and the like. These responses are sufficient to keep communicators sending messages, but a sender may misinterpret them as the receiver's agreement with his or her position, rather than as simple acknowledgments of receipt of the message.

3. **Active listening** is the third form. When receivers are actively listening, they restate or paraphrase the sender's message in their own language. Gordon (1977) provides the following examples of active listening:

SENDER: I don't know how I am going to untangle this messy problem.

RECEIVER: You're really stumped on how to solve this one.

TABLE 6.2 | Questions for Tough Situations

The Situation	Possible Questions
"Take it or leave it" ultimatums	"If we can come up with a more attractive alternative than that, would you still want me to 'take or leave' your offer?" "Do I have to decide now, or do I have some time to think about it?" "Are you feeling pressure to bring the negotiation to a close?"
Pressure to respond to an unreasonable deadline	"Why can't we negotiate about this deadline?" "If you're under pressure to meet this deadline, what can I do to help remove some of that pressure?" "What's magical about this afternoon? What about first thing in the morning?"
Highball or lowball tactics	"What's your reasoning behind this position?" "What would *you* think I see as a fair offer?" "What standards do you think the final resolution should meet?"
An impasse	"What else can either of us do to close the gap between our positions?" "Specifically what concession do you need from me to bring this to a close right now?" "If it were already six weeks from now and we were looking back at this negotiation, what might we wish we had brought to the table?"
Indecision between accepting and rejecting a proposal	"What's your best alternative to accepting my offer right now?" "If you reject this offer, what will take its place that's better than what you know you'll receive from me?" "How can you be sure that you will get a better deal elsewhere?"
A question about whether the offer you just made is the same as that offered to others	"What do you see as a fair offer, and given that, what do you think of my current offer to you?" "Do you believe that I think it's in my best interest to be unfair to you?" "Do you believe that people can be treated differently, but still all be treated fairly?"
Attempts to pressure, control, or manipulate	"Shouldn't we both walk away from this negotiation feeling satisfied?" "How would you feel if our roles were reversed, and you were feeling the pressure I'm feeling right now?" "Are you experiencing outside pressures to conclude these negotiations?"

Source: Adapted from Sam Deep and Lyle Sussman, *What to Ask When You Don't Know What to Say* (1993). Used by permission of the publisher, Prentice Hall/A Division of Simon & Schuster, Englewood Cliffs, NJ.

SENDER: Please, don't ask me about that now.

RECEIVER: Sounds like you're awfully busy right now.

SENDER: I thought the meeting today accomplished nothing.

RECEIVER: You were very disappointed with our session.

Athos and Gabarro (1978) note that successful reflective responding is a critical part of active listening and has these elements: (1) a greater emphasis on listening than on speaking, (2) responding to personal rather than abstract points (i.e., feelings, beliefs, and positions rather than abstract ideas), (3) following the other rather than leading him or her into areas that the listener thinks should be explored (i.e., allowing the speaker to frame the conversation process), (4) clarifying what the speaker has said about his or her own thoughts and feelings rather than questioning or suggesting what he or she should be thinking or feeling, and (5) responding to the feelings the other has expressed.

Active listening has generally been recommended for counseling communications, such as employee counseling and performance improvement. In negotiation, it may appear initially that active listening is unsuitable because, unlike a counselor, the receiver normally has a set position and may feel strongly about the issues. By recommending active listening we are not suggesting that receivers should automatically agree with the other party's position and abandon their own. Rather, we regard active listening as a skill that encourages others to speak more fully about their feelings, priorities, frames of reference, and, by extension, the positions they are taking. When the other party does so, negotiators will better understand the other's positions; the factors and information that support it; and the ways the position can be compromised, reconciled, or negotiated in accordance with their own preferences and priorities.

Role Reversal

Communication may also be improved through role reversal. Rapoport (1964) suggests that continually arguing for one particular position in debate leads to a "blindness of involvement," or a self-reinforcing cycle of argumentation that prohibits negotiators from recognizing the possible compatibility between their own position and that of the other party. While discussing active listening, we suggested that one objective was to gain an understanding of the other party's perspective or frame of reference. Active listening is, however, still a somewhat passive process. Role-reversal techniques allow negotiators to understand more completely the other party's positions by actively arguing these positions until the other party is convinced that he or she is understood. For example, someone can ask you how you would respond to the situation that he or she is in. In doing so, you can come to understand that person's position, perhaps accept its validity, and discover how to modify both of your positions to make them more compatible. Studies examining the impact and success of the role-reversal technique (e.g., Johnson, 1971; Walcott, Hopmann, and King, 1977) suggest the following conclusions:

1. Role reversal is effective in producing cognitive changes (greater understanding of the other party's position) and attitude changes (perceived similarities between the two positions).

2. When the parties' positions are fundamentally compatible with each other, role reversal is likely to produce acceptable results (cognitive and attitudinal change); when the parties' positions are fundamentally incompatible, role reversal may sharpen the perceptions of incompatibility and inhibit positive attitude change.

3. Although role reversal may induce greater understanding of the other party's position and highlight possible areas of similarity, it is not necessarily effective overall as a means of inducing agreement between parties.

In sum, role reversal may be a useful tool for improving communication and the accurate understanding and appreciation of the other party's position in negotiation. This may be most useful during the preparation stage of negotiation or during a team caucus when things are not going well. However, increasing understanding does not necessarily lead to easy resolution of the conflict, particularly when accurate communication reveals a fundamental incompatibility in the positions of the two sides.

Special Communication Considerations at the Close of Negotiations

As negotiations move toward a close with agreement in sight, negotiators must attend to two key aspects of communication and negotiation simultaneously: the avoidance of fatal mistakes and the achievement of satisfactory closure in a constructive manner.

Avoiding Fatal Mistakes

Gary Karrass (1985), focusing on sales negotiations in particular, has specific advice about communication near the end of a negotiation. Karrass enjoins negotiators to "know when to shut up," to avoid surrendering important information needlessly, and to refrain from making "dumb remarks" that push a wavering counterpart away from the agreement he or she is almost ready to endorse. The other side of this is to recognize the other party's faux pas and dumb remarks for what they are and refuse to respond to or be distracted by them. Karrass also reminds negotiators of the need to watch out for last-minute problems, such as nit-picking or second-guessing by parties who didn't participate in the bargaining process but who have the right or responsibility to review it. Karrass advises negotiators to expect such challenges and to be prepared to manage them with aplomb. Finally, Karrass notes the importance of reducing the agreement to written form, recognizing that the party who writes the contract is in a position to achieve clarity of purpose and conduct for the deal.

Achieving Closure

Achieving closure in negotiation generally involves making decisions to accept offers, to compromise priorities, to trade off across issues with the other party, or to take some combination of these steps. Such decision-making processes can be divided into four key elements: framing, gathering intelligence, coming to conclusions, and learning from feedback (Russo and Schoemaker, 1989). The first three of these elements we have discussed elsewhere; the fourth element, that of learning (or failing to learn) from feedback, is largely a communication issue, which involves "keeping track of what you expected would happen, systematically guarding against self-serving expectations, and making sure you review the lessons your feedback has provided the next time a similar decision comes along" (Russo and Schoemaker, p. 3). In Chapter 5, we discussed the decision traps that may result from perceptual and cognitive biases that negotiators will inevitably encounter. Although some of these traps may occur in earlier stages of the negotiation, we suspect that several of them are likely to arise at the end of a negotiation, when parties are in a hurry to wrap up loose ends and cement a deal.

Chapter Summary

In this chapter we have considered elements of the art and science of communication that are relevant to understanding negotiations. We began with model of two-party interaction that shows communication as a transactional process that cycles between the parties and is prone to error and distortion at various points. Such distortions are more likely to occur when communicating parties have conflicting goals and objectives or strong feelings of dislike for one another. Distortion may occur as information is encoded, transmitted, decoded, and interpreted. During all stages of the communication cycle between two parties, problems of "noise" or interference potentially affect the accuracy and clarity with which messages and responses are sent and received.

We then moved to a discussion of *what* is communicated during negotiation. Rather than simply being an exchange of preferences about solutions, negotiation covers a wide-ranging number of topics in an environment where each party is trying to influence the other. This was followed by an exploration of three issues related to *how* people communicate in negotiation: the characteristics of language, nonverbal communication, and the selection of a communication channel. We discussed at some length how the decision to negotiate in online environments (e.g., e-mail) alters negotiator behavior and outcomes.

In the closing sections of the chapter we considered ways to improve communication in negotiation, including improvement of listening skills and the use of questions, and special communication considerations at the close of negotiation, where we discussed avoiding last-minute mistakes and achieving closure.

Endnotes

[1] Clearly, communication can occur among more than two people, but the same general processes are expected to apply as to the two-person case, albeit with more complexity. For the sake of clarity, we will restrict our discussion to the two-person case in this chapter. The complexity of negotiations involving more than two parties is examined in detail in Chapter 13.

[2] See Roth and Malouf (1979); Schelling (1960); and Siegel and Fouraker (1960).

[3] For discussions of listening in general contexts, see Bostrom (1990); Wolff, Marsnik, Tacey, and Nichols (1983); and Wolvin and Coakley, (1988). For applications to business and organizational settings see Bone (1988); Lewis and Reinsch (1988); Rogers and Roethlisberger (1991); and Wolvin and Coakley (1991).

CHAPTER 7

Finding and Using Negotiation Power

Objectives

1. Understand different approaches to understanding power in negotiations and why power is critical to negotiation.
2. Explore different sources or bases of power in negotiation.
3. Consider different strategic approaches for negotiators who have more power and for dealing with others who have more power.

In this chapter, we focus on power in negotiation. By *power,* we mean the capabilities negotiators can assemble to give themselves an advantage or increase the probability of achieving their objectives. All negotiators want power; they want to know what they can do to put pressure on the other party, persuade the other to see it their way, get the other to give them what they want, get one up on the other, or change the other's mind. Note that, according to this definition, we have already talked about many power tactics in Chapters 3 and 4. The tactics of distributive bargaining and integrative negotiation are *leverage tactics*—tactics used to exert influence over the other party in the service of achieving the best deal for one or both parties.

In the next two chapters, we separate the concept of power from the use of influence. It is important to be clear about the distinction between the two. We treat power as the *potential* to alter the attitudes and behaviors of others that an individual brings to a given situation. Influence, on the other hand, can be thought of as *power in action*—the actual messages and tactics an individual undertakes in order to change the attitudes and/or behaviors of others. To put it concisely, power is potential influence, while influence is kinetic power (power in use) (French and Raven, 1959). We address power in this chapter and the use of influence in Chapter 8.

We begin by defining the nature of power and discussing some of the dynamics of its use in negotiation. We focus on the power sources that give negotiators capacity to exert influence. Of the many sources of power that exist (see French and Raven, 1959; Pfeffer, 1992), we consider three major ones in this chapter: information and expertise, control over resources, and one's position in an organization or network.

Why Is Power Important to Negotiators?

Most negotiators believe that power is important in negotiation because it gives one negotiator an *advantage* over the other party. Negotiators who have this advantage usually want to use it to secure a greater share of the outcomes or achieve their preferred solution. Seeking power in negotiation usually arises from one of two perceptions:

1. The negotiator believes he or she currently has *less power* than the other party. In this situation, a negotiator believes the other party already has some advantage that can and will be used, so he or she *seeks power to offset or counterbalance the other's advantage.*

2. The negotiator believes he or she needs *more power* than the other party to increase the probability of securing a desired outcome. In this context, the negotiator believes that added power is necessary to *gain or sustain one's own advantage in the upcoming negotiation.*

   Embedded in these two beliefs are significant questions of tactics and motives. The tactics may be designed to enhance the negotiator's own power or to diminish the other's power, and to create a state of either power equalization (both parties have relatively equal or countervailing power) or power difference (one's power is greater than the other's). The motive questions relate to why the negotiator is using the tactics. Most commonly, negotiators employ tactics designed to create power equalization as a way to level the playing field. The goal is to minimize either side's ability to dominate the relationship. This lays the groundwork for moving discussions toward a compromising or collaborative, integrative agreement. In contrast, negotiators also employ tactics designed to create power difference as a way to gain advantage or to block the other party's power moves. Such tactics enhance the capacity for one side to dominate the relationship, paving the way for a competing or dominating strategy and a distributive agreement. Box 7.1 presents a framework on the merits of using power as a negotiating tactic (compared with the focus on interests or an emphasis on "rights" in a dispute).

   In general, negotiators who don't care about their power or who have matched power—equally high or low—find that their deliberations proceed with greater ease and simplicity toward a mutually satisfying and acceptable outcome. In contrast, negotiators who do care about their power and seek to match or exceed the other's power are probably seeking a solution in which they either do not lose the negotiation (a defensive posture) or dominate the negotiation (an offensive posture).

   Power is implicated in the use of many of the competitive and collaborative negotiation tactics described earlier, such as hinting to the other party that you have good alternatives (a strong BATNA) in order to increase your leverage. Relatively few research studies have focused specifically on power and influence tactics in negotiation, and we integrate those that have into our discussion. However, much of the work on power discussed in this chapter is also drawn from broader studies of how managers influence one another in organizations, and we apply those findings to negotiation situations as appropriate.

A Definition of Power

In a broad sense, people have power when they have "the ability to bring about outcomes they desire" or "the ability to get things done the way [they want] them to be done"

One way of thinking about the role of power in negotiation is in relation to other, alternative strategic options. In Chapter 5 we introduced a framework developed by Ury, Brett, and Goldberg (1993) that compares three different strategic approaches to negotiation: interests, rights, and power.

- Negotiators focus on interests when they strive to learn about each other's interests and priorities as a way to work toward a mutually satisfying agreement that creates value.

- Negotiators focus on rights when they seek to resolve a dispute by drawing upon decision rules or standards grounded in principles of law, community standards of fairness, or perhaps an existing contract.

- Negotiators focus on power when they use threats or other means to try to coerce the other party into making concessions.

This framework assumes that all three approaches can potentially exist in a single situation; negotiators make choices about where to place their focus. But do negotiators really use all three? Should they? These questions were addressed in a study by Anne Lytle, Jeanne Brett, and Debra Shapiro (1999). They analyzed audiotapes of negotiations in a simulated contract dispute between two companies seeking to clarify their interdependent business relationship. Of the 50 negotiators who participated (25 tape-recorded pairs), some were students and some were employed managers, but all had five or more years of business experience.

Lytle and her colleagues found that most negotiators cycled through all three strategies—interests, rights, and power—during the same encounter. They also found that negotiators tended to reciprocate these strategies. A coercive power strategy, for example, may be met with a power strategy in return, which can lead to a negative conflict spiral and a poor (or no) agreement. They developed some important implications for the use of power in negotiation:

- Starting a negotiation by conveying your own power to coerce the other party could bring a quick settlement if your threat is credible. If the other party calls your bluff, however, you are left to either carry out your threat or lose face, both of which may be undesirable.

- To avert a conflict spiral and move toward an interests-based exchange, avoid reciprocating messages involving rights or power. Shift the conversation by asking an interests-related question. It may take several attempts to redirect the interaction successfully.

- If you can't avoid reciprocating negative behaviors (which may be a natural response, but not necessarily effective), try a "combined statement" that mixes a threat with an interests-oriented refocusing question or statement (e.g., "yes, we could sue you as well, but that won't solve our problem, so why don't we try to reach an outcome that helps us both?").

- Power tactics (and rights tactics) may be most useful when the other party refuses to negotiate or when negotiations have broken down and need to be restarted. In these situations, not much is risked by making threats based on rights or power, but the threat itself may help the other party appreciate the severity of the situation.

- The success of power tactics (and rights tactics) depends to a great extent on how they are implemented. To be effective, threats must be specific and credible, targeting the other party's high-priority interests. Otherwise, the other party has little incentive to comply. Make sure that you leave an avenue for the other party to "turn off" the threat, save face, and reopen the negotiations around interests. After all, most negotiators who make threats really don't want to implement them. As Lytle and her associates observe, "once you carry through with your threat, you frequently lose your source of power" (p. 48).

Source: Adapted from A. L. Lytle, J. M. Brett, and D. L. Shapiro, "The Strategic Use of Interests, Rights, and Power to Resolve Disputes," *Negotiation Journal* 15, no. 1 (1999), pp. 31–51.

(Salancik and Pfeffer, 1977). Presumably, a party with power can induce another to do what the latter otherwise would not do (Dahl, 1957; Kotter, 1979).

But there is a problem here: the definition we have developed so far seems to focus on power as absolute and coercive, which is too restrictive for understanding how power is used in negotiation. In fact, there are really two perspectives on power: power used to dominate and control the other (more likely in a distributive bargaining context) and power used to work together with the other (more likely in an integrative negotiation context; Coleman, 2000b). From the powerholder's point of view, the first perspective fits the Dahl *power over* definition, implying that this power is fundamentally dominating and coercive in nature. From the other party's point of view, this use of power implies *powerlessness and dependence* on the receiving end. The dynamics of this power relationship can range from "benign and supportive (as in many mentoring relationships) to oppressive and abusive (as with a dictatorial parent)" (Coleman, 2000b, p. 111).

From the second perspective, the actor's view of power suggests *power with* (Follett, 1942), implying that the power holder jointly develops and shares power with the other. The receiver experiences this power as *empowered and independent,* and its dynamics reflect the benefits of empowerment, such as better employee participation, broad delegation of authority, and a greater capacity to act with autonomy and personal integrity. This view of power fits a view of power that contrasts with Dahl's definition:

> an actor . . . has power in a given situation (situational power) to the degree that he can satisfy the purposes (goals, desires, or wants) that he is attempting to fulfill in that situation. Power is a relational concept; it does not reside in the individual but rather in the relationship of the person to his environment. Thus, the power of an actor in a given situation is determined by the characteristics of the situation as well as by his own characteristics. (Deutsch, 1973, pp. 84–85)

Deutsch (1973) notes a tendency for others to view power as an attribute of the actor only. This tendency ignores those elements of power that are derived from the situation or context in which the actor operates. As Deutsch suggests, the statement "A is more powerful than B" should be viewed from three distinct yet often interrelated perspectives: environmental power, or "A is more usually able to favorably influence his overall environment and/or to overcome its resistance than is B"; relationship power, or "A is usually more able to influence B favorably and/or to overcome B's resistance than B is able to do with A"; and personal power, or "A is usually more able to satisfy his desires than is B" (p. 85).

Let us consider two examples of power that illustrate these views:

1.   During economic downswings, labor unions can find themselves negotiating new contracts that delay wage increases or even reduce wages, which means giving hard-won concessions back to management—hardly something union officials want to do. They have usually done so when company officials have argued that unless wages go down, the firm will lay off thousands of employees, close a plant, move operations to another country, drop a line of business, or take some similar action. The union officials can be seen as making a rational or calculated decision to do something they ordinarily would not do (Dahl's definition), but in this case management is simply taking advantage of the shift in power within the economic environment. As markets shift, demand for products changes, costs rise, or less expensive (nonunion) labor becomes available in other areas.

2.   In contemporary organizations, heads of projects, teams, and task forces find that they must effectively influence other people without having the formal authority (direct reporting relationships) to give direct orders. As a result, managers have to master the use of "influence without authority" (Cohen and Bradford, 1989) to get their jobs done and meet group goals. The targets of this influence may be employees, peers, other managers, or the boss. Subordinates who approach their superior with a list of grievances about the job and tasks that cannot be done without the boss's compliance will receive scant attention. However, those who are able to use influence to get their boss's assistance without creating major problems for the boss may earn the boss's respect and accomplish their goals as well. In these kinds of situations, strong relationship and personal power skills are critical. In short, managers must learn to use relationship and personal power when environmental power, derived from a position in a formal organizational chart, is not available.

Before moving forward, we want to draw attention to the weakness of any discussion of power. It would be nice to be able to write a chapter that comprehensively reviews the power sources available to negotiators, the major configurations of power bases assembled as influence strategies, and the conditions under which each should be used. Unfortunately, such a task is not just daunting but impossible, for two principal reasons. First, the effective use of power requires a sensitive and deft touch, and its consequences may vary greatly from one person to the next. In the hands of one user, the tools of power can craft a benevolent realm of prosperity and achievement, whereas in the hands of another, they may create a nightmare of tyranny and disorder.[1] Second, not only do the key actors and targets change from situation to situation, but the context in which the tools of power operate changes as well. As a result, the best we can do is to identify a few key sources of power. Exactly how and when to use these tools, or in what combination, will be expanded more fully in the next chapter (See Box 7.2 for a few relevant observations).[2]

Sources of Power—How People Acquire Power

Understanding the different ways in which power can be exercised is best accomplished by looking first at the various sources of power. In their seminal work on power, French and Raven (1959) identified five major types: expert power, reward power, coercive power, legitimate power, and referent power. Most of these are relatively self evident in nature:

- *Expert power:* derived from having unique, in-depth information about a subject.
- *Reward power:* derived by being able to reward others for doing what needs to be done.
- *Coercive power:* derived by being able to punish others for not doing what needs to be done.
- *Legitimate power:* derived from holding an office or formal title in some organization and using the powers that are associated with that office (e.g., a vice president or director).
- *Referent power:* derived from the respect or admiration one commands because of attributes like personality, integrity, interpersonal style, and the like. A is said to have referent power over B to the extent that B identifies with or wants to be closely associated with A.

BOX 7.2   Some Thoughts about Power

- Power is in the eye of the beholder. For power to be effective, it does not necessarily have to be fully and completely possessed; rather, the actor must convey the appearance that he or she has power and can use it at will. Power is therefore somewhat self-fulfilling. If you—and others—think you have it, you have it. If you—and others—don't think you have it, you don't have it. Perceived power is what creates leverage, and many powerholders go out of their way to create the image of power as the critical element of effective influence (see Sun Tsu, 1983, for an excellent exposition of this point).

- The effectiveness of power and influence is ultimately defined by the behavior of the target person. What matters most is which tools and strategies actually work on that person. Does that individual comply, do what you want, or behave the way you want him or her to behave? When designing an influence strategy, you must pay attention to what you think will work with a particular target while also being sensitive to suggestions for alternative strategies.

- There is some indication that power is, in fact, corrupting—in Lord Acton's words, "Power tends to corrupt; absolute power corrupts absolutely." This may occur for several reasons. First, as just suggested, power is based on perception—creating the perception, or even the illusion, that you have power and can use it. In creating such an illusion, it is not uncommon for actors to deceive themselves as much as they deceive the target. Second, power can be intoxicating. This point is frequently lost on the naive and unskilled. Those who gain a great deal of power through rapid career success frequently overuse and eventually abuse it. Power brings a large resource base, privileged information, and the ability to control the fate of many others. In the hands of the unskilled, power can be dramatically destructive (Lewis, 1990; Stewart, 1992).

Many contemporary discussions of power are still grounded in this typology (and Raven has elaborated the typology several times since it was proposed over 45 years ago). In this chapter, we take a broader perspective on power as it relates to negotiation and aggregate the major sources of power into five different groupings (see Table 7.1):

- Informational sources of power.
- Personal sources of power.
- Power based on position in an organization.
- Relationship-based sources of power.
- Contextual sources of power.

As we regularly note, these categories are not rigid or absolute. Power can be created in many different ways in many different contexts, and a source of leverage can shift from one category to another over time. As we elaborate on these approaches, we also indicate how the French and Raven model has been revised and updated.

Informational Sources of Power

Within the context of negotiation, information is perhaps the most common source of power. Information power is derived from the negotiator's ability to assemble and organize

TABLE 7.1 | Major Sources of Power

Source of Power	Description
Informational	• Information: the accumulation and presentation of data intended to change the other person's point of view or position on an issue. • Expertise: an acknowledged accumulation of information, or mastery of a body of information, on a particular problem or issue. Expertise power can be positive (we believe the other because of their acknowledged expertise) or negative (we so distrust the other that their claimed expertise leads us to pursue a course of action opposite to the one they advocate).
Personality and individual differences	Power derived from differences in • Psychological orientation (broad orientations to power use). • Cognitive orientation (ideologies about power). • Motivational orientation (specific motives to use power). • Dispositions and skills (orientations to cooperation/competition). • Moral orientation (philosophical orientations to power use).

Position-based power	Power derived from being located in a particular position in an organizational or communication structure; leads to several different kinds of leverage:
	• Legitimate power, or formal authority, derived from occupying a key position in a hierarchical organization. However, legitimate power can also influence social norms, such as
	    Reciprocity, or the expected exchange of favors.
	    Equity, or the expected return when one has gone out of one's way for the other.
	    Dependence, of the expected obligation one owes to others who cannot help themselves.
	• Resource control, or the accumulation of money, raw material, labor, time, and equipment that can be used as incentives to encourage compliance or as punishments for noncompliance. Resource control is manifested in
	    Reward power, the use of tangible rewards or personal approval to gain the other's compliance.
	    Punishment power, the use of tangible punishments or withholding of personal approval to gain the other's compliance.

Relationship-based power	• Goal interdependence—how the parties view their goals Referent power—based on an appeal to the other based on common experiences, group membership, status, etc. Referent power can also be positive (we believe the other because we respect them) or negative (we so disrespect the other that we pursue a course of action opposite to the one they advocate). • Access to or control over information, resources supply flows, or access, derived from location within flows in a network.
Contextual power	Power derived from the context in which negotiations take place. Common sources of contextual power include • Availability of BATNAs. • Organizational and national culture. • Availability of agents, constituencies, and audiences who can directly or indirectly affect the outcomes of the negotiation.

BOX 7.3 The Power of Information in a Car-Buying Negotiation

Before the age of the Internet, many consumers approached buying a car with the same enthusiasm as visiting the dentist. Customers knew their role was to scoff at the asking price, threaten to walk away from the vehicle, and generally engage in tough negotiation postures in order to get the best deal. Still, after they drove the car off the lot, nagging doubts remained about whether or not they paid too much for their new car.

Savvy customers have always known that they should determine their real requirements for an automobile, find several cars that meet their objectives, determine the book value of each car, contact current owners to determine their satisfaction, and keep from becoming emotionally attached to a particular automobile. These strategies certainly have helped people prepare for negotiations with their local dealer. However, customers still had to rely largely on guesswork to determine what price offers would be acceptable to the dealership.

Today, however, price information on new and used cars is readily available through the Internet and other sources. Customers can enter negotiations with car dealers armed with accurate facts and figures about the car's cost to the dealership, the actual price for various options, prices in neighboring states, and the customer and dealer incentives in place at a given time. Car buyers who take the time to gather information about "real" prices report saving hundreds or even thousands of dollars on automobiles. This wealth of information gives consumers more power in negotiations with dealers. Ultimately, that power leads to lower prices on new automobiles (Blumenstein, 1997; McGraw, 1997).

facts and data to support his or her position, arguments, or desired outcomes. Negotiators may also use information as a tool to challenge the other party's position or desired outcomes or to undermine the effectiveness of the other's negotiating arguments. Even in the simplest negotiation, the parties take a position and then present arguments and facts to support that position. I want to sell a used motorcycle for $1,500; you say it is worth only $1,000. I proceed to tell you how much I paid for it, point out what good condition it is in and what attractive features it has, and explain why it is worth $1,500. You point out that it is five years old; emphasize the nicks, dents, and rust spots; and comment that the tires are worn and need to be replaced. You also tell me that you can't afford to spend $1,500. After 20 minutes of discussion about the motorcycle, we have exchanged extensive information about its original cost, age, use, depreciation, and current condition, as well as your financial situation and my need to raise cash. We then settle on a price of $1,300, including a "loan" of $300 I have given you. (See Box 7.3 on the ways that the power of information, now available through the Internet, has changed the ways people buy new cars.)

The exchange of information in negotiation is also at the heart of the concession-making process. As each side presents information, a common definition of the situation emerges. The amount and kind of information shared, and the way the negotiators share it, allow both parties to derive a common (and hopefully realistic) picture of the current condition of the motorcycle, its market worth, and the preferences of each side. Moreover, this information need not be 100 percent accurate to be effective; bluffs, exaggerations, omissions, and outright lies may work just as well. I may tell you I paid $2,200 for the bike when I paid only $2,000; I may not tell you that the clutch needs to be replaced. You may not tell me that you actually can pay $1,500 but simply don't want to spend that much or that you plan to buy this bike regardless of what you have to pay for it. (We return to these issues of bluffing and misrepresentation in Chapter 9 when we discuss the ethics of lying and deception.)

Through the exchange of information, a common definition of the situation emerges and serves as a rationale for both sides to modify their positions and, eventually, arrive at a mutually acceptable price. Negotiators in the motorcycle example may derive feelings of satisfaction about that settlement from two sources: the price itself and the feeling that the price is justified because of their revised view of the motorcycle and the other party. Thus, information exchange in negotiation serves as the primary medium for creating a common view of the situation, justifying one's own and the other's perspective, making concessions, and eventually explaining one's feelings about the agreement achieved.

The presentation of information is also a key source of power in negotiation. Raven (1993; Raven, Schwartzwald and Koslowski, 1998) argued that information can be presented in two ways: directly, in order to change the others' mind, or indirectly, through "overheard" communication or using techniques that seek to present information without directly confronting the target's current position or attitudes. We explore these "direct" and "indirect" approaches to persuasion in Chapter 8.

Power derived from expertise is a special form of information power. The power that comes from information is available to anyone who assembles facts and figures to support arguments, but expert power is accorded to those who are seen as having achieved some level of command and mastery of a body of information. Experts are accorded respect, deference, and credibility based on their experience, study, or accomplishments. One or both parties in a negotiation will give experts' arguments more credibility than those of nonexperts—but only to the extent that the expertise is seen as functionally relevant to the persuasion situation (Cronkhite and Liska, 1976, 1980). For example, someone knowledgeable about cars may not be an expert on motorcycles. Thus, a negotiator who would like to take advantage of his or her expertise will often need to demonstrate that this expertise (1) actually exists and (2) is relevant to the issues under discussion.

Power Based on Personality and Individual Differences

Personal Orientation   Individuals have different psychological orientations to social situations. According to Deutsch (1985, p. 74), three such orientations are paramount: "cognitive, motivational and moral orientations to a given situation that serve to guide one's behavior and responses to that situation." These are stable individual differences—personality traits, if you will—that affect how individuals acquire and use power. We now briefly discuss all of these orientations.

Cognitive Orientation   Burrell and Morgan (1979) suggest that individual differences in ideological frames of reference—one way to represent a cognitive orientation—are central to their approach to power. They identified three types of ideological frames:

- The unitary frame, characterized by beliefs that society is an integrated whole and that the interests of individuals and society are one, such that power can be largely ignored or, when needed, be used by benevolent authorities to benefit the good of all (a view common to many "communal" societies and cultures).

- The radical frame, characterized by beliefs that society is in a continual clash of social, political, and class interests, and that power is inherently and structurally imbalanced (a view common to Marxist individuals and cultures).

BOX 7.4

Power Doesn't Always Contribute to a Healthy Personality or a Healthy Use of Power

Psychologists have studied the ways that power can contribute to paranoia. *Paranoia* is a psychological disability in which the individual believes that he or she is the target of destructive actions by another person. Paranoid individuals feel a heightened sense of self-consciousness, believe that they are constantly being scrutinized and judged by others, and hence believe that their self-concept and self-esteem are threatened. Paranoid individuals suffer from high levels of distrust of others. This distrust is often "irrational" in nature, in that the individual experiences strong fear and suspicion of others, but there is no specific interactions or experiences to justify that distrust. In its most extreme cases, paranoia can be pathological, in that the individual distrusts almost all other people and persists in these beliefs, regardless of the actual words or behavior of these other parties.

Paranoia can arise from personality dispositions as well as situational circumstances. For example, several authors have examined the U.S. presidency of Lyndon Johnson. Kramer (1995) shows how Johnson had a profound distrust and suspicion of his political rivals, such as Robert Kennedy. This led Johnson to be highly vigilant about even the most minor of political threats and challenges. But the paranoia was also exacerbated by the escalation of the war in Vietnam and the strong, persistent voice of the antiwar movement encouraging him to withdraw U.S. troops from the conflict. As a result, Johnson significantly magnified the perceived power and threat of these adversaries and increased his resolve to not pursue any courses of action which might be seen as "giving in" to these critics. Unfortunately, as noted by Caro (2006), his response to the antiwar critics significantly diminished his legacy as a very talented politician and significant leader in the country's civil rights movement.

Sources: R. M. Kramer, "Power, Paranoia and Distrust in Organizations: The Distorted View from the Top." In R. J. Bies, R. J. Lewicki, and B. H. Sheppard, *Research on Negotiation in Organizations,* vol. 5 (Greenwich, CT: JAI Press, 1995), pp. 119–154; R. A. Caro, "Lessons in Power: Lyndon Johnson Revealed," *Harvard Business Review,* April 2006, pp. 47–52.

- The pluralist frame, characterized by beliefs that power is distributed relatively equally across various groups, which compete and bargain for a share of the continually evolving balance of power (a view common to many liberal democracies).

Each ideological perspective operates as a "frame" (see Chapter 5) or perspective on the world, shaping expectations about what one should pay attention to, how events will evolve, and how one should engage situations of power. The ideological perspective has also been shown to affect the way individuals process social information about power: "whether it is limited or expandable, competitive or cooperative, or equal or unequal" (Coleman, 2000b, p. 116), and how the orientation affects people's willingness to share power when they have authority. But having power doesn't always mean that it gets used in a healthy way (see Box 7.4).

Motivational Orientation A second orientation focuses on differences in individual motivations—that is, differences rooted more in needs and "energizing elements" of the personality rather than in ideology. McClelland (1975; McClelland and Burnham, 1976) identified individual differences in "power motive," or the disposition of some people to have high needs to influence and control others and to seek out positions of power and authority. More dramatically, in the era following World War II and the notorious empire-building dispositions of Hitler and Mussolini, personality theorists described "the authoritarian personality," as an individual who has a strong need to dominate others and yet, at the same time, to identify with and submit to those in high authority (Adorno, Frenkl-Brunswick, Levinson, and Sanford, 1950). These orientations are likely to play out in either the "power over" or "powerless" situations of power, depending on the status of the other party.

Dispositions and Skills   Several authors (e.g., Pfeffer, 1992; Frost, 1987) have suggested that orientations to power are broadly grounded in individual dispositions to be cooperative or competitive (e.g., the dual concerns model, Chapter 1, and individual differences in conflict management styles, Chapter 15). Competitive dispositions and skills may emphasize the "power over" approach and suggest that people with these dispositions maintain skills such as sustaining energy and stamina; maintaining focus; and having high expertise, strong self-confidence, and high tolerance for conflict. Cooperative dispositions and skills are more allied with the "power with" approach, emphasizing skills such as sensitivity to others, flexibility, and ability to consider and incorporate the views of others into an agreement. For example, one group of researchers encouraged students to recall a time when they felt powerful and then to see how this disposition translated to a negotiation. High-power individuals displayed a greater propensity to initiate negotiations and to make the first move in a variety of competitive situations, to actually make the first offer, and to gain bargaining advantage by making that offer (Magee, Galinsky, and Gruenfeld, 2007).

Moral Orientation   Finally, individuals differ in their moral views about power and its use. Coleman (1997) has noted that there is a significant positive relationship between people's implicit ideals regarding egalitarianism—a deep-seated belief in the ideal of equality of power for all—and their willingness to share power with low power parties. In Chapter 9, we show how differences in moral orientation broadly affect the use of ethical and unethical tactics in negotiation.

Power Based on Position in an Organization

We discuss two major sources of power based on position in an organization: (1) legitimate power, which is grounded in the title, duties, and responsibilities of a job description and "level" within an organization hierarchy; and (2) power based on the control of resources (budget, funding, etc.) associated with that position.

Legitimate Power   Legitimate power is derived from occupying a particular job, office, or position in an organizational hierarchy. In this case, the power resides in the title, duties, and responsibilities of the job itself, and the "legitimacy" of the officeholder comes from the title and duties of the job description within that organization context. Thus, a newly promoted vice president acquires some legitimate power merely from holding the title of vice president.

There are times when people respond to directions from another, even directions they do not like, because they feel it is proper (legitimate) for the other to direct them and proper (obligatory) for them to obey. This is the effect of legitimate power.

Legitimate power is at the foundation of our social structure. When individuals and groups organize into any social system—a small business, a combat unit, a union, a political action organization, a sports team, a task force—they almost immediately create some form of structure and hierarchy. They elect or appoint a leader and may introduce formal rules about decision making, work division, allocation of responsibilities, and conflict management. Without this social order, either the group can take little coordinated action (chaos prevails), or everyone is required to participate in every decision and group coordination takes forever. Social structures are efficient and effective, and this fact creates the basis for legitimate power. People are willing to give up their right to participate in every decision by vesting authority in someone who can act on their behalf (a president, leader, or spokesperson). By creating a group structure that gives one person a power base, group members generate a willingness within themselves to obey that person's directives.

People can acquire legitimate power in several ways. First, it may be acquired at birth. Elizabeth II has the title of Queen of England and all the stature the title commands. She also controls a great deal of the personal wealth of the monarchy. However, she has little actual power in terms of her ability to run the day-to-day affairs of Britain, a situation that has created controversy and resentment in recent years. Second, legitimate power may be acquired by election to a designated office: the President of the United States has substantial legitimate power derived from the constitutional structure of the American government. Third, legitimate power is derived simply by appointment or promotion to some organizational position. Thus, holding the title of Director or General Manager entitles a person to all the rights, responsibilities, and privileges that go with that position. Finally, some legitimate authority comes to an individual who occupies a position for which other people simply show respect. Usually, such respect is derived from the intrinsic social good or important social values of that person's position or organization. In many societies, the young listen to and obey the old. People also listen to college presidents or the members of the clergy. They follow their advice because they believe it is proper to do so. While clergy members, college presidents, and many others may have precious little they can actually give to individuals as rewards or use against them as coercive punishments, they still have considerable legitimate power (see Cialdini, 2001, on the illusions of authority).

The effectiveness of formal authority is derived from the willingness of followers to acknowledge the legitimacy of the organizational structure and the system of rules and regulations that empowers its leaders (Barnard, 1938). In short, legitimate power cannot function without obedience or the consent of the governed. If enough British citizens question the legitimacy of the Queen and her authority—even given the hundreds of years of tradition and law on which the monarchy is founded—her continued rule will be in serious jeopardy. If enough Catholics challenge the Pope's rulings on abortion, birth control, or other social policy, the Pope's authority will erode. If the President's cabinet members and key advisers are unwilling to act on presidential orders, then the President's effectiveness is nullified. When enough people begin to distrust the authority or discredit its legitimacy, they will begin to defy it and thereby undermine its potential as a power source.

Because legitimate power can be undermined if followers choose to no longer recognize the powerholder's authority, it is not uncommon for powerholders to accumulate other power sources (such as resource control or information) to fortify their power base. Resource control and information power frequently accompany a title, position, or job

definition. Legitimate power is often derived from manipulating these other sources of power. Military officers have known this for a long time. All military-style organizations (soldiers, police, etc.) still drill their personnel, even though military units no longer march into battle as they once did. There are several reasons for this: a drill is an easy place to give instructions, teach discipline and obedience, closely monitor large numbers of people, and quickly punish or reward performance. Drilling gets large numbers of people used to accepting orders from a specific person, without question. Those who follow orders are rewarded, whereas those who do not are quickly and publicly punished. After a while, the need for reward and punishment drops off, and it seems natural or legitimate for the soldier to accept orders from an officer without asking why or inquiring about the consequences.

Although we have been talking about organizational structures and positions as conferring "legitimacy," it is also possible to apply the notion of legitimacy to certain social norms or conventions that exert strong control over people (Raven, 1993; Raven, Schwartzwald and Koslowski, 1998). Examples include the following:

1. The legitimate power of reciprocity, a very strong social norm that suggests that if one person does something positive or favorable for the other, the gesture or favor is expected to be returned ("I did you a favor; I expect you to do one for me").

2. The legitimate power of equity, another strong social norm, in which the agent has a right to request compensation from the other if the agent goes out of his or her way or endures suffering for the other ("I went out of my way for you; this is the least you could do for me").

3. The legitimate power of responsibility or dependence, a third strong social norm that says we have an obligation to help others who cannot help themselves and are dependent on us ("I understood that the other really needed help on this and could not do it themselves").

Resource Control   People who control resources have the capacity to give them to someone who will do what they want and withhold them (or take them away) from someone who doesn't do what they want. Resources can be many things. Particular resources are more useful as instruments of power to the extent that they are highly valued by participants in the negotiation. In an organizational context, some of the most important resources are the following:

1. *Money,* in its various forms: cash, salary, budget allocations, grants, bonus money, expense accounts, and discretionary funds.

2. *Supplies:* raw materials, components, pieces, and parts.

3. *Human capital:* available labor supply, staff that can be allocated to a problem or task, temporary help.

4. *Time:* free time, the ability to meet deadlines, the ability to control a deadline. If time pressure is operating on one or both parties, the ability to help someone meet or move a deadline can be extremely powerful (we discussed deadlines in negotiation in Chapter 3).

5. *Equipment:* machines, tools, technology, computer hardware and software, vehicles.

6. *Critical services:* repair, maintenance, upkeep, installation and delivery, technical support, and transportation.

7. *Interpersonal support:* verbal praise and encouragement for good performance or criticism for bad performance. This is an interesting resource because it is available to almost anyone, does not require significant effort to acquire, and the impact of receiving it is quite powerful on its own.

Pfeffer and Salancik (1974), among others, stress that the ability to control and dispense resources is a major power source in organizations. Power also comes from creating a resource stockpile in an environment where resources appear to be scarce. In his book *Managing with Power* (1992), Jeffrey Pfeffer illustrated how powerful political and corporate figures build empires founded on resource control. During his early years in Congress, Lyndon Johnson took over the "Little Congress" (a speaker's bureau for clerical personnel and aides to members of Congress) and leveraged it into a major power base that led him to become Speaker of the House of Representatives and eventually President. Similarly, Robert Moses, beginning as the parks commissioner of New York City, built a power empire that resulted in the successful construction of 12 bridges, 35 highways, 751 playgrounds, 13 golf courses, 18 swimming pools, and more than 2 million acres of park land in the New York metropolitan area—a base he used to become a dominant power broker in the city.

Resources are generally deployed in one of two principal ways: as rewards and as punishments. French and Raven (1959) called these *reward power* and *coercion power.* Raven (1993; Raven, Schwartzwald and Koslowski, 1998) has further distinguished between these two to define both personal and impersonal forms. Personal forms of power derive from the personal attraction between the agent and the target. Thus, personal reward power is derived from the target being influenced because the agent liked them or showed them some form of social acceptance. Impersonal reward power, on the other hand, comes from the direct use of tangible rewards by the agent, such as pay, benefits, a promotion, or favorable consideration. Personal coercive power is in play when the target wants to avoid or minimize the agent's disliking or social rejection (being cold, distant, rejecting, etc.). Impersonal coercive power, on the other hand, comes from the direct use of coercive punishment by the other, such as denying a raise or promotion, giving the target unfavorable job assignments, and the like.

To use resources as a basis for power, negotiators must develop or maintain control over some desirable reward that the other party wants—such as physical space, jobs, budget authorizations, or raw materials—or control over some punishment the other seeks to avoid. As noted, these rewards and punishments could be tangible or intangible, such as liking, approval, respect, and so on. Successful control over resources also requires that the other party deal directly with the powerholder. Finally, the powerholder must be willing to allocate resources depending on the other's compliance or cooperation with the powerholder's requests. The increasing scarcity of resources of all kinds has led to the new golden rule of organizations: "whoever has the gold makes the rules." The potential use of reward and punishment power is most commonly expressed in negotiation as threats to punish and promises to reward, which we addressed in our discussion of distributive bargaining in Chapter 2.

Power Based on Relationships

Three types of power are discussed here: goal interdependence, referent power, and power based on relationship with others in personal and professional networks.

Goal Interdependence   How the parties view their goals—and how much achievement of their goal depends on the behavior of the other party—has a strong impact on how likely parties will be to constructively use power. Goal structure has consistently demonstrated a strong effect on negotiator's attitudes and behaviors by influencing the disposition parties take toward power. Cooperative goals tend to shape the "power with" orientation, even between superiors and subordinates; Tjosvold (1997) found that these goals induce "higher expectations of assistance, more assistance, greater support, more persuasion and less coercion and more trusting and friendly attitudes" (p. 297). Those with cooperative goals want others to perform effectively and achieve common objectives. In contrast, competitive goals lead the parties to pursue a "power over" orientation; to reinforce or enhance existing power differences; and to use that power to maximize one's own goals, often at the expense of the other (see also Deutsch, 1973; Howard, Gardner, and Thompson, 2007). For example, relationships and goal interdependence are key sources of power in salary negotiations (see Box 7.5).

Referent Power   As defined earlier, referent power is derived from the respect or admiration one commands because of attributes like personality, integrity, interpersonal style, and the like. A is said to have referent power over B to the extent that B identifies with or wants to be closely associated with A. Referent power is often based on an appeal to common experiences, common past, common fate, or membership in the same groups. Referent power is made *salient* when one party identifies the dimension of commonality in an effort to increase his or her power (usually persuasiveness) over the other. Thus, a negotiator might start getting to know the other in order to discover commonalities (home town,

BOX 7.5   **Power Relationships in Salary Negotiation**

Salary and negotiation expert Paul Barada from Monster.com points out that power is one of the most overlooked but important dynamics in negotiation. He says that power relationships aren't like blackjack, but there is one parallel: power will determine who has the better hand. The employer often has the better hand because he or she has something the candidate wants: the job opening, and there are probably lots of candidates who want the job (a good BATNA). But if the candidate has unique skills that the employer wants, or if there is a shortage of talent in a particular field, the candidate can have a lot of power (and hence a good hand). A job candidate can increase his or her power as follows:

- Determine what skills has, and which ones can be transferred to the job one has applying for.
- Do homework on the demand for those skills in various jobs and industries.

- Know what is a fair and reasonable salary for this job, given the market conditions and the geographic area in which the job is located.
- Be prepared to make a convincing set of arguments for the value one will bring to your new employer.
- Determine a fair compensation rate (target) and a threshold below which one will not go (walkaway point).

If the candidate determines that he or she does not have the appropriate skills, education or experience, he or she should consider how to gain those skills or experience to give him or her more power in job negotiations.

Source: P. W. Barada, "Power Relationships and Negotiation." (2008). http://www.career-advice.monster.com/salary-negotiation/Power-Relationships-and-Negotiation/home.asp.

---

college, favorite sports team, political perspective) that, when discovered, will hopefully create a bond between the parties that will facilitate agreement. Like expert power, referent power can also have negative forms. Negative referent power is often used, particularly when parties seek to create distance or division between themselves and others or to label the other. Thus, political rivals often label each other as "liberals" or "right wingers" in an effort to make the other a less attractive candidate in an upcoming election (Raven and Rubin, 1976).

Networks   The third type of relational power also comes from location in an organizational structure, but not necessarily a hierarchical structure. In this case, power is derived from whatever flows through that particular location in the structure (usually information and resources, such as money). The person occupying a certain position may not have a formal title or office; his or her leverage comes from the ability to control and manage what "flows" through that position. For example, before China modernized in the 1980s, automobile chauffeurs held enormous power even though their title was not prestigious. If a chauffeur did not like a passenger or did not feel like driving to a certain location, he could make life very difficult and impose serious consequences for the passenger (e.g., delayed departure time, driving very slowly, taking a roundabout route, etc.).

This example shows that even without a lofty position or title, individuals can become powerful because of the way their actions and responsibilities are embedded in the flows of information, goods and services, or contacts. For example, individuals such as clerks or data-entry operators, who have access to a large amount of information or who are responsible

FIGURE 7.1 | Comparing Organization Hierarchies and Networks

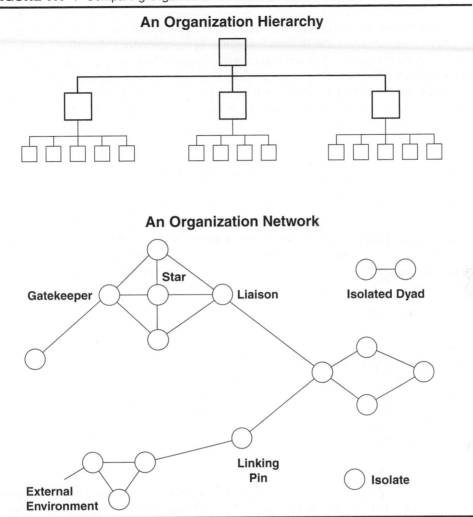

for collecting, managing, and allocating vital resources (money, raw materials, permissions and authorizations) may become very powerful (see Charan, 1991; Kaplan, 1984; Krackhart and Hanson, 1993). The job may not have a fancy title, a large staff, or a large corner office, but it can confer a significant amount of power by virtue of the amount of information and resources that pass through it.

Understanding power in this way is derived from conceptualizing organizations and their functioning not as a hierarchy, but as a network of interrelationships. Network schemas represent key individuals as circles or nodes and relationships between individuals as lines of transaction. (See Figure 7.1 for an example of a network as compared with an organizational hierarchy).

These lines *(ties)* connect individuals or groups *(nodes)* who interact or need to interact with each other in the organization. Through information and resources as the primary focus of transactions, personal relationships, referent power, and "pressure" may also be negotiated across network lines. In formal hierarchy terms, authority is directly related to how high the position is on the vertical organization chart and how many people report to that individual from lower levels. In network terms, in contrast, power is determined by location within the set of relationships and the flows that occur through that node in the network. Several key aspects of networks shape power: tie strength, tie content, and network structure (including node centrality, criticality, flexibility, and visibility).

Tie Strength   This is an indication of the strength or quality of relationships with others. Quality might be measured by how close you are, how much personal information you share with the other, or how much one person is willing to go out of his or her way for the other. Strength of ties between individuals can be determined by how often the parties interact, how long they have known each other, how close the personal relationship is with the other, how many different ways the two parties interact with each other, and how much reciprocity or mutuality there is in the relationship so that each contributes equally to the give-and-take. Stronger ties with another usually indicate greater power to have the other accede to requests.

Tie Content   Content is the resource that passes along the tie with the other person. This could be money or other resources, information, support, emotion, and the like. The more the content of the ties builds a strong personal relationship (rather than just a series of exchanges or transactions—also see Chapter 10) and the more they create trust and respect for each other, the stronger the tie will be (Ibarra and Andrews, 1993).

Network Structure   While tie strength and content relate to an individual relationship within a network, network structure refers to the overall set of relationships within a social system (e.g., a workplace, department, school, or other social environment). Some aspects of network structure that determine power in a role include:

1.   *Centrality*. The more central a node is in a network of exchanges and transactions, the more power that node's occupant will have. Centrality may be determined by the amount of information or total number of transactions that pass through a node or by the degree to which the node is central to managing information flow. In the network depicted in Figure 7.1, the star has greater centrality and therefore more power. Researchers have shown that being in the center of information flows—the workflow network, the informal communication network, and the friendship network—is particularly important to being promoted (see Brass, 1984). A new faculty member might decide to volunteer to head up the "speakers" program for faculty seminars because it would put him or her in the center of many communications about the weekly presentations.

2.   *Criticality and relevance*. A second source of network power is the criticality of the node. Although a large amount of information or resources may not flow through a particular node, what does may be essential to the organization's mission, major task, or key product. People who depend highly on others may become critical to the degree that they are charged with assembling information from many locations; that is, they may be in frequent contact with many important people and may be required to integrate information from those contacts into a recommendation, action strategy, or decision. In Figure 7.1, liaisons and linking pins perform this role. Employees who want to succeed rapidly are frequently counseled to find jobs with high centrality and criticality in an organization so they can get the experience and visibility necessary for rapid promotion. Being critical—even irreplaceable—is a core part of getting and maintaining power.

3. *Flexibility.* A third source of network power lies in the position's flexibility, or the degree to which the key individual can exercise discretion in how certain decisions are made or who gains access. Flexibility is often related to criticality (see the preceding discussion). A classic example of flexibility is the role of gatekeeper (Figure 7.1), the person in a network who controls the access to a key figure or group. Anyone who wants to get to the star has to go through the gatekeeper. If you want to see the boss, you have to get permission and access from the secretary.

4. *Visibility.* Nodes differ in their degree of visibility—that is, how visible the task performance is to others in the organization. Visibility is not necessarily the same thing as centrality or criticality. A negotiator who deals with his or her constituency in the same room has high visibility; if the negotiator gains significant concessions from the other party while being watched, the team will give that negotiator a great deal of affirmation. A node with high centrality and criticality may not be visible, but if it is not, it is much less likely to be recognized and rewarded. Visibility may also be determined simply by where a person's office or parking space is located, such as in the hallway where the president walks to lunch or near the location where the president parks his or her car. Pfeffer (1992) relates a story about a new faculty colleague who became well known simply by the proximity of his office to one of the few men's rooms in the building—most colleagues got to know him as they passed his office on their periodic trips to the lavatory.

5. *Membership in a coalition.* Finally, as a node in a network, you can be a member of one or more subgroups or coalitions. Coalitions often act together to represent a point of view or promote action or change; the more coalitions you belong to, the more likely you will be to find "friends" who can help you meet key people, obtain important (often "inside") information, and accomplish objectives. We say more about how coalitions work in negotiations in Chapter 12.

Contextual Sources of Power

Finally, while power can be located within individuals and their relationships, power is also based in the context, situation, or environment in which negotiations take place. While these forms of power often go unrecognized in the short term (because of our tendency to see power as an individual quality rather than embedded in the structure or context of a conflict), these sources are just as critical.

BATNAs In Chapters 3 and 4, we discussed the role of a best alternative to a negotiated agreement—that is, an alternative deal that a negotiator might pursue if she or he does not come to agreement with the current other party. The availability of a BATNA offers a ne-gotiator significant power because he or she now has a choice between accepting the other party's proposal or the alternative deal. Any viable BATNA gives the negotiator the choice to walk away from the current deal or to use the BATNA as leverage to strike a better agree-ment in the current discussions. Students who have two financial aid offers from different graduate schools will have significantly more power to increase the quality of that aid pack-age offer from either university than students who have only one financial aid offer, be-cause they can "play one off against the other." Knowledge of the other's BATNA can also help shape a negotiator's initial offer. Buelens and Van Poucke (2004) have shown that knowledge of the opponent's BATNA was by far the strongest determinant in shaping a manager's initial offer in a negotiation situation.

Several studies have reinforced the importance of a strong BATNA as a source of power. First, having a strong BATNA increases the likelihood that one will make the first offer (Magee, Galinsky, and Gruenfeld, 2007). Second, having a BATNA increases one's own outcomes as well as the other's outcomes, compared with not having a BATNA. Moreover, the better the BATNA, the more leverage a negotiator has over his or her opponent. Finally, negotiators with better BATNAs (compared with their oppo-nents) were able to claim a greater share of the resource pie (Pinkley, Neale, and Bennett, 1994). However, if one is concerned about integrative outcomes, the reverse is true: the smaller the perceived difference in power (as determined by the quality of alternatives), the better the integrative outcomes derived from the negotiation (Wolfe and McGinn, 2005).

Culture   Culture determines the "meaning system" of a social environment. That is, cul-ture is a system of basic assumptions, norms, and/or common values that individuals in a group or organization share about how to interact with each other, work together, deal with the external environment, and move the organization into the future (Schein, 1988). Culture often shapes what kinds of power are seen as legitimate and illegitimate or how people use influence and react to influence. For example, in one organization known to the authors of this book, the chief executive officer (CEO) introduced ideas for major changes in business strategy in management team meetings. Senior managers made very few critical comments about these ideas in the meeting, but they then actively expressed their disagreement with the idea in one-to-one conversations with each other or the CEO. This public lack of open-ness and honesty—a cultural value in this organization—contributed to many decisions that were apparently made by consensus, but then consistently undermined in private by the very people who were part of the decision. Changing this cultural value required a strong, concerted action by the CEO and other managers working together with a con-sultant over a number of months. Cultures often contain many implicit "rules" about use of power and whether "power over" or "power with" processes are seen as more or less appropriate.

National cultures also differ in the degree to which these "power over" or "power with" orientations are supported or encouraged. Hofstede (1980a, 1980b, 1989) identified "power distance" as a key dimension that distinguishes national cultures from each other. Cultures high in power distance accept inherent inequality in their social structure—that some people in the culture have "power over" others, such as religious or political leaders, elders, "wise men," and the like. In contrast, cultures low in power distance embrace a broad norm of "power with"—that decision-making power is spread broadly through the culture and that democratic decision making and delegation to those with expertise or unique skill is more acceptable than rule by a few. We explore this approach in greater depth in our treatment of international negotiation in Chapter 17.

Finally, culture—both organizational and national—often translates into deeply embedded structural inequalities in a society. The degree to which women, religious or ethnic groups, certain social classes, or other minority interests are treated unjustly in a society reflect longstanding historical evolution of power inequalities in social structures and institutions. Many significant social problems and negotiations about how to change them can be traced to the historical evolution of these dispositions within a culture, and they require significant effort and attention over many years to introduce meaningful change.

Agents, Constituencies, and External Audiences   Most negotiations that we describe in this book take place one-to-one—just you and the other negotiator. But negotiations become significantly more complex when negotiators are representing others' views (e.g., acting as an agent representing their organization or being represented by another person) and when there are multiple parties, the public media, and/or audiences present to observe, critique, and evaluate the negotiations. When all of these other parties are present in a negotiation, they can become actively involved to formally or informally pressure others as part of the negotiation process, which changes the power dynamics. We extensively discuss the effects of additional parties in Chapter 11.

Dealing with Others Who Have More Power

Thus far, we have been focusing on the numerous ways that negotiators can assemble and use power to their advantage in a negotiation. However, negotiators are often on the receiving end of that power. Very little research has focused on how parties can deal with others who have significantly more power (from one or more of the sources we have mentioned in this chapter). We end this chapter with some advice to negotiators who are in a low-power position, and we return to that advice in Chapter 18, where we specifically focus on negotiation "mismatches" and how low-power parties can deal with more powerful others who use strategy and tactics that makes them difficult. Watkins (2002) and others specifically address the problem of "dancing with elephants" (striking a deal with an opponent much bigger than you) and highlight ways that lower-power parties can deal with the big players in business deals and partnerships. Here is some of their advice:

1. *Never do an all-or-nothing deal.* Relying on a single party and creating a make-or-break deal with them leaves the low-power party highly vulnerable. For example, a small business that agrees to let Wal-Mart stores be its only customer runs the risk of being completely controlled by Wal-Mart. Low-power parties should attempt to diversify their risk by entering into deals with several other partners so that no single high-power player could wipe the low-power partner out. We comment more on this process when we discuss coalition dynamics in Chapter 12.

2. *Make the other party smaller.* In dealing with a high-power party, particularly if it is a group or organization, one should attempt to establish multiple relationships and engage in multiple negotiations. By dealing with a variety of different individuals and departments in the high-power party, one may be able to "divide and conquer" by diversifying the relationships and the multiple interests that may be served in working with these different subgroups.

3. *Make yourself bigger.* Similarly, low-power players should attempt to build coalitions with other low-power players so as to increase their collective bargaining power. Again, these coalition tactics are extensively discussed in Chapter 12. On the other hand, if a low-power player tries to "make itself bigger" by becoming more aggressive, he or she achieves significantly poorer outcomes than if he or she accepts the low-power position (Donohue and Taylor, 2007).

4. *Build momentum through doing deals in sequence.* Early deals can be done to build a relationship, strengthen the relationship with the high-power party, and perhaps acquire resources (information, technology, seed capital, etc.). Select those high-power targets that have the most to gain, and maximize visibility of those deals to other parties.

5. *Use the power of competition to leverage power.* This is a variation on the power of a BATNA. If you have something to offer, make sure you offer it to more than one high-power party. If you can get them competing against each other for what you want, some may actually do a deal with you simply to keep you from doing a deal with one of their competitors.

6. *Constrain yourself.* Tie your hands by limiting the ways that you can do business or who you can do business with. However, while these constraints might drive away your competition, they also have the liability of constraining you as well.

7. *Good information is always a source of power.* Seek out information that strengthens your negotiating position and case. Anticipate the information that would be most compelling or persuasive to the other side; organize it so that you can draw on it quickly and assemble it to be maximally persuasive.

8. *Ask lots of questions to gain more information.* Research shows that negotiators with less power ask more diagnostic than leading questions and constantly showed their willingness to cooperate—and that these behaviors resulted in better outcomes (de Dreu and Van Kleef, 2004).

9. *Do what you can to manage the process.* If the high-power party controls the negotiation process (the agenda, the cadence, the timing, and the location), he or she will do it in a way to assure outcomes he or she wants. If the low-power party controls the process, he or she is more likely to be able to steer the deal in an advantageous direction (Watkins, 2002).

Chapter Summary

In this chapter, we discussed the nature of power in negotiation. We suggested that there were two major ways to think about power: "power over," which suggests that power is fundamentally dominating and coercive in nature, and "power with," suggesting that power is jointly shared with the other party to collectively develop joint goals and objectives. There is a great tendency to see and define power as the former, but as we have discussed in this chapter and our review of the basic negotiation strategies, "power with" is critical to successful integrative negotiation.

We reviewed five major sources of power:

- Informational sources of power (information and expertise).

- Personal sources of power (psychological orientation, cognitive orientation, motivational orientation, certain dispositions, and moral orientation and skills).

- Position-based sources of power (legitimate power and resource control).

- Relationship-based power (goal interdependence and referent power and networks).

- Contextual sources of power (availability of BATNAs, availability of agents, and the organizational or national culture in which the negotiation occurs).

In closing, we wish to stress two key points. First, while we have presented many vehicles for attaining power in this chapter, it must be remembered that power can be highly elusive and fleeting in negotiation. Almost anything can be a source of power if it gives the negotiator a temporary advantage over the other party (e.g., a BATNA or a piece of critical information). Second, power is only the capacity to influence; using that power and skillfully exerting influence on the other requires a great deal of sophistication and experience. In the next chapter, we turn next to a detailed examination of how negotiators implement these power sources through the strategies and tactics of interpersonal influence.

Endnotes

1 Researchers have defined an individual difference called *communication competency* (Spitzberg and Cupach, 1984). Individuals who are high in communication competency are likely to have strong verbal ability, are able to strategize about the way they communicate from one situation to the next, and can easily take the perspective of the other party. Individuals who are high in communication competence are able to adapt to different situations and do what is most necessary and desirable in any given situation.

2 See, for example, Schreisheim and Hinkin, 1990; Yukl and Tracey, 1992; Cialdini and Goldstein, 2004. For one comprehensive approach to reconceptualizing the use of power in negotiation, see Kim, Pinkley, and Fragale, 2005.

8 CHAPTER

Influence

Objectives

1. Understand the principles of successful influence.
2. Explore the dynamics of the "two routes" to successful influence.
3. Consider the various influence tools and techniques that are available through each of the routes.
4. Gain a broader understanding of the variety of influence tools available to any negotiator.

In the last chapter we discussed power as the potential to alter others' attitudes and behaviors. In this chapter we turn to power's complement, *influence*—the actual strategies and messages that individuals deploy to bring about desired attitudinal or behavioral change. During negotiations, actors frequently need to convince the other party that they have offered something of value, their offer is reasonable, and they cannot offer more. Negotiators may also want to alter the other party's beliefs about the importance of her own objectives and convince her that her concessions are not as valuable as she first believed. Negotiators may portray themselves as likable people who should be treated decently. All these efforts are designed to use information, as well as the qualities of the sender and receiver of that information, to adjust the other party's positions, perceptions, and opinions; we call this group of tactics *influence*.

The pursuit of influence certainly can stem from and capitalize on power in the sense that if you have leverage over someone because of, say, your position of authority or your ability to confer rewards, you can use those things to influence—to get the other person to see or do something your way. But it is crucial to emphasize at the outset of this chapter that *achieving successful influence does not necessarily require having power over the individual(s) you seek to influence.* As we shall see, there are multiple routes to influencing someone else's attitudes or behavior, some of which benefit from having formal or informal power over the target of influence, but many of which don't.

People differ widely in their ability to use influence effectively. Some observers think that the ability to persuade is something with which people are born—something they either have or don't have. Although the natural persuasive abilities of people do differ, persuasion is as much a science as a native ability; everyone has the opportunity to improve persuasive skills. Our aim in this chapter is to discuss a variety of influence tools that are available to the savvy negotiator. To set the stage, we begin with an organizing framework that defines influence seeking in two broad categories that correspond to two different social–psychological avenues for achieving influence.

Two Routes to Influence: An Organizing Model

One way to think about how people are influenced by others is to draw upon a traditional model of communication that focuses on the content and characteristics as the *message* that a sender wants a receiver to believe, accept, or understand. For a long time this was the traditional way that psychologists analyzed influence and persuasion: effective influence occurs when a person is exposed to, pays attention to, comprehends, retains, and acts in accordance with the content of a message. By the 1980s, however, researchers came to understand that people can be influenced—their attitudes and behaviors can be changed—without them having to understand, learn, or retain the specific information contained in a message (Petty, Briñol, and Tormala, 2002). In fact, people can be influenced even when they are not actively thinking about the message itself (Petty and Briñol, 2008). This is not to suggest that the content of influence-seeking messages, like those used by negotiators to try to get the other side to see things his or her way, aren't important—they certainly are in many situations. It is, however, simplistic to think of influence only in terms of the verbal content of persuasive messages aimed by an influence seeker at an influence target.

An alternative way—the approach we choose here—is based on a more contemporary understanding of how influence and persuasion work. This approach, developed first in a stream of research by Richard Petty and John Cacioppo (1986a, 1986b),[1] suggests that there are two general paths by which people are persuaded:

- The first path occurs consciously and involves thinking actively about an influence-seeking message and integrating it into the individual's previously existing cognitive structures (thoughts, intellectual frameworks, etc.). Petty and Cacioppo have labeled this path to persuasion the *central route,* which "occurs when motivation and ability to scrutinize issue-relevant arguments are relatively high" (Petty and Cacioppo, 1986b, p. 131).

- The second route to persuasion, the *peripheral route,* is characterized by subtle cues and context, with less active thought and cognitive processing of the message. Persuasion via the peripheral route is thought to occur automatically (i.e., out of conscious awareness), leading to "attitude change without argument scrutiny" (Petty and Cacioppo, 1986b, p. 132). Because the information is not integrated into existing cognitive structures, persuasion occurring via this route is likely to last a shorter time than persuasion occurring via the central route (Petty and Cacioppo, 1986b). A simple example of peripheral-route persuasion is the listener who is convinced by the impressive credentials of the speaker rather than by the arguments the speaker is actually presenting.

For clarity of presentation, we represent elements from both paths in a single diagram (Figure 8.1). Many of the common elements used to increase leverage are part of the central route: the structure and content of the message or the relationship between sender and receiver. However, several influence strategies are designed to persuade through the indirect or peripheral route, such as enhancing the attractiveness and credibility of the source, invoking the principle of reciprocity (you should do something for me because I did something for you), or drawing on appeals to popularity (you should think this way because many others do).[2] The remainder of this chapter addresses the leverage factors presented in Figure 8.1. We organize this discussion according to the distinction between central and peripheral routes to influence.

FIGURE 8.1 | Two Routes to Influence

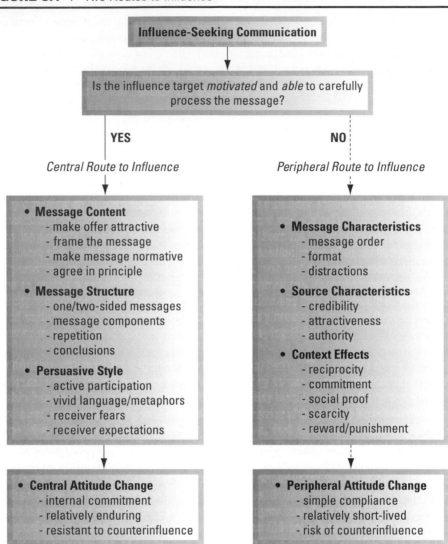

The effective use of influence, whether within a negotiation context or in other social settings, may be determined in part by an individual's stylistic talent as a "salesperson" or accomplished communicator, but we take the position that an understanding of the human psychology of influence is at least as important, if not more so. The negotiator who grasps the principles developed in this chapter will have at his or her disposal tools of influence that make it possible to elicit from others desirable and strategically useful attitudes and behaviors. Effective influence is not just a way for negotiators to claim more value for themselves; it can also help to persuade the other party to see possibilities for joint benefit, and to increase the other party's satisfaction with the deal that does ultimately result (Malhotra and Bazerman, 2008).

The Central Route to Influence: The Message and Its Delivery

Facts and ideas are clearly important in changing another person's opinions and perceptions, but the effectiveness of a persuasion effort depends on how the facts and ideas are selected, organized, and presented. There are three major issues to consider when constructing a message: the *content* of the message (the facts and topics that should be covered), the *structure* of the message (how the topics and facts should be arranged and organized), and the *delivery style* (how the message should be presented).

Message Content

When constructing arguments to persuade the other party, negotiators need to decide what topics and facts they should include. In this section, we discuss four questions negotiators need to consider when constructing persuasive arguments: (1) how to make offers attractive to the other party, (2) how to frame messages so the other party will say yes, (3) how to make messages normative, and (4) how to obtain agreements in principle.

1. Make the Offer Attractive to the Other Party   In structuring the message, negotiators should emphasize the advantage the other party gains from accepting the proposal (Michener and Suchner, 1971). Although this may seem obvious, it is surprising how many negotiators spend more time explaining what aspects of their offer are attractive to themselves than identifying what aspects are likely to be attractive to the other party. Experienced negotiators ensure that the other party understands what he or she will gain by accepting an offer. To do this well, negotiators need to understand the other party's needs. Salespeople often identify a customer's needs and requirements before they get down to the details of what a particular product or service can do for the purchaser. Labor negotiators often have preliminary, unofficial meetings with management at which both parties discuss the upcoming deliberations and signal the high-priority issues for the year. With information about the other party's needs and interests, negotiators can construct offers with highly appealing features.

When negotiators are on the *receiving* end of a proposal, they frequently choose not to talk about the attractive features of an offer but rather to highlight why certain features are undesirable. They try to argue that what the other party is trying to sell is not what they need, is inadequate, or does not meet their specifications. Thus, persuasion can be a struggle to define or evaluate the attractiveness of an offer. The negotiator making the offer stresses its attractive features, hoping to minimize further concessions. The receiver of the offer stresses its unattractive features, hoping to receive more concessions. The better a negotiator understands the other's real needs and concerns, the more he or she can anticipate the other's objections and structure the presentation to counteract them.

2. Frame the Message So the Other Party Will Say Yes   Advertisers discovered long ago that people who agree with one statement or proposal, even though it may be minor, are likely to agree with a second, more significant statement or proposal from the same person or on the same topic (Fern, Monroe, and Avila, 1986).[3] Hence, if you can get the other party to agree to something—almost anything—then you have laid the foundation for subsequent agreement. The task is to find something that the other party can agree with that puts him or her in the mind-set of saying yes. A real estate salesperson who gets potential buyers to agree that the house they are visiting is in a nice neighborhood or has a nice yard for their children has made the first step toward getting them to say yes to buying the house (even if it is not the ideal size, layout, or price).

3. Make the Message Normative   It is easy to assume that people are driven by simple and direct self-interest. There is plenty of evidence, however, to indicate that people are motivated to behave consistently with their values, that is, their religious, social, or ethical standards. These standards become part of people's self-image, a concept in their mind of what they are really like. People will go to considerable lengths to act or say things consistent with their self-image. At times, people act politely when in fact they are feeling quite hostile. People can act generously when they are actually financially strained and feel like being greedy (Reardon, 1981). They behave this way to preserve their self-image and to convince others that they are nice people (see our discussion of face saving in Chapter 10).[4]

A powerful argument in negotiation is to show the other person that by following a course of action (your proposal), he will be acting in accordance both with his values and with some higher (more noble, moral, or ethical) code of conduct. Politicians use normative messages to justify fiscal policies to promote domestic purchases (e.g., "buy American," "protect American jobs"), and interest groups use normative messages to either promote their points of view or demean other points of view (e.g., "save a tree," "tax and spend liberals"). At times, the simple statement "This is the right (or proper) thing to do" may carry considerable weight. People work hard to take responsibility for actions that lead to positive outcomes (Schlenker and Riess, 1979).

4. Suggest an Agreement in Principle   There are times when getting the other party to accept an "agreement in principle" may be a valuable step in a negotiation. For example, when there is bitter conflict between two parties who cannot seem to agree on anything, obtaining agreement on a general principle, such as a cease-fire, may be the first "yes" statement to which both parties can subscribe. In the negotiations between Israel and Egypt over the Sinai in the late 1970s, no details were settled about the fate of the Palestinians, but an agreement on the principle of Palestinian self-rule was reached. Although an agreement in principle is desirable when other options are blocked, it still takes a great deal of work to turn such an agreement into one that contains specific details and action proposals. Principles sound good, and most people may agree with what they advocate, but there is usually great uncertainty about how a principle applies to a specific situation. For example, to return to the Middle East and the question of Palestine, even if the parties agree to the principle of trading land for peace, there is still a great deal of work to do to specify which land and what kind of peace.

Message Structure

People are influenced not only by what negotiators say but also by how they arrange the words. Any writer or speaker faces the question of how to present material in the most logical or persuasive manner. How should arguments be arranged? Should counterarguments or opposing ideas be mentioned at all? There has been a considerable amount of research on the persuasive power of different message structures. Surprisingly, many of those elements that you might expect to have an important impact, such as the structure of logic in the message, have not been clearly shown to be important. Here we discuss four aspects of message structure that help to explain when and how persuasion occurs through the central route: (1) one- and two-sided messages, (2) message components, (3) repetition, and (4) conclusions.

1. One- and Two-Sided Messages   When negotiators try to persuade the other party it is because they believe that the other holds an opinion different from theirs. Many people deal with this problem by ignoring arguments and opinions that might support the other party's position—a *one-sided* approach. Many politicians not only do not mention their opponent's point of view but may never even mention their opponent's name. Advertisements for consumer products often refrain from identifying competing products by name or staging an open, direct comparison; although more common than it used to be, advertisers do not often refer explicitly to competitors and comparatively evaluate the features or qualities of competing products.

An alternate approach to ignoring the competition is to mention and describe the opposing point of view, and then show how and why it is less desirable than the presenter's point of view—a *two-sided* approach. The question then arises: Which of these approaches is most effective?

In general, *two-sided messages are considered to be more effective than one-sided messages* (Jackson and Allen, 1987). More specifically, two-sided messages appear to be most effective (1) when the other party is well educated, (2) when the other party initially disagrees with the position, (3) when the other party will be exposed to people who will argue points of view different from the position advocated, and (4) when the issue discussed is already familiar. In addition, two-sided arguments work best when the preferred argument is presented last (Zimbardo, Ebbesen, and Maslach, 1977). But there is a drawback: research has shown that a change in someone's attitude is more likely to produce a corresponding change in behavior when that person has been exposed to a one-sided message rather than a two-sided message (Glasman and Albarracín, 2006). In sum, when dealing with reasonably intelligent receivers, it is a mistake to ignore the impact of counterarguments. The other party will be formulating them as you speak, and it is an advantage to refute them by using two-sided messages. There is, however, the possibility that a two-sided argument will do a better job changing the other person's mind—which sometimes is all that's needed—than it will changing actual behavior.

2. Message Components   Big ideas or large propositions are hard to grasp and accept, especially when they are significantly different from your own. Negotiators can help the other party understand and accept their arguments by breaking them into smaller, more understandable pieces—a process known as "fractionating" (Fisher, 1964). It is even better if one can show that the component parts contain statements that the other party has already accepted or agreed with. For example, a company that is having trouble getting a union to accept a whole package of rule changes could break its presentation down into separate discussions of specific rules: transfers between departments within a plant, transfers between plants, temporary changes in work classifications, and so on. In one case, for example, a union was very interested in making changes to work rules to preserve job security; having already said yes to these changes, the union seemed more receptive to management's argument for other work rule changes. In addition, it is possible that breaking down complex arguments into smaller parts will lead the parties to see the possibilities to logroll, bundle, and trade off across issues (see Chapter 3) because the issues will be seen in sharper focus. If the goal is to find and capitalize on integrative potential, however, it is important that the parties not let splitting up of issues into smaller pieces lead to separate and final settlements on those piecemeal issues. To work as mechanisms for achieving mutual gains, logrolls, bundles, and trade-offs require that multiple issues be on the table and play. Integrative argeements are hindered if the parties take up, settle on, and dispense with individual issues one by one.

3. Repetition   We need only think of the regular blitz of typical television or radio advertisements to realize the power of repetition in getting a message across. Repetition encourages central-route processing, increasing the likelihood that the influence target will scrutinize the message, and thus enhances the likelihood that the message will be understood (Cacioppo and Petty, 1985). However, repeating a point is effective only for the first few times. After that, additional repetition does not significantly change attitudes (McGuire, 1973) and may become annoying and lead people to react against the message.

4. Conclusions   Sometimes writers or speakers will make an argument and then state the conclusion; other times, they will let listeners draw their own conclusions. Letting others draw their own conclusion (as long as it is the conclusion one wants drawn) can lead to a very effective presentation. Research suggests that when negotiating with people who are very intelligent or who have not yet made up their minds, leaving the conclusion open is a good approach (assuming your arguments up to this point have pulled them toward the "right" conclusion). In contrast, for people whose ideas are already well-formulated and strongly held, leaving the conclusion unstated risks leaving the most important part of the influence attempt undone. On balance, it is usually best not to assume that given a set of facts or arguments, the other party will reach the same conclusion you would reach; rather, draw explicit conclusions for listeners to ensure that they have understood the argument completely (Feingold and Knapp, 1977).[5]

Persuasive Style: How to Pitch the Message

When negotiators select a delivery style for the message they have constructed, they set the emotional tone and manner of their presentation. Some people are belligerent; others are solicitous and accommodating. Some people make speeches; others start a dialogue. Some present detailed facts and draw specific conclusions; others use metaphors and paint beautiful pictures with words. We now consider four major elements of persuasive style and how they affect successful persuasion: (1) active participation versus passive responding, (2) use of vivid language and metaphors, (3) use of threats to incite fears, and (4) violation of the receiver's expectations.

1. Encourage Active Participation   People are more likely to change their attitudes and beliefs for the long term when they are actively involved in the process of learning new material (Johnson and Eagly, 1990).[6] Good teachers know this—rather than lecture, they ask questions and start discussions. Teachers are even more effective when they can get students both intellectually and emotionally involved. Role-plays and cases can help negotiators make use of the power of active participation. Negotiators who can use active approaches are generally more persuasive than those who don't because an active approach requires the receiver to exert effort, which leads to involvement, which leads to attitude change.

It can be helpful to precede negotiations with a friendly and engaging dialogue. This extends beyond simple politeness; inquiring about an individual's day or mood and then responding accordingly can motivate him or her to cooperate (Howard, 1990). Dolinski, Nawrat, and Rudak (2001) demonstrated that when a request is preceded by a pleasant dialogue rather than simply a pleasant monologue, subjects were more willing to concede to the request. Furthermore, these findings generalized across a variety of different interactions and settings, even holding up when the subject declared being in a bad mood. As we mentioned in our discussion of communication in Chapter 6, the development of rapport between negotiators has a number of positive benefits for avoiding impasse and achieving integrative outcomes (e.g., Morris, Nadler, Kurtzbert, and Thompson, 2000; Swaab, Postmes, van Beest, and Spears, 2007). Engaging the other party in dialogue may lead them to perceive the situation as an interaction with an acquaintance, rather than a confrontation with a stranger (Dolinsky et al., 2001), and requests from acquaintances are more likely to be met with favor than those coming from strangers.

2. Consider Vividness and Intensity of Language   The vividness and intensity of the language negotiators use have a major effect on their persuasiveness. Saying "This is certainly the best price you will get" is more compelling than saying "This is quite a good price." Similarly, the statement "I don't feel like going out tonight" is not as intense as "You can't drag me out tonight with a team of horses." The intensity of language can also be increased through the use of colorful metaphors, swear words, or a change in intonation—from quiet to loud or loud to quiet (Bowers, 1964).

You might think that the most intense language would also be the most persuasive. On the contrary, language of relatively low intensity is at times more effective (Bowers, 1964). Evidence indicates that people react negatively to persuasive attempts using language they perceive as too intense (Burgoon and King, 1974). People under stress seem to be particularly receptive to messages using low-intensity language and more inclined to reject those using high-intensity language (Jones and Burgoon, 1975). The impact of language intensity is even more complex, however: research has shown that the effect of intense language depends in part on who uses it. Sources with high credibility can use more intense language than those who are not seen as credible (Burgoon and Stewart, 1975). It is also the case that an effective influencer will match his or her emotional fervor to the ability of the target of influence to receive and interpret the message (Conger, 1998). Bottom line: although there is a strong temptation to use intense language to make a point, it is often wise to moderate this impulse.

Metaphors and analogies are a particularly useful way to augment the vividness of a message in the service of persuasion (Bowers and Osborn, 1966; Conger, 1998). An auto salesperson can give a potential customer information about a car's engine, mileage, acceleration, and so forth, but for someone not concerned with the specific technical details can make these points by saying, "This car flies like the wind and doesn't guzzle gas." Using metaphors to excess may lead the other party to believe that you're filled with hot air (itself a metaphor!), but using them to summarize some facts or to create a visual impression can be valuable in persuasion. An important caution for negotiators, though: when using metaphors, be careful to choose analogies that are "correct" for the situation. This is especially challenging when negotiating across cultures because metaphors do not always translate well, and could leave the other party befuddle, or worse, insulted. (We discuss culture and negotiation fully in Chapter 16.)

3. Use Threats; Incite Fears   Messages that contain threats—threats of strikes by unions or lockouts by management, threats to harm the other party's reputation, or threats to break off negotiations—can be useful when a negotiator needs to underscore the absolute importance of a point being made. In essence, threats are if–then statements with serious negative consequences attached: "If you do X, then I will be forced to do Y."

Because of their dramatic nature and the emotional responses they can evoke, threats may be tempting to use (see Chapter 2). In fact, threats are probably used less frequently than one might expect, for several reasons. First, the other person's reaction to a threat is hard to predict. A second reason is that it is hard to know how menacing the threat appears to the other party. Often threats appear more powerful to the people who make them than they do to those on the receiving end. Third, a threatened party has the option to "call the bluff," forcing the negotiator who made the threat to carry it out. Often, following through on a threat will cost more than negotiators are willing to pay (Lytle, Brett, and Shapiro, 1999), and not following through can make a negotiator lose credibility. Finally, threats may produce compliance (a short-term change in behavior to avoid the consequences), but they do not usually produce commitment (a genuine and lasting change in attitude or belief). As we have pointed out, negotiating parties often want to reach an agreement they can live with. People can find many ways to avoid or undermine arrangements with which they were forced to comply but to which they are not committed.

How a threat is constructed and delivered can determine its effectiveness. Research suggests that threats can be effective if they increase the fear level of the recipient of the message (Boster and Mongeau, 1984; Sutton, 1982). Consider, for example, a manager who is negotiating with another about the flow of work between their two departments; the first manager intimates that if an agreement is not reached, the other manager will be portrayed to higher management as uncooperative. To be most effective, this kind of message should be accompanied by both a suggested alternative action that will reduce or eliminate the likelihood that the feared outcome will occur. Also, the effectiveness of a threat may depend on its timing and form. Sinaceur and Neale (2005) showed that threats made early in a negotiation are more effective when made *implicitly* (i.e., suggesting that there will be negative consequences without explicitly stating what that will entail). On the other hand, threats made late in the negotiation were more effective when they are *explicit*. Negotiators in this study saw explicit threats that came early and implicit threats that came later as unduly aggressive, which may explain their tactical ineffectiveness.

4. Violate the Receiver's Expectations   In *All the King's Men,* Robert Penn Warren (1946) describes a scene in which Willy Stark, the demagogic candidate for governor, is about to speak to a group of wealthy citizens to raise funds for his campaign. The citizens support neither his radical proposals nor his aggressive manner of speech. When he arrives, Stark is conservatively dressed and greets them in a quiet, relaxed manner. In a conversational tone, he proceeds to describe some modest proposals for social change, along with some sensible ways of financing them. His audience is at first surprised, then impressed, and finally won over. Stark is employing the technique of *violating expectations.* People who argue positions that are thought to be counter to their self-interest are generally more persuasive because they violate the receiver's expectation about what the sender should be advocating (O'Keefe, 1990). For instance, an automobile mechanic recently suggested that one of the authors of this book should use higher octane gas in his car to reduce maintenance and save money. This message was persuasive because the mechanic was arguing against his own self-interest (future auto repair revenue) when he suggested the change in fuel (his business does not sell gasoline).

Another way that receivers' expectations can be violated occurs when they expect one style of delivery from the speaker and then experience a very different style. For example, when one expects to be subjected to intense language (loud, volatile, provocative, etc.), one prepares defenses and counterarguments. If one instead encounters moderate, casual, reasonable language, one can relax one's defenses, listen to the message less critically, and be more likely to be persuaded (Miller and Burgoon, 1979). Great orators such as Winston Churchill and Martin Luther King Jr. used this style, frequently modulating the intensity of their voices to hold the audience's attention. Although this is not a stylistic tactic that everyone can use, skilled orators have a valuable tool at their disposal. This process can also work in reverse—an emotionally intense speaker may equally persuade audiences who were expecting quiet, controlled, highly rational discourse.

More generally, Barry (2001) proposed a model of interpersonal influence that revolves around violating expectations of influence targets as a way to increase one's effectiveness as an influencer. The model proposes that violated expectations will alter how the target of influence attends to an influence-seeking message. For example, if an influence seeker unexpectedly uses friendly tactics in what has up until now been a formal or aloof relationship, the target may become favorably disposed to comply and engage in diminished cognitive scrutiny of the message itself. Conversely, negative arousal created by (for example) an unexpectedly direct or assertive request may inhibit influence if the violation of expectations leads the target to scrutinize the message more closely. A clever study by Santos, Leve, and Pratkanis (1994) illustrated the compliance-gaining benefits of "unexpected" requests. Researchers acting as panhandlers asked some passers-by for a quarter (a "typical" request) and others for 17 cents or 37 cents (a "strange" request). Strange requests elicited significantly higher rates of compliance in the form of a willingness to give money, and they also elicited more questions from those approached about the reasons behind needing money.

Section Summary

In summary, negotiators need to take care when they construct a message to persuade another party to their point of view. Assuming the target of influence is motivated and able to pay attention to the persuasive appeal, then messages that are well reasoned, evidence-based, and logical will successfully persuade (Crano and Prislin, 2006). Aspects of the message content, message structure, and delivery style can all influence the extent to which a message meets these criteria and hence is persuasive. In other words, how one says something can be as important as what one has to say, and if the other party is not persuaded by the arguments, then perhaps the negotiator did not construct the message effectively. When messages are well crafted and influence does successfully occur through the "central route," the change in the target's attitudes is more likely to be long lasting and resistant to counterinfluence (Petty, Haugtvedt, and Smith, 1995).

Peripheral Routes to Influence

Thus far, we have focused on organizing the structure and content of the message in order to create leverage through the "central" route to influence (refer back to the left-hand side of Figure 8.1). In this section, we consider ways that a person can influence others through the "peripheral" route (the right-hand side of Figure 8.1). In such cases, the receiver attends less to the substance of persuasive arguments and is instead susceptible to more "automatic" influence through subtle cues. This usually occurs when the target of influence is either *unmotivated* or *unable* to attend carefully to the substance contained within a persuasive message (Petty and Briñol, 2008). As we suggested earlier, persuasion that occurs through the peripheral route is less likely to bring about real attitude change, more likely to last a shorter time, and more vulnerable to counterinfluence (Petty et al., 1995).

In our discussion of peripheral routes to influence we draw in part on the work of psychologist Robert Cialdini (2001), who argues that this type of persuasion can work almost automatically, like an eye blink or a startle response. Cialdini spent many years investigating why people comply with requests that, upon further reflection, they would rather not have agreed to. His research represents a skillful blend of laboratory investigation and observation of "compliance experts" such as salespeople, fund-raisers, and marketing and advertising experts. The insights that emerge are useful not only for achieving successful influence in negotiation and other contexts, but also for avoiding being a "victim" of these persuasive traps.

Our discussion of peripheral routes to influence considers three sets of strategies: message aspects, attributes of the persuader (the message "source"), and elements of the influence context.

Aspects of Messages That Foster Peripheral Influence

When targets of influence are unmotivated or unable to pay close attention to the influence seeker's message, they are susceptible to being influenced by message elements that exist apart from the actual arguments involved. We discuss three such elements here: the way in which the influence seeker chooses to order those arguments, the format through which arguments are conveyed, and the use of distraction to interfere with the target's ability to think effortfully about the arguments in play.

Message Order   In preparing a persuasive argument, negotiators usually have one major point, piece of information, or illustration that is particularly important or compelling. Where should it be placed in the message? At the beginning? In the middle? At the end?

Research tells us one thing clearly—do not place the important point in the middle of the message (Bettinghaus, 1966). So should it be at the beginning or at the end? When the topics are familiar, interesting, or controversial to the receiver, the important points should be made early, exposing the receiver to the *primacy effect:* the first item in a long list of items is the one most likely to be remembered. Thus, the negotiator should state messages that are attractive to the receiver early, before they present something the receiver may not want to hear. In contrast, when the topic is uninteresting, unfamiliar, or not very important to the receiver, the most critical point should be placed at the end of the message to take advantage of the *recency effect:* the tendency for the last item presented to be the best remembered. The recency effect should be considered when the message is likely to be contrary to the receiver's current point of view (Clark, 1984; Rosnow and Robinson, 1967).

Format   In our discussion of communication (Chapter 6), we addressed how negotiation is affected by the communication channels through which it can occur (face to face, telephone, e-mail, etc.). The same goes for influence, where certain arguments or appeals may be more or less effective depending on the channel in use or the format of the presentation (Barry and Fulmer, 2004). One way that a choice of message format can induce peripheral influence is if it elicits a snap judgment regarding the legitimacy of the argument. For instance, Herb Cohen (1980) suggests that written rules carry more weight than those given verbally. Thus, a principle could be seen as more credible or believable, and hence more likely to be adopted, if it is in a policy manual or the fine print of a contract than if it is merely expressed orally. A recent study by Guadagnoa and Cialdini (2007) found gender differences in the effectiveness of persuasion through different communication channels. Compared with men, women in the study were less receptive to persuasive messages sent by e-mail unless there was a prior relationship with the sender. Women also reported less liking for the communicator when e-mail was the vehicle for the influence attempt.

Distractions   One factor that makes the persuasion process complex is that people start to defend themselves against being influenced as soon as they suspect that someone is trying to persuade them. As they listen, part of their attention might be devoted to what is being said, but a large portion is also devoted to developing counterarguments (Brock, 1963; Festinger and Maccoby, 1964). Persuasion efforts are more effective if they can reduce the other party's efforts to develop defensive counterarguments. One way to do this is to have a *distraction* occur at the same time the message is sent. Distractions apparently absorb the effort that the other party normally would put into building counterarguments and leave the listener "vulnerable to the message appeals" (Reardon, 1981, p. 192). In other words, when receivers are distracted, they are less able to engage in issue-relevant thinking (Petty and Brock, 1981), and hence they may be more susceptible to processing peripheral cues that may push them toward a particular choice. For example, during an oral presentation of the economic advantages of an offer, a negotiator could produce papers with charts and graphs, hand them to the other party, and help that person turn from one chart to another as the oral presentation continues. Presumably, the charts and graphs absorb that part of the other party's attention that might normally go into formulating counterarguments. Distractions seem to inhibit the receiver's subvocalization (what people say to themselves as they hear a message). Sometimes subvocalizations are counterarguments, which occur when the receiver is opposed to or cautious about the message, but they can be supportive arguments as well. When receivers like what is being said (e.g., a friend trying to persuade you to take a second helping of chocolate cake), subvocalizations will encourage you to accept the offer. In a situation like this, a receiver who wants to protect him- or herself from temptation should in turn create distractions (Petty, Wells, and Brock, 1976).

Source Characteristics That Foster Peripheral Influence

When recipients of a persuasive message are unmotivated or unable to attend closely to the substance of the persuasive appeal, they become vulnerable to source effects. In other words, someone who is not paying close attention to the message may be unduly influenced by the characteristics of the person or organization delivering the message. A wide variety of source effects can potentially have an effect on the recipient of a persuasive message. We group them here into three broad categories: credibility, attractiveness, and authority.

Source Credibility   During a negotiation, both parties exchange information, opinions, and interpretations. What, and how much, should be believed? On one hand, there are often strong incentives for negotiators to mislead each other (see also Chapter 9 on ethics). On the other hand, negotiators have to accept and believe at least some of the information they are given, or successful negotiation is impossible. As a negotiator, you cannot check every fact and statement. The more information one is willing to accept from the other party without independent verification, the easier the task will be. The reverse is also true—the more credible you are to the other party, the more persuasive you will be.

To illustrate, let's assume that you are buying a house. The sellers tell you that they have three other parties coming to see the house this afternoon; two of them are being transferred to this area and have only one day to locate a house. If this is true, and you like the house, it would be to your advantage to make an offer now rather than delay your decision and possibly find that one of the afternoon visitors has bought the house. But are the sellers' statements true? No doubt the sellers know whether or not there are other potential buyers coming that same day; hence, there is no question that they are competent or qualified to have good information. The issue is whether or not they are credible.

There has been quite a lot of research over the last several decades demonstrating how and when the credibility of the source of an influence attempt matters (Pornpitakpan, 2004). Many factors contribute to source credibility. Here we discuss several that negotiators can control, beginning with the most important ones: qualifications, trustworthiness, and self-presentation.

1. Qualifications and Expertise   When people are determining how much to believe another person, they often ask, "Is this person in a position to possess the information he or she claims to have? Is he or she competent and qualified?" The stronger the person's perceived qualifications and expertise, the higher the credibility (Swenson, Nash, and Roos, 1984). Judgments about qualifications can substitute for judgments about the quality of the arguments that source is delivering—that's what makes source credibility a "peripheral" route to influence. Research studies have shown when people are not motivated to think deeply about the arguments they are hearing, they will let qualifications of the source of the argument determine whether or not to be persuaded, even when the arguments are weak (e.g., Chaiken and Maheswaran, 1994).

Expertise can be established in a number of ways. Sometimes your occupation, education, or past experiences will establish your qualifications and therefore the perception of your competence. At other times, there are no obvious ways to make your expertise known. Stereotypes can lead others to see you as lacking the requisite expertise to be credible. Some might see women as lacking knowledge about mechanical things; others might view men as underinformed about child care or cooking. In situations where you are unknown or apt to be viewed stereotypically, it's worth making an extra effort to establish qualifications and expertise. One way to do this is to work your education or credentials into the conversation (e.g., "In law school I learned that . . . "). Another is to cite credible sources of information (e.g., "A story in this morning's *New York Times* said . . . "). Finally, try asking questions or drawing conclusions that could only be derived from in-depth, firsthand knowledge or experience.

2. Reputation for Trustworthiness and Integrity   As the target of a persuasion attempt, it is natural to wonder, "Is this person reporting accurately what he or she knows? Is he or she personally believable or trustworthy? Is this a person of integrity?" (Berlo, Lemert, and Mertz, 1966). Integrity is character—the personal values and ethics that ground your behavior in high moral principles. Integrity is the quality that assures people you can be trusted, you will be honest, and you will do as you say. If people trust you with confidential information, you will not disclose that information to others. Finally, if you make an agreement, you will abide by its terms and conditions and follow through on it (Shapiro, Sheppard, and Cheraskin, 1992).

Conversely, people with a reputation for being dishonest or insincere have an extremely difficult time in negotiations—they tend not to be believed, even when they tell the truth. Research has shown that negotiators with reputations for self-interested behavior elicit negative reactions that can dampen the entire negotiation process, leading to poorer outcomes. Even when the negotiator is known to be an expert, a poor reputation tends to overshadow expertise (Tinsley, O'Conner, and Sullivan, 2002). A reputation for being dishonest is very difficult to change, so it is not surprising that professional negotiators work very hard to protect their reputation. While negotiators using a competitive strategy are often expected to inflate, magnify, and distort in order to present things in the best possible light for their side, a one-time success may contribute directly to future credibility problems. It is therefore critical for negotiators to consider the long-term consequences of their behavior if they are to be trusted by others (we introduced the role of trust in Chapter 3 and will explore it in greater depth in Chapter 10).

3. Self-Presentation   People appear more or less credible because of their presence—the way they present themselves to others. Someone who seems hesitant, confused, or uncertain when giving information is not as convincing as a person who appears calm, confident, and comfortable. A friendly, open person is easier to converse with (and easier to believe) than someone who is distant, abrasive, or haughty. A person with a dynamic vocal style and a strong delivery is often more persuasive than one without these attributes. Communicators can create a favorable presence in several ways. It is not an earth-shaking revelation to note that how you dress, speak, and behave will influence how credible you appear to others. What may not be as obvious is how you should adjust your appearance and style to increase (or avoid eroding) your credibility. Should you wear a suit for an interview, even if you usually wear jeans and a T-shirt? Should you adopt some of the local speech pronunciations and drop those that are native to you? Is a member of the clergy more effective in clerical garb or in street clothes? In general, researchers have found that it is best to be "normal" (Bettinghaus, 1980), meaning to act appropriately, naturally, and without affectation. A Harvard-educated politician with a New England accent who tries to spice his language with "Aw, shucks" and "y'all" in Texas will not appear normal; neither will a college student who drops in to buy a Porsche dressed in muddy boots and grimy work clothes.

4. First Impressions   Self-presentation can be especially important for establishing credibility early in a relationship or negotiation event. Put simply, first impressions matter. How people dress, behave, and speak can be enormously important in the first few minutes of meeting, especially with a stranger. When meeting others for the first time, people generally tend to evaluate them positively rather than negatively (Greenberg and Miller, 1966). People frequently remain open-minded during the first meeting; if they do form a first impression, they often err toward the positive viewpoint. Although this bias may seem to be an advantage in helping persuade someone you have recently met, keep in mind that it is probably working the other way as well.

5. Status Differences   Status is signaled by a variety of criteria: occupation, age, education level, the neighborhood where a person lives, dress, type of automobile, and the like. A president of a major corporation, for example, has more status than a university professor, but less than a Supreme Court Justice. Status confers credibility, which in turn can make someone influential, in several ways. First, status gives people visibility, which allows them to get attention and be heard. It also confers prestige, lending the image that certain people are worth listening to (Bettinghaus, 1980). However, a status difference may also increase resistance, because listeners may expect to be persuaded by a high-status communicator, and therefore increase their defenses against the effort. Persuaders need to decide whether they should enforce a status difference (act or dress consistently with their status) or minimize the difference by acting or dressing more like the listener.

6. Intention to Persuade   Does a negotiator initially come across as a huckster or as cool, poised, and polished? While people may give the benefit of the doubt in their initial judgment, the more they detect that a negotiator's mission is to influence their views, the more suspicious and resistant they may become. For instance, when the phone rings unexpectedly, it is often easy to identify the telemarketer who mispronounces your name and tries to involve you in friendly chit-chat ("How are you this evening?") while she eases into her prepared sales pitch ("I'm glad you're well. Do you ever have problems with . . . "). By the time she has gotten to the sales pitch, your defenses are most likely already well fortified. In contrast, communicating with natural enthusiasm, sincerity, and spontaneity may take the edge off persuasive communication, reduce defensive reactions, and enhance the speaker' credibility. Many skillful negotiators and persuaders may therefore assume a mild-mannered or even slightly confused demeanor to minimize the negative impact of a hard, persuasive style while giving or getting the information they need.

7. Associates Whom you associate with also can influence how you are perceived, in terms of both status and expertise. Judicious name dropping (i.e., mentioning well-known people who are also credible and prestigious) and even arranging for introductions or endorsements by people who can add to your reputation can be useful steps. There is, of course, a downside to invoking associates if it isn't done skillfully: the line between being perceived as admirably "well-connected" and as a shameless "name-dropper" can be a fine one indeed.

8. Persistence and Tenacity Persistence and tenacity are valuable personal qualities in a negotiator. Children are often considered great negotiators because they are so wonderfully persistent in pursuing what they want. Saying "no" usually does not stop the child from asking; children find all kinds of creative ways to persist in trying to achieve their objective (the candy bar, the toy, watching the TV show). From watching how children persist as negotiators, we can learn that part of persistence is doggedly pursuing the objective but that another part is finding new, unique ways to pursue the same request. The effective use of persistence doesn't mean pursuing your goals blindly and rigidly because you can be effectively rebuffed; instead, it means displaying creativity in finding novel approaches to pursuing the goal. Persistent people are comfortable being in a contentious mode with others—they don't fear conflict and try to escape simply because of a difference of opinion or views. They are persistent, but they are also flexible, redefining strategy and approach as times and conditions change.

Persistence can therefore help enhance a source's credibility to the extent that the target of the message isn't annoyed by that persistence, but rather comes to see it as a sign that the communicator is dedicated and tenacious. Box 8.1 presents an intriguing example of how hearing something repeatedly leads people to assume it must come from a credible source.

Source Attractiveness People will treat others better when they like them than when they don't (Roskos-Ewoldsen, Bichsel, and Hoffman, 2002). They are less likely to feel that attractive negotiators will be dishonest or attempt to coerce them (Tedeschi, Schlenker, and Bonoma, 1973). They are more likely to accept their influence, to believe them, and to trust them (Chaiken, 1986). Being nice and pleasant is a logical step to being more persuasive. Personal attractiveness may increase persuasiveness for a number of reasons. People may have a tendency to let their guard down and trust attractive people more readily. Attractive people may receive a lot of attention, or they may cause others to imitate them in order to be more like them (Trenholm, 1989). Personal attractiveness also increases liking (O'Keefe, 1990). An individual can enhance his or her personal attractiveness to a target of influence or a negotiating opponent in several ways, discussed next.

1. Friendliness A critically important attribute that a negotiator can have is the ability to be friendly and outgoing and to establish personal relationships with others—particularly the other parties in the negotiation. Warmth; empathy; and simple, direct, personal interest in others all help to soften the harder edges of other influence tactics. Rather than immediately getting down to business, successful negotiators use friendliness to make the other party feel comfortable and at ease, to get to know the other negotiator and show an interest

BOX 8.1

If a Message Is Believable, Does That Make the Source Credible?

Apparently so, to judge from a clever study conducted by researchers Alison Fragale and Chip Heath at Stanford University. Their experiment was part of a larger investigation of why rumors spread and what it is that leads people to believe that a rumor is accurate. A rumor is more believable, they assumed, when it is thought to come from a credible or trusted source. That seems logical enough, but does it work the other way around? Will people assume that if a message is believable then it must have come from a credible source?

To answer this question, Fragale and Heath presented experimental subjects with several "urban legends"—rumors—regarding food contamination. (Two of the allegations used in the study were "The wax used to line Cup-o-Noodles cups has been shown to cause cancer in rats" and "Jack-in-the-Box has fired two employees for spitting in customers' burgers before serving them".) The participants in the experiment saw some of the statements just two times, but they viewed some of them five times. Participants were then told that each of the allegations was originally reported in one of two places—*Consumer Reports* (a high-

credibility source) or the *National Enquirer* (a low-credibility source)—and were asked to say which they thought was most likely the source for each allegation.

Results showed that participants in the experiment were more likely to say an allegation came from *Consumer Reports* if they saw it five times than just two times. In other words, merely seeing the exact same rumor a few more times led people to infer that it came from a higher credibility source. If repetition leads to belief (the more you hear something, the more you believe it), then these studies show that people are more likely to assume that a "believable" message must come from a credible source. Ordinarily we assume that communicators try to enhance their credibility in order to get audiences to believe what they have to say; this research shows that in some situations if you can get them to buy your message, enhancement of your credibility may follow.

Source: Adapted from A. R. Fragale and C. Heath, "Evolving Informational Credentials: The (Mis)attribution of Believable Facts to Credible Sources," *Personality and Social Psychology Bulletin* (2004), pp. 225–36.

in his or her situation, and to discover things that both parties may have in common. As we mentioned earlier, requests are more favorably received when preceded by informal dialogue (Dolinski et al., 2001). Friendly, outgoing negotiators are also likely to use reward and praise to encourage and support the other party, whereas less friendly negotiators will be more likely to use criticism and verbal punishment.

2. Ingratiation Ingratiation involves enhancing the other's self-image or reputation through statements or actions, and thus enhancing one's own image in the same way (Jones, 1964; Vonk, 2002). Flattering another person by giving compliments is perhaps the most obvious form of ingratiation. Handing out flattery presumably induces others to like you and be more prone to accept your persuasive arguments (Gordon, 1996). Negotiators congratulate others on their excellent and thorough preparation, their considerate suggestions, or their willingness to listen or compromise or be reasonable. Compliments can be a potent means of ingratiation, not only because people like to receive them, but also because the norm of reciprocity leaves the other party with the obligation to return something for the compliment (Cialdini, 2001). And there is no denying its potential usefulness: Ellis and colleagues (2002) showed that ingratiation tactics used during a job interview positively influenced the reviewer's perception of the applicant, even moreso than the applicant's self-promotion tactics (Ellis, West, Ryan, and DeShon, 2002). Because it is an obvious option, ingratiation is used often; but if used poorly, it can backfire. When people are complimented for attributes they do not have or actions they know they did not perform well, or when the praise seems excessive, they are likely to become wary, wondering about the ingratiator's hidden agenda or ulterior motives.

3. Likability   The liking principle is quite straightforward: people you like have more influence over you (see our discussion of similarity under source factors earlier in this chapter). If you like the communicator, you are more likely to be persuaded by him or her and less likely to contest a weak or counterattitudinal argument (Roskos-Ewoldsen et al., 2002). However, research has shown that likability is less important than other credibility factors, such as expertise (Eagly and Chaiken, 1975).

The effects of the liking principle are insidious. Liking can occur through many different approaches, and defending against them all would be impossible. Deborah Tannen, in her well-known work on gender and communication differences (see Tannen, 1990), suggests that compared to men, women practice more "rapport-talk," in which their objective is to establish connections and negotiate the relationship, while, compared to women, men practice more "report-talk" in order to preserve status differences in some form of a hierarchical social order. Cialdini (2001) points out that it would be useless to try to prevent yourself from liking others. Rather, you should let the liking occur and then explore why you like the other person. If you find that you like the person more than you would typically like another person under similar circumstances, then it is time to be wary. Separating liking the other party from an evaluation of the deal should be enough to moderate the influence of the liking principle in your negotiations.

4. Helping the Other Party   There are many ways one party can help the other party in a negotiation: by doing a favor, allowing extra time, providing confidential information, complying with a request, or helping with a constituency. Negotiators can help the other party avoid being caught by surprise. For example, an automobile salesperson may say to the customer, "In a moment I'm going to take you in to talk to the sales manager about the amount we are going to allow on your present car. You may hear me say some unfavorable things about your car. Don't let that bother you—we'll still get the figure you and I agreed on." By "helping" you with his manager, the salesperson hopes you will help him by buying a new car from him. In another example, during negotiations on the sale of a large parcel of land to a major corporation, the seller privately told the company executive handling the negotiation about a forthcoming zoning change that would benefit the company. The executive got the credit for uncovering this inside information, and the seller was not materially affected one way or the other by sharing it (but got the deal).

5. Perceived Similarity   When meeting for the first time, people often try to find something they have in common. Perhaps they attended the same school, grew up in the same neighborhood, or have friends in common. The basic idea that we like those who are like us—known as the similarity-attraction hypothesis (Byrne, 1971)—is among the most robust and reliable findings in social psychology (e.g., Machinov and Monteil, 2002). (An alternative view—the dissimilarity-repulsion hypothesis [Rosenbaum, 1986]—is that we dislike those who are different, rather than liking those who are similar.) In a two-party

BOX 8.2 The Role of Anger and Compassion in Negotiation

Does the expression of emotion actually affect negotiation processes and outcomes? In one study, Keith Allred and his colleagues (Allred, Mallozzi, Matsui, and Raia, 1997) examined whether the expression of anger and compassion would exert influence on negotiation by affecting how the parties feel about each other, the outcomes each derived individually, and the amount of joint gain. The researchers found that expressing high anger and low compassion led negotiators to have less desire to work together in the future and to achieve fewer joint gains, but did not affect the ability of individual negotiators to reap greater gains for themselves. This was one of the first in a growing body of research studies examining the role of emotional expression and understanding within the negotiation process.

Source: Adapted from K. G. Allred, J. S. Mallozzi, F. Matsui, and C. P. Raia, "The Influence of Anger and Compassion on Negotiation Performance," *Organizational Behavior and Human Decision Processes* 70 (1997), pp. 175–87.

exchange such as a negotiation, the more similarities they find, the more bonds they establish, the better both parties feel, and the more receptive they will be to each other's messages and efforts at persuasion (Oldmeadow, Platow, Foddy, and Anderson, 2003). A useful negotiating tactic, therefore, is to identify and discuss experiences, characteristics, and opinions you hold in common with the other party. If you see pictures of a yacht on an office wall, you might mention your own interest in sailing. The other party's winter suntan might cue you to mention your own trips to the tropics or the ski slopes. But if it is to your advantage to find and explore commonalities in experience, attitude, and background with the other party, it is also to your disadvantage to highlight those areas where you differ. There is no point to starting a conversation on a politically controversial topic when you know or suspect that the other holds a different view.

6. Emotion   We discussed emotion earlier in this chapter in connection with the use of language to construct a message, but emotion can also be a source factor. Emotion combined with persistence leads to assertiveness and determination. Used effectively, emotion may enhance a message source's attractiveness by instilling in listeners the belief that the speaker holds appealing deep-seated values (this may also enhance the speaker's credibility).

As we discussed in Chapter 5, expressions of fear, anger, or enthusiasm can become an integral part of negotiations—particularly over issues about which you feel strongly (see Box 8.2). Emotion can be powerful because it offers a stark contrast to the expectation that negotiation is a cool, calm, rational exchange of information, driven by logical analysis of outcome maximization and economic valuation of alternatives. Yet negotiators frequently do not behave according to the principles of logic and economic rationality. In addition, when everyone else is being rational, it is frequently the person who expresses strong feelings, gets angry, or makes an impassioned speech in favor of a proposed solution who carries the day (Henderson, 1973). Union organizers, charismatic politicians, leaders of social movements, evangelists, and others whose aim is to organize and mobilize supporters all understand the importance of arousing emotion through their appeals.

An important aspect of the role of emotion in influence and negotiation is being aware that not everyone will respond to emotional appeals in the same way. Research (DeSteno, Petty, Rucker, Wegener, and Braverman, 2004) suggests that the use of emotion as a source of influence is most effective when the emotional overtones of the message match the receiver's emotional state. This study showed that individuals who were sad were most influenced by a message that conveyed sadness; likewise angry individuals were best influenced by an angry message. Another study linked receptivity to emotional arguments with personality traits. In this research (Haddock, Maio, Arnold, and Huskinson, 2008), people who are dispositionally oriented more toward cognitive rather than emotional processing were more receptive to cognitive (informational) arguments; others who by nature are more in need of emotionality were more receptive to emotional arguments.

Finally, be careful not to assume that your arguments will be better received if your target is in a good mood. Many influence-seekers probably figure it will help to put a listener in a good mood (maybe tell a joke or make a light-hearted comment), and then make the pitch. It sounds reasonable, but research shows that the connection between moods and receptivity to arguments is more complicated. Several studies have shown that people in a happy mood are less likely to scrutinize the content of an argument, whereas people in a negative mood are more likely to do so (Hullett, 2005 synthesizes this research literature). Accordingly, as Hullett observes, "attitude change resulting from strong arguments may be best accomplished when targeting people in bad moods" (p. 439). Solid arguments directed at "happy" people are likely to work when the (happy) person is already disposed to like or agree with the argument, but if you want your listener to truly scrutinize your message and be persuaded, putting them in a good mood beforehand is not necessary a successful strategy.

Authority   The principle of authority is quite simple: people with authority have more influence than those without authority. Researchers have long been interested in the effects of authority figures on human behavior. Stanley Milgram's (1974) classic studies of obedience to authority suggest that people will go to great lengths when their behavior is legitimized by an authority figure. Most people will obey the orders of a person wearing a uniform, even if there is no war or apparent emergency. This, too, is an effect of the principle of authority.

In negotiation, the principle of authority can be used in many ways. Cialdini (2001) observes that the use of a title, such as *doctor* or *professor,* gives the user more authority and thus more influence. A friend of one of the authors uses the title *doctor* whenever ordering airline tickets. He found out early in his career that airlines would telephone doctors when there was a flight delay but would ignore the other passengers. This simple illustration shows the esteem with which some titles (or positions) are held in society. Cialdini also suggests that authority is more than position; it can further lead to attributions of expertise. He tells the story of a waiter who, regardless of what patrons order, recommends something else on the menu that is cheaper because the original dish "is not as good tonight as it normally is" (pp. 198–99). In doing so, the waiter establishes his authority for later (more expensive) advice about the meal, such as expensive desserts (and perhaps also induces diners to reciprocate his generous advice when it's time to leave a tip).

Authority can take different forms and yield different outcomes. Researchers have distinguished between two broad uses of authority in influence-seeking: (1) authority based on one's personal expertise or credibility and (2) authority based on a person's legitimate position in an existing social hierarchy (Cialdini and Goldstein, 2004). The first form—expertise—has been labeled a "soft" influence tactic, whereas the second form—authority derived from one's position—is a "harsh" tactic (Koslowsky, Schwarzwald, and Ashuri, 2001). Koslowsky and colleagues, in a field study of influence behavior among nurses and

NON SEQUITUR   BY WILEY

From *The Wall Street Journal*. Used with permission of Cartoon Features Syndicate.

their supervisors, found that subordinates' compliance with requests and job satisfaction were higher when supervisors relied more on the use of soft tactics. These findings seem to suggest that establishing your personal expertise is preferred to highlighting differences in positional power, especially if the goal is not just simple short-term compliance, but longer term relational benefits as well.

Cialdini (2001, p. 197) offers the following advice for dealing with authority figures who may have influence over you. Ask two questions: "Is this authority truly an expert?" and "How truthful can you expect this expert to be?" The first question forces you to verify that the person really does have expertise in the situation and not just the appearance (title, attire) of expertise. The second question brings into focus the motive of the alleged authority. If someone, like the waiter just described, gives you some negative information before another suggestion, he or she may in fact be manipulating you into thinking that he or she is honest when this is not the case.

Aspects of Context That Foster Peripheral Influence

Finally, we explore aspects of the situation beyond the message itself and the sender of the message that create opportunities to pursue the peripheral route to influence. Five strategies are discussed: reciprocity, commitment, social proof, scarcity, and reward and punishment.

Reciprocity   The norm of *reciprocity* has been studied for years by philosophers, anthropologists, sociologists, and other social scientists. This norm suggests that when you receive something from another person, you should respond in the future with a favor in return. This norm is thought to be pan-cultural in that groups around the world appear to respect it (Gouldner, 1960). We alluded to the reciprocity norm in the previous section when discussing personal attractiveness of sources and some receiver factors.

The norm of reciprocity plays an important role in negotiations. Negotiators give concessions and expect concessions in return. When they treat the other party politely, they expect a corresponding politeness. The norm can also be used to obtain compliance from another negotiator. For instance, Negotiator A does a small favor for Negotiator B and later asks for a larger favor from B in return. The net advantage goes to A. Although one may think that the norm of reciprocity should apply only to favors of the same size, this does not appear to be the case. In fact, many sales pitches rely on giving the consumer a small gift early in an exchange and then asking for a large concession from the consumer later. In parts of Africa, particularly Nigeria, there is a custom of giving a small gift, called *dash,* to a potential customer soon after he or she has walked into a shop—before there has ever been a chance to identify the customer's needs. The shopkeeper will claim, legitimately, that it is a gift, no strings, yours to keep even if you turn and walk out of the shop at this minute. However, knowing human nature, the shopkeeper does not really expect this to happen and is rarely disappointed. The shopkeeper knows that people like to receive gifts and will develop positive feelings toward those who give them. Those who leave without buying often give the gift back, even though they know it is "free."

Similar opportunities exist in other negotiation situations. A compliment, such as a reference to the other party's positive behavior in a prior discussion, will make that person feel good and set the scene for him or her to act positively. Giving a quick concession on an issue that the other party wants will both please that party and create the implicit obligation for him or her to do the same. Too often negotiators begin by holding every advantage close to their chest and giving things away grudgingly, believing that this is the best way to succeed. Such rigid behavior is no more likely to lead to graceful and successful negotiation than it is to graceful and successful acting or public speaking. Flexibility and adaptability are necessary in all three.

Given the apparent powerfulness of the norm of reciprocity, how can the negotiator counter its effects? One possibility is to refuse all favors in a negotiation setting, but this would probably cause more problems than it resolves. For instance, refusing a cup of coffee from your host may remove the effects of the norm of reciprocity but at the same time may insult the host, especially if five minutes later you go out to get a cup of coffee yourself. Perhaps the other person was simply being polite. Perhaps he or she was setting a positive tone for the meeting. Or perhaps he or she was trying to use the norm of reciprocity to create a small sense of indebtedness.[7]

How should the negotiator respond to such favors? Cialdini (2001) suggests that you should respond politely to a favor and accept what is offered if it is something you want. If it becomes apparent that the favor was an attempt at manipulation, however, then you should redefine the event as a trick rather than a favor. This will remove the obligation of the rule of reciprocity because the "rule says that favors are to be met with favors; it does not require that tricks be met with favors" (Cialdini, 2001, p. 47).

Commitment   Researchers have long recognized that once people have decided something, they can be remarkably persistent in their beliefs. This process has been labeled *commitment* to a position, and it relies heavily on the common need that people have to appear consistent, both to themselves and to others. Most people are familiar with the bait-and-switch sales technique. Unscrupulous organizations advertise merchandise for sale at an incredibly low price but "run out" of stock by the time you arrive at the store. They then try to sell you alternate merchandise at a higher price. Why does this technique work? One reason is that once you have made the decision to purchase a product (a commitment), you almost automatically follow through with the commitment (even at a higher price). Thus, if you

BOX 8.3   **Commitment: A Cautionary Tale**

In his youth, one of the authors of this book decided to purchase a used MG sports car. He tells this story:

> After searching the city where I lived and finding only one car within my price range ($2,400), I test-drove the car, discussed the price with the salesman, made an offer to buy the car, completed most of the paperwork, was loaned the car overnight, and came back to sign the deal the next day. At this time the salesman embarrassedly told me that he was unaware the car had "electric overdrive" until his manager had told him, and that he could not sell the car for the agreed-on price. Rather, the salesman would have to charge an additional $350 for the overdrive. Of course, he would allow me to change my mind and not buy the car. I bought the car, but after driving away I was convinced that the salesman's bargaining strategy had been a manipulation to induce compliance. I could have confronted the dealer, but there was no proof that the dealer was dishonest (and who would believe a young consumer versus an established car dealer?). The consequences of this decision cost the dealership much more than the extra $350 it received for

the car. I told many of my friends to stay away from the dealer because of the way he did business. I didn't have any repairs done at the dealer after the warranty on the car expired.

If you think that an honest mistake occurred and the salesman really had forgotten the overdrive, his behavior during the warranty period should convince you that wasn't the case. The only repair needed under warranty was to replace the tachometer. The warranty stated that the dealer would pay for the parts and 50 percent of the labor. The salesman told me that replacing the tachometer in an MG was very difficult: the dashboard had to be removed, and many pieces under the dashboard had to be removed in order to pass the wires. He advised me that it would take six hours to install the part and suggested that I leave the car with them for the day. I didn't believe a word the salesman said. I diligently followed the mechanic around the car until he went into the service manager's office for a brief discussion. When he returned he replaced the tachometer in 15 minutes. After paying for half of the labor cost, I drove away, never to return!

went to the store to buy the product at the fantastic sale price of $49.95, you will be more likely to buy the alternative product at $64.95, even though that price may never have gotten you to the store in the first place. (See Box 8.3 for a cautionary tale involving commitment to the purchase of a car.)

Commitment strategies are very powerful devices for making people comply. One way to increase commitment is to write things down. Cialdini (2001) notes that encyclopedia companies that have customers complete their own order forms have a far lower cancellation rate than those companies that have salespeople write out the form. Why? Writing it themselves seems to increase the commitment that the customers feel. It is as if they say to themselves, "I wouldn't have written it down if I didn't want it, would I?" Many consumer-product companies have people write testimonials about their products in order to enter a drawing for a prize. Why? Apparently, writing testimonials increases the commitment to buy the product (Cialdini, 2001). Research has shown that even signing a petition can increase your compliance with a request to do something more intrusive several days later (Freedman and Fraser, 1966). Researchers have called this the foot-in-the-door technique (Clark, 1984).

How can commitment work in a negotiation? Usually, it is incremental. Agreement to innocuous statements early in the negotiation may be used as a foundation for further and further concessions. Frequently, our own words and behaviors are used to extract further concessions. In the car example in Box 8.3, the buyer was more than pleased to pay the extra $350 because in the drive-around period, he had shown the car to many friends and told them about the purchase. Because the salesman had been nice enough to let the buyer take the car overnight even before signing a contract, the only fair thing to do was to let the salesman off the hook for his mistake by paying $350 more!

Commitment strategies are difficult to combat. Frequently, one will have already been influenced and agreed to something before even realizing that manipulation has taken place. To some extent, being forewarned about these techniques is being forearmed. Cialdini (2001) suggests that your body will send two types of warning signals when these techniques are in use. Either you will feel uncomfortable when subtle commitments are being made, or something in the deal will just not seem quite right. If you encounter these thoughts or feelings when negotiating, look out for use of a commitment strategy by the other party. At the very least, be aware of all the agreements you strike during a negotiation, even those small, innocuous ones. They may be the setup for the next move.

Social Proof   The principle of *social proof* suggests that people look to others to determine the correct response in many situations. This principle suggests that people often behave in certain ways because everyone else is doing so. Cialdini (2001) identifies this as the principle that makes laugh tracks effective on television comedies (see Fuller and Sheehy-Skeffington, 1974). It also explains why marketers like to allude to previously satisfied customers; if other people used the product and liked it, then it must be good. Celebrities are hired to endorse products for similar reasons.

In negotiation situations, the principle of social proof can act as a powerful influence strategy. Salespeople will show lists of happy customers, knowing that few people will take the time to verify the list. ("If it wasn't true, why would the salesperson show me the list?") Sweepstakes advertisements highlight previous winners and feature celebrities. Negotiators will talk about how popular their new product is and how sales have really increased this year. Real estate agents will be sure that you are aware that many other people are interested in the house that you are considering buying (see Fishbein and Azjen, 1975).

The principle of social proof works because questionable information ("everyone thinks this product is good") is given weight in decisions. Cialdini (2001) suggests that the way to dilute its effectiveness is to identify the false information and give it the weight it deserves. In negotiations, this means careful preparation and being aware of "facts" about the others' advocated views that do not seem to match your preparation. When the other party offers "evidence" about the popularity of an item, do not automatically trust that the other party is being completely honest; rather, ask the other to substantiate the claims. Even when there is a shortage of an item, be sure that you are behaving in your own best interests. Frequently, a planned delay ("let me sleep on it") will be enough to separate the influence of social proof from your own needs and interests.

Scarcity   The principle of *scarcity* suggests that when things are less available, they will have more influence. Cialdini (2001) describes how common sales strategies rely on the scarcity principle. Frequently, salespeople will tell customers that they are not sure if the product the customers would like to purchase is currently in stock. Before making the trip to the stockroom they ask if they should grab one before another salesperson gets it. Typically shoppers will say yes and will feel relieved (or lucky) when the salesperson returns with the "last one" in the store. This is the scarcity principle at work; people are easier to influence when they feel that they are obtaining a scarce resource.

In negotiation situations, the scarcity influence strategy may be operating whenever there appears to be a great demand for a product. Some organizations deliberately keep their products in short supply to give the appearance that they are very widely sought (e.g., popular Christmas toys). Car dealers suggest that you not wait too long before deciding on the color car you want because they have very few cars left and they are selling fast. Any time negotiators talk about "exclusive opportunities" and "time-limited offers," they are using the scarcity principle. Censorship also results in scarcity; banning a specific book in the library is guaranteed to increase the demand for it. (See Brehm, 1976, for further discussion of this phenomenon, known as *psychological reactance.*) Finally, auctions also rely on the principle of scarcity by selling unique (one-of-a-kind) pieces to the highest bidder—the more scarce the item, the higher the bids.

The scarcity principle is difficult to combat when used effectively. It creates in the victim an activity trap focused on obtaining the item and effectively suspends cognitive evaluation of the broader situation (Cialdini, 2001). Cialdini suggests that people need to be aware of the emotional trappings that this principle arouses; when confronted with a strong emotional response to obtain a scarce good, they should carefully evaluate their reasons for wanting the item in the first place.

Use of Reward and Punishment   In Chapter 7, we indicated that control over resources was a strong source of power. These resources can be used in at least two major ways. First, negotiators can use *exchange*—the process of offering resources or favors (promises and assistance) to secure the other's compliance and cooperation. Exchange is clearly a close cousin of bargaining in that the user either directly or implicitly suggests reciprocity—in short, "If I do X for you, will you do Y for me?" Exchange relies on resources as the power base, particularly resources that can be translated into rewards for the other—favors, benefits, incentives, treats, perks, and the like. Thus, exchange frequently invokes the use of promises and commitments as persuasive tools—obligations that you are willing to make in exchange for the other's cooperation, compliance, or commitment to give you what you want. Finally, exchange transactions are often negotiated so that the other party completes his or her obligation now, but chooses not to ask you to complete your obligation until some point in the future, either defined or undefined. By doing so, you and the other party leave a series of chits or obligations out in your interpersonal marketplace, which you can call back in when you need them.

In his studies of successful managers and their use of power in organizations, Kotter (1977) emphasizes that a manager must recognize, create, and cultivate dependence among those around her—subordinates, peers, and even superiors—and convert these dependencies into obligations. Obligations may be created in several ways. Doing favors for people, recognizing and praising them for their accomplishments, helping people out, paying individual attention to them even when the job demands do not require it or they do not expect it, and dispensing extra funds for special projects in a tight-budget year are but a few examples of how resources can be controlled and measured to help people do their jobs better and to generate liking for the power holder.

A second way that negotiators attempt to use this power is through pressure—that is, by the threat of punishment. An influencer can make demands, suggest consequences about what will happen if the demands are not met, engage in frequent surveillance to determine whether the demands are carried out, remind the other person frequently about what is expected, and eventually follow through with the actual punishment if the demand is not met on time. A sales manager may cut a salesperson's pay for repeatedly failing to achieve sales target projections. A parent may deny a child television privileges for a week because she didn't clean up her room. A supplier may put a late charge on an overdue bill to a customer. Like rewards and the use of praise, coercion, or punishment can be as effective in the verbal form as in the withdrawal or denial of tangible resources. If the sales manager berates a salesperson for failing to make target sales quotas (rather than firing him or her), or if the parent yells at his child rather than denying television privileges, the impact may be just as great.

The conditions for the use of pressure are similar to those for the use of exchange and praise: the other party is dependent on the power holder in some way, the agent controls some form of resources that can be denied or taken away from the other party, and the punishment can be administered in a manner that will ensure the other party's compliance. According to Kipnis (1976, p. 104), one is better off with praise and rewards if the goal is to maintain the target's good will; criticism and sanctions are more appropriate when changing behavior is more important than maintaining goodwill.

The few empirical studies of power use in negotiation have found that, compared with those with low power, parties with high power tend to use more pressure tactics, such as threats, and make fewer concessions (Hornstein, 1965; Michener, Vaske, Schleiffer, Plazewski, and Chapman, 1975). When the power distribution between the parties was relatively small, the low-power party also showed a high degree of threat use and power tactics, creating an escalation between the parties that usually destroyed the negotiation (see also Vitz and Kite, 1970). There is also evidence that the use of power tactics varies cross-culturally. Tinsley (2001) found that negotiators from cultures that place a higher value on social hierarchy (Japanese, in this study) were more likely to use power tactics than negotiators from cultures having a greater emphasis on egalitarianism in society (Germans and Americans).

Pressure tactics produce, at best, short-term compliance with requests, but they also are likely to elicit resistance from the other party. Frequent use of pressure tactics alienates the other party and leads to very high resistance, in which case the agent must consistently escalate the severity of consequences for noncompliance and the willingness to invoke them. Pressure tactics should be used selectively and sparingly because their use is likely to corrode the relationship between the parties, and frequent use is likely to destroy it.

Section Summary

In this section, we examined several ways that persuaders can use the peripheral route to achieve influence. We discussed factors related to the message itself, characteristics of the message source, and aspects of the influence context that can result in influence. That last piece—context—is especially important because it complicates the influence situation, requiring the effective influence seeker to attend to additional social factors beyond just his or her relationship with the individual influence target. An example is the added complexity involved in seeking influence as part of negotiations that occur in large organizational settings (see Box 8.4).

BOX 8.4 Influence in Organizations

Michael Watkins (2001) discussed how influence operates when it occurs in the specific context of large organizations. He offered five key goals for effective persuasion in these settings:

1. *Mapping the influence landscape.* It is important to pinpoint who needs to be persuaded and what methods to employ to effectively influence the other party. Within an organization or social network, it is important to attend not just to the target of influence, but also to subgroups or coalitions that support the target. This also involves neutralizing opposition to your position.

2. *Shaping perceptions of interest.* An influencer can use framing techniques and persuasive strategies to influence others' beliefs about what they want. Successful persuasion can change a person's incentives in the negotiation, therefore facilitating desired outcomes. Compensation plans, mission statements, strategic plans, annual budgets, and the like are powerful media for influencing incentives in an organization.

3. *Shaping perceptions of alternatives.* Influencing another's perceptions of alternatives

to an agreement is also a powerful form of persuasion. This may involve focusing the target's attention on alternatives that highlight the value of your position, rather than those that detract from it.

4. *Gaining acceptance for tough decisions.* It is important to lay a framework within the organization for the acceptance of difficult decisions and their outcomes. When members of an organization feel involved in the decision-making process and perceive that process as fair, they are more likely to accept tough decisions.

5. *Persuading at a distance.* Because organizations are large and it is impossible to persuade one-on-one with all members, it is important to be able to persuade from a distance. Establishing reliable channels of communication, communicating important themes and messages through speeches and memos, and learning how to appropriately and creatively communicate an idea are important for mass persuasion in an organization.

Source: Adapted from M. Watkins, "Principles of Persuasion." *Negotiation Journal* 17 (2001), pp. 115–37.

Influence targets are particularly susceptible to peripheral forms of influence to the extent that they are unmotivated and/or unable to pay careful attention to the argumentative substance of the influence-seeker's message. Effective negotiators realize that a big part of their task is persuading the other party to view the situation as they do. Strategies that underlie peripheral routes to influence are an important part of a negotiator's arsenal for doing just that.

The Role of Receivers—Targets of Influence

We close this chapter with a discussion of the person who is the target of influence. Influence targets should not think of themselves as passive recipients who merely "consume" a persuasive message and then make an up-or-down decision whether to "buy" it or not. There are two prominent aspects to the influence target's role and options. First, targets should avoid becoming defensive and direct their energy instead toward ways to gain a great understanding of the goals and interests driving the other party's influence attempts. Second, there are a number of ways that negotiators who finds themselves on the receiving end of persuasive messages and strategies can resist the attempts at influence. We discuss each of these two aspects of the target's role in turn.

"No, Thursday's out. How about never—
is never good for you?"

Understanding the Other's Perspective

Negotiators on the receiving end of influence-seeking gambits will be much better equipped to make sound decisions about whether or not to be persuaded—and less likely to dig in and become defensive—if they have a through and nuanced understanding of where the other party is coming from. We present here three suggestions for achieving that kind of understanding.

1. Explore the Other's Point of View   Negotiators frequently give very little attention to the other party's opinions and point of view. This is unfortunate because it is very much to your advantage to understand what the other party really wants, how things look to him, and how he developed his position. One can explore the other party's perspective with questions designed to reveal his or her needs and interests. For instance, "Why are those important objectives for you?" "What would happen if you did not get everything you have asked for?" and "Have your needs changed since the last time we talked?" bring out more detailed information about the other party's position and interests. Exploring the other person's outlook not only provides more information, which can lead you to design solutions to meet both sides' needs, but helps you understand why the other party is trying to persuade you to think or act in a particular way. Be careful though of questions that attack rather than explore. Questions such as "How in the world can you say that?" and "Who in their right mind would believe that?" are likely to make the other party feel tense and defensive, turning the tone of the negotiation quite negative. (Recall from Chapter 6 our discussion and numerous examples of the use of questions in negotiations.)

2. Selectively Paraphrase   Paraphrasing ensures that both parties have understood each other accurately. If you haven't understood the other party, it gives her an opportunity to correct you. It is important to restate your understanding after being corrected, to make sure you have gotten it right. In addition, vocalizing the other person's ideas helps you remember them better than simply hearing them. Avoid literally repeating the other person's words; restate the message in your own words, starting with "Let me see if I understand the point you just made." When people have an important message to get across, they may talk vigorously and at length, often emphasizing the same point over and over. Once your paraphrasing indicates that the other person has been understood, he or she will usually stop repeating the same point and move on; hence, paraphrasing can be very helpful in moving a discussion forward.

You can also ask the other party to restate or paraphrase what you have said. You might say, "What I have said is very important to me, and I would appreciate it if you could restate what you understood to be my main points." This process accomplishes several things. First, it asks the other party to listen closely and recall what you have said. Second, it gives you the opportunity to check out the accuracy of his or her understanding. Third, it emphasizes the most important points of your presentation.

3. Reinforce Points You Like in the Other Party's Proposals   Negotiators are frequently ineffective because they respond only to what they dislike in the other party's statement or proposal and ignore the things they like. Responding in this way ignores a powerful means of shaping and guiding what the other party is saying. Several classical theories of behavior (e.g., exchange theory or learning and reinforcement theory) make the same basic point: people are more likely to repeat behavior that is rewarded than behavior that is not rewarded (Homans, 1961; Skinner, 1953).

The simplest way to reward people for what they say during a negotiation is to acknowledge and support a point they have made: "That's an interesting point," or "I hadn't heard that before." Nonverbal signals work as well—for example, a simple "mm-hmm" or a nod of the head. Statements and actions like these separate a key statement from other points the speaker has made. Second, compliment speakers when they make points you want emphasized, and express appreciation to them for considering your interests and needs. In a labor negotiation, for example, management might say to the union, "Your concern that toxic labor relations might make customers reluctant to give us long-term contracts is an important one." A third approach is to separate parts of a statement that you like from those parts you don't like, and encourage the other party to develop the favorable points. In negotiating the sale of a house, the buyer might say, "Let me focus on one of the points you made. An adjustment in price to cover needed repairs is a good idea. What repairs do you have in mind?"

Resisting the Other's Influence

In addition to the variety of things a negotiator can do to encourage, support, or direct the other's communication, there are three major things that listeners can do to resist the other's influence efforts: have good alternatives to a negotiated agreement, make a public commitment (or get the other party to make one), and inoculate yourself against the other's persuasive message.

1. Have a BATNA, and Know How to Use It   Several authors identify a BATNA (best alternative to a negotiated agreement) as a source of power (e.g., Pinkley, Neale, and Bennett,

1994; BATNAs were also described in Chapters 2, 4, and 7). There is no question that having a good BATNA enables a negotiator to walk away from a given negotiation, because it means that she can get her needs met and interests addressed somewhere else. Of course, a BATNA is a source of leverage at the negotiation table only if the other party is aware of it. To use a BATNA effectively, a negotiator must assess the other party's awareness that it exists and, if necessary, share that fact. This often must be done deftly—conveying the existence of a good alternative could be interpreted by the other party as an imminent threat to walk away. Keep in mind also that a BATNA can always be improved. Good negotiators will work to improve their BATNA before and even during an ongoing negotiation as a way to enhance their leverage. (We addressed the power of a BATNA in detail in Chapters 2 and 7.)

2. Make a Public Commitment   One of the most effective ways to get someone to stand firm on a position is to have him make a public commitment to that position. Union leaders have said to their rank and file such things as, "I will resign before I settle for a penny less than . . . " After making that statement, the union leader faces several pressures. One is the potential loss of face with union members that would come with backing away from that position—the leader may be unceremoniously thrown out of office if he or she does not actually resign. A second pressure is the threat to the leader's credibility with management in the future if there is no follow-through on the commitment. Finally, the leader may have his or her own cognitive inconsistency to deal with because failing to resign will be inconsistent with the earlier commitment.

Sometimes negotiators want the other party to make a public commitment, but not always. If you can get the other party to make a public statement that supports something you want, that party will be hard-pressed not to stand by the statement, even though he or she may have a desire to abandon it later on. Sometimes negotiators make a statement such as "I'm committed to finding an agreement that we can both benefit from," and then invite the other party to make a similar statement. At other times the inviting statement may be more direct: "Are you interested in selling us this property or not?" or "Let's agree that we are going to work together, and then get busy on the details of how to make it happen." Even better than eliciting statements of commitment to a point of view is enticing the other party to make a behavioral commitment. For example, retail merchants use down payments and layaway plans to get a behavioral commitment from customers when it is not possible to complete the total sale at that time. On the other hand, at times negotiators will want to prevent the other party from making public commitments to positions that might interfere with reaching an agreement. The other party may later need to back off the commitment to complete a deal. Although it might be tempting to taunt or scold the other party for making a commitment that cannot be kept, a savvy negotiator will realize that it may be in his or her interest to help the other party escape an ill-advised commitment in a face-saving way. This can be done by downplaying statements of commitment, not responding to them, or looking for a rationale to explain why the commitment no longer applies given changing assumptions or circumstances.

3. Inoculate Yourself against the Other Party's Arguments   One of the likely outcomes of listening carefully to the other party and exploring and understanding his or her point of view is that negotiators may change some of their own positions. At times they may not want to change their position, and therefore they may want to "inoculate" themselves against the other party's arguments (Pfau, Szabo, Anderson, Morrill, Zubric, and Wan, 2001). For instance, managers who must support organizational policies with which they disagree may want to inoculate themselves against subordinates' arguments by preparing and rehearsing counterarguments that can be used to refute the key points the other is likely to make.

There are three approaches for inoculating against the arguments of other parties:

1. Prepare supporting arguments *for your position only.*

2. Develop arguments *against your position only,* and then develop counterarguments; that is, find ways to refute them in the points you make.

3. Develop arguments *both for your original position and against your position,* and then develop counterarguments to refute both (a combination approach).

To illustrate, let's take the example of a director of admissions for a graduate program who will be meeting with an applicant to explain the school's decision not to accept the applicant. The admissions director could (1) develop arguments about why the student should not be admitted (e.g., the student's grades are not high enough), (2) develop arguments in favor of the student's perspective (e.g., the student took difficult courses at a very scholarly university), and (3) develop counterarguments to refute the student's arguments (e.g., the quality of the university and the rigor of the courses were taken into account when the admissions decision was made).

Research reveals that the best way to inoculate against being influenced is to use the combination approach (point 3)—developing arguments both for and against your position, and counterarguments to refute them (McGuire, 1964; Pfau et al., 2001). Developing arguments against your position only plus counterarguments (point 2) is also effective, but to a lesser extent. The least effective, by a large margin, is the first approach—developing arguments in support of your position only. Three further points emerge from research on inoculation. First, the best way to inoculate people against attacks on their position is to involve them in developing a defense. Second, the larger the number of arguments in any defense, the more effective it becomes. Third, asking people to make public statements supporting their original position increases their resistance to counterarguments.

Section Summary

Negotiators in the role of listener or target of influence can do many things to help blunt the persuasive force of an influence-seeking message that originates with the other party. By exploring the influence seeker's point of view, challenging the arguments set forth, and taking steps to actively resist the influence attempt, negotiators can minimize the chance that they will be swayed by weak arguments or "trapped" into the kind of shortcut persuasion that occurs through the peripheral route. Some key elements of resistance include making wise decisions about how and when to wield one's BATNA, knowing when to make public commitments, and inoculating oneself against anticipated arguments. In many situations, the other party will be persuasive because his or her arguments are solid and sensible. The key is approaching influence attempts with a focused and critical mind so that one is persuaded only when the arguments merit it. Understanding how persuasion works is certainly an essential step in becoming prepared to defend yourself against influence attempts across the negotiation table (Malhotra and Bazerman, 2008).

Chapter Summary

In this chapter, we discussed a large number of mechanisms of influence that one could use in negotiation. These tools were considered in two broad categories: influence that occurs through the "central route" to persuasion and influence that occurs through the "peripheral route" to persuasion. With respect to the central route, we addressed the content of the message, how messages are structured, and the style with which a persuasive message is delivered. Influence that occurs through the central route is likely to be relatively enduring and resistant to counterinfluence. With respect to the peripheral route, we considered tactics related to the construction of the message itself, as well as characteristics of the message source and elements of the influence context. When influence occurs through the peripheral route, the target may comply but will not necessarily make a corresponding attitudinal commitment; moreover, that compliance may be short-lived, and the target is generally more susceptible to counterinfluence.

In the last major section of the chapter, we considered how the receiver—the target of influence—can avoid being unduly persuaded by exploring the needs and interests of the other party or by resisting the persuasive effects of the message. Effective negotiators are skilled not only at crafting persuasive messages, but also at playing the role of skilled "consumers" of the messages that others direct their way.

We close with a cautionary note. This chapter has only touched on some of the more important and well-documented aspects of influence-seeking communication that can be used in bargaining. Negotiators usually spend a great deal of time devising ways to support and document their positions; they devote less time to considering how the information is presented or how to use qualities of the source and receiver to increase the likelihood that persuasion will be successful. Careful attention to source, target, and context factors, rather than just to message factors, is likely to have a positive impact on negotiator effectiveness.

Endnotes

[1] See also Chaiken (1987).

[2] Researchers have disagreed as to whether the two routes to persuasion are separate systems (e.g., Petty and Cacioppo, 1986a, 1986b) or compensatory systems (e.g., Chaiken, 1987). That is, it is not clear if the two routes to persuasion operate separately or if they work in conjunction. Some work (e.g., O'Keefe, 1990) seems to suggest that both processes operate at all times, but one is likely to be dominant. There is also disagreement about what to label the two routes and which research findings fit more precisely into which route. For sake of clarity, we have adopted Petty and Cacioppo's labels for the two routes: central and peripheral. It is also difficult to summarize and apply some concepts of persuasion because of contradictory research findings and the complex relationships between variables. Despite these weaknesses, this model of persuasion is comprehensive and helps organize a great deal of conflicting research on persuasion. The model does not provide exact prescriptions about how to persuade everyone in all circumstances. It does provide a clear way to think about the variables that have been found to influence persuasion. It helps clarify when persuasive tactics can work, although this does not mean that these factors will work in all circumstances. In many situations, influence is achieved through a skillful blend of many persuasive techniques.

[3] See also Freedman and Fraser (1966); Seligman, Bush, and Kirsch (1976).

[4] See also Bem (1972).

[5] See also Hovland and Mandell (1952); McGuire (1964).

[6] See also Johnson and Eagly (1989); Petty and Cacioppo (1990).

[7] Note that many public-sector bargaining laws prohibit negotiators from buying even a cup of coffee for each other. Negotiators need to be aware of the laws and norms that may have implications for compliance strategies. In addition, there are cross-cultural differences in refusing a gift, and negotiators need to prepare carefully for such instances when they negotiate across borders. (See Chapter 16 for more discussion of culture and negotiation.)

Ethics in Negotiation

Objectives

1. Understand whether there are commonly accepted ethical standards that apply to negotiations.
2. Explore the various factors that determine how ethics affect negotiation processes.
3. Consider the different types of ethically problematic tactics and how they are perceived.
4. Gain an understanding of how marginally ethical tactics will be received by others in a negotiation and how to detect others' use of deceptive tactics.

In this chapter, we explore the question of whether there are, or should be, accepted ethical standards for behavior in negotiations. This topic has received increased attention from researchers in recent years. It is our view that fundamental questions of ethical conduct arise in every negotiation. The effective negotiator must recognize when the questions are relevant and what factors must be considered to answer them. We want to be clear that it is not our intention to advocate a specific ethical position for all negotiators or for the conduct of all negotiations. Many treatises on business ethics take a strongly prescriptive or normative position, advocating what a person should or should not do. Instead, our aim in this chapter is to describe the ethical issues that arise in negotiations. We identify the major ethical dimensions raised in negotiations, describe how people tend to think about these ethical choices, and provide a framework for making informed ethical decisions. Along the way, we highlight research that has yielded worthwhile findings in this area.

But before we dive head first into all of that, let's set the stage with a few hypothetical dilemmas.

A Sampling of Ethical Quandaries

Consider the following situations:

1. You are trying to sell your stereo to raise money for an upcoming trip overseas. The stereo works great, and an audiophile friend tells you that if he were in the market for stereo equipment (which he isn't), he'd give you $500 for it. A few days later the first potential buyer comes to see the stereo. The buyer looks it over and asks a few questions

about how it works. You assure the buyer that the stereo works well. When asked how much, you tell the buyer that you have already had an offer for $500. The buyer buys the stereo for $550.

Is it ethical to have said what you said about having another offer?

2.   You are an entrepreneur interested in acquiring a business that is currently owned by a competitor. The competitor, however, has not shown any interest in either selling his business or merging with your company. To gain inside knowledge of his firm, you hired a consultant you know to call contacts in your competitor's business and ask if the company is having any serious problems that might threaten its viability. If there are such problems, you might be able to use the information to either hire away the company's employees or get the competitor to sell.

Is this an ethical course of action? Would you be likely to do it if you were the entrepreneur?

3.   You are a vice president of human resources, negotiating with a union representative for a new labor contract. The union refuses to sign a new contract unless the company agrees to raise the number of paid holidays from six to seven. Management estimates it will cost approximately $220,000 for each paid holiday, and argues that the company cannot afford to meet the demand. However, you know that, in reality, money is not the issue—the company simply doesn't think the union's demand is justified. To convince the union leaders that they should withdraw their demand, you have been considering these alternatives: *(a)* tell the union that the company simply can't afford it, without further explanation; *(b)* prepare erroneous financial statements that show that it will cost about $300,000 per paid holiday, which you simply can't afford; and *(c)* offer union leaders an all-expenses-paid "working" trip to a Florida resort if they will simply drop the demand.

Do any of the strategies raise ethical concerns? Which ones? Why?

4.   You are about to graduate from the MBA program of a leading university. You specialized in management information systems (MIS) and will start a job with a company that commercially develops Web pages. You own a personal computer that is a couple of years old. You have decided to sell it and buy new equipment later after you see what kinds of projects your employer has you working on. So you post a flyer on campus bulletin boards about the computer for sale. You have decided not to tell prospective buyers that your hard drive acts like it is about to fail and that the computer occasionally crashes without warning.

Is this ethical? Would you be likely to do this if you were this particular student?

5.   You buy a new pair of shoes on sale. The printed receipt states very clearly that the shoes are not returnable. After you get them home, you wear the shoes around the house for a day and decide that they just don't fit you correctly. So you take the shoes back to the store. The clerk points to the message on the receipt; but you don't let that deter you. You start to yell angrily about the store's poor quality service so that people in the store start to stare. The clerk calls the store manager; after some discussion, the manager agrees to give you your money back.

Is this ethical? Would you be likely to do this if you were this customer?

These situations are hypothetical; however, the problems they present are real ones for negotiators. People in and out of organizations are routinely confronted with important decisions about the strategies they will use to achieve important objectives, particularly when a variety of influence tactics are open to them. These decisions frequently carry ethical implications. In this chapter, we address the major ethical issues that arise in negotiation through consideration of these questions:

1. What are ethics, and why do they apply to negotiation?
2. What major approaches to ethical reasoning are relevant to negotiation?
3. What questions of ethical conduct are likely to arise in negotiation?
4. What motivates unethical behavior, and what are the consequences?
5. What factors shape a negotiator's predisposition to use unethical tactics?
6. How can negotiators deal with the other party's use of deception?

What Do We Mean by "Ethics," and Why Do They Matter in Negotiation?

Ethics Defined

Ethics are broadly applied social standards for what is right or wrong in a particular situation, or a process for setting those standards. They differ from morals, which are individual and personal beliefs about what is right and wrong. Ethics grow out of particular philosophies, which purport to (1) define the nature of the world in which we live and (2) prescribe rules for living together. Different philosophies adopt distinct perspectives on these questions, which means in practice that they may lead to different judgments about what is right and wrong in a given situation. The "hard work" of ethics in practice is figuring out how ethical philosophies differ from one another, deciding which approaches are personally preferable, and applying them to real-world situations at hand.

Our goal is to distinguish among different criteria, or standards, for judging and evaluating a negotiator's actions, particularly when questions of ethics might be involved. Although negotiation is our focus, the criteria involved are really no different than might be used to evaluate ethics in business generally. An ethical dilemma in business exists when a manager faces a decision "in which the financial performance (measured by the revenues, costs, and profits generated by the firm) and the social performance (stated in terms of the obligations to the individuals and groups associated with the firm) are in conflict" (Hosmer, 2003, p. 85). Analogously, an ethical dilemma exists for a negotiator when possible actions or strategies put the potential economic benefits of doing a deal in conflict with one's social obligations to other involved parties or one's broader community.

Many writers on business ethics have proposed frameworks that capture competing ethical standards (and as we shall see later, these typically map onto classical theories of ethical philosophy that have been around a long time). Drawing on some of these writers

(Green, 1994; Hitt, 1990; Hosmer, 2003), here are four standards for evaluating strategies and tactics in business and negotiation:

- Choose a course of action on the basis of results I expect to achieve (e.g., greatest return on investment).

- Choose a course of action on the basis of my duty to uphold appropriate rules and principles (e.g., the law).

- Choose a course of action on the basis of the norms, values, and strategy of my organization or community (e.g., the usual way we do things at this firm).

- Choose a course of action on the basis of my personal convictions (e.g., what my conscience tells me to do).

Each of these approaches reflects a fundamentally different approach to ethical reasoning. The first may be called *end-result ethics,* in that the rightness of an action is determined by evaluating the pros and cons of its consequences. The second is an example of what may be called *duty ethics,* in that the rightness of an action is determined by one's obligation to adhere to consistent principles, laws, and social standards that define what is right and wrong and where the line is. The third represents a form of *social contract ethics,* in that the rightness of an action is based on the customs and norms of a particular community. Finally, the fourth may be called *personalistic ethics,* in that the rightness of the action is based on one's own conscience and moral standards.

Applying Ethical Reasoning to Negotiation

Each of these approaches could be used to analyze the five hypothetical situations at the beginning of the chapter. For instance, in the first situation involving selling a stereo and the statement to a prospective buyer about the existence of another potential buyer:

- If you believed in *end-result* ethics, then you might do whatever was necessary to get the best possible outcome (including lie about an alternative buyer).

- If you believed in *duty* ethics, you might perceive an obligation never to engage in subterfuge, and might therefore reject a tactic that involves an outright lie.

- If you believed in *social contract* ethics, you would base your tactical choices on your view of appropriate conduct for behavior in your community; if others would use deception in a situation like this, you lie.

- If you believed in *personalistic* ethics, you would consult your conscience and decide whether your need for cash for your upcoming trip justified using deceptive or dishonest tactics.

What this example shows is that the approach to ethical reasoning you favor affects the kind of ethical judgment you make, and the consequent behavior you choose, in a situation that has an ethical dimension to it. These four approaches—think of them as ethical schools of thought—are the basis for our in-depth treatment of ethics in negotiation in the next major section of this chapter. First, however, allow us a brief digression on how ethics fits with other motives and bases for decisions about tactics and strategy.

Ethics versus Prudence versus Practicality versus Legality

Discussions of business ethics frequently confuse what is *ethical* (appropriate as determined by some standard of moral conduct) versus what is *prudent* (wise, based on trying to understand the efficacy of the tactic and the consequences it might have on the relationship with the other) versus what is *practical* (what a negotiator can actually make happen in a given situation) versus what is *legal* (what the law defines as acceptable practice) (Missner, 1980). In earlier chapters, we evaluated negotiation strategies and tactics by the prudence and practicality criteria; in this chapter, the focus is on evaluating negotiation strategies and tactics by ethical criteria.

There are other criteria that come into play. For example, Lax and Sebenius (1986) suggest that some people want to be ethical for intrinsic reasons—it feels better because behaving ethically allows them to see themselves as moral individuals or because certain principles of behavior are seen as moral absolutes. Others may judge ethical behavior in more instrumental terms—good ethics make good business. But no matter how reasonable the motives, it is still often that case that people's judgments about what is ethical or unethical in negotiation are not crystal clear. On the one hand, negotiators see some tactics as marginal—defined in shades and degrees rather than in absolutes. Reasonable people will disagree as to exactly where to draw the line between what is ethical and what is unethical for some tactics (e.g., bluffing about one's reservation price). On the other hand, negotiators show marked agreement that certain tactics are clearly unethical (e.g., outright falsification of information). Thus, although it may be difficult to tell a negotiator exactly what behaviors are ethical and unethical in any one circumstance, the subject of ethics is no less important. Examining ethics encourages negotiators to examine their own decision-making processes. In addition, sharpening the questions they ask will help negotiators create the opportunity for further studies on the complexity of ethical judgments (Lewicki, 1983; Raiffa, 1982).

Figure 9.1 presents a helpful way to think about what it means to comprehend and analyze an ethical dilemma. The figure shows a model of the process of analyzing a moral problem developed by Larue Hosmer (2003), a writer on business ethics. According to Hosmer, before one can ponder solutions, the first step is developing a complete understanding of the moral problem at hand. Looking at the left side of Figure 9.1, this means grasping the various subjective standards (norms, beliefs, values, etc.) in play among involved parties and recognizing the mix of potential harms, benefits, and rights that are involved in the situation. With the problem fully defined, the path to a convincing solution travels through the three modes of analysis shown on the right side of the figure: (1) a determination of economic outcomes of potential courses of action, (2) a consideration of legal requirements that bear on the situation, and (3) an assessment of the ethical obligations to other involved parties regarding what is "'right' and 'just' and 'fair'" (Hosmer, 2003, p. 87). This last element—ethical reasoning—benefits from a basic, working knowledge of ethical philosophy. In that spirit, we move now to a closer look at the four fundamental standards we identified above and their application to negotiator ethics.

Four Approaches to Ethical Reasoning

Those who write about business ethics tend to approach the subject from the perspectives of major philosophical theories (see Table 9.1). Drawing on this literature, we now take a closer look at the four ethical standards for making decisions in negotiation that we introduced above: end-result ethics, duty ethics, social contract ethics, and personalistic ethics.[1]

FIGURE 9.1 | Analytical Process for the Resolution of Moral Problems

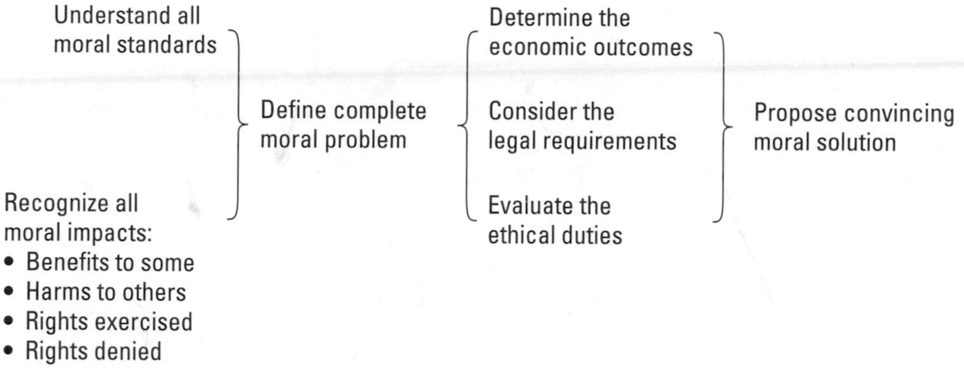

Understand all
moral standards

Define complete
moral problem

Determine the
economic outcomes

Consider the
legal requirements

Propose convincing
moral solution

Recognize all
moral impacts:
- Benefits to some
- Harms to others
- Rights exercised
- Rights denied

Evaluate the
ethical duties

Source: L.T. Hosmer (2003). *The ethics of management* (4th ed.). New York: McGraw-Hill/Irwin.

End-Result Ethics

Many of the ethically questionable incidents in business that upset the public involve people who argue that the ends justify the means—that is, who deem it acceptable to break a rule or violate a procedure in the service of some greater good for the individual, the organization, or even society at large. Several examples come to mind. Suppose a television network has convincing statistical evidence that a particular pickup truck was designed unsafely, so that in 1 test out of 10, it bursts into flame when hit in a side collision. To highlight this defect, the network producer decides to stage and videotape an accident. But because a collision may create a fire only 1 time in 10, and the producer can't afford to destroy 10 (or more) trucks, he decides to place detonators near the gas tank of the truck to be used. Thus, the exploding truck viewers would see would have been designed to "simulate" what (supposedly) happens to (supposedly) 1 truck out of 10. Is this unethical, even if the producer's goal is to warn viewers about the hazards of this truck model?

Consider a second example: a pharmaceutical company is convinced, as a result of early tests, that it has developed a dramatic new miracle drug that will cure some forms of cancer. But it cannot release the drug yet because it has to comply with government regulation that controls drug testing prior to widespread distribution, and thousands of lives may be lost before the government approves the drug. Is it unethical to keep the drug off the market while the regulatory testing goes on? Or is it unethical to release the drug before it has been thoroughly tested?

Those who would argue that the simulated truck test was appropriate and that the drug should be marketed argue for end-result ethics. In the negotiation context, when negotiators have noble objectives to attain for themselves or their constituencies, they will argue that they can use whatever strategies they want. They draw on a view of ethics known as *utilitarianism*. The originators of utilitarianism as a school of thought were Jeremy Bentham (see Bentham, 1789) and John Stuart Mill (see Mill, 1962). Utilitarians (end-result or "consequentialist" ethicists) hold that the moral worth of a particular action should be judged on the basis of the consequences it produces. Because they measure morality by the goodness

TABLE 9.1 | Four Approaches to Ethical Reasoning

Ethical System	Definition	Major Proponent	Central Tenets	Major Concerns
End-result ethics	Rightness of an action is determined by considering consequences.	Jeremy Bentham (1748–1832) John Stuart Mill (1806–1873)	• One must consider all likely consequences. • Actions are more right if they promote more happiness, more wrong as they produce unhappiness. • Happiness is defined as presence of pleasure and absence of pain. • Promotion of happiness is generally the ultimate aim. • Collective happiness of all concerned is the goal.	• How does one define happiness, pleasure, or utility? • How does one measure happiness, pleasure, or utility? • How does one trade off between short-term vs. long-term happiness? • If actions create happiness for 90% of the world and misery for the other 10%, are they still ethical?
Duty ethics	Rightness of an action is determined by considering obligations to apply universal standards and principles.	Immanuel Kant (1724–1804)	• Human conduct should be guided by primary moral principles, or "oughts." • Individuals should stand on their principles and restrain themselves by rules. • The ultimate good is a life of virtue (acting on principles) rather than pleasure. • We should not adjust moral law to fit our actions, but adjust our actions to fit moral law.	• By what authority do we accept particular rules or the "goodness" of those rules? • What rule do we follow when rules conflict? • How do we adapt general rules to fit specific situations? • How do rules change as circumstances change? • What happens when good rules produce bad consequences? • Are there rules without any exceptions?

(Continued)

TABLE 9.1 | *(Concluded)*

Ethical System	Definition	Major Proponent	Central Tenets	Major Concerns
Social contract ethics	Rightness of an action is determined by the customs and norms of a community.	Jean-Jacques Rousseau (1712–1778)	• People must function in a social, community context to survive. • Communities become "moral bodies" for determining ground rules. • Duty and obligation bind the community and the individual to each other. • What is best for the common good determines the ultimate standard. • Laws are important, but morality determines the laws and standards for right and wrong.	• How do we determine the general will? • What is meant by the "common good"? • What do we do with independent thinkers who challenge the morality of the existing social order (e.g., Jefferson, Gandhi, Martin Luther King)? • Can a state be corrupt and its people still be "moral" (e.g., Nazi Germany)?
Personalistic ethics	Rightness of an action is determined by one's conscience.	Martin Buber (1878–1965)	• Locus of truth is found in human existence. • Conscience within each person calls them to fulfill their human-ness and to decide between right and wrong. • Personal decision rules are the ultimate standards. • Pursuing a noble goal by ignoble means leads to an ignoble end. • There are no absolute formulas for living. • One should follow one's group but also stick up for what one individually believes.	• How could we justify ethics other than by saying, "it felt like the right thing to do"? • How could we achieve a collective definition of what is ethical if individuals disagreed? • How could we achieve cohesiveness and consensus in a team that only fosters personal perspectives? • How could an organization assure some uniformity in ethics?

Source: Derived from W. Hitt, *Ethics and Leadership: Putting Theory into Practice* (Columbus, OH: Battelle Press, 1990).

or badness of consequences, utilitarians believe that the way to maximize virtue is to maximize the best consequences for the largest number of people—usually in terms of happiness, pleasure, or utility. The highest moral conduct is to maximize the greatest good for the greatest number.

Debate about end-result ethics centers on several key questions. First, how do people (and which people) define happiness or pleasure or maximum utility, and how can each be measured? Second, how do actors trade off between short-term consequences and long-term consequences, particularly when the short-term results are damaging to the long-term results (i.e., good in the short run, bad in the long run) or vice versa? Third, if people cannot create utility for everyone, is it adequate for them to create it for a large number of people, even if other people will not benefit or will even suffer? How does utilitarianism balance the benefits for a majority with the protection of the rights of a minority? The debate on these and other questions related to end-result ethics is ongoing.

Duty Ethics

In contrast to end-result ethics, duty ethics emphasize that individuals ought to commit themselves to a series of moral rules or standards and make decisions based on those principles. A strong proponent of this view was the 18th-century philosopher Immanuel Kant (see Kant, 1963, 1964). The term *deontology*—derived from the Greek word for obligation—is used commonly to label this school of thought. Deontologists argue that a decision based on the utilitarian standards just discussed—that is, based on evaluation of outcomes—is flawed because outcomes may be too uncertain at the time of the decision. Besides, the ethical merits of an action should be linked more to the intentions of the actor than to the outcomes of the act (Hosmer, 1993). Kant proposed a series of principles (summarized into a few central tenets in Table 9.1) that serve as the standard by which each person may judge his or her own action. Kant argued that these principles are established on purely rational grounds and that the principles can be debated (and improved upon) as we improve upon the key tenets of rational science. One of his fundamental principles was that one should choose to act in ways that one would want everyone else to act, were they faced with the same situation and circumstances.

For example, let us suppose that a militant subgroup within a labor union has organized in protest over what it feels are critical questions of worker safety. When their initial attempts to bring their concerns to management are rebuffed, they walk out in a wildcat strike. Some other rank-and-file union members, who are not particularly affected by the safety rules in question, nevertheless support the strike because they think the strikers' concerns should be addressed by management. The strikers present a series of safety demands to management—if these demands are met, the strikers will return to work. Management agrees to meet the demands, and the strike ends. Management then immediately fires all the wildcatters for participating in the illegal strike and takes no action on the safety issues. The union leadership accuses management of unethical negotiating. In this situation, utilitarians might argue that management's tactic of agreeing to meet the workers' demands—even if that agreement was in bad faith—was necessary to end an illegal strike. The argument goes something like this: it is management's job (not the workers') to determine conditions of worker safety, and it is also management's job to take action against wildcat

Pepper . . . and Salt

THE WALL STREET JOURNAL

**"'Naughty or nice'—I was hoping for a
little more moral relativism."**

From *The Wall Street Journal*. Used with permission of Cartoon Features Syndicate.

strikes; both of these job definitions justify, in management's mind, the tactic of falsely agreeing to meet the wildcatters' demands and then firing them. Thus, the utility of ending the strike (the end) justified the deception (the means) in the negotiation.

In contrast, deontologists might argue that management has a responsibility to adhere to the principles of honesty and integrity—negotiating in good faith and not acting retributively against the strikers—because adhering to these principles over the long term will produce the best results for union–management relations, and no particular end can justify dishonest means. For example, in the truck fire scenario described earlier (which was, by the way, a real series of events involving an NBC network news program in 1993), the decision to stage the collision cost NBC's news department a great deal of negative publicity and credibility and cost both the producer and eventually the head of the NBC News Division their jobs—consequences that are extremely serious and may or may not be equivalent to the possibility of lives being lost in the dangerous pickup trucks.

These scenarios, and many others like them, constitute the grist of the debate between end-results ethics and duty ethics. When addressing means–ends questions in competition and negotiation, observers usually focus the most attention on the question of what strategies and tactics may be seen as appropriate to achieve certain ends. Are exploitative, manipulative, or devious tactics ever justifiable, even if they produce good ends for a large number of people? For example, in a hostage crisis, is it ethical for a government to agree to grant a terrorist immunity if he releases the hostages, even though the government has every intention of capturing and prosecuting the terrorist once his hostages are released? Many people would argue that end-result ethics win out here over duty ethics prescribing honesty and integrity, but there will also be detractors.

Clearly, deontology has its critics as well. Who sets the standards and makes the rules? What are the rules that apply in all circumstances? For example, those who believe strictly in the commandment (rule) "Thou shalt not kill" will argue that the commandment is the same regardless of whether the subject is murder, the death penalty for a convicted murderer, military combat, abortion (even to save the life of the mother), or assisted suicide (e.g., for terminally ill or suffering patients). What happens when two principles conflict? For example, if there are two obligations—one that says you should be considerate of others' feelings and another that says you should tell the truth—what do you do when you have to tell your best friend a truth that is painful and will hurt his or her feelings? How can the rules be adapted to specific situations, and what happens when the standards change over time? What happens when good rules produce bad circumstances? For example, cases of physician–assisted suicide result in moral conflict on both sides. The patient feels a moral dilemma between a right to make an autonomous decision to end his or her life with dignity and a moral prohibition against killing. Similarly, the doctor faces a moral dilemma between the mandate to save lives and "do no harm," and an obligation to relieve undue suffering for those whose lives cannot be saved. These and other questions and situations lead some to believe that an ethical emphasis on duties and rules creates more problems than it solves.

Social Contract Ethics

A third standard of ethics holds that the rightness of an action is determined by the customs and social norms of a community. This view is best articulated in the basic writings of Jean–Jacques Rousseau (1947). Rather than arguing that the utility of ends determines the standards, or that universal obligations should apply in all situations, social contract ethicists argue that societies, organizations, and cultures determine what is ethically appropriate and acceptable for themselves and then indoctrinate new members as they are socialized into the fabric of the community. In a sense, each member of the group agrees to an implied (or even explicit) social contract that explains what the individual is expected to give to the community, what the individual can get back from the community, and the social rules or norms that all members are expected to follow.

Social contract ethicists focus on what individuals owe to their community (country, organization, neighborhood, etc.) and what they can or should expect in return. As applied to negotiation, social contract ethics would prescribe which behaviors are appropriate in a negotiation context in terms of what people owe one another. For example, the context of a used-car negotiation may suggest that a buyer does not expect the truth from the salesperson, and therefore does not owe the salesperson the truth either. So when the salesperson lies about the reliability or gas mileage of the automobile that is for sale, the buyer should have no compunctions about lying about her interest in the car or her real intention to bring her friend back to take a closer look at it. In contrast, if a salesperson is establishing a long-term association with a customer, in this context—establishing an ongoing relationship with a valued partner who should be treated honorably and fairly now and in the future—the salesperson owes it to that customer to tell her the truth when he discovers defects in his products or when he will be late in shipping due to manufacturing errors and problems (Carlisle and Parker, 1989).

As we noted in Table 9.1, social contract ethics are also not without problems. How do we decide what implicit rules should apply to a given relationship, particularly when we have not explicitly spelled out those rules? Who makes these social rules, and how are they evaluated and changed? What happens when the existing social contract becomes corrupted over time (through collusion, monopolistic practices, etc.) such that it needs to be challenged by those who seek change and reform? Are new recruits to an organization bound by a contract that is unfulfilled or violated by the organization? These critical questions pose important challenges for those who advocate a social contract view of ethical decision making.

Personalistic Ethics

A fourth standard of ethics is that, rather than attempting to determine what is ethical based on ends, duties, or the social norms of a community, people should simply consult their own conscience. As argued most clearly by the philosopher Martin Buber (1958, 1963), the foundations for ethical behavior lie in the human conscience. Hitt (1990) offers an interesting example to highlight the tenets of this approach relative to the three earlier models:

> The setting is an outdoor hotel swimming pool on a warm July morning. At this particular time of day, there are only two persons present—a father who is fully clothed, sitting in a lounge chair beside the pool and reading the newspaper, and his five-year-old daughter, who is wading in the pool. While the father is engrossed in reading the sports page, he hears his daughter scream for help. She has waded into the deep end of the pool and is struggling to keep her head above water. At this moment, what is the right thing for the father to do? And what system of ethics will he use? If he chooses end-result ethics, he will compare the utilities associated with ruining his clothes, watch and billfold with those associated with saving his daughter's life. If he chooses rule ethics, he might first check to see if the hotel has posted any rules that prohibit a fully clothed person from entering the pool. And if he chooses social contract ethics, he might reflect on the social contract that he has with his family members. Obviously, he will choose none of these. He will jump into the pool immediately to rescue his daughter (pp. 121–22).

Hitt argues that the motivation to action is clearly the conscience of the father crying, "Act now!" The very nature of human existence leads individuals to develop a personal conscience, an internal sense of what is right and what one ought to do. Ultimately, these rules remain individual and personal, although they can be influenced by the social forces that lead people to reason ethically and learn to do the right thing—because, in this view, ethical judgments must be made by each individual; there are no absolutes. People must determine what is right and appropriate to do, on their own, and they should not impose their standards on others. Many of these forces are part of an individual's upbringing and are represented by what he or she learns at home, in school, and at religious institutions.

As applied to negotiation, personalistic ethics maintain that everyone ought to decide for themselves what is right based on their conscience (whatever it may say to them). Whether one lies, cheats, or steals, therefore, is ultimately a matter of individual conscience and not the nature of the ends, duties, rules, or narrow interpretations of the social contract. However, as you can well imagine, critics have argued that no one is as pure as Martin Buber. Individual conscience is too narrow and limited as a standard to apply to a broader social context (such as an organization). Finally, some critics would argue that social institutions (families, schools, houses of worship) have declined in their roles as teachers of character and developers of conscience; thus, it is not clear that younger members of society have a strong conscience by which they can act. In addition, personalistic ethics provide no mechanism for resolving disputes when they lead to conflicting views between individuals as to what is right or proper; conflicting views among individuals would lead to teams and organizations that have tremendous value rifts within them because there is no common set of ground rules and no mechanism for resolving value-based disputes.

Section Summary   In this section, we have reviewed four major approaches to ethical reasoning: end-result ethics, or the principles of utilitarianism; duty ethics, or the principles of deontology; social contract ethics, or the principles of community-based socially acceptable behavior; and personalistic ethics, or the principles of determining what is right by turning to one's conscience. Negotiators may use each of these approaches to evaluate appropriate strategies and tactics. We next explore some of the factors that tend to influence, if not dictate, how negotiators are disposed to deal with ethical questions.

What Questions of Ethical Conduct Arise in Negotiation?

Why do some negotiators choose to use tactics that may be unethical? The first answer that occurs to many people is that such negotiators are corrupt, degenerate, or immoral. However, that answer is much too simplistic. As we discussed in Chapter 5, people tend to regard *other people's* unsavory behavior as caused by disposition or personality, while attributing the causes of their *own* behavior to factors in the social environment (Miller and Ross, 1975). Thus, a negotiator might consider an adversary who uses an ethically questionable tactic unprincipled, profit-driven, or willing to use any tactic to get what he or she wanted. In contrast, when attempting to explain why you as the negotiator might use the same tactic, you would tend to say that you are highly principled but had very good reasons for deviating from those principles just this one time.

In this section we discuss negotiation tactics that bring issues of ethicality into play. We first discuss what we mean by tactics that are "ethically ambiguous," and we link negotiator ethics to the fundamental issue of truth telling. We then describe research that has sought to identify and classify such tactics and analyze people's attitudes toward their use. We also distinguish between active and passive forms of deception—lies of omission versus commission. The section concludes with a model that portrays the negotiator's decision-making process with respect to the possible use of such tactics.

Ethically Ambiguous Tactics: It's (Mostly) All about the Truth

Little needs to be said about the wide range of tactics available to a negotiator. We discussed many of these tactics in Chapters 2 and 3, when we discussed distributive bargaining and integrative negotiation, and in Chapter 8, when we discussed a variety of influence and persuasion tactics. Here we discuss what kinds of tactics are ethically ambiguous and how they can work to afford a temporary strategic advantage. Our use of the phrase *ethically ambiguous* reflects a carefully considered choice of words. One dictionary defines "ambiguous" as "open to more than one interpretation . . . doubtful or uncertain."[2] We are interested in tactics that may or may not be improper, depending on an individual's ethical reasoning and circumstances.

Most of the ethics issues in negotiation are concerned with standards of truth telling—how honest, candid, and disclosing a negotiator should be. That is, individuals must decide (according to one or more of the ethical theories presented earlier) when they should tell the truth (the whole truth and nothing but the truth) as opposed to engaging in some behavior short of telling the truth. The attention here is more on what negotiators *say* (communicate about) or what they say they will do (and how they say it) than on what they actually *do* (although negotiators may act unethically as well). Some negotiators may cheat (violate formal and informal rules—e.g., claiming that rules about deadlines or procedures don't apply to them) or steal (e.g., break into the other party's or competitor's database or headquarters to secure confidential documents or briefing memoranda), but most of the attention in negotiator ethics has been on lying behavior.

Most negotiators would probably place a high value on a reputation for being truthful. Yet what does being truthful mean? Questions about truth telling are straightforward, but the answers are not so clear. First, how does one define *truth?* Do you follow a clear set of rules, determine what the social contract is for truth in your group or organization, or follow your conscience? Second, how does one define and classify deviations from the truth? Are all deviations lies, no matter how small and minor they are? Finally, one can add a relativistic dimension to these questions: should a person tell the truth all the time, or are there times when not telling the truth is an acceptable (or even necessary) form of conduct? These are questions of major concern to negotiators (and philosophers since time immemorial!) who are trying to decide what they can and cannot say and still remain ethical.

A number of articles in business journals have addressed the ethical issues surrounding truth telling. For example, Carr (1968) argued in a controversial *Harvard Business Review* article titled "Is Business Bluffing Ethical?" that strategy in business is analogous to strategy in a game of poker. He advocated that, short of outright cheating (the equivalent of marking cards or hiding an ace up your sleeve), businesspeople ought to play the game as poker players do. Just as good poker playing often involves concealing information and bluffing (convincing others that you have the cards when you really don't), so do many business transactions. From time to time, most executives find themselves compelled, for their own interests or the interests of their companies, to practice some form of deception in their dealings with customers, suppliers, labor unions, government officials, or even other key executives. Through conscious misstatements, concealment of pertinent facts, or exaggeration—in short, bluffing—they seek to persuade others to agree with them. Carr argues that if an executive refuses to bluff periodically—if he or she feels obligated to tell the truth, the whole truth, and nothing but the truth all the time—he or she is probably ignoring opportunities permitted under the rules of business and is probably at a heavy disadvantage in business dealings (p. 144).

Carr (1968) further advocated a modified ethical act-based and rule-based relativism for standards of truth telling. Bluffing, exaggeration, and concealment or manipulation of information, he maintained, are legitimate ways for both individuals and corporations to maximize their self-interest. Such strategies may be either advantageous or disadvantageous. An executive might plead poverty in a contract negotiation with a key employee and thereby save a significant amount of money for the company. However, a similar cost-cutting focus might lead the same executive to fail to make safety or quality improvements on one of the company's products, which could have severe long-term business consequences. As you can well imagine, Carr's position sparked lively debate among *Harvard Business Review* readers. A number of critics argued that individual businesspeople and corporations should be held to higher standards of ethical conduct, and they took Carr to task for his position. Three decades later, Koehn (1997) challenged Carr's premise that negotiating is a game that legitimizes deceptive behavior, arguing that most games do not legitimize deception and that therefore Carr's logic is faulty. More recently, Allhoff (2003), in an essay titled "Business Bluffing Reconsidered," tried to strike a middle ground between Carr and Koehn, conceding Koehn's point that the game analogy may be faulty, but arguing that bluffing is permissible in certain forms within business negotiation "for the same reason that it is permissible in games, namely that the participants endorse the practice" (p. 287).

Questions and debate regarding the ethical standards for truth telling in negotiation are ongoing. As we pointed out when we discussed interdependence (Chapter 1), negotiation is based on information dependence (Kelley and Thibaut, 1969)—the exchange of information regarding the true preferences and priorities of the other negotiator. Arriving at a clear, precise, effective negotiated agreement depends on the willingness of the parties to share accurate information about their own preferences, priorities, and interests. At the same time, because negotiators may also be interested in maximizing their self-interest, they may want to disclose as little as possible about their positions—particularly if they think they can do better by manipulating the information they disclose to the other party (see Chapter 2). This results in fundamental negotiation dilemmas involving trust and honesty (Kelley, 1966). The dilemma of trust is that a negotiator who believes everything the other says can be manipulated by dishonesty. The dilemma of honesty is that a negotiator who tells the other party all of his exact requirements and limits will, inevitably, never do better than his walkaway point. As Rubin and Brown (1975) note, "To sustain the bargaining relationship, each party must select a middle course between the extremes of complete openness toward, and deception of, the other. Each must be able to convince the other of his integrity while not at the same time endangering his bargaining position" (p. 15).

As a final point on the subject of truth-telling, there is, beyond ethics, the matter of *legal* obligations to be truthful. Deception in negotiation can rise to the level of legally actionable fraud. The law on this subject (like on most subjects!) is complex and often hard to pin down. See Box 9.1 for a guide to the (il)legality of lying in negotiation.[3]

Identifying Ethically Ambiguous Tactics and Attitudes toward Their Use

What Ethically Ambiguous Tactics Are There?   Deception and subterfuge may take several forms in negotiation. Researchers have been working to identify the nature of these tactics, and their underlying structure, for almost 20 years (e.g., Lewicki and Robinson, 1998).[4] They have extensively explored the nature and conceptual organization of ethically ambiguous negotiating tactics. The general approach has been to ask students and executives to rate a list of tactics on several dimensions: the appropriateness of the tactic, the rater's likelihood of using the tactic, and/or the perceived efficacy of using the

Although a major focus in the ethics of negotiation is on the morality of using deception in negotiation, it also behooves the effective negotiator to be familiar with the *legality* of doing so. Richard Shell, a lawyer and professor who writes about and teaches negotiation, offered an interpretation of U.S. law in his article "When Is It Legal to Lie in Negotiation?"

Shell starts with a basic "common law" definition of fraud: "a *knowing misrepresentation* of a *material fact* on which the victim reasonably *relies* and which *causes* damage" (p. 94; emphasis added).

A closer look at the meaning of the key (italicized) words in this definition brings legal issues involving lying in negotiation into focus.

- A *misrepresentation*. An affirmative misstatement of something.

- A *knowing* misrepresentation. Shell says a misrepresentation is "knowing" when you know that what you say is false when you say it. Does this mean you can skirt liability by avoiding coming into contact with the knowledge involved? Shell says no—courts would regard that as reckless disregard for the truth.

- A *fact*. To be illegal, in theory, the thing being misrepresented generally has to be an objective fact. But in practice, Shell points out that misstating an opinion or an intention can get you into trouble if it builds on factual misrepresentation or is particularly egregious—especially if you know the falsity at the time you make the statement or promise.

- A *material* fact. Not all "facts" are objective or material. Shell says that by the standards of legal practice in the United States, demands and reservation points

are not regarded as "material" to the deal, so it is not actionable fraud to bluff about them. He cautions, however, that lying about alternatives or other offers or other buyers can get you into trouble. It's not clear that these are always material, but this kind of thing may be left up to a jury to decide if a claim of fraud went to trial.

- *Reliance/causation*. For a deceptive statement to be legally fraudulent, the receiver must prove that he or she relied on the information and that doing so caused harm.

Does this mean that illegal deception always involves affirmative statements that are false? Will silence protect you from legal liability? Shell says no: there are conditions under which you are legally bound to share truthful information. For instance, you are obligated to disclose in these situations:

- If you make a partial disclosure that would be misleading.

- If the parties stand in fiduciary relationship to one another.

- If the nondisclosing party has "superior information" that is "vital."

- In cases involving certain specialized transactions, such as insurance contracts.

Knowing the law is a good idea, but Shell cautions that splitting legal hairs to gain tactical advantage is unwise: "In negotiation, people who rely on the letter of legal rules as a strategy for plotting unethical conduct are very likely to get into deep trouble. But people who rely on a cultivated sense of right and wrong to guide them in legal matters are likely to do well" (p. 99).

Source: Adapted from G. Richard Shell, "When Is It Legal to Lie in Negotiations?" *Sloan Management Review* 32, no. 3 (1991), pp. 93–101.

Stu's Views   © 2002 Stu All Rights Reserved www.stus.com

TABLE 9.2 | Categories of Marginally Ethical Negotiating Tactics

Category	Example
Traditional competitive bargaining	Not disclosing your walkaway; making an inflated opening offer
Emotional manipulation	Faking anger, fear, disappointment; faking elation, satisfaction
Misrepresentation	Distorting information or negotiation events in describing them to others
Misrepresentation to opponent's networks	Corrupting your opponent's reputation with his or her peers
Inappropriate information gathering	Bribery, infiltration, spying, etc.
Bluffing	Insincere threats or promises

Sources: Adapted from R. Robinson, R. J. Lewicki, and E. Donahue, "Extending and Testing a Five Factor Model of Ethical and Unethical Bargaining Tactics: The SINS Scale," *Journal of Organizational Behavior* 21 (2000), pp. 649–664; and B. Barry, I. S. Fulmer, and A. Long, *Ethically Marginal Bargaining Tactics: Sanction, Efficacy, and Performance.* Presented at the annual meeting of the Academy of Management, Toronto, August, 2000.

tactic. Analyzing these questionnaire results, six clear categories of tactics emerged and have been confirmed by additional data collection and analysis (Robinson, Lewicki, and Donahue, 2000; Barry, Fulmer, and Long, 2000). These categories are listed in Table 9.2. It is interesting to note that of the six categories, two—emotional manipulation and the use of "traditional competitive bargaining" tactics—are viewed as generally appropriate and likely to be used. These tactics, therefore, while mildly inappropriate, are nevertheless seen as appropriate and effective in successful distributive bargaining. The other four categories of tactics—misrepresentation, bluffing, misrepresentation to opponent's network, and inappropriate information collection—are generally seen as inappropriate and unethical in negotiation.

Does Tolerance for Ethically Ambiguous Tactics Lead to Their Actual Use?   As we indicated earlier, much of the research on these tactics has asked people to respond to questionnaires about their judgment of the ethicality of certain tactics and what they would be likely to do in a negotiation. One researcher (Volkema, 2001) selected five specific tactics from the larger group of unethical tactics described in the previous section and made them available to participants in a competitive buyer–seller negotiation role-play. These five tactics were exaggerating an opening offer, pretending not to be in a hurry, hiding one's own bottom line, misrepresenting factual information, and making promises that could not be kept. Volkema measured each person's attitude toward using the tactics in general and using a specific tactic (judging whether it was appropriate or not), likelihood of using the tactics in general and using a specific tactic, and actual use of the tactic in the role-play. The findings from the study suggested the following:

- There is a positive relationship between an attitude toward the use of each specific tactic and the intention to use it.
- There is a positive relationship between an attitude toward the use of a specific tactic and actually using that tactic for four of the five tactics studied.
- Hiding the bottom line was the tactic most frequently used, exaggerating an opening offer was the second most commonly used, followed by stalling for time and misrepresenting information. Making empty promises was used only about 10 percent of the time.
- Hiding the bottom line improved negotiator performance in the role-play. Negotiators also believed that making empty promises, misrepresenting information, and exaggerating their opening offer improved their performance, although there was no direct evidence that their performance was actually better.

Is It All Right to Use Ethically Ambiguous Tactics?   The studies summarized here indicate that there are tacitly agreed-on rules of the game in negotiation. In these rules, some minor forms of untruths—misrepresentation of one's true position to the other party, bluffs, and emotional manipulations—may be seen by some negotiators as ethically acceptable and within the rules (but not by others). In contrast, outright deception and falsification are generally seen as outside the rules. However, we must place some strong cautionary notes on these conclusions. First, these statements are based on ratings by large groups of people (mostly business students); in no way do they, or should they, predict how any one individual negotiator will perceive and use the tactics or how any one target who experiences them will rate them. (We discuss reactions from the "victim's" perspective later in this chapter.) Second, these observations are based primarily on what people said they would do, rather than what they actually did (the Volkema study we just described is a rare exception). Perceptions and reactions may well be different when the parties are making decisions in an actual negotiation, rather than rating the tactics on a questionnaire removed from any direct experience with another person in a meaningful social context. Third, by engaging in research on ethically ambiguous tactics (as the authors of this book have) and reporting these results, we do not mean to endorse the use of any marginally ethical tactic. Instead, our objective is to focus debate among negotiators on exactly when these tactics might be appropriate or should be used. Finally, we acknowledge that this is a Western view, in which individuals determine what is ethically acceptable; in some other cultures (e.g., Asia), a group or organization would decide on ethics, while in other cultures (e.g., some nations with emerging free markets), ethical constraints on negotiated transactions may be minimal or hard to determine clearly, and "let the buyer beware" at all times!

Deception by Omission versus Commission

The use of deceptive tactics can be active or passive. To illustrate, consider a study by O'Connor and Carnevale (1997), who examined the tendency for negotiators to misrepresent their interests on a common-value issue—an issue for which both parties are seeking the same outcome. A negotiator using this tactic deceives the other party about what she wants on the common-value issue and then (grudgingly) agrees to accept the other party's preference, which in reality matches her own. By making it look as though she has made a concession, she can seek a concession from the other party in return. Overall, 28 percent of O'Connor and Carnevale's subjects misrepresented the common-value issue in an effort to obtain a concession from the other party. The researchers discovered that negotiators used two forms of deception in misrepresenting the common-value issue: misrepresentation by *omission* (failing to disclose information that would benefit the other) and misrepresentation by *commission* (actually lying about the common-value issue).

Schweitzer (1997; Schweitzer and Croson, 1998) also examined factors that affected the tendency of negotiators to lie about material facts. Students took part in a role-play involving the sale of a car with a defective transmission. Students could lie by omission— by simply failing to mention the defective transmission—or by commission—by denying that the transmission was defective even when asked by the other party. Far more students were willing to lie by omission (not revealing the whole truth) than by commission (falsely answering a question when asked). This finding points to an important insight into human nature: many people are willing to let another person continue to operate under false premises, but will stop short of assertively making a false statement themselves. It clearly reinforces the norm of caveat emptor (let the buyer beware), suggesting that it is up to each party to ask the right questions and be appropriately skeptical when accepting the other's pitch.

The Decision to Use Ethically Ambiguous Tactics: A Model

We conclude this section of the chapter with a relatively simple model that helps explain how a negotiator decides whether to employ one or more deceptive tactics (see Figure 9.2). The model casts a negotiator in a situation where he or she needs to decide which tactics to

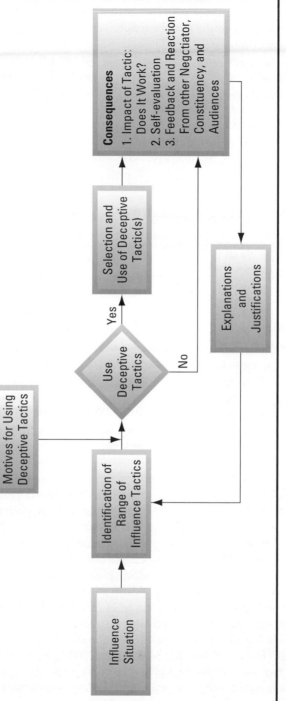

FIGURE 9.2 | A Simple Model of Deception in Negotiation

Influence Situation

Identification of Range of Influence Tactics

Intentions and Motives for Using Deceptive Tactics

Use Deceptive Tactics

Yes

No

Selection and Use of Deceptive Tactic(s)

Explanations and Justifications

Consequences
1. Impact of Tactic: Does It Work?
2. Self-evaluation
3. Feedback and Reaction From other Negotiator, Constituency, and Audiences

use to influence the other party. The individual identifies possible influence tactics that could be effective in a given situation, some of which might be deceptive, inappropriate, or otherwise marginally ethical. Once these tactics are identified, the individual may decide to actually use one or more of them. The selection and use of a given tactic is likely to be influenced by the negotiator's own motivations and his or her perception/judgment of the tactic's appropriateness. Once the tactic is employed, the negotiator will assess consequences on three standards: (1) whether the tactic worked (produced the desired result), (2) how the negotiator feels about him- or herself after using the tactic, and (3) how the individual may be judged by the other party or by neutral observers. Negative or positive conclusions on any of these three standards may lead the negotiator to try to explain or justify use of the tactic, but they will also eventually affect a decision to employ similar tactics in the future.

Why Use Deceptive Tactics? Motives and Consequences

In the preceding pages we discussed at length the nature of ethics and the kinds of tactics in negotiation that might be regarded as ethically ambiguous. Now we turn to a discussion of why such tactics are tempting and what the consequences are of succumbing to that temptation. We begin with motives, and motives inevitably begin with power.

The Power Motive

The purpose of using ethically ambiguous negotiating tactics is to increase the negotiator's power in the bargaining environment. As we discussed in Chapter 7, information is a major source of leverage in negotiation. Information has power because negotiation is intended to be a rational activity involving the exchange of information and the persuasive use of that information. One view of negotiation is that it is primarily an exchange of facts, arguments, and logic between two wholly rational information-processing entities. Often, whoever has better information, or uses it more persuasively, stands to "win" the negotiation.

Such a view assumes that the information is accuarate and truthful. To assume otherwise—that it is not truthful—is to question the very assumptions on which daily social communication is based and the honesty and integrity of the presenter of that information. Of course, raising such questions openly might insult the others and reduce the implied trust we placed in them. Moreover, investigating someone else's truthfulness and honesty is time and energy consuming. So any inaccurate and untruthful statements (i.e., lies) introduced into this social exchange manipulate information in favor of the introducer. Through the tactics we described earlier—bluffing, falsification, misrepresentation, deception, and selective disclosure—the liar gains advantage. In fact, it has been demonstrated that individuals are more willing to use deceptive tactics when the other party is perceived to be uninformed or unknowledgable about the situation under negotiation; particularly when the stakes are high (Boles, Croson, and Murnighan, 2000). The receiver either accepts the information at face value or has to decide whether there is a basis for challenging the other person's accuracy, credibility, and intentions (and/or must attempt to independently verify that information).

The *Boston Globe* investigated incidents of cheating during the late 1990s in the Boston Marathon and other similar competitions around the country. The report listed the following explanations:

1. Some cheaters were angry or disturbed, often demonstrating a pattern of erratic, unethical, or illegal behaviors.

2. More typically, cheaters were described as middle-aged males who were often successful in many parts of their lives and found it difficult not to be equally successful in racing.

3. Some people were categorized as "unintentional cheaters"; these were people who simply were caught up in the racing moment and did not fully realize what they were doing at the time.

4. Cheaters typically sought recognition rather than prize money or other material gain. Ironically, many reported that the negative publicity surrounding their cheating caused friends, neighbors, and even family members to view them negatively, even if they had never misbehaved before.

Source: Larry Tye, "They're Not in It for the Long Haul," *The Columbus (Ohio) Dispatch,* April 19, 1998, p. 10E.

Other Motives to Behave Unethically

The motivation of a negotiator can clearly affect his or her tendency to use deceptive tactics. (For example, see Box 9.2 for a discussion of the motives of cheaters in running.) When we consider individual differences in Chapter 15, we point out how motivational orientation—whether negotiators are motivated to act cooperatively, competitively, or individualistically toward each other—can affect the strategies and tactics they pursue. In the study cited earlier, O'Connor and Carnevale (1997) also manipulated the negotiators' motivational orientation to the situation, predisposing parties to either a competitive or a cooperative orientation toward the other. Competitive negotiators—those looking to maximize their own outcome, regardless of the consequences for the other—were more likely to use misrepresentation as a strategy. Cultural differences may also map onto motivational influences: Sims (2002) found that individuals in a highly individualistic culture (the United States) were more likely to use deception for personal gain than those in a more collectivist culture (Israel). (We say more about connections between culture and negotiator ethics later in the chapter.)

But the impact of motives may be more complex. In an early study on tactics, Lewicki and Spencer (1991) asked negotiators about their predisposition to use ethically ambiguous tactics. Different versions of the questionnaire explicitly told respondents to assume either a competitive or a cooperative motivational orientation toward the other party and to assume that the other party would be taking either a competitive or a cooperative motivational orientation. The authors predicted that competitive motivations would elicit the strongest endorsement of ethically ambiguous tactics. The results revealed that differences in the negotiators' *own* motivational orientation—cooperative versus competitive—did *not* cause differences in their view of the appropriateness of using the tactics, but the negotiators' perception of the *other's* expected motivation did! In other words, negotiators were significantly more likely to see the ethically ambiguous tactics as appropriate if they anticipated that the other party would be competitive versus cooperative. This finding suggests that negotiators may rationalize the use of marginally ethical tactics in anticipation of the other's expected conduct rather than take personal responsibility for using these tactics in the service of their own competitive orientation. Several authors (e.g., Batson and Thompson, 2001) have indicated that people may be more motivated to appear moral, rather than to actually act morally, because to act morally (e.g., act with integrity) may have a number of costs attached to it.

Earlier we discussed four philosophical approaches to the discussion of ethics in business: end-use, duty, social contract, and personalistic ethics. While these four approaches provide useful frameworks for scholars wishing to analyze ethical issues in business and other contexts, they also speak to the ways that individuals actually think about ethical dilemmas in practice. Perry and Nixon (2005) examined the extent to which an endorsement of each of these four philosophical frameworks predisposed individuals to engage in ethically ambiguous behavior during negotiations. They found that those who prefer an ends-based framework (utilitarian ethics) or a focus on community norms (social contract ethics) described themselves as more likely to engage in marginally unethical behavior such as making false promises or misrepresenting information. On the other hand, those inclined to adhere to rules and moral principles (duty-based ethics) were less comfortable with these tactics and, therefore, less likely to engage in ethically questionable practices.

The Consequences of Unethical Conduct

A negotiator who employs an unethical tactic will experience consequences that may be positive or negative, based on three aspects of the situation: (1) whether the tactic is effective; (2) how the other person, his or her constituencies, and audiences evaluate the tactic; and (3) how the negotiator evaluates the tactic. We discuss each in turn.

Effectiveness   Let us first consider the consequences that occur based on whether the tactic is successful or not. Clearly, a tactic's effectiveness will have some impact on whether it is more or less likely to be used in the future (essentially, a simple learning and reinforcement process). If using the tactic allows a negotiator to attain rewarding outcomes that would be unavailable if he had behaved ethically, and if the unethical conduct is not punished by others, the frequency of unethical conduct is likely to increase because the negotiator believes he or she can get away with it. Thus, real consequences—rewards and punishments that arise from using a tactic or not using it—should not only motivate a negotiator's present behavior but also affect his or her predisposition to use similar strategies in similar circumstances in the future. (For the moment, we will ignore the consequences of these tactics on the negotiator's reputation and trustworthiness, an impact that most deceptive negotiators unfortunately ignore in the short term.)

These propositions have not been tested in negotiating situations, but they have been tested extensively in other research studies on ethical decision making. For example, research by Hegarty and Sims (1978) appears to support both of these assertions. In that study, when research participants expected to be rewarded for making an unethical decision by participating in a laboratory-simulated kickback scheme, they not only participated but also were willing to participate again when a second opportunity arose. Moreover, when there were also strong pressures on the research subjects to compete with others—for example, announcing how well each person had done on the task and giving a prize to the one with the highest score—the frequency of unethical conduct increased even further.

NON SEQUITUR   **by WILEY**

Reactions of Others   A second set of consequences may arise from judgments and evaluations by the person who was the "target" of the tactic, by constituencies, or by audiences that can observe the tactic. Depending on whether these parties recognize the tactic and whether they evaluate it as proper or improper to use, the negotiator may receive a great deal of feedback. If the target person is unaware that a deceptive tactic was used, he or she may show no reaction other than disappointment at having lost the negotiation. However, if the target discovers that deception has occurred, he or she is likely to react strongly. People who discover that they have been deceived or exploited are typically angry. In addition to perhaps having "lost" the negotiation, they feel foolish for having allowed themselves to be manipulated or deceived by a clever ploy. As a result of both the loss and embarrassment, victims are inclined to seek retaliation and revenge. The victim is unlikely to trust the unethical negotiator again, may seek revenge from the negotiator in future dealings, and may also generalize this experience to negotiations with others. A strong experience of being exploited may thus sour a victim's perception of negotiation contexts in the future (Bies and Moag, 1986; Werth and Flannery, 1986).

These negative consequences were apparent in a study by McCornack and Levine (1990), who examined people's reactions to having been deceived (in many different types of relationships, not necessarily negotiating ones). They found that victims had strong emotional reactions to deception when they had an intimate relationship with the subject, when the information at stake was very important, and when they saw lying as an unacceptable type of behavior for that relationship (i.e., when strong expectations of truth telling were clearly violated). In a majority of cases, the discovery of the lie was instrumental in an eventual termination of the relationship with the other person, and in most cases the termination was initiated by the victim. The more the deception was serious, personal, and highly consequential for trust between the parties, the more destructive it was to the relationship. In a similar vein, there is also evidence that individuals who are deceptive are regarded as less truthful and less desirable for future interactions (Boles, Croson, and Murnighan, 2000). We will have more to say about negotiator reputation in Chapter 10, but it is worth emphasizing here that damage to one's reputation can be difficult to repair. A study by Schweitzer, Hershey, and Bradlow (2006) showed that the effects of untrustworthy actions on one's credibility can be remedied with subsequent truthful behavior, as long as the untrustworthy actions that breached trust did not involve deception. When deception was the cause of the rift, attempts to restore trust through an apology or other behavior apology were ineffective. In sum, although the use of unethical tactics may create short-term success for the negotiator, it may also create an adversary who is distrustful or, even worse, bent on revenge and retribution.

Reactions of Self   Very little systematic research has explored the third set of consequences: the negotiator's own reactions to the use of unethical tactics. Under some conditions—such as when the other party has truly suffered—a negotiator may feel some discomfort, stress, guilt, or remorse. This can lead a negotiator to seek ways to reduce the psychological discomfort. For example, Aquino and Becker (2005) found that individuals who had lied to their partner during the course of a simulated business negotiation made larger concessions later in the negotiation to compensate. This compensation for an earlier lie was especially common among study participants who rated themselves highly on "moral attributes" (e.g., honest, fairness, benevolence) and among those who told they were negotiating on behalf of an organization that "prides itself on being fair and honest in its business dealings." Of course, negotiators who see no problem with using deceptive tactics may be inclined to use them again and may begin to ponder how to use them more effectively. In Aquino and Becker's study, those who had no personal qualms about lying behaved no differently after lying than those who did not lie, meaning they were no more likely to compensate for the lie with a subsequent concession. On the one hand, although the use of ethically questionable tactics may have severe consequences for the negotiator's reputation and trustworthiness, parties seldom appear to take these outcomes into consideration in the short term. On the other hand, and particularly if the tactic has worked, the negotiator may be able to rationalize and justify the use of the tactic. We explore these rationalizations and justifications in the next section.

Explanations and Justifications

When a negotiator has used an ethically ambiguous tactic that may elicit a reaction—as we described earlier—the negotiator must prepare to defend the tactic's use to himself (e.g., "I see myself as a person of integrity, and yet I have decided to do something that might be viewed as unethical"), to the victim, or to constituencies and audiences who may express their concerns. The primary purpose of these explanations and justifications is to rationalize, explain, or excuse the behavior—to verbalize some good, legitimate reason why this tactic was necessary. Rationalization is often motivated by the desire to ease distress or dissonance over what the individual has just done (Aquino and Becker, 2005). There is an increasing stream of research on those who employ unethical tactics and the explanations and justifications they use to rationalize them. Most of the following rationalizations have been adapted from Bok (1978) and her excellent treatise on lying:

- *The tactic was unavoidable.* Negotiators frequently justify their actions by claiming that the situation made it necessary for them to act the way they did. The negotiator may feel that she was not in full control of her actions or had no other option; hence she should not be held responsible. Perhaps the negotiator had no intent to hurt anyone but was pressured to use the tactic by someone else.

- *The tactic was harmless.* The negotiator may say that what he did was really trivial and not very significant. People tell white lies all the time. For example, you may greet your neighbor with a cheery "Good morning, nice to see you" when, in fact, it may not be a good morning, you are in a bad mood, and you wish you hadn't run into your neighbor because you are angry about his dog barking all night. Exaggerations, bluffs, or peeking at the other party's private notes during negotiations can all be easily explained away as harmless actions. Note, however, that this particular justification interprets the harm from the actor's point of view; the victim may not agree and may have experienced significant harm or costs as a result.

- *The tactic will help to avoid negative consequences.* When using this justification, negotiators are arguing that the ends justify the means. In this case, the justification is that the tactic helped to avoid greater harm. It is OK to lie to an armed robber about where you have hidden your money to avoid being robbed. Similarly, negotiators may see lying (or any other means–ends tactic) as justifiable if it protects them against even more undesirable consequences should the truth be known.

- *The tactic will produce good consequences, or the tactic is altruistically motivated.* Again, the end justifies the means, but in a positive sense. As we stated earlier, a negotiator who judges a tactic on the basis of its consequences is acting in accord with the tenets of act utilitarianism—that the quality of any given action is judged by its consequences. Utilitarians may argue that certain kinds of lies or means—ends tactics are appropriate because they may provide for the larger good—for example, Robin Hood tactics in which someone robs from the rich to make the poor better off. In reality, most negotiators use deceptive tactics for their own advantage, not for the general good. In this case, others are likely to view these actions as less excusable than tactics that avoid negative consequences.

- *"They had it coming," or "They deserve it," or "I'm just getting my due."* These are all variations on the theme of using lying and deception either against an individual who may have taken advantage of you in the past or against some generalized source of authority (i.e., "the system"). Polls have noted an erosion of honesty in the United States— people increasingly think it appropriate to take advantage of the system in various ways, including tax evasion, petty theft, shoplifting, improper declaration of bankruptcy, journalistic excesses, and distortion in advertising (e.g., Patterson and Kim, 1991; Yankelovich, 1982).

- *"They were going to do it anyway, so I will do it first."* Sometimes a negotiator legitimizes the use of a tactic because he or she anticipates that the other intends to use similar tactics. Investigating Brazilian and American negotiators, Volkema and Fleury (2002) found that people were most willing to use deception when negotiating with a partner who had a reputation for being unethical. In other words, individuals who expect their partner to behave unethically were more likely to match that behavior. In an insightful study, Tenbrunsel (1998) also linked one's own inclination to deceive and judgments of the other party's integrity. She found that the more an individual was tempted to engage in misrepresentation, the more he or she believed that the other would also misrepresent information. Thus, one's own temptation to misrepresent creates a self-fulfilling logic in which one believes one needs to misrepresent because the other is likely to do it as well. At the same time, subjects in this study consistently rated themselves as more ethical than the other party, which suggests that people experience some combination of positive illusions about themselves and their own behavior, and negative illusions about the other and the other's likely behavior.

• *"He started it."* This is a variation on the anticipatory justification discussed in the last point. In this case, the rationale is that others have *already* violated the rules, therefore legitimizing the negotiator's right to violate them as well. In such cases, unethical tactics are employed in a tit-for-tat manner, to restore balance, or to give others their due. Justifications such as "An eye for an eye" or "He started it and I'm going to finish it!" are commonly heard as a defense for resorting to unethical tactics in these cases.

• *The tactic is fair or appropriate to the situation.* This approach uses a kind of moral (situational) relativism as a rationale or justification. Most social situations, including negotiations, are governed by a set of generally well-understood rules of proper conduct and behavior. For example, recall the earlier arguments of Carr (1968), that business is a game and that the game has a special ethos to it that legitimizes normally unethical actions. Bowie (1993) and Koehn (1997) have countered these arguments, contending that deceit in business is just as immoral as it is in other areas of life and that the game analogy of business no more legitimizes unethical conduct than other analogies. As a general matter, ethical relativism—the idea that moral standards shift with changing circumstances—frequently comes under fire as an unacceptable take on morality. As Hosmer (2003, p. 89) puts it, "If all ethical systems are equally valid, then no firm moral judgments can be made about individual behavior, and we are all on our own to do as we like to others, within economic limits and legal constraints." We leave it to the reader to decide if this is a good thing or a bad thing.

Research by Shapiro (1991) shows that these kinds of explanations matter in mitigating a victim's reactions to having been deceived. Her experimental subjects were supposedly working together to apply for a loan to support a new business venture. In the course of the simulation, subjects were told that the loan officer had caught their partner falsifying information on the loan application. The experimenter then manipulated the severity of the consequences for being caught in the deception (how much the subject lost as a result of the partner's deception), as well as how adequately the partner explained why the deception had occurred (the deception was unintentional, or selfishly motivated, or altruistically motivated). The findings indicate that the more a subject felt that the partner's explanation was adequate for the deception, the less he or she expressed feelings of injustice, disapproval, and punitiveness toward the partner. If subjects were mildly upset, the explanations had more impact than if the subjects were strongly upset. Moreover, explanations had the most impact when the partner stated that the deception was unintentional, less impact when the deception was altruistic, and the least impact when the deception was selfishly motivated.

As self-serving rationalizations for one's own conduct, explanations allow the negotiator to convince others—particularly the victim—that conduct that would ordinarily be wrong in a given situation is acceptable. Explanations and justifications help people rationalize the behavior to themselves as well. But there is a risk: we surmise that the more frequently negotiators engage in this self-serving process, the more their judgments about ethical standards and values will become biased, diminishing their ability to see the truth for what it is. The tactics involved may have been used initially to gain power in a negotiation, but negotiators who use them frequently may experience a loss of power over time. These negotiators will be seen as having low credibility or integrity, and they will be treated accordingly as people who will act exploitatively if the opportunity arises. Good reputations are easier to maintain than to restore once damaged.

What Factors Shape a Negotiator's Predisposition to Use Unethical Tactics?

Earlier we talked about the use of ethically ambiguous tactics in terms of the simple model presented in Figure 9.2. This model describes a rational calculation process in which the negotiator selects a tactic, uses the tactic, evaluates the consequences, and attempts to manage the consequences (if the tactic is detected) through explanations and justifications. A number of other factors can affect the sequences described in the model:

- The background and demographic characteristics of the negotiators.
- The personality characteristics and level of moral development of the negotiators.
- Elements of the social context (the situation in which the negotiators find themselves) that encourage or discourage unethical conduct.

In this section, we briefly mention how each of these factors might influence the predisposition to use ethically questionable tactics. The factors are included in an expanded version of the model, presented in Figure 9.3. As we discuss this model, it should be clear that the fundamental debate here is the "nature versus nurture" argument about what causes individuals to behave as they do. Many believe that making ethical decisions is completely determined by the moral standards of the individual actor; others, however, believe that situational factors (such as group and organizational norms, accountability pressures, and reward systems) can cause even ethical people to do unethical things. We expect the debate to continue for a long time. However, when social scientists try to hold individual differences constant, or randomize them across large groups of people, it is very clear that situational influences can predispose very ethical people to do marginally ethical things.

Demographic Factors

A number of survey-oriented studies on ethical behavior have attempted to relate differences in ethical conduct to differences in individual background, religious orientation, age, gender, nationality, and education. In general, these broad demographic studies have shown that individuals who are older or have a stronger commitment to some religious philosophy are less likely to behave unethically than younger or less religious individuals (e.g., Hassett, 1981). A few studies have investigated the relationship between demographic factors and the use of unethical tactics in negotiation. In reporting these research findings, *we are not suggesting that all people of a particular group will necessarily act in a specified manner.* Thus, for example, studies that show that young people tend to use more deceptive negotiating tactics than other people do not imply that every young person will use those tactics. We discuss these demographics because the trends appear to be reliable and consistent across a number of different ethical choice situations.

FIGURE 9.3 | A More Complex Model of Deception in Negotiation

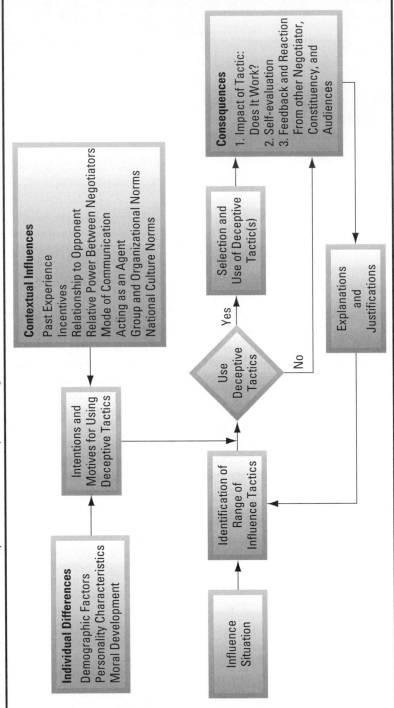

Sex   A number of studies have shown that women tend to make more ethically rigorous judgments than men. For example, Volkema (1999) found in comparing Brazilian and American women that those from both cultures were significantly more ethical than men, revealing less willingness to use ethically ambiguous negotiation tactics. Dawson (1997) asked men and women to respond to a number of decision-making scenarios involving ethics. Half the scenarios were relational, in that the actor's decision clearly affected the interests of others, while the other half were nonrelational, in that the consequences did not affect anyone else and were only matters of individual conscience. Dawson's results demonstrate that when making decisions about relational issues, women were significantly more ethical than men, but that there were no differences on the nonrelational situations. Hence, according to this study, women may make more ethical judgments, but only when the consequences of their decisions affect someone else.

Returning to the ethically ambiguous tactics described earlier in this chapter, Lewicki and Robinson (1998) and Robinson, Lewicki, and Donahue (2000) found that men were more likely to use some unethical tactics than women. This did not hold for tactics classified as "traditional competitive bargaining" (e.g., making an excessively high opening offer and stalling for time); there was no gender difference in the perceived appropriateness of these aggressive (but not deceptive) tactics.

However, a more recent study suggests differences may exist in the way that men and women are perceived as ethical decision makers. Schminke, Ambrose, and Miles (2003) created scenarios that described an individual (male or female) faced with an ethical dilemma, and they had participants rate their perceptions of that action as well as the ethical framework that the actor employed. Overall, female actors were perceived to be formalistic in their decision—they were thought to pay more attention to rules or principles than actual outcomes of the situation. In contrast, male actors were perceived to be more utilitarian—to give greater attention to net social good rather than rules or principles.

Age and Experience   In the Dawson (1997) and Volkema (1999) studies cited earlier, both men and women behaved more ethically as they aged. In the Anton (1990) study, where categories of deceptive tactics were rated, older parties tended to see bluffing as more acceptable and deception as less acceptable. Finally, Robinson, Lewicki, and Donahue (2008) report a strong negative correlation between age and the endorsement of unethical negotiating tactics. Overall, older individuals were less likely than younger ones to see marginally ethical tactics as appropriate. Moreover, they reported that individuals with more general work experience, and with more direct work experience, were less likely to use unethical negotiating tactics.

Professional Orientation   Anton (1990) compared ratings by MBA students, business alumni, and clergy of perceived appropriateness of categories of deceptive negotiation tactics. All groups indicated that traditional competitive bargaining and misrepresentation were ethically acceptable, but clergy were the most ethically conservative in their ratings. Deception was seen as moderately unethical, and all groups believed that outright falsification was highly unethical. Garcia, Darley, and Robinson (2001) conducted an interesting study of district attorneys and public defenders and their use of these tactics. They found that public defenders saw ethically ambiguous tactics as more appropriate than district attorneys, that both groups increased their approval of the tactics when they thought the other party was likely to use them, and that public defenders increased their approval as a "defensive move" more than district attorneys. Thus, these findings are actually more about which role a person plays—defender versus challenger of the status quo—than about the attorney role that they play.

Nationality and Culture   It is apparent that there are cultural differences in attitudes toward ethically ambiguous tactics in negotiation, although there are not enough research findings to create a coherent overall picture. Here are some of the findings (drawn from Elahee and Brooks, 2004; Lewicki and Robinson, 1998; Sims, 2002; Volkema, 1997, 1998, 1999; Volkema and Fleury, 2002):

- Americans and Asians were significantly more likely to use bluffing, and Eastern Europeans were less likely to do so.
- Students with a Middle Eastern heritage were more likely to endorse misrepresentation to an opponent's network, and Americans were less likely to do so.
- Managers from the United States and Brazil both rated traditional competitive bargaining tactics as acceptable, but managers from Brazil were more likely to rate other ethically ambiguous tactics involving deception or subterfuge as acceptable.
- Managers from the United States and Brazil were similar in their use of tactics involving third parties (e.g., information gathering or disseminating information through a network), but Brazilians were willing to be more deceptive in dealing with their immediate opponent.
- Mexican managers saw the same tactics as less appropriate than American managers did.
- People in a more individualistic culture (the United States) were more likely to use deception for personal gain than people in a more collectivist culture (Israel).
- Negotiators were more likely to endorse the use of ethically ambiguous tactics when negotiation with someone from another country than with someone from the same country.

The difficulty is knowing what to do with the information that comes from these research findings. Clearly there are cultural differences in perceptions of what is or isn't appropriate in negotiation—differences that we can uncover statistically in a research study looking at many individuals. But it is just as clearly hazardous—and wrong—to assume that because a researcher can find a cultural trend in a sample of many individuals that any one individual would actually behave in a certain way.

Not everyone acts in ways that are culturally representative; in fact, some negotiators may go out of their way to avoid doing so. An American attorney we know who negotiates business deals in Latin America tells us he has noticed that some Mexican negotiators he meets with will adopt an extreme U.S. style of interaction rather than exhibit communication patterns that are "typical" of Mexico, presumably to adapt to the American counterpart across the table. When it comes to negotiator ethics, differences across cultures may be a function not so much of different beliefs about ethics per se, but rather variations in the role of personal relationships in different societies. Rivers and Lytle (2007) illustrate this point: "A Chinese negotiator may not realize that a Western counterpart does not share their view of the importance of obligation to a friend and may be perplexed to be labeled 'unethical'

People who conduct business in countries other than their own encounter not only different languages but different cultural mores and practices as well. They may find that local business practices reflect ethical standards that are dictated by cultural norms that are dissimilar to their own. Such a situation can lead to an ethical dilemma: Which system of ethics should guide the interaction? Is it more appropriate to adopt the ethical system of the host country or to remain true to one's own ethical standards? Henry Lane, Joseph DiStefano, and Martha Maznevski argue that there are some guidelines for decision makers that bridge cultural differences. They offer this list of general advice that can guide businesspeople through interactions in a variety of cultural settings:

1. Identify the stakeholders that have an interest in or will be affected by the decision. This might include the home-country or host-country governments, suppliers, employees, unions, and customers. What are your responsibilities and obligations to each of these stakeholders?

2. Ask yourself whether you have the best information possible and whether it is reliable.

3. Do not avoid making ethical decisions that are your responsibility, but also do not accept responsibility for decisions that are not your responsibility.

4. Enter into dependent relationships with care. Be certain that you retain enough power to maintain your own standards.

5. Do the best for all involved stakeholders, fulfill your obligations, observe laws and contracts, do not use deception, and avoid knowingly doing harm (physical, psychological, economic, or social).

6. Remember the "billboard" or "light-of-day" test: when you drive to work tomorrow morning, would you be happy to see your decision on a billboard at the side of the road? Would your action appear reasonable then?

Source: Adapted from H. W. Lane, J. J. DiStefano, and M. L. Maznevski, *International Management Behavior,* 3rd ed. (Cambridge, MA: Blackwell, 1997).

when they are acting honorably within their ethical principles, and offer gift money to establish a stronger relationship. . . . Judging actions used by a culturally different other party as 'unethical' can elicit potent negative responses in a negotiator" (p. 23).

The complications involved in understanding ethics in cross-cultural negotiation are illustrated in Box 9.3. We return to a richer treatment of cross-cultural differences in Chapter 16.

Personality Differences

Researchers have sought to identify dimensions of personality that would successfully predict a person's predisposition to behave unethically. Selected findings are described next.

Competitiveness versus Cooperativeness Lewicki and Robinson (1998) found that students who rated themselves as aggressive were significantly more likely to use bluffing, misrepresentation, and a variety of other dishonest tactics than students who rated themselves as cooperative. Similarly, Robinson, Lewicki, and Donahue (2000) report that students who rated themselves as competitive were significantly more likely to use ethically ambiguous tactics than those who rated themselves as cooperative. It is also not surprising that individuals are more likely to lie to a competitor (Ross and Robertson, 2000).

Steinel and de Dreu (2004) examined how an individual's "social value orientation" influences his or her use of deceptive tactics using a mixed-motive decision game that resembles a prisoner's dilemma game. Social value orientations are preferences people have for acting cooperatively (a "pro-social" orientation) or competitively (a "pro-self" orientation) in a given situation. Not surprisingly, pro-social individuals in Steinel and de Dreu's study were more honest with a cooperative partner than were pro-self individuals. Interestingly, when interacting with a competitive partner, pro-social individuals used even more deceptive tactics than did pro-self actors. The researchers attributed this odd inconsistency to an "overassimilation" on the part of pro-social individuals. In other words, their reaction to competitive parties might have been a punitive effort to hold the other party responsible for his or her competitive orientation.

Machiavellianism   In Chapter 15, we discuss the personality variable called Machiavellianism. Machiavellians adhere to a pragmatic and expedient view of human nature—"The best way to handle people is to tell them what they want to hear" or "It is hard to get ahead without cutting corners here and there." A number of studies have shown that individuals who are high in Machiavellianism are more willing and able con artists, more likely to lie when they need to, better able to tell a lie without feeling anxious about it, and more persuasive and effective in their lies (Christie and Geis, 1970).[5] Machiavellianism thus appears to be a predictor of unethical conduct.

Locus of Control   Individuals differ in their locus of control—that is, the degree to which they believe that the outcomes they obtain are largely a result of their own ability and effort (internal control) versus fate, chance, or circumstance (external control). Studies have generally predicted that individuals who are high in internal control are more likely to do what they think is right (i.e., they have a stronger personal value system or ethical code) and to feel that they had more control over producing the outcomes they wanted to achieve in a situation in which there were temptations to be unethical. Evidence from studies of cheating and ethical decision making has supported this prediction (Lefcourt, 1982; Trevino and Youngblood, 1990), although it is important to note that locus of control seems most important when individuals can also exert control over outcomes. Thus, locus of control appears to be a moderately powerful contributor to ethical decision making, although it has yet to be tested as a factor in tactic selection in negotiation. We discuss its role in negotiation more generally in Chapter 15.

Moral Development and Personal Values

Many researchers have explored the relationship of an individual's level of moral development to ethical decision making. Kohlberg (1969) proposed that an individual's moral and ethical judgments are a consequence of achieving a particular developmental level or stage of moral growth. Kohlberg proposed six stages of moral development, grouped into three levels:

1. A preconventional level (Stages 1 and 2), where the individual is concerned with concrete outcomes that meet his or her own immediate needs, particularly external rewards and punishments.

2. A conventional level (Stages 3 and 4), where the individual defines what is right on the basis of what his immediate social situation and peer group endorses or what society in general seems to want.

3. A principled level (Stages 5 and 6), where the individual defines what is right on the basis of some broader set of universal values and principles.

The higher the stage people achieve, the more complex their moral reasoning should be and the more ethical their decisions should be. In addition, there may be gender-related differences in this ethical reasoning process—as noted earlier, women's ethical reasoning may be more relational and less individualistic than men's (Gilligan, 1982).

Many studies have demonstrated the power of measuring ethical orientation in this way (see Trevino, 1986; and Trevino and Youngblood, 1990, for reviews). The results have generally indicated that higher levels of moral development are associated with more ethical decisions, less cheating behavior, more helping behavior, and more resistance to authority figures who are attempting to dictate unethical conduct. Other studies have investigated value differences, defined more broadly. Glover, Bumpus, Logan, and Ciesla (1997) report on an extensive study of honesty/integrity and other values such as achievement, fairness, and concern for others on ethical decision making. In their study, fairness and achievement selectively predicted some ethical decisions, while honesty did not predict any ethical choices. These mixed findings are reasonably consistent with the growing literature that attempts to measure individual values and morality and relate them to ethical decisions. We are unaware of any studies examining the specific relationship between moral development and tendencies to use deceptive negotiating tactics.

Contextual Influences on Unethical Conduct

The last set of factors that should influence a negotiator's willingness to act unethically are contextual factors. We briefly examine a number of contextual elements: the negotiator's past experience with using unethical tactics, incentives to use the tactics, characteristics of the other party, the quality of the relationship with the other party, differences in power and status between the parties, modes of communication, whether a negotiator is acting as the principal actor or an agent, and the social norms that govern the negotiation process.

Past Experience   At least one study has shown that the simple impact of past experience—particularly failure—can increase the likelihood that a negotiator might attempt to use unethical tactics. Schweitzer, Ordonez, Douma (2004) gave students different kinds of goals (do your best, meet a specific goal, or exceed a specific goal), then asked them to solve puzzles and manipulated their success or failure at the puzzle task. First, having specific goals clearly influenced reporting of accomplishment; if told to "do your best," parties reported more honestly than if they had a specific goal to meet. Participants who had to meet specific goals were more likely to overstate their productivity than those who did not have specific goals, were more likely to overstate their success when their actual performance was closer to the goal, and were more likely to overstate in those situations where they thought they "deserved" the reward based on overall productivity.

Role of Incentives   A second factor that can influence a negotiator's tendency to use ethically ambiguous tactics is the role of incentives in place in a given situation. Tenbrunsel (1998) demonstrated that greater incentives influenced a negotiator's inclination to misrepresent to the other party, and they also enhanced the negotiator's expectation that the other party would misrepresent. However, it is difficult to determine whether the negotiator's heightened sensitivity to misrepresentation was due to an expectation that the other was going to misrepresent or was because the negotiator intended to misrepresent himself.

Characteristics of the Other Party   Negotiators may not necessarily plan to use deceptive or ethically ambiguous behavior during a negotiation, but may do so when it is perceived that the other party is vulnerable to such tactics. The work of Olekalns and Smith (2007) suggests that negotiators often use these tactics opportunistically. When a partner was perceived as benevolent, trustworthy, or having integrity, a negotiator was more likely to deceive him or her by omitting or misrepresenting information. The authors argued that this pattern may represent opportunistic betrayal, whereby negotiators use ethically ambiguous tactics because the potential cost of detection or punishment from the other party are low. Ironically, the authors also found that information was misrepresented more often when the other party was perceived as powerful. Power, in this context, was not defined as relative power, but rather as having a powerful disposition. In this circumstance, deception may not have been used opportunistically, but rather defensively. Olekalns and Smith argued that the perceived risk of exploitation is higher when the other party is powerful; hence the decision to distort information may be seen as a way of leveling the playing field.

Relationship between the Negotiator and the Other Party   Two aspects of the negotiator's relationship with the other party affect the tendency to use certain tactics: what the relationship has been like in the past and what the parties would like it to be in the future. The negotiators'*past* relationship will affect current behavior if the parties have been previously competitive or cooperative, are friends or enemies, feel indebted to each other, or hold grudges toward each other. For example, research by Gruder (1971) showed that negotiators were likely to make deceptive arguments, negotiate for a longer period of time, and make fewer concessions when they had previously experienced the other party as exploitative than when the other party had been cooperative. Similarly, Schweitzer (1997) demonstrated that students were more likely to lie to strangers than they were to friends, and they were particularly more likely to lie to strangers who did not ask any probing questions. An analogous argument can be made for a negotiator's expectations about how the other party will behave in the present or future. If you view the other party with suspicion—as exploitative, competitive, dishonest—you can then justify a relativistic approach to strategy and claim that anticipatory self-defense legitimizes your actions. However, you can see how this form of rationalization may be easily distorted by fear and suspicion and hence create a self-fulfilling prophecy to justify use of an unethical tactic. All a negotiator needs is to experience some mildly competitive or exploitative bit of behavior from the other party, or even to imagine that it is going to occur. Naturally, this will motivate the other party to seek revenge and act exactly as the negotiator anticipated.

A factor that can balance this self-fulfilling dynamic is whether the negotiator expects the relationship to be short term or long term. In the Lewicki and Spencer (1991) study discussed earlier, participants were told to expect either a short-term or long-term working relationship with the other party. Participants who expected to be in a short-term relationship were more likely to see ethically ambiguous tactics as appropriate than those expecting a long-term relationship, regardless of their own and the other party's motivations. This is consistent with research showing that the prospect of future negotiations with an individual is an important motivator to act ethically during negotiations (Volkema and Fleury, 2002). Taken together these are important findings, indicating that negotiators are more willing to use ethically precarious tactics if they do not anticipate having to live with the consequences of doing so.

Relative Power between the Negotiators   Another key situational factor is relative power—how much power one negotiator has relative to the other party. We discussed the link between power and ethics earlier in this chapter, observing that negotiators use deception as a way to gain temporary information power over the other party. In general, negotiators with relatively more power are more likely to use unethical tactics. For example, in one research study, negotiators with more power bluffed more often and communicated less with their counterpart than those with less power (Crott, Kayser, and Lamm, 1980). This result will seem paradoxical to some people. Why should negotiators with more power, who can presumably get what they want by using their power legitimately, use unethical tactics that increase their power even more? The answer may lie in an "intoxication" theory of power, which holds that power corrupts the thinking of the powerful; results confirming the theory have been consistently observed both in laboratory research and in the power dynamics between "haves" and "have nots" in society. A balance of power should lead to more ethical conduct than an imbalance does. (In Chapter 19, we investigate the role of third parties, such as mediators, who often must address power differences between disputants to produce a level playing field.)

Mode of Communication   Major changes in technology have affected the way negotiators can communicate with each other. As we discussed in Chapter 6, the evolution of e-mail, texting, instant messaging, and teleconferencing provides parties more ways to communicate back and forth than ever before (see Lewicki and Dineen, 2002, for a review of the overall impact of "virtuality" on negotiation). There is evidence that deception is viewed differently when it occurs over e-mail compared with other modes of communication (Zhou, Burgoon, Nunamaker, and Twitchell, 2004). The relevant question for us here is whether negotiators are more or less likely to use ethically ambiguous tactics when they are physically removed from each other (using phone, e-mail, voicemail, or instant messaging) than when they are face to face. Research thus far points to mixed results. Schweitzer, Brodt, and Croson (2002) suggest that negotiators lie more in face-to-face situations because they want to be able to monitor the other party's reactions—to make sure that the "lie" is having its intended effect. Yet others have argued that interpersonal bonds are weaker (Friedman and Currall, 2003) and there is less trust and more suspicion (Fortune and Brodt, 2000) among negotiators when they are not face to face. Face-to-face situations compel a negotiator to be more honest and cooperative because of the personal and emotional consequences of being caught in a lie in the face-to-face context (Thompson, 1998). Interestingly, though, it is plausible that e-mail is an advantageous medium when moral or ethical matters are themselves the actual subject of discussion. That's because an e-mail "conversation" features fewer interruptions, offers more time for reflection, and incorporates fewer emotional behaviors (van Es, French, and Stellmaszek, 2004). Clearly, more work is necessary on the intersection between negotiation ethics and communication channels to refine these ideas.

Acting as an Agent versus Representing Your Own Views   Acting as an agent for another party often puts you in a different ethical frame of mind than negotiating for yourself. As one author has put it,

> Many negotiators fail to understand the nature of negotiation and so find themselves attempting to reconcile conflicts between the requirements of negotiation and their own sense of personal integrity. An individual who confuses private ethics with business morality does not make an effective negotiator. Those who serve as agents in a negotiation must learn to be objective and to subordinate their own personal goals to the prime purpose of securing the best possible deal for their constituents. (Beckman, 1977, quoted in Lax and Sebenius, 1986, p. 363)

As we point out in Chapter 11, negotiators frequently find themselves representing others' views in negotiation rather than negotiating for their own personal goals and interests. A number of authors have suggested that when people act as an agent for someone else—particularly when the goals for that agent are to get the best possible agreement—they may be more willing to violate personal ethical standards (Bowie and Freeman, 1992). In essence, acting as an agent may release people from their own personal ethical code and allow them to create their own standard of legitimacy—that it is appropriate to do whatever is necessary to maximize the results for the constituent.

Group and Organizational Norms and Pressures   Many negotiators look to the social norms of a particular situation to decide how to behave. Norms are the informal social rules—the dos and don'ts—that govern social behavior. Research suggests that group and organizational norms and pressures may play a key role in legitimizing inappropriate behavior (although, again, this research has not specifically involved negotiating situations). Here are some key findings and observations:

• Studies have shown that different companies can have distinctly different ethical climates or cultures (Jackall, 1988; Victor and Cullen, 1988). Companies differ in how they value and endorse ethical conduct or appear to condone and tolerate marginally ethical behavior in the service of achieving corporate objectives at any price.

• A company as a whole may have a strong statement of corporate ethics and values, but job-related pressures within particular work groups, departments, or divisions may be such that ethically ambiguous behavior is not only tolerated but even condoned. The actions and practices of key managers within work groups or departments play a large role in determining what employees believe appropriate behavior (see Dineen, Lewicki, and Tomlinson, 2004, for one study; and Murphy, 1992, for a broader review). The more loyalty and commitment people feel toward an organization, the more likely they may be to suspend their own ethical judgment and engage in any and all behavior—even unethical or illegal behavior—to demonstrate that loyalty.

• Norms have to be "salient"—that is, immediate and relevant to the negotiator—to have an impact. In a study of the impact of ethical climate on negotiations, Aquino (1998)

Many corporations publish, for their employees and stakeholders, guides to what they regard as ethical business conduct or practice. It is not unusual for these corporate "codes of conduct" to mention negotiation practices, usually in connection with relationships with suppliers and customers. On the subject of negotiation, these codes typically do not go into the nuances of negotiator ethics as we have been discussing them in this chapter. Mostly they stick with sweeping statements that assert, in effect, "we are fair and honest." Here are a few examples from large U.S. companies.

Policies on Business Conduct, Pfizer Inc. (2003, p. 13):

At Pfizer, we are committed to fair competition. This means, among other things, abiding by all laws that apply to our marketing activities. Under these laws, it is illegal to use unfair methods of competition or unfair or deceptive acts or practices in commerce. This prohibition includes, but is not limited to: false or misleading advertising, or any other form of misrepresentation made in connection with sales.

Code of Ethics and Business Conduct, Lockheed Martin (2006, p. 23):

If you are involved in proposals, bid preparations, or contract negotiations, you must be certain that all statements, communications, and representations to prospective customers are accurate and truthful.

Statement of Ethics, Wal-Mart (2005, p. 17):

Wal-Mart bases its relationships with suppliers on lawful, efficient and fair business practices. . . . You must treat Wal-Mart suppliers with respect, fairness and honesty and not take undue advantage of a supplier by using Wal-Mart's business influence.

Code of Business Conduct, The Coca-Cola Company (2006, p. 20):

Consistent with the obligation we all have to act with integrity and honesty at all times, you should deal fairly with the Company's customers, suppliers, competitors and employees. No director, officer or employee should take unfair advantage of anyone through misrepresentation or any unfair business practice.

showed that when specific ethical standards were made salient and relevant to negotiators, the use of deception by negotiators diminished, and more ethical agreements ensued. Similarly, Ross and Robertson (2000) found that individuals were less likely to lie when their organization provided clear ethical guidelines about behavior. (Many corporations do provide guidelines on ethical behavior for their employees, although their coverage of ethics in negotiation rarely goes beyond broad statements touting the importance of honesty; see Box 9.4 for some examples.)

The pressure to obey authority is very strong, as anyone who has read about Stanley Milgram's famous obedience experiments will recall (Milgram, 1974). Such pressure is real in organizations, and social scientists have documented how thoroughly it can undermine individual integrity (e.g., Brief, 1992; Kelman and Hamilton, 1989). Moreover, the more complex an individual's moral reasoning capability, the more he or she perceives conflict between personal standards and typical organizational demands (Mason and Mudrack, 1997). In its most extreme forms, organizational pressure leads individuals to commit egregious crimes against humanity, such as the Holocaust during the 1940s, or the infamous My

BOX | 9.5 | *Making Ethical Decisions: Six Questions*

Making decisions in situations involving ethics may require a quick response to a complex set of issues. Author and consultant Michael Rion argues that managers can benefit from having at hand an efficient way of thinking through these kinds of situations. His system of guidelines for ethical decision making is built around asking yourself a series of questions about the situation at hand:

- Why is this situation bothering me?
- Who else matters in this situation and how are they affected by it?

- Is it *my* responsibility? What are my obligations?
- What is the *ethical* issue here (role of law/fairness/honesty/etc.)?
- What would others say about this situation?
- Am I being true to my values and those of my organization?

Source: Adapted from M. Rion, *The Responsible Manager: Practical Strategies for Ethical Decision Making* (West Hartford, CT: Resources for Ethics and Management, 1999).

Lai massacre in 1968 during the Vietnam war, or the events at the Abu Ghraib prison in Iraq in the early 2000s. Other authors (e.g., Street, Robertson, and Geiger, 1997) have argued that the pressures of escalating commitment, which (as we noted in Chapter 5) involve pressures to throw good money after bad or increase commitment to a failing course of action, may also predispose parties to commit ethically dubious actions that they might otherwise avoid.

Summary Research shows that a number of social forces can encourage negotiators to suspend their own personal and ethical standards and commit acts that are ethically questionable. These forces include:

- Acting as an agent for others and responding to their pressures to achieve.
- Viewing business dealings—such as negotiation—as a game (like poker or war) and therefore assuming that the rules of the game are the ones that should be applied.
- Being a member of a group, department, team, or organizational unit that values success and tolerates or even encourages bending or breaking the rules in order to achieve that success.
- Being so loyal to a group or organization that you are willing to do something you would not do as an individual, or convincing yourself that it is permissible to break the rules in order to be rewarded for your loyalty.
- Being willing to follow the direct or implied orders of senior officials in the organization who tell you to get a job done and not worry about how it gets done.

Any of these forces appear to be sufficient, under the right circumstances, to permit individuals to suspend their own good moral judgment in the service of doing what the organization appears to need, want, or request. Combining them can produce an even more lethal concoction of social pressures that permits people to rationalize their actions and do whatever is necessary. See Box 9.5 for a way to grapple with ethical dilemmas that arise unexpectedly.

How Can Negotiators Deal with the Other Party's Use of Deception?

People lie—quite frequently, in fact (Adler, 2007)—so a chapter such as this would be incomplete without briefly noting some of the things that you can do as a negotiator when you believe the other party is using deceptive tactics. (We will return to this issue in Chapter 17, when we examine a wide range of strategies for damage control. Table 9.3 presents some verbal strategies for trying to determine if others are being deceptive. And what if they are? Here are some options:

Ask Probing Questions   Many negotiators fail to ask enough questions, yet asking questions can reveal a great deal of information, some of which the negotiator might otherwise have intentionally left undisclosed (Schweitzer, 1997; Schweitzer and Croson, 1998). In an experimental simulation of a negotiation over the sale of a computer (Schweitzer and Croson, 2002), buyers were either strongly prompted to ask questions of the seller about the condition of the computer, or not prompted to ask questions. Across the board, asking questions about the condition of the computer reduced the number of the seller's deceptive comments (lies of commission). However, under some conditions, asking questions also increased the seller's use of lies of omission about other aspects of the computer. Thus, while questions can help a negotiator determine whether another is being deceptive, cross-examination may actually increase the seller's tendency to be deceptive in areas where questions are not being asked. (Refer back to Chapter 6 for a more extensive examination of asking good questions.)

Phrase Questions in Different Ways   Robert Adler (2007), a scholar in law and ethics, points out that what negotiators engaged in deception are usually doing is not outright lying (which risks liability for fraud); instead, "they dodge, duck, bob, and weave around the truth, assuming that their statements will be misconstrued or not challenged" (p. 72). A question posed a certain way may elicit an answer that is technically true, but skirts the actual truth the questioner seeks to uncover. Consider this example: as a prospective house buyer I ask, "How is the heating system?" and the seller replies, "It works fine," so I draw the conclusion that there's no problem. Alternatively, I could have asked, "When was the last time the heating system was inspected, and what was the result?" (and perhaps gone even further and asked for written documentation of the inspection). I might learn that although the system is in reasonable working order at the moment ("it works fine"), the inspection revealed it's on its last legs and will need replacement within the next year. Different question, different answer, and less of an evasion.

Force the Other Party to Lie or Back Off   If you suspect the other party is being cagey or deceptive about an issue but is not making a clear statement in plain language, pose a question that forces him or her to tell a direct lie (if the assertion is false) or else abandon or qualify the assertion. For instance, if the seller of a piece of property alludes to other interested buyers and implies there are other offers, ask a question about other offers in a clear way that calls for a yes or no answer. This can be a useful strategy because, as we noted earlier, research shows people are more inclined to lie by omission than by commission. Some people

TABLE 9.3 | Detecting Deception

Researchers have identified a number of verbal tactics that you can use to determine whether the other party is acting deceptively.

Tactic	Explanation and Examples
Intimidation	Force the other to admit he is using deception by intimidating him into telling the truth. Make a no-nonsense accusation of the other. Criticize the other. Hammer the other with challenging questions. Feign indifference to what he has to say ("I'm not interested in anything you have to say on the matter").
Futility portrayal	Emphasize the futility and impending danger associated with continued deceit: "The truth will come out someday," "Don't dig the hole deeper by trying to cover it up," "If you try to cover it up, it will only be worse in the future," "You are all alone in your deception."
Discomfort and relief	State the maxim, "Confession is good for the soul." Help the other reduce the tension and stress associated with being a known deceiver.
Bluffing	Lie to the other to make her believe you have uncovered her deception: "Your sins are about to be uncovered." Indicate that you know what she knows but will not discuss it.
Gentle prods	Encourage the other to keep talking so that he gives you information that may help you separate true facts from deceptions. Ask him to elaborate on the topic being discussed. Ask questions but indicate that you are asking because "other people want to know." Play devil's advocate and ask playful questions. Praise the other so as to give him confidence and support that may lead to information sharing.
Minimization	Play down the significance of any deceptive act. Help the other find excuses for why she was deceptive; minimize the consequences of the action; indicate that others have done worse; shift the blame to someone else.
Contradiction	Get the other to tell his story fully in order to discover more information that will allow you to discover inconsistencies and contradictions in his comments or reports. Point out and ask for explanations about apparent contradictions. Ask the speaker the same question several times and look for inconsistencies in his response. Present contradictions back and ask the speaker to explain. Put pressure on the speaker and get him to slip up or say things he doesn't want to say.
Altered information	Alter information and hopefully trick the other into revealing deception. Exaggerate what you believe is the deception, hoping that the other will jump in to "correct" the statement. Ask the suspected deceiver a question containing incorrect information and hope she corrects you.
A chink in the defense	Try to get the other to admit a small or partial lie about some information, and use this to push for admission of a larger lie: "If you lied about this one little thing, how do I know you have not lied about other things?"
Self-disclosure	Reveal a number of things about yourself, including, perhaps, dishonesty on your own part, hoping the other will begin to trust you and reciprocate with disclosures of dishonesty.

(Continued)

TABLE 9.3 | (*Concluded*)

Point of deception cues	Point out behaviors you detect in the other that might be an indication he is lying: sweating, nervousness, change of voice, inability to make eye contact, and so on.
Concern	Indicate your true concern for the other's welfare: "You are important to me," "I care deeply about you," "I feel your pain."
Keeping the status quo	Admonish the other to be truthful in order to maintain her good name. "What will people think?" Appeal to her pride and desire to maintain a good reputation.
Direct approach	"Simply tell me the truth." "Let's be honest here." "Surely you have no objection to telling me everything you know."
Silence	Create a "verbal vacuum" that makes the other uncomfortable and gets him to talk and disclose information. When he tells a lie, simply maintain direct eye contact but remain silent.

Source: Adapted from Pamela J. Kalbfleisch, "The Language of Detecting Deceit," *Journal of Language and Social Psychology* 13, no. 4 (1994), pp. 469–96.

are comfortable being cagey or misleading, but they will run headlong into their conscience if forced to flatly lie while looking someone in the eye. Conscience aside, this kind of question may also make the other party nervous about liability for fraudulent negotiator behavior. Hence the timely use of a sharp, direct question will induce some adversaries to back off rather than fib to your face. (Granted, the pathological liar may well rise to the challenge.)

Test the Other Party   Not sure if the other party is the kind of person who would lie? Adler (2007) suggests asking a question to which you already know the answer. If the answer you get is evasive or deceptive, you have learned something important about the other party and his or her trustworthiness. And when you do think your opponent's allegiance to the truth is shaky, Adler counsels taking good notes during the negotiation (and invite the other side to confirm the accuracy of your notes) in order to create and preserve accountability later.

"Call" the Tactic   Indicate to the other side that you know he is bluffing or lying. Do so tactfully but firmly, and indicate your displeasure. Keep in mind, however, that spotting lies is not always easy—see Box 9.6. Mistakenly calling the other party a liar or an unethical negotiator is certainly not the path to a constructive process and fruitful outcome.

Ignore the Tactic   If you are aware that the other party is bluffing or lying, simply ignore it, especially if the deception concerns a relatively minor aspect of the negotiation. Some may lie or bluff out of an expectation that this is what they "should" be doing—that it's part of the ritual or dance of negotiation—rather than out of a sinister sense of ethics or morality. We mentioned in Chapter 8 that negotiators at times make unwise commitments—statements they later regret promising things or ruling out options—and it is sometimes in the best interest of the other party to help that negotiator "escape" the commitment and save face. A similar logic can apply to deceptive statements when the motive is closer to naïveté than depravity: let it pass, avoid embarrassing the other person, and move on. (Table 9.3 has additional suggestions for dealing with situations where you suspect that the other party is engaged in deception.)

Although people in general are not particularly good at spotting lies, some people continue to believe that they can tell by looking into someone's face if that person is inclined to be dishonest or truthful on a regular basis. But how accurate are such assessments?

A study asked participants to view photographs of the same people as children, adolescents, and adults and to rate their attractiveness and honesty based on an assessment of their faces. These results were compared to self-reports of honest behavior provided by the people in the photographs. The results demonstrated that structural qualities of the face, such as attractiveness, "babyfaceness," eye size, and symmetry each individually contributed to perceptions of greater honesty in observers. The self-reports revealed that men who looked more honest early in life actually were more honest as they grew older. On the other hand, women whose behavior was less honest when they were young grew to appear more honest as they aged, even though their behavior did not change significantly. Study participants were able to correctly identify the most honest men in the group as they aged, but their assessment of women was largely inaccurate. The researchers concluded that men's faces accurately reflected their tendency toward honesty, but women's faces were not particularly valid indicators of their truthfulness.

Source: Adapted from L. A. Zebrowitz, L. Voinescu, and M. A. Collins, "Wide-Eyed and Crooked-Faced: Determinants of Perceived and Real Honesty across the Life Span," *Personality and Social Psychology Bulletin* 22 (1996), pp. 1258–69.

Discuss What You See and Offer to Help the Other Party Shift to More Honest Behaviors This is a variation on calling the tactic, but it tries to assure the other party that telling the truth is, in the long term, more likely to get him what he wants than any form of bluffing or deception will.

Respond in Kind If the other party bluffs, you bluff more. If she misrepresents, you misrepresent. We do not recommend this course of action at all, because it simply escalates the destructive behavior and drags you into the mud with the other party, but if she recognizes that you are lying too, she may also realize that the tactic is unlikely to work. Of course, if the other party's lies are so direct and extreme as to constitute legally actionably fraud, then it is not an approach you would want to mimic under any circumstances. In general, the "respond in kind" approach is best treated as a "last resort" strategy.

Chapter Summary

The process of negotiation raises frequent and critical ethical issues. In this chapter, we have discussed factors that negotiators consider when they decide whether particular tactics are deceptive and unethical. Although a lot of writing on negotiation is strongly normative about ethical dos and don'ts, we prefer an analytical approach that focuses on how negotiators actually make decisions about when and where to use specific tactics. Accordingly, we approached the study of ethically ambiguous tactics from a decision-making framework, examining the ethical overtones of the choices that negotiators make.

We began by drawing on a set of hypothetical scenarios to discuss how ethical questions are inherent in the process of negotiation. We then presented four fundamental approaches to ethical reasoning and showed how each might be used to make decisions about what is ethically appropriate in negotiations. We proposed that a negotiator's decision to use ethically ambiguous (or flatly unethical) tactics typically grows out of a desire to increase one's negotiating power by manipulating the landscape of (presumably accurate) information in the negotiation. We discussed the different forms that ethically ambiguous tactics take, and we reviewed relevant research about the use of those tactics.

Working from a simple model of ethical decision making, we analyzed the motives for and consequences of engaging in unethical negotiation behavior. We then expanded the model to identify individual differences and contextual factors that influence the likelihood that negotiators will use such tactics. Finally, we addressed how negotiators can respond to another party that may be using tactics of deception or subterfuge.

In closing, we suggest that negotiators who are considering the use of deceptive tactics should ask themselves the following questions:

- Will they really enhance my power and help me achieve my objective?

- How will the use of these tactics affect the quality of my relationship with the other party in the future?

- How will the use of these tactics affect my personal and professional reputation as a negotiator?

Negotiators frequently overlook the fact that, although unethical or expedient tactics may get them what they want in the short run, these same tactics typically lead to tarnished reputations and diminished effectiveness in the long run.

Endnotes

[1] See Boatright (2000); De George (2006); Donaldson and Werhane (2008); Green (1994); and Rachels (2003), for elaborations of these approaches.

[2] *The American Heritage Dictionary of the English Language* (3rd edition), 1992, © Houghton Mifflin.

[3] The accompanying box (9.1) on the legality of lying in negotiation addresses U.S. law. Obviously, legal systems vary from country to country, and so too will legal doctrine regarding deception and fraud in negotiation.

[4] See also Barry, Fulmer, and Long (2000); Lewicki (1983); Lewicki and Spencer (1990); Lewicki and Stark (1995); Robinson, Lewicki, and Donahue (2000).

[5] See also Braginsky (1970); Exline, Thibaut, Hickey, and Gumpert (1970); Geis and Moon (1981); Ross and Robertson (2000).

Relationships in Negotiation

Objectives

1. Understand how negotiation within an existing relationship changes the nature of negotiation dynamics.

2. Explore the different forms of relationships in which negotiation can occur.

3. Consider the critical roles played by reputations, trust, and fairness in any negotiating relationship.

4. Gain insight into how to rebuild trust and repair damaged relationships.

Up to this point in this text, we have described the negotiation process as though it occurred between two parties who had no prior relationship or knowledge of each other, came together to do a deal, and had no relationship once the deal was done. In other words, it was just a "snapshot" taken out of time and context. But this is clearly not the way many actual negotiations unfold. Negotiations occur in a rich and complex social environment that has a significant impact on how the parties interact and how the process evolves.

One major way that context affects negotiation is that people act within a relationship, and these relationships have a past, present, and future. In this chapter, we focus on the ways these past and future relationships impact present negotiations. Our treatment of relationships will come in two major sections. First, we examine how a past, ongoing, or future relationship between negotiators affects the negotiation process. This discussion challenges many of the general assumptions that have been made about the theory and practice of negotiation—assumptions that have not taken into account a relationship between the parties—and provides a critical evaluation of the adequacy of negotiation theory for understanding and managing negotiations within relationships. We present a taxonomy of different kinds of relationships and the negotiations that are likely to occur within them and broadly describe research studies that have examined negotiation processes within existing relationships. Finally, we look at three major themes—reputations, trust, and justice—that are particularly critical to effective negotiations within a relationship.

Our discussion of other social context factors continues in subsequent chapters. In Chapter 11 we examine negotiations when negotiators represent others' interests at the table—negotiating on behalf of others. In Chapter 12, we discuss the dynamics of coalitions—the ways negotiators aggregate together to exert collective influence and how they divide the resources once the coalition has achieved its goal. Finally, in Chapter 13, we examine how negotiators in groups and teams work together to negotiate complex decisions and agreements.

The Adequacy of Established Approaches to Research for Understanding Negotiation within Relationships

Traditionally, researchers have studied the negotiation process in two ways. On the one hand, they have studied actual negotiations with real negotiators in "live" field situations such as labor relations (Douglas, 1962; Friedman, 1994) and international relations (Ikle, 1964). On the other hand, researchers have simulated complex negotiations by simplifying them in a research laboratory. They create simplified negotiating games and simulations, find college students who are willing to be research participants, and explore negotiating problems and situations under controlled laboratory conditions. This latter approach has dominated the research process in the negotiation field for the past 40 years, for several reasons. First, this type of research is far easier to do than field research; it is simpler to create a bargaining game with college students and administer questionnaires than to study live negotiators in the middle of a real but often complex negotiation. It is also difficult to get parties who are actually in an intense negotiation to allow researchers to do interviews, ask questions, or publicly report actual successes and failures. Second, some research questions are best answered under controlled laboratory conditions because it would be impossible to simulate the same conditions repeatedly in actual negotiations. For instance, to study whether making threats increases antagonism in negotiation, one could hardly ask some negotiators in actual negotiations to make threats while others did not because it would not be genuine behavior if the parties were not predisposed to take that approach. Finally, compared with field situations, the laboratory setting allows researchers to collect data more efficiently, control extraneous factors in the environment, and be far more confident about the reliability and validity of the results.

There are, however, serious problems with this strong laboratory research tradition. Most of our conclusions about what is effective in *complex* negotiations have been drawn from studies using a limited set of fairly *simple* bargaining games and classroom simulations. Findings from simple laboratory research has been extensively used to prescribe how negotiators should behave in complex situations; thus, rather than just describe what people actually do in negotiations (real and simulated), many books (including this one) have used that theory to guide negotiators about what they *should* do and how they *should* negotiate. One can reasonably question whether such extensive prescriptions are fully accurate or appropriate, because most negotiations occur between people who are in a relationship with the other party and thus have a significant past history and expect to be together in the future. Only recently have researchers begun to examine actual negotiations in a rich relationship context in order to offer better prescriptions on how to negotiate when the parties are deeply embedded in a relationship.

Sheppard and Tuchinsky (Sheppard, 1995; Sheppard and Tuchinsky, 1996a) have discussed the inadequacy of existing theory to explain negotiation within ongoing relationships. They provided the following examples:

A recently married couple discusses whose parents they will be spending Christmas vacation with. Procter & Gamble and Wal-Mart discuss who will own the inventory in their new relationship. Price Waterhouse discusses a cost overrun with an extremely important audit client. Members of a new task force discuss their new roles only to discover that two wish to serve the same function. Each of these discussions could be modeled quite well as a single issue, distributive negotiation problem. There are two parties: A single, critical dimension and opposing positions. A great portion of each discussion will entail searching for the other's walkaway point and hiding of one's own. But the discussions are also more complicated than the single distributive problem (Sheppard and Tuchinsky, 1996a, pp. 132–33).

As we noted, the problem, they argue, is that researchers have been too quick to generalize from simple research studies ("transactional negotiations") to negotiating in complex relationships. Sheppard and Tuchinsky note several ways that an existing relationship context changes negotiation dynamics:

1. *Negotiating within relationships takes place over time.* In Chapter 3, we noted that one way of turning a distributive negotiation into an integrative one is for the parties to take turns in reaping a benefit or reward. Within a relationship, parties can do this easily. Husband and wife can agree to visit each other's parents on alternate holidays. Negotiators in a simple bargaining game cannot agree to do this because their relationship ends when the game is over. Hence, time becomes an important variable in negotiating in relationships; understanding how parties package or trade off issues over time may be critical to managing difficult situations.

2. *Negotiation is often not a way to discuss an issue, but a way to learn more about the other party and increase interdependence.* In a transactional negotiation, the parties seek to get information about each other so they can strike a better deal. The short time span of a transaction requires a party to either act simply on thier own preferences or to gather small bits of information about the other before deciding how to act. In a relationship, gathering information about the *other's* ideas, preferences, and priorities is often the most important activity; this information is usually used to learn about and understand the other's thinking, work habits, and so forth, and thus enhance the party's ability to coordinate activities and enhance the ongoing relationship. In short, in a transactional negotiation, the most important issue is usually the deal; in a relationship negotiation, the most important issue is preserving or enhancing the relationship. If given a choice between cleaning the kitchen or paying the bills (based on the job alone), I might readily choose the kitchen; but if my spouse has very strong preferences about "her" kitchen and how it should be cleaned, I will readily accommodate to bill paying. As we point out later in this chapter, learning about the other's preferences is central to developing trust, which is often the glue that holds relationships together, particularly in difficult circumstances.

3. *Resolution of simple distributive issues has implications for the future.* While time can be an asset, it can also be a curse. The settlement of any one negotiation issue can create undesired or unintended precedents for the future. How Procter & Gamble handles one inventory question may have implications for how similar inventory questions are handled in the future. Alternating holiday visits to their parents in the first two years does not mean the married couple can never change the visitation schedule or that they have to take turns on every issue on which they disagree. But they may have to discuss explicitly when certain precedents apply or do not apply and explain their decisions to others.

These negotiations may also shift the power and dependence dynamics in their future relationship. The more the parties learn about each other, the more they may become vulnerable or dependent on each other. For example, if Acme Company is having a difficult time with a challenging manufacturing problem, it may decide to form a strong relationship with one of its very large customers, Battle Corporation, which knows how to solve the problem because of its experience with similar problems in other suppliers. But Battle may insist that Acme sell its entire product inventory to Battle in order to make sure that Battle can benefit from helping Acme with its problem. Acme is now in a dependent relationship; it cannot go back to the market to other customers unless Battle agrees, and its dependence on Battle may lead its costs to rise, its quality to drop, or its competitiveness to decline. Acme will now be highly vulnerable as the demand for its product shifts, as technology changes, or as Battle begins to try to control other strategic issues in Acme's business. This is not an uncommon problem for relatively small firms supplying goods or services to much larger companies, such as Wal-Mart or the big auto makers; in these situations, the entire business viability of the supplier may depend on the whims of its one very large customer (Sheppard and Tuchinsky, 1996b; Yoshino and Rangan, 1995). These dynamics can create reputation problems for both Acme and Battle, and we explicitly address the impact of reputations later in this chapter.

4.   *Distributive issues within relationship negotiations can be emotionally hot.* If one party feels strongly about the issues or the other acts provocatively, the parties can become angry with each other. Expressing that anger clearly makes negotiating over other issues difficult (we discussed how emotion affects negotiation in Chapter 5). The parties may say things they don't mean, make hurtful comments, cut off discussions, and even refuse to speak further. At a minimum, the parties may have to cool off or apologize before they can proceed. In extreme cases, the parties can continue feuds for years, carrying emotional baggage from one fight to another that never gets resolved and never permits them to talk about issues important to the relationship. Many failed negotiations that end up in the courts—from small-claims cases and failed marriages to major organizational and international disputes—share a common history of bad feeling, failed communication, or a complete breakdown in the ability of the parties to solve their problems.

5.   *Negotiating within relationships may never end.* One of the advantages of negotiating in a game or simulation is that there is a defined end. In fact, many participants in laboratory negotiating experiments may develop a specific strategy for how they are going to play "the end game"; often, they abandon cooperative strategies in favor of getting the other on the last move. In many relationships, however, negotiations are never over; parties are often constantly trying to renegotiate old agreements or issues that were never firmly settled (or settled in favor of one party but not the other). This may have several consequences:

•   *Parties may defer negotiations over tough issues in order to start on the right foot.* If the married couple thought their relationship would be over in two years, they would make sure they each got what they wanted while they were married; in addition, they would probably negotiate a very specific agreement about who was to get what when the relationship was over. (Aware of the rising divorce rate in many countries, many couples intending to marry are increasingly turning to complex, legally binding prenuptial agreements to handle this problem.) But if the couple expects the marriage to last forever, they may simply mingle all of their assets and property in the hope that "everything will work out" in the future.

•   *Attempting to anticipate the future and negotiate everything up front is often impossible*. Two young entrepreneurs who decide to go into business together can't possibly anticipate all the dimensions of where their common efforts will take them or what issues they should consider if they decide to separate in five years. Who knows now how successful the business will be or what might be the most important issues? At best, all they can do is pledge to communicate with each other and discuss problems as they arise, or to agree to involve third parties as a peaceful means for resolving disputes (see Chapter 19).

•   *Issues on which parties truly disagree may never go away*. As we suggested earlier, some negotiations in relationships are never over. Two roommates who have different standards of cleanliness—one is neat, the other messy—may never settle the question of whose preference is going to govern the living arrangements in their apartment. The messy one will always be disposed to leave things out and around, while the clean one will always be bothered by things left out and around. As long as they live together, the issue may confront them; agreements about cleanliness may regularly get broken, even though they may go through a range of different possible solutions as they try to accommodate each other's preferences and habits.

6.   *In many negotiations, the other person* is *the focal problem.* A well-known prescriptive theory of integrative negotiation teaches that in order to be effective, negotiators must "separate the person from the problem" (Fisher, Ury, and Patton, 1991). But what happens if the other person *is* the problem? Return to some of our earlier examples: when one combines a set of emotion-laden issues with people who have major differences in values or preferred lifestyles, there is a recipe for a fight that goes beyond a single-issue negotiation. In the situation of the two roommates, the neatnik's passion for cleanliness may lead her to see the other's messiness not as a simple issue of lifestyle differences, but as intentional and even provocative: "She leaves a mess because she knows how angry I get when this place looks like a dump! She does it just to spite me!" This is no longer a problem of how often to clean or of whether one cares enough to tolerate the other's idiosyncrasies; this is now a problem of one party seeing the other as spiteful and provocative, causing the problem simply by her very coexistence in the living space. While the parties might engage in extensive efforts to "separate the person from the problem" and find viable solutions, the very fact that one party's existence, preferences, lifestyle, or behavior irritates the other can create an intractable negotiation problem for which permanent separation or relationship dissolution may be the only solution.

7.   *In some negotiations, relationship preservation is the overarching negotiation goal, and parties may make concessions on substantive issues to preserve or enhance the relationship.* A potential resolution to the "person-is-the-problem" negotiation is that one or both parties may actually make major concessions on substantive issues simply to preserve the relationship. Parties in traditionally distributive market transactions usually make concessions by starting high or low on an issue and moving toward the middle. Even logrolling concessions can be fairly well understood because the parties equate their benefits on two separate issues and then trade one off against the other. However, it is difficult to understand how parties trade off the value of the relationship against specific goals on tangible issues. Suppose I have a used car that has a market value of $5,000.

International negotiation expert Jeswald Salacuse (1998) suggests three important rules for negotiating a relationship:

- Don't rush prenegotiation. Spend ample time getting to know the other party, visiting with him, learning about him, and spending time with him. This process enhances your information gathering and builds a relationship that may include trust, information sharing, and productive discussions. In particular, North American executives have a tendency to rush through things in order to get down to business, which compromises this critical stage for relationship building.

- Recognize a long-term business deal as a continuing negotiation. Change and uncertainty are constants in any business deal. The

discussions do not end when the contract is signed; they continue as the parties perform according to the contract, during which time they often have to meet to work out problems and renegotiate specific parts of the agreement.

- Consider mediation or conciliation. Finally, consider the roles that can usefully be played by third parties. A third party can help monitor the deal, work out disagreements about contract violations, and assure that the agreement does not go sour because the parties cannot resolve differences in interpretation or enforcement.

Source: Adapted from J. Salacuse, "So, What's the Deal Anyway? Contracts and Relationships as Negotiating Goals," *Negotiation Journal* 14, no. 1 (1998), pp. 5–12.

However, I decide to sell it to my mother, who needs a car only for occasional trips around town or visits to her grandchildren. This is not a simple market transaction! Can I convince my mother that she should pay the same price that I would quote to a stranger off the street? Can I convince *myself* of that? Clearly, the value I place on the past and future relationships between my mother and me will dictate the answer to that question at least as much as (and quite possibly far more than) the market value of the car. In Chapter 1, we discussed *accommodation* as a strategic choice most likely to be pursued when the relationship with the other party is important but the substantive issues are not; accommodation is far more likely as a strategy in relationship negotiations than it is in market transactions.

In summary, we have identified several issues that make negotiating in relationships different from and more challenging than conducting either distributive or integrative negotiations between parties who have no past or intended future relationship. It is not always clear how the prescriptive lessons learned from market transactions apply to negotiation within relationships. Both negotiation theory and prescriptions need elaboration and refinement to take into account the importance of ongoing relationships (for example, see Box 10.1). We now turn to defining some of the parameters of relationships that make negotiations within them complex and challenging.

Forms of Relationships

Having identified a number of ways that negotiations within relationships may be different and more complex, we need to examine the properties of relationships that may affect how negotiations evolve.

The field of social psychology has studied relationships extensively and found several ways to describe them.[1] A characteristic of most relationships is that each party's actions are a major influential cause of the other party's behavior. How people react to that influence depends on what type of relationship they have (discussed later). Following Sheppard and Tuchinsky (1996b), we define the word *relationship* as a "pairing of entities that has meaning to the parties, in which the understood form of present and future interactions influences their behavior today" (p. 354). Two key assumptions accompany this definition: (1) the parties have a history and an expected future with each other that shapes the present interaction, and (2) the link between the parties themselves has meaning (i.e., the relationship itself has identity and meaning, above and beyond what each individual brings to it).

Four Fundamental Relationship Forms

Fiske (1991) argued that there were four fundamental types of relationships: communal sharing, authority ranking, equality matching, and market pricing. He defines them as follows:

1.   "*Communal sharing* is a relation of unity, community, collective identity, and kindness, typically enacted among close kin" (Fiske, 1991, p. ix). People are tied to one another by feelings of strong common group membership; common identity; and feelings of unity, solidarity, and belonging. Collective identity takes precedence over individual identity. The group is the most salient thing; a communal-sharing relationship is based on natural, generous, spontaneous feelings of kindness toward each other, which often derive from a sense of common roots, bonds, or blood. Such relationships are found in families, clubs, fraternal organizations, ethnic groups, and neighborhoods.

2.   "*Authority ranking* is a relationship of asymmetric differences, commonly exhibited in a hierarchical ordering of status and precedence, often accompanied by the exercise of command and complementary displays of deference and respect" (Fiske, 1991, p. ix). People follow the principles of organizational hierarchy; higher ranks dominate lower ranks. An authority-ranking relationship is one of inequality, in which high-ranked people control more things or people than others do, and are often thought to have more knowledge or mastery. Control in such relationships is not accomplished by coercion (force) but by acknowledging legitimate authority, in which those of lower rank submit willingly to those of higher rank (see Chapters 7 and 8). Examples include subordinates to bosses, soldiers to their commander, and negotiators to their constituents.

3.   "*Equality matching* is a one-to-one correspondence relationship in which people are distinct but equal, as manifested in balanced reciprocity (or tit-for-tat revenge), equal share distributions or identical contributions, in-kind replacement compensation, and turn-taking" (Fiske, 1991, p. ix). People in such relationships see each other as equal and separate, but often interchangeable; each is expected to both contribute equally to others and receive equally from others. This expectation is best represented by activities such as turn taking (where each person does the same function in turn), in-kind reciprocity (where each is expected to give the same and receive the same), or "distributive equality" (where each is expected to receive the same portion or allocation of outcomes). Equality-matching relationships occur within certain teams or groups whose members have to work together to coordinate their actions (recall the example of the roommates and their different housekeeping expectations earlier in this chapter). Similarly, when organizing a group dinner, each party may be asked to "bring a dish" that can be adequately shared with others, with the expectation that each party will bring enough for everyone.

4. "*Market pricing* is based on an (intermodel) metric of value by which people compare different commodities and calculate exchange and cost/benefit ratios" (Fiske, 1991, p. ix). The values that govern this kind of relationship are determined by a market system. Things are typically measured by some single quantitative calibration, such as utility points or dollars, and exchanges are measured in some ratio of price to goods. In this kind of relationship, people see others as interchangeable because the deal *is* more important than the relationship; parties will deal with anyone who can provide the same goods and services for a good price. In the preceding car example, I will sell the car to anyone who offers me my asking price because it is only the transaction that I care about. In market-pricing relationships, parties can attempt to change the ratio of price to goods in their own favor (maximize their utility) or they can seek what may be defined as a fair price.

The power of Fiske's (1991) typology is that it is a universally applicable "grammar of pairs" that can be used to understand social dynamics within and across societies around the world. Fiske demonstrates how this typology may be used to understand how people in different societies create and exchange things, make choices, create different social orientations, and make judgments. His definitions are basic to understanding different social motives that drive relationships, such as power, achievement, equality, and affiliation. Moreover, it is important to understand that *two parties may enact more than one form in their relationship*. As Sheppard and Tuchinsky (1996b) note, a brother and sister may engage in all four relational forms, depending on whether they are discussing the value of a toy one borrowed from the other and then broke, taking turns doing undesirable household chores, running to get a Band-Aid when the other gets hurt, or pulling seniority to claim privilege over who gets to select the TV channel. For another interesting application of negotiation across relationship forms, see Box 10.2.

Returning to the critique of negotiation research at the beginning of this chapter, much of the research has been dominated by the assumptions of a market-pricing relationship, a model heavily influenced by the work of economists, game theorists, and social psychologists with an "exchange" view of interpersonal behavior (Blau, 1964; Kelley, 1966). In the market-pricing paradigm, parties negotiate a price for a commodity, and how parties enact strategy and tactics consistent with this form of exchange is well understood. In authority-ranking relationships, actual "negotiations" have not been extensively studied, but there has been extensive study of the way bosses and subordinates use power and influence (see Chapters 7 and 8). Similarly, one might expect that negotiations in an equality-matching relationship might consist of discussions about what constitutes equivalence in outcomes, contributions, or resources, particularly when it is impossible to determine objectively true equivalence in treatment for all. (This is often a common problem in student teams when it comes to evaluating group member contributions to a report or project).

Conflict is common when family members go into business together. Conflicts over control, competing visions, succession, and inheritance are common. Parties often have conflicting expectations because they bring different relationship frames and expectations to the business—authority ranking (e.g., father–son), equality matching or communal sharing (brother–sister or cousin–cousin), and market pricing (significant economic issues in the business). And the problem becomes more complex because parties tend to avoid confrontation and hope the problem will go away, or address problems insensitively, rather than understand how to raise and productively resolve the conflicts.

Frank Sander and Robert Bordone suggest that integrative negotiation tools are most effective in resolving these disputes. Parties must consider all the interests involved, including the more covert (but equally important) strong emotions and relationship history that the parties bring to the dispute. They should consider options for dispute resolution that take into consideration different views fairness or the value of money. Finally, an acceptable BATNA might have to be considered within the family context, rather than going outside the family. They suggest four guidelines for making family business negotiations more productive:

1. *Prepare for complications.* Given the different frames/expectations people bring and the degree to which family relationships make "simple solutions" complex, be prepared to work hard on these issues.

2. *Strive for transparency.* Be ready to be honest and open about the conflict and the challenges it creates for satisfactory resolution within the family.

3. *Consider a neutral adviser.* The complexity of the issues and the strong emotions involved in these disputes almost require a neutral third party to help manage the conversation—a business analyst, mediator, family therapist, or even a trusted family friend.

4. *Anticipate upcoming problems.* Some typical family business conflicts—leadership succession, promotion and assignment, or changing the direction of the business—may be predictable. Anticipate that these problems will arise and, if possible, agree to a process on how they will be approached and discussed when the time arrives.

Ideas for ways to handle "difficult conversations" can be found in Chapter 18, and more information on neutral advisers and third parties can be found in Chapter 19.

Source: Adapted from F. E. A. Sander and R. C. Bordone, "All in the Family: Managing Business Disputes with Relatives," *Negotiation,* A Newsletter from Harvard Business School Publishing and the Program on Negotiation at Harvard Law School, 2006.

Negotiations in Communal Relationships

There has been a limited amount of negotiation research in communal-sharing relationships (see Tuchinsky, 1998, for one review). Studies have shown, however, that compared with those in other kinds of negotiations, parties who are in a communal-sharing relationship (or who expect to have future interaction):

- Are more cooperative and empathetic (Ben-Yoav and Pruitt, 1984b; Greenhalgh and Gilkey, 1993).
- Craft better quality agreements (Sondak, Neale, and Pinkley, 1995).
- Perform better on both decision making and motor tasks (Shah and Jehn, 1993).
- Focus their attention on the other party's outcomes as well as their own (Loewenstein, Thompson, and Bazerman, 1989).

Researchers have studied how to minimize inter-personal conflicts in working relationships and how to resolve them effectively when they do arise. They suggest that the key is to balance advocacy skills—what most managers are trained to do—with inquiry skills—the ability to ask questions—in order to promote mutual learning. Guidelines for balancing inquiry and advocacy include the following:

When advocating your own view,

- Make your reasoning explicit.
- Encourage others to explore your view.
- Encourage others to provide different views.
- Actively inquire into others' views that differ from your own.

When inquiring into others' views,

- State your assumptions clearly and acknowl-edge that they are assumptions.
- Share the "data" on which your assumptions are based.

- Don't ask questions if you are not genuinely interested in the others' responses.

When you arrive at an impasse,

- Ask what logic or data might change the others' views.
- Ask if there is any way you might jointly design a technique that might provide more information.

When you or others are hesitant to express views or experiment with alternative ideas,

- Encourage them (or yourself) to think out loud about what might be making it difficult.
- If mutually desirable, jointly brainstorm ideas about overcoming any barriers.

Source: Adapted from L. A. Hill (1997), "Building Effective One-on-One Work Relationships" (Harvard Business School Note 9-497-028); and P. Senge, *The Fifth Discipline: The Art and Practice of the Learning Organization* (New York: Doubleday Currency, 1990).

- Focus more attention on the norms that develop about the way that they work together (Macneil, 1980).
- Are more likely to share information with the other and less likely to use coercive tactics (Greenhalgh and Chapman, 1996; Greenhalgh and Kramer, 1990).
- Are more likely to use indirect communication about conflict issues and develop a unique conflict structure (Tuchinsky, 1998).
- May be more likely to use compromise or problem solving as strategies for resolving conflicts (Dant and Schul, 1992; Ganesan, 1993).

It is unclear, however, whether parties in close relationships produce better solutions than other negotiators do. Some studies found that parties who did *not* have a close rela-tionship produced better integrative solutions (Fry, Firestone, and Williams, 1983; Thompson, Peterson, and Brodt, 1996). It may be that parties in a relationship may not push hard for a preferred solution in order to minimize the conflict level in the relation-ship or, alternatively, may sacrifice their own preferences in order to preserve the rela-tionship (Barry and Oliver, 1996; Tripp, Sondak, and Bies, 1995). Senge (1990) and Argyris and Schön (1996) describe this tension as a process of balancing inquiry and ad-vocacy (see Box 10.3).

BOX | 10.4

Conflict Resolution in Intense, Complex Relationships

Psychologist John Gottman has been studying conflict resolution in marriages throughout his career. By videotaping thousands of couples as they talk about challenging problems in their marriages, he offers the following insights into what make a relationship effective:

1. Successful couples look for ways to stay positive, and say "yes" as often as possible. They constantly affirm the other's ideas, contributions, opinions and preferences. This is particularly important for men who often may not accept a woman's influence.

2. They embrace conflict as a way to work through differences, rather than try to avoid it or give in all the time. Typical conflicts in a relationship are about different preferences for working and relaxing, punctuality, and the way they resolve a dispute when they disagree about something important.

3. Good relationships are not only about how to fight, but how to repair a relationship after a fight. Humor, affection, apologies, and other

forms of "positive emotion" that allow for true "connection" with the other are critical. Gottman stresses that these are not large, complex events in a relationship—they are often brief, fleeting, and almost trivial moments but critical for relationship management.

4. Successful long-term relationships are characterized by continuing to stress what one likes, values, appreciates and respects in the other. In contrast, the best predictors that a relationship will not last are frequent incidents of criticism of the other, defensiveness when the other is critical, stonewalling and refusing to yield or compromise, and contempt or disgust for the other and their views. Gottman views contempt as the most toxic element that can quickly turn a relationship from good to bad.

Sources: Adapted from John M. Gottman, *The Seven Principles for Making Marriage Work;* and "Making Relationships Work: A Conversation with Psychologist John Gottman", *Harvard Business Review,* December 2007, pp. 45–50.

Finally, some research is beginning to explore the way parties in a relationship might enact different relationship forms, and the consequences of those differences. In a study of Israeli married couples who chose to participate in divorce mediation, men tended to use arguments that were based on principles of law and customary practice for handling problems and conflicts in the marriage dissolution, while women tended to use more arguments that were based on personal responsibility of parties to each other. Men tended to be more unemotional and reserved, while women tended to express deeper feelings of insult and pain. (Pines, Gat, and Tal, 2002). These results not only exemplify how parties might interpret a dissolving relationship in terms of the relationship form and appropriateness of ways to resolve the conflict, but also reveal gender differences in the approach to such relationships (see Chapter 14). For deeper insight into conflict management in relationships, see Box 10.4.

Section Summary

Much of the negotiation research reported in this volume is based on studies of negotiators in simulated market transactions—that is, simplified decision situations in which negotiators who have no past or future relationship with each other focus on key issues such as price and terms. But much actual negotiation occurs within established relationships, in which the past history and future expectations of the parties with each other significantly affects how they negotiate in the present. In this section, we indicated why negotiation within relationships is likely to be different from market transactions, discussed different forms that relationships could take, and reviewed what research has informed us about how a relationship context might shape negotiation behavior. In the next section, we show how issues of personal reputation, trust, and fairness significantly affect relationship negotiation.

Key Elements in Managing Negotiations within Relationships

Reputation, trust, and justice are three elements that become more critical and pronounced when they occur within a negotiation. In this section, we discuss how the effects of these elements become intensified in negotiations within relationships.

Reputation

Your reputation is how other people remember their past experience with you. Reputation is the legacy that negotiators leave behind after a negotiation encounter with another party. Reputation is a "perceptual identity, reflective of the combination of salient personal characteristics and accomplishments, demonstrated behavior and intended images preserved over time, as observed directly and/or as reported from secondary sources" (Ferris, Blass, Douglas, Kolodinsky, and Treadway, 2005, p. 215). Based on this definition, we can say several things about the importance of reputations:

• Reputations are perceived and highly subjective in nature. It is not how we would *like* to be known by others, or how we think we are known—it is what they *actually think* of us, and their judgment, that count. Once a reputation is formed, it acts as a lens or "schema" by which people form their expectations for future behavior (Fiske and Taylor, 1991) (refer back to our discussion of perception in Chapter 5).

• An individual can have a number of different, even conflicting, reputations because she may act quite differently in different situations. She may distributively bargain with the person who runs the yard sale down the road but be quite integrative with the person who regularly services her computer. While individuals can elicit different reputations in different contexts, most commonly a reputation is a single and consistent image from many different persons across many contexts—in most cases, there is generally shared agreement on who we are and how we are seen.

• Reputations are shaped by past behavior. On the one hand, we may know someone's reputation based on our own past experience with him (e.g., a history of cooperative or competitive behavior). On the other hand, our expectations may be shaped by the way the other behaves with other people. Thus, "direct" reputations (from our own experience) may be different from "hearsay" reputations (based on others' experience). Individuals tend to trust more those with better experiential reputations, and rely more on experiential reputations than hearsay reputations in deciding whether to trust another (Goates, 2008).

- Reputations are also influenced by an individual's personal characteristics and accomplishments. These may include qualities such as age, race, and gender; education and past experience; and personality traits, skills, and behaviors. All of these work together over time to create a broad reputation—how other people remember us in general—as well as a specific reputation that comes from how we, or others, have experienced this particular other person in the past.

- Reputations develop over time; once developed, they are hard to change. Our early experiences with another—or what we have heard about them from other people—shape our views of them, which we bring to new situations in the form of expectations about the other. These expectations are then confirmed or disconfirmed by the next set of experiences. Thus, first impressions and early experiences with others are powerful in shaping others' expectations; once these expectations are shaped, they become hard to change. A negotiator who develops a reputation as a distributive "shark" early on will thus have a difficult time convincing the current other negotiator that he is honest and trustworthy and wants to work toward a mutually acceptable agreement (Ferris et al., 2005).

- Others' reputations can shape emotional states as well as their expectations. Good hearsay reputations create positive emotional responses from others, and bad hearsay reputations elicit negative emotional responses from others (Goates, 2008).

Several studies tend to support the power of reputations in shaping these expectations. In one study, Glick and Croson (2001) created five reputation types (Liar/Manipulator, Tough but Honest, Nice and Reasonable, Cream Puff, and No Reputation) and presented them to students in a negotiation course. For 78 percent of the students, the other's reputation was a significant element in determining the strategy they used. Reputations also tended to dictate the type of strategy a negotiator used. Against a Liar/Manipulator, 61 percent of negotiators used distributive tactics and 10 percent used integrative tactics; against Tough but Honest negotiators, 49 percent used distributive tactics and 35 percent used integrative tactics; against Nice and Reasonable negotiators, 30 percent used distributive tactics and 64 percent used integrative tactics; while against Cream Puff negotiators, 40 percent used distributive tactics and 27 percent used integrative tactics.

These findings were generally confirmed in two additional studies on the impact of specific negotiator reputations. In one study, negotiators who knew that the other party had a strongly distributive reputation trusted the other party less, exchanged comparatively little critical information about key bargaining issues, and reaped poorer outcomes than those who were unaware of the other's reputation (Tinsley, O'Connor, and Sullivan, 2002). In contrast, knowing that the other party had a reputation for integrative negotiation (creating value) led negotiators to expect less deception from the other party; engage in a more candid discussion of specific needs, interests, and priorities; engage in significantly less nonnegotiation small talk; and be more optimistic about their ability to reach a mutually beneficial agreement (Tinsley and O'Connor, 2004). Thus, a "bad" (distributive, competitive) reputation can undermine your ability to be successful in a negotiation, not because of what you do, but because your reputation has negatively shaped the other's expectations of you. Similarly a "good" (integrative, cooperative) reputation can enhance your ability to be successful because your reputation has created positive expectations in the other party (c.f. Goates, 2008).

- Finally, negative reputations are difficult to "repair." The more long-standing the negative reputation, the harder it is to change that reputation to a more positive one. Reputations need to be actively defended and renewed in others' eyes. Particularly when an event is likely to be seen by others in a negative light, we must work hard to defend and protect our reputation and to make sure that others do not remember the experience in a negative way. How we account for past behavior, how we apologize and ask another person to overlook or discount the past, or how we use excuses or justifications to explain why we did something the other views as unfavorable will have a major impact on how others remember us and their experience with us. We say more about the role of apologies, excuses, and other "accounts" in the next section, on trust.

Trust

Many of the scholars who have written about relationships have identified trust as central to any relationship.[2] McAllister (1995) defined the word *trust* as "an individual's belief in and willingness to act on the words, actions and decisions of another" (p. 25). There are three things that contribute to the level of trust one negotiator may have for another: the individual's chronic disposition toward trust (i.e., individual differences in personality that make some people more trusting than others), situation factors (e.g., the opportunity for the parties to communicate with each other adequately), and the history of the relationship between the parties.

Early studies of trust envisioned it as a single unidimensional construct. However, more recent studies have shown that there are several different types of trust (c.f. Lewicki and Bunker 1995, 1996; Lewicki and Wiethoff, 2000). Lewicki and Wiethoff suggest that relationships of different depths (closeness) will be characterized by two[3] different types of trust: calculus-based trust and identification-based trust.

Calculus-Based Trust   Calculus-based trust is concerned with assuring consistent behavior: it holds that individuals will do what they say because (1) they are rewarded for keeping their word and preserving the relationship with others, or (2) they fear the consequences of not doing what they say. Trust is sustained to the degree that the punishment for not trusting is clear, possible, and likely to occur. Thus, the threat of punishment is likely to be a more significant motivator than the promise of reward.

This form of trust is most consistent with the market-pricing form of relationships or with the early stages of other types of relationships. In this context, the trustor basically calculates the value of creating and sustaining trust in the relationship relative to the costs of sustaining or severing the relationship. Compliance with calculus-based trust is often assured both by the rewards of being trusting (and trustworthy) and by the threat that if trust is violated, one's reputation can be hurt because the injured person will tell others that we can't be trusted.

Identification-Based Trust   The second type of trust is based on identification with the other's desires and intentions. At this level, trust exists because the parties effectively understand and appreciate each other's wants; this mutual understanding is developed to the point that each can effectively act for the other. Identification-based trust thus permits a party to serve as the other's agent in interpersonal transactions (Deutsch, 1949). The other can be confident that his or her interests will be fully protected and that no surveillance or monitoring of the actor is necessary. As the parties get to know each other and identification develops, the parties come to understand what they must do to sustain the other's trust. One comes to learn what really matters to the other and comes to place the same importance on those behaviors, qualities, expectations, and standards as the other does. This is the type of trust one might expect to see developed in communal-sharing relationships or in market-exchange relationships that transform into communal-sharing ones. Parties affirm strong identification-based trust by developing a collective identity (a joint name, title, logo, etc.); co-locating (living together in the same building or neighborhood); creating joint products or goals, such as producing a new product line or building a new living space together; and committing to commonly shared values, such that the parties are actually committed to the same objectives and can substitute for each other in external transactions. A suitable metaphor for identification-based trust may be a musical one, such as "harmonizing" or "jamming." Great identification-based trust can be seen in all kinds of relationships and teams. When people can anticipate each other's actions and intentions and flawlessly execute a great symphony, a complex surgery, a spectacular touchdown, a flawless relay race handoff, or an alley-oop pass to the basket with one second left on the clock, we see the product of strong, positive identification-based trust.

Trust Is Different from Distrust   A second important distinction that is emerging in the trust literature is the *distinction between trust and distrust* (Lewicki, McAllister, and Bies, 1998). If *trust* is considered to be confident positive expectations of another's conduct, *distrust* is defined as confident negative expectations of another's conduct—that is, we can confidently predict that some other people will act to take advantage of us, exploit our good faith and goodwill, or manipulate the relationship to their own personal ends. While early research tended to focus on trust as a single dimension—assuming that trust was on the high end and distrust or mistrust was on the low end of a continuum—understanding trust in complex personal relationships suggests that both trust and distrust can coexist in a relationship. Thus, I may trust my spouse to pick out a tie to go with my new suit, knowing that she has excellent taste, but not trust her to clean up my office, knowing that she has a tendency to throw away papers she thinks are worthless but I consider valuable. Distrust is increasing in today's work environment as a weak economy, corporate scandals, and the increasing discrepancy between chief executive and worker-level salaries continues to increase (see Box 10.5).

Combining the two types of trust with this distinction between trust and distrust leads us to be able to describe four types of trust:

Calculus-based trust (*CBT*) is a confident positive expectation regarding another's conduct. It is grounded in impersonal transactions, and the overall anticipated benefits to be derived from the relationship are assumed to outweigh any anticipated costs.

Calculus-based distrust (*CBD*) is defined as confident negative expectations regarding another's conduct. It is also grounded in impersonal transactions and the overall anticipated costs to be derived from the relationship are assumed to outweigh the anticipated benefits.

Consultants from Right Management have assessed the cost of losing employee trust. Organizations that don't "walk their talk"—valuing honesty and integrity as a key part of the culture—face high costs, including damage to the company's image, higher employee turnover, diminished ability to hire good talent, poor morale, and lower creativity and productivity. Ample evidence is available to show that high levels of trust, pride, and camaraderie are tied to organizational and financial success.

Despite the evidence, the trends indicate a decline in employee trust. In a survey of 202 organizations completed by the consultants in 2007, nearly 30 percent of employees said trust in their organizations had declined over the previous two years;

27 percent said levels were the same and 34 percent said trust had increased. Major causes of mistrust included managers withholding information, lying or telling half truths, not "walking their talk," demeaning employees, and not supporting employee development.

Recommended actions for improving trust between employees and managers included showing respect for employees as equal partners, sharing information, acting with honesty and integrity, and being committed to developing employee talents and skills.

Source: "The Cost of Losing Employee Trust," 2007, Right Management Consultants, 1818 Market Street, 33rd Floor, Philadelphia, PA 19103.

Identification-based trust (*IBT*) is defined as confident positive expectations regarding another's conduct. It is grounded in perceived compatibility of values, common goals, and positive emotional attachment to the other.

Identification-based distrust (*IBD*) is defined as confident negative expectations regarding another's conduct, grounded in perceived incompatibility of values, dissimilar goals, and negative emotional attachment to the other (Lewicki and Wiethoff, 2002).

Trust Building and Negotiations   These four forms of trust suggest clear action strategies for negotiators who wish to build trust with another party. These strategies are summarized in Table 10.1.[4] Note that if a negotiator is beginning a relationship with another party, or expects that the relationship with the other party will be no more than a market transaction, then the negotiator need only be concerned about developing and maintaining calculus-based trust, while managing calculus-based distrust. However, if the negotiator expects that the relationship could develop into a communal relationship, where identification-based trust would be more common, then the negotiator should establish calculus-based trust and also work to build identification-based trust. However, this process cannot be rushed, nor can it be one-sided. While one party can initiate actions that may move the trust-development process forward, the strongest trust must be mutually developed at a pace acceptable to both parties. Finally, if the negotiator senses that identification-based distrust is building, then he or she should work to both carefully manage the relationship and to minimize contact with the other.

Recent Research on Trust and Negotiation   Many researchers have explored trust in negotiation.[5] These early studies were often conducted with very primitive conceptualizations of trust and in reasonably primitive experimental settings; hence, the findings were rather limited in nature. As one might expect, this early research generally showed that higher levels of trust make negotiation easier, while lower levels of trust make negotiation more difficult. Similarly, integrative processes tend to increase trust, while more distributive processes are likely to

TABLE 10.1 | Actions to Manage Different Forms of Trust in Negotiations

How to Increase Calculus-Based Trust

1. Create and meet the other party's expectations. Be clear about what you intend to do and then do what you say.
2. Stress the benefits of creating mutual trust. Point out the benefits that can be gained for the other, or for both parties, by maintaining such trust.
3. Establish credibility. Make sure your statements are honest and accurate. Tell the truth and keep your word.
4. Keep promises. Make a commitment and then follow through on it.
5. Develop a good reputation. Pay attention to both your direct reputation and hearsay reputation. Work to have others believe that you are someone who has a reputation for being trusting and acting trustworthily.

How to Increase Identification-Based Trust

1. Develop similar interests. Try to be interested in the same things.
2. Develop similar goals and objectives. Try to develop similar goals, objectives, and scenarios for the future.
3. Act and respond like the other. Try to do what you know he or she would do in the same situation.
4. Stand for the same principles, values, and ideals. Hold similar values and commitments.
5. Actively discuss your commonalities and develop plans to enhance and strengthen them.

How to Manage Calculus-Based Distrust

1. Monitor the other party's actions. Make sure they are doing what they say they would do.
2. Prepare formal agreements (contracts, memoranda of understanding, etc.) that specify what each party has committed to do, and specify the consequences that will occur if each party does not fulfill their obligations.
3. Build in plans for "inspecting" and verifying the other's commitments. Specify how you will know if the other party is not living up to his or her agreements, and establish procedures for gathering data to verify those commitments.
4. Develop ways to make sure that the other party cannot take advantage of your trust and good will by invading other parts of your personal space. Be vigilant of the other's actions, and constantly monitor your personal boundaries.
5. Use formal legal mechanisms if there are concerns that the other might take advantage of you.

How to Manage Identification-Based Distrust

1. Expect that you and the other party will regularly disagree, see things differently, take opposing views, and stand for different ideals and principles.
2. Assume that the other party will exploit or take advantage of you if he or she has the opportunity. Monitor your boundaries with this person closely and regularly.
3. Check out and verify information, commitments, and promises the other party makes to you. Never take his or her word as given.
4. Minimize whatever interdependence you have with this party, and strongly manage the interdependencies that you have to have. Be vigilant of their efforts to take advantage of you or your goodwill. Be controlled and distant in what you say and how you say it to this person.
5. Minimize personal self-disclosure to this individual so as to not disclose information that could make you vulnerable. Do not share any confidences or secrets; assume you will be betrayed if you do.
6. Always assume that with this person, "the best offense is a good defense."

Source: Based on Lewicki and Stevenson, 1998; Lewicki, McAllister, and Bies, 1998; Lewicki and Wiethoff, 2000; Lewicki, 2006.

decrease trust.[6] Some of the more recent research on trust has revealed somewhat more complex relationships between trust and negotiation behavior. Here is a summary of those findings:

•   Many people approach a new relationship with an unknown other party with remarkably high levels of trust. Thus, while people in new relationships might be expected to start their trust of the other at "zero," in fact, most of us assume that the other can be trusted and are remarkably willing to trust the other even with very little information or knowledge about the other (Kramer, 1994; Myerson et al., 1996).

•   Trust tends to cue cooperative behavior. Parties who trust each other approach each other with cooperative dispositions (Butler, 1995, 1999). Thus, trust tends to cue a more communal orientation to a relationship and more cooperative behavior.

•   Individual motives also shape both trust and expectations of the other's behavior. Parties who are more cooperatively motivated report higher initial trust of the other party and more positive initial impressions of the other party than those who are individually motivated (Olekalns, Lau, and Smith, 2002).

•   Trustors, and those trusted, may focus on different things as trust is being built. Trustors may focus primarily on the risks of being trusted (e.g., how vulnerable they are), while those being trusted focus on the benefits to be received from the trust. Here we see a negotiator framing bias (Chapter 5) by both the sender and receiver that shapes how trust actions are viewed. Trustors are more likely to trust when the risk is low, but their willingness to trust does not seem to depend on the amount of benefit received by the person being trusted. However, the receiver is more likely to trust when the benefits to be received from the trust are high, but their trust does not seem to depend on the amount of vulnerability feared by the trustor. Moreover, each party reported that they were not particularly sensitive to the factors that affected their counterpart's decision (Malhotra, 2004). Thus, trust building might be greatly facilitated if parties could communicate more clearly and directly about the vulnerabilities to be felt or the benefits to be received, and how to manage these effectively.

•   The nature of the negotiation task (distributive versus integrative) can shape how parties judge the trust. In a more distributive context, trustors tend to focus on the risks they face, while those who are in a position to receive and then reciprocate the others' trust focus on the benefits that the trustors have provided them. Given the framing biases just mentioned, however, neither party tends to consider the other's point of view prior to making a decision whether to reciprocate the other's trust. As a result, the possibilities for trust to break down or not be completed may increase because neither party truly understands the risks or rewards as perceived by the other. More reciprocity occurs among individuals who are better at taking the perspective of the other in a negotiation, and reciprocity can be increased by coaching a negotiator to consider the views of the other party in their decision making (Malhotra, 2003).

•   Greater expectations of trust between negotiators leads to greater information sharing with the other party (Butler, 1999); similarly, greater expectations of distrust lead to less information sharing (Butler, 1995).

•   Greater information sharing tends to enhance effectiveness in achieving a good negotiation outcome, and less information sharing tends to diminish effectiveness in achieving a good outcome—although this effectiveness may *not* necessarily be the result of greater trust (Butler, 1999; Olekalns and Smith, 2001).

•   Distributive processes lead negotiators to see the negotiation dialogue, and critical events in the dialogue, as largely about the nature of the negotiation task (i.e., how to divide the pie). Distributive processes also lead people to judge the other party with negative characterization frames (see our discussion of frames in Chapter 5). Both of these perspectives tend to reduce trust. In contrast, integrative processes lead negotiators to see the dialogue as largely about interests, relationships, and positive affect and to see the other party with positive characterization frames; these perspectives tend to increase trust (Olekalns and Smith, 2001).[7]

•   Trust increases the likelihood that negotiation will proceed on a favorable course over the life of a negotiation. As described in Chapter 4, researchers have begun to examine turning points in negotiation—or key events, comments, or behaviors that turn the negotiation in a more positive (or more negative) direction. One study has generally shown that trust increases the likelihood of more facilitative turning points around interests and the relationship and decreases the number of inhibitory turning points around discussion of a distributive task or negative characterization of the other party. These processes subsequently lead to higher levels of trust at the end of the negotiation and lower levels of mistrust, and the process increased both calculus-based trust and identification-based trust. (Olekalns and Smith, 2001, 2005).

•   Face-to-face negotiation encourages greater trust development than negotiation online. There is evidence that parties anticipating an online negotiation expect less trust before the negotiations begin, are less satisfied with their negotiation outcomes, are less confident in the quality of their performance during the negotiation, trust the other less after the negotiation, and have less desire for a future interaction with the other party (Naquin and Paulson, 2003).

•   Negotiators who are representing others' interests, rather than their own interests, tend to behave in a less trusting way (be less trustworthy) and tend to expect that the other will be less trusting. As a result of being less trustworthy, negotiators engage in less give-and-take with the other party and expect the other party to engage in less give-and-take (Song, 2004).

•   In contrast to the increasing volume of research on the role of trust, persistent and pervasive distrust can significantly undermine negotiations. Kramer (2004) has investigated how "paranoid cognition"—a pervasive, irrational distrust of others, compounded by fear of exploitation, lack of confidence in others, and uncertainty regarding others motives—can significantly undermine interpersonal and group negotiations. Kramer offers a number of historical examples of political leaders whose paranoid distrust inhibited their ability to negotiate successfully.

Trust Repair   The preceding review of research clearly indicates that trust improves negotiation processes, leads to more integrative negotiations processes, and frequently produces better negotiation outcomes; and that *dis*trust hinders negotiation processes, leads to more distributive negotiations, and frequently diminishes strong negotiation outcomes. Because trust and positive negotiation processes and outcomes appear to be so critical, we

Pepper . . . and Salt
THE WALL STREET JOURNAL

LITZLER

**"Let's offer an apology but
without expressing contrition,
regret or responsibility."**

should comment on ways that broken trust can be repaired in order to return negotiations toward a more productive direction.

A number of studies have begun to investigate the ways that trust can be repaired.[8] A sampling of these results reveals the following:

- The more severe the breach of trust (the greater the costs incurred by the other party), the more difficult it is to repair trust and reconcile the relationship.

- If the parties had a good past relationship, it was easier to repair trust than if the past relationship had been poor.

- The sooner an apology occurs after the breach of trust, the more effective the apology is likely to be.

- The more sincerely an apology is expressed, the more effective it was in repairing trust.

- Apologies in which the actor took personal responsibility for having created the breach were more effective than those apologies in which the actor tried to blame external causes for the breach. Apologies were even more effective when the actor took personal responsibility *and* the apology was viewed as sincere.

- Apologies were more effective when the trust breach appeared to be an isolated event rather than habitual and repetitive for the other party (Tomlinson, Dineen, and Lewicki, 2004).

Recent studies have also shown that following a period of untrustworthy behavior, trust is more likely to be repaired if the trust violation was not accompanied by deception. Deception appears to harm trust far more than untrustworthy actions, and hence trust is much harder to repair if deception has occurred (Schweitzer, Hershey, & Bradlow, 2006).

Justice

The third major issue in relationships is the question of what is fair or just. Again, justice has been a major issue in the organizational sciences; individuals in organizations often debate whether their pay is fair, whether they are being fairly treated, or whether the organization might be treating some group of people (e.g., women, minorities, people from other cultures) in an unfair manner.

As research has shown,[9] justice can take several forms:

• *Distributive justice* is about the distribution of outcomes. Parties may be concerned that one party is receiving more than he or she deserves, that outcomes should be distributed equally, or that outcomes should be distributed based on needs (Deutsch, 1985). For example, Benton and Druckman (1974) showed that outcome fairness is often determined in a distributive negotiation as the point midway between the opening position of the two parties (what is often known as a "split-the-difference" settlement—see Chapter 2).[10] The presence of such an obvious settlement point appears to increase both concession making and the likelihood of settlement (Joseph and Willis, 1963). However, Sondak and Tyler (2001) showed that in important allocation decisions (such as who should work on Christmas or who should allocate a highly desirable parking place), many people would rather have a respected third party make the decisions than to resolve the problem by negotiation.

• *Procedural justice* is about the process of determining outcomes. Parties may be concerned that they were not treated fairly during the negotiation, that they were not given a chance to offer their point of view or side of the story, or that they were not treated with respect. Because negotiation is an environment in which parties are offered an opportunity to shape the outcome they receive, procedural fairness is generally high in most negotiations. Concerns about procedural fairness are more likely to arise when negotiators are judging the behavior of third parties. Tyler and Blader (2004) emphasize how important the procedural fairness of the third party is in viewing the third party as neutral, seeing them as trustworthy, accepting their decisions, and in the case of formal authorities such as police, voluntarily accepting their decisions and directives (see also Chapter 19).

• *Interactional justice* is about how parties treat each other in one-to-one relationships. Research has shown that people have strong expectations about the ways another party should treat them; when those standards are violated, parties feel unfairly treated. Bies and Moag (1986) argue that when the other party practices deception, is not candid and forthcoming, acts rudely, asks improper questions, makes prejudicial and discriminatory statements, or makes decisions or takes precipitous actions without justification, negotiators feel that fairness standards have been violated. Shapiro and Bies (1994) confirmed these predictions; they found that while negotiators who used threats were perceived as more powerful, they are also perceived as less cooperative and less fair because the parties felt unfairly treated.

• Finally, *systemic justice* is about how organizations appear to treat groups of individuals and the norms that develop for how they should be treated. When some groups are discriminated against, disfranchised, or systematically given poorer salaries or working conditions, the parties may be less concerned about specific procedural elements and more concerned that the overall system may be biased or discriminatory in its treatment of certain groups and their concerns. We will discuss the ways that these traditionally low-power groups respond in Chapter 12.

The issue of fairness is beginning to receive some systematic investigation in negotiation dynamics. The following conclusions can be drawn from a number of recent studies:

• Involvement in the process of helping to shape a negotiation strategy increases commitment to that strategy and willingness to pursue it (Jones and Worchel, 1992). This is the familiar "procedural justice effect," in that parties involved in the process of shaping a decision are more committed to that decision. Negotiators who helped develop a group negotiation strategy were more committed to it and to the group's negotiation goals.

• Negotiators (buyers in a market transaction) who are encouraged ("primed") to think about fairness are more cooperative in distributive negotiations. They make greater concessions, act more fairly and reach agreement faster, and have stronger positive attitudes toward the other party. They also demand fair treatment from the other party in return. However, when the other party did not reciprocate the negotiator's cooperative behavior, the negotiator actively retaliated and punished the other's competitive behavior. Thus, stating one's own intention to be fair and encouraging the other party to be fair may be an excellent way to support fair exchanges; but watch out for the negotiator whose fairness gestures are double-crossed (Maxwell, Nye, and Maxwell, 1999, 2003)!

• Similarly, parties who receive offers they perceive as unfair may reject them out of hand, even though the amount offered may be better than the alternative settlement, which is to receive nothing at all. Here we see the role of intangibles entering into a negotiation. Economists would predict that any deal better than zero should be accepted (if the only alternative is zero), but research has shown that negotiators will often reject these small offers (Pillutla and Murnighan, 1996). Clearly, a less-than-fair small offer creates feelings of anger and wounded pride, and negotiators will often act spitefully to sink the entire deal rather than accept a token settlement.

• Establishment of some objective standard of fairness has a positive impact on negotiations and satisfaction with the outcome. We discussed the role of setting an "objective standard" for fairness in Chapter 3 (Fisher, Ury, and Patton, 1991). Research by Kristensen (2000) has shown that among students who participated in a simulation of a corporate takeover, buyers who knew what a fair selling price would be for the company were more satisfied with those offered selling prices, more willing to buy the company, and more willing to do business with the other party in the future. Buelens and Van Poucke (2004) have shown that knowledge of an opponent's BATNA, as well as information about estimated market prices for the negotiated object, most strongly determine negotiator's judgments of fairness.

• Judgments about fairness are subject to the type of cognitive biases described earlier (Chapter 5). For example, most negotiators have an egocentric bias, which is the tendency to regard a larger share for oneself as fair, even if the obvious fairness rule is an equal split. Recent research has shown that this egocentric bias can be diminished by strong interactional justice. That is, recognizing the need to treat the other person fairly, and actually treating the other fairly, lead to a smaller egocentric bias, a more even split of the resources, quicker settlements, and fewer stalemates (Leung, Tong, and Ho, 2004).

• Not unsurprisingly, these egocentric biases vary across cultures. At least one study has shown that egocentric biases are stronger in cultures that are individualistic (e.g., the United States), where the self is served by focusing on one's positive attributes in order to stand out and be better than others, compared with more collectivist cultures (e.g., Japan) where the self is served by focusing on one's negative characteristics, so as to blend in with others (Gelfand et al., 2002). (We examine cultural differences in greater detail in Chapter 16).

Given the pervasiveness of concerns about fairness—how parties view the distribution of outcomes, how they view the process of arriving at that decision, or how they treat each other—it is remarkable that more research has not explicitly addressed justice issues in negotiation contexts. Several authors have studied how the actions taken by third parties are particularly subject to concerns about fairness (see Karambayya, Brett, and Lytle, 1992). Justice issues are also raised when individuals negotiate inside their organizations, such as to create a unique or specialized set of job duties and responsibilities. These "idiosyncratic deals" have to be managed effectively in order to make sure that they can continue to exist without disrupting others' sense of fairness about equal treatment (see Box 10.6). And they may not always be as fair as they seemed at the outset. One might expect that negotiated exchanges are seen as procedurally fair because the parties collectively make the decision, know the terms in advance, give mutual assent to the process, and make binding decisions. Yet at least one study has shown that after such agreements are struck, negotiators perceive their partners as *less* fair and are unwilling to engage in future exchanges with them. Thus, rather than making things more fair, negotiated exchanges may serve to emphasize the conflict between actors who are blind to their own biases and inclined to see the other party's motives and characteristics in an unfavorable light (Molm, Takahashi, and Peterson, 2003).

Finally, although we have identified these forms of justice (distributive, procedural, interactive, systemic) as separate entities, they are often intertwined. For example, many researchers have noted the relationship between procedural and distributive justice[11]: parties who feel that a given outcome is unfair are also likely to see that outcome as coming from an unfair procedure, and vice versa. Perceptions of distributive unfairness are likely to contribute to parties' satisfaction with the result of a decision, while perceptions of procedural unfairness are likely to contribute to the parties' dissatisfaction with the result or with the institution that implemented the unfair procedure (see Cropanzano and Folger, 1991).

Relationships among Reputation, Trust, and Justice

Not only are various forms of justice interrelated, but reputations, trust, and justice all interact in shaping expectations of the other's behavior. For example, when one party feels the other has acted fairly in the past or will act fairly in the future, he or she is more likely to trust the other (see Lewicki, Wiethoff, and Tomlinson, 2005). We would also predict that acting fairly leads to being trusted and also enhances a positive reputation. Conversely, several theoretical and empirical works have shown that when parties are unfairly treated, they often become angry and retaliate against either the injustice itself or those who are seen as having caused it.[12] Unfair treatment is likely to lead to distrust and a bad reputation. Trust, justice, and reputation are all central to relationship negotiations and feed each other; we cannot understand negotiation within complex relationships without prominently considering how we judge the other (and ourselves) on these dimensions.

Professor Denise Rousseau of Carnegie Mellon University has long studied the changing nature of employment relationships and "psychological contracts" between employees and employers. In a 2001 article, she discussed the "idiosyncratic deal"—the unique ways that employers may come to treat certain employees compared to others in the same office or environment. Many idiosyncratic deals are now negotiated in the workplace (e.g., educational leaves, flextime, working at home, working on one's own separate project while on the job, doing volunteer work on company time). While idiosyncratic deals were once available only to individuals with long seniority or to jobs with more discretionary job descriptions, Rousseau observes that idiosyncratic deals are much more common today, and they are not reserved only for a special few. Thus, while idiosyncratic deals are a new source of flexibility and innovation in the workplace, they also raise major concerns about fairness and consistent treatment of classes of employees. Here are some observations about idiosyncratic deals:

1. They are more common when workers

   - Are highly marketable (e.g., have a good BATNA in the job market).

   - Are willing to negotiate.

   - Have strong market and business knowledge.

   - Are located in small or start-up firms.

   - Work in more knowledge-oriented firms (specialize in information or services rather than specific products).

2. They are more common in certain countries, such as the United States, the United Kingdom, and New Zealand.

3. Idiosyncratic deals are more likely to work effectively when

   - There is a high-quality relationship between the worker and manager.

   - Responsibilities and role requirements are well understood and accepted.

   - Performance criteria are clear and well specified.

   - Workers trust the performance appraisal process.

   - There is shared understanding of performance criteria among co-workers.

   - Co-workers have mutually supportive relations.

   - Co-workers trust the manager.

   - When flexibility is limited, legitimate reasons are stated and clear. Such deals are viewed as a source of innovation that can be shared and adopted by others in the firm.

Source: D. Rousseau, "The Idiosyncratic Deal: Flexibility vs. Fairness?" *Organizational Dynamics* 29, no 4 (2001), pp. 260–73.

Section Summary   In this section, we have examined three core elements common to many negotiations within relationships: reputations, trust, and justice. Not only are these elements essential, but they also feed each other. Trust issues are central to relationships. While some amount of trust exists in market-transaction negotiations, trust is more critical to communal-sharing relationships in which the parties have some history, an anticipated future, and an attachment to each other. In addition, justice concerns are absolutely central to negotiation in relationships. Negotiations between many parties—husband and wife, business partners, or nations such as those in the Middle East—focus heavily on both fair solutions to distribution problems and fair processes for resolving those disputes. Finally, past evidence of trust and fairness—either from our own experience or from the experience of others—strongly shapes

BOX   10.7   JetBlue Apologizes

On February 14, 2007 (Valentine's Day in the United States), airline JetBlue suffered a major crisis. Two inches of snow and ice at New York's JFK airport lead to 1,000 flight cancellations, massive delays, and passengers stranded on planes for up to nine hours. The event received massive media visibility, and it took almost a week for JetBlue to resume normal operations. While other airlines also suffered service disruptions because of the storm, JetBlue received most of the visibility for the breakdown—largely because in its seven-year history it had inspired much higher expectations of good treatment from its loyal customers.

JetBlue founder and CEO David Neeleman was faced with the challenge of how to repair the public's trust in a way that would strengthen the strong brand identity that the company had created. In the week following the crisis, he appeared in every local and national news media. He accepted responsibility for bad decisions and organizational problems. He apologized repeatedly, promised refunds for stranded passengers, and promised to fix the problems that created the disaster. He also introduced a customer "bill of rights." Two weeks after the meltdown, 43 percent of a sample of people visiting JetBlue's Web site said the airline was still their number-one favorite.

In a time when most airlines enjoy very little customer confidence, Neeleman's successful handling of the crisis has been highlighted as an example of creating a trustworthy brand identity—and being able to sustain it in a time of crisis. Bruce Blythe, CEO of Crisis Management International, sums it up well: "The single most important thing that a company needs to show in a crisis is that it cares. That's not a feeling. It's a behavior."

Source: C. Salter, "Lessons from the Tarmac," *Fast Company,* May 2007, pp. 31–32.

whether negotiators have a positive or a negative reputation, which serves as a strong determinant of how negotiators shape their strategy with us in the future.

Not only are these elements critical to relationships, but as pointed out, building a relationship may be an essential critical component of being successful in negotiation. For one company's approach to building relationships in order to enhance sales, see Box 10.7.

Repairing a Relationship

There are many steps to repairing a relationship. Trying to overcome a bad reputation, rebuilding trust, or restoring fairness to a relationship are much easier to talk about than to actually do! Fisher and Ertel (1995) outline many of the steps to managing effective integrative negotiations and suggest the following diagnostic steps in beginning to work on improving a relationship:

1. *What might be causing any present misunderstanding, and what can I do to understand it better?* If the relationship is in difficulty, what might have caused it, and how can I gather information or perspective to improve the situation?

2. *What might be causing a lack of trust, and what can I do to begin to repair trust that might have been broken?* Trust repair is a long and slow process. It requires adequate explanations for past behavior, apologies, and perhaps even reparations (see Box 10.7).

3. *What might be causing one or both of us to feel coerced, and what can I do to put the focus on persuasion rather than coercion?* How can we take the pressure off each other so that we can give each other the freedom of choice to talk about what has happened and what is necessary to fix it?

4. *What might be causing one or both of us to feel disrespected, and what can I do to demonstrate acceptance and respect?* How can we begin to appreciate each other's contributions and the positive things that we have done together in the past? How can we restore that respect and value each other's contributions?

5. *What might be causing one or both of us to get upset, and what can I do to balance emotion and reason?* How can we surface the deeply felt emotions that have produced anger, frustration, rejection and disappointment? How can we effectively vent these emotions, or understand their causes, so that we can move beyond them?

These are important questions. If the relationship problem is not significant or long lasting, the parties may be able to work them out on their own. If the problem has persisted for a time, or the breakdown creates serious costs for one or both sides, third parties will probably have to intervene (see Chapter 19).

Chapter Summary

In this chapter, we explored the way that existing relationships shape negotiation. Much of negotiation theory and research is based on what we have learned in experimental research settings, consisting of two negotiating parties who don't know each other, don't expect to deal with each other in the future, and are engaged in a market transaction over price and quantity. Yet much of the professional negotiations conducted in business, law, government, communities, and international affairs occur in a context in which the parties have a past (and future) relationship and in which their relationship strongly affects the negotiation process.

In addition, we cannot assume that negotiators are involved only in arm's-length market transactions about the exchange of fees for goods and services. Many negotiations concern how to work (and live) together more effectively over time, how to coordinate actions and share responsibilities, or how to manage problems that have arisen in the relationship. In this chapter, we evaluated the status of previous negotiation research—which has focused almost exclusively on market-exchange relationships—and evaluated its status for different types of relationships, particularly communal-sharing and authority-ranking relationships. Within relationships, we see that parties shift their focus considerably, moving away from a sole focus on price and exchange to also attend to the future of the relationship, including the level of trust between the parties and questions of fairness, and to build strong positive reputations. We argue that most negotiations occur within these relationship contexts, and future work must attend to their unique complexities.

We turn next in Chapter 11 to another aspect of negotiations involving relationships: how things change when negotiators are representing the interests of others rather than their own interests and when more than two parties are actively involved in the negotiation process.

Endnotes

[1] See Holmes and Murray, 1996; Kelley et al., 1983; Reis and Patrick, 1996; and Rusbult and Van Lange, 1996.

[2] Greenhalgh, 2001; Greenhalgh and Chapman, 1996; and Tuchinsky, Edson Escalas, Moore, and Sheppard, 1994.

[3] Earlier papers by Lewicki and Bunker (1995, 1996) suggested three types of trust: calculus-based, knowledge-based, and identification-based. However, their more recent work has eliminated the knowledge-based form of trust, suggesting that knowledge of the other was more a component of the relationship itself than of trust. Thus, later theorizing only discusses calculus-based and identification-based forms of trust.

[4] See Lewicki, 2006.

[5] For example, Butler, 1991; Kimmel, Pruitt, Magenau, Konar-Goldbaud, and Carnevale, 1980; Lindskold, Bentz, and Walters, 1986; Schlenkler, Helm, and Tedeschi, 1973; and Zand, 1972, 1997.

[6] As we noted earlier, a problem with much of this research is that it tends to view trust as a simple, unidimensional construct characteristic of market exchanges (Kimmel et al., 1980; Tedeschi, Heister, and Gahagan, 1969). Because relationships are complex, multifaceted, changing over time, and often grounded in compatibility of personalities, interpersonal styles, and values, it would appear likely that the more complex models of trust we suggest in this chapter really operate in close communal relationships the same as in arm's-length market transactions.

[7] See Koeszegi (2004) for a description of the process of trust-building in interorganizational relationships.

[8] See Bottom, Gibson, Daniels, and Murnighan, 2002; Kim, Dirks, Cooper, and Ferrin, 2006; Schweitzer, Hershey, and Bradlow, 2006; and Tomlinson, Dineen, and Lewicki, 2004.

[9] See Sheppard, Lewicki, and Minton (1992); and Greenberg and Colquitt (2005) for reviews of justice issues in organizations; and Albin (1993) for a commentary on the role of fairness in negotiation.

[10] See also Lowenstein, Thompson, and Bazerman, 1989.

[11] See Ambrose and Arnaud, 2005; and Brockner and Wiesenfeld, 2005.

[12] See Greenberg, 1990; Sheppard, Lewicki, and Minton, 1992; and Skarlicki and Folger, 1997.

CHAPTER 11

Agents, Constituencies, Audiences

Objectives

1. Understand how negotiation dynamics change when additional parties are added to a two-person negotiation.

2. Explore how negotiation changes when a negotiator has to represent someone else's interests (i.e., be an agent) rather than (his or her) own.

3. Consider the critical actions and influence exerted by constituencies and audiences to a negotiation.

4. Gain specific advice on how constituencies should manage their agents and how agents manage their constituencies.

In this chapter, we explore how negotiation changes when (1) we move beyond simple one-to-one negotiations and add other parties to the process, and (2) negotiators act as agents in the process—that is, they are not necessarily presenting their own issues and interests, but are also representing the views of others who may or may not be at the table. This situation is called an *agency relationship*.

Our objective is to examine how adding negotiators makes the social environment significantly more complex and dynamic. We examine the ways that negotiations change when negotiators are representing the interests of others rather than arguing for their own interests. Within this larger context, individuals and groups attempt to exert both direct and indirect pressures on negotiators to advocate their interests. A second dimension of complexity, therefore, is the type of influence strategies that negotiators use, and the different types of influence attempts that occur as the number of parties increases.

The Number of Parties in a Negotiation

An important aspect to consider in negotiation is how the number of parties—either at the table, influencing what happens at the table, or affected by what happens at the table—affects the dynamics of negotiating. The simplest negotiation form is a negotiating dyad. This structure occurs when two isolated individuals—*negotiators*—negotiate for their own needs and interests. Each member of the dyad is responsible only for expressing his or her own positions and needs and for working with the other party to arrive at an agreement. Each has the full power to decide on the acceptable outcome and finalize the deal.

Negotiations become more complex when there are more than two negotiators. If a family is trying to decide where to spend a summer vacation, each party—Mom, Dad, the two children, and Grandma—has his or her own preferences and priorities. Although each is responsible for expressing his or her own positions and needs, the agreement has to reflect the views of all parties (some parties with low status or power may be forced to go along with the agreement by the others). When there are more than two negotiators, there is a strong possibility that some parties will form alliances, searching for strength in numbers or in the coincidence of their interests. We explore the dynamics of these alliances in Chapter 12 on the topic of coalitions.

Negotiation can also occur within or between *teams* of negotiators. A team is two or more parties on the same side who are collectively advocating the same positions and interests. The *intra-team* dynamics (e.g., whether some members have more power or status than others) will affect the *inter-team* negotiation process. Moreover, as the number of negotiators increases, the likelihood of finding common ground and thereby satisfying all interests usually decreases. We discuss the care and planning necessary to conduct effective intra-team negotiations in Chapter 13.

Negotiation also increases in complexity with the addition of *agents* and *constituencies*. Often negotiators act not only for themselves but also for others. In these situations, we will describe the negotiator as an *agent* and the individuals he or she is representing as a *constituent* (also called a *principal*). A constituent is one or more parties who have designated someone else (the agent) to represent his or her positions and interests in a negotiation. Two common examples of an agent and a constituent (principal) are an attorney and a client and a salesperson and her boss or manager. Constituents usually do not participate in the actual negotiations (although they may be present); rather, they choose agents both to advocate their interests to the other negotiator and to report back accurately on what has transpired during the deliberations.

Finally, negotiation becomes most complex when *bystanders, audiences,* and *third parties* also are active in the negotiation. *Bystanders* are those who may have some stake in a negotiation and who care about the substantive issues or the process by which a resolution is reached, but who are not formally represented at the table. Bystanders frequently follow the negotiation, express public or private views to the negotiators about the potential outcomes or the process, and in some way are affected by what happens. An *audience* is any individual or group of people who are not directly involved in or affected by a negotiation, but who have a chance to observe and react to the ongoing events and who may at times offer input, advice, or criticism to the negotiators. Bystanders and constituents can also serve as audiences. So, too, can members of negotiating teams who are not actively engaged in dialogue with the other party. Finally, we describe *third parties* as bystanders who may be drawn into the negotiation specifically for the purpose of helping to resolve it. Third parties often can reshape a polarized situation into a constructive agreement. Bystanders can be effective as third parties if they have the necessary skills and are seen as neutral. We examine the key roles played by bystanders and audiences later in the chapter and by third parties in Chapter 19.

It is important to understand that although we have distinguished these different roles, negotiating parties may, in fact, assume more than one role during the life of a negotiation.

Agents can become constituents or bystanders, and so on. We now explore how agents, constituents, audiences, and bystanders can change the nature of negotiation.

How Agents, Constituents, and Audiences Change Negotiations

There are often parties to a negotiation who are not active participants in the process because others are negotiating on their behalf. The interests of these parties are represented by an agent; they will be affected by the outcome achieved by the agent, and/or they may observe the agent's behavior and perhaps offer comments, critiques, or evaluations of the process or outcome. When these circumstances occur, the negotiator must redirect some of his or her attention away from the other negotiator and toward these other parties. We broadly describe the attention paid to these additional parties—regardless of who they are—as *audience effects.*

In this section, we first examine the different types of audiences that can exist in negotiation and the consequences that audiences have on a negotiator's behavior. We then examine the different ways in which negotiators can manage their audiences so as to be more effective in dealing with the audience and with the other negotiator.

Audiences: Team Members, Constituents, Bystanders, and Others

There are many different kinds of audiences and audience effects. We identified the primary ones in the preceding introduction. Initially, we include all the roles delineated—negotiating team members, constituents, bystanders, and even neutrals (everyone except the focal negotiators)—as audiences because they can all serve the function of constituents, observers, and commentators relative to the focal negotiators' behavior.

One form of audience is the *additional team members* who are present with the negotiator at the deliberations. Members of a negotiating team may take on one or more important roles: chief spokesperson, expert or resource person on a specific issue, advocate for a particular subgroup with a stake in the outcome, legal or financial counsel, statistician or cost analyst, recording secretary, or observer. Team members may agree to play a special role in negotiation, but they may also shift into another role as the negotiation evolves. The most frequent role shift is from being the chief negotiator to being a passive observer who is silent while others are speaking. The observer may be taking notes, listening to the discussion, preparing to make comments to be introduced later on, or simply evaluating and judging the actions of those who currently hold the floor. Negotiators also direct their comments toward observers on the other side. So, for example, while a member of one team (chief spokesperson) may appear to be talking directly to a member of the other team (the other chief spokesperson), the purpose of the conversation may be to influence the other team's legal expert (also at the table) on some point.

Team members can play multiple roles. Team members can do as much to influence and shape a spokesperson's behavior as what the opposing negotiator says or does. Figure 11.1 represents a simple negotiation between two pairs of negotiators—on each side, one may be the primary spokesperson (N1) while the other (N2) assists, but within each side, N1 and N2 may change roles at any time. In this example, imagine the focal negotiators are a renowned rock singer Athena and her manager, negotiating a performance contract with the president

FIGURE 11.1 | Each Negotiator with a Partner

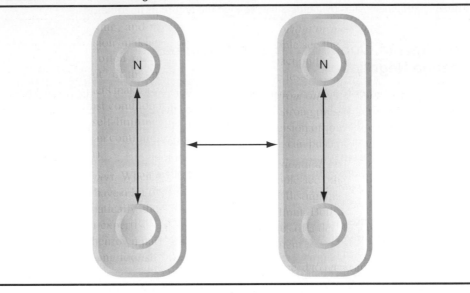

and general manager of Glitzy Productions Inc., a media company organizing the halftime show for the next Super Bowl (Figure 11.2).

Another type of audience is a *constituency*. A constituency is one or more parties whose interests, demands, or priorities are being represented by the focal negotiator at the table. The term *constituency* usually applies to politics; elected officials are usually accountable to the voters who elected them (their constituency). For attorneys or accountants or consultants, their constituents are their clients. The social structure of this negotiation is represented in Figures 11.3, 11.4, and 11.5. In Figure 11.3, the negotiator (the manager) has a constituent who is also a team member (Athena the rock star) and is present during the negotiation; in Figure 11.4, the negotiator represents a constituent who is outside of the negotiating setting (e.g., Athena did not attend the meeting but will have to authorize the deal); in Figure 11.5, the negotiator represents a group of constituents (Athena's nine-member band—the Greek Gods—plus media promoters, equipment managers, bodyguards, and the like).

As these figures suggest, negotiators who have constituents are usually involved in two distinctly different relationships—and often in two separate and distinct negotiations. The first negotiating relationship is between the agent and constituent (sometimes called "negotiating at the back table"; see Docherty and Campbell, 2005). The two must decide on their collective view of what they want to achieve in the negotiation (fee for the appearance, advertising and promotion, etc.) and the strategy and tactics of how to get it. This is often a tense negotiation in itself, particularly if the two parties differ on their goals for the negotiation or the strategy and tactics they should use. Once the two agree on their goals, the constituent then delegates some power and authority to the agent to achieve the goals in discussions with the other negotiator. Constituents expect that their agents will accurately and enthusiastically represent the collective interests of the constituent in the deliberations,

FIGURE 11.2 | Athena and her Manager versus the President and General Manager of Glitzy Productions

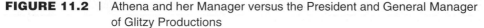
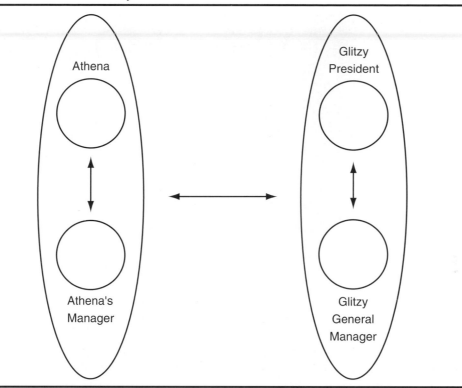

periodically report back as negotiations evolve, and eventually report back the outcomes at the end of the process. Constituents therefore expect to profit (or lose) as a direct result of the agent's effectiveness, and they often select their agent based on his or her ability to achieve their goals (more on this later in the chapter).

The second negotiating relationship maintained by the agent is with the other agent—the opposing negotiator—as the two negotiators attempt to reach a viable and effective agreement. These negotiations usually take place at the "front table" (Docherty and Campbell, 2005). Reaching an agreement may require the agent to compromise at the front table on the goals set with his or her constituency at the back table and then to explain and justify those compromises back to the constituent. Because agents may be unable to both completely satisfy their constituent and achieve an agreement with the other party, representing a constituent creates unique pressures and conflicts for agents. These pressures and conflicts are discussed in detail throughout this chapter.

A third type of audience is composed of external bystanders and observers. Remember that negotiating team members themselves can act as bystanders and observers. In addition there may be many bystanders whose interests may not be directly represented in the negotiation, or present at the table, but who are affected by the negotiation outcome or have a

FIGURE 11.3 | Negotiator with a Constituent Who Is Present versus Other Negotiator

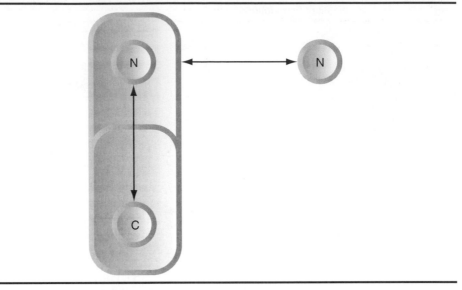

FIGURE 11.4 | Negotiator with a Constituent Who Is Not Present versus Other Negotiator

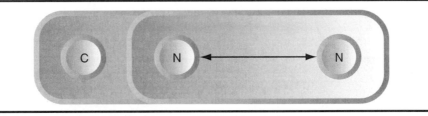

vantage point from which to observe it and some strong need to comment on the process or the emerging outcome. Figure 11.6 represents this most socially complex environment for a negotiation. In our example, this may include other groups negotiating with Glitzy Productions (e.g., other performing artists, groups that will manage the acoustics, set designers, security, etc.) and observers/bystanders (such as the entertainment media, the Super Bowl organization, the TV network that will be covering it, and the like). The public nature of this negotiation offers a context in which many parties are watching and evaluating the negotiation, but it also offers many ways for the negotiator to use these audiences to bring indirect leverage to bear on the other negotiator. We examine some of these tactics later in this chapter.

Characteristics of Audiences We can describe the major characteristics of audiences in several ways (Rubin and Brown, 1975). First, audiences vary according to whether they are physically *present at or absent from* the negotiation. Some observers (like team members) may be present during negotiations and directly witness the events that occur; others may

FIGURE 11.5 | Negotiator with Several Constituents versus Other Negotiator

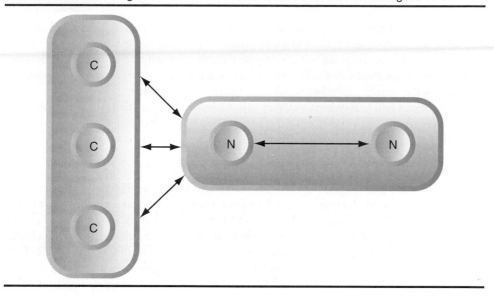

FIGURE 11.6 | Negotiators Representing Constituencies with Input from Audiences

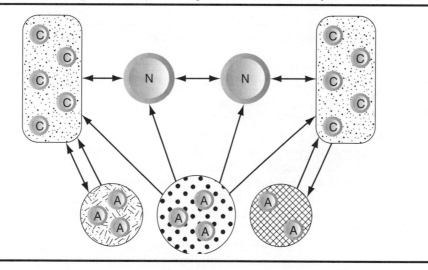

be physically removed and learn about what happens only through reports and accounts. Whether an audience is present or absent affects how a negotiator behaves; he or she may say one thing with the audience present and another with the audience absent. In addition, when audiences are absent, agents must report to them what happened in the negotiation; when the audience has no real way of independently knowing what happened, these accounts may not be completely accurate.

Second, audiences may or may not be dependent on the negotiators for the outcomes derived from the negotiation process. Audiences who are *outcome-dependent* derive their payoffs as a direct result of the negotiator's behavior and effectiveness. In our rock concert example, the compensation paid to other groups negotiating with Glitzy Productions— warm-up acts, musicians, and so on—may be directly affected by the agreement between Athena and Glitzy Productions. In contrast, a *nondependent* audience will not be directly affected by the results. Although members of the general public may be interested in the contract Athena and Glitzy arrive at, they will be less directly affected by the settlement, except perhaps through the ticket prices they must pay. Other bands who learn of the terms of the contract may also use the contract as a benchmark to demand higher pay for themselves.

A third major way in which audiences affect negotiations is by the *degree of their involvement* in the process. Audiences may become *directly* involved in the negotiation process; when they do, the complexity of the interaction increases in a number of ways, depending on who the audience is, what is at stake, how much power the audience has, and what kind of a role the audience chooses to play. In international affairs, the United States has often become involved in another country's or region's local disputes—the Middle East, Eastern Europe, the former Yugoslavian republics, and emerging African nations. U.S. involvement has occurred in almost every form and variation—from expressing a preference for a particular strategy, process, or outcome; to attempting to facilitate negotiations and work out internal difficulties; to becoming militarily involved, and either taking sides or keeping parties separate to help achieve a peaceful resolution.

Audiences also give periodic *feedback* to the negotiators, evaluating their effectiveness and letting them know how they are doing. Feedback may be verbal, in the form of personal conversations and advice, notes, messages, or letters, or it may be nonverbal, in the form of smiles and nods of affirmation or scowls and frowns of disapproval. Feedback may be directed toward the positions that a negotiator has taken, concessions made, agreements reached, or behavior during the deliberations.

In contrast to this direct involvement, audiences may also be *indirectly* involved in the negotiation. Indirect involvement occurs when audiences make their own wishes and desires known through the communication of their ideas but do not directly try to influence the course of an ongoing negotiation. Again, there are numerous examples in international negotiations as well as labor and political disputes. In some circumstances, the United States makes its views known on how other countries should conduct their affairs through public statements or private informal communication, but does not directly try to influence those actions. Consumers are often encouraged to boycott a store or product (e.g., grapes, lettuce) to support a labor union and back its demands. Indirect communication also provides a large amount of feedback to the other party, indicating the degree to which the audience approves or disapproves of the agent's words and actions.

Audiences may vary in several other ways: identity (who they are and what they stand for), composition (the number and type of different points of view represented), size (which may affect their level of power), relationship to the negotiator (emotional ties, amount of informal control they can exercise over the negotiator), and role in the negotiation situation (readiness to try to influence directly the negotiator's behavior, style, or content of communication). In short, as soon as the negotiation setting is expanded to three or more parties, the nature and complexity of their interaction increases. Audiences play several different roles and attempt to shape the progress of negotiation in many ways. In addition, as the type of relationship among the parties changes from market transaction to some other form (see Chapter 10), the negotiation issues, strategies, and processes may change as well.

Before we discuss audiences in more detail, we will summarize the most important principles about audiences and the significant ways in which they influence an agent's behavior.

Audiences Make Negotiators "Try Harder" and "Act Tougher"   Research has shown that the presence of an audience increases negotiator aspirations—that is, the negotiators "try harder" when they know they are being watched. Merely being aware that they are under surveillance can motivate negotiators to act tough. In one experiment, Carnevale, Pruitt, and Britton (1979) told some subjects in an experimental negotiation that they were being watched by their constituents through a one-way window, while others believed they were not being watched. Negotiators who believed they were under surveillance were significantly more likely to conduct their negotiations in a distributive bargaining manner and to use threats, commitment tactics, and put-downs of their opponents to gain advantage (see Chapter 2). They were in turn less likely to pursue integrative bargaining strategies, and they obtained lower joint outcomes than negotiators not under surveillance. Druckman (1994), after reviewing a number of research studies on the impact of constituencies, suggests that inflexibility in public negotiations is largely due to pressures on group representatives to adopt tough postures. Time pressures can also significantly affect this inflexibility. Mosterd and Rutte (2000) found that when negotiators are negotiating only for themselves, time pressure makes the negotiator act less competitively and a higher proportion of the negotiations ended in successful agreement. In contrast, when negotiators are negotiating on behalf of their constituencies, time pressures results in *more* competitive interaction and a higher proportion of impasses.

Negotiators Seek a Positive Reaction from an Audience   The presence of an audience also motivates negotiators to seek a positive evaluation from the audience and to avoid a negative one. Thus, an audience increases aspirations because negotiators try to impress them in order to receive a beneficial evaluation. Tjosvold (1977) reported that agents who received a strong affirmation of personal effectiveness from their constituents resisted compromising toward the other agent's position in order to maintain their image of competence to their constituents. Thus, when there is a trade-off between a positive self-image and an agreement with the other party, a favorable self-image for the negotiator may dominate.

Pressures from Audiences Can Push Negotiators into "Irrational" Behavior   In addition to the mere presence of an audience, the presence of a salient audience—one valued for its opinions and supportive comments—affects a negotiator even more dramatically. A classic study by Brown (1968) reveals the power of feedback from a salient audience on a negotiator's subsequent behavior. In Brown's experiment, high school students played a competitive negotiation game with someone they thought was another student, but who was in fact an ally of the experimenter playing a preprogrammed strategy. In all cases, the preprogrammed strategy was aggressive and exploitative—thus, the students lost a lot of money in the early part of the game. The students then received contrived feedback messages from a group of their "peers" (whom they thought had been observing the first round), telling them either that they looked weak and foolish as a result of the way that they had been exploited in the first game, or that they looked good and strong in the first round because they had played fair. Students then played a second round of the game, during which they were given the choice of using either a retaliatory strategy to get back at the opponent who took advantage of them (a strategy that would also cost them a great deal of money to execute), or a second strategy that did not involve retaliation, thus ignoring the challenge to their self-esteem created by the negative messages from the audience. The experiment, therefore, required the subjects to choose between pursuing a strategy in which they made money but lost face (image and self-respect) in front of the audience or peers or one in which they retaliated against the opponent and restored their image with the important audience, but at great financial cost. As Brown summarized,

> The results were striking: publicly humiliated subjects—those who received the derogatory feedback—were far more likely to retaliate, and with greater severity and self-sacrifice—than subjects who received the more favorable feedback. . . . Of special interest is the fact that when asked why they chose severe retaliation, 75 percent of the subjects who did so reported that they didn't want to look foolish and weak as a result of having been exploited, and that they retaliated in order to reassert their capability and strength. (Rubin and Brown, 1975, p. 45)

In a follow-up study, Brown tested whether knowledge of the costs of retaliation was important in getting subjects to engage in retaliatory behavior. In one variation, the audience knew how much cost the subject endured in order to retaliate. In a second variation, the audience did not know the costs. The results of these two variations demonstrated clearly that retaliation was greatest when the audience told the subject that he looked foolish and the audience did *not* know how much it cost the subject to retaliate. Brown's research highlights the classic face-saving dilemma for negotiators: to preserve one's image to an audience, often at high costs not known to the audience, or to lose face but conserve resources. The research clearly shows that negotiators are most aggressive when there is a high need to regain a positive image with an audience that does not know the amount it costs for the negotiator to do so.

Brown's study has several important implications for understanding the power of an audience over a negotiator. First, the student subjects in the study did not know the specific identity of anyone in the audience—only that they were from the same high school. The student negotiators never saw the audience, which was only vaguely identified as an important group. Thus, even audiences who are viewed only as a somewhat-important group to please can exert powerful influences over a negotiator's behavior by simply telling negotiators that they look weak and foolish. A second finding was that some students retaliated against the other party even when there was no audience present. This suggests that the opposing negotiator may act as an audience as well. Negotiators who believe that the opposing negotiator made them look foolish or has evaluated their behavior as weak and ineffective may try to regain a positive evaluation as "tough," even from their adversary. (See Box 11.1, which represents a simple negotiation between two pairs of negotiators.) Anyone who has ever played a "friendly" game of tennis, golf, basketball, or touch football with some competitive friends will recognize that much of the banter, teasing, verbal

A 2001 news article featured sports agents in the Columbus, Ohio, area. The area is a fertile ground for budding agents, who seek to represent Ohio State athletes moving into professional sports, as well as professional hockey players, coaches, broadcasters, and musicians. Among their insights:

- Competition for top players is very heavy. The number of potential agents—registered and unregistered—far exceeds the number of eligible athletes in any given year.

- Many agents choose not to represent first-round football draft picks. "The only way to compete is to cheat," says agent and attorney Bret Adams. "If you don't cheat, you're not going to get the first-round draft picks. You either break the rules, or you sell your soul, by doing things that you normally wouldn't." "Cheating" includes signing players to contracts while they still have amateur status, giving gifts to players (cash, cars, investment funds), and the like. Adams chooses to represent coaches and broadcasters, who are less in demand and require him to stay within ethical boundaries.

- Depending on the sport, some agents don't get involved in any of the salary negotiations. For example, in representing golfers in the Ladies Professional Golf Association, agents are only responsible for signing endorsements—with golf equipment manufacturers, soaps, shoe companies, and so on.

- While many agents are attorneys and are bound by a legal code of ethics, others define their business as a "ministry" and follow religious principles to guide their conduct.

- Commissions vary significantly depending on whom the agent is representing. In 2001, National Football League contracts capped the agent's compensation at 3 percent of the player's contract, but endorsements can go up to 15 percent on a football player's contract and to 20 to 25 percent for a Ladies Professional Golf Association contract.

- Many states are now passing regulations that limit what agents can do—requiring them to register with a state agency; placing language into the agent's contract with the player that spells out the consequences of rule violation for the player, including loss of college eligibility; and posting a security bond that could pay damages to athletes and universities if the agent misbehaves.

Extensive processes for educating coaches, athletes, their parents and families, and agents themselves are the best mechanisms for preventing agent abuse, but every year there are a few widely publicized incidents that indicate that problems still persist.

Source: Adapted from J. Caton, "Big League Agents," *Columbus Monthly,* June 2001, pp. 54–60.

---

harassment or "trash talking" that occurs is designed to undermine the opponent's self-confidence or to challenge him or her to play better. While this is usually done with good-natured humor, the banter can quickly turn serious if a comment is made too sharply or misinterpreted, and it can both seriously unsettle the opponent and hurt the relationship. One can thus imagine the impact of a message to a negotiator from the other party that he or she was "easy to beat." Not only is the other party embarrassed by losing, but the embarrassment will be magnified by the taunting. Such comments are the fuel for revenge and long-standing, deep-seated animosity.

Brown's research shows how important face saving is to negotiators whose behavior is highly public, visible, and subject to a great deal of feedback from audiences. For example,

BOX 11.2

"Face Threat Sensitivity" Seen as Roadblock to Agreement and Joint Gain

A group of researchers has recently validated and updated Brown's classic research findings on the power of face saving. Several interesting findings were recently reported by these researchers:

1. Individuals differ in the degree to which they are sensitive to face-saving dynamics, which these researchers call "face threat sensitivity." Individuals who are stronger in face threat sensitivity are more likely to agree with the following three statements:

   a. "My feelings are hurt easily."

   b. "I don't respond well to direct criticism."

   c. "I am pretty thin-skinned."

2. In a simulated negotiation experiment, buyers and sellers were less likely to reach an agreement that was in the interest of both parties when the seller was higher in face threat sensitivity.

3. In a simulated negotiation of a job interview, both recruiters and job candidates reached an employment contract that contained less joint gain when the candidate was higher in face threat sensitivity. Moreover, those candidates who reported higher face threat sensitivity described themselves as more competitive, and this competitiveness mediated the relationship between higher face threat sensitivity and lower joint gain.

It is clear that face threat sensitivity can be a powerful factor in determining negotiation outcomes.

Source: J. White, R. Tynan, A. Galinsky, and L. Thompson, "Face Threat Sensitivity in Negotiation: Roadblock to Agreement and Joint Gain," *Organizational Behavior and Human Decision Processes* 94 (2004), pp. 102–24.

Wheeler (1999) studied sports agents who represented their clients in salary and contract negotiations, examining the impact of this representation process on agents' perceptions of their reputations. He found that agents who felt that their reputations were at stake as part of the negotiation were more likely to take higher risks, set higher walkaway points for the negotiation, and have higher impasse rates than agents without their reputations at stake (for a somewhat different view, see Box 11.2). Other examples come to mind from international relations, politics, and labor relations. Decades ago, President Lyndon Johnson characterized the United States's presence in South Vietnam as one of a "pitiful, helpless giant," which soon led to the massive military buildup in Southeast Asia in order to "win" a war that would not humiliate American military capability at home and abroad (but ultimately did). Not only was this effort to "free" South Vietnam ultimately unsuccessful—thus sustaining the actual loss of face that Johnson and others had dreaded—but also the loss was incurred at a huge cost in dollars, military equipment, and human lives, the magnitude of which was disclosed to the American public only long after the war ended. More recently, strong face-challenging language was used in 1990 between Iraqi president Saddam Hussein and U.S. president George H. W. Bush, leading to the senior Bush's escalation of the war with Iraq following its invasion of Kuwait. A decade later, following the horrific attack on the World Trade Center in New York City and the Pentagon in Washington, D.C., U.S. president George W. Bush used his description of an "axis of evil" promoting terrorism in the world that must be eliminated as a means of building and sustaining support for military actions that the United States would take to fight terrorism. This war became a defining issue in the 2004 election between George W. Bush and John Kerry, and procedures for withdrawing troops from Iraq without "appearing to have surrendered" was a source of constant debate during President Bush's second term and well into the 2008 elections.

Finally, tragic twists to face-saving dynamics can also occur when audiences are only indirectly involved. For example, in the mid-1990s, a spokesperson for the state of Ohio's Prison Corrections Department questioned the credibility of a group of prisoners in a prison riot who were holding prison guards as hostages and threatening the hostages' safety. When asked by the press whether the prisoners' threats were real, the spokesperson dismissed the threats, stating that "prisoners threaten to kill hostages all the time." Soon after these comments, the prisoners actually killed a guard—perhaps just to prove that their threat was a credible one and to save face with their own constituents inside and outside the prison.

Audiences Hold the Negotiator Accountable   Audiences maintain control over negotiators by holding them accountable for their performance and by administering rewards or punishments based on that performance. This accountability occurs under two dominant conditions: (1) when a negotiator's performance is visible to the audience so that the audience is able to judge how well the negotiator performs and (2) when the audience is dependent on the negotiator for their outcomes. An audience that is dependent on a negotiator's performance for their outcomes will generally insist that he or she be tough, firm, demanding, and unyielding in the struggle to obtain the best possible outcome for them. Failure to perform in this manner in the eyes of the audience may lead to public criticism of the negotiator, with the expectation that this criticism will embarrass him or her into performing in ways that guarantee a larger payoff for the audience. This was nicely demonstrated in a study reported by Breaugh and Klimoski (1977). Some agents had been members of a group that developed a negotiating position, while other agents were "outsiders" who had not helped to develop the position. After negotiations concluded, the agents had to go back and "sell" the negotiated agreement to their constituents (back-table negotiations). Agents who had been team members had a far more difficult time selling the agreement than the outsiders because of their earlier participation in developing the group's position.

Continued characterizations of a negotiator as weak or soft, or as someone who sells out, may lead to unfortunate but predictable outcomes. First, the negotiator may become increasingly inflexible or retaliatory to demonstrate to the constituency that he or she is capable of defending their interests. Second, the negotiator may try to be a more loyal, committed, and dedicated advocate of the constituency's preferred outcomes and priorities in order to regain their good favor and evaluation. Finally, the negotiator may resign, judging him- or herself incapable of representing the constituency's best interests. Remarkably, the status level of the agent does *not* seem to affect the pressures. One might expect that high-status agents would believe that they had more flexibility and autonomy to decide what was best for their constituents. However, high-status members of a group (e.g., senior-level managers or formally designated leaders) do not appear to negotiate more quickly, do not achieve fewer deadlocks in the negotiating process, and do not attain better agreements than low-status members (Klimoski and Ash, 1974; Kogan, Lamm, and Trommsdorf, 1972). As a result, the presence of accountability pressures leads to longer, more time-consuming negotiations than when accountability pressures are absent.[1]

The effects of accountability to constituents do not have to be all bad, however. Constituents can keep negotiators from making extreme or outrageous commitments that might get them in trouble later. For example, Kirby and Davis (1998) had constituents monitor the investment decisions of managers in a simulated production game. The results of the experiment indicated that monitored managers were less likely than nonmonitored ones to escalate their commitment to unproductive courses of action and less likely to pursue risky investment strategies. Thus, accountability can deter individuals from pursuing risky decisions that may have long-term destructive consequences. And Fassina (2004) points out that constituents can clearly develop at least two different kinds of contracts with their agents. The first is a *behavior contingent* contract, in which the agent is primarily paid based on how he or she behaves in the role, versus an *outcome contingent* contract, in which the agent is primarily paid based on the type of results he or she achieves. "Combined" contracts that specify both behaviors and outcomes are also possible. Fassina shows how aspects of the specific negotiation—expertise, emotional strain, the zone of possible agreement and other issues—can help determine which form of contract is preferable and how those different contracts might lead to different negotiating behaviors displayed by the agent.

Tactical Implications of Social Structure Dynamics: The Negotiator's Dilemma

The presence of an audience—particularly an outcome-dependent audience—creates a paradox for negotiators because of two sets of pressures. One set comes from the constituency and team, leading the agent to be tough, firm, unyielding, and supportive of the constituency's demands. The other set comes from the opposing negotiator and calls upon the negotiator to be flexible, conciliatory, and willing to engage in give-and-take. (See again Figure 11.6, which depicts these pressures simultaneously pushing the negotiator from opposite directions.) Cutcher-Gershenfeld and Watkins (1999) have noted that these dynamics create a dilemma of trust.[2] Agents enter negotiations with the challenge of representing the interests of their constituents (goals established at the back table) but bring their own interests as well. There is often a tension between how much they can pursue their own interests versus the interests of their constituents, and the negotiator must resolve this tension. The dilemma is that the more trust constituents put in a representative, the more autonomy and freedom the representative will feel to "create value" with other negotiators; the more they are involved in creating value, the more difficult it may be to go back and persuade constituents that the "new" solution truly represents the original interests of the constituents. (Note how the type of contract an agent has with his or her constituents—outcome versus behavioral—might help resolve some of this tension.)

The basic dilemma, then, is to determine how negotiators can satisfy both the constituency's demands for firmness (and a settlement favorable to their interests) and the other party's demand for concessions (and a settlement favorable to the other party or to their mutual gain). The answer is that negotiators must build relationships with *both* the constituency and the other party. On the one hand, the relationship with the constituency must be cultivated on the basis of complete support for their demands and willingness to advocate these demands in negotiation. On the other hand, the relationship with the other party must be developed through stressing the similarity of the parties' collective goals or fate and the desirability of establishing and maintaining a productive working relationship to reach a positive outcome. However, each of these relationships must be developed privately, outside the visibility of the other group. Privacy ensures that negotiators can conduct deliberations with the other party without accountability pressures. Maintaining privacy may require a certain degree of duplicity by negotiators, in that they must promise loyalty and dedication to each group out of view of the others. It is possible, however, to achieve this through carefully describing to each group what the negotiator is promising.

Typically, negotiators first meet with the constituency to define their collective interests and objectives (the back table). They then meet with opposing negotiators at the front table in private so that they can candidly state their constituents' expectations but also make necessary concessions without looking weak or foolish to the constituents. Finally, a negotiator returns to the back table to sell the agreement to them, persuading them that it was the best outcome possible under the circumstances. Successful management of a constituency therefore requires negotiators to control the visibility of their negotiating behavior. Negotiators who do not have such control are going to be on public display all the time. Every statement, argument, concession, and mistake will be in full view of the constituents who may pick it apart, critique it, and challenge it as possibly disloyal. Such potential pressure is highly undesirable and is likely to lead negotiators to appeal to the constituents rather than to find an agreement.

Managing constituencies is a very important but quite delicate process. In the following sections, we summarize this process by offering two forms of prescriptive advice: first, to negotiators who have constituencies to manage and, second, to those constituencies who must manage an agent.

Advice to Agents on Managing Constituencies and Audiences

Clarify the Role Expectations and Performance Contract   As noted earlier, Fassina (2004) has suggested that constituents can negotiate either behavior contracts and/or outcome contracts with their agents. Behavior contracts simply require the agent to perform a specific set of behaviors (e.g., for an attorney, to provide adequate representation in a legal matter), while outcome contracts reward the agent for achieving certain outcomes (e.g., having the opponent drop the lawsuit). If the constituents do not specify how the agent is being evaluated or rewarded, the agent should ask directly so that he or she knows what to do and to eliminate misunderstandings. Bottom, Holloway, Miller, Mislin, and Whitford (2006) have demonstrated that crafting a strong and clear outcome contract can provide assurance to the principal that the agent will be strongly motivated to achieve negotiation goals without having to regularly monitor the agent.

Rau and Feinauer (2006) point out that in some situations, agent roles can be even more complex. For example, in considering the role that a human resource professional (agent) might play in helping a new recruit obtain a good starting salary with a company, the agent might behave as

- A *bargainer* (act as an advocate for the company and distributively bargain over salary with the new recruit).

- An *advocate* (act as a surrogate agent for the new recruit to make sure the recruit gets the best starting salary possible from the company).

- A *mediator* (act more as a go-between between the company and the new recruit to make sure that a satisfactory agreement is achieved).

- A *fact-finder* (simply make sure that information is flowing clearly between the company and the new recruit, in the hopes that they can reach agreement on their own).

Clearly, these options suggest that human resource (HR) professionals acting as agents can vary their roles considerably based on their contracts with their employers *and* on their own interpretation of what is best for themselves, the new recruits, and the companies. In some cases, agents become more like third parties than advocates (see Chapter 19).

Clarify Authority to Make Agreements   In addition to clarifying role and performance expectations, agents should also clarify how much authority they have to accept the opposing negotiator's offer *without* consulting the constituents. Subramanian (2006) points out that a negotiator should understand this in advance so as to not violate his or her constituent's expectations, and so as to not bind his or her constituent to a deal that may later be deemed unacceptable. We point out later that agents should also determine how much authority the opposing negotiator has.

Manage Constituency Visibility and Communication   Agents can control both the visibility of their behavior and the communication process with constituents, audiences, and the other party by employing tactics that appear to enhance their commitment to their bargaining position. A few of the most common tactics are described here.

Limit One's Own Concessions by Making Negotiations Visible to the Constituency
Because negotiators who negotiate in full view of their constituencies are less likely to make concessions than negotiators who deliberate in private, negotiators strengthen their position by enhancing their visibility with their constituency. Negotiators typically go public when they want to remain firm. For example, a negotiator may insist on allowing the constituency to be present for all negotiations, knowing that most concessions are made when parties deliberate in private. As a result, observable negotiations will limit the agent's search for solutions and are likely to increase the frequency of impasse. They will also likely result in shifting priorities to issue-by-issue, short-term goals rather than long-term interests (King and Zeckhauer, 1999; Kurtzberg, Moore, Valley, and Bazerman, 1999).

Use the Constituency to Show Militancy   A second way that a constituency can be used tactically is to make the constituency visible and let them demonstrate that they are more extreme, radical, committed, and inflexible than the agent. Community groups that want to inspire public officials to enact change often insist that the officials come to an open meeting, in which community spokespersons confront the officials with their concerns or grievances. Those invited to speak at the meeting are often the most demanding or militant. Militants may be deliberately invited to let the other party know that concessions will not come easily and that the only way agreement will be reached is if the other party makes major concessions. In addition to intimidating the other party, this tactic can have another benefit for the agent. A barely-under-control militant constituency may not only intimidate the other party but also allow the agent to seem like a nice, pleasant, reasonable person in contrast.

Pepper . . . and Salt

THE WALL STREET JOURNAL

"OK, let me go pretend to talk to my manager."

From *The Wall Street Journal.* Used with permission of Cartoon Features Syndicate.

It is natural to prefer to deal with nice, pleasant negotiators rather than angry, militant ones. As a result, a negotiator can look more cool, calm, and rational than the out-of-control constituency simply by contrast. If the negotiator then says, "Either you deal with me and my demands or you work with someone else from my constituency who is far more irrational than me," the negotiator is likely to gain significant ground with the other party. This is a variation of the classic good cop/bad cop negotiating tactic discussed in Chapter 2.

Use the Constituency to Limit One's Own Authority   A third way that a negotiator can use a constituency tactically is to show the other party that the constituency has limited the negotiator's authority to make certain concessions. This tactic may be used either as a bluff or because of a genuine limit on authority. As a bluff, the negotiator leads the other party to believe that all concessions must be cleared with the constituency. As a genuine tactic, the negotiator's constituency has actually defined limits to what the negotiator can decide on his or her own. In banks, for example, new loan officers may be able to approve very few loans on their own signature, whereas the bank's senior loan officer has a wider latitude. While the senior loan officers could easily approve certain loans on their own authority, they may use their constituency (the bank's loan committee) both for protection (to make sure that the loan is not granted foolishly) and also to pressure the borrower into meeting certain terms and conditions.

Negotiators must be careful about revealing how much authority and autonomy they really have. On the one hand, it might seem that limiting authority would give a party a distinct advantage. Every minor deviation from the originally stated position would have to be approved, a process that is very tedious and time-consuming. If the other party is in a hurry, he or she may choose to make concessions to avoid the delay. On the other hand, the tactic may backfire. Not only is it very frustrating for the other party to wait while every minor change and concession is reviewed and approved, but it also frustrates the agent, who may feel embarrassed by his or her powerlessness. This mutual frustration eventually may lead to a complete breakdown in negotiations. Because negotiation is understood as the process of making concessions toward mutual agreement, encountering a negotiator who cannot make any concessions on his or her own violates expectations and creates anger. This may lead the other party to demand that the constituency send a representative who has the power to negotiate an agreement. Jackson and King (1983) argue that if constituencies really want to get an agreement, they should send their highest status member (e.g., the CEO or president), or invest more authority in the negotiator when the group prefers to have a deal emerge.

Use Great Caution in Exceeding One's Authority Negotiators who overextend their authority or exceed the limits set by their constituency may be unable to persuade the constituency that the achieved settlement is a good one. This is often a problem in union–management relations, particularly when the union group is militant and has very high aspirations. After a long and arduous negotiation, a union negotiating team reaches a tentative settlement with management. But the union rank-and-file, who may have inflated expectations, rejects the proposed contract offer at the back table. This rejection vote is tantamount to a vote of "no confidence" in the negotiator. Sometimes negotiators in this position resign; at other times they return to negotiate with heightened belligerence to prove their toughness to their constituency, which jeopardizes the possibility of any effective agreement with the other party. In the extreme, negotiators may be willing to endure extremely high personal costs—a long strike, personal fines, jail sentences, and negative public opinion—to restore their image with the constituency.

For example, in the 1981 strike of the Professional Air Traffic Controllers Organization (PATCO) against the Federal Aviation Authority (FAA), the PATCO leader, Robert Poli, spent several months negotiating a new package on behalf of his organization. When the deal was finally presented to the union for a ratification vote, 90 percent of the membership rejected the tentative contract as inadequate. So Poli returned to the FAA and attempted to gain a better package, but the FAA wouldn't budge, and after two weeks of unsuccessful debate, PATCO called a strike. The strike (an illegal action by a government worker) led the FAA and the administration of President Ronald Reagan to (1) fire all the striking controllers from their jobs; (2) obtain federal injunctions and impose fines of several million dollars per day against the union and its leadership; (3) jail some union members and officials, including Poli; (4) impound the union's strike fund; and (5) ban all striking controllers from any further employment with the U.S. government, either as controllers or in any other federal job. In the early days of this confrontation, 90 percent of the union supported Poli's taking them out on strike and going to jail. Poli was put in the difficult position of either leading the union in its militant demands (and becoming a hero-martyr in going to jail for them) or affirming that the deal he struck with the FAA was a good one and being rejected by his union. As it turned out, the animosity from this dispute lingered for a long time: it was 12 years later before President Bill Clinton finally declared that fired air traffic controllers could be rehired.

Increase the Possibility of Concession to the Other Negotiator by Reducing Visibility to Constituencies If increased audience visibility heightens the likelihood that negotiators will take tougher stands, be less flexible, and make fewer concessions, than a negotiator who wishes to be more flexible and conciliatory would want negotiations to be less visible. There are three approaches to accomplishing this objective:

1. *Establish "privacy" prior to the beginning of negotiations.* It is important to establish negotiating ground rules before the actual process begins. One rule that should be considered is that the negotiations at the front table will be conducted in private, that no media or public interviews will be granted, and that contact with the other party's constituency and visibility to audiences will be strictly controlled. To keep the negotiations private, parties may select a remote location in neutral territory, where their meetings will not be too obvious or visible. When the time comes for announcements about progress or achievements, both parties can make them jointly, coordinating their communications. Needless to say, if the other party wishes the negotiations to be held in a public environment—where communication with constituencies is easy and audiences have a direct view—setting the terms and conditions for the visibility of the negotiation should be the first item on the negotiation agenda. Given the many ways in which people can communicate these days—cell phones, text messaging, fax, electronic mail, etc.—finding and maintaining true privacy in a negotiation can be a real challenge, but it can be done.

2. *Screen visibility during negotiations.* If negotiators have not agreed beforehand to a location that is private and secure, there are other options for screening out unwanted observers from sensitive discussions. One of the simplest ways is to have some discussions with the other agent occur informally, on a strictly unofficial basis. These discussions can occur during coffee breaks, walks around the building, or even in the exercise room or bar of a hotel. Key representatives may agree to meet for breakfast before the day's formal deliberations begin or for cocktails afterward. During such meetings, parties can speak more candidly off the record, or they can hint about their bottom-line position or signal their willingness to make certain concessions: "We've been sitting in that room for a long time, and you know, if your side is willing to name a proposal something like the following [insert the specific details here], my people would probably be willing to go along with it." Druckman and Druckman (1996) have shown that negotiators with opposing positions were more flexible when media coverage was limited and when talks were held in a "peripheral location" where proceedings could be less formal and less visible to audiences and constituents.

Heads of state who negotiate major peace treaties, arms-limitation talks, and trade agreements are frequently photographed at dinners, receptions, or walks in the garden. Although a large portion of such functions is public and ceremonial, private time is frequently part of them as well.[3] Every formal gathering between heads of state and heads of organizations is also an opportunity for informal contact.

In some cases, the meeting may be planned but very secretive. In one industry, for example, labor negotiations occurred every two years. Before starting formal talks, the union president and the company president met for dinner in a distant city half a continent away and broadly discussed the key issues that would be raised in the negotiations. Although the union president could lose his job if the rank and file were to become aware of this meeting, both presidents considered the meeting invaluable to keeping an informal communication channel open between them and permitting them to maintain a personal connection in the midst of the confrontational negotiations that would occur for the next few months.

Other kinds of information can also be privately exchanged in these informal venues. Negotiators can grumble and complain, brag about their constituency and its support, or even let the other party overhear their conversations with their own constituents. All these tactics give the other side information about what is really possible without saying it directly during the formal negotiation.

3. *Be aware of time pressure.* Not unsurprisingly, time pressure in negotiation may also increase competitive behavior, particularly when the negotiator is accountable to a constituency. Research indicates that when negotiators are not representing the views of constituents, time pressure tends to make negotiators act less competitive (Mosterd and Rutte, 2000). However, when negotiators are acting as agents of others, time pressure results in more competitive dynamics and a higher rate of impasse.

Establish a Reputation for Cooperation   Finally, agents can establish a strong reputation for being cooperative, both with those they represent and with the other agent. For example, Gilson and Mnookin (1994) have suggested that lawyers can both effectively represent their clients and establish sound relationships with other attorneys:

> Our message is that the relationship between opposing lawyers and their capacity to establish credible reputations for cooperation have profound implications for dispute resolution: If the payoff structure establishes cooperation as the most desirable strategy and supportive institutional structures exist, lawyers may be able to damp conflict, reduce transaction costs and facilitate dispute resolution. (p. 564)

However, concern for reputations can create a problem for agents. Agents who feel that their reputations are at stake in a negotiation may be more likely to take risks, display more contentious behavior, set higher walkaway prices, and have higher impasse rates than agents who do not feel that their reputations are at stake (King and Zeckhauser, 1999; Kurtzberg, Moore, Valley, and Bazerman 1999).

Communicate Indirectly with Audiences and Constituents   Negotiators can often create the observability/accountability dynamics described earlier by communicating indirectly. Indirect communications are efforts by the negotiator to bring the opinions of audiences and constituents to bear on the other party. Informal communication takes place in several ways:

Communicate through Superiors   The technique of communicating through superiors is frequently used when negotiators are representatives of two hierarchically structured organizations (e.g., a company and a union or two companies engaged in a business deal) and when one or both negotiators are dissatisfied with the progress of negotiations or the behavior of the other party. To manage their frustration and dissatisfaction, they may go to their own superiors and ask them to contact their counterpart in the opposing organization. The situation is represented in Figure 11.7. A salesperson, A (acting as an agent for her company) is frustrated in her negotiations with a buyer over a major sales contract. The buyer, D, wants a major price concession because of the volume of product being purchased. The salesperson isn't authorized to reduce the price, so she finally talks to her boss, B, the vice president of sales, who then approaches the buyer's senior

FIGURE 11.7 | Indirect Communication between Negotiators through Their Bosses

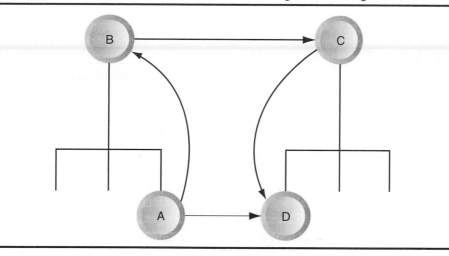

purchasing manager, C. The senior purchasing manager spends several hours describing the details of competitive bids that the company has received from other sellers (their BATNAs) and explains why the seller must reduce their price or lose the business. B is convinced that the price decrease is necessary and finally authorizes the salesperson to sell the product at a considerably discounted price without losing her incentive bonus for completing the sale.

Such indirect processes work under several conditions. First, the tactic's effectiveness depends on a social structure in which the negotiator represents an organization or group that has some formal hierarchy of power—and the other party also works in a similar structure (refer back to our dicussion of authority-ranking relationships in Chapter 10). Negotiations between agents representing most formal private- and public-sector organizations fit this description. Second, the chief negotiator should *not* be the person with the most authority, such as the president, chairman, or (in this case, the vice president of sales). The reason chief executives should not negotiate is not because they are too busy doing other things. Rather, conducting negotiations through an agent who is not the senior person allows the organization to limit its concessions by limiting the negotiator's power and authority to make decisions. Senior executives should become involved only when negotiations are extremely delicate, critical, or symbolically significant to the well-being of the organization and its relationships with other organizations. (In our example, if the vice president of sales thought that the buyer was bluffing when demanding a price decrease, he could simply tell the salesperson to hold firm—but he might run the risk of losing the business to a competitor.) Usually, much of the preliminary groundwork has been laid by subordinates and chief negotiators. In international relations, for example, contacts between nations occur on several diplomatic levels: diplomatic aides, chief diplomats, Secretary positions, etc. The heads of state become directly involved in only the most delicate, symbolic, or politically important negotiations.

FIGURE 11.8 | Indirect Communication through an Intermediary

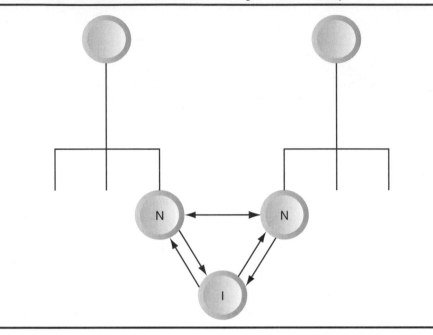

The effectiveness of executing this tactic depends on indirect communication originating from someone the other party either trusts or is less well-defended against. When the indirect communication comes from superiors, it may be even more effective because the communicator has high status, reputation, and visibility. Thus, in the previous illustration, the senior purchasing manager has to make a compelling case for the price required price decrease; if the case is not made well, or if the sales vice president thinks it is a bluff, the tactic will not work. In this context, if the senior purchasing manager (who is indeed an agent) can be seen not as a "bargainer" but more as a "fact-finder" (presenting neutral information about the buyer's choice alternatives and what will influence them), the vice president of sales may be more likely to accept and believe the financial information than if the same information were presented by the buyer during the negotiation.

Communicate through Intermediaries   Negotiators communicate through intermediaries when they need to make informal contact with the other party, an opposing negotiator, or a constituency (see Figure 11.8). Here the approach is made through an external contact who can serve as an intermediary or communication conduit. Those selected are usually chosen for a valid reason—past experience in working together; a personal friendship or relationship; or a personal reputation for credibility, trustworthiness, impartiality, and integrity. The tactic is most often used under two circumstances: when a negotiator wants to feel out the opposing group to attempt to gain information about what the other party really wants or when deliberations are deadlocked and need to be unfrozen. In our Super Bowl halftime show negotiation, suppose that the booking agent for Glitzy Productions, Maurice, is frustrated in his discussions with Athena's agent. Maurice thinks Athena would agree to the deal if only he could talk to Athena directly, but Athena's agent won't permit that. So Maurice goes to Athena's current boyfriend, Justin, and asks Justin to take a new offer directly to Athena. Here, Justin becomes an important *intermediary* (I) in brokering the deal.

Pruitt (1994, 1995; also see Salacuse, 1999) has proposed a branching-chain model of interorganizational negotiation. This model employs the concept of influence networks (see our discussion of the power in networks in Chapter 7) and suggests that negotiations between organizations take place between organizational members and interested intermediaries across and within organizational boundaries. At the ends of the chains are major stakeholders, while all other members of the chain are intermediaries of one form or another (diplomats, former and current leaders, friends and allies of each key party), who try to reconcile the needs and values of the different stakeholders. Examining several cases drawn from U.S. State Department negotiations, Pruitt offers a number of interesting ideas about the ways in which chains can be mobilized to achieve negotiation goals that cannot be achieved by the stakeholders themselves.

Political scientists have dubbed this process "back-channel diplomacy." Wanis-St. John (2002) conducted an elaborate study of back-channel diplomacy in the Israeli–Palestinian peace negotiations from 1991 to 1998. He particularly studied the treatment of the negotiable issues, the role of secrecy, the exclusion of key parties that results because of secrecy, the role of third parties, and other dynamics. The major conclusion is that decision makers use back-channel diplomacy to control many of the uncertainties that affect negotiations, but that are particularly salient for negotiations in violent international conflicts. These uncertainties include the cost of entry into the negotiations, the effect of spoilers in the peace process, the absence of key information about other parties' interests and preferences that may be needed to decide how to negotiate, and the impact of the negotiation outcome on the decision makers. In the short term, back-channel diplomacy helps manage these uncertainties by achieving early breakthroughs where front channels often fail. However, because back-channel diplomacy is secretive and may exclude certain parties, the factors that make it successful in the short term may turn sour in the long term as "spoilers" work to corrupt the agreement, and those who were not involved in the early deliberations may ultimately reject or sabotage those agreements later on.

Similar to the tactic of communicating through superiors, the effectiveness of informal contact depends on engaging the right individuals: ones who are not subject to the same accountability pressure that binds formal group representatives so they can use informal communication channels that may eventually clear blockages in the formal links.

Communicate Directly to the Other Party's Constituency   In a third form of indirect communication (see Figure 11.9), one agent seeks to bypass the other agent and communicate directly with that agent's constituency to persuade those involved to change their position or the instructions they are giving their representative. The agent himself may initiate this tactic, usually when he believes that negotiations are deadlocked, that the other negotiator is not communicating effectively with her constituency, or that the other agent is not representing her constituency's interests clearly. Thus, the agent attempts to eliminate the other agent and communicate directly with the other's constituency. In labor–management

FIGURE 11.9 | Indirect Communication through a Constituency

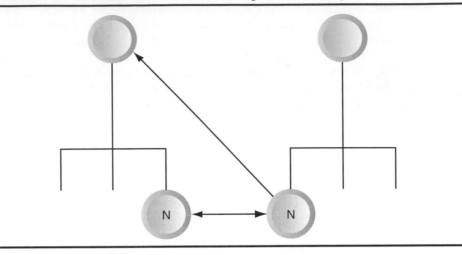

negotiations, for example, management representatives frequently prefer to speak or write directly to the rank-and-file rather than go through the union leadership. The intent may be to ensure that management's position is clearly heard and understood, but this may also subtly undermine the credibility and effectiveness of the union leadership. In international relations, one country's political message may be broadcast on the other country's news media, or "propaganda" messages may be included with gifts of food, medical supplies, and the like. The tactic, of course, may also be initiated by the other negotiator. In this case, the opponent usually extends the invitation because she believes her credibility or integrity is being questioned and wants the agent to hear the message directly from her constituency. In our rock concert example, instead of going to Justin, Maurice shows up at one of the band's rehearsals and tries to talk directly to Athena and her musicians about the offer.

However, it should be clear that direct communication with the other party's constituency—particularly without the approval of the other agent—will likely be viewed as an inflammatory tactic. Negotiators who are undermined by their opponents in this way are likely to become defensive and rigid. The immediate impact on the negotiator's constituency, however, is less clear. They may perceive this tactic as one intended to undermine their leadership's effectiveness and respond by rallying around their leadership more strongly. At other times, particularly when a constituency may already have doubts about the effectiveness of its own agent, direct, open, accurate communication from the other negotiator may serve to undermine their confidence in their agent even further.

Communicate Directly to Bystanders   An agent may also try to manipulate the opinion of bystanders and to mobilize their support, either to enhance their own position or to undermine the other party's position (see Figure 11.10). Communication through bystanders may occur (1) as an explicit and conscious tactic to exert influence on the other party, but through circuitous channels; (2) as an effort to build alliances and support for one's own

FIGURE 11.10 | Negotiating through Constituents, Audiences, and Bystanders

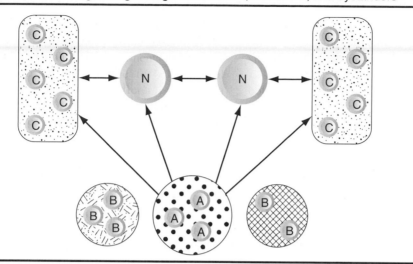

position; or (3) as a result of the natural tendency for conflict to proliferate and envelop innocent bystanders. In all cases, agents are public about their demands. They will tell anyone who will listen how fair, legitimate, just, and appropriate their position is, and how unfair, unjust, illegitimate, and inappropriate the other party's position is. The agent's hope is that unaligned parties will openly side with them, lend strength and credence to their arguments, and their dissatisfaction and displeasure to the other party (thus undermining the strength and credibility of the other party's arguments). In our rock concert example, Maurice might go directly to the entertainment news media, announce that the rumored plan to have Athena and the Greek Gods perform at the Super Bowl halftime show is in serious jeopardy, and indicate that Athena's fans should text message Athena and encourage her to accept Glitzy Productions' "very reasonable" offer. (Also see Box 11.3 on involving constituencies.)

Communication through audiences—particularly the media—is extremely common in major community, environmental, and intergovernmental negotiations. Most of these conflicts are well known for first having a "public" phase in which the negotiators address their arguments to audiences rather than to one another. In this phase, the media—radio, television, and newspaper—play an integral role by serving as both an audience themselves and a communication vehicle to reach other audiences. Media relations and image management often become ends in themselves; strong negotiators can consciously stage their performance before radio microphones or television cameras in order to win public opinion to their side, which will then put pressure on the other party to concede.

Communication through the media can also be used to reach one's own constituency. The quickest and most efficient way of letting one's own constituency know the exact elements of one's negotiating posture and commitment to this posture is to represent that position in the media—although, admittedly, many agents have learned that the media may

BOX 11.3 — The Importance of Involving Constituencies in Solving Community Problems

When a Canadian regional government commission proposed to solve its budget problem by selling parklands known as the national capital area's "Emerald Necklace" (Greenbelt), residents in affected neighborhoods feared their open space would fall into the hands of developers. They launched an all-out campaign to block this sale of the "family jewels."

Closed-door negotiations among government officials soon produced a solution that seemed to avoid the residents' worst fears while accomplishing the commission's goals of slashing costs. However, by excluding the public in crafting a solution, these behind-the-scenes arrangements may have so aroused public cynicism about this process that the regional commission would find it even more difficult to rally political support for future planning challenges.

This future failure, disguised as today's success, offers a clear lesson to public-dispute facilitators about the value of involving the public in the design of a consensus-building process.

Source: From a description of a parkland dispute in Ottawa, Canada, Richard Jackman, "Back Room Politics Solve Today's Problem—but Create Tomorrow's?" *Consensus,* April 1996, pp. 1, 12.

---

not get the facts right either. This approach is likely to be used when an agent wants to communicate firmness and toughness in a position—and not as likely to be used when the agent wants to communicate concession-making or flexibility. Many environmental disputes play out this way; after failing to adequately influence a government agency or company about an issue, the aggrieved group "takes their case to the public" through newspaper or television coverage.

Communication may also be designed to activate and win over interested audiences who will communicate directly with the other party. An example can be found in the major speeches given by heads of state in most democratic countries. Once the head of state delivers the speech, various political leaders and all forms of special interest groups who will be affected by the key issues begin to put their spin on the speech and cast it in negative or positive terms.

The effectiveness of communicating through audiences is determined by several factors. First, the success of the tactic depends on the degree to which an audience's outcome hinges directly on the negotiator's effectiveness and how severe the consequences are likely to be. This degree and severity of effect can vary from outcomes that directly affect the audience in a dramatic way to those that only minimally and indirectly affect the audience. If I live in Canada, a strike by farm workers in the United States may not affect me very strongly, particularly if I can purchase fruit and vegetables grown locally or if I eat very few fruits and vegetables. On the other hand, if I have school-age children, a strike by school bus drivers in my local area is likely to affect me and my family very directly.

The second factor in the effectiveness of communicating through audiences is the degree to which the audience is organized as a coherent unit. An audience may be directly and seriously affected by the results of a particular negotiation but unable to exert leverage on the negotiations because they have no means for determining their collective sentiments or making decisions among themselves. Even a very large group of people is unlikely to have significant impact on the negotiations if their reaction cannot be brought to bear on the negotiators themselves. The many families who may be grossly inconvenienced by a strike of school bus drivers cannot easily organize to provide alternate transportation for all, nor can they bring much pressure on the strikers. Interestingly enough, the media are increasingly providing opportunities for such "disorganized majorities" to have a voice. The last decade has seen a dramatic rise in radio and television talk shows, and weblogs, featuring hosts and authors who stir controversy over politically charged topics and provide both airtime and bait to their listening audiences. Call-in talk shows have been credited with being one of the only vehicles by which average citizens can have a say in governmental and public affairs, and in many cases they have stirred significant public support or opposition for key political issues. Web-based chat rooms, weblogs, and media polls have also become popular vehicles for airing public opinion.

Having stated that audiences cannot have impact without some form of communication leverage, we must note that the reverse is also true: well-organized audiences can have significant effects on the outcome of negotiations even if their total size is small. The effectiveness of particular political lobbies and "special interest groups" in state and federal government of all political persuasions and special interest orientations is testimony to the strength of organization. For example, numerous public opinion polls support government action on issues such as gun control, political campaign financing limits, and environmental protection legislation. But lobbyists who may oppose these changes succeed not because of size, but because of their ability to strategically block such changes with key legislators, lawsuits, and procedural and technical delays.

Finally, appeals to audiences will be effective to the degree that the negotiator is sophisticated in the use of media relations. To someone who is naive in using the media as an effective but indirect negotiating tool, media relations may involve no more than appearing before a camera or microphone and reading a prepared statement. However, as we implied in Chapter 8, the content of one's message, particularly on television, often is considerably less important than the visual presentation and the performance. Portraying an image of confidence, control, and steadfast determination is essential. The negotiator needs to be well dressed, well spoken, and in control of the situation. Further, he or she needs to be able to respond to hostile or loaded questions effectively. Finally, an agent may wish to be surrounded by his or her constituency—the rank-and-file, supporters, close advisers—who will openly demonstrate their solidarity and support. Effective politicians in all industries and contexts have learned how to use the media to get their message across and win the hearts and minds of key audiences.

Build Relationships with Audiences, Constituents, and Other Agents   At the beginning of this chapter, we suggested that negotiators who are intent in building or strengthening a relationship with the other party should negotiate differently than if the negotiation is a simple, one-time market transaction. The same principles are true for how negotiators should manage relations with constituents, audiences, and opposing agents. Rather than undermining the other party's support, negotiators should try to develop personal relationships with the other party. The underlying assumption should be that it is easier (and definitely more pleasant) to work with and persuade a friendly counterpart than an unfriendly one. Individuals who see themselves as similar to each other, who are attracted to each other, or who are likely to experience a common fate are more likely to change their attitudes toward each other (refer back to our discussion of source and receiver factors of influence in Chapter 8). In addition, building a personal

relationship will permit the agent to get the message across to a less defensive, less antagonistic adversary. Thus, the better the relationship between an agent and other agents, the more the final agreement will represent long-term interests rather than short-term gains (Kurtzberg, Moore, Valley, and Bazerman 1999; McKersie, 1999). In essence, the agent is attempting to convert the relationship context from more market transaction to more communal (Chapter 10).

Many of the tactics we described earlier in this chapter can be applied in this setting. Some negotiators meet informally outside the context of negotiations. Shared cocktails, a meal, or even a coffee break are obvious opportunities for promoting friendliness, easy conversation, and cordiality. When parties drop their formal negotiator roles and meet as individual people, they can discover their commonality and develop their liking for each other. The agenda for both sides is usually not to conduct formal deliberations, but to communicate openly, build trust that will alleviate the tension and conflict inherent in formal deliberations, and keep negotiations from ending in deadlock or an angry walkout. But even in these conversations, parties are still negotiating.

In addition to developing a relationship based on shared personal interests or genuine liking, agents may also stress their common fate—namely, the accountability pressures put on them by their constituencies. If both agents feel strongly pressured by their constituencies, they are likely to stress their common fate as a way to build the relationship. Thus, "You and I are in this together," "We both have our constituencies to deal with," "We want to achieve the best for all of us," and "We want to develop an agreement based on mutual respect that we can live with successfully in the future" are all statements that typify the opening stages of negotiation (see our discussion of stages in Chapter 4). Many experienced negotiators refer to these expressions of common fate as the "harmony-and-light speech." They may believe that the other party is using such expressions merely as a tactical ploy to soften them up before presenting tough demands. Although that allegation may be true, all of the flattering, optimistic, "happy talk" that opens many formal negotiations does play a critical role. Even if the speech is ritualistic, it communicates that the other party is interested in building a personal relationship. Moreover, the absence of the speech may indicate that the parties are so adamant in their positions or so angry at each other that they cannot bring themselves to make the speech. This may be a clear sign that the negotiations will be tense and are likely to become deadlocked.

A further purpose of informal meetings is to permit each party to get a sense of the other's objectives. In many negotiations, chief negotiators meet before the formal deliberations, much like the corporate and labor leaders we described earlier. The purpose of this meeting is usually twofold: to sense what the other side's major demands will be and to develop a relationship and an open channel of communication that can be used regardless of how tense the negotiations become. Such meetings are usually held privately because publicizing the event might lead other managers or union members to view the meeting as collusion. However, some negotiators may choose to publicize the event to demonstrate a spirit of cooperation.

Finally, a strong relationship between agents should allow the negotiators to do a better job of coordinating their actions in presenting their settlements back to their constituents. The better the relationship, the better able the agents will be to present their agreement back to constituents in a way that makes it appear to meet both sides' interests, even if this is not truly the case (Kurtzberg et al., 1999; McKersie, 1999).

When to Use an Agent

This chapter has contained a great deal of advice to negotiators on the ways that negotiations change when more people become involved and when agents, constituents, audiences, and bystanders begin to play their roles. In Table 11.1, we summarize the conditions under which a negotiator might wish to employ an agent and when a negotiator may choose to "go it alone."

"Look, I'm not saying it's going to be today.
But someday—someday—you guys will be happy that you've taken along a lawyer."

TABLE 11.1 | When to Use an Agent and When to Negotiate for Yourself

When to Use an Agent

1. When the agent has distinct or unique knowledge or skills in the issues or the negotiation context (e.g., a lawyer or accountant) that are essential to achieving an agreement.

2. When the representative has better negotiation skills than you do (this judgment requires clear self-reflection on your part to recognize relative competence)!

3. When you strongly care only about the outcome, and not the relationship. Experts agree that we often give in more quickly when negotiating for ourselves.

4. When the agent has special friends, relationships, or connections that he or she can use to contact the right people to access critical decision makers to get a deal done. (This access or connections are the type of relationship power that we discussed in Chapter 7). These special friends and relationships may be used to gain information the negotiator would not necessarily obtain on his or her own, or they may be used to access and persuade others who cannot be accessed through direct contact.

5. When you are very emotionally involved in an issue or problem and need to be represented by someone who is less likely to get emotionally sidetracked by the discussion.

6. When you want the flexibility to use negotiation tactics that require several parties, such as the good cop/bad cop or limited-authority tactics described in Chapter 2. These tactics are more common in the context of a distributive negotiation.

7. When your natural conflict management style is to compromise, accommodate, or avoid. Even if agents have the same conflict management style as you, because of agency dynamics, they will be tougher as your agent than if they were negotiating for themselves.

8. In negotiations with higher stakes to gain if you do well and/or higher costs to incur if you do poorly.

When to Negotiate for Yourself

1. When you want to develop or reestablish a strong personal relationship with the other negotiator and/or you want them to develop a strong personal relationship with you. Trust is best built and cultivated one-to-one, without the agents. It is not uncommon for parties in a lawsuit to dismiss the attorneys and attempt to cut a deal on their own.

2. When you need to repair a damaged relationship. Explanations and apologies for past behavior, and promises for future performance, are better delivered personally than through an agent.

3. When you want to learn a lot about them before you craft an agreement by using informal meetings, dialogue and conversation, etc.

4. When your negotiation skills are better than those of any available agent. Again, modesty and unbiased self-perception are required to make this judgment.

5. When hiring an agent may be too costly or time consuming. Schotter, Zeng, and Snyder (2000) argue quite convincingly that there is a substantial increase in inefficiency when bargaining through an agent.

6. When the "image" of being represented by an agent may make the other side suspicious, defensive, or less likely to agree. Most of us would probably not use an agent to negotiate a pay increase with our boss.

7. When the agent is too emotionally involved, defensive, adamant, and caught up in game playing of his or her own and is endangering the agreement because of his or her own emotional investment and commitment. For example, attorneys may become so caught up in legal technicalities and the like that they are unable to have a productive conversation on the specific aspects of the deal.

Source: Adapted and extended from J. Rubin and F. Sander, "When Should We Use Agents? Direct vs. Representative Negotiation," *Negotiation Journal* 4 (1988), pp. 395–401.

Managing Agents

While most of our prescriptive advice has been to the negotiator in managing one's audience and constituents, we should also spend some time describing how a constituency can effectively manage its agent. Much of this advice can be extracted from our earlier discussion of the impact of audiences on agents—the impact of competing interests, pressures for accountability and face saving, deadlines, and so on. We also draw on Fisher and Davis (1999) and their advice to constituencies on managing agents, particularly those attempting to achieve an integrative outcome:

1. Check out the agent's credentials and qualifications. Interview them, find out their experience, check references, and decide whether you and the agent are compatible.

2. Spend time getting to know the agent. Make sure that your "contract" with the agent, and your expectations, are clear.

3. At the outset, the agent should have no authority to make a binding commitment on any substantive issues.

4. At the outset, the agent should have the discretion to design and develop an effective overall negotiation process.

5. The constituent should focus most of his or her communication to the agent on interests, priorities, and alternatives, rather than specific settlement points.

6. The constituent should establish clear expectations about the frequency and quality of reporting back to the constituent.

7. The agent's authority should expand as the agent and constituent gain insight about the other parties through the negotiation process.

8. Specific and direct instructions to the agent by constituents should be put in writing and be available to show to the other side when necessary.

9. The constituent should instruct the agent on exactly what the agent can disclose in negotiation—interests, ranges of acceptable settlement, key facts, the principal's identity (sometimes kept secret in business or real estate deals), and so on. Craft a behavior or outcome contract that both of you are clear about, and be ready to clarify if it appears that there has been miscommunication or misunderstanding.

Chapter Summary

Sometimes negotiation is a private affair between two parties. At other times, however, there are audiences to a negotiation, and the presence of an audience has both a subtle and a direct impact on negotiations.

Three types of audiences may be encountered. First, when teams of people (rather than individuals) negotiate, the chief negotiators provide much of the actual dialogue. Although these two usually speak directly to one another, they also use their own and opposing team members as an audience. We address these dynamics extensively in the next chapter.

A second type of audience is the constituency the negotiator represents. A husband or wife negotiating for a new house represents a family, division heads on a companywide budget committee negotiate what portion of capital resources their departments will have for the coming year, sales or purchasing people negotiate for their companies, and diplomats negotiate for their countries. The audiences in each case have a stake in the outcome of the negotiation and benefit or suffer according to the skills of their representatives.

The third type of audience is bystanders. Bystanders see or hear about the negotiations and form favorable or unfavorable opinions of the settlement and the parties involved. Bystanders may or may not be indirectly affected by the course and outcome of the negotiations.

Audiences influence negotiators through two different routes. One is that negotiators desire positive evaluations from those who are in a position to observe what they have done. The other is that audiences hold negotiators responsible for the outcomes of negotiations. They can reward negotiators by publicly praising them and punish negotiators by firing them. They can intrude and change the course of negotiations—as when the public requires mandatory arbitration or fact-finding in some disputes. They make their preferences known—for example, by talking to the press—thereby putting pressure on one or both negotiators through the impact of public opinion and support.

Audiences can have both favorable and unfavorable effects on negotiations. Sometimes negotiators try to use an audience to their advantage, as when they try to pressure the other party into taking a more flexible or desirable position; they may also try to prevent an audience from having influence when they think it might be undesirable for their position. Although there are many different ways of influencing an audience, all involve controlling the visibility or communication with that audience. In this section, we suggested four basic strategies to influence audience effects:

1. Limit concessions by making actions visible to one's constituency, thereby putting oneself in a position that the other party will recognize as difficult to change.

2. Increase the possibility of concessions on the part of both sides by cutting off the visibility of negotiations from the audiences.

3. Communicate indirectly with the other negotiator by communicating with his or her audiences.

4. Facilitate building a relationship with the other negotiator by reducing visibility and communication with both parties' audiences.

Finally, we offered suggestions for constituents that they can use to manage their agents in negotiation. These include processes for managing agent authority, helping the agent understand the constituent's primary interests and alternatives, giving the agent discretion to manage the process, and establishing the process for frequent reporting between agents and constituents.

When negotiations move from a private to a public context, they become more complex and more formal. In setting strategy, a negotiator needs to consider whether negotiations should be held privately or involve audiences in various ways. To ignore this social context is to ignore a potent factor in determining negotiation outcomes.

Endnotes

[1] See Benton (1972); Breaugh and Klimoski (1977); Haccoun and Klimoski (1975); and Klimoski (1972).

[2] In Chapter 1, we noted a dilemma of trust that most negotiators face: how much to trust and believe what the other says (Kelley, 1966). To trust and believe everything the other says puts the negotiator under the other's control, but to trust and believe nothing the other says precludes any agreement. A comparable dilemma of trust exists between agents and constituents.

[3] Blessing's 1988 play, *A Walk in the Woods,* is an interesting re-creation of the way President Jimmy Carter shaped the Camp David accords between Israel and Egypt through a number of informal discussions with Prime Minister Menachem Begin and President Anwar Sadat.

CHAPTER 12

Coalitions

Objectives

1. Understand what coalitions are and why they are important in negotiation.
2. Explore how coalitions form and develop and what makes them strong or weak.
3. Consider how coalitions and their members make decisions about negotiation issues.
4. Gain practical advice on how to build and maintain coalitions.

In Chapters 10 and 11, we focused on the social context of negotiation and developed two major themes: (1) that negotiation dynamics become more complex when there is an ongoing relationship between the parties and (2) that negotiation dynamics also become more complex when negotiators represent other parties. We considered negotiators as agents representing the interests of others at the table, and the dynamics between agents and their constituents. In this chapter and the one that follows, we extend the analysis to three situations that involve multiple parties. Our focus now is on situations in which multiple (more than two) parties are negotiating with one another, with the parties each striving to achieve their own individual objectives. In this chapter we examine how parties ally into *coalitions* to achieve these objectives. In Chapter 13, we look at negotiation involving multiple parties and negotiations in which multiple individuals comprise each party.

In this chapter, we present an overview of what a coalition is and describe the different forms that coalitions take. We then analyze how and why coalitions form and develop, the nature of coalition decision making, and the role of power and leverage in coalitions. The chapter concludes with some practical advice for building and maintaining coalitions. Done well, coalitions are not just convenient vehicles for the pursuit of self-interest through short-term alliances with expedient partners, but can be ways to achieve beneficial and lasting outcomes for all parties at the negotiating table and for the larger social systems (e.g., organizations, communities) within which coalition politics exist. Our hope is that this chapter helps you become more proficient in the art and science of building and maintaining constructive coalitions, and also become better "consumers" of the coalition politics that swirl around you in multiparty negotiation and dispute resolution.

Let's begin with an example illustrating the variations in complexity that occurs when multiple parties are involved.

A Situation with More Than Two Parties

A negotiation situation becomes more complex when more negotiators are added (see Figure 12.1). For example, let's consider a student who wants to sell a used stereo system. He posts a notice on the bulletin board in the student union, providing details about the stereo and a suggested price. Two interested students call. Let us now assume three different variations on this situation:

- In the first case, the two potential buyers are roommates. One roommate has agreed that she will do the talking and try to negotiate the best deal with the seller, while the other one stays silent but comes along for moral support.

- In the second case, the two buyers do not know each other. The seller can sell to the first one who calls, sell to the first one who shows up at his apartment, or ask the two to come at the same time and try to play the two off against each other. In this case, each buyer's offer on the stereo becomes the seller's alternative for the stereo (assuming the alternative offer is an acceptable one), and the seller can, in effect, auction the stereo off to the highest bidder.

- In the third case, the two buyers show up at the door together, exchange greetings, and discover that they live in the same dormitory. They also discover that they were both asked to come at the same time by the seller and figure out that the seller is probably trying to get them to bid against each other. So they agree to make a lowball offer on the stereo and not increase their bids by more than a few dollars. They hope that if they try to hold the price down but offer to pay cash on the spot, they can get the seller to sell the stereo now.

FIGURE 12.1 | A Seller and Two Buyers

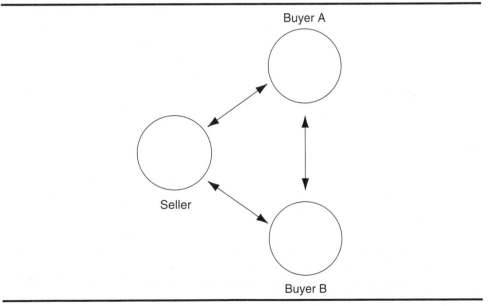

These are three different variations on a three-party negotiation. The first case resembles the typical agency relationship situation we described in Chapter 11. One buyer is representing the other, and we have two negotiations occurring: one between the buyer and the seller and one between the buyer and her roommate. In the second case, the seller is conducting a sequenced series of one-on-one transactions; he gets one to bid, then goes to the other with the bid and asks her to raise it; thus, he is using each potential buyer as his alternative while he tries to get them to compete in an auction. The seller's success in this case relies heavily on the buyers' unwillingness or inability to communicate with each other. In the third case, the seller is about to be unwittingly compromised by the buyers. Having discovered the seller's intent to get them to compete, the buyers are motivated and able to collude in order for both to hold the price down and to punish the seller for trying to structure the deal as an auction. If the buyers are successful, they may be able to purchase the stereo at a bargain price (although they still may face a negotiation between themselves over who actually gets the stereo or the terms of its use). In this chapter we are focusing on this third situation—what happens when the parties form coalitions or subgroups in order to strengthen their bargaining position through collective action.

What Is a Coalition?

A *coalition,* simply defined, is a collection of two or more parties within a larger social setting who work together to pursue mutually desirable goals (Guo and Lim, 2007; Murnighan, 1986). So, for example, in a four-party negotiation, two parties might come together as a coalition to try to influence the outcome in a way that makes the two of them happy, even if that means the other parties' interests are given less emphasis.

There has been extensive research on coalitions. Much of this work has been done in laboratory settings with experimental bargaining games or simulations of voting behavior, but some has consisted of applied studies that analyze coalition formation in real-world settings. One particularly appealing context for studying coalitions is complex organizations, where decisions are often made by coalitions of people. Venerable theories of organizational governance and management[1] refer to the group of people who direct and manage the organization as the "dominant coalition." This usually includes those with the highest rank, such as a president or executive officer, but may also include consultants, senior advisers, attorneys, or others who may not have a major title but have significant influence over the organization's goals and direction.

Pearce, Stevenson, and Porter (1986) suggest that coalitions have these attributes.

- *Coalitions are interacting groups of individuals.* People who may want the same thing but do not specifically interact (the second stereo example) are excluded from this analysis. Coalition members will communicate with each other about pertinent issues. Usually, most people in a coalition are aware of those who belong and those who do not belong.

- *Coalitions are deliberately constructed and issue oriented.* In a coalition, the parties are intentionally joining to accomplish some specific purpose that serves their interests. Once interaction concerning these issues ceases to occur, the coalition no longer exists as an active entity.

- *Coalitions exist independent of formal structure.* A coalition is not necessarily a formal group, such as a department, team, or task force (whose members may unite because they have been created by design in the organization), although a department or team could also informally band together around a common purpose or objective. But the origins of a coalition are informal, based on the interests of the parties rather than created by formal organizational designation.

- *Coalitions lack formal structure.* Because coalitions lack formal organizational designation and legitimacy, they also lack any internal hierarchy or formal legitimate authority. Informal leadership and roles may evolve as the coalition persists and grows, however.

- *Coalitions focus on goals external to the coalition.* For the most part, coalitions form to exert influence on a person or body external to the coalition. This may be another individual or group inside their organization (but who is not in the coalition), or an individual or group outside their organization.

- *Coalitions require concerted member action.* A coalition requires the commitment of its members to focus their action collectively on an intended target. The members may act in concert or may focus on refraining from action (e.g., an organized protest of some form), but the objective is to achieve collectively what they cannot accomplish individually.

An essential aspect of a coalition is that its members are trying to achieve outcomes that satisfy the interests of the coalition, not those of the larger group within which the coalition is formed; at times, though, the two may be compatible (Polzer, Mannix, and Neale, 1998).

Types of Coalitions

Coalitions take many forms. We draw here on Cobb's (1986) inventory of the different types of coalitions that exist.

1. A *potential coalition* is an emergent interest group. It has the potential to become a coalition by taking collective action but has not yet done so. Two forms of a potential coalition can also be identified, latent and dormant:

   - A *latent coalition* is an emergent interest group that has not yet formed into an operating coalition.

   - A *dormant coalition* is an interest group that previously formed but is currently inactive.

   Potential coalitions can be of interest both to coalition members and to those they oppose; if one can identify what might lead a supportive or opposing coalition to form (or to invigorate a dormant one), one can select courses of action that might be more or less likely to activate that coalition.

2. An *operating coalition* is one that is currently operating, active, and in place. Two forms are common, established and temporary:

   - An *established coalition* is relatively stable, active, and ongoing across an indefinite time span. It may continue because the members represent a broad range of interests, because the issues are never fully resolved, or because they are in constant opposition to another established coalition that is taking action. For example, in most governmental systems there are established coalitions of liberals, conservatives, and moderates who are engaged in ongoing debates across a range of issues and involving a large cast of actors and operatives.

- A *temporary coalition* operates for a short time and is usually focused on a single issue or problem. These groups form for the express purpose of exerting collective action; when their objectives are met, they disband. Often, however, people in temporary coalitions discover that they have a number of other common interests that are more persistent or long term; thus, temporary coalitions often transform into established ones.

3. A *recurring coalition* is one that may have started as temporary but then determined that the issue or problem does not remain resolved; hence, the members need to remobilize themselves every time the presenting issue requires collective attention in the future. For example, a citizen's group that successfully opposed the location of a fast-food restaurant in a certain neighborhood may discover that the issue does not completely go away and that they need to remobilize when a massive convenience store subsequently seeks a building permit for the same site.

How and Why Coalitions Form and Develop

When Do Coalitions Form?

Coalitions Form All the Time   In families, parents may be seen as acting in a unified front, creating major obstacles for children who want to influence them about extending curfew times or lightening the load of household chores. Parents often align with one or more of their children in order to exert pressure on the other parent; "Go tell your mom that it would be great to order in Thai food," says Dad (who doesn't feel like making dinner that night) to the oldest child. Similarly, coalitions form constantly in political organizations where people are mobilizing their efforts to support or oppose any number of legislative agendas. The same occurs in business organizations, where parties get together to support or oppose an action being planned by the organization's formal leadership. In each of these contexts, the fundamental dynamic is the same: parties come together to pool their efforts and resources in pursuit of common or overlapping goals.

Coalition Formation Can Be Analyzed in Different Ways   Coalitions have been studied within a variety of social science disciplines, including economics, sociology, psychology, and political science (among others). Sociologists tend to look at real-life collectivities and movements as landscapes for coalition building. For example, Netta Van Dyke (2003) used historical archives to examine the conditions under which coalitions formed both within and across social movement boundaries. Van Dyke looked at 2,644 protest events that occurred on college campuses between 1960 and 1990. Findings suggested that single-movement coalitions are more likely to form when resources are available and when local threats are present. In contrast, psychologists and economists often explore coalition dynamics through laboratory "games," where individuals possess resources that may have to be pooled in order to realize some desired outcome. The focus is often on how individual actors can form the smallest possible "winning" coalition and the payoffs that each player can obtain from participating in that coalition (Murnighan, 1982). Control over resources is the basis for two critical pieces of the coalition formation process: what each member brings to the coalition, and what each member should receive if the coalition forms.

A Classic Coalition Game   To understand when and why coalitions form, we examine a classic coalition problem: the 4–3–2 game (Murnighan, 1978, 1982). In this game, three players are given an unequal number of votes in order to collect a prize (e.g., a pool of money). Andrea (A) has four votes, Barbara (B) has three votes, and Cecilia (C) has two votes. To collect the prize, they must assemble at least five votes; thus, no player can claim the prize without forming a coalition with another player, and each player must use all her votes at once. The players can communicate with one another (sometimes by talking, sometimes only by sending written messages); their job is to determine whom to ally with and then how they are going to split the prize. Not surprisingly, the most important factor that determines who aligns with whom is how they decide to split the money. Based on a series of research studies, Murnighan (1986, 1991; Murnighan and Brass, 1991) reports the following findings:

•   The 3–2 (Barbara–Cecilia) coalition is the most common. This result usually occurs because Andrea (with four votes) argues that she contributes the most to the coalition and hence should receive the largest share of the outcomes. Either because Andrea's demands are seen as excessive (they may be), or because Barbara and Cecilia feel badly treated by Andrea, or because Barbara and Cecilia recognize that they can pool the fewest votes to get the whole pot, Barbara and Cecilia tend to form a coalition most often.

•   Once the 3–2 coalition arises, it appears to be stable. That is, on a large number of repeated trials, the Barbara–Cecilia coalition will continue to dominate. Barbara and Cecilia will choose each other to the consistent exclusion of Andrea. The most common distribution of the pool is 50/50 or a small advantage to Barbara (with three votes).

•   Occasionally, stable coalitions are broken. This is most likely to occur because Andrea makes a very attractive offer to Barbara or Cecilia that lures one of them away from the Barbara–Cecilia pattern. Interestingly, research results show that if Andrea wants to break the Barbara–Cecilia coalition, she should make Barbara or Cecilia a dramatically good offer (e.g., a 10/90 split). In fact, however, Andrea seldom does this; she may make marginally better offers than she did before, but usually the improvement is so minimal that it does not cause Barbara or Cecilia to defect from their prior agreement.

When Andrea is successful, she is more likely to get Barbara to defect than Cecilia (Murnighan, 1986). Murnighan speculates that this may be due to Barbara's inflated ego—"I'm getting a better deal, probably because I deserve it," she thinks, "and why shouldn't I deserve an even better deal?" (Murnighan, 1991, pp. 131–132). The result may also be due to the increased loyalty of Cecilia to a deal in which she is getting consistently less than the other and has to rationalize continued involvement; hence, she may be less likely to defect.

If a defection occurs, what happens next? The defector (assume Barbara), who probably got a big incentive to defect (e.g., a promise of a large share of the pot), now may insist that she continue to receive the bonus. This action is usually seen as greedy by Andrea, even though Andrea encouraged the greediness by offering the hefty bonus to begin with! As a result, Andrea may reject Barbara in future deals because of Barbara's greediness. Moreover, Cecilia is still mad at Barbara for defecting from the stable B–C relationship. Hence, Barbara, who was tempted to defect and took the opportunity, may now be rejected by both sides, who then ally with each other in an Andrea–Cecilia coalition. This coalition may persist for a long time, often until Barbara is able to put a highly tempting offer on the table that will break the Andrea–Cecilia coalition.

A "Real-World" Example   There are a number of real-world parallels to the coalition dynamics found in the 4–3–2 game. For example, the first formulation of the European Economic Community (EEC), in 1957, included the charter members Germany, France, Italy, the Netherlands, Belgium, and Luxembourg. Germany, France, and Italy were very large and economically powerful; Belgium and the Netherlands were weaker than the "big three" but more economically powerful than Luxembourg. In the first EEC treaty, each government had voting power proportional to its economic and physical size (four votes each for Germany, France, and Italy; two votes each for Belgium and Netherlands; and one vote for Luxembourg). Some decisions required unanimous votes, while others required only a majority vote (four out of six countries). These requirements produced a tremendous amount of coalition behavior. When the votes needed to be unanimous, even the smallest countries could exert strong control over the decision because they could block any deal that came along. In contrast, when the votes only needed to be a majority, smaller countries could ally with larger countries, and it was even possible for all the small countries to be excluded if the big three decided to get together. These dynamics did not fundamentally change until the EEC expanded its membership in 1973. When Denmark, Ireland, and the United Kingdom entered the EEC, the proportional votes held by each party changed, as did the total number of votes necessary to carry a majority and take action (Murnighan, 1991).

The Nature of Coalition Inputs   In general, people form coalitions to preserve or increase their resources. As Murnighan (1986) notes, there can be several different types of resources: money, information, natural resources, discretion (the ability to make decisions without consulting others), and so on. In the situations we have been discussing—both the 4–3–2 game and the real-world example of the formation of the EEC in the 1950s—the resources involved were potential votes that individual parties brought to a decision-making process. Early research on coalitions in laboratory situations tended to define resources as votes (Gamson, 1961), but studies of voting behavior are often difficult to generalize when the votes don't translate into any real power to control anything.

It is important to keep in mind, however, that the resources that serve as coalition inputs take many other forms, depending on the specific context involved. In organizations, for example, coalitions realistically form around key resources such as information, money, or control over the future direction of the group or organization. Coalition inputs may also include other kinds of resources: the amount of effort one has exerted, the ability or skill one contributes to the task or problem, or the level of expertise one has obtained. Effort, ability, and skill may be as critical to the coalition as control over specific resources; for example, in the formation of joint ventures in organizations, ability, skill, and expertise are often as critical as money, plant capacity, or raw materials.

Coalitions can also form around a shared sense of social identity, which arises when two or more parties see themselves as part of common social categories. Those categories can involve the kinds of large social groupings that are routinely the basis for group identity and social stereotyping (e.g., gender, race, nationality, etc.), or they can involve categories that emerge as individuals become acquainted and group interaction occurs (e.g., strong vs. weak contributors, or individuals in common task roles; Swaab, Postmes, and Spears, 2008). Note that when coalitions form purely around social identities, they are not really "rational." In other words, they aren't formed on the basis of the substance of the negotiation—on the shared ability of coalition partners to influence the outcome through collective control of resources—so the coalition will not necessarily help the allied parties achieve their negotiation objectives. Nonetheless, negotiators are humans, and humans tend to form alliances with others who are similar to them, making identity-based coalitions an inevitable possibility in multiparty interaction.

For an interesting example involving somewhat unusual inputs into coalition formation, see Box 12.1 on the role of coalitions in string quartets.

The "Tragedy of the Commons"   The coalition games and examples we have discussed to this point involve actors forming coalitions to achieve some desired outcome that meets shared objectives. However, coalitions also form in order to avoid a poor outcome that will occur if individuals act alone in a self-interested manner. A classic statement of this type of problem (called a social dilemma or a commons dilemma) is an anecdote developed by Garrett Hardin (1968) known as "The Tragedy of the Commons" drawn from 17th-century village life in England. Murnighan (1991) relates the story:

> Near the center of the town was a common area that everyone in the town could use. Picnics, county fairs, and summer weddings often took place on the commons. Early on, there were no rules about this area. All the townspeople could use the commons in any way they pleased. Unfortunately, a herdsman in one end of the town realized that he could expand his herd without having to buy more land if he grazed his cows on the commons. This way he could make the most of his own farmland and maximize his returns on his now larger herd. Once one herdsman started, the others in the town realized what a beneficial plan this was and they too began to graze their cattle on the commons. Before long, of course, the commons was reduced to a barren field, with no grass, no attraction for anyone, and no social activity. When it rained, the commons was a pool of mud. No one even thought of getting married there anymore. As Hardin put it, "Ruin is the destination toward which all men rush, each pursuing his own best interest in a society that believes in the freedom of the common. Freedom in a common brings ruin to all." (pp. 141–142)

The reader will recognize that the term *social dilemma* applies to a number of major contemporary issues—air and water pollution, use of natural resources, charitable contributions, voting (or not voting) in elections. In each situation, if a large enough number of people reason that their behavior or vote will not make a significant difference, then a major social problem ensues. For instance, a New England lobster fisherman may wish to

Coalition Dynamics in String Quartets BOX 12.1

Researchers Keith Murnighan and Donald Conlon studied the group dynamics and coalition politics that occur in string quartets. Their analysis was based on interviews with musicians in 80 string quartets in England and Scotland.

In a string quartet, four musicians—two violinists, a viola player, and a cellist—must play together so that their music sounds like it is played by a cohesive unit. But each group, because of the individual talents of its members and their collective work together, develops its own idiosyncratic style; thus, two quartets playing the same piece of music can sound quite different from each other. There is a lot of debate, discussion, and negotiation among the players, driven in part by roles and reputations:

- The first violin is usually the strongest player and the driving force behind the group; he or she usually carries the tune for the group, and much of the best music is written explicitly for this role. Therefore, it is not uncommon for the first violinist to develop a big ego.

- The second violin always has to follow the first and is usually seen as a weaker player whose job is to play "second fiddle" and support the first violinist.

- Viola players are often seen as the flakiest and most unconventional; it is assumed that many of them began playing the violin early in their career, couldn't make it in the strong competition with other top violinists, and switched to the viola as a less demanding instrument.

- Finally, cellists are seen as playing a background role; they often play the bass notes, which set a foundation for the rest of the group.

- Compared with the first violinist, the remaining three are often referred to as the "bottom" of the quartet, whose job it is to complement and show off what the first violinist can do.

Based on their interviews, Murnighan and Conlon determined that coalition dynamics are most common in the bottom and middle of the quartet. The first and second violins often form an alliance because they play the same instrument. In contrast, the researchers observed that the cellist is rarely excluded from any coalition, even though he or she plays a larger instrument, one that is not held under the chin. Moreover, other differences within the coalition can drive the dynamics (e.g., if one member is female and the others are male, or if three live together in a different part of the city, or if one person's ability and/or commitment to the group creates a significant problem for the other three).

Applying principles of coalitions to these very specialized groups sheds light on how we negotiate the inherent conflicts and coalitions that lie beneath the surface of groups of all kinds.

Source: Adapted from J. K. Murnighan and D. E. Conlon, "The Dynamics of Intense Work Groups: A Study of British String Quartets," *Administrative Science Quarterly* 36 (1991), pp. 165–86.

continue fishing to support a family; if all fishing in the same waters (in the "commons") continues unabated, however, there will be little lobster left for future generations. Commons dilemmas can be avoided only if a large number of people accept some responsibility for doing their part to avoid taking advantage of an unlimited good, so that others may also be able to share that resource in the future.

Unfortunately, commons dilemmas often become an unending downward spiral. However, research shows that communication between the individuals involved (Orbell, Van de Kragt, and Dawes, 1988), education about the resource in question (Roch and Samuelson, 1997), and asking individuals to commit publicly to conserve resources

(Dickerson, Thibodeau, Aronson, and Miller, 1992) can increase prosocial responses to commons dilemmas. In addition, those who feel included and respected by their social group are more likely to behave in ways that benefit the group as a whole (De Cremer, 2002). These potential strategies for inducing cooperation highlight the important effect that coalitions can have during times of group conflict.

How Do Coalitions Develop?

Through a series of studies, Murnighan and his colleagues (Murnighan, 1986; Murnighan and Brass, 1991) offer a detailed assessment of the coalition formation process. The following steps and activities seem to be the most critical.

Coalitions Start with a Founder   The founder is the person who initiates the coalition. Typically, founders are those who recognize that they cannot get what they want through existing channels by themselves. Coalition founders usually identify an agenda or course of action that must be accomplished or achieved. In terms of leverage (see Chapters 7 and 8), the founder develops some form of action agenda, vision, or commitment and persuades others to join him or her in pursuing it.

Discussions with others often take the form of a negotiation. In some cases, persuasion efforts alone may be successful—that is, simply by describing the agenda, or by portraying it in glowing and enthusiastic terms, the founder may be able to win the others' support. In other cases, the persuasion effort is not sufficient, and the founder may have to offer tangible rewards or benefits to get others to join the coalition. This is where the negotiation process really takes place. Murnighan and Brass (1991) suggest that early in the coalition-building process, founders may have to offer a disproportionate share of profits or benefits to potential partners. In other words, founders may have to offer an unequal or inequitable share to early prospects. This is done because the prospects may be unwilling to take the risk and make the commitment to join the coalition without some kind of significant incentive. One apparent paradox of being a founder, therefore, is that early in the coalition-building process the founder may have to give away a lot in order to apparently gain a little. This process does not continue indefinitely, however; as the coalition builds and strengthens, other prospective partners will have more interest in joining on their own, and the founder's power position shifts from weakness (having to give away a lot to gain supporters) to strength (being able to dictate what new members must give in order to join the coalition).

Murnighan and Brass (1991) suggest that there are two key propositions that affect the founder's ability to build a coalition:

•   Successful founders have extensive networks. In Chapter 7, we discussed the power of having a network and being in a key position within a network. Successful founders usually have a strong network of friends and associates whom they know and whom they can approach when they need support for a particular agenda. As we mentioned in Chapter 11, multiparty negotiations often look like branching chains, and negotiators often work through the chains to eventually make contact with the other party and establish the basis for a more formal meeting or discussion (Pruitt, 1994, 1995).

BOX 12.2

How do coalition leaders define success? What qualities of leadership are believed to contribute to that success? To answer these questions, researchers Terry Mizrahi and Beth Rosenthal (2001) interviewed 70 current and former coalition leaders from 40 distinct coalitions that mobilized for some social change initiative in the New York/New Jersey area. Participants were asked about their goals, strategies, structural and organizational techniques, and decision-making processes.

Results showed that coalition leaders defined success in a number of different ways. The majority of leaders interviewed felt that success comes from achieving one's goals and gaining recognition from targets for social change. Others defined success in terms of "gaining new consciousness of the issue," "creating lasting networks," and "attaining longevity."

Regardless of how these leaders defined success, the overwhelming majority believed that commitment to the goal of the coalition and competent leadership were the most important elements for success. Other important factors in coalition success cited by participants fell into two categories:

- *Internal* elements (under the coalition's control): process, structure, strategies, and available resources.

- *External* elements (outside the coalition's control): political climate, the target of influence, and timing.

A common theme raised was the importance of exchange within the coalition. Many leaders believed that it is important for members to receive something from the coalition in order for them to give back. "The more resources that members gave and received, the more they stayed committed" (p. 73). Thus, reciprocity was seen as key to success.

Asked what personal attributes make an effective leader of a coalition, participants responded that persistence, persuasiveness, and negotiation and facilitation skills were among the most important qualities.

Source: Adapted from R. Mizrahi and B. B. Rosenthal, "Complexities of Coalition Building: Leaders' Successes, Strategies, Struggles, and Solutions," *Social Work* 46 (2001), pp. 63–78.

- Founders' benefits from early coalitions are likely to be small. Because others will be skeptical of lending their support to the coalition, a founder needs to give early partners enough to make it worth their while. As we noted earlier, founders don't immediately benefit from early support; in fact, they may become worse off until several other people join the coalition and it builds some momentum.

Coalition building is a particularly important enterprise in the world of social movement activism. Box 12.2 describes a study of coalition success seen through the eyes of coalition leaders in social change settings.

Coalitions Build by Adding One Member at a Time   Coalitions do not come together in a single, defining event; instead, coalitions are built by adding individuals one at a time. The founder or an early ally is instrumental in driving this process. Contacts may be made simply through friends or acquaintances with whom the founder meets on a regular basis. Proximity and convenience influence who is approached, but neither may be enough. This is where another key negotiation principle comes in—the founder can benefit significantly in coalition building if he or she understands the others' interests. A founder who knows what others want or need—and who can explain how coalition membership may deliver on those needs—has powerful tools for attracting new partners. The nature of these wants and needs, and resources one can use to build and leverage them, can be multifaceted and complex. Discussions with others may be tentative, with the founder trying to find out what the others might want instead of making explicit offers; he or she may then get the process started by making such offers, based on one or more of several criteria:

- The other has something important to bring to the coalition that will enhance its strength.

- The other wants less than other people do in order to be a member of the coalition. (The less the other demands, the more desirable he or she may be as a coalition prospect, but a person who demands little may also not be seen as valuable or critical to have on board.)

- The founder can make some form of promise or commitment to the other about future rewards or benefits to be derived. Sometimes these commitments are clear, explicit, or even written; in other situations, they may be vague and oblique. A founder who can get away with making nonspecific promises clearly maintains more control than if the commitments are clear, specific, and costly.

Coalitions may also require opportunities to form—opportunities for side conversations apart from the table of a multiparty negotiation. When the parties don't know each other (or each other's interests) very well prior to coming together to negotiate, it may be hard to identify and solidify coalition partners unless you have the chance to caucus with them away from the main table. Recent research shows that opportunities for side conversations in small groups give rise to norms of coalition formation and also give greater voice to minority points of view (Swaab, Phillips, Diermeier, and Medvec, 2008). These researchers suggest that group leaders think carefully about whether they want to allow or encourage side conversations, and the same advice is relevant for those who control process features of a multiparty negotiation.

Coalitions Need to Achieve Critical Mass   Coalitions continue to grow through pairwise discussions and matching processes. How big they get is determined by a number of factors, but at some point, they reach a "joining threshold"—a level in which a minimum number of people are on board—and others begin to join because they recognize that their current friends and associates are already members. Founders and their early supporters make lots of contacts with other people, trying to determine others who might be interested in joining as well as the "price" of such membership. There is a point at which a coalition, having reached a critical mass (Schelling, 1978), finds that further growth is easier, but at the same time less necessary (Murnighan and Brass, 1991). From that point forward, the coalition may continue to accumulate more members, "especially in particularly politicized, turbulent environments" (Murnighan and Brass, 1991, p. 292).

Coalitions Exclude   Coalitions don't just add members; they also *exclude* members. A study by van Beest, Wilke, and van Dijk (2003) explored the role of the excluded player in coalition formation. Actors left out of a coalition may be worse off as a result; van Beest and colleagues cite the examples of a merger of two firms that hurts an excluded competitor and of the creation of a free trade organization that hurts countries not participating. But actors left out may, in some circumstances, be better off, such as when two firms form a coalition to market a product in a context where other firms in the same line of business benefit from publicity surrounding the merger. In their experiment, van Beest and colleagues predicted and found that individuals forming coalitions are motivated not only to pursue personal gain, but also to maintain personal relationships and minimize harm that may be caused to excluded individuals. Experimental participants were less likely to form smaller coalitions that excluded an individual when the excluded person received lower payoffs because of it.

The exclusion of parties from coalitions may depend in part on the communication channels through which multiparty negotiation and coalition politics play out. A new study by Swaab, Kern, Diermeier, and Medvec (in press) looked at exclusion in a three-person game, where deals were possible with only two parties. Groups that interacted face-to-face were less likely to exclude a party than groups that interacted through a text-based online communication system. Publicness of communication also mattered: even when groups interacted online, exclusion was less likely when side conversations were not allowed. These researchers conclude that if computer-based communication is the only available channel, and if cooperation rather than exclusion is desired, then those in charge of the process should limit interaction to public settings and discourage or disallow private side conversations.

Weak Ties Can Be Strong   Earlier, we discussed the strength-is-weakness dynamic in coalitions—that coalition founders will go to those who are the weakest for support, often because the weakest may need to be in the coalition most and will demand the least payoff from joining the coalition. A related dynamic involves the founder's network. Founders usually have a large and diverse network of initial contacts and associates whom they can contact for potential membership. Research has shown that those founders who have a large, diverse network of weak ties are often in a better position to form a coalition than those who have a small, uniform network of strong ties (Granovetter, 1973; Kadushin, 1968).[2] Paradoxically, those who have a few strong ties, with high frequency of interaction and high multiplexity, already have a small coalition that demands a lot of their attention. In organizational settings, veto players (senior managers or those in formal authority positions) are unlikely to be founders because they will not be willing to give much away and will have difficulty selling others on membership. In contrast, veto players are more likely to wait until others approach them with initiatives and "bide their time until offers become attractive enough to accept" (Murnighan and Brass, 1991, p. 293). The founder may use this approach early on, but in a tentative manner, because at some point the founder probably wants to bring the veto player on board. Founders, on the other hand, have extensive networks of weak ties with several other parties, often bring on those who have their own extensive networks (thereby extending the "network reach" of possible members), and use these ties to make contacts and build support.

Many Successful Coalitions Form Quietly and Disband Quickly   Coalitions do not have to be permanent, large, or public to be effective. In fact, if they do become permanent and public, their members tend to be seen as the opposition, as naysayers, or as people who are known for challenging the formal leader or established structure. In contrast, successful coalitions are often drawn together quickly around key issues and mobilize simply for the purpose of endorsing or blocking a particular course of action. The coalition seldom meets formally; instead, pairs and subgroups may meet informally (over lunch, by e-mail) to exchange ideas, share information and rumors, and perhaps develop a common mind-set about what is going on and how it is happening. When a critical action or decision is forthcoming, they mobilize to work together, then go back to their own individual activities and environments when either the objective is achieved or the critical moment passes. Note, by the way, that communication channels may play a role in the ability of coalitions to form and disband efficiently. In Chapter 6 we discussed how negotiation processes are affected when interaction occurs through different channels (face-to-face, telephone or teleconference, e-mail, and so forth). Although coalition formation and interaction can occur through any medium, research does point to the challenges involved when online media, such as e-mail, are used in multiparty negotiation (Kurtzbert, Dunn-Jensen, and Matsibekker, 2005). The more parties involved in a situation ripe for coalition formation, the more difficult it may be to identify common interests, and promising coalition partners, when using socially impoverished media like text-based messaging or e-mail.

Murnighan and Brass (1991) identify several reasons it is risky for a coalition to remain intact after the successful resolution of an issue:

- *Revenge of the vanquished.* If a coalition "wins" and is identified, the nonwinners may eventually want payback. Revenge can eventually pit coalitions against each other so that each one's sole objective is to keep the other side from succeeding. This is a common dynamic in legislative bodies around the world, as various liberal and conservative groups attempt to block each other's initiatives and agendas.

- *Turmoil within.* Public acknowledgment of the coalition may also lead to turmoil within the coalition that could damage future coalition activity. For example, if the coalition is comprised of people who all have strong egos, most will want to take more than their share of the credit for the coalition's success. If the coalition is informal, all can take credit and feel good; if the coalition's activity becomes public, actual contributions may become known and some members will be recognized as actually having contributed very little, which could then lead to in-fighting and threaten the coalition's viability.

- *Desire for anonymity.* Some coalition members may prefer anonymity. The more publicly identified they become with the coalition, the more others may see their future actions as motivated by coalition membership and not by their own interests. They may lose the option to join other coalitions, and they may lose personal effectiveness because they are assumed to be puppets of the coalition's leadership. For this reason, many coalition members do not want to be known as being political or publicly associated with other coalition members, and they definitely want to be able to keep their options open to form other associations as their interests may dictate in the future.

Standards for Coalition Decision Making

Coalition decision rules emphasize the criteria that parties will use to determine who receives what from the results of the coalition's efforts. Decision rules focus on the standards for which members of the coalition will advocate and how the output or results should be allocated. Decision rules tend to parallel three standards of fairness: equity, equality, and need. Those advocating an *equity* standard argue that anyone who contributed more should receive more, in proportion to the magnitude of the contribution. Those advocating an *equality* standard argue that everyone should receive the same, and those advocating a *need* standard argue that parties should receive more in proportion to some demonstrated need for a larger share of the outcome (see also Chapter 10).

In general, *parties tend to argue for the standard that is most likely to serve their individual needs.* For example, returning to the 4–3–2 game we introduced earlier, Andrea, as the player with four votes, will probably argue for the equity standard—that she should receive the larger share of any pool because she contributes more votes. Cecilia, as the player with only two votes, might argue for equality, because she stands to make more in an equal split with either Andrea or Barbara than she would from an equitable split. Barbara, as the swing player, might argue for equality if she was trying to form a coalition with Andrea, but might argue for equity when negotiating with Cecilia. If one player had a very strong need—for example, a need for money to repair her car so she could get to her job—that argument might prevail if she could convince the other two of the strength and validity of her need, relative to their needs, to get either an equitable or equal split of the resource pool.

Power and Leverage in Coalitions

Chapters 7 and 8 addressed the general nature of power and leverage in negotiations. The dynamics of power and influence are central aspects of the formation and maintenance of coalitions because coalitions tend to arise in situations where multiple actors have competing and partially overlapping interests. Leverage issues in coalitions are discussed from two perspectives: the issue of strength versus weakness in coalitions and the types of power that underlie coalition formation.

Where Is the Strength in Coalitions?   The more resources a party holds or controls, the more likely he or she is to be a critical coalition member. Such a person will be a central figure to pulling the coalition together, dictating its strategy, and influencing the distribution of the resource pool. This is known as the *strength-is-strength* argument. Note that this centrality directly parallels the type of centrality we discussed in Chapter 7: formal and informal power that comes from one's position in a hierarchy and in a network structure. Coalition players with strength often become the center of communication networks that form in the process of both shaping the coalition and deciding on the distribution of the pool (Murnighan and Volrath, 1984).

Sometimes, however, the goal is to form the smallest possible winning coalition; in these circumstances, those parties who have relatively fewer resources in a coalition may be stronger. This is true because their relatively weaker resource position leads them to ask for less from the winning pool, and hence they are more desirable to have as coalition partners (Murnighan, 1978). Thus, when any winning coalition obtains the same payoff, and the structure of the situation indicates that two given actors are interchangeable (either one can contribute the same amount to the dominant coalition), those actors who appear to contribute the fewest resources, have the least power, or exert the least influence will have an advantage. This result is often referred to as the *strength-is-weakness* argument (Murnighan, 1986). As Murnighan notes, "When anyone will do, interchangeability favors those who appear weak. Thus, a supervisor who needs any supportive voice for a new group strategy will almost certainly attempt to convince the weakest, most agreeable group member to concur" (p. 161). Murnighan cautions, however, that although this may lead to adoption of the proposed strategy, a coalition based on weak members may, with its lack of dedicated support, undermine the implementation of that strategy.

How Is Power Related to Coalition Formation?   Polzer, Mannix, and Neale (1995, 1998) have identified three key types of power in multiparty negotiations: strategic, normative, and relational. Discussion of these types of power provides a convenient summary of the coalition-formation process:

•   *Strategic power* emerges from the availability of alternative coalition partners. If negotiators have good alternatives, then they can walk away from any unacceptable deal and approach others who may be able and willing to discuss a better deal. The more resources a given potential partner brings to a coalition, or the greater variety in resources or types of inputs, the more that partner can add to the coalition, and the more power he or she will have in contributing to the coalition and dictating what the coalition should look like.

•   *Normative power* derives from what parties consider to be a fair or just distribution of the outcomes and results of a coalition. In essence, the party that proposes the rule or principle of what constitutes a fair distribution of the outcomes has more normative power. One party may argue for an equal distribution, the other for an equitable distribution, and a third for a distribution based on need; the party whose arguments ultimately shape the allocation rule used by the group has the most normative power.

•   *Relationship-based power* is shaped by the compatibility of preferences between two or more parties. As we noted in Chapter 10, parties who see each other as having common or compatible interests are more likely to begin and preserve a relationship with each other. The parties' compatibility may be based on shared or complementary interests (mutual gain), common ideology, or simply liking each other and enjoying being together.

In studies examining these three sources of power (Polzer, Mannix, and Neale, 1995, 1998), negotiators playing the role of one of three divisional vice presidents in a research and development firm were asked to allocate funding from two resource pools. The value of the first resource pool varied depending on which two of the three players were included in the final agreement on the pool; their varying power was based on the size of the division they represented. Thus, strategic power was manipulated by who could coalesce with whom to get the pool. Normative power was manipulated by the degree to which each division, if it received the resources, could use the resources to best contribute to the overall mission of the organization. Finally, relationship power was manipulated through the second pool, in which parties had more or less compatible preferences on negotiation issues. The results indicate that *relationship power from compatibility of interests was the overriding source of power*. As the authors note:

> Players who had compatible interests were able to achieve higher individual outcomes from both portions of the task. This was true even when compatible players did not form exclusive

two-way coalitions. These findings indicate that compatible players formed internal coalitions, acting as allies against the incompatible third party—not necessarily to lock the third party out of the final agreement, but to force him or her to accept a reduced share of both resource pools. (Polzer, Mannix, and Neale, 1995, p. 128)

Polzer and colleagues also note that relationship dynamics can significantly affect the formation and stability of coalitions. Parties in relationships tend to see themselves as aligned in the future; thus, they incorporate a temporal aspect into their relationship and expect that if their interests are not being met now, they certainly will be in the future. As a result, they work together without requiring the certainty of immediate payoff. In addition, they see themselves as having compatible preferences, which means a common interest in seeing both parties achieve their respective goals. Finally, parties in relationships develop trust, which means greater confidence in the other's behavior and intentions, and greater recognition of opportunities to work together. For negotiators in multiparty situations, the lesson here is that personal relationships with other parties can be just as useful, and sometimes even more useful, than just identifying overlaps in strategic priorities.

How to Build Coalitions: Some Practical Advice

We conclude this section with a practical approach to coalitions developed by Peter Block (1987), who proposed a strategy of empowerment and positive politics in organizations. Empowerment, Block states, "comes from acting on our enlightened self-interest. Politics is the pursuit of self-interest, and positive politics is the pursuit of enlightened self-interest" (p. 105). Enlightened self-interest, according to Block, occurs when people

- Pursue activities that have meaning to themselves and to others.
- Are needed.
- Genuinely contribute to the organization and its purpose.
- Act with integrity and tell the truth about what they see happening.
- Treat others well and have a positive impact on them.
- Strive to be as good and productive as they can at what they do.

Parties who pursue enlightened self-interest are likely to use authentic tactics with others. Authentic tactics are actions grounded in the principles of enlightened self-interested just listed. The contrast with authentic tactics would be expedient, dubiously ethical actions (such as those discussed in Chapter 9) taken exclusively in the service of one's own self-interest, to the exclusion of concerns about what others want or how they are treated. Block argues that authentic tactics require parties to do the following:

1. *Say no when they mean no.* Rather than hedging a position, refusing to make commitments, sitting on the fence, or being nice to everybody regardless of beliefs, parties need to let others know where they stand.

2. *Share as much information as possible.* Authentic tactics require parties to tell everything they know so that they can maximize what others know, maximize the common pool of information, and increase the ability of the parties to arrive at a solution that is in their individual and collective interests. As Block notes, this might mean sharing the entire budget, rather than only a small part; sharing complete financial data; involving people extensively in proposed changes and giving them this information early in the process; letting people know about possible failures early on so they can plan to avert them or minimize the impact; and letting people know where they stand and how their job performance is rated so they can make informed decisions about their lives and future.

3.   *Use language that describes reality.* Instead of using language that obscures, masks, or disguises what is really going on, parties should use language that is straightforward and clear. Politicians are frequently criticized for refusing to answer questions clearly or fully or for failing to give complete and accurate accounts of what has happened. Instead of using language that describes reality, politicians skillfully use language that distorts, obscures, misleads, or places the blame elsewhere (see Kurtz, 1998).

4.   *Avoid repositioning for the sake of acceptance.* Parties should not shift their position, endorsement, or support simply to make it more acceptable, palatable, or consistent with what is "hot" or current. Such repositioning is often scorned as "the flavor of the month" program; cheap efforts at better employee relations; or an effort to polish up old, tired ideas and present them as new ones. For example, companies have often been accused of retreading the same fundamental management programs with new names and slogans, depending on what is hot—corporate culture, quality, productivity, leadership, and so on. Politicians accuse each other of taking old jobs or social welfare programs and giving them new names and buzzwords. The more often this happens— and people recognize it—the more it breeds cynicism about whether real change is desired or feasible.

Block (1987) sees the dominant driving force for a coalition as vision—getting people collectively to endorse a view of greatness for their unit and organization that others will buy into. However, recall that relationships, common interests, or normative rules can also provide the organizing principle for building a coalition. Political action begins the moment parties try to move from articulating a vision to implementing it; parties begin to talk about their ideas and desires to other people and test out how those others react. As this occurs, Block suggests, you can think about other prospective coalition partners along two dimensions:

*   Are they in high or low agreement with your objectives?
*   Do they generate from you high or low levels of trust?

In Figure 12.2, these two dimensions are joined to define and illustrate five possible roles for coalition partners: allies, opponents, bedfellows, fence sitters, and adversaries. The description of each is drawn from Block (1987).

Allies   Allies are parties who are in agreement with a negotiator's goals and vision, and whom the negotiator trusts. The preferred strategy with allies is to treat them as friends; to let them know exactly what is envisioned and planned; and, because allies can help a negotiator compensate for the areas where he or she feels weakest, to share vulnerabilities and doubts. In addition, a negotiator trusts an ally, believing that person will tell the truth and will act in the negotiator's best interests.

FIGURE 12.2 | Trust/Agreement Matrix

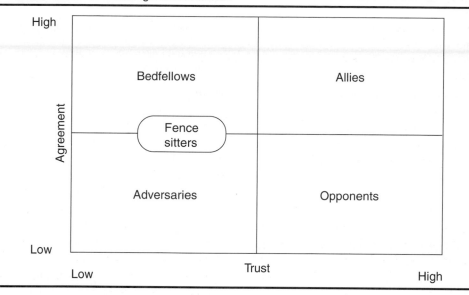

Source: Peter Block, *The Empowered Manager: Positive Political Skills at Work* (San Francisco: Jossey-Bass, 1987). Used with permission of the author.

Opponents   Opponents are people with whom a negotiator has conflicting goals and objectives, but who can be trusted to be principled and candid in their opposition. They challenge, ask tough questions, don't accept glib answers, and constantly push the negotiator to be better and stronger at advocating a specific course of action. Negotiators expect that opponents will play by the rules and play to win. As Block points out, when people play a game against someone, they want the other person to perform well in order to push them to perform well; when they win, they want to feel that they have played against someone who also tried as hard as possible, and that therefore their victory was deserved.

Bedfellows   Bedfellows are parties with whom a negotiator has high agreement on the vision or objectives but low to moderate levels of trust. The low levels of trust arise because either one or both sides don't share information, don't tell the whole truth, play it cagey, and say what they think the other wants to hear rather than the truth. Note that bedfellows can be created either by the other party's actions or by one's own actions; if negotiators are less than open and honest with the other party, or think the other party will be less than open and honest in return, trust levels tend to decrease.

Fence Sitters   Fence sitters are parties who will not take a stand one way or the other on a given issue. They fear taking a position because it could lock them in, be politically dangerous, make enemies out of those they don't ally with, or expose them to risk. They also may truly not know what they want to do. As a result, the negotiator can have little trust in fence sitters because it is not clear where they stand, and they may be actively trying to maintain that ambiguity.

BOX | 12.3 | **Action Strategies for Building Relationships in Coalitions**

Author Peter Block has prescriptive advice for building a coalition with each of the five types of partners he identifies. His major suggestions can be outlined as follows.

With allies:

- Affirm your agreement on the collective vision or objective.
- Reaffirm the quality of the relationship.
- Acknowledge the doubt and vulnerability that you have with respect to achieving your vision and collective goal.
- Ask for advice and support.

With opponents:

- Reaffirm that your relationship is based in trust.
- State your vision or position.
- State in a neutral way what you think their position or vision is.
- Engage in some kind of problem solving.

With bedfellows:

- Reaffirm the agreement.
- Acknowledge the caution that exists.

- Be clear about what you want from bedfellows in terms of their support.
- Ask bedfellows what they want from you.
- Try to reach an agreement on how the two parties are going to work together.

With fence sitters:

- State your position on the project.
- Ask where they stand.
- Apply gentle pressures.
- Encourage them to think about the issue and tell you what it would take to gain their support.

With adversaries:

- State your vision or goals.
- State in a neutral way your understanding of your adversary's position.
- Identify your own contribution to the poor relationship between you and your adversary.
- End the meeting by restating your plan but making no demands.

Source: Peter Block, *The Empowered Manager: Positive Political Skills at Work* (San Francisco: Jossey-Bass, 1987).

Adversaries Adversaries are low in agreement, but unlike opponents, whom negotiators trust to conduct themselves with dignity, adversaries cannot be trusted. Efforts to speak to adversaries usually lead to a failure to agree and a failure to develop trust, reinforcing their adversary status. Many people become preoccupied with adversaries, often because the failure to negotiate with them reveals weaknesses and defects in their ability to manage relationships. In addition, adversaries often behave in ways parties find unacceptable; therefore, the goal is either to win over the adversary or to destroy the adversary. Unfortunately, as Block notes, it doesn't work this way. The more you focus on trying to convert or pressure other people, the stronger they become, the more they threaten you, and the more you become obsessed with them. Kramer (2002) has shown how a long-term focus on adversaries can lead to paranoia and dysfunctional behavior in organizations.

Block (1987) suggests that it is possible to build a coalition with each of these five types, but that one has to use a different strategy in each case. His prescriptive advice is summarized in Box 12.3.

Chapter Summary

In this chapter, we have addressed the nature of coalitions and explored the processes by which they are formed, led, maintained, and ultimately disbanded. We suggested that coalition formation occurs when there are more than two negotiating parties and is most likely when parties need to add the resources or support of others to enhance the likelihood of achieving their own individual outcomes. We discussed when, why, and how coalitions form; addressed how they work (and don't work) once formed; and considered the role of power and leverage in coalition politics. Finally, we offered some advice to those who are building a coalition, particularly regarding how one can think about potential partners, and what should be the agenda in conducting negotiations with those partners.

We conclude with a cautionary note about the importance of underlying relationships among the parties to a dispute that may involve the formation of coalitions. As Murnighan (1991) notes, much of the earlier work on coalitions

ignored one important factor: whether the people who form coalitions together can actually work with each other effectively. . . . Whom you choose as a partner depends on the potential payoffs that can result from that partnership. Those payoffs include the interpersonal benefits you get from your work interactions. . . . More generally, you may maximize your monetary outcome in all your negotiations, but if you also sour all your interpersonal relationships, you'll end up rich and lonely. There's more to bargaining (and life) than winning negotiations, especially if you pay the price of alienating the other person. Burn enough personal bridges and the very opportunity to negotiate will disappear. (p. 137)

These issues of relationships between the parties—past, present, and future—clearly have an impact on how the parties select their coalition partners and whether those partnerships are likely to endure or to shift as economic incentives change.

Discussion

1. In multiparty negotiation situations where coalitions are possible, what kinds of process choices would you make for the interaction? Would you prefer to establish a norm that all conversation occurs at the main table with all parties involved, or would you allow side conversations and caucuses involving some but not all parties? Under what conditions would you prefer one of the other approach? What are the benefits and drawbacks of each?

2. Consider a negotiation with three parties, where only two are needed to make a deal happen but

where all three must be involved in implementation of the agreement after it is reached. If you are part of a "winning" coalition of two parties that excludes the third from the deal, what can you do to ensure the excluded party's cooperation in the outcome after the agreement is reached? Are there steps you could have or should have been taken during the negotiation to increase the chances that the third party will cooperate post-settlement?

Endnotes

[1] See Cyert and March (1963); March (1962); and Thompson (1967).

[2] In this context, the strength of ties is determined by the frequency and multiplexity of interaction that founders have with members of their network. *Interaction* frequency means the number of times

that two parties interact. *Uniplexity/multiplexity* means the number of different ways that the parties interact with each other. If parties only work on a single project together, the relationship is uniplex; if parties work together on different projects, see each other socially, and often eat lunch together, the relationship is multiplex.

13 CHAPTER

Multiple Parties and Teams

Objectives

1. Understand the ways negotiations become more complex when there are more than two negotiators at the bargaining table.
2. Describe the key elements of an effective group as they apply to negotiation processes in groups.
3. Spell out the key stages in managing an effective multiparty negotiation.

In the previous two chapters, we focused on the way negotiation changes when additional parties are added to the context. In Chapter 11, we examined how negotiation changes when negotiators act as agents and represent the interests of others. In Chapter 12, we examined the ways that three or more parties negotiate by forming into subgroups (coalitions) and how those coalitions can exert influence on others. In this chapter, we extend the analysis to two situations that involve multiple parties:

1. Multiple parties are negotiating with one another and attempting to achieve a collective or group consensus. We discuss this kind of team or group decision making as a process of multiparty negotiation.
2. Multiple individuals are present on each "side" of the negotiation—in other words, the parties to a negotiation are teams against teams, rather than individuals.

The Nature of Multiparty Negotiations

We define a *multiparty negotiation* as one in which more than two parties are working together to achieve a collective objective. To illustrate the nature of a multiparty negotiation, let's extend the example used at the beginning of Chapter 12 (a student is selling a stereo system and puts up notices in the dorm and dining areas). However, now assume that there is not one seller, but four roommates who jointly own and are selling the stereo system. A year ago, each put in $200 to buy the system; now they have different preferences for what they should do with it. Aaron (A) wants to sell it and simply split up the money because he wants to buy a new bike for himself; Bill (B) wants to sell it and buy a newer but inexpensive stereo system; Chuck (C) wants to sell it and buy a super-high-quality system that will require each of them to chip in a lot more money; and Dan (D) doesn't want to sell it at all and thinks the whole thing is a dumb idea. Each party has his own preferences and priorities, and the roommates must collectively decide what to do as a

FIGURE 13.1 | A Multiparty Negotiation

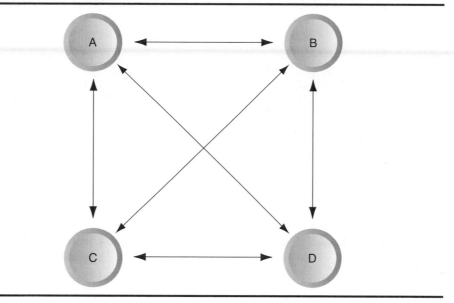

group if and when the system is sold. They might agree to make a single collective decision about what to do next, or they might agree to align together in subgroups to pool their money, or each might go his separate way. When the parties agree to hold a meeting to discuss the options and make a collective decision, this is a multiparty negotiation that involves unique dynamics in a collective decision-making process.

The general model for a multiparty negotiation is represented in Figure 13.1. Each of the parties (there can be three or more) is representing his or her own interests. In a different situation (e.g., they might be representatives of different departments meeting together as a task force), they could be representing the interests of others (see Figure 13.2). Most of the complexities described in this section increase linearly, if not exponentially, as more parties, constituencies, and audiences are added.

In this chapter, we note the factors that make multiparty negotiations more difficult to manage than one-on-one negotiations. We comment on some of the key stages and phases of multiparty deliberations. For each phase, we consider a variety of strategies that can be used to manage multiparty negotiations effectively. We show the ways that multiparty negotiations are complex and highly susceptible to breakdown and show that managing them effectively requires a conscious commitment from the parties and a facilitator as they work toward an effective multiparty agreement.[1]

Differences between Two-Party Negotiations and Multiparty Negotiations

Multiparty negotiations differ from two-party deliberations in several important ways. In every case, the differences are what make multiparty negotiations more complex, challenging, and difficult to manage.

FIGURE 13.2 | A Multiparty Negotiation with Constituents

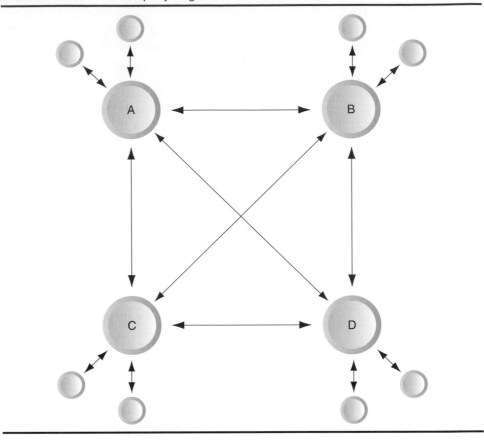

Number of Parties   The first difference is the most obvious one: multiparty negotiations have more negotiators at the table. Thus, negotiations simply become bigger. This creates challenges for managing several different perspectives and ensuring that each party has adequate time to speak and be heard. Each party may be acting as a principal—that is, representing his or her own interests (Figure 13.1)—or an agent—representing the interests of at least one other party (the constituency; Figure 13.2). (Refer back to our discussion of these roles in Chapter 11.) In addition, parties may have different social roles outside the negotiation (e.g., president, vice president, director, board chairman) that may lead to either equal or unequal levels of power and status in the negotiation (see Chapter 7). If the parties are all equals (e.g., all vice presidents), the exchange within the negotiation should be more open than if one party has higher status or power than the others. For instance, if one party is the president and the others are vice presidents, we can expect the president to control and dominate the process more actively.

Informational and Computational Complexity   A second difference in multiparty negotiations is that more issues, more perspectives on issues, and more total information (facts, figures, viewpoints, arguments, documentary support) are introduced. "One of the most fundamental consequences of increasing the number of parties is that the negotiation situation tends to become less lucid, more complex, and therefore, in some respects, more demanding. As size increases, there will be more values, interests, and perceptions to be integrated or accommodated" (Midgaard and Underal, 1977, p. 332, as quoted in Kramer, 1991). Keeping track of all this information, the perspectives of each side, and the parameters into which a solution must fit becomes a major challenge for the negotiators. Therefore, it is even more critical that negotiators spend time in more thorough preparation prior to a negotiation, rather than trying to keep track of issues and trade-offs as the negotiation is evolving.

Social Complexity   A third difference is that as the number of parties increases, the social environment changes from a one-on-one dialogue to a small-group discussion. As a result, all the dynamics of small groups begin to affect the way the negotiators behave. First, how the process evolves may depend on the motivational orientation of the parties toward each other. One study found that parties with a cooperative (versus an individualistic) motivational orientation were much more likely to achieve a higher-quality outcome in their deliberations and that cooperatively motivated parties were more trusting and engaged in less argumentation than individualistic ones (Weingart, Bennett, and Brett, 1993). This orientation also seemed to affect the way the parties discussed the issues (discussed later).

Second, social pressures may develop for the group to act cohesively, yet the members are in conflict with each other and cannot be cohesive unless they can find an acceptable solution. Members compare themselves with one another, evaluate themselves against one another, and try to use a variety of influence tactics to persuade one another toward their point of view (see Chapter 8 for a description of these tactics). Strong pressures for conformity develop as members pressure other members to adopt a common perspective or definition of the problem or to endorse a particular solution. In addition, the group can develop dysfunctional group dynamics. For example, if pressures to keep the group cohesive are strong, the group may attempt to avoid or minimize conflict by downplaying their differences or not working through them adequately to reach an effective solution. Janis's (1982, 1989) research on policy-making and decision-making groups has shown that these efforts to minimize and avoid conflict can frequently lead to disaster. Fiascoes such as the U.S. invasion of the Bay of Pigs in Cuba during the Kennedy administration (Janis, 1982) or NASA's decision to launch the Challenger space shuttle (Tompkins, 1993) were caused by dynamics in the key decision-making groups that left group members hesitant to create conflict and express their real reservations about going ahead with the project (see Box 13.1). This hesitancy led to an illusion of consensus in which each party believed that he was the only dissenting member in a fairly strong emerging agreement about what actions to take. Afraid to express their dissent for fear of looking weak and foolish (note the face-saving dynamics—see Chapter 11), group members self-censored their reservations and concerns, thereby reinforcing the apparent surface consensus and leading to a decision with disastrous consequences.

Procedural Complexity   A fourth way in which multiparty negotiations are more complex than two-party ones is that the process they have to follow is more complicated. In one-on-one

BOX 13.1   **Space Shuttle Challenger**

On January 28, 1986, the space shuttle Challenger exploded 73 seconds into its flight. All those on the flight were instantly killed, including civilian passengers specially recruited for the trip. Subsequent investigations placed part of the blame for this tragedy on leaders at the National Aeronautics and Space Administration (NASA) who failed to create a communication environment that allowed their subordinates to discuss openly potential technical difficulties. If communication had been more open, the Challenger might not have been lost.

In his book-length report on the Challenger disaster, Philip Tompkins (1993) noted that workers at NASA knew their director did not like to hear bad news. He had a tendency to "kill the messenger," particularly when faced with technical information that might necessitate delays in the launch schedule. Consequently, his subordinates communicated with him in a passive, nondirective style. In the days prior to Challenger's launch, engineers met to discuss potential technical difficulties with the flight based on the colder-than-usual weather. These technical professionals concluded

that launching the Challenger might be dangerous in cold-weather conditions. However, because meetings at NASA did not generally promote open exchange of ideas and debate, the indirect warnings they issued were ignored. Some professionals testified after the accident that they were intimidated by senior administrators at NASA and did not feel they could bring problems to the table for discussion. Instead, they relied on hints and technical memos to try to get their message across without angering their superiors.

Tompkins wrote that one purpose of his book was "to point out the value of communication, the dangers of defensiveness and unwillingness to face open appraisal" (p. 110). The Challenger disaster aptly demonstrates the tragedy that can strike if all members of a work team cannot speak openly in meetings and negotiations. Many who have studied this disaster have also pointed out that the dynamics Tompkins describes are dramatically similar to the characteristics of "groupthink" (Janis, 1982).

Source: Adapted from P. K. Tompkins, *Organizational Communication Imperatives: Lessons of the Space Program* (Los Angeles: Roxbury Publishing Company, 1993).

negotiations, the parties simply take turns in presenting their issues and perspectives, challenging the other's perspectives, or moving the negotiation along from its early stages to the later ones. When more parties are involved, the procedural rules become far less clear. Whose turn is it to do what? How do the parties coordinate where they are in the negotiations (e.g., opening statements, presentation of viewpoints, moving toward agreement)? There are several consequences of this procedural complexity. First, negotiations will take longer (Sebenius, 1983), so more time must be allowed. Second, the greater the number of parties, the more complex and out of control the process can become—particularly if some parties choose to adopt a strategy of tough positional bargaining and dominate the process in an effort to railroad through their particular viewpoints (Bazerman, Mannix, and Thompson, 1988). Third, as a result of the first two elements, negotiators will probably have to devote explicit discussion time to how they will manage the process to arrive at the type of solution or agreement they want. Finally, the parties must decide how they want to approach multiple issues on the table. Weingart, Bennett, and Brett (1993) reported that parties who discussed multiple issues simultaneously—considering all the issues at once and looking for ways to trade one off against another—achieved higher—quality agreements and increased the likelihood of achieving agreement compared with groups that approached the issues sequentially (one at a time, in a fixed or negotiated sequence). Groups that approached issues simultaneously also exchanged more information and had greater insight into the preferences and priorities of the other parties at the table.

Strategic Complexity   Finally, multiparty negotiations are more strategically complex than two-party ones. In one-on-one negotiations, the negotiator need only attend to the behavior of the other negotiator; strategy is therefore driven by the negotiator's objectives, the other party's actions, and the tactics they each use. The strategic and tactical options of two-party negotiations were discussed in Chapters 3, 4, and 5.

In a group negotiation, complexity increases significantly. The negotiator must consider the strategies of all the other parties at the table and decide whether to deal with each of them separately or as a group. The actual process of dealing with each of them usually evolves into a series of one-on-one negotiations—but conducted within the view of all the other group members. Viewed in this manner, this series of one-on-one negotiations can have several consequences.

First, these exchanges are subject to the surveillance and audience dynamics described in Chapter 11. In this context, negotiators will be sensitive to being observed and may feel the need to be tough to show their firmness and resolve (both to the other party and to bystanders or audiences). As a result, the social milieu may lead negotiators to adopt distributive strategies and tactics—even if they did not intend to do so—simply to show their toughness and resolve to others. The short-term result is that negotiators in the group may become strongly positional unless specific actions are taken to manage the group beyond this competitive escalation. A related dynamic is that once the parties have become strongly positional, negotiators will have to find satisfactory ways to explain modification of their positions—concession making or movement toward compromises and consensus—to their constituencies without the face-threatening dynamics discussed earlier. Even without constituencies, negotiators will not want to lose face with the other negotiators present. This will be particularly true in the situation shown in Figure 13.2, when negotiators have constituencies.

Second, negotiators who have some way to control the number of parties at the table (or even in the room) may begin to act strategically, using this control to serve their objectives. The tactic used will be determined by the strategic interests to be served by adding other parties. Additional parties may be invited to add support or credence to the negotiator's position, to provide "independent" testimony or support to a point of view, or simply to present a show of force. For example, when communities are in dispute about whether to build a new shopping center or school, change a zoning law, or present a new tax package, it is not uncommon for the agents who will publicly speak about the issue to pack the audience with a large number of supporters who will occasionally show their enthusiasm and support (or opposition) for a position. (Recall the discussion in Chapter 11 of enlisting audience support to pressure an opponent.) Thus, negotiators can strategically add parties to the negotiation, either to enhance their perceived power through sheer numbers or the prestige of the supporters or to present some credible threat about the consequences that will occur if the negotiators do not get their way.

Third, negotiators can explicitly engage in coalition building as a way to marshal support. Coalition dynamics were described in Chapter 12. Parties may explicitly or implicitly agree to support each other's positions in order to add collective weight to their combined view and then use this coalition to either dominate the negotiation process or shape the desired settlement. Coalitions may be explicitly formed prior to negotiations or during negotiation recesses and breaks, or they may emerge as the discussion proceeds. Two or more parties may begin to realize that they have compatible views and agree to help each other achieve their separate objectives as the group objective is attained.

Members of coalitions can exert their strength in multiparty negotiations in a number of ways: by expressing solidarity with each other, by agreeing to help each other achieve their common or individual objectives, by dominating discussion time, and by agreeing to support each other as particular solutions and negotiated agreements emerge. Murnighan (1986) has suggested that the emergence of consensus in decision-making groups proceeds as a "snowballing coalition." As noted earlier, coalitions are built one party at a time. Thus, in a group discussion, as parties share information and then deliberate possible solutions, a few people will emerge with a common perspective and then tacitly or explicitly agree to support each other's views. Other individuals then negotiate with the emerging coalition to incorporate their own views. Those who may be unwilling to negotiate or modify their views are eventually rejected and left out of the group decision.

The risk for those on the outside of an influential coalition is that they will not be an active participant in the discussions, some of which may occur in caucuses away from the main negotiating table. A study by Kim (1997) demonstrated that negotiators who are excluded from part of a multiparty negotiation receive a lesser share of the outcome than those who are present for the duration. Kim's findings showed that this is particularly damaging to the excluded party when he or she misses the second half of the discussion. The lesson seems to be that simply being present when key discussions occur is important, especially in the later stages as the parties hone in on a final settlement.

Polzer, Mannix, and Neale (1995, 1998) have argued that relationships are the most significant force in shaping which parties will enter coalitions with each other in a multiparty negotiation. When a relationship is in place, parties extensively incorporate the time dimension into their deliberations and side negotiations with each other. Thus, what the parties have done for each other in the past, and/or what they think they can do for each other in the future, has a strong impact on the current discussions. In addition, as we noted in Chapter 10, relationships may lead the parties to have similar preferences, to have strong concern for the others and a desire to help the others achieve their outcomes, and to create and sustain strong trust among group members.

Section Summary

There are five ways in which the complexity increases as three or more parties simultaneously engage in negotiation. First, there are simply more parties involved in the negotiation, which increases the number of speakers, increases the demand for discussion time, and increases the number of different roles the parties may play. Second, more parties bring more issues and positions to the table; thus, more perspectives must be presented and discussed. Third, negotiations become socially more complex—social norms emerge that affect member participation, and there may be stronger pressures to conform and suppress disagreement. Fourth, negotiations become procedurally more complex, and the parties may have to negotiate a new process that allows them to coordinate their actions more effectively. Finally, negotiations become more strategically complex because the parties must monitor the moves and actions of several other parties in determining what each will do next. In addition, the possibility of coalitions increases the likelihood that decisions will not be made by a comprehensive negotiated consensus but by some subgroup that can dominate the discussion and decision-making processes.

What Is an Effective Group?

Multiparty negotiation looks a lot like group decision making because it involves a group of parties trying to reach a common solution in a situation where the parties' preferences may diverge. Consequently, understanding multiparty negotiation means, in part, understanding the attributes of an effective group. Schwartz (1994) suggests that effective groups and their members do the following things:

1. *Test assumptions and inferences.* In effective groups, each individual member makes his or her assumptions and inferences clear by articulating them and checking them out with others. Unchecked assumptions and inferences can lead to unfounded conclusions.

2. *Share as much relevant information as possible.* In a competitive negotiation, parties are likely to use information strategically—sharing very little with other parties while attempting to gain much information from others. However, effective groups require the type of information sharing that occurs in integrative negotiation in order to maximize the information available to the group to find solutions that meet the interests of all parties. Thus, parties should discuss their interests, but not disclose their walkaway or BATNA.

3. *Focus on interests, not positions.* As in an integrative negotiation, group deliberations should use procedures that surface the underlying interests of individual members, rather than just their stated positions: sharing information, asking questions, and probing for underlying interests or needs.

4. *Explain the reasons behind one's statements, questions, and answers.* Disclosing interests requires that we be clear to others about what is most important and that we indicate the reasons *why* those things are important.

5. *Be specific—use examples.* Parties should attempt to talk in specific terms about directly observable behaviors, people, places, and events. Generalities can lead to misunderstandings or ambiguity that can send problem solving off the track.

6. *Agree on the meaning of important words.* Participants should be careful to fully explain and define key words or language that may be part of the agreement. For example, if group members agree that all decisions will be made by *consensus,* they should all have the same definition of what will constitute "consensus" in the group—voting procedures, general support by most members, or full support by 100 percent of the members.

7. *Disagree openly with any member of the group.* If parties withhold their disagreement, conflict is forced underground, which may ultimately lead to an inability to reach consensus or to implement a plan to which the group might agree. Disagreement can be productive without being offensive.

8. *Make statements, then invite questions and comments.* Diversity of viewpoints should not just be reserved for disagreeing with another, but it should also be invited *from* others: encourage others to clarify their own understanding of your interests and needs.

9. *Jointly design ways to test disagreements and solutions.* Develop a process for confirming facts, verifying interpretations of events, and surfacing the reasons for disagreements so that problem solving can move forward. This process can be facilitated by anyone who is not directly involved in the central debate. We return to this point later in the chapter.

10. *Discuss undiscussable issues.* Groups often have a number of issues that they consider undiscussable: group members who are not performing up to expectations (or who are behaving badly) or challenges to a boss in the room. Getting these issues on the table may be critical for the group to be productive. One approach is to discuss openly the undiscussability of an important norm, rule, or problem and to state the implied consequences of discussing that topic openly. As Schwartz notes, "If members can be assured that their fears will not be realized, they will be more willing to talk openly about previously undiscussable issues" (p. 82).

11. *Keep the discussion focused.* Team leaders should make sure that the conversation stays on track until everyone has been heard. Develop an agenda, and have the chair manage the process to ensure that discussions don't wander all over the map.

12. *Do not take cheap shots or otherwise distract the group.* Distractions, sarcasm, irrelevant stories, and humor are all distractions that take the group off task and off focus. Although some of this behavior is perhaps inevitable, both in groups that like each other a lot and those that have strong conflict, effective groups try to keep distractions to a minimum.

13. *Expect to have all members participate in all phases of the process.* All group members must be willing to contribute to all phases of the group process—sharing relevant information, working to help the group arrive at a solution, or helping manage the process.

14. *Exchange relevant information with nongroup members.* If outsiders are invited in as experts or important sources of information, they should be fully briefed on the group's ground rules for operation and asked to comply with them.

15. *Make decisions by consensus.* Although it is not always possible for groups to make unanimous decisions, groups should strive for consensus whenever possible. We return to discuss group decision rules later in the chapter.

16. *Conduct a self-critique.* Finally, in between decisions or major deliberations, groups should spend some time in a postmortem evaluating their process and effectiveness. Paradoxically, groups that do not work well together seldom take the time to evaluate their process, probably because they hope to avoid the anticipated conflict that might arise from discussing the dysfunctionality. Not surprisingly, not discussing the dysfunctionality usually makes it worse.

In summary, many of the principles of an effective decision-making group can be readily applied to a group negotiation. We now turn to exploring techniques that can be used to manage multiparty negotiations more effectively.

Managing Multiparty Negotiations

Given the additional complexity that occurs in a multiparty negotiation, what is the most effective way to cope? Touval (1988), who examined many multiparty and treaty negotiations in international diplomacy, outlined three key stages that characterize multilateral negotiations: the prenegotiation stage, managing the actual negotiations, and managing the agreement stage. In addressing these three stages, we also identify what a single negotiator can do when:

- The individual is simply one of the parties in a multiparty negotiation and wants to ensure that his or her own issues and interests are clearly incorporated into the final agreement.

- The individual wants to ensure that the group reaches the highest quality and best possible final agreement.

- The individual is responsible for managing a multiparty negotiation process to ensure that many of the strategic and procedural complexities are effectively managed.

The Prenegotiation Stage

This stage is characterized by a great deal of informal contact among the parties. During this stage, the parties tend to work on a number of important issues: who is at the table, whether coalitions can be formed, what roles group members will take, understanding the consequences of no agreement, and constructing an agenda.

Participants The parties must agree on who is going to be invited to the talks. If the group is already an intact one, this is an easy question. However, many complex international negotiations give a great deal of time to the question of who will be recognized and who can speak for others. Issues about participants can be decided on the basis of the following:

- Who must be included if a deal is to be reached (key coalition members)?
- Who could spoil the deal if they were excluded (possible veto players)?
- Whose presence is likely to help other parties achieve their objectives (desirable coalition members)?
- Whose presence is likely to keep other parties from achieving their objectives (key coalition blockers)?
- Whose status will be enhanced simply by being at the table? (This was often a key issue in the Palestinian–Israeli talks in the Middle East and in the Paris Peace Talks to end the Vietnam War—when the Viet Cong were invited to the table as a fully recognized party.)

Coalitions We discussed coalitions in detail in Chapter 12. It is not uncommon for coalitions to exist before negotiations begin or for coalitions to organize in anticipation of the meeting of all the parties. Naturally, coalitions will form to either promote or block a particular agenda.

TABLE 13.1 | Roles Commonly Played by Members of a Group

Task-Oriented Roles	Relationship-Oriented Roles	Self-Oriented Roles
Initiating/offering—offering new ideas	Encouraging—supporting others' comments, contributions	Blocking—act negatively, active and frequent disagreement with others
Information seeking—asking others for their views	Harmonizing—smoothing over conflict, reinforcing "we-ness" of the group	Recognition seeker—draw the group's attention to themselves, seek approval from others
Opinion seeking—asking others for their opinions, judgments	Compromising—shifting one's own position in order to find a middle ground of opinion between people	Dominator—speak frequently, dominate the conversation, manipulate the group toward their preferred outcome
Elaborating—clarifying, expanding on the topic	Gatekeeping—encouraging participation from those who do not speak often, discouraging participation from those who speak frequently	Avoider—remain quiet and disengaged, withhold contributions on either task or relationship issues
Evaluating—offering judgments about the topic	Standard setting—Asking for or offering standards for judging the team's effectiveness	
Coordinating—pulling together ideas proposed by others		
Energizing—creating excitement about the topic being discussed		

Source: Based on K. D. Benne and P. Sheats. "Functional Roles of Group Members," *Journal of Social Issues* 4 (1948), 41–49.

Defining Group Member Roles   If the group already has a structure, then roles—leaders, mediators, recordkeepers, and so on—will already have been determined. But if the group has not met before, then parties may begin to jockey for key roles. Some may want to lead, participate actively, and promote a particular agenda; others may wish to stay silent and be invisible; still others may wish to take a third-party role such as mediator or facilitator (see Chapter 19). Group members can play a number of different roles in a group. Table 13.1 describes three types of roles that members can play—*task roles,* which move the group along toward a decision or conclusion; *relationship roles,* which manage and sustain good relationships between group members, and *self-oriented roles,* which serve to bring attention to the individual group member, often at the expense of group effectiveness.

Understanding the Costs and Consequences of No Agreement   Brett (1991) suggests that negotiators need to understand the costs and consequences that will ensue if the group fails to agree. Earlier in this volume, we made that suggestion to negotiators in one-on-one encounters, in the discussion of a BATNA (cf. Chapters 2, 3, and 4). For example, suppose a group of vice presidents in a computer company is trying to decide which models of a new line of personal computers should be built next year, and the quantities of each one. To make this decision effectively, they must include in their decision options a consideration of what will happen if they fail to agree on what to do. Will someone else (i.e., the president) step in and decide for them? How will the president feel about the group if the members can't agree? Are the costs of impasse the same for every negotiator? Usually this is not the case—different agents have different costs associated with no agreement. For example, if the vice presidents cannot agree, the president may mandate the model line and quantities, which may have greater costs for the engineering and manufacturing departments (which would have to change over) than for the marketing and sales departments (which would have to design a new marketing and ad campaign regardless of what was done). The group members with the better impasse alternatives are likely to have more power in the negotiation because they care less about whether the group reaches a particular solution relative to no agreement. Finally, do group members perceive their agreement and no-agreement options accurately? There is much evidence that negotiators are prone to perceptual biases that lead them to believe they are better than others (refer back to Chapter 5), their options are better than others' options, they are more likely to achieve their outcomes than others, and they have more control over shaping an outcome than others (Taylor and Brown, 1988; Tyler and Hastie, 1991). In multiparty negotiations, these biases are likely to affect negotiators by inflating their sense of power and ability to win—leading them to believe that the no-agreement alternative is much better than it really is. Reality checking with others is important in keeping these biases under control: are group members really willing to live with the possible costs of no agreement, and at what point will the group be ready to endorse that possibility?

Learning the Issues and Constructing an Agenda   Finally, parties spend a great deal of time familiarizing themselves with the issues, absorbing information, and trying to understand one another's interests. They also spend time constructing an agenda. There are many reasons an agenda can be an effective decision aid:

- It establishes the issues to be discussed.
- Depending on how the issues are worded, it can also define how each issue is positioned and framed (refer back to our discussion of framing in Chapter 5).
- It can define the order in which issues are discussed.
- It can be used to introduce process issues (decision rules, discussion norms, member roles, discussion dynamics), as well as substantive issues, simply by including them.
- It can assign time limits to various items, thereby indicating the importance of the different issues.

In addition to creating an agenda, parties in the process might also agree to abide by a set of "ground rules"—ways to conduct themselves during the negotiation. LoFasto and Larson (2001) propose the Connect Model as a proven approach to building effective team relationships. Table 13.2 overviews the four key requirements and steps in this process model.

The Formal Negotiation Stage—Managing the Group Process and Outcome

Much of the multiparty negotiation process is a combination of the group discussion, bilateral negotiation, and coalition-building activities described earlier in this volume. It also incorporates a great deal of what we know about how to structure a group discussion so as to achieve an effective and endorsed result. The following approaches are likely to ensure a high-quality group decision.

TABLE 13.2 | The Connect Model and the Requirements for Building a Relationship

Four Requirements	Process Model
1. Can we agree to have a constructive conversation?	**C**ommit to the relationship—signal that you are ready to work on the problem and it is worth doing. **O**ptimize safety—you will do your best to not make the other feel defensive, and you will try to appreciate the other's point of view.
2. Can our conversation be productive enough to make a difference?	**N**arrow the discussion to one issue—identify one issue at a time in a nonthreatening way. **N**eutralize defensiveness—minimize using words, terms, or descriptions that make the other defensive.
3. Can we understand and appreciate each other's perspective?	**E**xplain and echo each perspective—tell the other what you observe, how it makes you feel, and the long-term consequences.
4. Can we all commit to making improvements?	**C**hange one behavior each—agree that each of you is going to change one behavior. **T**rack it!—determine ways to monitor progress.

Source: From F. LoFasto and C. Larson, *When Teams Work Best* (Thousand Oaks, CA: Sage Publications, 2001), p. 51.

Appoint an Appropriate Chair Multiparty negotiations will proceed more smoothly when it is clear to everyone involved who is chairing or facilitating the process. Often this role will be played by one of the interested parties, but multiparty negotiations can be greatly facilitated by the presence of a neutral chairperson who can implement many of the tactics described here. When feasible, the parties should seriously consider designating a chair who has little stake in the specific outcome but a strong interest in ensuring that the group works toward achieving the best possible outcome. As a practical matter, it is frequently the case that the chair will be drawn from within the circle of interested parties. Keep in mind that if a chairperson is also advocating a particular position or preferred outcome, it will be most difficult for that individual to act or be seen as neutral because the solution the person wants to obtain on the issues is likely to compromise (or be perceived to compromise) his or her neutrality or objectivity with respect to facilitating the process. See Box 13.2 for an inventory of constructive approaches to acting as a chair in multiparty negotiations.

Use and Restructure the Agenda A critical way to control the flow and direction of negotiation is through an agenda. Either the chair or the parties to the negotiation may introduce and coordinate the agenda. An agenda adds a high degree of structure, organization, and coordination to a discussion. Agendas provide low-power or disadvantaged groups a vehicle for getting their issues heard and addressed, assuming that they can get them on the agenda. However, the manner in which an agenda is built (by collective consensus at the beginning of a meeting versus by one person prior to the meeting) and who builds it will have a great deal of impact on the flow of the negotiation. Unless group members feel comfortable challenging the person who introduces a preemptive agenda, the agenda will go unquestioned and hence the implicit discussion structure and format it suggests will prevail. Negotiators entering a multiparty negotiation for which an (unacceptable) agenda has been created in advance should consider letting other parties know ahead of time that they

Chairing a Multiparty Negotiation BOX 13.2

Chairpersons of multiparty negotiations must be sensitive to keeping tight control over the group process while not directly affecting the group's outcome. When a group wants to achieve a consensus or unanimous decision, the responsibility of the chair is to be constantly attentive to the group process. Some pointers for how to chair a multiparty negotiation effectively include these:

1. Explicitly describe the role you will take as chair. Be clear that you are there only to manage process and that the group will determine the outcome.

2. Introduce the agenda or build one based on the group's issues, concerns, and priorities. Make sure the group has an opportunity to discuss, modify, or challenge the agenda before you begin.

3. Make logistical arrangements that will help the negotiation process. Does the physical setup of the room offer the best possible configuration for constructive discussion? Arrange for a flip chart, whiteboard, or overhead projector to write down issues and interests. Many negotiators find they benefit from common visual access to issues, proposals, and other information during the discussion.

4. Introduce necessary ground rules or let the parties suggest them. How long will the group meet? What is the expected output or final product? Will minutes be taken? Will the group take breaks? Where will negotiations take place? How and when can group members consult with their constituents?

5. Create or review decision standards and rules. Find standards for what parties believe will be a fair or reasonable settlement. What criteria will be used to assess whether a particular solution is fair, reasonable, and effective? How will the group ultimately decide to adopt an agreement?

6. Assure individual members that they will have an opportunity to make opening statements or other ways of placing their individual concerns and issues on the table. Be clear that once parties are familiar with the issues, simultaneous discussion of several issues can take place. This will permit trade-offs among issues rather than forcing a compromise on each individual issue.

7. Be an active gatekeeper. Make sure that people have a chance to speak and that the more vocal people do not dominate so that the less vocal people become silent and drop out. Ask the more vocal people to hold back and explicitly invite the more silent people to make comments and input. Often, as a group moves toward some form of agreement or consensus, some people participate less. Make sure that they have chosen not to participate, rather than simply dropped out because they don't think their views are worthwhile or important.

8. Listen for interests and commonalities. Encourage people to express interests, mirror them back, and encourage people to identify not only what they want, but also why they want it. Listen for priorities and concerns. Once the issues and interests have been identified, explicitly set aside a time for inventing options. Use brainstorming and other group decision-making techniques to generate options and evaluate them.

9. Introduce external information (studies, reports, statistics, facts, testimony from experts) that will help illuminate the issues and interests. Ask for hard data to support assertions (but be careful to refrain from engaging in aggressive "cross-examination" that will compromise your neutrality).

10. Summarize frequently, particularly when conversation becomes stalled, confused, or tense. State where you think the group is, what has been accomplished, and what needs to be done. Paraphrasing and summarizing brings the group back to reality and back on task.

BOX 13.3   Why Group Members Give Up

Researchers Paul Mulvey, Jack Veiga, and Priscilla Elsass (1996) note that group members are quite cynical about group decision making, and many report that they find group decision making so frustrating and tedious that they often raise the white flag and privately "check out" of the group rather than working hard to help others make a good decision. Here are some of the most common reasons group members engage in "self-limiting behavior" (quietly giving in rather than continuing to participate in the group discussion):

- *The presence of a perceived expert.* When they think that others in the group have a lot of expertise—and, more problematically, these group members show off their expertise—members will strongly limit their own participation, usually for fear of looking foolish in front of the expert.

- *The presence of a compelling argument.* When one or more people make a very strong, persuasive, and convincing argument—and particularly when it is made after a lot of fruitless discussion—other people will self-limit.

- *Lacking confidence in one's ability to contribute.* If someone is not extremely confident

about his or her own views, and doesn't want to take a risk, he or she will self-limit.

- *An unimportant or meaningless decision.* When people see the decision as having little or no impact on their operations, they will contribute less.

- *Pressure from others to conform to the group decision.* Strong pressures to align with the team's decision or join a coalition, or fear of retaliation, can push people to find their place.

- *A dysfunctional decision-making climate.* When people see other group members as frustrated, disorganized, or floundering, they may self-limit. Both weak leadership and the early stages of a decision process can lead to this judgment.

The authors proceed to recommend several strategies that team leaders can use—many of which are noted later in this section—to ensure that members do not drop out of the conversation early and create a false consensus.

Source: Adapted from P. W. Mulvey, J. F. Veiga, and P. M. Elsass, "When Team Members Raise a White Flag," *Academy of Management Review* 10, no. 1 (1996), pp. 40–49.

---

view the agenda itself as open to discussion or change. In other words, make sure that possible modifications to the agenda are part of the agenda.

Although an agenda may add needed structure to a complex negotiation, a drawback is that it may artificially partition related issues; as a result, issues may be discussed separately rather than coupled or traded off to exploit integrative potential. The parties using an agenda must be sensitive to the implicit structure it imposes, and they must be willing to challenge and reconfigure it if doing so will facilitate the emergence of an integrative, consensus-based agreement.

Ensure a Diversity of Information and Perspectives   A third way to facilitate the negotiation is to ensure that the group receives a wide variety of different perspectives about the task and different sources of information. Because the nature of the information changes depending on the group's task—for example, designing and implementing a change, finding the best possible solution to a problem, or simply finding a solution that is politically acceptable to several constituencies—it is difficult to prescribe what information is critical and how to ensure that the group is exposed to it. This can simply be a matter of making sure that the voices of all participants are heard (see Box 13.3 for insight on why some group members become silent in a group deliberation). In a study of cross-functional teams, Lovelace, Shapiro, and Weingart (2001) found that the effect of disagreement on task performance depended on (1) how the task disagreement was being communicated—collaboratively or contentiously, (2) how free team members felt to express task-related doubts, and (3) how effective the team's leader was assumed to be. More collaborative communications were likely to be associated with greater innovativeness, while an absence of contentious communications was associated with a team's freedom to express doubts about how the task should be approached. Thus, effective management of the process of sharing diverse views on the task is critical to achieving effective sharing of a diversity of views and perspectives on the problem.

Ancona and Caldwell (1988) suggest four group-member roles that may be useful during this information management phase: scouts, ambassadors, coordinators, and guards. Scouts patrol the environment and bring in relevant external information—reports, statistics, findings, and others' experience. Ambassadors represent a formal link to some important constituency (e.g., senior management); they help to acquire the resources the group needs to continue to operate and provide some limited information about the group's activities to constituencies (enough to give the constituency an idea about events and deliberations but not so much as to divulge private or confidential discussions). Coordinators provide a formal link between the group members and the constituencies they represent—frequently, negotiators are themselves the coordinators of input from their constituency into the group deliberations. Finally, guards are designated to keep some information inside the group and ensure that there are no leaks or premature disclosures of key information or discussions. Clearly, group members can play more than one role and can rotate roles in the course of a multiparty negotiation.

If there is a chair, he or she can ensure that the group receives input from each group member; that various constituencies and stakeholders have an opportunity to provide input (through written comments or opportunities for open testimony before the group); and that relevant reports, documents, or statistical analyses are circulated and discussed. Manz, Neck, Mancuso, and Manz (1997) suggest key process steps that a chair can implement to ensure having an effective, amicable disagreement on a team:

1. *Collect your thoughts and composure before speaking.* Avoid the temptation to "shoot from the hip" with emotion rather than reasoned arguments.

2. *Try to understand the other person's position.* In Chapters 6 and 10, we discussed techniques such as listening skills, mirroring, and role reversal to understand the other.

3. *Try to think of ways that you both can win.*

4. *Consider how important this issue is to you.* Is this your most important issue in the negotiation? Can you afford to sacrifice all or part of your position on this issue for gains elsewhere?

5. *Remember that you will probably have to work together with these people in the future.* Even out of anger and frustration, don't use tactics that will make you regret the conversation tomorrow.

Ensure Consideration of All the Available Information   One way to ensure that the group discusses all available information is to monitor discussion norms. Discussion norms reflect the way the group engages in sharing and evaluating the information introduced (Brett, 1991).

Although it would be highly desirable to do so, groups seldom consider in advance what discussion norms they are going to follow. In most cases, this failure is probably due to a lack of understanding about how much deliberations can be improved by following norms and rules that will enhance discussion. Several group norms can undermine an effective discussion:

- *Unwillingness to tolerate conflicting points of view and perspectives.* There may be many reasons for this: one or more members dislike conflict, are afraid that conflict will be uncontrollable, or see conflict as destructive to group cohesiveness. But as we noted earlier, the absence of conflict can also lead to disastrous decisions.

- *Side conversations.* Side conversations between two or three members of a group can sometimes be beneficial and sometimes detrimental. While people can often have a more comfortable conversation with one or two other people compared with an entire group, side conversations can also destroy the sense of unity in the group and the ability to come to agreement when consensus is critical. When a decision can benefit from unique perspectives and creative input, side conversations can be beneficial; however, when a group must remain unified and collectively embrace the outcome, side conversations may create more disruption and reduce the likelihood of achieving that unity (Swaab, Phillips, Diermeier, and Medvec, 2008).

- *No means for defusing an emotionally charged discussion.* Unless there is a way to release it, anger, frustration, or resentment can become mixed in with the substantive issues and hamper the group's efforts. Although a great deal of negotiation literature suggests that parties should simply be calm and rational at all times, doing so is simply not humanly possible. The more the parties care about a particular issue and are invested in it, the more likely it is that emotions will creep in. Vehicles must exist to allow the parties to vent their emotions productively.

- *Coming to a meeting unprepared.* Unfortunately, preparation for a meeting often consists of either no preparation at all or simply preparing one's own position. Attention to the others' positions or to assessing underlying interests and priorities requires thorough preparation.

Several strategies may be used to manage each of these three potentially destructive discussion norms. The parties must generate and exchange ideas in a manner that permits full exploration and allows everyone to have some input, yet avoids some of the destructive conflict and emotions that can occur. Bazerman, Mannix, and Thompson (1988) reviewed several group decision-making and brainstorming techniques that are frequently used to achieve this objective.

The Delphi Technique   A moderator structures an initial questionnaire and sends it out to all parties, asking for input. Parties provide their input and send it back to the moderator. The moderator summarizes the input and sends it back to the parties. Parties then evaluate the report, make further input, and return it to the moderator. Over a number of rounds, through the questions and inquiries shaped by the moderator, the parties can exchange a

- **No criticism is allowed.** No other member can say whether an idea is good or bad.

- **Questions can be asked only for clarification of an idea.**

- **Free-wheeling is a plus.** Wild and crazy ideas are welcome, and in fact they may help trigger other ideas from team members. Don't worry about whether the idea you voice is good, bad, silly, or realistic; just say it.

- **Go for quantity.** The more ideas you get from team members, the better this team effort will be.

- **Combine and improve ideas.** It is certainly fine to build on someone else's idea.

Source: C. C. Manz, Christopher P. Neck, James Mancuso, and K. P. Manz, *For Team Members Only* (New York: AMACOM, 1997), p. 135.

great deal of information and share different perspectives. The advantages are that the group has little face-to-face interaction, does not get bogged down in personal hostility or inefficient communications, and can go through several iterations. The limitations are that the real priorities and preferences of group members may not be expressed, and the way the problem is defined and shaped early in the process can greatly determine the outcome. The parties may miss opportunities to expand the pie of resources, redefine the problem in an important way, or truly evaluate important tradeoffs. Thus, the Delphi technique may tend to generate compromise settlements rather than truly creative, integrative solutions.

Brainstorming   In brainstorming, the parties are instructed to define a problem and then to generate as many solutions as possible without criticizing any of them. We discussed brainstorming in Chapter 3. Box 13.4 offers a list of critical rules to be used in brainstorming.

Nominal Group Technique   The nominal group technique typically follows brainstorming. Once the brainstormed list of solution options is created, group members can rank, rate, or evaluate the alternatives in terms of the degree to which each alternative solves the problem. The leader collects, posts, and records these ratings so that all group members have an opportunity to formally evaluate the options and vote on the ones they consider to be most effective.

Manage Conflict Effectively   As implied by many of the suggestions offered throughout this section, groups must generate many ideas and approaches to a problem—which usually creates conflict—while not allowing that conflict to either disrupt the information flow or create personal animosity. When done well, conflict is a natural part of group life that improves members' ability to complete tasks, work together, and sustain these relationships. When done poorly, conflict actively disrupts all of these processes. Jehn and Mannix (2001) have studied the development and management of conflict over time in high-performance task groups. They examined three kinds of conflict typical to work groups: relationship conflict (interpersonal incompatibilities; dislike among group members; and feelings of tension, friction, annoyance, frustration, and dislike), task conflicts (awareness of difference in viewpoints about the group's task), and process conflict (awareness of controversies about how task accomplishment will proceed—who will do what, how much one should get from a result, etc.). High-performing teams were characterized by low, but increasing, levels of process conflict; low levels of relationship conflict with a rise near the deadline; and moderate levels of task conflict at the midpoint of the interaction. Those teams that were able to create this ideal conflict profile had similar preestablished work-related value systems among the group members, high levels of trust and respect, and open discussion norms around conflict during the middle stages of the interaction.

In a related study, Benfar, Peterson, Mannix, and Trochim (2008) studied conflict resolution procedures in effective and ineffective teams. They discovered that groups that maintain or improve their top performance over time share three conflict resolution strategies: (1) they focus on the content of the interactions with the other party rather than the other party's delivery style, (2) they explicitly discuss the reasons behind any decisions reached in accepting and distributing work assignments, and (3) they assign work to members who have relevant task experience rather than assigning them based on convenience or volunteering. Effective groups both anticipate that they will have to deal with conflict and have developed multiple strategies for dealing with them when they arise.[2]

Review and Manage the Decision Rules In addition to monitoring the discussion norms and managing the conflict processes effectively, the parties also need to manage the decision rules—that is, the way the group will decide what to do (Brett, 1991). In decision-making groups, the dominant view is to assume that the majority rules and, at some point, take a vote of all members, assuming that any settlement option that receives more than 50 percent of the votes will be the one adopted. Obviously, this is not the only option. Groups can make decisions by dictatorship (one person decides); oligarchy (a dominant minority coalition decides); simple majority (one more person than half the group decides); two-thirds majority; quasi-consensus (most of the group agrees, and those who dissent agree not to protest or raise objections); and true unanimity, or consensus (everyone agrees). Determining the group's decision rule before deliberations begin also significantly affects the group process. For example, if a simple majority will make the decision in a five-person group, then only three people need to agree. Thus, any three people can get together and form a coalition during or even prior to the meeting. In contrast, if the decision rule will be consensus, or unanimity, then the group must meet and work hard enough to ensure that all parties' interests are raised, discussed, and incorporated into the group decision. Deciding whether a coalition-building strategy or a complete sharing of positions, interests, and problem solving is necessary requires significantly different approaches.

Table 13.3 summarizes the three different negotiating strategies and the related tactics, decision rules, goal orientations, and decision aids. Each of the three strategies—maximizing individual gain, entering into a coalition, or pursuing mutual gain (consensus or unanimity decision rules)—is outlined, along with the tactics, decision rules, goal orientations, and decision aids that accompany each. As the chart reveals, any one set of elements can drive the others—decision rules or goals can drive the approaches, or vice versa. Thus, negotiators would do well to understand the decision rules and goal orientations before selecting a strategy and set of tactics. Similarly, negotiators need to understand the consequences of adopting an approach (strategy and tactics) that may not fit the related decision

TABLE 13.3 | Tactics, Decision Rules, Goal Orientations, and Decision Aids for Mutual, Coalition, and Individual Gain

Mutual	Coalition	Individual
Tactics		
1. Share own and elicit others' interests	1. Seek similar others and construct an alternative that meets your interests	1. Open with a high, but not outrageously high, demand
2. Consider many alternatives; be creative; look for ways to use available resources	2. Recruit just enough members to control the group's decision	2. Argue the merits of your alternative; do not reveal your interests
3. Don't just compromise, make trade-offs	3. Encourage interpersonal obligations among coalition members	3. Appear unable or unwilling to concede
4. Encourage positive relations		4. Encourage positive relations
		5. Use threats, time deadlines, and promises, if necessary
Decision Rules		
Consensus	Oligarchy	Dictator
Unanimity	Majority	
Goal Orientation		
Cooperative	Cooperative or Individual	Individual
Decision Aids		
Packaging	Packaging	
Search models	Search models	

Source: From J. Brett, "Negotiating Group Decisions," *Negotiation Journal,* July 1991, pp. 291–310. Used with permission of Plenum Publishing Corporation.

rules and goal orientations, because mismatches are likely to produce frustration, poor group process, and perhaps suboptimal outcomes.

Strive for a First Agreement   Finally, if the objective is consensus or the best quality solution, negotiators should not strive to achieve it all at once. Rather, they should strive for a *first agreement* that can be revised, upgraded, and improved. As we have discussed, the additional complexity of multiparty negotiations increases the complexity of the events, the likelihood of communication breakdown, and the likelihood that the parties will negotiate more positionally (either because of the competitive dynamics or the consequences of audience or constituency dynamics). Given these conditions, achieving true consensus among the parties becomes much more difficult, even if a true consensus solution exists. As a result, it is often better to set a more modest objective for these negotiations: to reach a preliminary agreement or a tentative consensus that can then be systematically improved through "renegotiation," using the first agreement as a plateau that can be modified, reshaped, tweaked, and improved upon in a follow-up negotiation effort.

The drawback, of course, is that many group members may be satisfied with the first solution—either because it already incorporates their views or because the difficulty of achieving it may sap their enthusiasm for exerting any time and energy to improve it. First agreements typically reflect the position of a group's majority or the views of a small number of powerful group members (Brett, 1991; Nemeth, 1986, 1989). These parties may not be open to dissenting views that would otherwise stimulate consideration of a wider set of possible alternative outcomes. As Brett (1991) notes:

> Majority and powerful individuals, however, are often intolerant of dissent. After all, why should they risk losing control over the group decision by providing an opportunity for dissent? A second agreement resolves this dilemma. It preserves the control of the powerful party—if no better agreement is forthcoming, the first agreement will stand. It also protects the interests of both the majority and the minority, letting them reveal information about their weaknesses and hidden agendas without fear that the group will use the information against them. At their best, second agreement deliberations encourage the sharing of minority points of view, the questioning of assumptions, the discussion of decision ramifications, the search for superior alternatives and the testing of consensus. (p. 294)

This resistance to further deliberations by parties who are happy with the first agreement may be overcome by taking a break after the first agreement is reached, encouraging the group to critique and evaluate the first agreement, and explicitly planning to come back with a commitment to try second-agreement negotiations (renegotiations). In addition, if the group has been through a great deal of divisive and unproductive conflict to reach the first agreement, then the renegotiations must specifically attend to changing and managing the conflict process. As Brett (1991) states, effectively attending to this process may also allow a group to achieve a high-quality outcome in their first negotiation effort. Finally, "first agreements" can serve as an anchor (see Chapter 5), which might make it difficult for a group to move toward some significantly different solution once the first agreement has been reached.

Manage Problem Team Members   Finally, the behaviors of individual team members may be a source of difficulty for group process. Members may show up late for meetings, fail to prepare adequately, distract the group with side comments and humor, or neglect to put in their fair share of work. Unfortunately, there is a tendency for many groups to try to ignore these individuals rather than to address their behavior and try to change it. Manz et al. (1997) suggest the following tactics for dealing with problem team members:

1. Be specific about the problem behavior—offer clear, specific examples.
2. Phrase the problem as one that is affecting the entire team, rather than just you. Use "we" instead of "you," which sounds much more accusatory and is likely to make the other defensive.
3. Focus on behaviors the other can control. The purpose is not to criticize or embarrass, but to focus on specific behaviors that the individual can control and modify.

*"And now at this point in the meeting I'd like to shift
the blame away from me and onto someone else."*

4.   Wait to give constructive criticism until the individual can truly hear and accept it. Consult with the problem person in private, and when he or she is not pressured to go elsewhere or deal with some major problem.

5.   Keep feedback professional. Use a civil tone and describe the offending behavior and its impact specifically. Make the tenor of the conversation adult to adult, not parent to child.

6.   Make sure the other has heard and understood your comments. Ask him or her to repeat or rephrase so that you know you have been heard.

In Chapter 17, we also address strategies for dealing with other negotiators whose behavior can be called difficult.

The Agreement Stage

The third and final stage in managing multiparty negotiations is the agreement stage. During the agreement stage, the parties must select among the alternatives on the table. They are also likely to encounter some last-minute problems and issues, such as deadline pressures, the discovery of new issues that were not previously addressed, the need for more information on certain problems or concerns, and the tendency for some parties to threaten veto power while they lobby to get their specific pet idea or project included in the final group agreement. Many of the tactics to be used in this stage are similar to the ones we prescribed in Chapters 3 and 4. Four key problem-solving steps occur during this phase (Schwartz, 1994):

• *Select the best solution.* The group must weigh the alternatives they have considered and either select a single alternative or combine alternatives into a package that will satisfy as many members as possible.

• *Develop an action plan.* This increases the likelihood that the solution will be implemented completely, effectively, and on time. For example, a good action plan might include a list of key steps, the objectives to be achieved at each step, when the step should be started and completed, what resources are needed to complete the step, and who has responsibility for completing the step. Working on this plan can also cause ambiguities or omissions from the earlier discussion to surface, thus preventing greater conflict down the road when implementation has begun.

• *Implement the action plan.* This is likely to take place after the group disbands or outside the scope of the group, but it needs to follow the guidelines established by the group. Without an effective action plan, the problems that might have been recognized at this point are sure to occur.

• *Evaluate outcomes and the process.* Conducting an evaluation of the process and the outcome can be critical for surfacing data about the group's working effectiveness. This evaluation need not occur at the same time or place as the decision meeting, but it should not be deferred or omitted. If team members are unwilling to raise criticisms publicly, anonymous questionnaires can be completed, summarized, and sent back to the group by the leader or a neutral facilitator, who can then use the data to highlight specific concerns about faulty process or incomplete outcomes. For example, in hostage negotiations, the police hostage team specifically debriefs after every incident to determine what they can learn and how to perform more effectively in the future (see Box 13.5).

What the Chair Can Do to Help   In addition to the list of chair responsibilities outlined in Box 13.2, here are some things a group facilitator can do to keep the group moving toward a successful completion:

• *Move the group toward selecting one or more of the options.* Use the process rules we discussed earlier, as well as the wide variety of techniques for achieving an integrative agreement presented in Chapter 3. Listen for the emergence of the "snowballing coalition" among key members (see Chapter 12). Permit and encourage packaging and trade-offs among multiple issues or modification of the first agreement or tentative agreement reached earlier. If the decision is particularly laden with conflict, pursue a first agreement with the understanding that the group will take a break and come back to renegotiate the agreement at a later date.

In an application of coalition negotiation, authors Bahn and Louden (1999) point out that hostage negotiation is often mistakenly seen as two-person exchange between the hostage-taker and the hostage negotiator. Instead, hostage negotiation represents a team effort that involves an elaborate coalition of individuals, each with his or her specific role, all working to ensure the safety of those involved.

The authors presented an example of a two-day hostage situation at an urban hospital. During the 48-hour standoff, 250 police department personnel were deployed, ranging in duties from traffic control officers to the police commissioner. In addition, government employees were present, along with 25 tactical team members and 8 trained hostage negotiators. The authors described this effort as highly interdependent, with each individual depending on the others to fulfill her mission.

After the hostage event is over, team members get together to discuss and process the outcomes of the negotiation. Discussions are meant to be constructive, focusing on what could have been done better and what needs to be changed for future hostage situations. Meetings also serve as a forum for team members to decompress and vent their frustrations after an intense experience.

Source: C. Bahn and R. J. Louden, "Hostage Negotiation as a Team Enterprise," *Group* 23 (2) (1999), pp. 77–85.

- *Shape and draft the tentative agreement.* Write it down. Work on language. Write the wording on a whiteboard, flip chart, or overhead projection that can be displayed to the entire group, so that all can see it and edit it freely. Test to make sure all parties understand the agreement and its implications and consequences. Remember that the person who does the writing often has more power than others because he or she gets to write the agreement in his or her own language and may bias or selectively remember some points and omit others.

- *Discuss whatever implementation and follow-up or next steps need to occur.* Make sure that individuals who have a role in this process understand what they need to do. Make assignments to individuals to ensure that key action steps are designed and executed. Schedule a follow-up meeting. Plan for another meeting in the future to evaluate how the agreement is working.

- *Thank the group for their participation, their hard work, and their efforts.* If the discussion has been particularly difficult or required a large time commitment, a small group

THE CHRONICLE OF HIGHER EDUCATION

V S HIXSON
VIVIAN SCOTT HIXSON

"Okay. The resolution is that since nobody on the committee took notes last week, and nobody can remember what happened, what we did last week probably didn't matter. All in favor say 'Aye.'"

Used by permission of Vivian Scott Hixson.

celebration and formal thank-you notes or gifts may be in order. Have dinner or a party together to celebrate all the hard work.

• *Organize and facilitate the postmortem.* Have group members discuss the process and the outcome and evaluate what they might do better or differently the next time. This will ensure learning for both the group members and the chair.

Interteam Negotiations

In this final section of the chapter, we examine negotiations where the parties are working in teams rather than as single individuals. We use the term *inter-team negotiation* to describe these situations: two or more co-negotiators sharing interests and priorities who negotiate with two or more co-negotiators on the other side who share their own interests and priorities (Shapiro and Von Glinow, 1999). In Chapter 11 we discussed how additional team members at the negotiation table provide an audience that influences the roles individuals assume during the negotiation. Here we address a broader set of questions about negotiation processes when teams are present:

• Do teams behave differently than individuals?

• How does the presence of two or more people change the way one party interacts with the other party and advances its own interests?

• Are teams more likely to act competitively, or are they more inclined to pursue cooperative strategies that would lead to integrative outcomes?

Only a small number of research studies have investigated these issues. We can summarize the findings of these studies in four broad conclusions.

Integrative Agreements Are More Likely When Teams Are Involved   A study by Thompson, Peterson, and Brodt (1996) compared negotiations between teams, negotiations between individuals, and (mixed) negotiations where a team negotiates against an individual. They found that joint profits for the two parties are greater when at least one of the parties is a team. Part of the explanation was that teams exchange more information than solo negotiators, which increases the likelihood that integrative potential can be discovered and exploited. Even when a team negotiates against a solo negotiator, the positive benefits of team negotiation occur. Polzer (1996) showed that the benefit of teams for achieving integrative outcomes might depend on *experience:* when negotiators were novices, the presence of teams reduced the integrativeness of settlements. However, when trained negotiators were involved, the presence of teams led to more integrative outcomes. In general, however, the presence of at least one team seems to trigger behaviors that enhance integrativeness. As Thompson and colleagues (1996, p. 75) state, "team negotiation initiates a process of information exchange that is mutually beneficial for all parties."

Teams Are Sometimes More Competitive Than Individuals and May Claim More Value
A substantial research tradition in game theory has shown that groups tend to be highly competitive in their dealings with other groups (e.g., McCallum, et al., 1985). Does this extend to the realm of negotiation? Research efforts to explore this issue have yielded mixed

findings. In one study of the effects of negotiating teams on competition, cooperation, and trust, Polzer (1996) found that when teams are present in negotiations, there is more contentiousness and less trust between the parties. Other studies, however, failed to find differences between the competitiveness of negotiating teams versus individuals (O'Connor, 1997; Thompson et al., 1996).

Competitiveness aside, are teams better than individuals at the distributive component of negotiation—claiming the value that the parties have created? Research to date points to an advantage for teams. In one of the key recent studies of team negotiations that we have discussed (Thompson et al., 1996), teams claimed more value than solo negotiators in one experiment, but not in another involving the same negotiation task. Polzer (1996) found that teams did better than the individuals against whom they were negotiating in mixed (team versus solo) matchups. One partial explanation lies in Polzer's finding that negotiating teams were perceived as having more power than individuals. These studies point to two implications for an individual facing a negotiating team on the other side: (1) be attentive to the possibility that the team will be aggressive in pursuing its interests and claiming value, and (2) avoid the trap of assuming that the other party has disproportionate power merely because it elected to send a team to negotiate.

Accountability Pressures Are Different for Teams Compared to Individuals   As we discussed in Chapter 11, individual negotiators are more likely to behave in a more competitive manner when they are accountable to constituents than when accountability pressures do not exist. This occurs, at least in part, because negotiators feel a need to show "toughness" when the people on whose behalf they are negotiating can observe their performance. However, a study by O'Connor (1997) reveals that teams of negotiators do not respond in the same way to constituent surveillance. In her experiment, accountability increased the competitive behavior of solo negotiators to a significantly greater degree than it did for negotiating teams. O'Connor's findings suggest that the pressures created by accountability are distributed and diffused among the members of a negotiating team, leading individual team members to perceive less responsibility for the outcomes that result from the negotiation.

The Relationship among Team Members Affects Negotiation Process and Outcomes
Peterson and Thompson (1997) examined what happens when teams comprised of friends negotiate against teams of strangers. Not surprisingly, they found that teams of friends were more cohesive as a group, and more focused on maintaining their relationship, than were teams of strangers. For teams of strangers, more cohesiveness was associated with improved negotiating performance. Peterson and Thompson found that the relationship among team members affected how information was used to reach a negotiated outcome. Specifically, when individuals on the team had unique information about the team's interests and preferences, teams of strangers were able to claim more of the joint profit on the table than were teams of friends. The issue of accountability also played a role in Peterson and Thompson's study. When teams of strangers were accountable for their negotiating performance (to a supervisor), they did better (claimed a greater share of joint profit) than did teams of friends who were similarly accountable. Taken as a whole, these findings indicate that relationships among team members complicate the ways that teams use information

and tactics to work toward a negotiated settlement. As a general matter, Peterson and Thompson found that teams of strangers outperform teams of friends under some conditions, but that teams of friends never outperform teams of strangers. We do not conclude that it is necessarily "bad" for individuals negotiating as a team to be friends or acquaintances, but it does appear that when team members have a preexisting friendly relationship, they need to be especially vigilant about not allowing those friendships to interfere with the pursuit of optimal outcomes. Teams of strangers, on the other hand, may be able to improve their performance by taking the time to become a more cohesive operating unit before entering the negotiation.

Chapter Summary

Most negotiation theory has been developed under the assumption that negotiation is a bilateral process—that there are only two focal negotiators or teams of negotiators opposing each other. Yet many negotiations are multilateral or group deliberations—more than two negotiators are involved, each with his or her own interests and positions, and the group must arrive at a collective agreement regarding a plan, decision, or course of action. In this chapter, we explored the dynamics of two forms of multiparty negotiations: when multiple parties must work together to achieve a collective decision or consensus and when two or more teams are opposing each other in a negotiation.

One theme that runs through all forms of multiparty negotiation is the need to actively monitor and manage negotiation process situations that are significantly more complex than two-party negotiations. We present here a brief set of questions that any participant in negotiations involving coalitions, multiple parties, or teams should keep in mind:

- What are the consequences of the parties failing to agree due to the increased complexities? What happens if there is no agreement?

- How will the parties involved actually make a decision? That is, what decision rules will be used? Why are these the best possible rules?

- How can the parties use iterations—multiple rounds of discussion—to achieve their objectives? (This may be particularly appropriate when the decision rule is consensus—or the best-quality agreement—because consensus may not be achievable in a single iteration.)

- Do we need a designated chair or facilitator? Should it be a neutral outsider, or can one of the parties fill this role? What tactics can a facilitator use to manage group process in order to ensure that the best decision is reached? (These tactics might include ensuring that the group is exposed to a variety of information sources, managing the process to make sure that the group considers and discusses all available information thoroughly, and structuring the group's agenda with care.)

If these issues are raised and thoughtfully considered, the parties involved are considerably more likely to feel better about the process and to arrive at an effective outcome than if these factors are left to chance.

Endnotes

[1] These sections draw heavily on the work of Bazerman, Mannix, and Thompson (1988); Brett (1991); and Kramer (1991), who provide excellent overviews of the problems and challenges of multiparty negotiation.

[2] For additional ideas on managing conflict in groups, see Cloke and Goldsmith (2005).

CHAPTER 14

Individual Differences I: Gender and Negotiation

Objectives

1. Understand the distinction between sex and gender.
2. Explore alternative conceptual approaches to gender and social interaction.
3. Consider differences in how men and women negotiate, and in how they are treated by others in negotiation.
4. Gain ways to overcome negotiation disadvantages that result from gender differences and stereotypes.

Some people are better negotiators than others. What characteristics of individuals make a difference in negotiation? How do the best negotiators behave, think, or feel that make them different from average negotiators? Researchers have been examining the effects of individual differences on the process and outcome of negotiations for years, and we devote the next two chapters to an examination of these differences. We confess right at the start that some of the research findings in this area are fragmented, contradictory, or difficult to apply in practical settings. However, research on this topic has yielded some important insights, and we spend this chapter and the next one discussing some new research findings that appear to be particularly promising in this area.

In this chapter we focus exclusively on the individual difference that has received more attention from negotiation researchers than any other: gender differences. In Chapter 15 we examine a range of other individual difference factors, including personality traits and abilities. All of these things—gender, personality traits, native abilities—are what psychologists think of as "stable" individual differences, meaning they are attributes that change only very gradually over time, if at all. If these aspects of individuals are stable and unchangeable, then are they worth worrying about? Some scholars (e.g., Bazerman, Curhan, Moore, and Valley, 2000) question the value of exploring individual differences in negotiation because (1) they don't predict negotiation processes and outcomes as well as situations do, and (2) in any event, stable individual differences are generally not under the individual negotiator's control.

Both of these assertions are correct, but they don't necessarily annul the value of examining individual differences in negotiation. We point to three ways that negotiators can benefit from an understanding of the role of individual differences. First, although negotiators may not be able to choose their own traits or abilities, there are many situations (e.g., in business or professional life) in which a manager has the opportunity to choose a negotiator from among multiple candidates who differ from each other on relevant attributes. Second, as we show in these two chapters, we can link some individual differences to liabilities or disadvantages for the negotiator that can be compensated for through awareness and concerted effort. Third, a grasp of the benefits and drawbacks of relevant individual differences can help the negotiator diagnose the other party's talents, tendencies, and limits, and adjust strategy and tactics accordingly.

Our examination in this chapter of gender differences, which some might prefer to call sex differences, will begin by distinguishing between the terms *sex* and *gender*. We then examine research on gender differences in negotiation. This will involve, first, a review of theoretical perspectives on why one might expect differences. We then look at the empirical research evidence. There have been some exciting new research developments in this area in the last few years, giving us a clearer picture of the underlying psychology of gender in negotiation. Some of that research points to gender differences that can put a negotiator at a disadvantage. We close this chapter with some suggestions for overcoming gender-based disadvantages in negotiation.

Defining Sex and Gender

The terms *sex* and *gender* in common usage outside of scientific circles are seemingly treated as synonyms. However, the distinction is important to biologists, psychologists, and other scientists; hence we take this opportunity to make the distinction clear and to justify the usage we will adopt in this chapter.

Sex refers to the *biological* categories of male and female. As one standard dictionary of English puts it, *sex* is "the property or quality by which organisms are classified as female or male on the basis of their reproductive organs and functions."[1] *Gender* refers to *cultural* and *psychological* markers of the sexes—the aspects of role or identity (rather than biology) that differentiate men from women in a given culture or society. This is more than just a semantic difference. Those who investigate sex differences believe that differences are rooted primarily in biology, whereas investigators who examine gender lean toward social explanations for differences in behavior (Deaux, 1985). Few investigators would support purely biological (nature) or purely social (nurture) explanations of behavior; rather, it is a difference in focus or in the balance of implicit assumptions underlying the research.

Most of the empirical research on male/female differences in negotiation has examined sex differences (i.e., compared men and women), but has posited theoretical aspects of gender to account for differences found. For instance, a typical experiment may compare how males and females bargain in integrative negotiations. If differences are found, they are interpreted in relation to gender (e.g., men and women are socialized differently as children and adolescents, and this explains an aspect of adult bargaining behavior).

Consistent with this pattern, the trend seems to be for negotiation researchers to rely predominantly on the term *gender*. For example, a comprehensive review of sex/gender/negotiation research by two leading scholars in this area (Kray and Babcock, 2006) refers almost exclusively to gender in describing both existing research findings and their conceptual underpinnings and implications. One of these authors explains that research in this vein is for the most part examining socialized differences, not differences that can be traced to biological causes or markers; hence, the term *gender* is appropriate and preferred.[2] We agree, so we emphasize throughout this chapter the term and the concept of *gender,* given its primacy as the underlying theoretical explanation for the research discussed.

Research on Gender Differences in Negotiation

The search for gender differences is the most researched individual difference topic in negotiation. Until recently, this research tended to yield contradictory findings; some research suggests that there is little or no difference between male and female negotiators,[3] whereas other research documents significant differences between male and female negotiators.[4] Two large-scale meta-analytic reviews[5] of the literature on gender differences in negotiation have concluded that women behave more cooperatively in negotiation than men (Walters, Stuhlmacher, and Meyer, 1998) and that men tend to negotiate better outcomes than women (Stuhlmacher and Walters, 1999). For both of these conclusions, however, the differences, while statistically significant, are small.

There might be no simple answer to the question of how gender influences negotiation, but recent studies are shedding light on differences that do exist and on why it can be hard to find them in broad-brush comparisons of male and female negotiators. In a nutshell, the *situation* matters: given certain circumstances, gender differences emerge; in other circumstances, they are elusive. To pursue this, our discussion here begins with theoretical critiques of previous research on sex and gender in negotiation and then reviews recent empirical work that is beginning to yield some interesting findings.

Male and Female Negotiators: Theoretical Perspectives

Although gender differences have long been of interest in the study of bargaining and other forms of interpersonal interaction, this subject was injected with new life in the 1990s with the application of feminist theory to negotiation.[6] This work clearly delineates that negotiation is a gendered activity (Kolb and Putnam, 1997), whereas the focus of much negotiation theory is on autonomous people who work to achieve instrumental outcomes (Gray, 1994). These theorists identify several key aspects of negotiation that have been undervalued by negotiation theory and research (see Harding, 1986, for a general discussion). For instance, until fairly recently, the focus on the instrumental value of negotiating has led to the neglect of the importance of relationships in negotiation. Because relationships may influence how negotiations are perceived, framed, and conducted, researchers' inattention to relationships may have undervalued their importance in understanding negotiation dynamics (Gray, 1994).

The view that seems to prevail among researchers is that there are differences in how males and females negotiate but that these differences are difficult to detect (Kolb and Coolidge 1991). In addition, researchers have only recently begun to address the critical question of *how* gender influences negotiation. Does it affect negotiator preferences? Strategies and tactics? Concessions? Outcomes? Situational factors combine with gender to influence these variables in complex ways, making it difficult for gender to have the generalized influence it is expected to have.

If the prevailing view is that male and female negotiators differ, then what are the differences that are theoretically presumed to exist? Scholars writing on this subject have argued that several important factors affect how women and men approach negotiations.

1. Relational View of Others   Women are more aware of the complete relationship among the parties who are negotiating and are more likely to perceive negotiation as part of the larger context within which it takes place than to focus only on the content of the issues being discussed (Kolb and Coolidge, 1991). Consequently, women may place a greater emphasis on interaction goals (the interpersonal aspects of the negotiations), whereas men are driven more by task-specific goals (Kray and Babcock, 2006). This could have important implications for how male versus female negotiators attend to the other party versus the issues on the table. As we said in Chapter 3, learning how the other party perceives the situation may be just as important as attending to substantive needs and interests that are discussed during the negotiation.

2. Embedded View of Agency   Kolb and Coolidge (1991) argue that women tend not to draw strict boundaries between negotiating and other aspects of their relationships with other people but instead see negotiation as a behavior that occurs within relationships without large divisions marking when it begins and ends. In contrast, men tend to demarcate negotiating from other behaviors that occur in the relationship and to signal the beginning and end of the negotiations behaviorally. Because women are more likely to see negotiations as flowing naturally from the relationship, they may be less likely "to recognize that negotiations are occurring unless they are specifically demarcated from the background against which they occur" (Kolb and Coolidge, 1991, p. 265).

3. Beliefs about Ability and Worth   An individual's expectations and perceived self-worth affect how he or she approaches the negotiation table. One possible explanation for gender differences in salary negotiation outcomes is that women are more likely to see their worth as determined by what the employer will pay (Barron, 2003). It has also been demonstrated that men expect to earn more than women over the course of their career (Major and Konar, 1984). In addition, women may feel less comfortable operating in the social context of negotiation in general (Small, Gelfand, Babcock, and Gettman, 2007), which in turn could undermine self-confidence that good outcomes are achievable.

4. Control through Empowerment   Women and men perceive and use power in different ways. Women are more likely to seek empowerment where there is "interaction among all parties in the relationship to build connection and enhance everyone's power" (Kolb and Coolidge, 1991, p. 265). Men can be characterized as using power to achieve their own goals or to force the other party to capitulate to their point of view. While women's conceptualization of power may make them more comfortable than men with integrative versus distributive negotiation, the fit is not perfect.

5. Problem Solving through Dialogue   Women and men use dialogue in different ways, a tendency that first appears in very young children (Sheldon and Johnson, 1994). Women "seek to engage the other in a joint exploration of ideas whereby understanding is progressively clarified through interaction"; they also alternatively listen and contribute, and this results in "the weaving of collective narratives that reflect newly-emerging understanding" (Kolb and Coolidge, 1991, p. 266). Contrast this with men, who use dialogue *(a)* to convince the other party that their position is the correct one and *(b)* to support various tactics and ploys that are used to win points during the discussion.

6. Perceptions and Stereotypes   How the negotiator perceives and "frames" the process of negotiation may have important effects on negotiation behavior. In Chapter 5 we discussed perceptual frames and stereotypes as influences on the negotiation process. Kray and Babcock (2006) refer to the notion that men have an advantage in negotiation as a "dominant cultural stereotype." For the female negotiator, this may mean a reputation that precedes her. Negative stereotypes about female bargainers shape expectations and behaviors by both men and women at the negotiating table.

Empirical Findings on Gender Differences in Negotiation

Earlier we mentioned a couple of large-scale reviews of research pointing to conclusions that women behave more cooperatively than men, while men reap better outcomes, but we cautioned that these effects are small in magnitude. A more compelling and useful perspective on gender differences emerges when we look beyond broad-brush inferences, and focus on specific cognitive and behavioral processes. In this section we research on five of those processes: (1) how men and women think about negotiation, (2) how they communicate in negotiation, (3) how they are treated within negotiation, (4) how they respond to tactics, and (5) how they are influenced by stereotypes.

1. Men and Women Conceive of Negotiations in Different Ways   There is a growing body of evidence that male and female negotiators have very different views of what it means to negotiate and what the process of negotiation is about. We discuss here a few ways this can occur.

How Conflict Is Framed: Relationship versus Task Orientation   Robin Pinkley (1990, 1992) explored how disputants interpret, or "frame," conflict situations.[7] In her research people remembered and described a recent dispute in which they were involved. Pinkley found that disputants use three dimensions to interpret conflicts: relationship versus task, emotional versus intellectual, and compromise versus win. Women were more likely to perceive conflict episodes in relationship terms, whereas males were more likely to perceive the task characteristics of conflict episodes. The focus on relationships and task characteristics was also related to better relationship outcomes and task outcomes, respectively. (There were no differences between male and female perceptions of conflict on the other two dimensions.)

How Conflict Is Framed: Competition versus Collaboration   Linda Babcock and Sara Laschever (2003), addressing the gender divide in negotiation, argue that from birth, men are taught to uphold the masculine norms of competition and superiority: ". . . superiority is central to our society's definition of maleness" (p. 103). They contend that women learn, quite early, that competing and winning against a man can threaten his socially defined masculinity. Similarly, women are groomed to maintain social harmony and are often punished for self-promotion or competitive behavior as a violation of femininity (Rudman, 1998; Rudman and Glick, 1999). In a review of research on gender in negotiation, Kray and Babcock (2006) argue that gender differences are most evident when negotiation is portrayed as a competition rather than a collaborative effort. Work by Deal (2000) illustrated this point by demonstrating that men are more likely than women to intentionally use information that helps their own position but harms another's position in a competitive negotiation context. However, in a collaborative negotiation context, this gender difference disappeared. In a related study, Bowles, Babcock, and McGinn (2005) showed that women achieved poorer outcomes than men when negotiating on their own behalf but actually outperformed men when advocating on behalf of another individual. Together these results suggest that women suffer in situations where they are expected to fill the social role of a deferential, cooperative female, but thrive in setting in which these pressures are lifted. It is important to mention that in both studies the performance of male negotiators were unaffected by manipulations of context.

Is the Situation Perceived as a Negotiation Opportunity? In a situation that could, but need not, involve negotiation, does an individual perceive and act on it as a negotiation opportunity? Research evidence suggests that there are significant differences between men and women in their *propensity to negotiate*. Deborah Small and colleagues (2007) in a recent study found marked gender differences in propensity to negotiate. They told their participants that they would receive between $3 and $10 for their performance on a word task. Upon completing the task, all participants were told "Here's $3. Is $3 OK?" Most participants said OK, but males were far more likely (eight times more!) than females to seek more money. This difference was found when there were no social cues involving negotiation (i.e., no mention by the experimenter of the word *negotiation* as an option), but persisted when participants were explicitly told in a follow-up experiment that negotiation was an option. Interestingly, though, in a variation of the experiment where some participants were told that they could "*ask* for more money" and others were told they could "*negotiate*

for more money," the gender gap in propensity to negotiate disappeared in the "ask" condition. Women, these results indicate, view negotiating for things more negatively than asking for things. Small and colleagues concluded that "The prospect of negotiating may inhibit women from initiating negotiation more so than the differently framed prospect of asking" (p. 610). Further evidence that women are less apt to initiate negotiations came in a survey by Babcock, Gelfand, Small, and Stayn (2006), who asked working adults to think of the last time they had initiated a negotiation. Men reported that two weeks had elapsed on average since initiating negotiation, whereas for women the average was more than twice that time.

Outcome Expectations   In addition to the tendency to overlook the potential for negotiation more often than men, there is also evidence to suggest that women expect lower outcomes from a negotiation. Bowles and her colleagues (2005) ran an experiment in which participants played the part of a manufacturer negotiating the price of supplies. The researchers varied the amount of information made available to the negotiators. Some participants, in a "low-ambiguity" condition, were given information about their superiors thought to be a desirable outcome. Other negotiations, in a "high-ambiguity" condition, did not receive this information. The results showed that when expectations were ambiguous, male buyers expected to pay 10 percent less and offered 19 percent less than did female buyers. Male participants went on to conclude deals at prices that were 27 percent lower on average than those negotiated by female participants. On the other hand, when ambiguity was low (buyers given specific information about performance expectations), the information provided about expected outcomes was enough to overcome these gender differences.

2. Men and Women Communicate Differently in Negotiation   Watson and Kasten (1988) examined how men and women perceive communication behaviors that occur during negotiations. In a simulated negotiation study with managers as participants, Watson and Kasten found that women perceived male behavior as more assertive than men did. The important implication here is that the same behavior may elicit significantly different perceptions and reactions depending on the gender of the other party who is the target/perceiver of the behavior. In a similar vein, aggressive and competitive tactics are viewed differently when employed by women rather than men (Bowles, Babcock, and Lai, 2007; Dreher, Dougherty, and Whitely, 1989). A possible interpretation of these findings would be that society (American society, anyway) promotes competition among males, yet discourages it among females.

Differences in perceptions of communication may translate into differences in behavioral style and strategy when negotiating. For example, one study showed that men and women discuss different things when they negotiate. Halpern and Parks (1996) used a low-conflict bargaining simulation to examine how same-sex pairs of men and women negotiated. They found that men were more likely to discuss positions than women, whereas women were more likely to reveal personal information and feelings than men. In addition, men and women chose different examples to buttress their arguments during the negotiation.

Gender differences in communication vary with contextual aspects of the negotiation situation. We mention two here. First, evidence points to differences between men and women depending on the *communication channel* in use for negotiation. In a recent compilation of research findings from several studies, Stuhlmacher, Citera, and Willis (2007) concluded that women are more likely to be contentious or hostile in virtual negotiations (e.g., via e-mail) than in face-to-face negotiation. There was no difference between the two channels of communication for male negotiators. Stuhlmacher and colleagues explain this in terms of social roles and how those are highlighted or diluted by communication methods. The role of a negotiator, they argue, is fundamentally masculine with its focus on competition and winning. Virtual negotiation "makes the gender of the negotiator less salient (compared to face-to-face negotiation) because there are fewer status and social cues" (p. 333), reducing the attention paid by female negotiators to the status of their opponent and increasing their attention to the substance of the interaction.

A second situational factor that appears to bring out gender differences is *surveillance*: who is watching the negotiators negotiate. As we discussed in Chapter 11, surveillance effects are important because negotiators in many situations are observed by constituents or others to whom they are accountable for their actions and outcomes. Research on surveillance points to gender effects, but unfortunately without clarity: one study found that men made greater demands and were rated as more dominating when observed by women (Cantrell and Butler, 1997), while another found negotiators acting more contentiously when the observers were men (Pruitt, Carnevale, Forcey, and Van Slyck, 1986). Gender seems to influence these outside social perceptions of assertive or cooperative behavior, but a clear picture of how and when that occurs awaits further study.

3. Men and Women Are Treated Differently in Negotiation   Not only do women and men perceive negotiations in different ways, but there is evidence that women in negotiations are often treated worse than men during negotiations (Whittemore, 1996). We consider research findings from two different domains: negotiating the purchase of a new car and salary negotiations. See Box 14.1 for an interesting experimental example.

Automobile Negotiations   Ian Ayres and Peter Siegelman (1995; also see Ayres, 1991) conducted an intriguing experiment that documented how men and women are treated during negotiations for a new car. They assigned different pairs of negotiators (black female/white male, black male/white male, white female/white male) to shop for a new car at 153 Chicago-area car dealerships. A white male negotiator participated in all pairs. Each negotiator in the pair separately visited the same car dealership on different days and bargained for a new car (negotiators chose the particular car for each negotiation from a list; no cars were actually purchased). Negotiators, who received two days of training before visiting their first car dealer, followed a set script during the negotiations and were similar in terms of age, education, dress, economic class, occupation, and attractiveness. The key outcomes of interest in the study were estimates of dealer profit from the initial and final offers that negotiators received. Dealer profits were calculated as the difference between published list prices of the cars and the offers received by the negotiators (dealer fixed costs were ignored in the study).

Sara Solnick (2001) published the results of a study comparing the behavior of men and women in a common two-person negotiation simulation known as the "ultimatum game." Here's how the game worked in Solnick's experiment.

Each pair plays the game for $10 of real money. The first player (the "offerer") proposes a division of the $10 between the two. The second player (the "recipient") independently indicates a division amount that he or she would find minimally acceptable. If the share of the $10 offered by the first player exceeds the minimum acceptable amount stated by the recipient, then the division is accepted, and both players receive their share of the money. If the offer does not exceed the recipient's minimum, then both players receive nothing. The offerer does best for him- or herself by proposing a split that only just exceeds the recipient's minimum.

Participants knew the gender of the other person in their pair. Men and women in the role of the offerer did not differ in the size of the divisions that they proposed. However, offers did vary according to the gender of the offer recipient. On average, offerers tendered $4.89 to men, but only $4.37 to women. According to Solnick, this may suggest that offerers expected women to demand less payment than men.

Interestingly, however, a comparison of the minimum acceptable amounts stated by recipients shows that women demanded *higher* minimum offers than men. Solnick also found that recipients of both genders stated higher acceptable minimum amounts when paired with female offerers compared with male offerers. Solnick interprets this to mean that people may expect more generosity or fairness from women than from men.

The moral of the story seems to be that negotiators often harbor and act upon questionable assumptions that women will demand less and concede more. As Solnick observes, this may help explain findings that women are offered higher prices than men in new car negotiations (Ayers and Siegelman, 1995) and that men receive higher gains than women in salary negotiations (Gerhart and Rynes, 1991). Negotiators—especially women—need to be careful not to allow dubious assumptions to interfere with the successful pursuit of desirable outcomes at the bargaining table.

Source: S. J. Solnick, "Gender Differences in the Ultimatum Game," *Economic Inquiry* 39 (2001), pp. 189–200.

Ayres and Siegelman (1995) found that the offers negotiators received from the car dealers differed significantly depending on the negotiators' gender and race (see Table 14.1). White males received the most favorable offers, followed in order by white females, black females, and black males. When the bargaining process (number of bids and counterbids) was examined, Ayres found that differences in the opening offers accounted for the majority of the differences in the final offers that the negotiators achieved. Concession rates and the length of the negotiation were not found to differ significantly across the gender and race of the negotiators. Finally, the gender and race of the salesperson had no effect on the results of the Ayres and Siegelman study; that is, women and blacks (versus white men) did not gain any advantage by dealing with a female or black salesperson.

The results of the Ayres and Siegelman (1995) study suggest that people are treated differently when they bargain for new cars—women and blacks may start negotiations at a less favorable position than white males. It is not clear why women and blacks are treated this way—it could be racism, sexism, or opportunistic behavior by the car dealers (dealers may believe that women and blacks are willing to pay more than white males for the same

TABLE 14.1 | Average Car Dealer Profit

Experimenter	Initial Offer		Final Offer	
	Profit	Markup	Profit	Markup
White male	$1,019	9.2%	$ 564	5.2%
White female	1,127	10.3	657	6.0
Black male	1,954	17.3	1,665	14.6
Black female	1,337	12.2	975	7.2

Note: Profit figures are estimates that Ayres and Siegelman calculated from published list prices of the new cars.

Source: Adapted from I. Ayres and P. Siegelman, "Race and Gender Discrimination in Bargaining for a New Car," *American Economic Review* 85 (1995), pp. 304–21.

product). Note that there was no evidence that the negotiation process was different for women and blacks compared with white males; the differences in the final deals obtained were present in the opening offers made to the different negotiators, and these differences carried through to the final offers. Consider what this means to the typical negotiator in the Ayres and Siegelman study. Negotiators received the same average concession from the car dealers during the negotiation, so in a relative sense, they believed that they negotiated good deals. It is only when the results are compared across groups (which typically would not occur, because most people simply don't know a large number of other people who are buying the same car at the same time) that differences based on gender and race become clear.

Salary Negotiations   Research on salary negotiations by job seekers documents how men and women may receive different treatment and outcomes during negotiations. Some differences in outcomes result from different degrees of willingness to even try to obtain a better salary. We mentioned earlier a gender difference in propensity to initiate negotiations; research has shown that this difference in propensity can play out with dramatic effects in the arena of job and salary negotiation. In a survey of new graduates from a master's degree program, researcher Linda Babcock found that only 7 percent of female graduates asked for a higher salary rather than accepting the employer's initial offer; in contrast, 57 percent of male graduates asked for more money (Babcock and Laschever, 2003). This occurred even though career services professionals at the school had advised students to negotiate job offers. Students who did negotiate increased their starting salaries by an average of 7.4 percent, which just about matched the overall disparity (7.6 percent) between male and female starting salaries. Babcock and Laschever (2003) in their aptly titled book, *Women Don't Ask,* point out that neglecting to initiate even a single salary negotiation can cascade over the length of a career into a significant financial loss. As an illustration they point to a 22-year-old woman who accepts a $25,000 job offer as presented, and a man of the same age who negotiates the offer up to $30,000. If the two of them receive identical 3 percent raises for the rest of their careers through age 65, the man's earnings over 38 years will exceed the woman's by more than $360,000. Saved and invested at 3 percent interest, these extra earnings will compound by age 60 to $568,000 more in the bank for the man than the woman.

This is, as Babcock and Lashever put it, "an enormous return on investment for a one-time negotiation" (p. 5).

Even when both men and women do initiate negotiations over salaries, there is evidence that women fare worse. In a study of MBA graduates, Gerhart and Rynes (1991) found that males received a higher monetary payoff for negotiating their salary than did females, even though men and women were equally likely to negotiate. To rule out other possible explanations, Gerhart and Rynes statistically controlled for the effects of industry, college major, grade point average, and business experience on the salaries received. Gender differences in negotiated salaries may emerge from differences in how negotiators define the bargaining zone, which inevitably influences the offers that individuals will make and accept. One study presented evidence that, compared with men, women anticipating a hypothetical salary negotiation reported lower pay expectations and set lower targets and resistance points (Kaman and Hartel, 1994).

4. Similar Tactics Have Different Effects When Used by Men versus Women   One of the most compelling gender differences in negotiation is not concerned with how men and women behave differently, but with how the same behaviors of male and female negotiators are *perceived* differently. Here are brief descriptions of two studies that make this point persuasively (and perhaps disturbingly).

Exchange Tactics   The results of a study by Dreher, Dougherty, and Whitely (1989) suggest that not only do men and women receive different outcomes during salary negotiations, but that the same tactic may have opposite effects on salary negotiation outcomes, depending on whether it is used by a male or a female employee. Dreher and his colleagues found that the use of exchange tactics (reminding supervisors of previous favors and offering to make sacrifices) had a positive effect on the outcome of salary negotiations of male employees and a negative effect on the outcome of salary negotiations of female employees. That is, women using the same negotiation tactic that men used were less successful than men. Dreher and his colleagues surmise that women who use exchange tactics "may violate stereotypic expectations about appropriate female behavior" (1989, p. 547) and are therefore penalized for using this tactic.

Aggressive Tactics   Bowles, Babcock, and Lai (2007) investigated reactions to people who negotiate aggressively. Participants in the study read a résumé and interview notes from a job candidate. The gender of the candidate was varied as well as whether or not the candidate attempted to negotiate for specific job benefits. Aside from these two manipulations, participants saw exactly the same information. Results showed that both male and female candidates were less likely to be hired when they bargained aggressively. However, females were 3.5 times less likely to be hired when aggressive. In short, women were punished far more severely than men for exactly the same action.

5. Gender Stereotypes Affect Negotiator Performance   In an important series of studies, Kray, Thompson, and Galinsky (2001) examined how the performance of male and female negotiators varies depending on the kinds of sex-role stereotypes that are activated in a particular situation. They theorized a link between classic gender stereotypes about how men and women claim resources and perceptions of how men and women will perform in negotiation. Their analysis draws upon a social psychological theory of "stereotype threat" (Steele, 1997). Stereotype threat refers to performance anxiety that afflicts individuals in certain social categories (e.g., race, gender) who fear that their performance will confirm a negative stereotype. Kray and colleagues (2001) argued that people who are consciously aware of certain gender stereotypes will act in ways that confirm these stereotypes during negotiation. Here are a few key findings from their studies of this phenomenon.

Stereotypes Undermine the Performance of Female Negotiators   When stereotype threat is activated—by telling negotiators that the bargaining task is diagnostic of one's ability as a negotiator—women do worse because of the negative stereotypes that are active, and men do better because of the positive stereotypes in play (Kray, Thompson, and Galinsky, 2001). In contrast, when negotiators were told explicitly that the task was *not* diagnostic of ability, there were no differences in the performance of male and female negotiators. Thus, to the extent that men do better in negotiation than women (e.g., Stuhlmacher and Walters, 1999), Kray and her colleagues have shown that the activation of stereotypes about performance—which may or may not have any basis in fact—is part of the reason why.

The Negative Effect of Stereotypes about Gender Differences Can Be Overcome
Although stereotypes can undermine the performance of female negotiators, there is also evidence that negative stereotypes of women at the bargaining table can sometimes *improve* performance. In another part of the same study described above, Kray and colleagues (2001) found that after explicitly mentioning that masculine traits lead to better performance, women actually outperformed men in mixed-gender negotiations. Instead of fulfilling the negative connotations of this stereotype, the women in this experiment reacted against it and began negotiating more aggressively.

The Activated Stereotype May Matter More than the Actual Gender of the Negotiator   Putting aside the actual gender of the negotiator, a study by Kray, Reb, Galinsky, and Thompson (2004) found that more powerful negotiators (those with a better alternative in the form of a higher BATNA) obtained higher outcomes when a masculine stereotype—one that stressed that aggressiveness and self-interest were important for negotiator success—was explicitly activated. When a feminine stereotype was activated, negotiators of both sexes achieved more integrative outcomes. It may be that when explicit stereotypes are in play, negotiators use this information to evaluate their own strengths and weaknesses and therefore act more consistently with this stereotype, even if it means acting contrary to the stereotypes of one's own gender.

Overcoming the Disadvantage of Gender Differences

Much of the research we have described in this chapter places female negotiators at a disadvantage, suggesting that differences in process choices and styles, combined with the pernicious effects of stereotypes, leaves women worse off at the negotiation table. Following Kray and Babcock (2006), we mention here three categories of interventions that help to overcome some of the liabilities of gender or otherwise "level the playing field" for women in the realm of negotiation. Ultimately, overcoming these liabilities, like overcoming troublesome or harmful tendencies in judgment and perception (discussed in Chapter 5), is largely a matter of cultivating awareness that these tendencies exist and developing the ability to avoid the traps that they can set for unwary negotiators.

Motivational Interventions   It is an unfortunate reality that many people, even accomplished professionals, continue to view men's and women's abilities differently and apply double standards in judging the actions of others. Women, for example, are more likely than men to be sanctioned for behavior that looks like self-promotion; hence, female negotiators more than male negotiators may find themselves trying to juggle the management of others' impressions with the pursuit of good results. As a consequence of that impression management motive, women may accept lower outcomes than men. Kray and Babcock (2006) suggest that a way to break this pattern is to emphasize the mutual dependency of both parties in the negotiation relationship. In other words, dilute the double standard by making the negotiation less about self-promotion for each party; reframe it as an occasion for parties to come together to solve a shared problem.

Sex differences in negotiation performance have been found to result from gender stereotypes about male and female ability and behavior. One way to overcome the influence of gender stereotypes on negotiation performance is to connect those stereotypes explicitly with negotiation outcomes. Kray, Reb, Galinsky, and Thompson (2004), for example, found that activating masculine stereotypes—simply mentioning to negotiators that there is a male gender advantage (favoring assertive, self-interested behavior typical of males)—led negotiators to behave more competitively, consistent with that stereotype. In a second experiment, Kray and colleagues (2004) instead activated feminine stereotypes, telling participants that skilled negotiators "have a keen ability to express their thoughts verbally, good listening skills, and insight into the other negotiator's feelings" (p. 406). This led negotiators to do a better job exploiting integrative potential and achieving joint payoffs. The point is that activating stereotypes—making people consciously aware of them and their supposed effects on outcomes—can motivate negotiators to behavior in ways that overcome gender differences in performance, and in some cases even led women to outperform men (Kray, Thompson, and Galinsky, 2001). In short, activating a negative stereotype may motivate a person to disprove it.

Cognitive Interventions   Having a powerful mind-set can be an important tool in negotiation. By "powerful mind-set" we mean an awareness of the role of power in the situation and its relation to tactics and outcomes. Galinsky, Gruenfeld, and Magee (2003) showed that such mind-sets make a difference in behavior: power becomes action. In negotiation, approaching the negotiation with a powerful frame of mind can lead to higher outcomes for the female negotiator, who might otherwise be at a disadvantage. Small and colleagues (2007) showed that although women tend to be more intimidated than men by the prospect of negotiating, this can be overcome when women first are induced to think about power (in their experiment, by having participants describe a "situation in which you had control and influence over others"). "When women are primed to experience power," these researchers concluded, "their aversion to negotiating is diminished such that they react much more like men typically do (p. 609). Other ways to change the mind-sets of female negotiators, according to Kray and Babcock (2006), include focusing on things that negotiators have in common that transcend gender, such as their common goals or identities; redefining what it means to be a good negotiator to include stereotypically feminine attributes; and increasing perceptions of control through structured training.

Situational Interventions   Power differences may well be responsible for many of the differences observed between male and female negotiators (Watson, 1994b). Yet according to Kray and Babcock (2006), power is an equalizing factor in a negotiation in the sense that men and women tend to use it similarly and benefit from it equally. Given equal power, they perform equally well. Accordingly, overcoming gender differences may require diluting structural imbalances of power in negotiation situations. One way to do this is to alter the social roles that women assume in a negotiation to "reduce the extent to which women feel constrained to conform to gender role" (p. 36).

Keep in mind also that power in negotiation, as we discussed in Chapter 7, is often a function of alternatives to a negotiated settlement: the person who comes to the table with better alternatives is, other things equal, the more powerful party. Kray, Reb, Galinsky, and Thompson (2004) showed that the pernicious effects of gender stereotypes can be overcome by making parties consciously aware of them, but their findings also showed that stereotypes may persist if there is a significant power imbalance between the parties. In other words, it isn't necessarily enough for a negotiator to know about harmful stereotypes and behave during a negotiation in ways that run counter to them; negotiators also need to be doing important power-enhancing background work: amassing information that fortifies your positions and your arguments, expanding and improving your alternatives to a negotiated settlement, and using these resources to persuade the other party that your position is one of strength.

In closing, the assumption that negotiators benefit when they exhibit stereotypically male attitudes and behaviors (assertiveness, competitiveness, and the like) is built on a fundamentally false premise. Negotiation is not inherently an activity where the parties benefit from assertive or contentious behavior. Rather, there are some negotiation situations where competitiveness is appropriate, others where cooperation is essential, and still others (most, we would argue) where there is a blend between competitive and cooperative impulses and motives. Gender stereotypes and simplistic assumptions about sex roles get in the way of what really matters for effective negotiation: the ability to accurately perceive the situation and your opponent and to make sound tactical choices that are not clouded by unwarranted stereotypes and irrelevant assumptions. Given research suggesting that women may be disadvantaged as negotiators, especially in business and other professional settings where gendered role assumptions and stereotypes persist, Box 14.2 presents some practical suggestions for managing negotiation in those settings.

Practical Advice for Negotiating the Gendered Workplace

BOX 14.2

A trade publication for business professionals recently offered some sensible advice for women whose jobs in the contemporary workplace involve negotiation—which at one time or another is just about everyone. We list some of their suggestions here, along with a few of our own. (Most, it turns out, are good advice for negotiators of all genders!)

- Rely on research. Determine what matters to others involved in the negotiation. "Equip yourself with information."

- Make a business case to support your arguments, especially when it's your own salary at stake. Determine how your role adds to the firm's bottom line and adds value to the business. The more concrete and specific your case, the less likely it is that others will resort on stereotypes in reacting to your approach.

- Make a concerted effort to improve your negotiation skills, and practice. Invite a trusted colleague or friend to role-play the interaction before an upcoming important negotiation.

- Combat stereotypes in your own dealings with others. Research shows that women as well as men can harbor stereotypes that will put women at a disadvantage.

- Don't try to replicate the stereotypically male style of negotiation. Double standards endure: the reality is that aggressive women may still draw negative reactions, even as these attributes are admired in men.

- But don't go too far the other way, taking on the stereotypically female role of nurturer. Strive for a reasonable middle ground that capitalizes on talents and strengths that come naturally without either playing to stereotypes or overcompensating for them. Women (and men!) who are oriented toward cooperation and relationship building can use these to their advantage, especially when the situation is one that will reward cooperation over competition.

Source: Adapted from E. Agnvall, "Women and Negotiation," *HRMagazine* 52 (December 2007), pp. 69–73.

Chapter Summary

A growing body of evidence suggests that women and men behave differently in negotiation situations and are treated differently both before and during negotiations. Taken at face value, these findings tend to suggest that women are at a disadvantage when they negotiate simply because they are women. This disadvantage may manifest itself in several elements of the negotiation process: aspirations, opening offers, aggressiveness of interaction, concessions, and outcomes, among others. Yet having noted these potential disadvantages, it is important to keep in mind that the broad-brush differences that researchers have uncovered between male and female negotiators are quite small in statistical magnitude.

The more important findings are those that speak to the underlying theoretical basis for gender differences in negotiation. Several arose over the course of this chapter, including differences in emphasis on relationships in negotiation, views of the embeddedness of negotiation in broader social contexts, beliefs about ability and worth, notions of how to use power, and ways of framing negotiations. The empirical research on gender differences in negotiation suggests a number of important principles: men and women conceive of negotiations in different ways, communicate differently in negotiation, and are treated differently in negotiation; the tactics used by men versus those used by women have very different effects; and perceptual stereotypes have important effects on how men and women negotiate.

Many of the gender differences that we have discussed are open to various alternative explanations.

417

Recent trends in research on gender in negotiation are promising because of the renewed interest in the subject and rejuvenated attention to theoretical explanations. Our understanding of gender differences will continue to benefit from studies that go beyond simple empirical documentation of differences to explore the underlying social and psychological mechanisms that account for how men and women experience negotiation differently.

A final point: we began this chapter by distinguishing between the terms *sex* and *gender,* and we observed that negotiation research has emphasized gender rather than sex in describing both existing research findings and in discussing conceptual underpinnings

and implications. This research has, however, relied exclusively on the use of biological sex (i.e., males versus females) to test and measure differences, rather than assessing gender roles (e.g., masculine or feminine sex role identity) as a predictor variable. We are not aware of studies in the negotiation literature that directly compare individuals by sex roles. This is a weakness in the field to the extent one believes that sex role identity is a theoretically important factor in understanding individual differences in negotiation.

Gender is, of course, just one of many possible individual differences with a role in negotiation processes and outcomes. In the next chapter we discuss several others.

Endnotes

[1] *The American Heritage Dictionary of the English Language,* 3rd edition, 1992, © Houghton Mifflin.

[2] Personal communication with L. Kray, June 29, 2004.

[3] See, for example, Carnevale and Lawler (1987); Pruitt, Carnevale, Forcey, and Van Slyck (1986); and Putnam and Jones (1982).

[4] See, for example, Kimmel, Pruitt, Magenau, Konar-Goldband, and Carnevale (1980); Neu, Graham, and Gilly (1988); Pruitt and Syna (1985); Stuhlmacher and Walters (1999); Walters, Stuhlmacher, and Meyer (1998); and Watson and Kasten (1988).

[5] In a meta-analytic literature review, empirical results from many studies on the same subject are combined in order to create a broad statistical estimate of the effect or relationship that the underlying studies investigated. Meta-analysis is a way to capitalize statistically on the fact that the studies being reviewed together provide a much more robust sample than any one of them does individually.

[6] For examples, see Gray (1994); Kolb and Coolidge (1991); Kolb and Putnam (1997); Northrup (1995); and Watson (1994a).

[7] See also Pinkley and Northcraft (1994).

CHAPTER 15

Individual Differences II: Personality and Abilities

Objectives

1. Understand why personality and ability differences in negotiation have been difficult to uncover.
2. Explore specific personality traits that influence negotiation behaviors and processes.
3. Consider the role of native cognitive and emotional abilities in negotiation encounters.
4. Gain insight into how behaviors of expert negotiators differ from those of less experienced negotiators.

In the last chapter we examined in depth one particular individual difference: gender. In this chapter we look more broadly at the range of other differences that have been studied in connection with negotiation. We begin with a brief review of early research on individual differences. We then focus on more recent research on individual differences and negotiation, segmenting our discussion into two major categories: (1) dimensions of *personality* that appear to have an influence on negotiation and (2) the role of native *abilities* in negotiation, including cognitive ability and the relatively new domain of emotional intelligence. The chapter then concludes with an alternative approach to studying negotiator characteristics, one that examines how the behaviors of superior negotiators differ from those of average negotiators.

Early Research on Individual Differences and Negotiation

Research examining the effects of individual differences in negotiation dates back to the 1950s. Studies through the 1960s and 1970s examined biographical variables such as age, gender, race, culture, and socioeconomic status; personality factors such as risk-taking propensity, locus of control, cognitive complexity, tolerance for ambiguity, and social motives; and attitudes such as interpersonal trust and cooperativeness. Unfortunately, many findings were disparate, inconclusive, and sometimes directly contradictory (Rubin and Brown, 1975).[1] Many find it intuitively apparent that some individual characteristics are important in negotiation, so why were research findings so inconclusive? We briefly mention four explanations here.

1. The Effects of Individual Differences Are Subtle and Elusive   Although individual differences may predispose bargainers to behave in certain ways, key situational factors such as the nature of the bargaining problem, the relative power between negotiators, pressures from constituencies, or simply the behavior of the other negotiator may matter more. To put it another way, it's not that individual differences aren't potentially important; it's that aspects of situations determine whether or not individual differences can emerge and have a measurable effect during negotiation. For example, consider the type of negotiation problem: there is evidence that certain types of people may be successful in negotiation situations with integrative potential, while other types of people may perform well in win–lose negotiations (Barry and Friedman, 1998). Or consider the power dynamics involved: one study found that the personality traits of more powerful negotiating parties were more influential than traits of less powerful parties because "powerful individuals have the freedom to 'call the shots' as they wish, and therefore their traits have the capacity to shape their own behavior and the social environment" (Anderson and Thompson, 2004, p. 137).

2. The Wrong Kind of Task Was Investigated   A good deal of early research employed a simple, two-choice Prisoner's Dilemma game, which typically involved experimental subjects who could not see each other or speak to each other, and whose "negotiating" consisted of making simple choices between cooperative and competitive decision options. Limited and constrained interaction of this form is hardly comparable to the complex verbal and nonverbal communication processes that occur in face-to-face negotiation. Research settings must be rich enough to allow the impact of personality and other individual differences to emerge.

3. The Wrong Individual Differences Were Investigated   The study of individual differences in social psychology has come a long way since the 1970s. Inconsistent results in early research may reflect an overly simplistic view of the kinds of traits and characteristics that would matter in negotiation. With respect to personality, for instance, there is more attention now to aggregating traits into broader underlying dimensions of disposition, and these broader clusters of traits do a better job predicting behavior. There is also now among psychologists a much better understanding of connections between mental and emotional abilities and behavior, as we will discuss later in this chapter.

4. Research Methods Were Flawed or Inconsistent   Methods varied considerably from one study to the next in early research on individual differences in negotiation. As a result, contradictory findings may be a result of different research designs, methods, and experimental bargaining problems. One particularly important issue is sampling—the question of who is studied. The effects of certain personality predispositions may go undiscovered if research is limited to homogeneous populations of research subjects who do not possess that predisposition, or who all possess it to a roughly equivalent extent. Most experimental negotiation studies have been conducted with volunteer university populations, usually students enrolled in psychology or management courses. This particular population may be so homogeneous with respect to age, socioeconomic background, and other demographic or dispositional characteristics that true differences in negotiation style may not be readily identified.

We include this discussion of the early research legacy of ambiguous findings because they set the tone for more contemporary work on this subject. Conceptual approaches to individual differences are now more sophisticated, methods are better and more diverse, and psychologists know more about the structure of personality and the nature of individual abilities. Still, the early research of the 1950s, 1960s, and 1970s matters as a kind of cautionary tale. Our methods and theories may be better, but the fact remains that the effects of individual differences can be subtle and hard to detect and, at times, are properly understood only in conjunction with aspects of the negotiation situation. These lessons of early research are still important, as we see in the two major sections in this chapter on personality and on individual abilities.

Personality and Negotiation

Personality traits are stable tendencies to think, feel, or behave in certain ways that can be identified and measured. Consider, for example, the trait of extraversion (versus introversion). You probably know some extraverted people—those who are consistently gregarious and assertive, and you probably know some introverts—people who are typically quiet, reserved, and less gregarious. People differ on all kinds of attributes; for instance, at any given time one person may be happy and another angry. But those kinds of descriptors don't amount to personality traits unless, like extraversion, they are markers of *stable* ways of thinking or acting that can usefully *predict* other aspects of individual or social behavior. Personality traits are sometimes referred to as "dispositions," and we use these terms interchangeably here.

Although it seems like an obvious and intuitive insight that people have different personalities and that variations in personality affect how things go in certain situations, there has actually been—over the past few decades—quite a bit of controversy among scholars in psychology and organizational behavior about the overall importance of dispositions. To simplify the debate, on one side are those who argue that the study of personality is theoretically thin and that dispositional effects are less important than situations in predicting attitudes and behaviors (e.g., Davis-Blake and Pfeffer, 1989). On the other side are those who concede that situations matter but insist that dispositions by themselves are significant predictors of relevant behaviors (e.g., House, Shane, and Herold, 1996). Many psychologists have come to regard the debate as a "false dichotomy" (Funder, 2001, p. 200): research offers ample evidence that personality traits are sufficiently stable and can be as predictive of important behaviors as situations. In short, dispositions and situations both matter.

In this section, we review eight approaches to studying personality that have shown promise as predictors of negotiation behavior. These include (1) conflict style, (2) social value orientation, (3) interpersonal trust, (4) self-efficacy and locus of control, (5) self-monitoring, (6) Machiavellianism, (7) face threat sensitivity, and (8) the "Big Five" personality factors.

Conflict Management Style

Dealing with conflict is a central part of the negotiating process. In Chapter 1, we identified five modes of behavior that are commonly used to deal with conflict: contending, problem solving, inaction, yielding, and compromising. We also examined the effect on outcomes that would be created by choosing one style over another; we did not, however,

FIGURE 15.1 | Thomas-Kilmann Conflict Styles

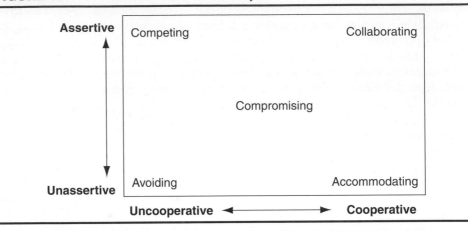

Source: Adapted from K. Thomas and R. H. Kilmann (1974). *Thomas Kilmann Conflict Mode Survey.* Tuxedo Junction, NY: Xicom. Used with permission.

examine the reasons that one style is chosen over another. A negotiator may use rational criteria to make this choice, such as selecting the style that is assumed to be most likely to lead to the desired outcomes. It is also possible, however, that people use styles consistently because they have a personality predisposition to do so. As discussed in Chapter 1, there are two levels of concern underlying the five conflict management styles. One is the degree of concern a party shows for his or her own outcomes; the other is the degree of concern the party shows for the other's outcomes. Thomas (1976) proposed that two personality dimensions can represent these two levels of concern:

1. The degree of *assertiveness* that a party maintains for his or her own preferred solutions or outcomes.

2. The degree of *cooperativeness* a party shows toward working with the other party to achieve mutual goals.

Bringing these two dimensions together (see Figure 15.1), Thomas identified five major conflict management styles:

- A *competing* style—high on assertiveness and low on cooperativeness.

- An *accommodating* style—low on assertiveness and high on cooperativeness.

- An *avoiding* style—low on both assertiveness and cooperativeness.

- A *collaborating* style—high on both assertiveness and cooperativeness.

- A *compromising* style—moderate on both assertiveness and cooperativeness.

Research by Thomas and colleagues (Kilmann and Thomas, 1977; Thomas, 1976, 1977) has supported the premise that conflict management styles in a given situation result both from the strategic choices an individual makes and from individual tendencies to use

Taking Conflict Personally—An Individual Difference BOX 15.1

Researchers Judith Dallinger and Dale Hample (1995) have determined that individuals differ in the degree to which they take conflict personally—that is, how they experience strong negative emotional reactions to specific conflict management incidents and episodes. People who take certain conflicts personally are more likely to feel threatened, anxious, damaged, devalued, and/or insulted by a particular conflict event. The researchers argue that taking conflict personally is both a *state* (a temporary feeling associated with a particular event) and a *trait* (an enduring predisposition that differs across individuals). Research findings suggest that

- Those who are more likely to take conflict personally are more likely to have noncon-

frontational (avoiding or accommodating) styles of managing conflict.

- Those who are more likely to take conflict personally prefer supervisors who have a compromising conflict management style.

- Those who are more likely to take conflict personally are more likely to feel persecuted by, and have a higher stress management reaction to, those supervisors who use a forcing (competing) conflict style, and they are much less satisfied with this supervisor.

Source: J. M. Dallinger and B. D. Hample, "Personalizing and Managing Conflict," *International Journal of Conflict Management* 6, no. 3 (1995), pp. 273–89.

certain styles regardless of the situation. Research exploring the model's two dimensions (assertiveness and cooperativeness) has generally been supportive.[2] Although little research has explored the effects of negotiator choice of conflict management styles on actual negotiation behavior (see Butler, 1994), studies where conflict styles were experimentally manipulated have generally supported the model.[3] Broadly speaking, the Thomas–Kilmann model represents a simple yet coherent model for viewing the effect of disposition on bargaining and conflict management behavior.

It is easy to surmise how particular conflict style tendencies might lead to particular behaviors, give certain kinds of conflict situations. If the stakes for winning are high and outcomes are derived through individual effort, then individuals with strong competing modes should dominate the situation; if outcomes are derived from joint efforts, then individuals with a strong collaborative mode should dominate. In contrast, if the stakes are low for an individual, then that individual should be more likely to ignore the conflict (avoiding mode) or allow the other to reap what little resources are available (accommodating mode). It also appears that people have a self-serving view of the value and effectiveness of these conflict styles: In a study examining strategic approaches to a hypothetical conflict situation (Gross and Guerrero, 2000), individuals regarded a competing style as inappropriate for *others* to use, but appropriate and effective for *their own* use in the situation.

Individual differences in conflict management style have been correlated with other dispositions. For example, Thomas (1976) suggests that individuals high in a competing style are lower in risk taking, more internally controlled, higher on needs for power and control, and lower on needs for affiliation. Similarly, individuals strong in collaboration are thought to be more task-oriented, creative, and capable of dealing with complexity. There has not been much direct empirical research connecting conflict styles with other stable personality traits, although Box 15.1 does present one interesting example.

Social Value Orientation

Social value orientations are preferences that people have regarding the kinds of outcomes they prefer in social settings where interdependence with others is required (McLintock and Liebrand, 1988). Some people have a *pro-self* or egoistic orientation, which means they are primarily concerned with personal outcomes and unconcerned with outcomes obtained by the other party; others have a *pro-social* or cooperative orientation, which means a preference for outcomes that benefit both self and others with whom they are interdependent (de Dreu, Weingart, and Kwon, 2000). A pro-social orientation is, in essence, a tendency to act in a collaborative conflict management style (refer back to Figure 15.1).

Negotiation is clearly an example of the kind of social interdependence in which these social value orientations can play a role. Research on this issue shows that pro-self individuals behave distributively, adopting a style that is relatively tough and contentious, with more emphasis on bargaining over positions than exploring underlying interests that might yield mutual gain (Steinel and de Dreu, 2004).[4] Pro-socials on the other hand, being more concerned with the well-being of others, are more oriented toward problem solving and reciprocal cooperation. As a result, pro-social negotiators achieve more integrative outcomes (higher joint gain) than pro-self negotiators (de Dreu et al., 2000). This is not to suggest that pro-self negotiators are incapable of reaching integrative solutions, but they are less likely to (especially when a negotiation pairs two pro-self individuals at the same table), and they may use some different tactics to get there (Olekalns and Smith, 2003).

There is evidence that pro-self negotiators are happier with the agreements that they reach. Gillespie, Brett, and Weingart (2000) found that judgments of satisfaction after the negotiation were higher for pro-socials. They explained their finding this way: "Pro-social negotiators who are focused on themselves and the group have two sources of satisfaction, so they may be more easily satisfied than individualistic negotiators who are only focused on themselves and therefore have only one source of satisfaction" (p. 792). Gillespie and colleagues also speculated that if pro-socials set lower goals for themselves in negotiation, then they will be more easily satisfied compared with others (e.g., pro-self negotiators) who might set tougher goals.

Differences in negotiation behavior and outcomes that result from social value orientation are significant, but they can be diluted by aspects of the bargaining situation. In one recent study (Giebels, de Dreu, and van de Vliert, 2003), pro-social individuals negotiated more collaboratively than egoistic individuals, as previous studies have shown. However, when both parties in the negotiation had an exit option (i.e., both had a good alternative to a negotiated agreement), pro-social individuals made more threats, exchanged less information, and reached lower joint outcomes. Thus, with good alternatives mutually available, the differences between pro-social and pro-self negotiators tended to dissipate.

Pro-social versus egoistic motives in negotiation can be rooted either in stable individual differences (a reliable tendency to act that way, like a personality trait) or in elements of a particular situation (e.g., when negotiators are directed or encouraged to act selfishly or cooperatively). For the most part, the effects of these social motives on negotiation behavior appear to be generally the same regardless of whether they derive from individual disposition or from situational demands (de Dreu et al., 2000).[5]

"Dickie Wilson attacked my values."

Interpersonal Trust

As we discussed in Chapter 1, one of the fundamental dilemmas in negotiation is the degree to which negotiators should trust the other party. Negotiators must gather information and determine how much the other party is likely to be deceptive or deceitful—by misrepresenting true positions, distorting relevant facts, or introducing spurious information and positions. In addition, the trustworthiness of the other party may change over time, depending on whether negotiations are beginning or near the end, and depending on whether the negotiation has proceeded cooperatively or competitively.

Although we might conceptualize trust as an attitude that shifts with changing relationships and circumstances, interpersonal trust also functions as a personality variable with important effects in social relationships. According to research by Julian Rotter (1980), individuals differ in their level of *interpersonal trust*—defined as "a generalized expectancy held by an individual that the word, promise, oral, or written statement of another individual or group can be relied upon" (p. 1). Interpersonal trust, according to Rotter, is determined by the experiences that people have in dealing with others. If people have had experiences when they have trusted others, and this trust has been rewarded by reciprocal trust and productive relationships, then generalized interpersonal trust should be high. In contrast, if people have had their trust punished by others through exploitation, deception, and dishonesty, then interpersonal trust is likely to be low.[6]

The implications for negotiation of a dispositional tendency to trust others are significant.[7] High trusters believe that others will be trustworthy and that they need to be trustworthy themselves; hence, they are more likely to impose high moral standards on themselves and behave ethically. In contrast, low trusters believe that others cannot be trusted to observe the rules and therefore may feel less pressure themselves to tell the truth. Interestingly, though, high trusters are not necessarily more easily deceived than low trusters. One might think that high trustors are more apt to believe communications from others without questioning their validity, but studies summarized by Rotter (1980) indicate that the high-trust individual is no more prone to gullibility than the low-trust individual.

There is a "self-fulfilling prophecy" aspect to dispositional trust. Someone with high interpersonal trust is likely to approach the other person, in attitude and style, in a way that signals trust (Chaudhuri, Khan, Lakshmiratan, Py, and Shah, 2003). The other party, searching for cues about appropriate behavior in this situation, may respond in kind with trusting behavior, leading to a cooperative relationship between the parties. In contrast, a low-trust individual who communicates suspicion and mistrust may lead the other party to respond in kind with low self-disclosure, dishonesty, and mistrust. This will tend to reinforce the initial low-trust orientation and lead to a less cooperative relationship between the parties. One shouldn't assume, however, that low trusters will always be outwardly suspicious; Chaudhuri and colleagues (2003) found that low trusters sometimes exhibit trusting behaviors as a way to exploit the other party and maximize self-interest.

Self-Efficacy and Locus of Control

Self-efficacy is a judgment about one's ability to behave effectively in a given situation (Gist, Stevens, and Bavetta, 1991). The ability to do well at a task is a function of both motivation to be effective and ability to perform at a high level. A more formal definition of self-efficacy captures both of these elements: self-efficacy refers to "people's beliefs in their capabilities to mobilize the motivation, cognitive resources, and courses of action needed to exercise control over events in their lives" (Wood and Bandura, 1989, p. 364). Self-efficacy has been found to influence performance through the setting of higher goals and the adoption of more analytic strategies.

Self-efficacy plays an important role in complex interpersonal behavior, including negotiation. For example, a negotiator's self-efficacy predicts the likelihood that he or she will choose to negotiate, rather than accept mediation (Arnold and O'Connor, 2006). In research using a salary negotiation simulation, Marilyn Gist and her colleagues (1991) found that people with higher levels of self-efficacy obtained higher salaries in the simulation.[8] Self-efficacy led to higher outcomes in the salary negotiation because people higher in self-efficacy were also more likely to set higher goals before the negotiation (also see Brett, Pinkley, and Jacofsky, 1996). There is also evidence that one's perceived level of competence at the task of negotiation may increase the likelihood that collaborative problem solving will occur. Alexander, Schul, and McCorkle (1994), in a study of industrial managers participating in a sales negotiation simulation, found that individuals high in task-specific self-esteem (one's perceived degree of competence in performing a task) engaged in more cooperative, problem-solving behaviors. This extends to the perceived efficacy of using distributive or integrative bargaining tactics within a negotiation. Those who believe themselves more competent at using distributive or integrative tactics employed these strategies more often and achieved higher outcomes in distributive or integrative problems, respectively (Sullivan, O'Connor, and Burris, 2006).

A construct conceptually related to self-efficacy is *locus of control,* which refers to the extent to which people perceive that they have control over events that occur (Rotter, 1966). Those who attribute the cause of events to external reasons (e.g., luck) have a high external locus of control, while those who attribute the cause of events to internal reasons (e.g., ability) have a high internal locus of control. In a distributive negotiation task, Ford (1983) found that "internals" had higher resistance points than "externals." In addition, Ford found a tendency for teams composed of internals to be more likely to stalemate during negotiations. Greenhalgh and Neslin (1983) found that externals were more likely to prefer an impasse than a moderately favorable settlement. While neither study found a direct effect of locus of control on negotiation outcomes, a study of distributive negotiations in four-person networks with a sample of female college students by Stolte (1983) suggests that internals may negotiate better outcomes than externals, especially when they are in noncentral positions in networks. Taking these findings as a whole, locus of control appears to influence negotiator aspirations, preferences, and negotiation outcomes.

Self-Monitoring

Self-monitoring refers to the extent to which people are responsive to the social cues that come from the social environment (Snyder, 1974, 1987). High self-monitors are attentive to external, interpersonal information that arises in social settings and are more inclined to treat this information as cues to how they should behave. Low self-monitors are less attentive to external information that may cue behavior and are guided more in their behavioral choices by inner, personal feelings. One can think of self-monitoring as the extent to which people monitor the external social environment for cues about how they are supposed to behave.

Jerry Jordan and Michael Roloff (1997) examined the effects of self-monitoring on planning for negotiation. In their integrative negotiation simulation, high self-monitors were more likely to plan the impressions that they wanted to make on the other negotiator (e.g., to appear friendly), to plan to use logrolling during the negotiation (see Chapter 3), and to consider more strategies while planning. Self-monitoring also had an effect on the outcome of the negotiation, with high self-monitors negotiating outcomes that helped them achieve higher percentages of their goals than low self-monitors.

These findings indicate that self-monitoring is an important individual difference that influences negotiation. One might be tempted to think of self-monitoring as a tendency that is not particularly appealing; an example would be the insecure person who constantly adjusts his or her own actions to conform to what he or she thinks is appropriate for the situation. But having the motivation to monitor the social context, read it accurately, and adjust to it appear to be real assets in negotiation. Self-monitoring seems important during planning, but it may also interact with other factors, such as the other party's behavior, to influence negotiation process and outcomes (see Ohbuchi and Fukushima, 1997).

Machiavellianism

Another stream of research that links personality to bargaining behavior is work by Christie, Geis, and their associates on the concept of "Machiavellianism." After extensive study of the writings of Niccolo Machiavelli and similar political philosophers, Christie and Geis (1970) developed an attitude scale based on Machiavelli's classic writings. Those scoring high in Machiavellianism (high Machs) tend to be cynical about others' motives, more likely to behave unaltruistically and unsympathetically toward others, and less willing to change their convictions under social pressure. High Machs are thought to be more likely to tolerate behavior that violates social norms and are more inclined to advocate the use of deception interpersonally.

In numerous studies, Christie and Geis explored the relationship between a Machiavellian orientation and behavior in various situations. We describe a few of these experiments here because of their applicability to negotiation processes. (See Christie and Geis, 1970, for more detailed descriptions of these and other studies of Machiavellianism.)

- One experiment created opportunities for subjects to dissuade another person from cheating, expose the cheater to the experimenter, refrain from using unethically obtained information, confess bad behavior to the experimenter, and lie about their own behavior. High Machs initially tried harder to persuade the other not to cheat and initially resisted using unethically obtained information in the experimental task. But high Machs were no different from low Machs in the frequency of lying before being directly accused by the experimenter. Once accused, high Machs maintained their ability to lie with far greater credibility. They confessed less and were able to maintain more direct, convincing eye contact with the experimenter while lying than were low Machs.

- A second experiment explored the willingness of subjects to engage in manipulative behavior when they were in a high-power position. High Machs attempted significantly more manipulative behaviors than low Machs, in both the total number and variety. They told bigger lies, were more verbally distracting, and were more innovative in the manipulative techniques employed. Finally, high Machs enjoyed their manipulative, high-power role.

- A third experiment described behavior in a game structured to allow players to join coalitions in order to win. Compared with other players, high Machs displayed a more opportunistic sense of timing with regard to making or breaking a coalition, and they more clearly controlled the initiation of bids and the structure of the coalition negotiations. High Machs initiated more offers, decisively dissolved coalitions when they were not advantageous, and were sought after by others to be in coalitions. As a result, high Machs were usually a member of the winning coalition and seldom lost the game or were shut out of points.

A few studies since Christie and Geis's experiments have directly examined the influence of Machiavellianism on negotiation. An experiment by Fry (1985) found that high Machs did better than low Machs in distributive negotiation.[9] Interestingly, Fry found that low Machs change their negotiation style as a function of the Machiavellianism of the other negotiator: when negotiating with a high Mach, low Machs made fewer offers and were less effective negotiators than when negotiating with low Machs. High-Mach negotiators did not change their negotiation style as a function of the other party's Machiavellianism. Lastly, Barry, Fulmer, and Long (2000) included Machiavellianism in their study of people's attitudes toward the use of ethically questionable negotiation tactics. Barry and colleagues found that high Machs were more likely to approve of the use of deceptive tactics (making false promises, misrepresenting interests) in negotiation. Taken together, these findings suggest that high Machs are willing to use a variety of tactics to pursue their objectives, and in doing so may intimidate the other party into adjusting strategy in ways that make the latter worse off.

Face Threat Sensitivity

The concept of "face" refers to the value people place on their public image or reputation. The everyday expressions "losing face" and "saving face" describe situations in which a person fears a decline in that reputation or encounters an opportunity to avoid such a decline. Researchers have recently begun to explore the notion that sensitivity to threats to face is a stable aspect of an individual's personality. In other words, some of us are by disposition more susceptible to reacting in a negative way to threats to face—more thin-skinned, you might say. A study by Judith White and her colleagues (White, Tynan, Galinsky, and Thompson, 2004) explored how this trait—they call it *face threat sensitivity* (FTS)—might work as an element of the personality of negotiators. Face is important in negotiation, they argue, because threats to one's image will make a negotiator competitive in a situation that might otherwise benefit from cooperative behavior. In two studies, White and colleagues found that negotiating dyads with at least one high-FTS negotiator (someone who scores high on sensitivity to face threats) were less likely to create value that could benefit both parties and less likely to reach cooperative settlements. Although these studies did not pinpoint exactly how and why high FTS interferes with integrative potential, the authors offer some plausible explanations. One is that a high FTS negotiator is more likely to perceive the other party's actions as a potential threat, leading to negative feelings, mistrust of the other party, and more competitive behavior. Another is that the opponent of the high FTS negotiator may see that person as " 'high maintenance,' requiring more care and trouble than he/she is worth" (p. 118). Research exploring predispositions to react to threats to self-image is a worthwhile direction for the study of individual differences in negotiation research because, as White and colleagues put it, "Face concerns exert a gravitational pull on negotiators: powerful, inexorable, invisible" (p. 120).

The "Big Five" Personality Factors

One way of moving the study of personality toward a more unified and coherent position, and away from numerous studies of a multitude of seemingly unrelated traits, is to focus on a very few key personality categories, or factors, under which most individual traits can be subsumed. This is what personality psychologists had in mind when they developed the Five-Factor Model of personality (e.g., Goldberg, 1993), also known as the "Big Five." The personality factors that comprise the Big Five include these (Barrick and Mount, 1991, pp. 3–5):

- Extraversion—being sociable, assertive, talkative.
- Agreeableness—being flexible, cooperative, trusting.
- Conscientiousness—being responsible, organized, achievement oriented.
- Emotional stability—being secure, confident, not anxious.
- Openness—being imaginative, broad-minded, curious.

Research by Barry and Friedman (1998) examined how the Big Five personality factors are related to negotiator behavior and outcomes. Their study looked at both distributive and integrative negotiation situations, focusing on the first three of the five factors listed. With respect to distributive bargaining (a price negotiation simulation), Barry and Friedman found that negotiators higher in extraversion and agreeableness were more likely to do worse for themselves. One reason is that these negotiators were more susceptible to the trap of "anchoring," which occurs when one party's extreme offer biases the other party's view of the underlying structure of the situation. For example, imagine that Jack makes an extreme opening offer; to the extent that Jill, after hearing Jack's offer, reframes her view of her own aspirations and probability of success and concedes more than she otherwise would have, she is said to have been "anchored" by Jack's opening. Barry and Friedman argued that anchoring is a greater risk for extraverted and agreeable negotiators because of their greater focus on the maintenance of social relations. Importantly, however, their findings showed that these effects of personality were lessened when negotiators had high aspirations for their own performance. To put it another way, a high degree of motivation to do well overcame the liability of certain personality traits in negotiation.

Barry and Friedman found that these elements of personality did not affect how well negotiators did in a separate experiment involving a more complex integrative bargaining simulation. In that situation, personality was less important than the cognitive ability (intelligence) of negotiators (we discuss the role of abilities later in this chapter). Unexpectedly, they found no role for negotiator conscientiousness in either distributive or integrative settings. It is widely assumed, and we agree, that successful negotiators are better planners, are more attentive, are more organized, and have higher aspirations—the very characteristics one might expect from a person high in the personality trait of conscientiousness. However, we have yet to see research evidence connecting the disposition to be conscientious with negotiation behaviors or outcomes.

Section Summary

In this section, we discussed the role of personality in negotiation in terms of a variety of dispositional traits, including conflict style, social value orientation, interpersonal trust, self-efficacy, locus of control, self-monitoring, Machiavellianism, and face threat sensitivity. Recent convergence by many personality psychologists around the Five-Factor Model (the "Big Five") has brought into focus the question of whether personality traits are best viewed separately or in clusters of related traits. The Five-Factor Model is an appealing way to analyze personality because it reduces many personality traits that exist into a limited and manageable set of broad categories. On the other hand, narrow traits may do a better job predicting negotiation behavior than these broad personality factors because the aggregation of traits into factors masks important relationships between specific traits and specific strategies (Moberg, 1998). It seems likely that future research on personality in negotiation will continue to struggle with this tension between the specific and the general.

Personality is also potentially important in negotiation because people view the actions of other parties through a lens of personality. A study by Morris, Larrick, and Su (1999) found that although interests and positions determine much of what happens in negotiation, negotiators tend to interpret the behavior of their negotiating counterparts in terms of personality. For example, negotiators who lack sufficient information about the other party's situation may resort to inferences about the other party's agreeableness or cooperativeness as a way to understand what is happening. The result is *misperception*—negotiators inappropriately explain the actions of others in personality terms even though elements of the situation are actually responsible. Clearly, a full understanding of the role of personality in negotiation requires attention not just to how someone's personality affects his or her actions, but also to how we use or misuse personality to explain the actions of others with whom we negotiate. Context is also a critical issue that deserves more attention. Consider, for instance, national cultures: personality traits may function in one culture very differently than in another. Liu, Friedman, and Chi (2005) showed that "Big Five" traits, such as agreeableness and extraversion, affect American negotiators but not Chinese, while other factors, such as harmony, affect Chinese negotiators but not Americans. With international negotiations growing in importance as globalization expands, there is much yet to learn about the intersection of personality and culture in negotiation.

Abilities in Negotiation

Are smarter people or those more capable in certain cognitive or emotional domains better negotiators? What does it mean to be "smart"? In this section, we examine the relationship between three kinds of abilities and negotiation behavior: (1) cognitive ability, which is the traditional conceptualization of intelligence; (2) the more recently developed concept of emotional intelligence; and (3) perspective-taking ability.

Cognitive Ability

Cognitive ability refers to "a very general mental capability that, among other things, involves the ability to reason, plan, solve problems, think abstractly, comprehend complex ideas, learn quickly and learn from experience" (Gottfredson, 1997, p. 13). Cognitive ability, which is synonymous with the general notion of intelligence, has been shown to influence reasoning, decision making, information processing capacity, learning, and adaptability to change, particularly in novel or complex situations.[10] These aspects of thinking and mental processing are clearly related to much of what goes on the cognitive (as opposed to the emotional) side of negotiation. To the extent that negotiation entails the navigation of complex problem-solving tasks, it is reasonable to expect that individual cognitive ability may predict negotiation processes and outcomes (Fulmer and Barry, 2004).

There has been only limited research attention to the role of cognitive ability in negotiation. A few early studies involving experimental bargaining games, such as the Prisoner's Dilemma, produced mixed and inconclusive findings. However, a different picture emerged when studies examined cognitive ability in more complex integrative negotiation settings. Barry and Friedman (1998) found a strong link between negotiator cognitive ability and the integrativeness of settlements reached by participants in a complex commercial real estate negotiation simulation. Similarly, Kurtzberg (1998) found that cognitive ability predicted the ability of negotiators to reach integrative settlements in a simulation about a syndication contract for a television program. Smarter negotiators, it appears, have an advantage in moving the parties toward recognizing and exploiting joint gain.

Integrative complexity is a term psychologists use to refer to the complexity of cognitive rules that a person employs to process information. Those who are high in integrative complexity are able to make distinctions between different dimensions of a problem and to understand how these dimensions are related to one another. People who are low in this ability tend to perceive the world in "black and white" and often display more authoritarian personality characteristics (Tibon, 2000).

Researchers have looked at integrative complexity as a factor related to effectiveness in political crises and international diplomacy. Here are a few select findings:

- Low integrative complexity is associated with more competitive conflict resolution strategies, while high integrative complexity

is associated with the use of more cooperative strategies and more integrative agreements (Walker and Watson, 1994).

- Suedfeld and Bluck (1988) analyzed documents from nine international crises in the 20th century to show that leaders' integrative complexity decreased in the three months prior to committing a surprise attack, whereas no such decrease was found prior to committing to a peaceful agreement.

- An analysis of U.S. congressional transcripts prior to and during the 1991 Persian Gulf war revealed that members of Congress in favor of the use of force in Iraq were less cognitively complex than those who voted against the attack (Wallace, Suedfeld, and Thachuk, 1993).

What about purely distributive negotiation situations? Do negotiators with high cognitive ability do better? Barry and Friedman (1998) explored this issue using a distributive bargaining task in which a manufacturer and supplier negotiate the price of a component. They found no link between intelligence and performance. However, this finding should be regarded with caution because the task in their study was a very basic, single-issue negotiation. The possible role of negotiator intelligence in distributive bargaining situations of greater complexity remains unexplored. Box 15.2 provides a related application of the role of intelligence in negotiation.

Emotional Intelligence

In recent years psychologists have proposed that other forms of intelligence beyond general cognitive ability may exist as stable abilities. One in particular that has attracted a good deal of attention since the early 1990s is the notion of emotional intelligence (EI). Researchers define *emotional intelligence* as encompassing a set of discrete but related abilities: (1) the ability to perceive and express emotion accurately, (2) the ability to access emotion in facilitating thought, (3) the ability to comprehend and analyze emotion, and (4) the ability to regulate appropriately one's own emotions and those of others (Mayer and Salovey, 1997). A book written by a journalist in the mid-1990s (Goleman, 1995) made strong claims about the role of emotional intelligence in a broad range of social domains and attracted widespread attention in the popular press. Some academics criticized those claims as misleading, and overstated (Mayer, Salovey, and Caruso, 2000), others have questioned the research methods behind those claims (Landy, 2005), and still others have questioned whether the very concept of EI has any scientific validity at all (Locke, 2005). Nonetheless, interest in EI has continued to grow among

scholars who see it as appropriately rooted in the scientific analysis of human emotion (Ashkanasy and Daus, 2005). It is fair to say, as a general matter, that the concept of emotional intelligence has resonated with both researchers and the lay public as a way to capture variations in how people analyze and use emotion in social life.

As we discussed in Chapter 5, interest among negotiation researchers in emotional aspects of negotiation has risen in recent years. To the extent that the concept of EI captures stable and measurable tendencies involving the perception, comprehension, and regulation of emotion, it may be an important individual difference for the study of negotiation (Ogilvie and Carsky, 2002). Making this case, Fulmer and Barry (2004) argued that an emotionally intelligent negotiator's ability to sense and regulate emotion will confer several advantages: better information gathering about the other party's interests; more accurate risk assessment; and more effective management of one's own emotions and inducement of desired emotions from the other party. Negotiators high in EI may be better able to use emotions to influence the negotiation outcome—part of a process that Thompson, Nadler, and Kim (1999) referred to as *emotional tuning*.

To date, only a few studies have empirically investigated the role of EI in negotiation. The work that has been done clearly suggests that people high in EI tend to create a more positive negotiation experience, both for themselves and for the other party (Foo, Elfenbein, Tan and Aik, 2004; Mueller and Curhan, 2006). However, the link between EI and negotiation outcomes—are emotionally intelligent negotiators "better" negotiators?—is less clear. Two studies have examined the effect of an individual's EI on individual and joint outcomes in two-party negotiations (Elfenbein, Foo, White, Tan, and Aik, 2007; Foo et al.,

2004). The findings from both suggest that high-EI negotiators are more effective at creating value in a negotiation, suggesting EI may be an asset in reaching integrative deals. These two studies reported conflicting findings, however, on the issue of whether EI helps the individual negotiator claim more of that value for him- or herself (in other words, reach a better deal). More research is needed to fully understand the role of EI in negotiation and to resolve lingering questions about the best way to measure EI (Conte, 2005; Van Rooy and Viswesvaran, 2004).

Perspective-Taking Ability

Negotiators need to perceive, understand, and respond to arguments that the other party makes during negotiations. The ability to take the other person's perspective, especially during planning for negotiation, should enable negotiators to prepare and respond to the other party's arguments. Perspective-taking ability is defined as "a negotiator's capacity to understand the other party's point of view during a negotiation and thereby to predict the other party's strategies and tactics" (Neale and Northcraft, 1991, p. 174). As a fundamental example, distributive negotiators who better understand the resistance point of the other party will have a strategic advantage during negotiations (a point made first by Walton and McKersie, 1965, in their now classic treatise on bargaining). Negotiators who understand the other party's perspective will be more likely to form arguments that convince the other party and should also be more likely to find an agreement that satisfies the other party. The ability to see the other party's point of view is especially important during integrative negotiation as the negotiator strives to understand the other party's needs and interests and works to craft an agreement that satisfies the interests of both parties.

Neale and Bazerman (1983) investigated the importance of perspective-taking ability in a study of the effect of arbitration on distributive contract negotiations. They found that negotiators with higher perspective-taking ability negotiated contracts of higher value than did negotiators with lower perspective-taking ability. Their findings pointed to a link between perspective-taking ability and concession rate: negotiators high in perspective-taking ability appear to be able to increase the concessions that the other party is willing to make. It appears that perspective takers are better able to uncover the underlying interests shared by two parties and to come to more creative solutions because of their ability to understand the goals and interests of the other party (Galinsky, Maddux, Gilin, and White, 2008). This is particularly important for arriving at integrative solutions. Perspective-taking ability has been shown to predict joint outcomes as well as individual outcomes. In fact, merely thinking about perspective taking prior to an integrative negotiation can lead to higher joint outcomes (Kemp and Smith, 1994).

Given that negotiation is fundamentally about resolving conflict through interdependence and communication, it seems plausible to assume that perspective-taking ability is an important individual difference in social interaction, one that is generally beneficial in negotiation and other situations involving the resolution of conflict. However, in a fascinating series of experiments, Epley, Caruso, and Bazerman (2006) demonstrated that perspective taking can be a double-edged sword. In several tasks involving allocations of limited resources within groups, they found that individuals who took time to think about what others would believe is fair were more apt to say that fairness for themselves involves taking a smaller share of resources. In other words, taking the others' perspective made one less likely to

Power Corrupts Perspective Taking?

BOX 15.3

Are powerful people self-centered and focused on their own desires and objectives, and less attuned to the needs of others? Researchers Adam Galinsky, Joe Magee, Ena Inesi, and Deborah Gruenfeld think the answer is yes—that individuals having power or feeling powerful are less able to move beyond their own experience and imagine the motivations, needs, and emotions of others. They explored this hypothesis by inducing feelings of power in some experimental subjects and then testing their ability to read others' emotions.

In their experiment, half of the participants (the high-power condition) were told to recall and write about a past incident in which they had power over someone else. Other studies have shown this to be a reliable technique for inducing a sense of power in experimental subjects. The other half of their participants (a control condition) were told to recall and describe what their day yesterday was like. All participants then performed a task that involved looking at a number of images of faces, each of which expresses an emotion, and indicating for each face which of four emotions (happiness, fear, anger, and sadness) is on display.

The researchers anticipated that high-power participants, being less inclined to attend to how others experience the world and feel about things, would do worse at reading the emotions expressed by faces in the images. And that's exactly what happened: those who were induced to feel powerful (merely by writing an essay in the high-power condition) made significantly more errors judging the facial emotions in the images than did participants in the control condition.

Because study participants were not aware of a connection between the manipulation of power (inducing feelings of power for half the subjects) and the subsequent task involving detecting emotions, the researchers reasoned that the loss of perspective taking that accompanies power is at least partially a nonconscious process. "We believe that power leads not to a conscious decision to ignore other individuals' perspectives," they concluded, "but rather to a psychological state that makes perspective taking less likely" (p. 1072).

Source: Adapted from A. D. Galinsky, J. C. Magee, M. N. Inesi, and D. H. Gruenfeld, "Power and Perspectives Not Taken," *Psychological Science* 17 (2006), pp. 1068–74.

judge what is fair in egocentric terms. That seems sensible enough, but here's the rub: perspective takers may have *judged* fairness in a *less* self-interested way, but when the time came to actually make an allocation decision, they *behaved* in a *more* self-interested way—they took more of the available resources for themselves! How to explain this surprising paradox? The researchers were able to show that it happened because the act of considering the perspective of others led people to contemplate the possibility that others will probably act more selfishly, leading the "perspective taker" to arrive at a decision to act selfishly in return (they call this "reactive egoism"). Does this make perspective taking a bad thing? No, but Epley and colleagues do say it points to the value of explicitly highlighting the parties' mutual interests and their need for cooperation as a way to capitalize on the benefits of perspective taking without incurring the negative (selfish) behavior. They concluded: "Sometimes considering others' perspectives can increase the very egoistic behavior that perspective taking was designed to reduce. Care should be taken when suggesting that people should look beyond their own perspective, as those who look into the minds of others may not like what they see" (p. 887).

A social condition that may cloud or reduce people's ability to understand others' perspective in the first place is the exerience of having power or feeling powerful; see Box 15.3 for a clever experimental illustration.

An Alternative Approach: Studying Successful Negotiators

Some research seeks to uncover negotiation effectiveness by analyzing the actual behaviors of superior negotiators, rather than identifying their personality traits or native abilities. The implicit assumption underlying this research is that individuals who can understand and apply the behavior of successful negotiators will become better negotiators themselves. That assumption rests, in turn, on an even more basic premise: that negotiation is a skill that can actually be improved rather than just a fixed ability that you either have or you don't. To put it another way, are good negotiators born or made? It may seem apparent that as authors of a textbook on negotiation, we side with the view that negotiation is a skill that can be developed.

The position one takes on this question—whether negotiators are born or made—is more than just an intellectual diversion. Recent research by Laura Kray and Michael Haselhuhn (2007) shows that one's view on this issue is strongly related to negotiation outcomes. In a series of experiments, Kray and Haselhuhn contrasted the negotiation behavior and performance of individuals who believe that negotiating abilities are fixed (they labeled people with this belief "entity theorists") with individuals who believe that negotiating ability can be changed and improved (they called these people "incremental theorists"). In some studies they manipulated these beliefs by having experimental participants read (supposedly) expert opinions about whether good negotiators are born or made. In other studies they simply measured these beliefs, tapping participants' actual views on the subject. In all cases, they found that incremental theorists—people holding beliefs that negotiation is a malleable skill—outperformed entity theorists by a wide margin. The advantage was found in both claiming value (distributive negotiation) and creating value (integrative negotiation). Why should these beliefs about negotiation ability matter so much? The answer, Kray and Haselhuhn argue, is that incremental theorists benefit from "a willingness to expend effort in the face of challenges, even when the chances for success appear small. Armed with a goal to learn and master the negotiation domain, incremental theorists are willing to stare potential failure in the face and plow through it with continued perseverance" (p. 62).

If there is value in believing that negotiation is a skill that can be developed, there is also value in trying to understand the actions of people who are already good at it. Three approaches have been used to study the behavior of successful negotiators: (1) comparing superior and average negotiators in actual negotiations, (2) comparing expert and amateur negotiators in simulated negotiations, and (3) comparing experienced and naive negotiators in simulated negotiations. Each of these approaches has strengths and weaknesses; none of them is ideal. However, this research does provide some interesting insights about how superior negotiators behave.

A comprehensive study comparing superior and average negotiators in actual negotiations was conducted by Neil Rackham (1980), who compared the behavior of labor relations negotiators in 102 actual negotiation sessions. He found important differences between superior and average negotiators during prenegotiation planning, face-to-face negotiations, and postnegotiation review. The results of this study are summarized in Table 15.1. While the results of Rackham's study may not be fully applicable to negotiations outside of labor relations, they provide sensible advice for all negotiators.

TABLE 15.1 | Behaviors of Superior Negotiators Identified by Rackham (1980)

During Prenegotiation Planning

Considered more outcome options for the issues being discussed.

Spent more time looking for areas of common ground.

Thought more about the long-term consequences of different issues.

Prepared their goals around ranges rather than fixed points.

Did not form their plans into strict sequential order.

During Face-to-Face Bargaining

Made fewer immediate counterproposals.

Were less likely to describe their offers in glowingly positive terms.

Avoided defend–attack cycles.

Used behavioral labeling, except when disagreeing.

Asked more questions, especially to test understanding.

Summarized compactly the progress made in the negotiation.

Did not dilute their arguments by including weak reasons when they were trying to persuade the other party.

During Postnegotiation Review

Reserved time to review what they learned from the negotiation.

Source: Adapted from N. Rackham (1980), "The Behavior of Successful Negotiators," Huthwaite Research Group. Reprinted in R. J. Lewicki, D. M. Saunders, and J. W. Minton (eds.), *Negotiation: Readings, Exercises, and Cases,* 3rd ed. (New York: McGraw-Hill, 1999).

Margaret Neale and Greg Northcraft (1986) compared the performance of expert and amateur negotiators in a simulated negotiation market. This task gives buyers and sellers the opportunity to negotiate with any other seller or buyer in the market, but each buyer–seller pair may make only one deal. There is typically not enough time in market simulations for all possible buyer–seller pairs to make a deal. The expert negotiators in the study were professional negotiators with average formal experience of more than 10 years. The amateur negotiators were graduate and undergraduate college students. Neale and Northcraft found that while both experts and amateurs were more likely to reach integrative solutions as the market progressed, experts were more integrative at the beginning of the negotiations than were amateurs. Experts also tended to receive higher average outcomes than amateurs, although this difference was not very strong.

A couple of studies have investigated the effects of experience on subsequent negotiation outcomes. O'Connor, Arnold, and Burris (2005) explored how experience in one negotiation encounter influences the quality of negotiated outcomes in subsequent encounters. Their findings were straighforward: those whose first negotiation ended in impasse (no deal) were more likely to reach another impasse in their next negotiation. Moreover, those who reached an impasse the first time but reached a deal the second time arrived at agreements of lower quality compared to those who successfully reached a deal the first time. These results held regardless of whether the second negotiation was with the same opponent or not, whether negotiation occurred face-to-face or online, or whether the time interval between negotiations was short (15 minutes) or long (one week).

Leigh Thompson (1990a) examined the effects of a particular kind of experience—prior opportunities to engage in integrative bargaining—on judgments, behaviors, and outcomes in negotiation. Thompson formed two groups of negotiators. In the experienced negotiator group, negotiators increased their experience by bargaining with a different person in seven different integrative negotiation simulations. In the naive negotiator group, negotiators had either little or no previous experience with integrative negotiation, and only one opportunity to increase their experience in the study. Thompson found that experienced negotiators made more accurate judgments about the other party's priorities as they gained experience and that the likelihood of negotiating favorable agreements increased with experience, especially when negotiating with a naive negotiator who had no previous experience with the simulation.

In summary, research examining successful negotiators suggests that expert, experienced, and otherwise superior negotiators behave differently from average negotiators in several ways. We hasten to add, however, that studying expertise and experience in negotiation is challenging because it is difficult for researchers to gain access to actual negotiations (Rackham, 1980, is a rare example). When researchers do find opportunities to study professional negotiators in action, the act of observing poses its own problems because observational methods can easily change the process under study. (People being observed often find it difficult to ignore their watchers and may change their behavior from what it would otherwise be unobserved.) Although researchers can study negotiator experience with more precision and control in laboratory simulations, these experimental methods lack the richness of actual negotiations. The most appropriate approach may be a combination of laboratory studies and field work.

A Concluding Note

In closing, we wish to revisit and reinforce observations we made at the start of Chapter 14—the first of the two chapters on individual differences—about the value of understanding how personal differences are connected with negotiation processes and outcomes. As we noted in Chapter 14, it is true that the characteristics of individuals generally do not predict negotiation processes and outcomes as well as the characteristics of situations, and it is also the case that stable individual differences for the most part cannot be controlled or altered by an individual negotiator. We believe, nonetheless, that individual differences matter for several reasons. One is that although negotiators can't "choose" their abilities or traits, there are times when a leader or manager can choose a negotiator, and in making that choice may have access to information about relevant personal attributes of candidates. Another is that some individual differences point to disadvantages for which the savvy negotiator can compensate—perhaps by becoming aware of the disadvantage and seeking to overcome it through concerted effort, or perhaps by assembling a negotiating team that capitalizes on others' strengths in order to limit one's own weaknesses. It is also the case that understanding how individual differences affect negotiators for better or worse can help us improve how we perceive, interpret, react to, and act upon the other party's actions and strategies.

Chapter Summary

In this chapter we reviewed early and contemporary research on the effects of individual differences—personality traits and abilities—on negotiation. Early research found clear and simple effects to be elusive. In many cases, the research methods were inadequate to allow personality differences to emerge; in other cases, personality differences were obscured by major structural differences in the bargaining situation (the nature of the bargaining problem, relative power of negotiators, constituency pressures, etc.), or personality and structure interacted to produce complex effects.

More recent studies have overcome some of these liabilities. We discussed several aspects of personality that have some promise for characterizing differences among negotiators, including conflict management style, social value orientation, interpersonal trust, self-efficacy, locus of control, self-monitoring, Machiavellianism, face threat sensitivity, and the Five-Factor Model. We then examined the role of abilities in negotiation, including cognitive ability, emotional intelligence, and perspective-taking ability. There is some evidence that smarter negotiators (higher cognitive ability) are better able to find and exploit integrative potential. Although empirical evidence on the role of emotional intelligence in negotiation is still emerging, there is reason to believe that emotionally intelligent negotiators may have some strategic advantages. Research links perspective-taking ability to the development of integrative outcomes, although the underlying process through which this occurs has not been clearly illuminated.

We also explored a behavioral approach to studying individual differences was also examined. Rather than searching for underlying personality dimensions, this approach concentrates on describing how expert or accomplished negotiators behave and compares it with the actions of less experienced or less effective negotiators. Research using this approach has the potential to provide unique information about how people can learn to negotiate more effectively.

Although the study of individual differences continues to pose significant challenges, we see a future for research in this area. Researchers must be careful, however, to measure differences rigorously and to analyze behavior across diverse negotiation situations. Positive trends in research on individual differences include a focus on how personality effects vary depending on situational factors (also called the interactionist approach; see, e.g., Cantrell and Butler, 1997; Ohbuchi and Fukushima, 1997) and movement beyond the study of simple distributive negotiation tasks to consider more complex integrative situations (e.g., Barry and Friedman, 1998; Kray, Thompson, and Galinsky, 2001).

We noted at the outset of Chapter 14 (on gender and negotiation), and again in this chapter, that some researchers are skeptical about the importance of individual differences. Although the concerns are legitimate, we believe that some may have closed the book prematurely on the effects of individual differences on negotiation and that individual differences can have an important effect on the process and outcome of negotiation. It is true that negotiators cannot "change" their personalities or other stable individual differences, but they can learn to compensate for the limitations these characteristics might bring and to capitalize on behavioral tendencies that may follow from the characteristics of other parties. Moreover, constituencies and organizations frequently make choices about who will negotiate on their behalf; in these circumstances, individual differences can play an important role in negotiator selection.

Endnotes

1. Rubin and Brown (1975) reviewed 200 empirical studies of background, demographic, and personality factors that might contribute to differences in bargaining outcomes. Other detailed reviews of early research include Hermann and Kogan (1977) and Terhune (1970).

2. See, for example, Kabanoff, (1987); Pruitt and Rubin (1986); Rahim (1983); Ruble and Thomas (1976); van de Vliert and Kabanoff (1988); and van de Vliert and Prein (1989).

3. See Ben-Yoav and Pruitt (1984a, 1984b); Carnevale and Keenan (1990); O'Connor (1997); O'Connor and Carnevale (1997); and Pruitt, Carnevale, Ben-Yoav, Nochajski, and Van Slyck (1983).

4. See also de Dreu and van Lange (1995); Olekalns and Smith (1999); and Olekalns, Smith, and Kibby (1996).

5. An exception to the idea that trait motives and state motives have similar effects is the satisfaction with outcomes

that negotiators experience after a deal is reached. In the study of satisfaction mentioned earlier (Gillespie, Brett, and Weingart, 2000), the finding that pro-self negotiators were less satisfied afterward held for measured (stable-trait) motives, but there was no effect for induced motives (instructing the negotiator to be pro-self or pro-social).

[6] Rotter and his colleagues developed a test for diagnosing an individual's level of interpersonal trust and used the scores to measure levels of interpersonal trustworthiness. More detailed description of these and other studies of interpersonal trust can be found in Rotter (1967, 1971, 1980).

[7] See Ross and LaCroix (1996), for a review of research on trust and negotiation.

[8] See also Stevens, Bavetta, and Gist (1993); Stevens and Gist (1997).

[9] There is one study, Greenhalgh and Neslin (1983), that reported a contrary finding—that high Machs tended to negotiate inferior outcomes compared with low Machs.

[10] See, for example, Gottfredson (1997); Lepine, Colquitt, and Erez (2000); Ree and Earles (1991); and Schmidt and Hunter (1998).

CHAPTER 16

International and Cross-Cultural Negotiation

Objectives

1. Understand how international and cross-cultural negotiations are different from domestic or same-culture negotiations.
2. Explore different definitions and meanings of a culture.
3. Consider how culture affects negotiation dynamics.
4. Gain strategies that negotiators can adapt to another party's cultural style.

Although there has been an interest in international negotiation for centuries, the frequency of international negotiation has increased rapidly in the past 20 years (Hopmann, 1995; Weiss, 2006). People today travel more frequently and farther, and business is more international than ever before. For many people and organizations, international negotiation has become the norm rather than an exotic activity that only occurs occasionally. Numerous books and articles—from both academic and practitioner perspectives—have been written about the complexities of negotiating across borders, be it with a person from a different country, culture, or region. Although the term *culture* has many possible definitions, we use it to refer to the shared values, beliefs, and behaviors of a group of people. Countries can have more than one culture, and cultures can span national borders. As we discussed in Chapters 1 and 10, negotiating is a social process that is embedded in a much larger context. This context increases in complexity when more than one culture or country is involved, making international negotiation a highly complicated process (Sebenius, 2002a).

So much has been written on this topic that we cannot summarize it all in one chapter, and those seeking more information about international and cross-cultural negotiation are encouraged to consult one of several important literature reviews.[1] Recent topics addressed in this area include studies of negotiations in newly developing economies,[2] intracultural comparisons of negotiators from several different countries,[3] negotiation in China (examined by numerous researchers),[4] and international diplomacy and trade negotiations.[5] Our goal in this chapter is to present a broad overview of the international and cross-cultural negotiation field, as well as to highlight and discuss some of the most recent and interesting work that has been written on this topic.

BOX 16.1   Cross-Cultural Negotiations within the United States

I had a client in West Virginia who bought from me for several years. He had a family business that he'd started in a small town with his grandfather, and it had now grown to be the major employer in the town. We had developed quite a close relationship. Every few months, I would make a trip up from North Carolina to see him, knowing after a while that he would need to place an order with me as long as I spaced our visits out every few months. When we got together, at first we would talk about everything but business, catching up with each other. I would ask him about his life, the business, his family, the town, etc., and he would ask me about my work and the company and life in the big city in North Carolina where I lived and worked. Once we'd caught up with each other, we would get down to some business, and this was often after lunch. Each and every time, it would take a few hours of this and that, but I'd always leave with an order, and it was always a pleasant break, at least for me, from my usual hectic pace.

One day I phoned in preparation for my next trip, to see if he would be in, to arrange a convenient day, and he told me that he'd like me to meet a friend of his next time I was up there to visit him. His friend, he said, was interested in some of the things my company was selling, and he thought I should meet him. Of course I was delighted, and we arranged a convenient day for the three of us to meet.

When I arrived at my client's office, his friend, Carl, was already there. We were very casually introduced, and my client began explaining Carl's work, and how he thought what my company sold could be useful to him. Carl then took over and spoke a little about what he did, and I thought for a moment that we were going to go straight into business talk. However, in just a few moments, the conversation among the three of us quickly turned back to discussions of life in town, North Carolina, our respective families, and personal interests. It turned out that Carl liked to hunt, and he and my client began regaling me with stories of their hunting adventures. I'd hunted a little, and shared my stories with them. One thing led to another, and soon we were talking about vacations, the economy, baseball—you name it.

Occasionally, we would make a brief journey back to the business at hand, but it always seemed to be in conjunction with the small talk, like how the tools we manufactured were or were not as precise as the mechanisms on the guns we used for hunting, things like that. I realized that quite a lot of information about our mutual work, my company, their needs, and their work was being exchanged in all this, even though business was never directly addressed. I remember the first few meetings my client and I had had with each other many years ago—how we learned about each other this way then, too. I was struck with how quaint it felt now, how different it was from the way I usually had to sell, and yet how much I enjoyed working like this!

Well, our discussions went on this way through the rest of the morning, weaving some business back and forth through the larger context of informal chit-chat about each other and our lives. Just before lunch, my client leaned back and began what seemed to be a kind of informal summary of who I was and what I did, and how what I did seemed to him to be just the thing that Carl and his company could use. Carl agreed, and my client asked him, almost on my behalf, how much he wanted to order, and Carl thought for a moment and gave me the biggest order I ever got from West Virginia. "Now that that's done," my client said, "how about some lunch?" We all went to the same place we always go to when I'm in West Virginia, talking about life and things and some business. By midafternoon I said I had to be heading home. We all agreed to stay in touch. We've been in touch ever since, and now I've got two clients to visit whenever I'm in West Virginia.

Source: D. A. Foster, *Bargaining across Borders: How to Negotiate Business Successfully Anywhere in the World* (New York: McGraw-Hill, 1992), pp. 108–09. Reproduced with the permission of The McGraw-Hill Companies.

It is important to recognize that this book has been written from a North American perspective, and that this cultural filter has influenced how we think about negotiation, what we consider to be important aspects of negotiation, and our advice about how to become a better negotiator (Brett and Gelfand, 2004). This chapter also reflects our own cultural filter, both in our choices about what we discuss and because we use Americans as the base from which to make comparisons to other cultures.[6] That is not to say that all Americans share the same culture (see Box 16.1). In fact, there is evidence that people from countries as similar as the United States and Canada negotiate differently (see Adler and Graham, 1987; Adler, Graham, and Schwarz, 1987). Within the United States and Canada, there are systematic regional and cultural differences (e.g., among English and French Canadians, and among Hispanics, African Americans, Southerners, New Yorkers, and other groups in many areas of the United States). At some level, however, Americans do share (more or less) a common culture that is different from that of other countries. While recognizing the differences within the United States, we use some common aspects of American culture in our discussion of international and cross-cultural negotiation.

This chapter is organized in the following manner. First we discuss the art and science of cross-cultural negotiation. Next, we consider some of the factors that make international negotiation different, including both the environmental context (macropolitical factors) and the immediate context (microstrategic factors). We then turn to a discussion of the most frequently studied aspect of international negotiation: the effect of culture, be it national, regional, or organizational. We discuss how culture has been conceptualized and discuss four approaches to culture used by academics and practitioners. Next we examine the influence of culture on negotiations, discussing this from managerial and research perspectives. The chapter concludes with a discussion of culturally responsive strategies available to the international negotiator. Boxes throughout the chapter present examples of factors to think about when negotiating with people from other cultures.[7]

International Negotiation: Art and Science

The notion that negotiation is both art and science is especially valid at the cross-cultural or international level. The science of negotiation provides research evidence to support broad trends that often, but not always, occur during negotiation. The art of negotiation is deciding which strategy to apply when and choosing which models and perspectives to apply to increase cross-cultural understanding. This is especially challenging because cross-cultural and international negotiations add a level of complexity significantly greater than within-culture negotiations. There are two implications of this complexity for this chapter.

First, we present many different models and perspectives on cross-cultural negotiation. They vary in comprehensiveness and usefulness across different situations. No one model will explain every cross-cultural negotiation situation—there is simply not the level of knowledge to create such a model, and likely never will be. This complexity is a source of frustration for many cross-cultural negotiators, who would like clearer practical guidance when negotiating across borders.

No simple cookbook exists. The models and approaches we present in this chapter allow cross-cultural negotiators to build a strong portfolio of tools to draw upon when they are

Consider, by way of broad illustration, the following situation. You are seated across from a male negotiator from a culture very different from your own. In the course of the negotiations, he makes an unexpectedly large concession. While you are pleased by this behavior, you probably also wish to explain and understand it. There are several distinct possibilities.

First, the other negotiator may have made his concession because of the kind of person he is. That is, something about his personality led him to do what he did, in which case he might be expected to behave this way under lots of other circumstances. Second, it may be something about the particular conflict that the two of you are engaged in; this, the problem over which you are negotiating, may be one that invites or tolerates large concessions. Third, the explanation may have to do with the unique interaction created by the two of

you working together; thus, had your opposite number been seated across from someone else, perhaps his negotiating behavior would have been very different. Finally in this listing of explanations for the other side's negotiation behavior is the possibility of culture. Perhaps people from his culture tend to be rather conciliatory in negotiation.

Each of these possible reasons—and others no doubt—could explain why another negotiator behaves in particular ways. We suspect, however, that culture is far more likely than other possibilities (at least in international settings) to be invoked as the dominant explanation. When in doubt we tend to begin with the assumption that culture or nationality is *the* source of the behavior, when, in reality, all of the above sources may be implicated.

Source: Jeffrey Z. Rubin and Frank E. A. Sander, "Culture, Negotiation and the Eye of the Beholder," *Negotiation Journal* (1991), pp. 249–50.

negotiating cross-culturally. From practice, reading and studying the effects of these tools negotiators will be able to hone their artistry in the domain of cross-cultural negotiation.

The second implication of the complexity of cross-cultural negotiation is the tendency for negotiators to undervalue the amount of *within-culture variation* that exists. It is important to remember that negotiation outcomes, both domestically and internationally, are determined by several different factors. While cultural differences are clearly important, negotiators must guard against assigning too much responsibility to them (Rubin and Sander, 1991; Sebenius, 2002b; Weiss, 2003). Dialdin, Kopelman, Adair, Brett, Okumura, and Lytle (1999) have labeled the tendency to overlook the importance of situational factors in favor of cultural explanations the *cultural attribution error* (also see Huang and van de Vliert, 2004; Matsumoto and Yoo, 2006). Consider the scenario described in Box 16.2. It is possible that any one of the potential causes, or any combination of them, could explain the negotiator's behavior. It is also important to recognize that even though culture describes group-level characteristics, it doesn't mean that every member of a culture will share those characteristics equally, and it is very difficult to predict an individual's behavior on the basis of cultural differences (Avruch, 2000; Sebenius, 2002b; Weiss, 2006). In fact, there is likely to be as wide a variety of behavioral differences *within* cultures as there is between cultures (Rubin and Sander, 1991). Although knowledge of the other party's culture may provide an initial clue about what to expect at the bargaining table, negotiators need to be open to adjusting their view very quickly as new information is gathered (Adler, 2002).

In summary, cross-cultural and international negotiations are much more complex than domestic negotiations. This complexity is also a source of energy, excitement, and frustration when negotiating across borders and will challenge negotiators to understand the science of negotiation while developing their artistry.

What Makes International Negotiation Different?

Phatak and Habib (1996) suggest that two overall contexts have an influence on international negotiations: the environmental context and the immediate context (see Figure 16.1). The *environmental context* includes environmental forces that neither negotiator controls that influence the negotiation. The *immediate context* includes factors over which negotiators appear to have some control. Understanding the role of factors in both the environmental and the immediate contexts is important to grasping the complexity of international negotiation processes and outcomes.

Environmental Context

Salacuse (1988) identified six factors in the environmental context that make international negotiations more challenging than domestic negotiations: political and legal pluralism, international economics, foreign governments and bureaucracies, instability, ideology, and culture. (Culture has received by far the most attention by those examining international negotiation, and it is discussed in a separate section later in this chapter.) Phatak and Habib (1996) have suggested an additional factor: external stakeholders. These factors can act to

FIGURE 16.1 | The Contexts of International Negotiations

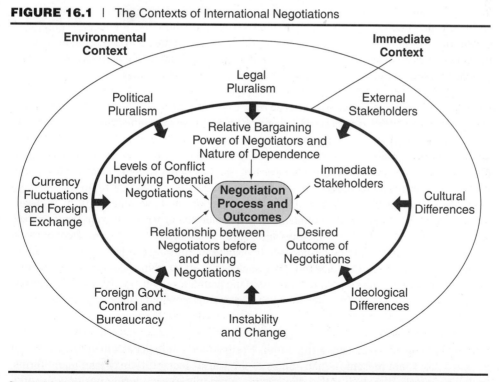

Source: Adapted from A. V. Phatak and M. H. Habib, "The Dynamics of International Business Negotiations," *Business Horizons* 39 (1996), pp. 30–38; and J. W. Salacuse, "Making Deals in Strange Places: A Beginner's Guide to International Business Negotiations," *Negotiation Journal* 4 (1988), pp. 5–13.

limit or constrain organizations that operate internationally, and it is important that negotiators understand and appreciate their effects.

Political and Legal Pluralism   Firms conducting business in different countries are working with different legal and political systems. There may be implications for taxes that an organization pays, labor codes or standards that must be met, and different codes of contract law and standards of enforcement (e.g., case law versus common law versus no functioning legal system). In addition, political considerations may enhance or detract from business negotiations in various countries at different times. For instance, the open business environment in the former Soviet republics in the 1990s is quite different than the closed environment of the 1960s, and conducting business in China today is quite different than even 10 years ago.

International Economics   The exchange value of international currencies naturally fluctuates, and this factor must be considered when negotiating in different countries. In which currency will the agreement be made? The risk is typically greater for the party who must pay in the other country's currency (Salacuse, 1988). The less stable the currency, the greater the risk for both parties. In addition, any change in the value of a currency (upward or downward) can significantly affect the value of the agreement for both parties, changing a mutually valuable deal into a windfall profit for one and a large loss for the other. Many countries also control the currency flowing across their borders. Frequently, purchases within these countries may be made only with hard currencies that are brought into the country by foreign parties, and domestic organizations are unable to purchase foreign products or negotiate outcomes that require payment in foreign currencies.

Foreign Governments and Bureaucracies   Countries differ in the extent to which the government regulates industries and organizations. Firms in the United States are relatively free from government intervention, although some industries are more heavily regulated than others (e.g., power generation, defense) and some states have tougher environmental regulations than others. Generally, business negotiations in the United States occur without government approval and the parties to a negotiation decide whether or not to engage in an agreement based on business reasons alone. In contrast, the governments of many developing and (former) communist countries closely supervise imports and joint ventures (see Brouthers and Bamossy, 1997; Derong and Faure, 1995; Pfouts, 1994), and frequently an agency of the government has a monopoly in dealing with foreign organizations (Salacuse, 1988). In addition, political considerations, such as the effect of the negotiation on the government treasury and the general economy of the country, may influence the negotiations more heavily than what businesses in developed countries would consider legitimate business reasons.

Instability   Businesses negotiating within North America are accustomed to a degree of stability that is not present in many areas of the world. Instability may take many forms, including a lack of resources that Americans commonly expect during business negotiations (paper, electricity, computers), shortages of other goods and services (food, reliable transportation, potable water), and political instability (coups, sudden shifts in government

policy, major currency revaluations). The challenge for international negotiators is to anticipate changes accurately and with enough lead time to adjust for their consequences. Salacuse
(1988) suggests that negotiators facing unstable circumstances should include clauses in their
contracts that allow easy cancellation or neutral arbitration and consider purchasing insurance
policies to guarantee contract provisions. This advice presumes that contracts will be honored
and that specific contract clauses will be culturally acceptable to the other party.

Ideology   Negotiators within the United States generally share a common ideology about
the benefits of individualism and capitalism. Americans believe strongly in individual
rights, the superiority of private investment, and the importance of making a profit in business (Salacuse, 1988). Negotiators from other countries do not always share this ideology.
For example, negotiators from some countries (e.g., China, France) may instead stress
group rights as more important than individual rights and public investment as a better allocation of resources than private investment; they may also have different prescriptions for
earning and sharing profit. Ideological clashes increase the communication challenges in
international negotiations in the broadest sense because the parties may disagree at the
most fundamental levels about what is being negotiated.

Culture   One does not have to leave the United States to see the influence of culture on
negotiations (see Box 16.1). Clearly it is challenging when the fundamental beliefs about
what negotiation is and how it occurs are different. The critical role that culture plays in international and other cross-cultural negotiations will be discussed at length later in this
chapter; here we mention some highlights.

People from different cultures appear to negotiate differently (e.g., Graham and Mintu-
Wimsat, 1997; Metcalf, Bird, Shankarmahesh, Aycan, Larimo, and Valdelamar, 2006;
Metcalf, Bird, Peterson, Shankarmahesh, and Lituchy, 2007). In addition to behaving differently, people from different cultures may also interpret the fundamental processes of negotiations differently (such as what factors are negotiable and the purpose of the negotiations).
According to Salacuse (1988), people in some cultures approach negotiations deductively
(they move from the general to the specific) whereas people from other cultures are more
inductive (they settle on a series of specific issues that become the area of general agreement; see Palich, Carini, and Livingstone, 2002; Xing, 1995). In some cultures, the parties
negotiate the substantive issues while considering the relationship between the parties to be
more or less incidental. In other cultures, the relationship between the parties is the main
focus of the negotiation, and the substantive issues of the deal itself are more or less incidental (see Tinsley, 1997). There is also evidence that preference for conflict resolution
models varies across cultures (Tinsley, 1997, 1998, 2001).

External Stakeholders   Phatak and Habib defined external stakeholders as "the various people and organizations that have an interest or stake in the outcome of the negotiations" (1996,
p. 34). These stakeholders include business associations, labor unions, embassies, and industry associations, among others (see Sebenius, 2002a). For example, a labor union might oppose
negotiations with foreign companies because of fears that domestic jobs will be lost. International negotiators can receive a great deal of promotion and guidance from their government
via the trade section of their embassy and from other business people via professional associations (e.g., a Chamber of Commerce in the country in which they are negotiating).

Immediate Context

At many points throughout this book we have discussed aspects of negotiation that relate to immediate context factors, but without considering their international implications. In this section, we will discuss the concepts from the Phatak and Habib (1996) model of international negotiation, highlighting that the immediate context can have an important influence on negotiation (Lin and Miller, 2003).

Relative Bargaining Power   One aspect of international negotiations that has received considerable research attention is the relative bargaining power of the two parties involved. Joint ventures have been the subject of a great deal of research on international negotiation, and relative power has frequently been operationalized as the amount of equity (financial and other investment) that each side is willing to invest in the new venture (see Yan and Gray, 1994, for a review). The presumption is that the party who invests more equity has more power in the negotiation and therefore will have more influence on the negotiation process and outcome. Research by Yan and Gray (1994) questions this perspective, however, and suggests that relative power is not simply a function of equity, but appears to be due to management control of the project, which was found to be heavily influenced by negotiating. In addition, several factors seem to be able to influence relative power, including special access to markets (e.g., in current or former communist countries), distribution systems (e.g., in Asia, where creating a new distribution system is so expensive that it may be a barrier to entering markets), or managing government relations (e.g., where the language and culture are quite different).

Levels of Conflict   The level of conflict and type of interdependence between the parties to a cross-cultural negotiation will also influence the negotiation process and outcome. High-conflict situations—those based on ethnicity, identity, or geography—are more difficult to resolve.[8] Ongoing conflicts in Zimbabwe, the Middle East, and Sudan are but a few examples. There is historical evidence, however, that civil wars concluded through a comprehensive, institutionalized agreement that prohibits the use of coercive power and promotes the fair distributions of resources and political power lead to more stable settlements (Hartzell, 1999). Also important is the extent to which negotiators frame the negotiation differently or conceptualize what the negotiation concerns (see Chapters 4 and 5 for extended discussions of framing), and this appears to vary across cultures (Abu-Nimer, 1996), as do the ways in which negotiators respond to conflict (Ohbuchi and Takahashi, 1994; Tinsley, 1998; and see Weldon and Jehn, 1995, for a review). For example, Fisher, Ury, and Patton (1991) discuss how conflicts in the Middle East were difficult to deal with for several years because the different parties had such different ways of conceptualizing what the dispute was about (e.g., security, sovereignty, historical rights). Diplomatic "back-channel" negotiations conducted in secret may help resolve high conflict situations, but their success is not guaranteed (Wanis-St. John, 2006).

Relationship between Negotiators   Phatak and Habib (1996) suggest that the relationships developed among the principal negotiating parties before the actual negotiations will also have an important impact on the negotiation process and outcome. Negotiations are part of the larger relationship between two parties. The history of relations between the parties will influence the current negotiation (e.g., how the parties frame the negotiation), just as the current negotiation will become part of any future negotiations between the parties. (See Chapter 10 for a detailed discussion of this point.)

Desired Outcomes   Tangible and intangible factors also play a large role in determining the outcomes of international negotiations. Countries often use international negotiations to achieve both domestic and international political goals. For instance, one of the main goals of the North Vietnamese during the Paris Peace Talks to end the war in Vietnam was to be recognized formally by the other parties to the negotiation. Similarly, in recent ethnic conflicts around the world, numerous parties have threatened that unless they are recognized at the formal negotiations they will disrupt the successful resolution of the conflict (e.g., Northern Ireland). Ongoing tension can exist between one party's short-term objectives for the current negotiations and its influence on the parties' long-term relations. In trade negotiations between the United States and Japan, both sides often settle for less than their desired short-term outcomes because of the importance of the long-term relationship (see Phatak and Habib, 1996).

Immediate Stakeholders   The immediate stakeholders in the negotiation include the negotiators themselves as well as the people they directly represent, such as their managers, employers, and boards of directors (Phatak and Habib, 1996). Stakeholders can influence negotiators in many ways (see Chapter 10). The skills, abilities, and international experience of the negotiators themselves clearly can have a large impact on the process and outcome of international negotiations. In addition, the personal motivations of the principal negotiators and the other immediate stakeholders can have a large influence on the negotiation process and outcomes. People may be motivated by several intangible factors in the negotiation, including how the process or outcome will make them look in the eyes of both the other party and their own superiors, as well as other intangible factors like their personal career advancement (Phatak and Habib, 1996).

Section Summary

In summary, models such as Phatak and Habib's (1996) are very good devices for guiding our thinking about international negotiation. It is always important to remember, however, that negotiation processes and outcomes are influenced by many factors, and that the influence of these factors can change in magnitude over time (see Stark, Fam, Waller and Tian, 2005; Yan and Gray, 1994). The challenge for every international negotiator is to understand the simultaneous, multiple influences of several factors on the negotiation process and outcome and to update this understanding regularly as circumstances change. This also means that planning for international negotiations is especially important, as is the need to adjust as new information is obtained through monitoring the environmental and immediate contexts.

Conceptualizing Culture and Negotiation

The most frequently studied aspect of international negotiation is culture, and the amount of research on the effects of culture on negotiation has increased substantially in the past 20 years.[9] There are many different meanings of the concept of culture (see Avruch, 2000), but all definitions share two important aspects. First, culture is a group-level phenomenon. That means that a defined group of people shares beliefs, values, and behavioral expectations. The second common element of culture is that cultural beliefs, values, and behavioral expectations are learned and passed on to new members of the group.

Robert Janosik (1987) identified four ways that culture has been conceptualized in international negotiation: as learned behavior, as shared values, as dialectic, and in context. While there are similarities and differences among the four approaches, each stresses the importance of understanding how culture affects negotiation.

Culture as Learned Behavior

One approach to understanding the effects of culture documents the systematic negotiation behavior of people in different cultures. Rather than focusing on why members of a given culture behave in certain ways, this pragmatic, nuts-and-bolts approach concentrates on creating a catalogue of behaviors that foreign negotiators should expect when entering a host culture (Janosik, 1987). Many popular books and articles on international negotiation treat culture as learned behavior, providing lists of dos and don'ts to obey when negotiating with people from different cultures. For instance, Solomon (1987) suggests that international negotiators should recognize that Chinese negotiators will begin negotiations with a search for broad principles and building a relationship. This will be followed by a long period of assessment in which the boundaries of the relationship will be explored; a decision about whether or not to strike an agreement will eventually be made, and this agreement will form the foundation for further concessions and modifications. Research consistent with this perspective has examined the effects of culture on displaying emotion during negotiation (George, Jones, and Gonzalez, 1998) and on face-saving behavior (Ogawa, 1999; Ting-Toomey and Kurogi, 1998).

Culture as Shared Values

The second approach to conceptualizing culture concentrates on understanding central values and norms and then building a model for how these norms and values influence negotiations within that culture (Faure, 1999; Sebenius, 2002a). Cross-cultural comparisons are made by finding the important norms and values that distinguish one culture from another and then understanding how these differences will influence international negotiation.

Hofstede's Model of Cultural Dimensions   Geert Hofstede (1980a, 1980b, 1989, 1991) conducted an extensive program of research on cultural dimensions in international business. Hofstede examined data on values that had been gathered from more than 100,000 IBM employees around the world, and more than 50 cultures were included in the initial study. Statistical analysis of these data suggests that four dimensions could be used to describe the important differences among the cultures in the study: individualism/collectivism, power distance, career success/quality of life, and uncertainty avoidance.[10] Cultures ranking in the top 10 on each of these dimensions are listed in Table 16.1, and each dimension is discussed next.

1. Individualism/Collectivism   The individualism/collectivism dimension describes the extent to which a society is organized around individuals or the group. Individualistic societies

TABLE 16.1 | Cultures Ranking in the Top 10 on the Cultural Dimensions
Reported by Hofstede (1991)

Individualism	Power Distance	Quality of Life	Uncertainty Avoidance
1. United States	1. Malaysia	1. Sweden	1. Greece
2. Australia	2. Guatemala	2. Norway	2. Portugal
3. Great Britain	Panama	3. Netherlands	3. Guatemala
4. Canada	4. Philippines	4. Denmark	4. Uruguay
Netherlands	5. Mexico	5. Costa Rica	5. Belgium
6. New Zealand	Venezuela	Yugoslavia	El Salvador
7. Italy	7. Arab countries	7. Finland	7. Japan
8. Belgium	8. Ecuador	8. Chile	8. Yugoslavia
9. Denmark	Indonesia	9. Portugal	9. Peru
10. France	10. India	10. Thailand	10. Argentina
Sweden	West Africa		Chile
			Costa Rica
			Panama
			Spain

Source: Based on G. Hofstede, *Culture and Organizations: Software of the Mind* (London: McGraw-Hill, 1991).
Reproduced with permission of The McGraw-Hill Companies.

encourage their young to be independent and to look after themselves. Collectivistic societies integrate individuals into cohesive groups that take responsibility for the welfare of each individual. Hofstede suggests that the focus on relationships in collectivist societies plays a critical role in negotiations—negotiations with the same party can continue for years, and changing a negotiator changes the relationship, which may take a long time to rebuild. Contrast this with individualistic societies, in which negotiators are considered interchangeable and competency (rather than relationship) is an important consideration when choosing a negotiator. The implication is that negotiators from collectivist cultures will strongly depend on cultivating and sustaining a long-term relationship, whereas negotiators from individualistic cultures may be more likely to swap negotiators, using whatever short-term criteria seem appropriate.

2. Power Distance   The power distance dimension describes "the extent to which the less powerful members of organizations and institutions (like the family) accept and expect that power is distributed unequally" (Hofstede, 1989, p. 195). According to Hofstede, cultures with greater power distance will be more likely to concentrate decision making at the top, and all important decisions will have to be finalized by the leader. Cultures with low power distance are more likely to spread the decision making throughout the organization, and while leaders are respected, it is also possible to question their decisions. The consequences for international negotiations are that negotiators from comparatively high power distance cultures may need to seek approval from their supervisors more frequently, and for more issues, leading to a slower negotiation process.

3. Career Success/Quality of Life   Hofstede found that cultures differed in the extent to which they held values that promoted career success or quality of life. Cultures promoting career success were characterized by "the acquisition of money and things, and not caring for others, the quality of life, or people" (Hofstede, 1980a, p. 46). Cultures promoting quality of life were characterized by concern for relationships and nurturing. According to Hofstede (1989), this dimension influences negotiation by increasing the competitiveness when negotiators from career success cultures meet; negotiators from quality of life cultures are more likely to have empathy for the other party and to seek compromise.

4. Uncertainty Avoidance   Uncertainty avoidance "indicates to what extent a culture programs its members to feel either uncomfortable or comfortable in unstructured situations" (Hofstede, 1989, p. 196). Unstructured situations are characterized by rapid change and new situations, whereas structured situations are stable and secure. Negotiators from high uncertainty avoidance cultures are less comfortable with ambiguous situations and are more likely to seek stable rules and procedures when they negotiate. Negotiators from low uncertainty avoidance cultures are likely to adapt to quickly changing situations and will be less uncomfortable when the rules of the negotiation are ambiguous or shifting.

Hofstede's model has become a dominant force in cross-cultural research in international business, although the model is not without its skeptics (see, e.g., Kale and Barnes, 1992; Schwartz, 1994; Triandis, 1982). The most important criticism of the model is that the research was conducted with a sample of participants that was not truly representative of the richness of different cultures because there were proportionally too many males, members of the middle class were overrepresented, the education levels were higher than average, and the participants came from one company (IBM). In other words, there is some concern that Hofstede's model underestimates the true richness of value differences across cultures.

Hall's Model of Cultural Values   The work of cultural anthropologist Edwin Hall (1959; 1976; Hall and Hall, 1990) has been very influential in conceptualizing cultural values. Hall specified a limited number of cultural values that could be used to understand differences between cultures, and two of them have been applied to international negotiations: *communication context* and *time and space*. Hall argued that cultures can be differentiated on the basis of whether they engage in low- or high-context communication. Low-context cultures tend to communicate directly, with meaning clearly and explicitly conveyed through words themselves. On the other hand, high-context cultures tend to communicate less directly, with meaning inferred from the surrounding context. Hall's second dimension, time and space, refers to differences between cultures in how they relate to, manage, and schedule events. Hall suggested that some cultures were *monochronic* in that they prefer to organize and schedule things sequentially, while other cultures are *polychronic* in that they are characterized by the simultaneous occurrence of many different activities. Negotiators from cultures with different time expectations will find it quite frustrating to negotiate with each other unless they understand the traditions of the other negotiator.

Schwartz's 10 Cultural Values   The work of Shalom Schwartz and his colleagues provides a very comprehensive example of the culture-as-values perspective (see Figure 16.2).[11] Schwartz concentrated on identifying the motivational goal underlying cultural values and

FIGURE 16.2 | Schwartz's 10 Cultural Values

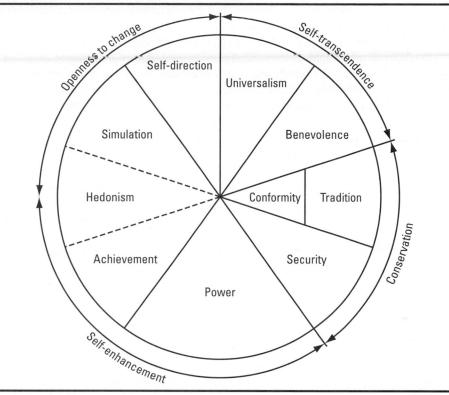

found 10 fundamental values (see the values within the circle in Figure 16.2). These 10 values may conflict or be compatible with each other, and the values on the opposite side of the circle from a given value are most likely to be in conflict. Schwartz also proposed that the 10 values may be represented in two bipolar dimensions: openness to change/conservatism and self-transcendence/self-enhancement (see the outer wheel in Figure 16.2). Schwartz's cultural values and the two bipolar dimensions provide the most comprehensive exploration of cultural values to date, and they have been validated with extensive research. While this work has been slow to appear in the study of cross-cultural negotiation, references to it have started to appear (see Gelfand and Dyer, 2000; Kozan and Ergin, 1999). The advantage of Schwartz's 10 values is the richness with which they can be used to describe a culture. The disadvantage is while this richness may increase cultural understanding, it does not provide clear managerial advice about negotiating across cultures. The presumption is that negotiators who better understand another culture will be more successful negotiating within that culture.

Section Summary

The culture-as-shared-value perspective provides explanations for why cross-cultural negotiations are difficult and have a tendency to break down. For example, a central value in the United States is individualism. Americans are expected to make individual decisions, defend their points of view, and take strong stands on issues that are important to them.

Contrast this with a central value of the Chinese—collectivism (see Faure, 1999, for systematic analysis of the effects of culture on the Chinese negotiation style). Chinese negotiators are expected to make group decisions, defend the group above the individual, and take strong stands on issues important to the group. When Americans and Chinese negotiate, differences in the individualism/collectivism cultural value may influence negotiation in many ways. For instance, (1) the Chinese will likely take more time when negotiating because they have to gain the consensus of their group before they strike a deal; (2) Chinese use of multiple lines of authority will lead to mixed signals about the true needs of the group, and no single individual may understand all the requirements; and (3) because power is shared by many different people and offices, it may be difficult for foreigners to identify their appropriate counterpart in the Chinese bureaucracy (Pye, 1992).

Despite the influence and importance of the culture-as-values perspective, there is some concern that variation *within* cultural value dimensions is underrecognized. For instance, Miyahara, Kim, Shin, and Yoon (1998) studied preferences for conflict resolution styles in Japan and Korea, both of which are collectivist cultures. Miyahara and colleagues found significant differences between Japanese and Koreans, with Koreans reporting more concern about avoiding impositions and avoiding dislike during conflict resolution, while Japanese reported more concern about obtaining clarity. For these reasons, interpretations of the effects of cultural value dimensions on negotiations should be treated with caution.

Culture as Dialectic

The third approach to using culture to understand international negotiation identified by Janosik (1987) recognizes that all cultures contain dimensions or tensions that are called *dialectics.* These tensions are nicely illustrated in parables from the Judeo-Christian tradition. Consider the following examples: "too many cooks spoil the broth" and "two heads are better than one." These adages offer conflicting guidance for those considering whether to work on a task alone or in a group. This reflects a dialectic, or tension, within the Judeo-Christian tradition regarding the values of independence and teamwork. Neither complete independence nor complete teamwork works all the time; each has advantages and disadvantages that vary as a function of the circumstances (e.g., the type of decision to be made or task to be addressed). According to Janosik (1987), the culture-as-dialectic approach has advantages over the culture-as-shared-values approach because it can explain variations within cultures (i.e., not every person in the same culture shares the same values to the same extent). The culture-as-dialectic approach does not provide international negotiators with simple advice about how to behave in a given negotiation. Rather, it suggests that negotiators who want to have successful international negotiations need to appreciate the richness of the cultures in which they will be operating.

Theoretical work by Gelfand and McCusker (2002) provides a similar way to examine the effects of culture on negotiation through examining *negotiation metaphors* rather than dialectics. They define negotiation metaphors as "coherent, holistic meaning systems, which have been developed and cultivated in particular socio-cultural environments, [and] *function* to interpret, structure, and organize social action in negotiation" (Gelfand and McCusker, 2002). Cultural negotiation metaphors help people understand things that happen in negotiation and "make sense" of them. Gelfand and McCusker suggest that *negotiation as sport* is the dominant metaphor for understanding negotiation in the United States, where negotiators concentrate on their own performance and winning and negotiations are episodic. Contrast this with the dominant negotiation metaphor in Japan, *negotiation as ie* (traditional household). The fundamental challenge of *ie* is continuity and succession; negotiators concentrate on relationships and survival of the group, and negotiations are a continuous part of a larger whole. The greater the difference in cultural negotiation metaphors, the more likely it will be that negotiators will not understand each other, and the challenge of having a positive negotiation outcome increases.

The culture as dialectic perspective starts with a deep understanding of a culture and uses that understanding to create negotiation metaphors to have a rich understanding of how negotiations unfold within a culture. Negotiators with stronger understanding of the negotiation metaphor within a culture are more likely to succeed in negotiations.

Culture in Context

Proponents of the fourth approach to using culture to understand international negotiations recognize that human behavior is not determined by a single cause. Rather, all behavior may be understood at many different levels simultaneously, and a social behavior as complex as negotiation is determined by many different factors, one of which is culture. Other factors that may be important determinants of negotiation behavior include personality, social context, and environmental factors (Rubin and Sander, 1991). Proponents of the culture-in-context approach recognize that negotiation behavior is multiply determined, and using culture as the sole explanation of behavior is oversimplifying a complex social process. Kumar and Worm (2004) make this point succinctly: "while negotiations are always in the present they are influenced by what looms in the past and are constrained by the shadow of the future" (p. 305).

Recent theory and research in international negotiation has taken a culture-in-context approach. For instance, Tinsley, Brett, Shapiro, and Okumura (2004) proposed a *cultural complexity theory* in which they suggest that cultural values will have a direct effect on negotiations in some circumstances and a moderated effect in others. Values are proposed to have a direct effect when they have strong effects across several different contexts (e.g., American individuality), whereas values that have a moderated effect are those that have different contextual instigators in the culture. For example, France has both monarchical and democratic traditions, both of which can influence negotiation behavior depending on the context (Brett et al., 1998). Fang (2006) suggests that traditions of Mao, Confucius, and Sun Tzu provide multiple influence on Chinese negotiators that can vary by context. Another example of the culture-in-context approach comes from Adair and Brett (2003), who found that communication patterns were different for negotiators from high- and low-context cultures at different stages of the negotiation.

The culture-in-context models are becoming more and more complex in order to explain nuanced differences in cross-cultural negotiations. As this complexity increases, however, they become less useful for practitioners of cross-cultural negotiation to put into practice (Janosik, 1987). Their strength, however, is in forging a deeper understanding of how cross-cultural negotiations work and using that understanding to prepare and engage more effectively in international negotiation.

The Influence of Culture on Negotiation: Managerial Perspectives

Cultural differences have been suggested to influence negotiation in several different ways. Table 16.2 summarizes 10 different ways that culture can influence negotiations.[12] Each is discussed in turn next.

Definition of Negotiation

The fundamental definition of negotiation, what is negotiable, and what occurs when we negotiate can differ greatly across cultures (see Ohanyan, 1999; Yook and Albert, 1998). For instance, "Americans tend to view negotiating as a competitive process of offers and counteroffers, while the Japanese tend to view the negotiation as an opportunity for information-sharing" (Foster, 1992, p. 272).

Negotiation Opportunity

Culture influences the way negotiators perceive an opportunity as distributive versus integrative. Negotiators in North America are predisposed to perceive negotiation as being fundamentally distributive (Thompson and Hastie, 1990b). This is not the case outside North America, however, as there appears to be a great deal of variation across cultures in the extent to which negotiation situations are initially perceived as distributive or integrative (Salacuse, 1998). Cross-cultural negotiations are influenced by the extent that negotiators in different cultures have fundamental agreement or disagreement about whether or not the situation is distributive or integrative.

Selection of Negotiators

The criteria used to select who will participate in a negotiation is different across cultures. These criteria can include knowledge of the subject matter being negotiated, seniority, family connections, gender, age, experience, and status. Different cultures weigh these criteria differently, leading to varying expectations about what is appropriate in different types of negotiations. For instance, in China it is important to establish relationship connections

TABLE 16.2 | 10 Ways That Culture Can Influence Negotiation

Negotiation Factors	Range of Cultural Responses		
Definition of negotiation	Contract	◄----------►	Relationship
Negotiation opportunity	Distributive	◄----------►	Integrative
Selection of negotiators	Experts	◄----------►	Trusted associates
Protocol	Informal	◄----------►	Formal
Communication	Direct	◄----------►	Indirect
Time sensitivity	High	◄----------►	Low
Risk propensity	High	◄----------►	Low
Groups versus individuals	Collectivism	◄----------►	Individualism
Nature of agreements	Specific	◄----------►	General
Emotionalism	High	◄----------►	Low

Source: Based on Foster (1992), Hendon and Hendon (1990), Moran and Stripp (1991) and Salacuse (1998).

Never touch a Malay on the top of the head, for that is where the soul resides. Never show the sole of your shoe to an Arab, for it is dirty and represents the bottom of the body, and never use your left hand in Muslim culture, for it is reserved for physical hygiene. Touch the side of your nose in Italy and it is a sign of distrust. Always look directly and intently into your French associate's eye when making an important point. Direct eye contact in Southeast Asia, however, should be avoided until the relationship is firmly established. If your Japanese associate has just sucked air in deeply through his teeth, that's a sign you've got real problems. Your Mexican associate will want to embrace you at the end of a long and successful negotiation; so will your Central and Eastern European associates, who may give you a bear hug and kiss you three times on alternating cheeks. Americans often stand farther apart than their Latin and Arab associates but closer than their Asian associates. In the United States people shake hands forcefully and enduringly; in Europe a handshake is usually quick and to the point; in Asia, it is often rather limp. Laughter and giggling in the West Indies indicates humor; in Asia, it more often indicates embarrassment and humility. Additionally, the public expression of deep emotion is considered ill-mannered in most countries of the Pacific Rim; there is an extreme separation between one's personal and public selves. Withholding emotion in Latin America, however, is often cause for mistrust.

Source: D. A. Foster, *Bargaining across Borders: How to Negotiate Business Successfully Anywhere in the World* (New York: McGraw-Hill, 1992), p. 281. Reproduced with the permission of The McGraw-Hill Companies.

early in the negotiation process, and selection of the appropriate negotiators can help with this (see Zhu, McKenna, and Sun, 2007).

Protocol

Cultures differ in the degree to which protocol, or the formality of the relations between the two negotiating parties, is important. American culture is among the least formal cultures in the world. A familiar communication style is quite common; first names are used, for example, while titles are ignored. Contrast this with other cultures. Many European countries (e.g., France, Germany, England) are very formal, and not using the proper title when addressing someone (e.g., Mr., Dr., Professor, Lord) is considered insulting (see Braganti and Devine, 1992). The formal calling cards or business cards used in many countries in the Pacific Rim (e.g., China, Japan) are essential for introductions there. Negotiators who forget to bring business cards or who write messages on them are frequently breaching protocol and insulting their counterpart (Foster, 1992). Even the way that business cards are presented, hands are shaken, and dress codes are observed are subject to interpretation by negotiators and can be the foundation of attributions about a person's background and personality.

Communication

Cultures influence how people communicate, both verbally and nonverbally. There are also differences in body language across cultures; a behavior that may be highly insulting in one culture may be completely innocuous in another (Axtell, 1990, 1991, 1993). To avoid offending the other party in negotiations, the international negotiator needs to observe cultural rules of communication carefully. For example, placing feet on a desk in the United States signals power or relaxation; in Thailand, it is considered very insulting (see Boxes 16.3 and 16.4 for

BOX | 16.4 | Cross-Cultural Miscommunication

Although many multinational organizations have extensive experience in overseas markets, some problems persist. Language and cultural differences make it difficult to translate slogans and ideas effectively in new environments. For example:

- In Taiwan, the Pepsi slogan "Come alive with the Pepsi Generation" translated into "Pepsi will bring your ancestors back from the dead."

- In Chinese, Kentucky Fried Chicken's "Finger-lickin' good" became "Eat your fingers off."

- Salem cigarette's slogan, "Salem—Feeling Free" became "When smoking Salem, you feel so refreshed that your mind seems to be free and empty" in Japan.

- When Chevrolet introduced the Nova in South America, they were apparently unaware that in Spanish "No va" means "It won't go."

- When Parker Pen marketed a ballpoint in Mexico, the slogan was supposed to inform customers that the pen "won't leak in your pocket and embarrass you." However, the company used the word *embarazar* for *embarrass*. Mexican consumers read the advertisement as "It won't leak in your pocket and make you pregnant."

- In Italy, a campaign for Schweppes tonic water translated the name as "Schweppes Toilet Water."

Source: Anonymous.

more examples). Clearly, there is a lot of information about how to communicate that an international negotiator must remember in order not to insult, anger, or embarrass the other party during negotiations. Culture-specific books and articles can provide considerable advice to international negotiators about how to communicate in various cultures; seeking such advice is an essential aspect of planning for international negotiations.[13]

Time Sensitivity

Cultures largely determine what time means and how it affects negotiations (see Macduff, 2006; Mayfield, Mayfield, Martin, and Herbig, 1997). In the United States, people tend to respect time by appearing for meetings at an appointed hour, being sensitive to not wasting the time of other people, and generally holding that "faster" is better than "slower" because it symbolizes high productivity. Other cultures have quite different views about time. In more traditional societies, especially in hot climates, the pace is slower than in the United States. This tends to reduce the focus on time, at least in the short term. Arab-speaking Islamic cultures appear to focus more on event-time than clock-time where "in clock-time cultures people schedule events according to the clock; in event-time cultures, events schedule people" (Alon and Brett, 2007, p. 58). Americans are perceived by other cultures as enslaved by their clocks because they watch time carefully and guard it as a valuable resource. In some cultures, such as China and Latin America, time per se is not important. The focus of negotiations is on the task, regardless of the amount of time it takes. The opportunity for misunderstandings because of different perceptions of time is great during cross-cultural negotiations. Americans may be perceived as always being in a hurry and as flitting from one task to another, while Chinese or Latin American negotiators may appear to Americans to be doing nothing and wasting time. Ilai Alon and Icanne Brett propose five tactics for managing differences in time sensitivity (see Box 16.5).

1. Spend extra time preparing for cultural differences.

2. Commit the time to building and maintaining relationships.

3. Plan your actions according to clock-time, but allow for wide margins to accommodate for event-time.

4. Prepare argumentation in advance, using precedents, models, and history.

5. Try to avoid language that might suggest that the parties have full control over future events.

Source: I. Alon and J. M. Brett, "Perceptions of time and their impact on negotiations in the Arabic-speaking Islamic world." *Negotiation Journal, 23,* (2007), pp. 55–73.

Risk Propensity

Cultures vary in the extent to which they are willing to take risks. Some cultures tend to produce bureaucratic, conservative decision makers who want a great deal of information before making decisions. Other cultures produce negotiators who are more entrepreneurial and who are willing to act and take risks when they have incomplete information (e.g., "nothing ventured, nothing gained"). According to Foster (1992), Americans fall on the risk-taking end of the continuum, as do some Asian cultures, while some European cultures are quite conservative (e.g., Greece). The orientation of a culture toward risk will have a large effect on what is negotiated and the content of the negotiated outcome. Negotiators in risk-oriented cultures will be more willing to move early on a deal and will generally take more chances. Those in risk-avoiding cultures are more likely to seek further information and take a wait-and-see stance.

Groups versus Individuals

Cultures differ according to whether they emphasize the individual or the group. The United States is very much an individual-oriented culture, where being independent and assertive is valued and praised. Group-oriented cultures, in contrast, favor the superiority of the group and see individual needs as second to the group's needs. Group-oriented cultures value fitting in and reward loyal team players; those who dare to be different are socially ostracized—a large price to pay in a group-oriented society. This cultural difference can have a variety of effects on negotiation. Americans are more likely to have one individual who is responsible for the final decision, whereas group-oriented cultures like the Japanese are more likely to have a group responsible for the decision. Decision making in group-oriented cultures involves consensus and may take considerably more time than American negotiators are used to. In addition, because so many people can be involved in the negotiations in group-oriented cultures, and because their participation may be sequential rather than simultaneous, American negotiators may be faced with a series of discussions over the same issues and materials with many different people. In a negotiation in China, one of the authors of this book met with more than six different people on successive days, going over the same ground with different negotiators and interpreters, until the negotiation was concluded.

Nature of Agreements

Culture also has an important effect both on concluding agreements and on what form the negotiated agreement takes. In the United States, agreements are typically based on logic (e.g., the low-cost producer gets the deal), are often formalized, and are enforced through the legal system if such standards are not honored. In other cultures, however, obtaining the deal may be based on who you are (e.g., your family or political connections) rather than on what you can do. In addition, agreements do not mean the same thing in all cultures. Foster (1992) notes that the Chinese frequently use memorandums of agreement to formalize a relationship and to signal the start of negotiations (mutual favors and compromise). Frequently, however, Americans will interpret the same memorandum of agreement as the completion of the negotiations that is enforceable in a court of law. Again, cultural differences in how to close an agreement and what exactly that agreement means can lead to confusion and misunderstandings.

Emotionalism

Culture appears to influence the extent to which negotiators display emotions (Salacuse, 1998). These emotions may be used as tactics, or they may be a natural response to positive and negative circumstances during the negotiation (see Kumar, 2004). While personality likely also plays a role in the expression of emotions, there also appears to be considerable cross-cultural differences, and the rules that govern general emotional displays in a culture are likely to be present during negotiation (Salacuse, 1998).

In summary, a great deal of practical advice has been written about the importance of culture in international negotiations. Although the word culture has been used to mean several different things, it is clearly a critical aspect of international negotiation that can have a broad influence on many aspects of the process and outcome of international negotiation. We now turn to examining research perspectives on how culture influences negotiation.

The Influence of Culture on Negotiation: Research Perspectives

A conceptual model of where culture may influence negotiation has been developed by Jeanne Brett (2001) (see Figure 16.3). Brett's model identifies how the culture of both negotiators can influence the setting of priorities and strategies, the identification of the potential for integrative agreement, and the pattern of interaction between negotiators. Brett suggests that cultural values should have a strong effect on negotiation interests and priorities, while cultural norms will influence negotiation strategies and the pattern of interaction (Brett, 2001). Negotiation strategies and the pattern of interaction between negotiators will also be influenced by the psychological processes of negotiators, and culture has an influence on these processes.

Effects of Culture on Negotiation Outcomes

Researchers initially explored the fundamental question of how culture influences negotiation outcomes. Two approaches were taken to explore this question. In the first approach, researchers compared the outcomes of the same simulated negotiation with negotiators from several different cultures who only negotiated with other negotiators from their own culture. The goal of these *intracultural* studies was to see if negotiators from different cultures reached the same negotiation outcomes when presented with the same materials. The other approach to explore how culture influenced negotiation outcomes was to compare intracultural and *cross-cultural* negotiation outcomes to see if they were the same. Researchers investigated this by comparing negotiation outcomes when negotiators negotiated with people from the

FIGURE 16.3 | How Culture Affects Negotiation

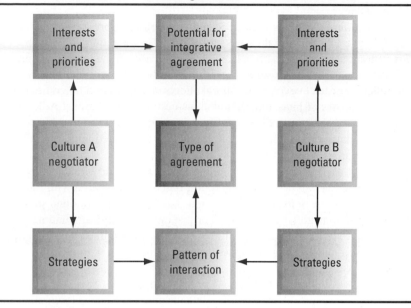

Source: J. M. Brett, *Negotiating Globally* (San Francisco: Jossey-Bass, 2001).

same culture with outcomes when they negotiated with people from other cultures. For example, did Japanese negotiators reach the same negotiation outcomes when negotiating with other Japanese negotiators as they did with American negotiators?

A series of research studies comparing intracultural negotiations in several different cultures was conducted by John Graham and his colleagues (for a review of these studies see Graham, 1993), using a very simple buyer–seller negotiation simulation in which negotiators have to decide on the prices of three products (televisions, typewriters, air conditioners). Graham and his colleagues found no differences in the profit levels obtained by negotiators in different cultures, including comparing the United States with Japan (Graham, 1983, 1984), China (Adler, Brahm, and Graham, 1992), Canada (Adler and Graham, 1987; Adler, Graham, and Schwarz, 1987), Brazil (Graham, 1983), and Mexico (Adler, Graham, and Schwartz, 1987).

Research has found, however, that negotiators in collectivist cultures are more likely to reach integrative outcomes than negotiators in individualist cultures. For instance, Lituchy (1997) reported that negotiators from a more collectivist culture (Japan) reached more integrative solutions than negotiators from a more individualist culture (the United States). Arunachalam, Wall, and Chan (1998) found that negotiators from a more collectivistic culture (Hong Kong) reached higher joint outcomes on an integrative negotiation task than did negotiators from a more individualistic culture (the United States).

Research by Jeanne Brett and her colleagues has used a richer negotiation simulation and also identified differences in negotiation outcomes by negotiators in different cultures. For instance, Brett, Adair, Lempereur, Okumura, Shihkirev, Tinsley, and Lytle (1998) compared intracultural negotiators in six different cultures (France, Russia, Japan, Hong Kong, Brazil,

United States) and found differences in joint gains achieved. In addition, Dialdin, Kopelman, Adair, Brett, Okumura, and Lytle (1999) reported differences in individual gains for negotiators from five different cultures (United States, Hong Kong, Germany, Israel, Japan). These two studies suggest that culture does have an effect on negotiation outcomes, but there were complex patterns across cultures. It is likely that differences in the negotiation process across cultures, and not the cultures per se, are responsible for the different outcomes (discussed next).

The other approach to exploring cultural effects on negotiation outcomes compared the negotiation outcomes of intracultural and cross-cultural negotiations. Adler and Graham (1989) found that Japanese and English-Canadian negotiators received lower profit levels when they negotiated cross-culturally than when they negotiated intraculturally; American and French-Canadian negotiators negotiated the same average outcomes in cross-cultural and intracultural negotiations. These results support Adler and Graham's hypothesis that cross-cultural negotiations will result in poorer outcomes compared with intracultural negotiations, at least some of the time. In addition, Adler and Graham found some differences in the cross-cultural negotiation process. For instance, French-Canadian negotiators used more cooperative strategies in cross-cultural negotiations than in intracultural negotiations, and American negotiators reported higher levels of satisfaction with their cross-cultural negotiations (versus intracultural negotiations).

Studies by Natlandsmyr and Rognes (1995), Lituchy (1997), and Brett and Okumura (1998) extend Adler and Graham's results. Natlandsmyr and Rognes found that when negotiating intraculturally, Norwegian negotiators reached higher joint outcomes than Mexican negotiators. During cross-cultural negotiations, however, the Mexican–Norwegian dyads reached agreements closer to the intracultural Mexican dyads than to the intracultural Norwegian dyads. Natlandsmyr and Rognes report that the progression of offers that Mexican and Norwegian negotiators made was different, and they suggest that culture may have a significant effect on the negotiation process. Lituchy (1997) found that Japanese intracultural negotiators reached more integrative solutions than were reached by Japanese–American cross-cultural negotiators, and Brett and Okumura (1998) found that Japanese and American negotiators had lower joint gains when negotiating cross-culturally than when negotiating with each other intraculturally.

In summary, research suggests that culture does have an effect on negotiation outcomes, although it may not be direct, and it likely has an influence through differences in the negotiation process in different cultures. In addition, there is some evidence that cross-cultural negotiations yield poorer outcomes than intracultural negotiations. Considerable research has been conducted to understand why. We review two broad approaches to examining this question next. First, considerable work has used dimensions of cultural values (Hall, Hofstede, Schwartz) to compare and contrast negotiations that occur in different cultures. More recently, researchers have turned to examining the effect of culture on the psychological states of negotiators, including how it affects judgment biases and implicit theories of negotiation.

Effects of Culture on Negotiation Process and Information Exchange

Graham and his colleagues found significant differences in the negotiation strategies and tactics in the cultures they studied (also see Graham, Evenko, and Rajan, 1992). For instance, Graham (1983) concluded that "in American negotiations, higher profits are achieved by making opponents feel uncomfortable, while in Japanese negotiations, higher profits are associated with making opponents feel comfortable" (p. 63). In addition, Graham (1983) reports that Brazilian negotiators who used powerful and deceptive strategies were more likely to receive higher outcomes; these strategies were not related to the outcomes attained by the American negotiators. Further, Adler, Graham, and Schwartz (1987) report that representational strategies (gathering information) were negatively related to profits attained by Mexican and French-Canadian negotiators, whereas these strategies were unrelated to the profits that American negotiators received. Finally, although Adler, Brahm, and Graham (1992) found that Chinese and American negotiators used similar negotiation strategies when they negotiated, their communication patterns were quite different—the Chinese asked more questions, said "no" less frequently, and interrupted each other more frequently than did American negotiators. Adair, Weinport, and Brett (2007) also found different communication patterns in the use of offers during negotiation whereby Japanese negotiators used offers early to find out information while Americans used offers later to consolidate information.

Cai (1998) demonstrated how individualism/collectivism influenced negotiation planning: negotiators from a more collectivist culture (Taiwan) spent more time planning for long-term goals, while negotiators from a more individualistic culture (the United States) spent more time planning for short-term goals. Gelfand and Christakopoulou (1999) found that negotiators from a more individualistic culture (the United States) made more extreme offers during the negotiation than did negotiators from a more collectivist culture (Greece).

Adair and colleagues (2004) found considerable difference in direct information sharing, with negotiators from the United States most likely to share information directly. In addition, they found that while U.S. and Japanese negotiators both maximized their joint gains, they took different paths to do so. U.S. negotiators used *direct information exchange* about preferences and priorities and referred to similarities and differences between the parties to achieve joint gains. Japanese negotiators used *indirect information exchange* and inferred the preferences of the other negotiator by comparing several different offers and counteroffers, and they justified their trade-offs with persuasive arguments. It is instructive to note that Russian and Hong Kong negotiators did not achieve high joint gains for different reasons: "Hong Kong negotiators did not exchange enough information and Russian negotiators were too focused on power" (Adair et al., 2004, p. 105).

Adair, Kopelman, Gillespie, Brett, and Okumura (1998) examined the effect of information sharing on joint gains in negotiation in a cross-cultural context and found that negotiators from culturally similar countries (United States, Israel) were more likely to share information during negotiation than negotiators from less culturally similar countries (United States, Japan), and those differences in information led to higher joint gains for negotiators from the culturally similar countries.

Adair, Okumura, and Brett (2001) examined negotiation outcomes and information sharing in both intracultural (within the United States and within Japan) and cross-cultural (United States–Japan) negotiations. They found that both U.S. and Japanese intracultural negotiators reached higher joint gains than cross-cultural negotiators. The way that intracultural negotiators achieved these gains, however, was different for the U.S. and Japanese negotiators. Intracultural U.S. negotiators were more likely to share information directly and less likely to share information indirectly than were intracultural Japanese negotiators.

In cross-cultural negotiations, Japanese negotiators adapted to U.S. normative behaviors, and Japanese cross-cultural negotiators were more likely to share information than Japanese intracultural negotiators. This increased direct information sharing by Japanese negotiators did not translate into higher joint gains in cross-cultural negotiations, however.

Adair (2002, 2003) extended the research on the importance of culture on information sharing in negotiation by comparing integrative behavior sequences in intracultural negotiations from several high- and low-context cultures and in cross-cultural negotiations from two mixed-context cultures.[14] Adair (2003) found that culture led to different communication patterns in intracultural negotiations, with negotiators from low-context cultures tending to use direct communication while negotiators from high-context cultures used more indirect communication. In cross-cultural negotiations, direct integrative sequences of information exchange led to higher joint outcomes, which suggests that *both* negotiators need to exchange information integratively in order for cross-cultural negotiations to reach a successful conclusion.

Rosette, Brett, Barsness, and Lytle (2004) examined how culture influenced intracultural and cross-cultural e-mail negotiations with negotiators from high-context (Hong Kong) and low-context (United States) cultures. They found that Hong Kong negotiators achieved higher joint gains in e-mail negotiations than in face-to-face negotiations, while there was no difference in the joint gains achieved for U.S. negotiators. The higher joint gains appear to be the result of the use of higher opening offers and more multiple-issue offers by Hong Kong negotiators when conducting e-mail negotiations. In the cross-cultural e-mail negotiation, Hong Kong negotiators achieved higher individual outcomes than U.S. negotiators, apparently as a function of more aggressive opening offers. There were no differences in the number of multiple-issue offers between Hong Kong and U.S. negotiators in the cross-cultural negotiation, likely due to negotiators reciprocating offers during the negotiation. The Rosette et al. (2004) study suggests that culture has an effect on the process of e-mail negotiations, which in turn appears to influence negotiation outcomes.

In summary, culture has been found to have significant effects on several aspects of the negotiation process, including how negotiators plan, the offers made during negotiation, the communication process, and how information is shared during negotiation.

Effects of Culture on Negotiator Cognition

Researchers have recently turned their attention to discovering how culture influences the psychological processes of negotiators (Gelfand and Dyer, 2000; Morris and Gelfand, 2004), and researchers are working to understand how culture influences the way that negotiators process information during negotiation and how this in turn influences negotiation processes and outcomes.

Gelfand and Realo (1999) found that accountability to a constituent influenced negotiators from individualistic and collectivistic cultures differently. They found that accountability led to more competition among individualists but to higher levels of cooperation among collectivists. In addition, there were differences in negotiator cognitions: individualists had more competitive behavioral intentions and thoughts before negotiating, acted less cooperatively during negotiations, and perceived the other party more negatively after the negotiation.

Gelfand, Nishii, Holcombe, Dyer, Ohbuchi, and Fukuno (2001) explored how people from a collectivist culture (Japan) and an individualist culture (the United States) perceived the same conflict. They found that the Japanese were more likely to perceive the conflicts as involving compromise than were the Americans. Gelfand and associates also found that Japanese and Americans used different frames to make sense of some conflicts. For instance, the Japanese framed some conflicts as *giri violations* (breaches in social positions), while the Americans never used that frame. The Gelfand et al. study suggests that there are some universal ways of framing conflict (e.g., compromise–win) but there are also significant culturally specific ways (e.g., *giri* violations).

Another way to explore the influence of culture on negotiator cognition is to examine the extent to which well-known cognitive effects identified in Western cultures occur in other cultures. Gelfand and Christakopoulou (1999) found that negotiators from an individualistic culture (the United States) were more susceptible to fixed-pie errors (see Chapter 5) than were negotiators from a more collectivist culture (Greece). In a series of creative studies examining the self-serving bias of fairness[15] in other cultures, Gelfand and colleagues (2002) found that the self-serving bias was far stronger in an individualist culture (United States) than a collectivist culture (Japan). Wade-Benzoni, Okumura, Brett, Moore, Tenbrunsel, and Bazerman (2002) reported a similar finding for cultural differences in how asymmetric social dilemmas (i.e., the tension between self and group interests) are managed in the United States and Japan. The study found that the Americans provided less cooperative solutions and expected others to be less cooperative than Japanese participants. Finally, Valenzuela, Srivastava, and Lee (2005) report that members of a collectivist culture (Korea) are less prone to making fundamental attribution errors during negotiation than are members of an individualistic culture (the United States).

In summary, it appears that several aspects of negotiator cognition are significantly influenced by culture and that negotiators should not assume that findings on negotiator cognition from Western negotiators are universally applicable to other cultures (Wade-Benzoni, Okumura, et al., 2002).

Effect of Culture on Negotiator Ethics and Tactics

Researchers have recently turned their attention to examining ethics and negotiation tactics in cross-cultural negotiations by exploring the broad question of whether negotiators in different cultures have the same ethical evaluation of negotiation tactics (see Rivers and Lytle, 2007, for a review). For instance, Zarkada-Fraser and Fraser (2001) investigated perceptions of Lewicki and Robinson's (1998) negotiation tactics (see Chapter 9) with negotiators from six different cultures. They found significant differences in the tolerance of different negotiation tactics in different cultures, with Japanese negotiators more intolerant of the use of misrepresentation tactics than negotiators from Australia, the United States, Britain, Russia, and Greece. Volkema and Fleury (2002) examined the responses of Brazilians and Americans to Lewicki and Robinson's ethics questionnaire and found similar evaluations of the level of acceptability of the negotiation tactics in Brazil and the United States, but American negotiators reported that they would be more likely to use the tactics, especially exaggerating their opening offers, than Brazilian negotiators. Elahee and colleagues (Elahee and Brooks, 2004; Elahee, Kirby, and Nasif, 2002) explored the influence of trust on the use of Lewicki and Robinson's tactics by American, Mexican, and Canadian negotiators. They found that negotiators who trusted the other party were less likely to use questionable negotiation tactics. Elahee et al. also found that Mexican negotiators were least likely to trust foreign negotiators and more likely to use tactics like bluffing and misrepresentation in cross-cultural than intracultural negotiations. Canadian and American negotiators reported no difference in the likelihood of using these tactics in cross-cultural and intracultural negotiations.

Effect of Culture on Conflict Resolution

Kim and Kitani (1998) demonstrated how individualism/collectivism influenced preference for conflict resolution styles in romantic relationships as partners from a more collectivist culture (Asian Americans) preferred obliging, avoiding, and integrating conflict management styles, while partners from a more individualistic culture (Caucasian Americans) preferred a dominating conflict management style. Similarly, Pearson and Stephan (1998) found that negotiators from a more collectivist culture (Brazil) preferred accommodation, collaboration, and withdrawal compared with negotiators from a more individualist culture (the United States), who had a stronger preference for competition (also see Ma, 2007; Mintu-Wimsatt, 2002; Oetzel and Ting-Tomey, 2003). Smith, Dugan, Peterson, and Leung (1998) found that within collectivistic countries disagreements are resolved based on rules, whereas in individualistic countries conflicts tend to be resolved through personal experience and training. In addition, Smith and colleagues (1998) found that "out-group" disagreements were less likely to occur in high-power distance cultures than lower-power distance cultures.

A study by Mintu-Wimsatt and Gassenheimer (2000) provided further evidence of the effects of individualism/collectivism on conflict resolution styles—they found that exporters from the Philippines (a high-context culture that is more collectivist) preferred less confrontational problem solving than did exporters from the United States (a low-context culture that is more individualistic). Gire (1997) found that negotiators from both a more individualistic culture (Canada) and a more collectivist culture (Nigeria) preferred negotiation to arbitration as a conflict management procedure. Negotiators from the more collectivist culture had an even stronger preference for negotiation than did negotiators from the more individualistic culture, who found arbitration more acceptable than negotiators from the more collectivist culture. In addition, Arunachalam, Wall, and Chan (1998) found that mediation had a stronger effect on negotiation outcomes with negotiators from a more individualistic culture (the United States) than those with negotiators from a more collectivist culture (Hong Kong).

Section Summary

There has been considerable research on the effects of culture on negotiation in the last decade. Findings suggest that culture has important effects on several aspects of negotiation, including the outcomes of negotiation, the negotiation process, information exchange, negotiator cognition, negotiator perceptions of ethical behavior, and preferences for conflict resolution. The research is difficult to summarize however, because it explores many different cultures, samples and topics and the findings are occasionally contradictory.

There are some who now suggest that similar models of negotiation may be more pancultural than originally thought (Ma, 2006; Ma and Jaegar, 2005; Metcalf, Bird, and Dewar,

2008), as well as suggesting that cultures may shift their negotiation patterns as economies develop and nations modernize (Wang, Jing, and Klossek, 2007). More research will need to be done to verify if this apparent pattern is due to the effects of globalization, better measurement of negotiation variables or the misspecification of negotiation models that have missed differences that actually exist (Metcalf et al., 2008).

Culturally Responsive Negotiation Strategies

Although a great deal has been written about the challenge of international and cross-cultural negotiations, far less attention has been paid to what negotiators should do when faced with negotiating with someone from another culture. The advice by many theorists in this area, either explicitly or implicitly, has been, "When in Rome, act as the Romans do" (see Francis, 1991 and Weiss, 1994, for reviews of the oversimplification of this advice). In other words, negotiators are advised to be aware of the effects of cultural differences on negotiation and to take them into account when they negotiate. Many theorists appear to assume implicitly that the best way to manage cross-cultural negotiations is to be sensitive to the cultural norms of the other negotiator and to modify one's strategy to be consistent with behaviors that occur in that culture.

Several factors suggest that negotiators should *not* make large modifications to their approach when negotiating cross-culturally, however:

1. Negotiators may not be able to modify their approach effectively. It takes years to understand another culture deeply, and negotiators typically do not have the time necessary to gain this understanding before beginning a negotiation. Although a little understanding of another culture is clearly better than ignorance, it may not be enough to enable negotiators to make effective adjustments to their negotiation strategy. Attempting to match the strategies and tactics used by negotiators in another culture is a daunting task that requires fluency in their language as well as deep cultural understanding. Even simple words may be translated in several different ways with different nuances, making the challenge of communicating in different languages overwhelming (see Adachi, 1998).

2. Even if negotiators can modify their approach effectively, it does not mean that this will translate automatically into a better negotiation outcome. It is quite possible that the other party will modify his or her approach too. The results in this situation can be disastrous, with each side trying to act like the other "should" be acting, and both sides not really understanding what the other party is doing. Consider the following example contrasting typical American and Japanese negotiation styles (also see Box 16.6). Americans are more likely to start negotiations with an extreme offer in order to leave room for concessions. Japanese are more likely to start negotiations with gathering information in order to understand with whom they are dealing and what the relationship will be. Assume that both parties understand their own and the other party's cultural tendencies (this is a large assumption that frequently is not met). Now assume that each party, acting out of respect for the other, decides to "act like the Romans do" and to adopt the approach of the other party. The possibilities for confusion are endless. When the Americans gather information about the Japanese, are they truly interested or are they playing a role? It will be

BOX 16.6   A Simple "Hai" Won't Do

When a TV announcer [in America] reported Bill Clinton's comment to Boris Yeltsin that when the Japanese say yes they often mean no, he gave the news with an expression of mild disbelief. Having spent my life between East and West, I can sympathize with those who find the Japanese yes unfathomable. However, the fact that it sometimes fails to correspond precisely with the Occidental yes does not necessarily signal intended deception. This was probably why the announcer looked bewildered, and it marks a cultural gap that can have serious repercussions.

I once knew an American who worked in Tokyo. He was a very nice man, but he suffered a nervous breakdown and went back to the United States tearing his hair and exclaiming, "All Japanese businessmen are liars." I hope this is not true. If it were, all Japanese businessmen would be driving each other mad, which does not seem to be the case. Nevertheless, since tragedies often arise from misunderstandings, an attempt at some explanation might not be amiss.

A Japanese yes in its primary context simply means the other person has heard you and is contemplating a reply. This is because it would be rude to keep someone waiting for an answer without supplying him with an immediate response.

For example: A feudal warlord marries his sister to another warlord. (I am back to TV.) Then he decides to destroy his newly acquired brother-in-law and besieges the castle. Being human, though, the attacking warlord worries about his sister and sends a spy to look around. The spy returns and the lord inquires eagerly, "Well, is she safe?" The spy bows and answers, "Hai," which means yes. We sigh with relief, thinking, "Ah, the fair lady is still alive!" But then the spy continues, "To my regret she has fallen on her sword together with her husband."

Hai is also an expression of our willingness to comply with your intent even if your request is worded in the negative. This can cause complications. When I was at school, our English teacher, a British nun, would say, "Now children, you won't forget to do your homework, will you?" And we would all dutifully chorus, "Yes, mother," much to her consternation.

A variation of hai may mean, "I understand your wish and would like to make you happy but unfortunately . . ." Japanese being a language of implication, the latter part of this estimable thought is often left unsaid.

Is there, then, a Japanese yes that corresponds to the Western one? I think so, particularly when it is accompanied by phrases such as "sodesu" (it is so) and "soshimasu" (I will do so).

A word of caution against the statement "I will think about it." Though in Tokyo this can mean a willingness to give one's proposal serious thought, in Osaka, another business center, it means a definite no. This attitude probably stems from the belief that a straightforward no would sound too brusque.

When talking to a Japanese person, it is perhaps best to remember that although he may be speaking English, he is reasoning in Japanese. And if he says, "I will think about it," you should inquire as to which district of Japan he hails from before going on with your negotiations.

Source: This article by Reiko Hatsumi first appeared in *The New York Times,* April 15, 1993. Copyright © 1995 by The New York Times Company. Reprinted by permission.

clear that they are not acting like Americans, but the strategy that they are using may not be readily identified. How will the Americans interpret the Japanese behavior? The Americans have prepared well for their negotiations and understand that the Japanese do not present extreme positions early in negotiations. When the Japanese do present an extreme position early in negotiations (in order to adapt to the American negotiation style), how should the Americans interpret this behavior? The Americans likely will think, "That must be what they really want, because they don't typically open with extreme offers." Adopting the other party's approach does not guarantee success, and in fact it may lead to more confusion than acting like yourself (where at least your behavior is understood within you own cultural context).

3.   Research suggests that negotiators may naturally negotiate differently when they are with people from their own culture than when they are with people from other cultures (Adler and Graham, 1989; Natlandsmyr and Rognes, 1995). The implications of this research are that a deep understanding of how people in other cultures negotiate, such as Costa Ricans negotiating with each other, may not help an American negotiating with a Costa Rican (see Drake, 1995; Weldon and Jehn, 1995).

4.   Research by Francis (1991) suggests that moderate adaptation may be more effective than "acting as the Romans do." In a simulation study of Americans' responses to negotiators from other countries, Francis found that negotiators from a familiar culture (Japan) who made moderate adaptations to American ways were perceived more positively than negotiators who made no changes or those who made large adaptations. Although these findings did not replicate for negotiators from a less familiar culture (Korea), more research needs to be conducted to understand why. At the very least, the results of this study suggest that large adaptations by international negotiators will not always be effective.

Recent research findings have provided some specific advice about how to negotiate cross-culturally. Rubin and Sander (1991) suggests that during preparation, negotiators should concentrate on understanding three things: (1) their own biases, strengths, and weaknesses; (2) the other negotiator as an individual; and (3) the other negotiator's cultural context. Brett and her colleagues (1998) suggest that cross-cultural negotiators should go further and ask themselves a series of questions about how culture may influence information sharing and the negotiation process (e.g., Does this culture share information directly or indirectly? Is it monochronic or polychronic?). Learning about how another culture shares information and structures the negotiation process may help negotiators plan more strategically for the negotiation (Adair et al., 2004). Finally, Adair, Okumura, and Brett (2001) suggest that both parties in a cross-cultural negotiation need to be prepared to communicate in the other party's culturally preferred method of direct or indirect communication in order to increase the chances of a successful negotiation outcome.

Stephen Weiss (1994) has proposed a useful way of thinking about the options we have when negotiating with someone from another culture. Weiss observes that negotiators may choose from among eight different culturally responsive strategies. These strategies may be used individually or sequentially, and the strategies can be switched as the negotiation progresses. When choosing a strategy, negotiators should be aware of their own and the other party's culture in general, understand the specific factors in the current relationship, and predict or try to influence the other party's approach (Weiss, 1994). Weiss's culturally responsive strategies may be arranged into three groups, based on the level of familiarity (low, moderate, high) that a negotiator has with the other party's culture. Within each group there are some strategies that the negotiator may use individually (unilateral strategies) and others that involve the participation of the other party (joint strategies).

Low Familiarity

Employ Agents or Advisers (Unilateral Strategy)   One approach for negotiators who have very low familiarity with the other party's culture is to hire an agent or adviser who is familiar with the cultures of both parties. This relationship may range from having the other party conduct the negotiations under supervision (agent) to receiving regular or occasional advice during the negotiations (adviser). Although agents or advisers may create other challenges (see Chapter 11), they may be quite useful for negotiators who have little awareness of the other party's culture and little time to prepare.

Bring in a Mediator (Joint Strategy)   Many types of mediators may be used in cross-cultural negotiations, ranging from someone who conducts introductions and then withdraws to someone who is present throughout the negotiation and takes responsibility for managing the negotiation process (see Chapter 19). Interpreters will often play this role, providing both parties with more information than the mere translation of words during negotiations. Mediators may encourage one side or the other to adopt one culture's approaches or a third cultural approach (the mediator's home culture).

Induce the Other Negotiator to Use Your Approach (Joint Strategy)   Another option is to persuade the other party to use your approach. There are many ways to do this, ranging from making a polite request to asserting rudely that your way is best. More subtly, negotiators can continue to respond to the other party's requests in their own language because they "cannot express themselves well enough" in the other's language. Although this strategy has many advantages for the negotiator with low familiarity, there are also some disadvantages. For instance, a Japanese party may become irritated or insulted by having to make the extra effort to deal with a Canadian negotiator on Canadian cultural terms. In addition, the other negotiator may also have a strategic advantage because he or she may now attempt more extreme tactics and excuse their use on the basis of his or her "cultural ignorance" (after all, negotiators can't expect the other party to understand everything about how they negotiate).

Moderate Familiarity

Adapt to the Other Negotiator's Approach (Unilateral Strategy)   This strategy involves negotiators making conscious changes to their approach so that it is more appealing to the other party. Rather than trying to act like the other party, negotiators using this strategy maintain a firm grasp on their own approach but make modifications to help relations with the other party. These modifications may include acting in a less extreme manner, eliminating some behaviors, and adopting some of the other party's behaviors. The challenge in using this strategy is to know which behaviors to modify, eliminate, or adopt. In addition, it is not clear that the other party will interpret modifications in the way that negotiators have intended.

Coordinate Adjustment (Joint Strategy)   This strategy involves both parties making mutual adjustments to find a common process for negotiation. Although this can be done implicitly, it is more likely to occur explicitly ("How would you like to proceed?"), and it can be thought of as a special instance of negotiating the process of negotiation. This strategy requires a moderate amount of knowledge about the other party's culture and at least some facility with his or her language (comprehension, if not the ability to speak). Coordinate adjustment occurs on a daily basis in Montreal, the most bilingual city in North America (85 percent of Montrealers understand both English and French). It is standard practice for businesspeople in Montreal to negotiate the process of negotiation before the substantive discussion begins. The outcomes of this discussion are variations on the theme of whether the negotiations will occur in English or French, with a typical outcome being that either party may speak either language. Negotiations often occur in both languages, and frequently the person with the best second-language skills will switch languages to facilitate the discussion. Another outcome that occasionally occurs has both parties speaking in their second language (i.e., the French speaker will negotiate in English while the English speaker will negotiate in French) to demonstrate respect for the other party. Another type of coordinate adjustment occurs when the two negotiating parties adopt aspects of a third culture to facilitate their negotiations. For instance, during a trip to Latin America, one of the authors of this book conducted discussions in French with a Latin American colleague who spoke Spanish and French, but not English. On a subsequent trip to China, negotiations were conducted in French, English, and Chinese because each of the six participants spoke two of the three languages.

High Familiarity

Embrace the Other Negotiator's Approach (Unilateral Strategy)   This strategy involves completely adopting the approach of the other negotiator. To be used successfully, the negotiator needs to be completely bilingual and bicultural. In essence, the negotiator using this strategy doesn't act *like* a Roman; he or she *is* a Roman. This strategy is costly in preparation time and expense, and it places the negotiator using it under considerable stress because it is difficult to switch back and forth rapidly between cultures. However, there is much to gain by using this strategy because the other negotiator can be approached and understood completely on his or her own terms.

Improvise an Approach (Joint Strategy)   This strategy involves crafting an approach that is specifically tailored to the negotiation situation, other negotiator, and circumstances. To use this approach, both parties to the negotiation need to have high familiarity with the other party's culture and a strong understanding of the individual characteristics of the other negotiator. The negotiation that emerges with this approach can be crafted by adopting aspects from both cultures when they will be useful. This approach is the most flexible of the eight strategies, which is both its strength and weakness. Flexibility is a strength because it allows the approach to be crafted to the circumstances at hand, but it is a weakness because there are few general prescriptive statements that can be made about how to use this strategy.

Effect Symphony (Joint Strategy)   This strategy allows negotiators to create a new approach that may include aspects of either home culture or adopt practices from a third culture. Professional diplomats use such an approach when the customs, norms, and language they use transcend national borders and form their own culture (diplomacy). Use of this strategy is complex and involves a great deal of time and effort. It works best when the parties are familiar with each other and with both home cultures and have a common structure (like that of professional diplomats) for the negotiation. Risks of using this strategy include costs due to confusion, lost time, and the overall effort required to make it work.

Chapter Summary

This chapter examined various aspects of a growing field of negotiation that explores the complexities of international and cross-cultural negotiation. We began the chapter with a discussion of the art and science of negotiation. Next we considered some of the factors that make international negotiations different. Phatak and Habib (1996) suggest that both the environmental and the immediate context have important effects on international negotiations. We then discussed Salacuse's (1988) description of the environmental factors that influence international negotiations: (1) political and legal pluralism, (2) international economics, (3) foreign governments and bureaucracies, (4) instability, (5) ideology, and (6) culture. We added one more environmental factor—external stakeholders—from Phatak and Habib (1996). Phatak and Habib's five immediate context factors were discussed next: (1) relative bargaining power, (2) levels of conflict, (3) relationship between negotiators, (4) desired outcomes, and (5) immediate stakeholders. Each of these environmental and immediate context factors acts to make international negotiations more difficult, and effective international negotiators need to understand how to manage them.

Next, we turned to a discussion of how to conceptualize culture. Robert Janosik (1987) suggests that researchers and practitioners of negotiation use culture in at least four different ways: (1) culture as learned behavior, (2) culture as shared values, (3) culture as dialectics, and (4) culture in context. We then examined two perspectives on how cultural differences can influence negotiations. From the managerial perspective, we discussed 10 ways that culture can influence negotiation: (1) the definition of negotiation, (2) the negotiation opportunity, (3) the selection of negotiators, (4) protocol, (5) communication, (6) time sensitivity, (7) risk propensity, (8) groups versus individuals, (9) the nature of agreements, and (10) emotionalism. From the research perspective, we examined the effect of culture on negotiation outcomes, negotiation process and information exchange, negotiator cognition, negotiator ethics, and conflict resolution.

The chapter concluded with a discussion of how to manage cultural differences in negotiation. Weiss presents eight different culturally responsive strategies that negotiators can use with a negotiator from a different culture. Some of these strategies may be used individually, whereas others are used jointly with the other negotiator. Weiss indicates that one critical aspect of choosing the correct strategy for a given negotiation is the degree of familiarity (low, moderate, or high) that a negotiator has with the other culture. However, even those with high familiarity with another culture are faced with a daunting task if they want to modify their strategy completely when they deal with the other culture.

Endnotes

[1] For example see Binnendijk (1987); Brett (2001); Fisher, Schneider, Borgwardt, and Ganson (1997); Foster (1992); Gelfand and Dyer (2000); Habeeb (1988); Hendon and Hendon (1990); Kremenyuk (1991); Lukov (1985); Mautner-Markhof (1989); Reynolds, Siminitiras, and Vlachou (2002); and Weiss (1996, 2004). For earlier work, see Fayerweather and Kapoor (1976), Hall (1960), and Van Zandt (1970).

[2] For example see Arino, Abramov, Rykounina, and Vila (1997); Brouthers and Bamossy (1997); and Pfouts (1994).

[3] For example see Husted (1996), Natlandsmyr and Rognes (1995), and Zarkada-Fraser and Fraser (2001).

[4] For instance see Drake (1995); Fan (2002); Ghauri and Fang (2001); Kumar and Worm (2003); Leung and Yeung (1995); Lin and Miller (2003); Palich, Carini, and Livingstone (2002); Shi and Wright (2001); Tjosvold and Sun (2001); and Tse, Francis, and Walls (1994).

[5] For example see Druckman (2001), Bush (2003), and Martinez and Susskind (2002).

[6] Descriptions of the American negotiation style may be found in Druckman (1996), Koh (1996), LePoole (1989), and McDonald (1996).

[7] For more examples see Acuff (1993), Hendon and Hendon (1990), and Kennedy (1985).

[8] See Agha and Malloy (2002), Isajiw (2000), Ross (2000), Rubinstein (2003), Stein (1999), and Zartman (1997).

[9] For reviews of this work see Brett (2001) and Gelfand and Dyer (2000).

[10] Hofstede labeled career success/quality of life as masculine–feminine, but we have adopted gender neutral labels for this dimension (Adler, 2002). Subsequent research by Hofstede and Bond (1988) suggested that a fifth dimension, labeled Confucian Dynamism, be added. Confucian Dynamism contains three elements: work ethic, time, and commitment to traditional Confucian values. The dimension has received little attention in the negotiation literature (cf., Chan, 1998).

[11] See Schwartz (1992, 1994), Schwartz and Bilsky (1990), and Smith and Schwartz (1997).

[12] This box and the discussion that follows is based on the work of Foster (1992), Hendon and Hendon (1990), Moran and Stripp (1991), Salacuse (1998), and Weiss and Stripp (1985).

[13] For example see Binnendijk (1987), Graham and Sano (1989), Pye (1992), and Tung (1991).

[14] The low-context cultures included in the study were the United States, Sweden, Germany, and Israel; the high-context cultures were Japan, Hong Kong, Thailand, and Russia; and the mixed-context cultures were United States–Japan and United States–Hong Kong.

[15] Negotiator definitions of fairness are influenced by what would benefit themselves (see Chapter 5).

Managing Negotiation Impasses

Objectives

1. Understand why some conflicts and negotiations are difficult to resolve successfully.

2. Explore fundamental mistakes that negotiators make that increase the likelihood of impasse.

3. Consider a series of major tools and approaches that negotiators can use to break and resolve impasses.

After months of negotiation about a joint venture in the oil and gas industry, one party broke off discussions abruptly. It is not clear why this happened, and the party has refused repeated requests to schedule a meeting. Two colleagues on the same floor of a computer consulting company are no longer speaking to each other. This has started to cause problems with some clients, who have commented that the level of service from the organization is slipping and that telephone calls are not being returned. There are numerous examples from international conflicts where negotiations have reached an impasse. Some have restarted negotiations and managed through the impasse, while others remain deadlocked (see Box 17.1).

Negotiations break down and stall for many reasons. In this chapter, we address situations in which negotiations become especially difficult, often to the point of impasse, stalemate, or breakdown. Parties can become angry or entrenched in their positions. Perceptions become distorted, and judgments are biased. The parties stop communicating effectively and instead blame each other. One party has a conflict management style that is not compatible with the other. Perceptions are so different that the parties do not believe there is any possible compatibility between them, or they cannot find a middle ground where agreement is possible. In short, destructive conflict processes override the negotiation, and the parties cannot proceed.

The chapter is organized into three major sections. First, we discuss the nature of negotiations that are difficult to resolve. We examine the nature of impasses—what makes negotiations intractable—and discuss four elements that make negotiations difficult to resolve: the types of issues, the parties, the negotiation environment and the negotiation setting. In the second section, we explore fundamental mistakes that negotiators make that cause negotiation impasses. Finally, we discuss strategies that negotiators can use to resolve impasses, get negotiations restarted, and back on track to productive outcomes.

BOX 17.1

Illustrative Cases	Historical Impasse	Current Impasse
Rebounded to outcome	Bosnia Northern Ireland Mali Mozambique	Cyprus Israel-Palestine Sri Lanka Colombia
Remained deadlocked or reverted to war	Nagorno-Karabakh Angola Rwanda	

Source: B. I. Spector, "Resiliency in negotiation: Bouncing back from impasse." *International Negotiation, 11,* (2006), pp. 273–286.

The Nature of Difficult-to-Resolve Negotiations and Why They Occur

It is not uncommon for negotiations, especially distributive ones, to become contentious to the point of breakdown. In extreme cases, conflict escalates and interpersonal relations can become strained and even nasty. What are the characteristics of difficult-to-resolve negotiations? Several things can go wrong. We begin this section by discussing impasse as a way to understand difficult negotiations, and we examine what causes negotiations to become intractable and reach impasse.

The Nature of Impasse

We define difficult-to-resolve negotiations broadly as being at *impasse*. Impasse is a condition or state of conflict in which there is no apparent quick or easy resolution. When impasse exists, the parties are unable to create deals that satisfy their aspirations and expectations (Ross and Stillinger, 1991).

• *Impasse is not necessarily bad or destructive (although it can be).* There are numerous reasons negotiations can be at impasse, and there are very good reasons parties sometimes choose to stay at impasse until a viable resolution can be recognized (Mayer, 2000).

• *Impasse does not have to be permanent.* Impasse is a state of a negotiation that means that conflict is not resolvable given the current content, context, process, or people involved in the discussion. Thus, if the content, context, process, or people are altered in some way—either intentionally or simply by the passage of time and change of circumstances—the negotiation can move out of impasse and into resolution.

• *Impasse can be tactical or genuine.* Tactical impasse occurs when parties deliberately refuse to proceed with negotiation as a way to gain leverage or put pressure on the other party to make concessions (Mayer, 2000). Ross and Stillinger (1991) suggest that this sort of intransigence occurs when "one or both parties in a conflict . . . [believes] that a willingness to forgo immediate gains in trade (and thereby deprive its adversary of similar gains) will win for itself even more favorable terms in future negotiations" (p. 391). Genuine impasse, in contrast, occurs "when the parties feel unable to move forward without sacrificing

475

something important to them . . . usually, disputants experience this kind of impasse as beyond their control, and they feel they have no acceptable choice but to remain there" (Mayer, 2000, p. 171). Impasses that begin as tactical may become genuine (Mayer, 2000).

• *Impasse perceptions can differ from reality.* The difference between tactical and genuine impasse may be perceived rather than real—but even if it is perceived, that may be real enough for the parties to believe they are at impasse. The perception of impasse can be created by an intransigent negotiator who is looking to extract concessions from the other party. Intransigence can be defined as a party's unwillingness to move to any fallback position through concession or compromise. Such toughness in negotiating may lead to short-term gain if agreement ensues, but toughness that calls forth toughness in response may well lead to no agreement whatsoever, making such a tactic a "powerful but dangerous card for a negotiator to play" in negotiations (Brams and Doherty, 1993, p. 706).

What Causes Impasses and Intractable Negotiations?

Negotiations evolve as time passes and the issues, parties, and context change. A negotiation becomes more *tractable* when it becomes easier to resolve and *intractable* when it is more difficult to resolve. Intractable negotiations may persist over a long period of time, and when there is no further progress they are at *impasse.* Putnam and Wondolleck (2003) suggest that intractable conflicts vary along four dimensions:

1. *Divisiveness*—the degree to which the conflict divides people such that they are "backed into a corner" and can't escape without losing face.

2. *Intensity*—the level of participant involvement, emotionality, and commitment in a conflict.

3. *Pervasiveness*—the degree to which the conflict invades the social and private lives of people.

4. *Complexity*—the number and complexity of issues, the number of parties involved, the levels of social systems involved in the conflict, and the degree to which it is impossible to resolve one issue without resolving several others simultaneously.

The characteristics that increase the likelihood of impasse are listed in Box 17.2. These characteristics can lead to an atmosphere charged with anger, frustration, and resentment. Channels of communication, previously used to exchange information and supporting arguments for each party's position become closed or constrained. Negotiators use communication to criticize and blame the other, while simultaneously attempting to limit the same type of communication from the other party. The original issues at stake have become blurred and ill defined, and new issues may have been added. Negotiators have become identified with positions on issues, and the conflict has become personalized.

The parties tend to perceive great differences in their respective positions. Conflict heightens the magnitude of these differences and minimizes areas of perceived commonality and agreement. As anger and tension increase, the parties become locked into their initial negotiating positions. Rather than searching for ways to make concessions and move toward agreement, the parties become firmer in stating their initial demands, and they resort to threats, lies, and distortions to force the other party to comply. One party will usually meet threats with counterthreats and retaliation. Those on the same side tend to

Characteristics That Increase or Decrease the Likelihood of Impasses

BOX 17.2

Increase

- The parties themselves are unorganized, loosely connected, and lacking structure.

- The social system from which the parties come is ill defined, dispute resolution procedures are chaotic and uncertain, and there is an absence of clear governing authority.

- There are fundamental value differences on the key issues.

- The conflict repeatedly escalates: the parties grow in size, the number of issues expands, and the costs of resolution increase. Parties are polarized against each other, and conflict repeatedly spirals.

Decrease

In contrast, the following characteristics make a negotiation more tractable:

- The parties themselves are well organized; group members communicate clearly, and the parties have clearly defined roles and agree on a common mission.

- The social system from which the parties come is clearly structured; there are clear procedures and rules for resolving disputes; and clear, legitimate authority exists.

- There is general consensus on underlying values, but a disagreement on how resources are to be allocated.

- The conflict frequently de-escalates: the negotiation remains contained and focused, the parties are strongly committed to finding a mutually acceptable resolution, and cycles of high conflict are frequently broken up by long cycles of relative peace and calm.

Source: L. Putnam and J. Wondolleck "Intractability: Definitions, Dimensions and Distinctions." In R. J. Lewicki, B. Gray, and M. Elliott, *Making Sense of Intractable Environmental Disputes* (Washington, DC: Island Press, 2003).

view each other favorably. They see the best qualities in the people on their side and minimize whatever differences exist, yet they also demand conformity from their team members and will accept a militant, autocratic form of leadership. If there is dissension in the group, it is hidden from the other party; group members always attempt to present a united front to the other side.[1]

Next we discuss four dimensions that cause negotiations to reach impasse—characteristics of the issues, the parties, the negotiation environment, and the negotiation setting.

Characteristics of the Issues

The first dimension that can cause negotiations to reach impasse are characteristics of the issues. Three characteristics that can have a particularly important influence are value differences, high-stakes distributive bargaining, and risk to human health and safety.

- *Value differences.* Many negotiations that reach impasse can be traced to fundamental value differences between the parties. Value differences vary from minor differences in preferences to major differences in ideology, lifestyle, or what is considered sacred and critical. The critical question is how individuals or groups with distinct differences in values choose to deal with these differences—by attempting to force their views on others or by supporting efforts to accommodate and respect others. Many of the most intractable conflicts in society—ethnic, religious, political, economic, legal, and environmental—are rooted in core value differences (see Dingwall, 2002). Wade-Benzoni, Hoffman, Thompson, Moore, Gillespie, and Bazerman (2002) argue that differences in ideology are the result of differences in core values, and these differences are significant barriers that can derail negotiations.

- *High-stakes distributive bargaining.* Negotiation impasses may also result from distributive bargaining when there is no apparent overlap in the bargaining range. As we noted in Chapters 2 and 7, parties may have inflated their negotiating positions to the point that there is no apparent zone of agreement; the costs of settling are seen as higher than the costs of protracting the dispute; the parties have locked themselves into public postures from which they are unwilling to back down; and the parties are inclined to use power to force the other side to back down. Many of these impasses are very responsive to the tactics we describe later in this chapter.

- *Risk to human health and safety.* Finally, some negotiations—particularly those in the area of health and the environment—reach impasse because the threat to human welfare is clear and apparent, and because the issues themselves are rooted in complex science that is difficult for the layperson to understand, much less believe and blindly trust. Environmental cleanup, nuclear power, disposal of toxic waste, pollution control, and related issues create intense debate and deeply felt argument.[2] Burgess and Burgess (1995) note that negotiating parties often compete in "bidding wars" of one-upmanship over who has the greatest concern for public health and safety.

Characteristics of the Parties

The second set of factors that cause negotiations to be difficult to resolve are characteristics of the parties. We discuss five characteristics of the parties that may play a role: how people define themselves, how people compare themselves to others, perceptions of power, revenge and anger, and conflict management styles.

How One Defines One's Self   Many impasses originate because of the way parties define themselves. Issues of *identity* are central to many difficult-to-resolve negotiations. Identity is determined by the way that individuals answer the question "Who am I?" (Hoare, 1994, p. 25). People may answer this question in a variety of ways, depending on the social groups to which they belong and how they understand themselves to be.[3] Rothman (1997) suggests that conflict is likely to occur when people's identities are threatened because such threats challenge people's fundamental sense of who they are. Examples from global and domestic affairs abound (see Box 17.1). Appeals for ethnic self-determination or a national homeland, the correction of perceived institutionalized discrimination against aggrieved minorities, and the universal extension of human or political rights are all causal elements in intractable negotiations. Harold Saunders (2003) suggests that the psychological processes involved in group identity are among the strongest causes of impasses. Moreover, as we noted in Chapter 5, parties often frame a negotiation around an identity issue when they believe that one outcome of the conflict could be to either strengthen or weaken their sense of identity (Gray, 2003a). The influence of the definition of self is not limited to international affairs. Negotiators often adopt a stance based on role (e.g. defender of the underdog) or a personal definition of ethics that is strongly related to self. These stances readily lead to impasses when confronted with another party who does not share these characteristics.

Comparing One's Self to Others   If issues of identity focus on the question "Who am I?" then issues of social comparison reflect the way individuals define "Who are they?" (Gray, 2003a). The development of one's social identity is often inextricably linked to the process of comparing oneself to others. When we define ourselves by virtue of the groups to which we belong, we also begin to define others as members of groups to which we do not belong. Moreover, parties in conflict tend to fall into a psychological trap called the *fundamental attribution error*—tending to blame others when things go wrong, but taking personal credit for successes; conversely, they tend to see others' successes as due to luck, but failures as due to others' defects and deficiencies (Ross, 1997).

Babcock, Wang, and Loewenstein (1996) examined the effect of this social comparison process as it occurs in negotiation impasses, with two principal findings. First, negotiators chose comparison groups to reflect a supportive, self-serving bias for their own positions by comparing themselves to others whose positions make their own demands seem fair and reasonable. Second, negotiation breakdowns or impasses were positively correlated with perceived differences between the negotiators' chosen comparison groups. In short, the greater the perceived differences between the comparison groups, the greater the likelihood of a breakdown. While the first finding could be based on an intentional, strategic choice, the second finding is consistent with our earlier comments regarding extreme positions, perceptual differences, and resultant impasses.

Comparing with others can frequently lead to negotiation impasse in highly structured and departmentalized organizations. The marketing department spends money they don't have, operations is slow to produce new products, and so forth. These groups see the world differently and when under stress can easily lead to impasse because of misinterpretations of communication based on group membership.

Perceptions of Power   Negotiators may believe that they can exercise coercive power to levy costs on the other party or to force that party to accept a settlement that is not in his or her best interest (we examined power at length in Chapter 7). The effectiveness of such a tactic, in the short run and without regard to its effect on the long-term negotiation relationship, clearly depends on the other party's belief that the negotiator has such power and will use it (Brams and Doherty, 1993; de Dreu, 1995). Negotiators in such confrontations are likely to develop a tendency to see each other as extreme, biased, and self-interested. If the other party is perceived to be politically or philosophically the opposite, and if good manners lead one or both of you to avoid mutual disclosure of your views on volatile subjects, the level of negotiation difficulty is likely to rise. Keltner and Robinson (1993) found such negotiations to be marked by excessive length, few agreements overall, and, in retrospect, little perceived cooperation.

According to Smyth (1994) impasses often result from the perceived need to negotiate simultaneously about change in power and the applicable, appropriate institutions for maintaining that power shift. For instance, when social identification is strong (as it is, for example, among Serbs in the former Yugoslav republics or among Israelis and Palestinians in the Middle East), the consequent in-group/out-group bias often leads one or both parties to demonize the other and to discount the validity and acceptability of the other's bargaining position. This often results in an unwillingness to deal with the other party at all. Third-party strategies to manage this are discussed in Chapter 19. It is in the nature of intergroup negotiations that some adjustment of each party's own identity, or the rigor with which it is defended, must be made in order for negotiations to proceed productively (Ring and Van de Ven, 1994). In short, there has to be some give on both sides (particularly the high-power side) and a willingness to at least consider that the other party may have a legitimate interest and a valid perspective.

Revenge and Anger   Impasse may also result from an expression of fear and anger (Adler, Rosen, and Silverstein, 1998) or from a desire to seek revenge on the offending party (Kim and Smith, 1993). The escalation of conflict through revenge seems to be driven by three factors: an interest in retribution to correct injustice, the need to stand up and express one's self-worth, and the wish to deter future instances of undesirable behavior (Kim and Smith, 1993). These emotions and motivations, in turn, exacerbate the tendency for conflict to escalate and for negotiations to break down completely. Pruitt, Parker, and Mikolic (1997) propose that escalation often occurs in response to persistent annoyance of one party by another, while Jones and Remland (1993) suggest that escalation might also be explained by "nonverbal status displays" (p. 119). Such displays are meant to express power, dominance, or relative status in face-to-face conflicts in order to degrade the other party's physical or intellectual presence. For instance, negotiators can refuse to meet in the same room with the other party (degrading physical presence) or refuse to acknowledge questions from the other party during negotiations (degrading intellectual presence).

Conflict Management Styles   Finally, impasses may also result from too little engagement in the negotiation, rather than too much. Mayer (2000) observed that parties often prefer to avoid conflict in a number of creative ways:

- Aggressive avoidance ("Don't start with me or you will regret it")—intimidate others to keep them away.
- Passive avoidance ("I refuse to dance")—try to ignore the other.
- Passive aggressive avoidance ("If you are angry at me, that's *your* problem")—put the blame on the other party and walk away.
- Avoidance by claiming hopelessness ("What's the use . . . ?").
- Avoidance through surrogates ("Let's you and she fight")—deflect the conflict to an agent or representative to take the other on.
- Avoidance through denial ("If I close my eyes, it will all go away")—make believe it isn't there.
- Avoidance through premature problem solving ("There is no conflict—I fixed everything").
- Avoidance by folding ("OK, we'll do it your way; now can we talk about something else?").

Note that these eight different approaches can be used individually or combined together. The function is to avoid engaging in the conflict in a productive way, which may in and of itself perpetuate the impasse until the other party, or the circumstances, change in some way (Mayer, 2000). We discussed avoidance as a strategy in Chapter 1 and as a personal style in Chapter 15.

Characteristics of the Negotiation Environment

The third dimension that can cause negotiations to reach impasse includes characteristics of the negotiation environment. It is important that negotiators clearly understand what they are negotiating because this may be different for both parties (Fortgang, Lax, and Sebenius, 2003). For instance, one party may be interested in only the current contract while the other is interested in creating a long-term strategic partnership. When negotiators learn that they have very different understandings about what they are negotiating, the risk of impasse increases.

Another environmental factor that can lead to impasse is the *renegotiation* of existing agreements. Salacuse (2001) suggests that renegotiations of existing agreements occur frequently and are in response to three situations: (1) postdeal negotiations, (2) intradeal negotiations, and (3) extradeal negotiations. *Postdeal* negotiations are negotiations that occur as an existing agreement is expiring. For instance, when a contract between a purchaser and supplier is coming to completion, both parties have the opportunity to negotiate a new agreement. *Intradeal* negotiations occur when an agreement states that negotiations should be reopened at specific intervals. For instance, two parties to a joint venture could agree to renegotiate certain contract provisions every 12 months to ensure that the agreement is working well. *Extradeal* negotiations occur when it appears that there is a violation of the contract, or in the absence of a contract reopening clause. For instance, negotiations that result from one party missing a payment to the other would be an extradeal negotiation.

While all three types of renegotiations can lead to impasse, extradeal negotiations have the largest probability of doing so because they are generally the result of a large shift in the environment, such as a sudden increase in oil prices, unforeseen changes in government policy, or political instability that has a much larger effect on one party than the other. The negatively affected party clearly has more motivation to reopen negotiations, while the less affected negotiator may feel hostile, that a "deal is a deal," and see no need to negotiate (Salacuse, 2001).

Characteristics of the Negotiation Setting

The fourth set of reasons that negotiations reach impasse involve characteristics of the negotiation setting, which includes temporal issues, relational issues, and cultural issues. The influence of culture on negotiation is discussed in Chapter 16. Very little has been written about how the negotiation setting leads negotiators to impasses. Experienced negotiators understand, however, that changing the negotiation setting—the physical location in which it occurs—can be an important tactic for getting negotiations back on track. For instance, changing from one hotel or city to another can be used as a symbol for a new start to negotiations and a signal that the previous approach was left at the old location. Alternatively, changing from a more formal space—such as a formal conference or board room—to an informal space—such as a living room, lounge, or restaurant—can make people more comfortable and change the interpersonal dynamics. Even more importantly, replacing an aggressive member of the negotiating team with a more collaborative member, either temporarily or permanently, can signal the other party that one is also willing to change the substance of the negotiation. Lax and Sebenius (2003) suggest further that "negotiating with the wrong parties, or about the wrong set of issues, involving parties in the wrong sequence, or at the wrong time" can all lead to impasses (p. 66). Finally, timing is critical in a negotiation (see Chapter 2). Compromises that are presented too early may be rejected outright, but if they can be repackaged and presented later for exploration, they may be able to break an impasse (Eliasson, 2002).

Section Summary

In this section, we reviewed four dimensions that cause negotiations to be difficult to resolve: characteristics of the issues, the parties, the negotiation environment, and the negotiation setting.

Fundamental Mistakes That Cause Impasses

We now turn to exploring mistakes that negotiators make that increase the likelihood of negotiation impasses and how these errors can derail negotiations. Sebenius (2001) outlines six fundamental mistakes that negotiators make that can derail the negotiation process and result in impasses:

1. *Neglecting the other side's problem.* A lack of understanding of what the other side needs to receive from the negotiation or what they are trying to accomplish will make negotiations much more difficult to resolve and increase the likelihood of impasses. Negotiators who do not ensure that they are working to craft an agreement that satisfies the needs of both parties are making a mistake that can derail negotiations.

2. *Too much of a focus on price.* An overemphasis on price will make negotiations much more difficult to resolve and can result in impasse. Negotiators need to remember that there is almost always more to a negotiation than just price, and they need to pay attention to both tangible and intangible factors.

3. *Positions over interests.* Negotiations require both creating value and claiming it. Negotiators who focus too early on claiming value, or who do so in too aggressive a manner, are making a mistake that will make negotiations more difficult to resolve and increase the probability of impasse. As Sebenius (2001) suggests, "the pie must be both expanded and divided" (p. 91) or the negotiator is making an error that could derail negotiations.

4. *Too much focus on common ground.* A key aspect of negotiation is interdependence (see Chapter 1), which means that parties need to have enough in common to strike a deal. It can be very difficult to reach agreement with identical other parties, however, because without differences there is little reason to negotiate. Negotiators who focus too much on what they have in common with each other and not enough on their differences are making a mistake and will lose the opportunity to find the creative solutions that make deals work. Unless enough value is created to make a deal attractive, a negotiation will be more difficult to resolve simply because there is not enough motivation to complete the agreement.

5. *Neglecting BATNAs.* Strong BATNAs are an important tool in negotiation, and they give a negotiator the power to drive a positive outcome (Sebenius, 2001). Negotiators who do not work to improve their BATNA are making a mistake because neglecting BATNAs will reduce one's power in the current negotiation and may actually make it more difficult to reach an agreement.

6. *Adjusting perceptions during the negotiation.* Negotiators need to use information that they gather throughout the negotiation to adjust their view of the situation, potential agreements, and the other negotiator. Negotiators who do not adjust their perceptions accurately are making a mistake that will make the negotiation more difficult to resolve. This is a challenging mistake to correct because many biases in negotiation occur unconsciously (see Chapter 5), although they still have the power to derail a negotiation to impasse.

Another mistake that negotiators make during negotiations is that they do not proactively manage the negotiation process itself. Research by Deborah Kolb and Judith Williams (2000, 2001) suggests that a major reason negotiations are not successful is that negotiators fail to manage what they have labeled the *shadow negotiation,* a negotiation about the negotiation process that occurs within the substantive negotiation. Shadow negotiation "doesn't determine the 'what' of the discussion, but the 'how.' Which interests will hold sway? Will the conversation's tone be adversarial or cooperative? Whose opinions will be heard? In short, how will bargainers deal with each other?" (Kolb and Williams, 2001, pp. 89–90). Negotiators who do not manage the shadow negotiation will find that they either cannot get the negotiation started, or they cannot get their issues discussed, and this increases the likelihood of impasse. For instance, before negotiating the content of a merger the parties should discuss how they want to work together and set norms for how the discussion should occur.

In a related vein, Ron Fortgang, David Lax, and James Sebenius (2003) suggest that negotiators need to manage the *social contract* in addition to the economic issues under discussion or the negotiation may derail. The social contract has two components. The *underlying* social contract determines what the negotiation is about. For instance, is the discussion to determine a series of contracts or a deep strategic relationship? The *ongoing* social contract is concerned with "how we make decisions, handle unforeseen events, communicate, and resolve disputes" (Fortgang et al., 2003, p. 68). Negotiators who neglect managing the social contract of a negotiation are making a mistake that could lead to negotiation impasses.

Finally, Barbara Gray (2003b) suggests that another reason negotiations reach impasse is that negotiators allow their emotions to determine their reaction to the other party rather than responding in a measured way to the situation. Instead of "separating the people from the problem" (Fisher, Ury, and Patton, 1991), Gray suggests it is important that negotiators understand their internal emotional responses to the other party—when they are strong, an internal psychological aspect may be driving the response. For instance, if Sam is always late for their negotiation meetings, Mary, who is fastidiously on time, may interpret this pattern as a lack of respect. Sam, on the other hand, may be late because he has to travel farther to the meetings across town and with his tightly packed schedule he cannot arrive on time. In fact, Sam may see it as a sign of disrespect that he always has to travel farther to

BOX | 17.3 | Process Signals to Monitor to Avoid Impasses

1. Monitor the interactive quality of the process, noting how each statement and action is linked to the next. Recognize that what you intend will never be perfectly read.

2. Pay special attention to the multiple levels of the negotiation, noting how identity and role are positioned as well as the substance. Note, too, how emotion is expressed or suppressed.

3. Be attuned to the other party's verbal and nonverbal cues. Pitch of voice, speed of conversation, pauses, and verbal stumbles can all signal internal emotions. Changes in physical behaviors may also mark transitions.

4. Be cautious in interpreting the behavior of others, however. Explore alternative explanations

of what is taking place. Do not assume that others would respond as you might.

5. Face up to the fact when you are caught in unproductive cycles, rehashing old arguments and advocating old solutions.

6. Recognize your own trigger points, particularly things that make you lose perspective.

7. Anticipate change by imagining different scenarios. Remember that past is not necessarily prologue.

Source: G. M. Green and M. Wheeler, "Awareness and action in critical moments." *Negotiation Journal, 20,* (2), (2004), pp. 349–364.

the meetings. Thus, Mary's emotional response may have more to do with her own internal emotional state than Sam's behavior. For instance, she may have been raised by parents who were very strict about honoring time commitments. Negotiators who do not understand how their emotions can influence their reactions to the other party are making a mistake that can derail negotiations.

Preventing Impasses

Gillian Green and Michael Wheeler (2004) suggest that there are critical moments in negotiations before they unfold. One of the best ways to resolve an impasse is to avoid having one occur. It may be possible to avoid an impasse at the last moment by being very aware of changes in the negotiation process. Green and Wheeler (2004) suggest seven things to be especially aware of that may signal an impending impasse (see Box 17.3).

How to Resolve Impasses

The first two sections of this chapter focused on what causes negotiations to be difficult to resolve and approach impasse. We now turn to examining how to manage impasses, which need to be resolved on three levels: cognitive, emotional, and behavioral (Mayer, 2000):

1. *Cognitive resolution* is needed to change how the parties view the situation. For parties to achieve cognitive resolution, ". . . they must *perceive* that the key issues have been resolved, think that they have reached closure on the situation, and view the conflict as part of their past as opposed to their future . . ." (Mayer, 2000, p. 98). Cognitive resolution is often difficult to achieve because people tenaciously hang onto beliefs and perceptions in spite of new data to the contrary. New information and explicit reframing are key to achieving cognitive resolution.

- Get or share more information. Ask more questions and recognize the value in answering your counterpart's questions.

- Switch objective criteria. For example, a home buyer may switch justification from focusing on a home's market value to the seller's profits.

- Prioritize needs and interests. Make a list to stay focused.

- Brainstorm options. Explore creative solutions.

- Set deadlines. Agreeing to deadlines increases the likelihood parties will act and move.

- Temporarily put aside the issue. Set it aside and revisit after gaining some momentum by agreeing on minor issues.

- Take a break. Time away from the table can help parties regain composure and reassess issues.

- Move up the chain. If your counterpart doesn't have the authority to concede anymore, ask to speak with the boss.

- Pick a fair alternative process. For example, asking an independent third party to arbitrate or mediate can help.

- Concede. While possibly your last choice, it may still be in your interest if making no deal leaves you worse off.

Source: M. Latz, *Gain the Edge: Negotiating to Get What You Want* (New York: St. Martins Press, 2004).

2. *Emotional resolution* involves changing how parties feel about the impasse and the other party, as well as reducing the amount of emotional energy they put into the negotiation. When parties have emotionally resolved an impasse they no longer experience strong negative feelings, relations with the other are less intense, and they have reached some kind of emotional closure on the conflict. Emotional resolution often involves trust rebuilding, forgiveness, and apology.

3. *Behavioral resolution* explicitly addresses what people will do in the future and how agreements they make about the future will be realized. Behavioral resolution agreements should specify ways that the parties can stop difficult conflict dynamics, specify reparations, and include mechanisms for instituting new behaviors that prompt resolution.

There are many ways to start to break an impasse (see Box 17.4). The key is to find a way to restart the process (Spector, 2006). This may be difficult and the first attempts may fail.

In this section, we describe six strategies that can be used to resolve impasses. These strategies tend to focus on behavioral and cognitive resolution, but they also have an influence on emotional resolution:

1. Reaching agreement on rules and procedures.
2. Reducing tension and synchronizing the de-escalation of hostility.
3. Improving the accuracy of communication, particularly improving each party's understanding of the other's perspective.
4. Controlling the number and size of issues in the discussion.
5. Establishing common ground where parties can find a basis for agreement.
6. Enhancing the desirability of the options and alternatives that each party presents to the other.

There is no standard recipe for resolving impasses, nor is there a standard approach that works every time. Researchers studying the nature of conflict and its resolution have suggested a wide array of different dispute resolution techniques that can be applied in several ways.[4] We suggest that it is frequently productive to resolve negotiation impasses by using these strategies in the order presented here. This means starting with attempts to agree on ground rules and to reduce tension, followed by efforts to improve the accuracy of communication and to control the proliferation of issues. Finally, the parties should move to establish common ground and enhance the attractiveness of each other's preferred alternatives. This approach is by no means firm and inflexible; many impasses have been successfully resolved by invoking the steps in a different order. However, the order in which we present these approaches is one that third parties frequently use to resolve impasses, so we believe it will also be the most effective if employed by the negotiators themselves. If the impasse cannot be broken and productive negotiations started, then third-party intervention may become necessary (see Chapter 19).

Agreement on the Rules and Procedures

Parties can try to manage impasses by obtaining mutual agreement about the rules that will govern the negotiation. Escalated conflict tends to exceed its original bounds; as parties become more upset, they may be more likely to resort to more extreme tactics to defeat the other. Efforts at effective conflict de-escalation and control may require the parties to rededicate themselves to basic ground rules for how they will manage the impasse. Establishing ground rules might include the following steps (see also Dukes, Piscolish, and Stephens, 2000):

- Determining a site for a meeting (changing the site or finding a neutral location).
- Setting a formal agenda outlining what may or may not be discussed and agreeing to follow that agenda.
- Determining who may attend the meetings. (Changing key negotiators or representatives may be a signal of the intention to change the negotiation approach.)
- Setting time limits for individual meetings and for the overall negotiation session. (As we have pointed out, progress in negotiation is often paced according to the time available; therefore, setting limits is likely to yield more progress than not setting them.)
- Setting procedural rules, such as who may speak, how long they may speak, how issues will be approached, what facts may be introduced, how records of the meeting will be kept, how agreements will be affirmed, and what clerical or support services are required.
- Following specific dos and don'ts for behavior (e.g., don't attack others).

Finally, the parties may agree to set aside a short period during negotiations to critique how they are doing. This mechanism designates a specific time for the parties to evaluate their own progress. It provides time to reevaluate ground rules, change procedural mechanisms, or perhaps even change negotiators. This process provides the opportunity for the parties to correct the procedural mechanisms that will allow them to make greater progress on their substantive disagreements (Walton, 1987).

Reducing Tension and Synchronizing De-escalation

Unproductive negotiations can easily become highly emotional. Parties are frustrated, angry, and upset. They are strongly committed to their viewpoints and have argued strenuously for their preferred alternatives, seeing themselves as firm, principled, or deserving. The other side, behaving the same way, is seen as stubborn, bull-headed, inflexible, and unreasonable. The longer the parties debate, the more likely it is that emotions will overrule reason—name-calling and verbal assaults replace logic and reason. When the negotiation becomes personalized, turning into a win–lose feud between individuals, all hope of a productive discussion is lost. Several approaches for resolving impasses are directed at defusing volatile emotions.

Separating the Parties   The most common approach to de-escalating conflict is to stop meeting. Declare a recess, call a caucus, or agree to adjourn and come back later when there has been a chance to unwind and reflect. The parties should acknowledge explicitly that the purpose of the caucus is to allow tempers to cool so the dialogue will become less emotional. Each party should also agree to return with a renewed effort to make deliberations more productive—either by simply regaining composure or by attempting a new or different way to address the issue that created the anger.

The parties may be separated for a few minutes or hours to several days or weeks. Variations in the time period are related to the level of hostility, as well as to unique situational circumstances. Parties may use the time to check with their constituencies, gather new information, and reassess their position and commitments.

Tension Management   Tension is a natural by-product of negotiations. Negotiators should be aware that it is bound to occur, and they should know how to manage it. Some negotiators who are sensitive to increases in tension know how to make a witty remark or crack a joke that causes laughter and releases tension. Others know that it is sometimes important to let the other party ventilate pent-up anger and frustration without responding in kind. Skilled negotiators recognize that allowing the other party the opportunity for a catharsis will often clear the air and may permit negotiations to return to a calmer pace.

Source: © CartoonResource.com.

Acknowledging the Other's Feelings: Active Listening   When one party states her views and the other openly disagrees, the first negotiator often hears the disagreement as more than just disagreement. She may hear a challenge, a put-down, an assertion that her statement is wrong or not acceptable, an accusation of lying or distorting of the facts, or another form of personal attack. Whether or not this is the message that was intended is beside the point; the negotiator has to deal with the way it was received. Understandably, such misinterpretations escalate conflict. As discussed above, negotiators need to have a good understanding of their own reactions during negotiation (Gray, 2003b). Negotiators who overreact to the other party are likely responding to something inside themselves, and they need to learn to manage this or it will become a liability during the negotiation process.

There is a difference between accurately hearing what the other party said and agreeing with it. One can let the other party know that both the content and emotional strength of his or her message have been heard and understood, but that does not mean that one agrees with it. This technique is called *active listening,* and it is frequently used in interviews and therapy settings as a way of encouraging a person to speak more freely (Rogers, 1961). Communication processes were discussed in more detail in Chapter 6. Rather than challenging and confronting the other negotiator's statements by bolstering one's own statements and position, negotiators can respond with statements that probe for confirmation and elaboration. Comments may include: "You see the facts this way," "You feel very strongly about this point," and "I can see that if you saw things this way, you would feel threatened and upset by what I have said." Again, these statements do not indicate that a negotiator agrees with the other party; rather, they communicate that the other has been accurately heard and understood.

Synchronized De-escalation   Charles Osgood (1962), writing about the cold war and disarmament, suggested a unilateral strategy for conflict de-escalation called "graduated and reciprocated initiatives in tension reduction" (GRIT). One party decides on a small concession that both parties could make to signal their good faith and desire to de-escalate. The concession should be large enough to be interpreted as an unambiguous signal of the desire to change the relationship, but not so large that if only one side acts it would be weak or vulnerable. The party should then make a public announcement stating:

1. Exactly what the concession is.

2. That the concession is part of a deliberate attempt to reduce tension.

3. That the other side is explicitly invited to reciprocate in a specified form.

4. That the concession will occur on a stated time schedule.

5. That each party commits to make the concession without knowing whether the other will reciprocate.

The party who initiated the de-escalation then makes the concession. The specific concession should be something that is obvious, unambiguous, and subject to easy verification. For instance, a union may state that in order to start a positive negotiation process they will return to the table next Monday but they expect management to be ready to negotiate in good faith. Making it public and symbolic also helps. If the other party does not respond, then the initiator follows through with the action and repeats the sequence, selecting a simple, low-risk concession in an effort to attract the other into synchronized de-escalation. If the other does respond, then the initiator proposes a second action, slightly riskier than the first, and once again initiates the sequence. As the synchronized de-escalation takes hold, the parties can both propose larger and riskier concessions that will bring them back into a productive negotiating relationship. In a variation of this approach to de-escalation, a negotiator invites the other party to make a small initial concession, providing a short list of options from which that party may choose. Such a proposal is accompanied by a promise to respond in kind, choosing their concession from a list to be provided by the other party (Ross and Stillinger, 1991).

Improving the Accuracy of Communication

The third step in conflict reduction is to ensure that both parties accurately understand the other's position. (For a broader treatment of communication processes in negotiation, see Chapter 6.) When conflict becomes heated, communication efforts concentrate on managing emotions and directing the next assault at the other. Effective listening decreases. Both parties think they know what the other side is going to say and no longer listen. During impasses listening becomes so poor that the parties are frequently unaware that their positions may have much in common. Rapoport (1964) labeled this the "blindness of involvement" because it inhibits the development of trust and the problem-solving process. Several approaches can be used to rectify this situation (see Box 17.5)

Role Reversal   It is often easy to see the logic, rationale, and potential common ground when one is an outsider. Recognizing them when one is personally involved in a conflict, however, is another matter. Role reversal can help negotiators place themselves in the other party's shoes and look at the issue from his or her perspective. For instance, a manager can take the position of an employee, a salesperson that of a customer, a purchasing agent that of a supplier. Negotiators can play out scenarios in their imagination, ask a friend or colleague to assume the other role and act out a dialogue, or, more effectively, include role reversal as part of a unilateral strategy preparation process. Although role reversal will not identify exactly how the other party thinks and feels about the issues, the process can provide useful and surprising insights. (For example, see Box 17.6 on managing offensive comments.)

During negotiations, one side often tries to encourage the other to reverse roles. He may plead, "Look at this from my perspective. What you're suggesting puts me in this position, and how could you expect . . . ?" A variation on this occurs when one party tells the other, "If I were in your shoes, I would . . ." If role reversal gives the negotiator an accurate understanding of the other's perspective and shows that a previous view was wrong, it gives the negotiator a chance to correct specific misperceptions. Accurate communication gives the negotiator a broader, more integrated view of the negotiation. Role reversal also provides the negotiator an opportunity to explore how a planned action may affect the relationship. For instance, a member of management taking labor's role may discover that some of management's arguments or tactics may have an ineffective or undesirable effect, leading management to drop the tactics before they cause problems (Johnson and Dustin, 1970).

BOX 17.5   Language Strategies to Facilitate Communication

Linguist Deborah Tannen argues that Americans live in an argument culture, where the language we use in talking about issues reflects a preference for adversarial relationships. The words we choose to describe our interactions shape our perceptions of the experience. Consequently, when we refer to the "opponent" in a "debate," we shape our communication as adversarial and are more likely to escalate the conflict.

Tannen proposed the following naming alternatives to help defuse the argument culture:

Instead of This . . .	Say This . . .
Battle of the sexes	Relations between women and men
Critique	Comment
Fight	Discussion
Both sides	All sides
Debate	Discuss
The other side	Another side
Having an argument	Making an argument
The opposite sex	The other sex
War on drugs	Solving the drug problem
Litigation	Mediation
Provocative	Thought-provoking
Most controversial	Most important
Polarize	Unify
Attack-dog journalism	Watchdog journalism
Automatic opposition	Genuine opposition
Focus on differences	Search for common ground
Win the argument	Understand another point of view
The opposition party	The other party
Prosecutorial reporting	Investigative reporting
The argument culture	The dialogue culture

Source: From Deborah Tannen, "How to Turn Debate into Dialogue," *USA Weekend,* February 27–March 3, 1998, pp. 4–5.

One purpose of role reversal is to highlight areas of commonality and overlap between positions; however, this cannot be achieved unless such compatibilities actually exist and at least one party moves toward them by suggesting ideas. When no actual compatibility exists, role reversal may simply sharpen the differences between the parties. Although some negotiators find that a lack of compatibility inhibits attempts to resolve the negotiation, others prefer to be aware of it so they can find other means to break the impasse. To negotiate integratively, both parties need accurate knowledge of the other's goals. If the parties' goals are completely incompatible, integrative negotiation is impossible, and the sooner that is

When you are on the receiving end of offensive comments in a negotiation setting, your first response may be to offend back, or to stalk off in anger and displeasure. For important negotiations, though, this creates the risk of denying you (as well as the other parties) any mutual gains from the exchange, as well as diverting your attention from the issues that brought you to the table in the first place. Andrea Schneider (1994) suggests that your basic options when faced with offensive comments involve first trying to understand why the offense occurred and then deciding what to do about it. To understand the behavior, she suggests four steps:

- Check your assumptions.
- Check the data on which your assumptions are based.
- Seek and evaluate other data, even (or especially) if those data tend to disconfirm your assumptions.

- Evaluate and adjust your assumptions, as appropriate.

Once your assumptions seem correct and appropriate, then decide whether to handle the behavior by:

- Ignoring it (just act like it never occurred).
- Confronting it (i.e., counterattack: "That's racist," or "How juvenile").
- Deflecting it (i.e., acknowledge it and move on—a sense of humor often helps here).
- Engaging it (talk with the other party about his or her purpose in being offensive, and about your reaction to the offense).

Source: Adapted from A. K. Schneider, "Effective Responses to Offensive Comments," *Negotiation Journal* 10 (1994), pp. 107–15.

discovered, the better. As we showed in Chapter 2, the existence of a negative settlement range has serious consequences for the distributive bargaining process, and it is best to be identified. Thus, role reversal can be a powerful tool for uncovering the true goals of both parties and determining how the negotiation should proceed.

Imaging Imaging is also a method for gaining insight into the other party's perspective. In the imaging process, parties in conflict are asked to engage in the following activities separately:

1. Describe how they see themselves.
2. Describe how the other party appears to them.
3. State how they think the other party would describe them.
4. State how they think the other party sees themselves.

The parties then exchange this information, in order. The two sets of statements frequently reveal both similarities and differences. Imaging usually produces animated discussion as the parties clarify and substantiate what they have said or heard. A common result is that the parties recognize that many apparent differences and areas of conflict are not real, and thus they begin to understand those that are real. Alderfer (1977) gives an example of imaging in negotiations between top executives who met to work out an organizational structure for a new firm that resulted from a merger of two organizations. Executives from both sides were deeply concerned that they would be outmaneuvered by the other and would lose their power as a result of the merger. A consultant suggested having an imaging meeting prior to actual negotiations. This meeting sharply altered the perceptions of both parties, and successful integrative negotiations became possible.

The successful use of role reversal or imaging techniques can accomplish several things. First, they can clarify and correct misconceptions and misinterpretations. In addition, they bring to the surface both parties' interests, goals, and priorities, as well as limitations, which can then be used in the negotiation process. One or both sides often gains an understanding of the other side's true needs. Finally, these processes set a positive tone for the negotiation. Negotiators find they can make their needs and concerns heard and not be interrupted. This reduces defensiveness and encourages people to listen. Most people begin the negotiation process with a rather clear idea of what they need from the other party; in this phase, they learn more about what the other needs from them. Joint problem solving moves from being an unattainable ideal to an achievable process.

Controlling Issues

The fourth step to conflict resolution is to control the number of issues under discussion. As conflict intensifies, the size, number, and complexity of the issues expand. Although small conflicts have issues that can be managed satisfactorily one at a time, large conflicts become unwieldy and less amenable to easy resolution. The challenge for negotiators in impasses, therefore, is to develop strategies to contain issue proliferation and reduce the negotiation to manageable proportions. We discuss several strategies below.

Fractionate the Negotiation   *Fractionating* is a method of issue control that involves dividing a large conflict into smaller parts (Fisher, 1964). According to Fisher, fractionating can involve several actions: reducing the number of parties on each side; controlling the number of substantive issues discussed; stating issues in concrete terms rather than as principles; restricting the precedents involved, both procedural and substantive; searching for ways to narrow the big issues; and depersonalizing issues, separating them from the parties advocating them. These approaches work as follows:

1. Reduce the Number of Parties on Each Side   When there is an impasse, both parties try to build alliances for strength or to bring their constituencies into the negotiation to have more clout at the table. Additional parties, such as lawyers, experts, or parties with formal authority, are often brought in for the information or the leverage they can provide (12 ways to manage dueling experts are presented in Box. 17.7). The sheer number of parties in the negotiation can increase the complexity of the negotiation substantially (more parties bring more perspectives on the issues, more time is needed to hear each party, therefore more opportunities for disagreement, etc.). One way to manage an impasse that has escalated is to reduce the number of participants. Having fewer negotiators present, or even limiting the discussion to two individuals, will increase the chances of reaching a settlement.

2. Control the Number of Substantive Issues Involved   A second way to fractionate a conflict is to keep the number of issues small enough to manage. When conflict builds to impasse, the size and number of issues proliferate. Some negotiations escalate to the

1. Try to convince the other party that your expert is better.

2. Have experts jointly explain why they have different advice.

3. Have each expert answer a list of written questions.

4. Have the experts sign a joint explanation.

5. Jointly choose a third expert to attend the negotiation.

6. Have the third expert write a nonbinding decision.

7. Have the third expert write a binding decision.

8. Create doubt by introducing new or hypothetical facts.

9. Split the difference between the experts.

10. Logroll across experts.

11. Choose randomly between the experts.

12. Refer the decision to a binding third party (arbitrator, judge).

Source: J. H. Wade, "Dueling experts in mediation and negotiation: How to respond when eager expensive entrenched expert egos escalate enmity." *Conflict Resolution Quarterly, 21,* (4), (2004), pp. 419–436.

point where there are too many issues to manage constructively. At the same time, limiting negotiations to very few issues also raises problems. Single-issue negotiations are frequently harder to manage because they quickly lead to win–lose polarization over the issue. In such circumstances, it is often important to expand the number of issues so both sides can see themselves as having gained. The number of issues can be expanded by defining the issue broadly enough so that resolution can benefit both sides or by coupling the issue with another issue so that each party can receive a preferred settlement on at least one issue. (We discussed defining the bargaining mix, bundling and packaging issues, and inventing options in Chapters 2, 3, and 4.)

3. State Issues in Concrete Terms Rather than as Principles   Negotiation issues become difficult to control when events or issues are treated as matters of principle. Small conflicts can rapidly become intractable disputes when their resolution is not treated as an isolated event but instead is made consistent with a broader policy or principle. Negotiators may view any deviation from policy as a threat to that policy. Because it is far more difficult to change broad policy than to make a concession on a single issue, negotiations become challenging quickly. For example, an employee needs to take her child to the doctor during her work hours and requests an excused absence from the company. The company does not have a policy that permits employees to take time off for this reason, and the employee's supervisor tells her she has to take sick leave or vacation time instead. "It's a matter of principle," the manager asserts. Resorting to arguments of principle and policy is often a tactic used by high-power parties against any change from the status quo; the longer the discussion remains at the level of policy or principle, however, the less likely it is that it will become specific enough to be successfully resolved.

There are times, of course, when a single event is indicative of a new principle or policy. When this is the case negotiations should specifically address the policy or principle. Frequently people are reluctant to address principles because they know negotiations over principles are difficult and lengthy. Attempting to negotiate a concrete issue when the negotiation really should address the broader principle, however, may result only in frustration and a sense of futility. If this occurs, it is wise to face the underlying issue and raise it directly. There are at least two tactics that can be used:

- Question whether the issue needs to be addressed at the principle or policy level. Inquire about the link between the specific issue and the broader principle or policy. If none exists, and one party wants to look at the matter from a principle or policy level, suggest that the immediate concrete issue be handled and discussed separately from the underlying principle or policy.

- Identify that exceptions can be made to all policies and that principles and policies can be maintained even if exceptions are made under special circumstances. The parties may be willing to agree that this specific case might be one of those times.

4. Restrict the Precedents Involved, Both Procedural and Substantive   Another opportunity to fractionate the negotiation occurs when the parties treat concessions on a single issue as creating a substantive or procedural precedent. When a substantive precedent is at stake, the party may feel that to concede on the issue at this time will render him or her vulnerable to conceding on the same issue, or a similar issue, in the future. To return to our previous example, the manager may argue that if she grants the employee an excused absence in this case, when no policy exists, then she will be obligated to grant permission to every other employee making the same request. Belief in the power of substantive precedents is strong, but it may be possible to restrict the negotiation so that it has no precedent value and the agreement applies only to the current situation. Ideally, some aspect of the current situation is unique so that the fractionation may occur. Procedural precedents are at stake when parties agree to follow a process they haven't followed before. In the employment example, the manager may not want to give the employee the excused absence because the employee did not submit any proof that she was, in fact, taking a child to the doctor. So they could agree that the employee will return with some evidence that the doctor's visit was made.

Issues of precedent can be as difficult to manage as issues of principle. Negotiators trying to move conflict toward de-escalation and resolution should try to prevent single issues from being translated into major questions of precedent. Focusing the dialogue on the key issue and persisting in arguments that concessions on this issue at this time do not have to set any precedents—substantive or procedural—is a way to undermine the power of precedent and to return the negotiation to a course leading toward agreement.

5. Search for Ways to Divide the Big Issues   Negotiators should try to find ways to slice a large issue into smaller pieces, known as using *salami tactics* (Fisher, 1964). Issues that can be expressed in quantitative measurable units are easy to slice. For example, compensation demands can be divided into cents-per-hour increments, or lease rates can be quoted as dollars per square foot. When working to fractionate issues of principle or precedent, parties may use the time horizon (when the principle goes into effect or how long it will last) as a way to fractionate the issue. It may be easier to reach an agreement when settlement terms don't have to be implemented until months in the future. Another approach is to vary the number of ways that the principle may be applied. For example, a company may devise a family emergency leave plan that allows employees the opportunity to be away from the company for a period of no longer than three hours, and no more than once a month, for illness in the employee's immediate family.

6. Depersonalize Issues: Separate Them from the Parties Advocating Them   Positional bargaining can create conflict over the issues and enhance tension in the relationship between negotiators. People become identified with positions on issues, and vice versa. Effective negotiation requires separating the issues from the parties, not only by working to establish a productive relationship between the parties, but also by trying to resolve the issues in a fair and impartial way independent of the relationship between the parties with conflicting views. Fisher, Ury, and Patton (1991) elaborate on this point, suggesting that effective integrative negotiation is tough on the negotiating problem but soft on the people. We expect this to be even more important when negotiations are at impasse.

Establishing Common Ground

Parties in escalated conflict tend to magnify perceived differences and to minimize perceived similarities (Pruitt and Rubin, 1986). The parties see themselves as further apart and having less in common than may actually be the case. A fifth step that parties can take to de-escalate conflict is to establish common ground and focus on common objectives. Several approaches are possible: establishing superordinate goals, aligning against common enemies, establishing common expectations, managing time constraints and deadlines, reframing the other party's view, building trust, searching for semantic solutions, and using analytical reasoning. As we discussed in Chapter 3, these approaches might also be viewed as efforts to reframe the conflict away from a focus on differences and toward a focus on common areas. In general, as the conflict de-escalates it becomes possible to move to an approach that accommodates a mix of distributive and integrative strategies, and to reduce the use of purely distributive approaches.

Superordinate Goals   Superordinate goals are common goals; both parties desire them, and both parties must cooperate to achieve them (see Box 17.8). In a corporation, for example, people perform different jobs that have different objectives (e.g., marketing, manufacturing, distribution), yet they must work together or the business will not survive. A local city council may disagree with community members about the ways to spend limited funds for community development; however, the two sides may be able to agree if they write a joint grant proposal that will provide enough money to meet the majority of their objectives. Two entrepreneurs may be in a heated conflict over how to resolve a design problem in a new product, but if they share the common objective of resolving the problem in time to present their case to a group of venture capitalists who could fund the enterprise, they may improve their chances of finding a solution.

To have a constructive impact on negotiations, superordinate goals must be wanted by both parties and must not be seen as benefiting one more than the other. Johnson and Lewicki (1969) showed that when one party introduced superordinate goals that were closely related to the issues of conflict that party often became caught up in the conflict dynamics and lost their effectiveness. Random events or events created by neutral third parties generate better superordinate goals than those sought or planned by the parties involved. For example, disasters such as floods, storms, blackouts, and fires—witness the

Disputes over the use of water are common among environmentalists, water recreation enthusiasts, and industry. Early in 1996, the Deerfield River Hydroelectric Project in Vermont was simply another battle site in this longstanding, multiparty war. More recently, however, creative negotiation has transformed the heated discussions over the Deerfield project into cooperative ventures that have benefited most of the parties involved.

Each of the stakeholders in this dispute brought different priorities to the negotiation table. The rafting and canoeing companies wanted the power company to agree to a regular schedule of water release into the Deerfield River so they could coordinate recreation activities with their clients. Fishing enthusiasts felt that the flow into the river should be continuous and steady so that regular cycles of fish breeding and migration would be undisturbed. Local environmental groups wanted the power company to set aside land for conservation to offset damage that might be caused by the water release. Finally, local towns worried that the use of land for conservation would reduce their property tax revenue. Ultimately, it was a lose–lose situation for

the power company: There was no activity they could envision that would satisfy all constituents.

The typical strategy for the power company would have been to divide and conquer, asking that the federal government or court agree to the proposed release schedule as originally presented simply because the other parties could not agree. But they noted the potential for long, costly court battles and appeals, coupled with the risk that the final settlement may not be to their liking, and opted instead to renew negotiation efforts.

Ultimately, the company agreed to spend $7 million to protect both fish and land, while agreeing to coordinate release of white water with local recreation companies. Local towns are thrilled with the increase in sales tax revenue that accompanies an increase in recreational activity. More important, the lines of communication in Vermont remain open. The stakeholders in this dispute realized that they shared a common goal: protection of the Deerfield River.

Source: N. Ulman, "Unlikely Allies: Pact for River's Use Unites Conservationists and a Power Company," *The Wall Street Journal,* May 20, 1996, pp. A6, A9.

impact of the World Trade Center and Pentagon attacks of September 11, 2001—bring people and communities together with a common purpose of survival; the same impact can be seen in negotiations.

Common Enemies   A common enemy is a negative type of superordinate goal. The parties find new motivation to resolve their differences to avoid intervention by a third party, or to pool resources to defeat a common enemy. Political leaders of all persuasions invoke outside enemies, such as the other political party, to bring their own constituencies together. Managers who are in conflict learn that if they don't resolve their differences themselves, their boss will make the decision for them. Labor and management may behave more collaboratively when threatened with binding arbitration, declining market share, foreign competition, or government intervention. Common enemies have the capacity to establish common ground between parties, who can then work to resolve impasses.

Common Expectations   We noted earlier in this chapter that parties can manage the social context by devising ground rules to govern their conflict. When ground rules are poorly chosen and mismanaged, however, they become part of the conflict rather than a process for effectively managing it. For example, ground rules are often introduced in a directive manner;

they are formal, limiting, and prohibitive, trying to prevent people from doing the wrong things rather than encouraging people to do the right things. They are also not consistently applied, deviations are handled arbitrarily, and there is no agreed-upon procedure for revising them.

A more effective process is to move from ground rules to what Dukes, Piscolish, and Stephens call "higher ground" by creating common and shared expectations. The act of doing this—a process for how the parties will move forward—is called "creating a group covenant" (Dukes, Piscolish, and Stephens, 2000). A group covenant addresses differences, clarifies expectations, and establishes ground rules to move the group forward. There are six key elements to this process:

1. Establish the need for creating shared expectations.

2. Educate and inspire people to create a new covenant that all will agree to follow.

3. Envision desired outcomes for the future, and then develop common ground rules that will enable the group to reach them.

4. Promote full participation by giving everyone a voice in the process.

5. Be accountable by honoring the agreements contained in the new covenant.

6. Evaluate, modify, revise, and recommit to these new principles as necessary (Dukes, Piscolish, and Stephens, 2000, p. 83).

Manage Time Constraints and Deadlines   While time can be a source of power and leverage in many negotiations (see Chapter 7), it can also be an impediment. Gersick (1988, 1989) suggests that time and timing are critical aspects of effective group process. Not only should parties try to agree to a time schedule for moving discussions along, but they should also realize that under the time pressure of an approaching deadline, any substantive issues that remain unresolved may surface, changing one or both parties to a more competitive, less collaborative frame of mind. In addition, while people may feel that they become more creative as deadlines approach, research evidence suggests that in fact the opposite occurs (Amabile, Haelley, and Kramer, 2002). Research shows that negotiators reach better agreements when they have more time to negotiate (de Dreu, 2003). The remedies for managing time constraints and deadlines to de-escalate impasses are straightforward:

- Conduct thorough and open problem diagnosis and issue identification to clarify the motives of both parties.

- Address and identify the clearly distributive issues early enough so they are not a surprise as the deadline approaches.

- Be generous in estimating the time necessary to conclude the negotiation, allowing extra time to manage difficult or linked issues.

- Recognize tentative deadlines for what they are, consider benchmarking progress against the time allotted, and let both sides reconsider tentative settlements before closing the discussion.

- Consider the possibility of extending a deadline set early in the negotiation. If the deadline is not movable, pay additional attention to timing, pacing, and especially benchmarking progress.

Reframe the Parties' View of Each Other   In Chapter 4, we discussed the power of frames to shape the way the parties view each other, the issues, and the conflict management process. Lewicki, Gray, and Elliott (2003) provided detailed examples of how frames shape and misshape the ways parties perceive difficult-to-resolve environmental disputes and the processes available for their resolution. In an examination of several ways that disputes can be reframed, Lewicki and colleagues suggest that parties must be able to gain perspective on the dispute. This perspective-taking requires standing back from the negotiation, observing it, and reflecting on it in a way that allows parties to recognize that there is more than one way to view the other party, the issues, and the process of resolving it (see Schön and Rein, 1994). Many of the processes we describe in this chapter presume that the parties are able to engage in this perspective-taking on their own. If they are unable, however, then these suggestions will be difficult to employ, and the help of a third party may be required (see Chapter 19).

Build Trust   Strong, constructive bargaining relationships are typically marked by conditions of high trust (characterized by hope, faith, confidence, assurance, and initiative) and low distrust (characterized by the absence of fear, skepticism, and cynicism), and are accompanied by low vigilance and low monitoring behaviors between the parties (Lewicki, McAllister, and Bies, 1998; Lewicki and Stevenson, 1998). Healthy interdependence,

"Is every contract dispute settled by a dance-off?"

characterized by strong trust and either low distrust or the effective management of any distrust that exists will support the pursuit of mutually beneficial opportunities. The collaborative ideal of high trust/low distrust refers to each party's expectation that the other will cooperate, be predictable, and be committed to solving the problem (Ross and LaCroix, 1996). Such attitudes and behaviors are critically important to moving parties to create value in negotiations and to move beyond impasses. The trust produced by successful collaboration—based on enhanced knowledge of the other party and his or her needs—reinforces itself through multiple iterations of bargaining situations (e.g., Lewicki and Stevenson, 1998; Shapiro, Sheppard, and Cheraskin, 1992). Trust was discussed more extensively in Chapter 9.

Search for Semantic Resolutions   Negotiations where the parties are negotiating over specific words and ideas—deciding on contract language, setting policy, or establishing memoranda of agreement—can lead to an impasse over key words, phrases, and expressions. Sometimes these discussions can be reduced to irrelevant linguistic hairsplitting, yet to the parties involved the wording is significant in both meaning and intent. Discovering how parties attach different meanings to some words, and exploring language that can accommodate both sides, is another approach to moving beyond impasse.

Use Analogical Reasoning   Spector (1995) suggested applying creative decision-making approaches to negotiation, especially in difficult or intractable cases.[5] Going beyond basic creativity heuristics such as brainstorming, role-playing, and role reversal, Spector proposes that the metaphorical process of analogical reasoning (the illustrative use of analogies) provides considerable power to reframe intractable conflict. *Analogical reasoning* is defined as the inferential process by which a resemblance, similarity, or correspondence, perceived between two or more things in some respect, suggests that they will probably agree in other ways as well.[6] When using analogies, the problem is restated in terms of something very familiar. By comparison and through different lenses, new ideas and options may be generated (Spector, 1995, p. 87).

This might be a particularly fruitful remedy for impasse problems since "the way a dispute is framed can constrain the options for resolution" (p. 82). Several kinds of analogies may prove useful:

- *Direct analogies,* in which the problem is placed or examined in a totally different field of information (e.g., "This conflict is like a can of worms").

- *Fantasy analogies,* in which the problem is restated in terms of a party's fantasized or wished-for state (e.g., "I wish I could sweep this thing away like a pile of dust").

- *Personal analogies,* in which a party puts herself in the problem situation, attempting to identify with it or empathize with those in the situation ("You must feel like a large picture in a small frame").

- *Symbolic analogies,* in which a different, often graphic image is conjured up to focus attention and provide a starting point for more open discussion ("This conflict reminds me of trying to land an airplane whose landing gear won't go down") (p. 88).

The desired outcome—fresh ideas and new perspectives—becomes possible when parties use the analogy to develop a new or amended cognitive orientation to the problem.

Enhancing the Desirability of Options to the Other Party

The sixth step parties can use to de-escalate a conflict is to make their desires and preferences appear more palatable to the other. As conflict escalates, the parties may lock into a rigid position on an issue. Moreover, as this position is interpreted and reinterpreted over time, negotiators try to remain consistent with the original position. If the other party does not comply with a negotiator's position, the negotiator's tendency is to escalate tactics or increase the magnitude of threats for noncompliance. These actions make impasse more likely.

Roger Fisher (1969) suggests that most influence situations can be characterized by a demand (what you want) and offers and threats (the consequences of meeting or not meeting the demand). Fisher suggests that negotiators tend to emphasize demands and threats, and this emphasis is greatly misplaced and self-destructive. Rather, negotiators should direct their efforts to the following question: how can we get the other party to make a choice that is best for us, given that our interests diverge? This approach is largely a matter of focusing on the other's interests rather than one's own. One powerful way to do this is to focus on *why* the other party wants what they want (Malhotra and Bazerman, 2007). Understanding why the other party takes positions and holds interests allows negotiators to create new options that may get an impasse back on track. Like role reversal, it requires negotiators to focus less on their own position and more on clearly understanding and addressing the other party's needs. Moreover, once those needs are understood, negotiators should move toward the other party, instead of trying to get the other party to come to them. This can be done in most cases by making offers rather than demands and threats. Fisher suggests several alternative strategies, which are discussed below.

Give the Other Party a "Yesable" Proposal   A negotiator should direct effort to understanding the other side's needs and devising a proposal that will meet those needs rather than emphasizing one's own position and letting the other party suggest alternatives that can be approved or overruled. Fisher calls this a "yesable" proposal, one to which the only answer can be "Yes, it is acceptable." To succeed, however, this approach requires negotiators to consider what the other party wants or would agree with, rather than exclusively considering their own goals and needs.

Ask for a Different Decision   Rather than making demands more general, negotiators should endeavor to make demands more specific. Negotiators must determine what specific elements of their demands are most palatable or offensive to the other party, then use this information to refine the demand. "Ask for a different decision," asserts Fisher (1969). Reformulate, repackage, reorganize, or rephrase. Fractionate, split, divide, or make more specific. Making demands more specific is not making them more rigid; rather, specific demands can be reformulated to meet the other's needs. Fisher, Ury, and Patton (1991) recommend that successful negotiators be skilled at inventing options for mutual gain (see Chapter 3). Inventing and refining ways in which both parties can succeed, and providing a variety of these options to the other party, greatly enhances the likelihood that both parties can select a desirable option.

Sweeten the Offer Rather than Intensifying the Threat   Negotiators can also make options more palatable by enhancing the attractiveness of accepting them. Again, this is a matter of placing emphasis on the positive rather than the negative. In the language of traditional carrot-and-stick tactics for motivating workers, the approach should make the carrot more attractive rather than enlarging the stick. Promises and offers can be made more attractive in several ways: maximizing the attractive qualities and minimizing the negative ones, showing how the offer meets the other party's needs, reducing the disadvantages of accepting the offer, making offers more credible (i.e., you will do what you promise to do), or setting deadlines on offers so they expire if not accepted quickly. Many would argue that these are common sales tricks akin to time-limited rebates, discount coupons, two-for-the-price-of-one offers, "today only" sales, and extra-added-attraction elements. They are! Negotiators can and should use the same techniques that salespeople use to move their products. Some of these techniques were described more fully in Chapter 8 under the topic of influence.

Use Legitimacy or Objective Criteria to Evaluate Solutions   Finally, negotiators may insist that alternative solutions be evaluated by objective criteria that meet the tests of fairness and legitimacy. Negotiators on all sides should be able to demonstrate that their demands are based on sound facts, calculations, and information and that preferred solutions are consistent with those facts and information. This procedure will frequently require disclosing and sharing those facts, rather than disguising and distorting them. "Here's how we arrived at our proposal. Here are the facts we used, the cost data we used in our estimates, the calculations we made. You can verify these by the following procedures." The more these data are open to public verification and demonstrated to be within the bounds of fairness and legitimacy, the more convincing it will be that the position is independent of the negotiator who advocates it, and the more persuasive the position will be in achieving a settlement.

Section Summary

In this section, we reviewed six major strategies that negotiators can use to get derailed negotiations back on track and return to a more productive flow of events: agreeing on the ground rules, reducing tension, improving communication, controlling issues, finding common ground, and making options more attractive for joint resolution. Taken together, these strategies create a large portfolio of alternatives that negotiators can pursue to manage derailed discussions, enhance deteriorating communications, and find ways to invent acceptable solutions. These techniques are ways that parties can work together to overcome intractability and improve the odds that successful resolution can occur.

Chapter Summary

Through several different avenues—breakdowns in communication, escalation of anger and mistrust, polarization of positions and refusal to compromise, issuing ultimatums, or even avoiding conflict—negotiations can hit an impasse. Productive dialogue stops. The parties may continue talking, but the communication is usually characterized by trying to sell or force one's own position, talking about the other's unreasonable position and uncooperative behavior, or both. When these breakdowns occur, the parties may simply agree to recess, cool off, and come back tomorrow. More commonly, however, the parties break off negotiation and walk away angry and upset. Although they may privately wish there was some way to get back together, they usually don't know how to start the reconciliation.

This chapter explored various reasons that conflicts become difficult to resolve and likely to reach impasse. We discussed the fundamental nature of difficult-to-resolve conflicts and discussed four dimensions that make them difficult to resolve: the characteristics of the issues, the parties, the negotiation environment, and the negotiation setting. We then examined several common mistakes that negotiators make that result in derailed negotiations and impasses. Finally, we suggested six strategies that the parties could use to attempt to resolve a dispute on their own:

- Reach agreement on the ground rules of the negotiation.

- Reduce tension by separating themselves from one another through cooling-off periods, releasing tension, talking about emotions and feelings, or attempting to synchronize de-escalation of the conflict.

- Improve the accuracy of communication by role reversal or mirroring the other's statements.

- Keep the number of issues under control so that issues are managed effectively, new issues are not carelessly added, and large issues are divided into smaller ones.

- Search for common ground through exploring superordinate goals, identifying common enemies, using effective time management, developing common expectations through a covenant, building trust, searching for semantic solutions, and using analogical reasoning.

- Enhance the desirability of the options and alternatives for both parties by providing "yesable" proposals, asking for different decisions, sweetening offers, and using objective criteria to evaluate solutions.

The tools we discussed are broad in function and in application, and they represent self-help for negotiators in dealing with stalled or problematic exchanges. None of these methods and remedies is a panacea, and each should be chosen and applied with sensitivity to the needs and limitations of the situations and of the negotiators involved. Their successful application requires a significant amount of interpersonal communication skill. A truly confrontational breakdown, especially one that involves agreements of great impact or importance, sometimes justifies the introduction of individuals or agencies who themselves are not party to the dispute. Third-party interventions are discussed in detail in Chapter 19.

Endnotes

[1] Characteristics of the conflict resolution process are discussed in more detail in Adler, Rosen, and Silverstein (1998); Blake and Mouton (1961a, 1961b, 1961c); Corwin (1969); Harvey (1953); and Keltner and Robinson (1993).

[2] Environmental negotiations are discussed in detail in Sauer, Dvorak, Lisa, and Fiala (2003) and Wade-Benzoni, Hoffman, et al. (2002).

[3] See Gray (2003a); Hogg, Terry, and White (1995); and Smyth (1994).

[4] For more detailed discussion, see Deutsch (1973); Deutsch and Coleman (2000); Pruitt and Rubin (1986); Susskind, McKearnan, and Thomas-Larmer (1999); and Walton (1987).

[5] For a discussion of creative thinking see De Bono (1990), Sternberg (1988), Von Oech (1992), and Whiting (1958).

[6] Analogical reasoning and other aspects of negotiation have been examined by Loewenstein, Thompson, and Gentner (1999); and Loewenstein, Thompson, and Gentner (2002).

CHAPTER 18

Managing Difficult Negotiations

Objectives

1. Understand how to manage the social contract.
2. Consider how to respond when the other party responds distributively, has more power, or presents you with an ultimatum.
3. Learn different approaches a negotiator can use when dealing with difficult people.

Michele is having a terrible dispute with her neighbor in the condo next door. The neighbor, who recently moved into the apartment, brought a large German shepherd dog with him that barks *all* the time. Michele is a writer who needs to work at home, but the dog is so distracting that she cannot get anything done. Michele has talked to the neighbor, who has apologized for the problem but has done nothing to keep the dog quiet. Since then, the neighbor won't speak to her or respond to her messages. He won't even answer the door when she knocks, even though she knows he is home. Michele is considering filing a nuisance complaint with the police and taking the neighbor to court.

Jose and his co-worker Max are at it again. They both work as Web site administrators for a major marketing firm. Max just can't seem to get to work on time in the morning, and Jose always has to cover for him on the Web site problems that cropped up overnight. Max always stays later than Jose, but there is much less work in the late afternoon than first thing in the morning. Jose and Max have talked about it; Max promises to get to work earlier, and for a few days he is fine, but then he slips back into his old pattern. Jose doesn't want to report him to the boss, but he doesn't see any other alternative.

Simon, a manufacturer's representative for a machine tool company, finds that a client's recent expansion has resulted in Simon having to follow the client into another sales representative's territory. Simon is sure that the problem can be worked out to everyone's satisfaction and advantage, but so far the other sales rep seems to not want to give up a piece of his "turf"—in fact, he seems to act like it's some sort of contest and wants to play games.

In this chapter, we turn to situations where parties are using *different* models to guide their negotiation because they have diagnosed the situation differently, possess different levels of negotiation sophistication, or prefer different approaches to negotiating. We believe that many negotiators are not very familiar with collaborative negotiation and use it less frequently than they should. One goal of negotiators should be to ensure the broader application of integrative negotiating under appropriate circumstances in order to produce better agreements. We direct our discussion and advice to negotiators who wish to negotiate collaboratively but find they must deal with others who are reluctant to do so—who wish, intend, or are actively trying to be distributive. We call them "difficult" people.

Negotiators always run the risk of encountering other parties who, for any number of reasons, are difficult negotiators. That difficulty may be *intentional,* the result of a clear strategic, behavioral, or philosophical choice by the other party. It may also be due to *inadequate skill,* including faulty diagnosis of negotiation opportunities—the other party just doesn't see any value or potential for a collaborative approach or doesn't know how to craft and pursue such an approach. In this section, we address methods negotiators can use when dealing with an intentionally difficult party. We then proceed to explain the skills and behaviors needed to defend against such parties and/or to convert them to use a more productive negotiation process. In simple terms, the collaborative party is trying to change the social contract or proactively manage the shadow negotiation introduced in Chapter 17 (see Fortgang, Lax, and Sebenius, 2003; Kolb and Williams, 2001). In essence, the goal is to convince the other party to move from distributive to integrative negotiations. There are several challenges to negotiators who want to convert a distributive bargainer towards a more collaborative approach. We begin by discussing how to manage the social contract and shadow negotiation. Next, we turn to a discussion of how to respond to the other party's hard distributive tactics, which is followed by a discussion of the options available to negotiators who are faced with another party who is more powerful. We then discuss possible tactics to use with generally difficult negotiators, examine how to respond to ultimatums, and conclude the chapter with a discussion of how to manage difficult conversations.

Managing the Shadow Negotiation and Social Contract

Managing the shadow negotiation and social contract is fundamentally concerned with determining *what* ground the negotiation is going to cover and *how* the negotiators are going to work together (Fortgang, Lax, and Sebenius, 2003; Kolb and Williams, 2001). The *shadow negotiation* occurs in parallel with the substantive negotiation and is concerned with how the negotiation will proceed. Who will have influence and power? What is acceptable behavior? Who is included or excluded from the discussion? Frequently these matters are not decided in the open but occur "in the shadows." The result of this ongoing shadow negotiation is a *social contract* regarding how the negotiation will proceed, who has influence and power, and what the boundaries of the negotiation are.

The social contract and shadow negotiation are concerned with what the negotiation is about and how decisions are made. Negotiators need to be clear in their own minds where the boundaries of the current negotiation are and should be. If the discussion is too narrow or too broad, then this needs to be explicitly addressed and corrected. When the other party has a different implicit or explicit understanding of the negotiation, then negotiators need to discuss this and work to create alignment in the social contract. This alignment can occur by convincing the other party to agree with your view of the situation, changing your expectation to match theirs, or reaching an agreement about the parameters of the social contract. In other words, the social contract should be discussed and negotiated, not assumed.

It is important that negotiators consider the shadow negotiation carefully before meeting with the other party so that they are clear in their own minds about the scope of the negotiation and understand how they would ideally like to work with the other party. For instance, do they want to be more or less collaborative? How important is time pressure? Is this a one-time deal, or is this discussion part of a longer relationship? It is also important that negotiators monitor the shadow negotiation once the substantive negotiation has started—because if the shadow negotiation is ignored, it has the potential to lead to poorer outcomes or even to derail the talks.

Deborah Kolb and Judith Williams (2001) interviewed hundreds of executives about their negotiation experiences, especially with respect to the shadow negotiation. Kolb and Williams suggest that negotiators ignore shadow negotiations at their peril because the unaddressed shadow negotiation can lead to negotiations that are "blocked or stalled—undermined by hidden assumptions, unrealistic expectations, or personal histories" (p. 90). They identify three strategic levers available to help people navigate the shadow negotiation: power moves, process moves, and appreciative moves (see Box 18.1).

Power Moves

Power moves are designed to bring reluctant bargainers back to the table. There are three kinds of power moves: incentives, pressure tactics, and the use of allies. *Incentives* draw the attention of the other party to the importance of the negotiation and help them recognize that they will benefit from negotiation. *Pressure tactics* force the other party to realize that the status quo is unacceptable, and they make the costs of not negotiating very explicit. Finally, enlisting the support of *allies* can provide assistance to help the other party see the advantage of negotiating.

Process Moves

Process moves are designed to alter the negotiation process itself through adjustments to the agenda, sequencing, decision rules, and the like. For example, a competitive mind-set may favor those who speak loudest or longest, or who like bluffing and gamesmanship. A negotiator who is uncomfortable with this dynamic can try to reframe the process, for example, by redefining something that was a competition over resources into a collaborative group allocation decision based on need.

Appreciative Moves

Appreciative moves are designed to break cycles of contentiousness that may have led to deteriorating communication, acrimony, or even silence. Examples of appreciative moves are tactics that help the other party save face in an argument, maintain dialogue and information exchange in the face of pressures to disengage, or invite new perspectives into the discussion to try to break a logjam or reverse a skid toward stalemate.

BOX 18.1 The Shadow Campaign

A single strategic move seldom carries the day. In combination, however, such moves can jump-start workplace negotiations and keep them moving toward resolution.

Consider the case of Fiona Sweeney, the new operations chief. She had neither the authority nor the personal inclination to order the sales and production divisions of her company to cooperate. Instead, she fashioned a series of strategic moves designed to influence the negotiations.

Power Moves

Having established her credibility with sales by increasing the turnaround time on expense-account reimbursements, Sweeney knew she needed to up the ante for maintaining the status quo, which created hardships for production and was frustrating customers. It was particularly important to bring pressure to bear on the sales division, because the informal reward systems, and many of the formal ones, currently worked to its benefit. To disturb the equilibrium, Sweeney began to talk in management meetings about a bonus system that would penalize the sales division whenever it promised more than production could deliver. Rather than immediately acting on this threat, however, she suggested creating a cross-divisional task force to explore the issues. Not surprisingly, sales was eager to be included. Moreover, the CEO let key people know that he backed Sweeney's proposal to base bonuses on profits, not revenues.

Process Moves

Sweeney then moved to exert control over the agenda and build support for the changes she and the CEO envisioned. She started an operations subgroup with the heads of quality control and production, mobilizing allies in the two areas most directly affected by the sales division's behavior. Soon they developed a common agenda and began working in concert to stem the influence of sales in senior staff meetings. On one occasion, for example, Sweeney proposed assigning a low priority to orders that had not been cleared by the operations subgroup. Quality control and production roundly supported the suggestion, which was soon implemented. Through these process moves, Sweeney built a coalition that shaped the subsequent negotiations. But she did something more.

Power and process moves often provoke resistance from the other side. Sweeney prevented resistance from becoming entrenched within the sales division through a series of appreciative moves.

Appreciative Moves

To deepen her understanding of the issues sales confronted, Sweeney volunteered her operations expertise to the division's planning team. By helping sales develop a new pricing-and-profit model, she not only increased understanding and trust on both sides of the table, but she also paved the way for dialogue on other issues—specifically the need for change in the company's decision-making processes.

Most important, Sweeney never forced any of the players into positions where they would lose face. By using a combination of strategic moves, she helped the sales division realize that change was coming and that it would be better off helping to shape the change than blocking it. In the end, improved communication and cooperation among divisions resulted in increases in both the company's top-line revenues and its profit margins. With better product quality and delivery times, sales actually made more money, and production no longer had the burden of delivering on unrealistic promises generated by sales. Customers—and the CEO—were all happy.

Source: D. M. Kolb and J. Williams, "Breakthrough Bargaining," *Harvard Business Review* (2001), pp. 89–97.

Section Summary

The concepts of the shadow negotiation and social contract are compelling ways to think about the often hidden yet crucial power plays that occur in negotiation alongside haggling over positions and arriving at agreements. Negotiators who want to change to a more collaborative process should actively manage the shadow negotiation and social contract process.

Responding to the Other Side's Hard Distributive Tactics

By *hard tactics,* we mean the distributive tactics that the other party uses in a negotiation to put pressure on negotiators to do something that is not in their best interest. The temptation to use hard tactics is inherent in the distributive model: try to get information, but don't share it; work to convince the other party of the value of staying in the deal, or enhance the perception of the cost of leaving it rather than working to create value; and so on. Distributive tactics were discussed in Chapter 2, where we also discussed strategies for responding to these tactics. To summarize briefly, as a party managing a negotiation mismatch, you can respond to these tactics in the following ways: call them on it, ignore them, respond in kind, or offer to change to more productive methods.

Call Them on It

Negotiators should tell the other party that they are aware of what he or she is doing when they use hard tactics by identifying the tactic and raising it to the level of open discussion. This should be done tactfully but firmly. Negotiators may indicate their displeasure with the tactic and explain why it is interfering with a positive discussion and preventing the negotiation from progressing. Sometimes, the embarrassment value of such an observation is sufficient to make negotiators disavow the tactic and stop using it. Discussing the tactic is a good first step to converting negotiators to more win–win negotiating.

Ignore Them

A tactic that is ignored is essentially a tactic defeated; even if it is recognized later, it does not have the power to bring undue pressure to bear. Unfortunately, some bargainers continue to bargain distributively and ignoring their tactics may not be enough to give them the message that a more collaborative approach to the negotiation is possible. Yama (2004) presents several responses from a hard bargaining sales context that ignore buyers' aggressive bargaining tactics while refocusing the negotiation on the sellers' value proposition (see Box 18.2).

Respond in Kind

The possibility of responding to a hard tactic with a hard tactic was discussed in Chapter 2. While this is appropriate in some circumstances, responding in kind is likely to escalate the conflict. Hence, responding in kind is not consistent with the goal of trying to convert the other party to use a more collaborative approach and should not be considered in this situation.

Offer to Change to More Productive Methods

Negotiators may announce that they have identified the other party's behavior and suggest a better way to negotiate. Fisher, Ury, and Patton (1991), in advising well-intentioned bargainers

Aggressive Bargaining Technique	Value-Based Response
Early request for price quote	Probe buyer's needs. Quote list pricing or a w-i-d-e range.
Focus on seller's cost and profit margins	Communicate ways you lower costs for the buyer through unique elements of your offer.
Constrained by buyer's budget	Identify items that can either be trimmed from the proposal or shared with other budget centers.
Provide a discount to win future business	Explain your perspective that future business is based on value delivery today.
Price discounts based on past service failure	Seek to understand the issue and its impact, then fix it without providing a price discount.
Requests for additional items at no charge	Explain the offering menu and that items purchased outside the scope of the agreement are priced "à la carte."

Source: E. Yama, "Buying hardball, playing price." *Business Horizons, 47,* (5), (2004), pp. 62–66.

not to let themselves be victimized, suggest a comprehensive strategy: "Recognize the tactic, raise the issue explicitly, and question the tactic's legitimacy and desirability—negotiate over it" (p. 130). The logic of this advice lies in the assumption that once the aggressive negotiator understands that (1) their behavior is understood and (2) continuing this behavior will entail certain costs (including the possibility that you will walk away from the negotiation), he or she will (hopefully) respond to a suggestion for a more integrative exchange.

Section Summary

In summary, we recommend that negotiators who are trying to convert the other party from using hard distributive tactics to a more collaborative approach should respond by calling the other on the tactics and offer to change to more productive methods if the distributive bargaining persists. Ignoring the tactics may work for a while, but responding in kind is not likely to be helpful in this situation.

Responding When the Other Side Has More Power

Relative power can be a good predictor of how a conflict will evolve. Other things being equal, when power is unequal, the more powerful party can achieve his or her goals more readily. Power imbalances in negotiation can represent clear dangers to the satisfaction of the needs of both parties and to the collaborative process. First, high-power parties tend to pay little heed to the needs of low-power parties, who either don't get their needs met or use disruptive, attention-getting tactics that make collaboration very difficult (Donohue and Kolt, 1992). Second, low-power parties are not usually in a position to trigger and advance an integrative process. Integrative negotiation requires a tolerance of change and flexibility, which often requires negotiators to give up some control over outcomes; low-power parties "have less to give, and thus less flexibility to offer the other party" (Donohue and Kolt, 1992, p. 107). Negotiators should consider four tactics when dealing with a party with more power:

1. Protect themselves.
2. Cultivate their best alternative to a negotiated agreement (BATNA).
3. Formulate a trip wire alert system.
4. Correct the power imbalance.

Negotiators can *protect themselves* by keeping in mind that they have real interests, that negotiation may be the preferred approach of achieving those interests, and that excessive accommodation to the high-power party will not serve them well over the long term. In other words, low-power parties should remember their resistance point and try to stick to it. That said, while knowing the resistance point will provide a clear measure of minimum acceptability (lowest price, maximum monthly payment, etc.), too strict adherence to it may deprive negotiators of creativity and flexibility, which are critical components to the design of an integrative outcome. It may also limit their ability to use information that emerges during the exchange (Fisher, Ury, and Patton, 1991). Thus, lower power parties need to protect their bottom line but also be open to creative approaches that may allow them to achieve their interests in other ways.

When in the low-power position, it is very important that negotiators *cultivate their BATNA,* which represents the best outcome that they can accomplish without the current negotiation. Many negotiators bargain without a clear definition of their BATNA; we pointed out in Chapters 2 and 3 that the lack of such a critical reference point gives negotiators less power and limits what they can achieve in the current negotiation (Fisher, Ury, and Patton, 1991). Even after negotiations have started, negotiators should continue to try to improve their BATNA, especially when dealing with another party that has more power. For example, a job seeker who is discussing a weak offer with a particular employer should continue to cultivate alternatives by pursuing other employment opportunities.

Keep in mind that cultivating a BATNA also has important perceptual elements: does the other party perceive that your BATNA is worthwhile and you are likely to accept it if sufficiently favorable negotiation terms are not available? A low-power negotiator is strengthened to the extent that his or her alternatives improve, but it may not be enough simply to have an improved alternative. The other party must be aware that the alternative exists and must recognize its strength in relation to the preferred outcome. Negotiators can also help the other party see that his or her BATNA is not really as good as he or she thinks it is. Negotiators should work to identify what unique aspects they bring to the negotiation situation that gives them a competitive advantage over other providers. For example, perhaps you understand the needs and processes of the other party better than your competitors, so the other party's BATNA may not be as good as they are claiming.

A clear, strong BATNA may also be reinforced by additional measures. Low-power negotiators are advised to *formulate a trip wire alert system* that serves as an early warning signal when bargaining enters the "warning" zone close to the walkaway option or the BATNA (Fisher, Ury, and Patton, 1991). The trip wire tells the negotiator to exercise special caution and pay increased attention to the negotiation in progress. Given that negotiations often become intense and engrossing at such points, it might be appropriate to assign a co-negotiator to watch for the warning zone and to notify the involved negotiator at the critical time.

The next option involves dealing with an existing power imbalance. The fourth option for dealing with more powerful parties is to *correct the imbalance.* Three approaches to this are possible: low-power parties taking power, high-power parties giving power, and third parties managing the transfer and balance of power. The first approach, power-taking, is typically not feasible in negotiations. Using disruptive or attention-getting actions to try to assume power typically contributes to a distributive exchange, generating in-kind responses from the high-power party. As we pointed out in Chapter 7, however, power in negotiation is multifaceted, and power may be gained on dimensions different from those currently held by the high-power party.

The second approach is for the high-power party to transfer power to the other party. Such actions include sharing resources, sharing control over certain processes or outcomes (e.g., the shadow negotiation, agendas, or decisions), focusing on common interests rather than solely on the high-powered party's interests, or educating the low-power party about what power he or she does have and how to use it more effectively (Donohue and Kolt, 1992). One may question why high-power parties would ever choose to transfer power to the other party. The answer is complex, but there are good reasons. First, sharing power facilitates the integrative negotiation process and leads to a better agreement. Second, when one party does have power over the other, frequently the best outcome the high-power party can achieve is compliance rather than enthusiastic cooperation. Finally, no power imbalance exists forever, and when low-power parties gain a power base or a BATNA, they are likely to either sever the relationship or to engage in some form of revenge. Sharing power is a proactive way to prevent these outcomes.

Finally, the third approach—using a third party to manage power transfer—is feasible and is commonly used. We discuss the use of mediators and other third parties in detail in Chapter 19.

The Special Problem of Handling Ultimatums

One particularly troublesome hard tactic distributive negotiators use is ultimatums. An *ultimatum* is an attempt "to induce compliance or force concessions from a presumably recalcitrant opponent" (Kramer, Shah, and Woerner, 1995, p. 285). Ultimatums typically have three components: (1) a demand; (2) an attempt to create a sense of urgency, such that compliance is required; and (3) a threat of punishment if compliance does not occur (George, 1993). For example, one particular type of ultimatum is the *exploding offer,* in which one party presents the other with a classic no-win, use-it-or-lose-it dilemma. An exploding offer has a specific time limit or deadline attached to it, forcing the other party to decide on a less-than-ideal offer or run the risk of going without anything (Robinson, 1995). Such offers have several other components, including:

• A clear asymmetry of power between the parties.

• A pressure-inducing test of faith for the receiver.

• A restricted set of options.

- A lack of consideration and respect for the offerer by the respondent.

- An apparent lack of good faith on the offerer's part. (Robinson, 1995, pp. 278–79)

The strategic logic of this type of ultimatum often involves an attempt to force a negotiator into a premature agreement, thereby bringing an early end to a negotiation process that might eventually produce a more equitable outcome for the receiver. It might also have the effect of limiting the negotiator's ability to comparison-shop among multiple competing offers or possible BATNAs. Exploding offers have become popular among some organizations recruiting graduating university students. These organizations may offer competitive, or even slightly better, financial packages to graduates but only allow 24 or 48 hours for students to decide or the offer is withdrawn. Typically, these organizations are very early in the recruiting process and their motive is to lock-in their preferred candidates and prevent them from considering other offers. While many university career centers actively discourage exploding offers, the practice persists.

While an initial analysis of ultimatums might suggest that such a take-it-or-leave-it tactic might be successful, given that something (anything) must be preferable to nothing (a failed negotiation), empirical studies have not found this to be so (Guth, Schmittberger, and Schwarze, 1982; Guth and Tietz, 1990). Conflicts involving ultimatums often fall prey to escalation problems, as noted elsewhere in this chapter, through severe action–reaction spirals. Reactions to the making of ultimatums seem to go beyond the violation of simple fairness concerns, in that they

> are motivated by asymmetric moral imperatives. Most offerers define the situation as the opportunity for . . . gain; they tend to be blatantly strategic. Many respondents, on the other hand, owing to their relatively powerless situation, define the situation morally. . . . This asymmetry can lead to disagreement and unhappiness for both parties—for the offerer, following a rejection, or for the respondent, in accepting an offer that he or she feels is unfair (Murnighan and Pillutla, 1995, p. 265).

The pervasive unhappiness resulting from the use of such ultimatums can taint future dealings between the parties, sometimes permanently.

Robinson (1995) has developed one possible response to ultimatums, which he calls the "farpoint gambit" (after the name of a maneuver on a *Star Trek* episode). The success of the response hangs on the ability to say "Yes, but . . ." to an ultimatum. Robinson cautions—and we agree—that this approach is a last resort; other remedies should be exhausted first. When first presented with an ultimatum, negotiators should probably try a reasonable approach: be forthright in addressing the ultimatum; make sensible, reasonable counteroffers; or attempt to engage the offerer in joint problem solving. If that fails, Robinson suggests "an exploding offer can be defused by *embracing* it" (p. 282)—that is, agree to the ultimatum provisionally, subject to some qualifying event or condition. Robinson advises that the farpoint gambit only be used when all three of the following conditions exist:

1. When the initiator is perceived as behaving unethically and ignores appeals to reason.

2. When the respondent is truly interested in the basic offer but needs more time to consider it.

3. When there are issues central to the deal that genuinely need clarification.

Responding When the Other Side Is Being Difficult

When the other side presents a pattern of clear difficult behavior, two possibilities exist. On the one hand, it is possible that the negotiator does not know any other way to negotiate, but might be responsive to suggestions for changing his or her behavior. On the other hand, it may be that the other party has a difficult personality and acts consistently inside and outside the negotiation context. In most cases it is likely that not enough is known about the other party to make the distinction. In this section, we review several approaches for dealing with difficult negotiators. The first, proposed by Ury (1991), suggests a broad-based approach that may be used with any other party who is being difficult, including one using hard distributive tactics. The second, based on the work of Bramson (1981), suggests several different strategies for dealing with negotiators who have particularly difficult styles. Finally, the third approach is by Weeks (2001), who outlines the importance of preparation and management when confronted with the need to have a difficult conversation with another person.

Ury's Breakthrough Approach

William Ury (1991) conceptualizes obstacles set by the other party as challenges that can be addressed through specific strategies described in a five-stage "breakthrough approach." Ury suggests creating a favorable negotiation environment by regaining mental balance and controlling one's own behavior; helping the other party achieve similar balance and control; changing the approach from a distributive to an integrative one; overcoming the other party's skepticism by jointly crafting a mutually satisfactory agreement; and achieving closure through firm, even-handed use of negotiating power. Ury argues that his approach operates on the principle of acting counterintuitively. This requires negotiators to behave directly opposite to what they might naturally do in difficult situations. When the other

"How did the negotiations go?
Take a wild guess."

Source: © CartoonResource.com

party stonewalls or attacks, people often feel like responding in kind. When others insist on their position, negotiators often want to reject it and assert their own. When others exert pressure, negotiators are inclined to retaliate with direct counterpressure. In trying to break down the other party's resistance, however, these counterpressure responses actually increase it. In contrast,

> The essence of the breakthrough strategy is indirect action. You try to go around his resistance. Rather than pounding in a new idea from the outside, you encourage him to reach from within. Rather than telling him what to do, you let him figure it out. Rather than trying to break down his resistance, you make it easier for him to break through it himself. In short, breakthrough negotiation is the art of letting the other person have it your way. (Ury, 1991, p. 9)

Ury proposes a five-step process for this counterintuitive pattern of responding (the titles of the steps are adapted from Ury's strategies for managing difficult negotiations; see Table 18.1).

Step 1: Don't React—Go to the Balcony   A natural reaction to aggressive tactics is to strike back, give in, or break off negotiations. These behaviors do not serve the negotiator's tangible interests, let alone move the process in an integrative direction. The challenge to this obstacle is to not react, thereby avoiding the destructive effect that reacting naturally has on the process. Instead, Ury recommends that negotiators should "go to the balcony"— that is, psychologically remove themselves from the interaction so that they become an observer to their own interaction with the other party. The advantages of going to the balcony are it:

- Provides some distance from the conflict and from one's own emotions.

- Creates breathing space, allowing negotiators to cool off so their response can be more reasoned.

- Creates an opportunity for negotiators to understand the situation in the broader context and to remind themselves why they are there in the first place.

TABLE 18.1 | Ury's Strategies for Managing Difficult Negotiations

Steps	Barriers to Cooperation	Challenges	Strategies
Step 1	Your natural reaction to the other side's competitive behavior	Don't react	Go to the balcony
Step 2	Other's negative emotions	Disarm them	Step to the side
Step 3	Other's positional behavior	Change the game	Don't reject, reframe
Step 4	Other's skepticism about benefits of agreement	Make it easy for them to say yes	Build them a golden bridge
Step 5	Other's perceived power	Make it hard to say no	Bring them to their senses, not their knees

Source: Adapted from "Strategy Table," from *Getting Past No* by William Ury. Copyright © 1991 by William Ury. Used by permission of Bantam Books, a division of Random House, Inc.

Step 2: Disarm Them—Step to Their Side   Negative and attacking behavior in negotiation tends to breed more of the same from the other party. Tensions heighten and damaging exchanges tend to escalate. Confrontation and impending impasse typically elicit negative emotions for both sides. The negotiator's challenge is to act counterintuitively—to deflect or sidestep the other party's negative behavior, disarming him or her through positive, constructive communication. The strategy of stepping to the other side conveys the compelling image of "coming around" the table to listen to and acknowledge the other party's legitimate points, needs, and concerns. This strategy of disarmament includes:

- Active listening.
- Acknowledging the other party's points, without necessarily conceding their truth or accuracy.
- Recognizing points of understanding and overlap that might provide the foundation for subsequent agreement.
- Acknowledging the other party personally as a mark of recognition and respect for his or her authority, sensitivity, and competency.
- Expressing one's own views clearly and considerately.

Step 3: Change the Game—Don't Reject, Reframe   Framing the problem is an important step in preparing for any negotiation (see Chapter 4). Given the obstacle of the other party's positional behavior, the challenge at this stage is to change the negotiation by proactively reframing his or her tactics. A reframing strategy includes the following active behaviors:

- Asking open-ended, problem-solving questions.
- Reframing the other party's tactics. For example, if presented with a stone wall, ignore it, test it, or reinterpret it as just wishful thinking. If attacked, ignore it, deflect it from you to the problem, or recast it in less confrontational terms that highlight common goals and interests.
- Negotiating directly and openly the rules of the negotiation process.

Step 4: Make It Easy to Say Yes—Build Them a Golden Bridge   This is the persuasive stage of the process, wherein the challenge and opportunity for negotiators is to make it easy for the other party to say yes to an offer (see, Fisher, 1969). According to Ury (1991, p. 89), the four most common objections from the other party to your proposals are:

- They're not my idea.
- They don't address one of my basic interests.
- They might cause me to lose face or look bad to some important constituency.
- They require too big of an adjustment for me (i.e., "you want too much, too fast").

The proposed strategy is to close the gap between negotiators by building a golden bridge to entice the other party to cross over to agreement by:

- Involving him or her in the actual design of an agreement that addresses the interests and challenges of all parties.

- Satisfying his or her unmet needs as much as possible without jeopardizing meeting your needs or the basic fabric of the agreement.

- Recognizing and being empathetic to the range of personal and organizational demands and expectations that he or she faces.

- Helping him or her to save face and deal with constituencies by providing justifications for the agreement—for example, that conditions have changed, a third party recommends this, or an objective standard of fairness supports this outcome.

- "Going slow to go fast" (Ury, 1991, p. 105), walking him or her through complex agreements step by step and not demanding closure until everyone is ready.

Step 5: Make It Hard to Say No—Bring Them to Their Senses, Not Their Knees
Throughout the first four stages, the other party may believe in his or her superior power or wits. Having made it easy for the other party to say yes, negotiators must now address the challenge of making it hard for them to say no. Confronting power plays with power plays will most likely return the negotiation to the competitive dynamics the parties have worked to change. A better strategy is to bring the other negotiators to their senses without bringing them to their knees. The components of this strategy are to:

- Pay attention to one's own BATNA, strengthening it and making sure the other party knows what it is.

- Help the other party think about the consequences of not reaching an agreement.

- If necessary, actually use one's own BATNA, being careful to anticipate and defuse the other's reaction to what may be perceived as a punitive move.

- Keep sharpening the other's choice—refer back to the attractive terms that got the other party to cross the bridge and help them maintain their focus on the advantages of completing the deal.

- Fashion a lasting agreement, thinking through and planning for implementation.

Ury's breakthrough approach is an active strategy that negotiators can use to deal with another party that is being difficult. Care must be taken when using this approach because in an emotionally charged negotiation, these tactics have the potential to make matters worse if they are not applied subtly and with care. That said, Ury's approach does provide a powerful way to manage difficult people in a nonconfrontational manner.

Responding to Difficult People

Sometimes problems in negotiation can be traced to difficulties in the other party's behavioral style. The subject of how to deal with difficult people in the workplace has received increasing attention in recent years from several authors (e.g., Bernstein and Rosen, 1989; Bramson, 1981, 1992; Solomon, 1990). These authors make several important points. First, everyone can exhibit difficult behaviors or be difficult to deal with at times; some people, however, are *invariably* difficult, and their behavior follows predictable and identifiable patterns. Second, what is difficult behavior to one person may not be difficult for another. Labeling an action "difficult" may say as much about the receiver

BOX 18.3

Why, You No Good, Uncooperative, Double-Dealing, . . . Etc.

Emotions are frequently an aspect of difficult, high-stakes negotiation. When emotions run wild, however, they can be detrimental to the process, distorting perceptions and diverting attention from the real issues. Adler, Rosen, and Silverstein (1998) looked at the problem and effects of fear and anger in negotiations, and they suggest some tactics for managing such emotions. Regarding your *own* emotions, negotiators can:

- Determine which situations tend to trigger inappropriate anger.

- When angry, decide whether or not to display your anger.

- Use behavioral techniques to reduce your anger (e.g., taking a break, counting to 10).

- Express your anger and disappointment effectively (e.g., openly and in a nonaccusatory fashion).

- Avoid the negotiator's bias ("I'm fair and reasonable, you're not . . .").

- Try to promote trust.

Regarding the *other party's* emotions, negotiators can:

- Defuse emotional buildups by direct confrontation ("You seem angry; are you?").

- Assess the real significance of emotional displays (Is it an act? A distributive dirty trick?).

- Address the other's anger directly, perhaps apologizing for a comment or pointing out the effects of a bad situation.

- Respond to the other's anger strategically (call a break, use silence to "wait him out," make a modest concession, etc.).

- Help the other party save face, especially when losing face contributed to his or her anger.

- Consider engaging a mediator when you anticipate anger rising.

Source: R. S. Adler, B. Rosen, and E. M. Silverstein, "Emotions in Negotiation: How to Manage Fear and Anger," *Negotiation Journal* 14, no. 2 (1998), pp. 161–79.

as it does about the sender. Person A may have a great deal of difficulty contending with a very aggressive negotiator, whereas Person B has little difficulty with that person. Third, difficult people behave the way they do because it achieves results for them. Their behavior gives them control, feels comfortable, and lets them get their way. By giving in to it, negotiators reinforce the behavior, providing the difficult person ample reasons to continue behaving in ways that have worked in the past. Difficult people also may continue their behavior because they honestly are not aware of the long-term costs to people and organizations that must contend with them.

It is possible to cope with invariably difficult people—contending with their behavior on equal behavioral terms—as opposed to giving in to them; accepting their behavior; or getting them to change their values, beliefs, or attitudes. In short, negotiators must effectively counterbalance the potential power these behaviors give to those who use them. Box 18.3 offers a general framework for coping with a difficult other party. Relating to difficult people in negotiation or other highly charged, results-oriented exchanges is a critically important skill. We encourage anyone wishing to go beyond the basics presented here to refer to Bramson (1981), Solomon (1990), and Ury (1991) to build their skills and insights in this area.

Having Conversations with Difficult People

There are many topics that people find difficult to discuss with others, including both negative situations like discussing poor performance with an employee that may lead to a dismissal and positive situations such as providing praise for a job well done (Weeks, 2001). While people differ in the type of situations that they find stressful, whatever the topic it is much harder to discuss when the other party is a difficult person. Weeks suggests that there are two fundamental stages to dealing with a stressful conversation: preparation and managing the conversation.

Preparation   The best place to begin preparing for difficult conversations is to really understand your comfort level in dealing with them (Weeks, 2001; also see Gray, 2003b; Stone, Patton and Heen, 1999). Some people are more comfortable discussing negative situations like a poor performance appraisal than others. Other people are more comfortable with delivering praise than others. The key here is to understand your own comfort level and to know how you react to different difficult conversations. For instance, if someone gets aggressive, raises his or her voice, and threatens you during a negotiation is your natural response to withdraw, push back, or to analyze the situation? It is important to understand your natural response to difficult situations so that it is not vulnerable to being taken advantage of by the other party (Weeks, 2001). Stone, Patton, and Heen (1999) have created a useful checklist for a five-step process of having difficult conversations that starts with solid preparation before starting the conversation (see Box 18.4).

There are at least three things you can do once you are aware of your likely response to an upcoming difficult conversation. First, you can *visualize* how the conversation will unfold—meaning think about the order of the conversation, how the other person may respond, and how you will respond back. You should consider multiple pathways because it may not be possible to predict with complete accuracy what direction the conversation will take. Second, you can *practice* the upcoming difficult conversation with a neutral party (Weeks, 2001). This person should not have the same reactions to others as you do in order to provide a different perspective on the upcoming difficult conversation. The practice can involve role-playing "what if he or she says this" and should include an honest appraisal by the neutral friend of how the other party may interpret your responses. Finally, the third thing that can be done during preparation is to construct a team that has a wide variety of strengths and weaknesses when dealing with difficult others. This is likely limited in practice to more complex negotiations, but often people can take someone with them to a difficult conversation to provide emotional support and to help with the postdiscussion interpretation.

Managing Difficult Conversations   Weeks suggests that there are three important elements to the successful management of difficult conversations: *clarity, tone,* and *temperate phrasing.* Each is discussed in detail here.

Clarity   Clarity means to use language that is as precise as possible when managing a difficult conversation. There is a natural tendency to use euphemisms and to speak indirectly, especially in a difficult conversation where there is bad news (Weeks, 2001). Clarity is important because the precision of using words to express exactly what is thought and

BOX 18.4   A Difficult Conversations Checklist

Step 1: Prepare by Walking through the Three Conversations

1. Sort out what happened.

   - Where does your story come from (information, past experiences, rules)? Theirs?

   - What impact has this situation had on you? What might their intentions have been?

   - What have you each contributed to the problem?

2. Understand emotions.

   - Explore your emotional footprint, and the bundle of emotions you experience.

3. Ground your identity.

   - What's at stake for you *about you?* What do you need to accept to be better grounded?

Step 2: Check Your Purposes and Decide Whether to Raise the Issue

- *Purposes:* What do you hope to accomplish by having this conversation? Shift your stance to support learning, sharing, and problem-solving.

- *Deciding:* Is this the best way to address the issue and achieve your purposes? Is the issue really embedded in your identity conversation? Can you affect the problem by changing your contributions? If you don't raise it, what can you do to help yourself let go?

Step 3: Start from the Third Story

1. Describe the problem as the difference between your stories. Include both viewpoints as a legitimate part of the discussion.

2. Share your purposes.

3. Invite them to join you as a *partner* in sorting out the situation together.

Step 4: Explore Their Story and Yours

- Listen to understand their perspective on what happened. Ask questions. Acknowledge the feelings behind the arguments and accusations. Paraphrase to see if you've got it. Try to unravel how the two of you got to this place.

- Share your own viewpoint, your past experiences, intentions, feelings.

- Reframe, reframe, reframe to keep on track. From truth to perceptions, blame to contribution, accusations to feelings, and so on.

Step 5: Problem-Solving

- Invent options that meet each side's most important concerns and interests.

- Look to standards for what *should* happen. Keep in mind the standard of mutual caretaking; relationships that always go one way rarely last.

- Talk about how to keep communication open as you go forward.

Source: D. Stone, B. Patton, and S. Heen, *Difficult conversations: How to discuss what matters most.* New York, Penguin Books, (1999).

felt in a difficult conversation is likely to make the conversation unfold as positively as possible under the circumstances. Delivering the message in a clear and concise manner allows people to understand the message as clearly as possible and to start to make sense of the information. As Weeks (2001) states, ". . . there's nothing inherently brutal about honesty. It is not the content but the delivery of the news that makes it brutal or humane" (p. 117). In other words, receiving bad news is difficult enough without having the additional stress of having to interpret an unclear message as well.

Tone   Tone is the nonverbal aspect of the conversation and it includes "intonation, facial expressions, conscious and unconscious body language" (Weeks, 2001, p. 117). It is important to strike a neutral tone when having a stressful conversation, especially if it is about bad news. Taking a gloating or an aggressive tone will not only interfere with the other person's comprehension during a difficult conversation, it will also likely lead to an escalated conversation that is even more difficult. In addition, people are very sensitive to tone, and a negative tone along with bad news will likely increase their motivation for revenge in the future.

Temperate Phrasing   Temperate phrasing involves choosing language carefully to deliver a message that will not provoke the other side. Instead of telling the other party to "shut up and listen," one can say "may I finish my sentence before we move onto the next topic." Provocative language may provide some flair to the conversation in the short term and allow one to impress or hurt the other party, but the goal during difficult conversations is to ensure that the other party hears and understands the message as clearly as possible. Temperate phrasing is an important way to increase the probability of that happening.

Chapter Summary

There are times when negotiators confront a situation where the other party is using a different negotiating model, and this needs to be managed. This chapter examined what negotiators can do when they are in an integrative mode, and the other party is being competitive or "difficult." We began the chapter with a discussion of managing the social contract and shadow negotiation, two important and related concepts that negotiators need to manage proactively. They are concerned with managing the *how* of the negotiation, rather than the *what*. We then turned to a discussion of how to respond when the other side persists in using hard distributive tactics and how to respond when the other side has more power. The chapter concluded with a discussion of tactics to use with generally difficult negotiators, responding to ultimatums, and how to manage difficult conversations.

There are two important themes that ran through this chapter. First, preparation for dealing with negotiation mismatches is critical. This preparation not only involves a thorough understanding of the situational dynamics, but it also requires a deep, critical self-analysis of one's likely response to stressful negotiation situations. In addition, we recommend that you carefully consider how the other party is behaving and how you are responding to their behavior. The second theme running through the chapter is the importance of actively processing information about the negotiation as it unfolds. It is not enough to concentrate on the content of the discussions. When dealing with a difficult other party, negotiators need to be even more vigilant about the process of the negotiation, managing the shadow negotiation and social contract proactively and being careful with the tone of the discussion.

The tools that we discussed in this chapter take considerable practice to master. Their application is as much an art as a science, and even the best negotiators will be pushed to their limits when dealing with difficult other parties. That said, they can provide rewards if they are applied judiciously and with sensitivity to the needs and limitations of the situations and of the negotiators involved.

Third-Party Approaches to Managing Difficult Negotiations

Objectives

1. Understand the benefits and liabilities of involving a third party to assist in resolving a negotiation.

2. Explore the major approaches that third parties use: arbitration, mediation, and process consultation.

3. Consider more informal approaches used by third parties to resolve disputes.

4. Gain an understanding of alternative dispute resolution systems used by organizations.

There is a long history of third parties helping others resolve disputes or reaching decisions for them when they cannot. Third parties may become involved because of a legal requirement (e.g., to manage a labor dispute or strike), diplomacy (to prevent a war between countries), as part of a contractual obligation (e.g., a dispute about a late delivery of merchandise), or because the parties have asked for help. Third parties become involved when negotiators have tried all other options and are not making progress, when mistrust and suspicion are high, or when the parties cannot take actions toward defusing conflict without being misinterpreted and mistrusted by others.

In this chapter we describe the typical roles that third parties play and how they can contribute to resolving conflict. We begin by discussing how the addition of third parties changes the negotiation process. This is followed by an examination of the types of third-party interventions, with special attention paid to three formal third-party roles: arbitration, mediation, and process consultation. We then discuss informal third parties and conclude the chapter with an examination of the institutionalization of third-party processes through the establishment and maintenance of alternative dispute resolution (ADR) systems.

Adding Third Parties to the Two-Party Negotiation Process

Third parties work to manage conflict and help resolve disputes through several different approaches and techniques. Often, third parties only need to implement some of the dispute resolution techniques reviewed in Chapter 17, such as aiding the reduction of tension, controlling the number of issues, enhancing communication, establishing common ground, and highlighting decision options to make them more attractive. As we discuss, some third-party approaches use more of these techniques than others.[1]

The negotiation process we have described throughout this book presumes two or more parties working face-to-face without the direct involvement of others. Their personal involvement can create a deep understanding of the issues and a commitment to resolve their differences in a constructive manner. As long as this direct form of negotiation remains productive, it is best to allow it to proceed without the involvement of other parties. As we have described, however, negotiations are often tense and difficult, and they can lead to frustration and anger. Negotiation over critical issues may reach an impasse, leaving the parties unable to move beyond a particularly difficult point. When passions are high and the parties are deadlocked, third-party intervention may be the only way to get negotiations back on track. We believe that third-party intervention should be avoided as long as negotiations have a chance of proceeding unaided—that is, as long as progress is occurring or is likely to occur within reasonable limits of time and other resources. When intervention becomes advisable, however, it should be done in a timely and thoughtful manner.

The negotiators themselves may seek third-party intervention, or it may be imposed from the outside by choice, custom, law, or regulation. In addition, informal third parties may impose themselves on a situation and bring in the perspective of someone who is not part of the dispute per se, but is nonetheless interested in its resolution. The third party may be a manager, friend, or peer of the negotiators. As a rule, interventions that are not sanctioned by the parties—or reinforced by a third party's expertise, friendship, or authority—are unwelcome and ineffective (see Arnold and O'Connor, 1999). Uninvited third parties may find themselves bearing the brunt of hostility from one or both parties in a negotiation, regardless of the third party's intention or motivation. For example, law enforcement officers who attempt to intervene in domestic disputes, if only to separate the parties and cool down the situation, often find that the battling parties unite in turning on the officers as unwelcome outsiders. Many law enforcement agencies, in fact, caution officers to respond to domestic disputes in pairs in order to separate the disputants and to protect the officers' safety.

Benefits and Liabilities of Third-Party Intervention

Benefits   Third parties can provide and on occasion enforce the stability, civility, and forward momentum that negotiators need to address the problems that remain to be solved—especially those problems that are central to the negotiation and that have stalled or derailed discussions. Third-party interventions can yield several other benefits, including:

- Creating breathing space or a cooling-off period.
- Reestablishing or enhancing communications.
- Refocusing on the substantive issues.
- Remedying or repairing strained relationships.

- Establishing or recommitting to time limits and deadlines.
- Salvaging sunk costs.
- Increasing levels of negotiator satisfaction with and commitment to the conflict resolution process and its outcomes.

Even if the relationship between the parties is so damaged that future exchanges will be extremely difficult, third parties may enable the parties to reduce hostility, manage their emotions, and achieve some closure on the key issues (Jones and Bodtker, 2001). In addition, many organizations adopt and support alternative dispute resolution (ADR) systems and conflict management skills training for their employees. Such commitments may result in a constructive, collaborative work environment, leading to greater individual and organizational effectiveness (Costantino and Merchant, 1996).

Liabilities and Limitations   Third-party interventions also have some liabilities and limitations. The involvement of third parties signals that the negotiation process has stalled. Intervention by a third party may signal that the parties have failed to build relationships or to manage their interdependence positively. This is especially true when parties turn to arbitration (see our later discussion) because parties lose control over determining their outcomes. Arbitration can also be viewed as the result of the negotiators' agreement to disagree and a willingness to surrender control over the outcome of their dispute. In contrast, the dominant purpose of other types of third-party interventions such as mediation and process consultation (also discussed later) is to enhance the parties' dispute resolution skills. Their goal is to allow the parties to maintain control over outcomes while the third party manages the process of their interaction. Each type of third-party intervention has its own particular advantages and disadvantages, depending on the context.

When Is Third-Party Involvement Appropriate?

Serious negotiators must make a realistic effort to resolve their own disputes. In labor–management negotiations, for example, failure to bargain in good faith has been codified as an unfair labor practice under U.S. labor law [N.L.R.A., Sections 8(a)(5) and 8(b)(3)]. In general, though, negotiators initiate third-party interventions when they believe they can no longer manage the situation on their own. When one negotiator requests intervention, that process must be acceptable to the other parties. If only one party recognizes a need for third-party intervention, he or she may have to persuade the other party to agree. Someone with power or authority over the negotiators may also impose interventions, particularly when a failure to resolve the dispute threatens to lead to significant costs for the affected organization or individuals. A list of conditions under which negotiators might seek third-party involvement is presented in Table 19.1. Judicial decisions share many characteristics of arbitration, while legislative decisions are heavily influenced by coalitions; further discussion of both, as well as extralegal decisions, is beyond the scope of this book.

Which Type of Intervention Is Appropriate?

Numerous different third-party interventions are available to negotiators. Moore (1996) suggests that approaches to conflict management and resolution can be placed on a single

TABLE 19.1 | Conditions Where Third-Party Intervention May Help

- Intense emotions appear to be preventing a settlement.
- Poor communication is beyond the ability of the negotiators to fix it.
- Misperceptions or stereotypes hinder productive exchanges.
- Repeated negative behaviors (anger, name-calling, blaming others, etc.) create barriers between the parties.
- There is serious disagreement over the importance, collection, or evaluation of data.
- There is disagreement as to the number or type of issues under dispute.
- Actual or perceived incompatible interests exist that the parties are unable to reconcile.
- Unnecessary (but perceived-as-necessary) value differences divide the parties.
- There is an absence of a clear, agreed-on negotiation procedure or protocol, or established procedures (such as caucuses or cooling-off periods) are not being used to their best advantage.
- Severe difficulties occur in getting negotiations started or in bargaining through an impasse.

Source: Adapted from C. Moore, *The Mediation Process: Practical Strategies for Resolving Conflict,* 2nd ed. (San Francisco: Jossey-Bass, 1996), pp. 13–14. Also see Arnold and Carnevale (1997).

continuum (see Figure 19.1), in which the styles are in increasing order according to the amount of coercion used by third parties to convince negotiators to accept and endorse the third-party settlement. Under conditions of very low coercion, the parties don't engage in the issues themselves, choosing to avoid them or to discuss them informally. At the other extreme, third parties with the force of law of legitimate authority may impose settlements, or the parties may go outside the bounds of the legal and regulatory system by using violent or nonviolent pressure tactics directly on the other.

Thibaut and Walker (1975) presented an important framework suggesting that negotiators may surrender control over neither, either, or both the process of the dispute (the *how*) and the outcome of the dispute (the *what;* see Figure 19.2). Parties are negotiating when they retain both process and outcome control (lower right cell), as addressed in the other chapters of this book. Negotiators who surrender both outcome and process controls have completely withdrawn from the discussion (upper left cell), indicating their willingness to have the dispute managed by an otherwise uninvolved person who will manage the dispute and determine its outcome in whatever manner he or she sees fit. The remaining

FIGURE 19.1 | Continuum of Conflict Management and Resolution Approaches

Decisions Made by Negotiators				Decisions Made by Private Third Parties		Decisions Made by Legal (Authoritative) Third Parties		Extralegal Decisions	
Conflict avoidance	Discussion and problem solving	Informal negotiation	Mediation	Administrative decision	Arbitration	Judicial decision	Legislative decision	Nonviolent direct action	Violence

——— Increased coercion and more likelihood of win–lose decisions ⟶

Source: Adapted from C. Moore, *The Mediation Process: Practical Strategies for Resolving Conflict,* 2nd ed. (San Francisco: Jossey-Bass, 1996), p. 7, Table 1.1.

FIGURE 19.2 | Categories of Third-Party Intervention

Level of Negotiator Control over Outcome

	Low	High
Low	Autocracy	Mediation
High	Arbitration	Negotiation

Level of Negotiator Control over Procedure

Source: Adapted from B. H. Sheppard, "Third Party Conflict Intervention: A Procedural Framework," in B. M. Staw and L. L. Cummings, eds., *Research in Organizational Behavior,* vol. 6 (Greenwich, CT: JAI Publishing, 1984), pp. 141–90; and J. Thibaut and L. Walker, *Procedural Justice: A Psychological Analysis* (Hillsdale, NJ: Lawrence Erlbaum Associates, 1975).

two mixed situations are arbitration and mediation (both discussed in detail later in this chapter). Mediation is the most common third-party intervention and negotiators surrender control over the process while maintaining control over outcomes. Mediation can be highly effective in many disputes,[2] while helping preserve an important benefit of negotiation: The parties retain control over shaping the actual outcome or solution, which enhances their willingness to implement it. Our corollary to the rule "No third-party involvement unless necessary," then, is "If involvement is necessary, use a minimally intrusive intervention" (one toward the left side of the chart in Figure 19.1), such as mediation.

Procedure-only third-party interventions support the needs of negotiators who want guidance or procedural assistance but wish to maintain control over the choice and implementation of the outcome. Frustrated negotiators may feel they just want an end to the dispute, but completely abdicating control to a third party could have several detrimental effects (see the discussion of arbitration later in this chapter). In addition, negotiators may not know how to screen potential third parties to predict what they will do, or the negotiators may be at the mercy of whatever help is most conveniently available. Failure to use a third-party intervention when appropriate is just as wasteful and damaging to the negotiation process as using the wrong intervention method (e.g., arbitration rather than mediation, when negotiator commitment to outcomes is critical for a lasting resolution), or even using the right method at the wrong time (e.g., before negotiators have exhausted the unassisted methods we outlined in Chapter 17 or after expressed anger and personal attacks have soured one or both parties on the entire process—see also Conlon and Fasolo, 1990).

The same issues of propriety and timeliness apply to uninvited interventions, such as when a manager chooses to intervene in a dispute between two subordinates. The third party has the advantage of being potentially more objective than the disputants about the choices of whether to intervene and what intervention to use. Naive third parties are less likely to be objective or impartial, however, because they may have a personal feeling or belief about what is right for this situation, as opposed to having a specific or direct interest in helping to resolve the dispute solely by working "to reconcile the competing interests of the two parties" (Moore, 1996, p. 17). Finally, research by Conlon and Ross (1993) suggests that partisan third parties—who lack impartiality due to a prior relationship with one or both parties or who have a clear bias to settle the dispute more in favor of one side than the other—could have a significant negative effect on disputant satisfaction regarding the third-party intervention. The third party must keep in mind the likely effect of the intervention on the negotiators—on their willingness and ability to address and manage disputes more effectively in the future.

Third-party interventions, particularly arbitration, may have strong negative consequences such as decreasing the ability of the parties to negotiate effectively and increasing their dependency on third parties (see Beckhard, 1978). Third parties need to use moderation: (1) to borrow the medical dictum, "First, do no harm," and (2) to intervene only when necessary and control only as much as necessary to enable the parties to find resolution. In other words, don't let the intervention make the situation worse, do use surgery when needed, and don't use surgery when simple first aid would be sufficient. This advice assumes an overriding value in the negotiators' ability to interact constructively; it also assumes that immediate resolution of the dispute is not critical. To the extent that the negotiators will have little or no interaction in the future or that timeliness is critical, relatively more controlling interventions may be acceptable or necessary (see the midrange of Figure 19.1). Quite often, however, neither of these conditions applies; we discuss choice processes in these less drastic situations in more detail later in this chapter.

Types of Third-Party Intervention

In the following sections, we discuss several different types of third-party intervention. Third-party intervention may be formal or informal. *Formal* interventions are designed intentionally, in advance, and they follow a set of rules or standards; they are used by judges, labor arbitrators, divorce mediators, referees, and group facilitators (e.g., psychologists or organization development practitioners). *Informal* interventions are incidental to the negotiation; a manager or a concerned friend, for example, may become involved in someone else's dispute. While it is important to know whether the third party is following a clear, public, specified set of procedures or "making it up on his own," the proliferation of hybrid forms of dispute resolution, both formal and informal, has blurred this traditional separation.

Formal Intervention Methods

There are three fundamental types of formal third-party interventions: arbitration, mediation, and process consultation.[3] We review the objectives, style, and procedural impact of each approach and describe how each affects negotiation. This section concludes with an examination of two hybrid types of third-party interventions: mediation-arbitration (med-arb) and arbitration-mediation (arb-med).

BOX 19.1 Arbitration with a Twist

Arbitration

Arbitration allows negotiators to have considerable control over the process but they have little or nonexistent control over outcomes (see Figure 19.2). It is the most recognized form of third-party dispute resolution because of its high-profile use in labor relations and the setting of compensation and benefits of professional athletes. The goals of negotiation and arbitration are very different (Posthuma and Dworkin, 2000). Parties negotiate to reach an agreement, while arbitration resolves a disagreement by having a neutral third party impose a decision. The process is very straightforward: parties in dispute, after having reached a deadlock or a time deadline without successful resolution of their differences, present their positions to a neutral third party. The third party listens to both sides and then decides the outcome of the dispute (Elkouri and Elkouri, 1985; Prasow and Peters, 1983). Arbitration is used widely in disputes between organizations (Corley, Black, and Reed, 1977) and management and labor unions (Elkouri and Elkouri, 1985), and it has become the accepted process for resolving global commercial disputes (Beechey, 2000; Swacker, Redden, and Wenger, 2000).

There are several different forms of arbitration. First, arbitrators may hear and rule on a *single issue* under dispute, or on multiple issues in a *total settlement package* (Feigenbaum, 1975). Second, arbitration may be voluntary or binding. Under *voluntary arbitration,* the parties submit their arguments to an arbitrator, but they are not required to comply with the arbitrator's decision. In contrast, *binding arbitration* requires the parties to comply with the decision, either by law or by contractual agreement. In labor–management contract disagreements, the arbitrator's ruling typically amends an existing agreement and becomes part of the agreement for the remaining life of the contract. A third variation concerns the arbitrator's flexibility. At one extreme, arbitrators are free to craft and reach any resolution they deem appropriate; at the other, their choice is severely constrained, as in *final-offer* arbitration, in which the arbitrator must choose, without amendment, one of the positions presented by the disputing parties (see McAndrew, 2003; Pecorino and Van Boening, 2001). In labor–management settings, management frequently attempts to control this situation by requiring the arbitrator to neither add nor detract from the labor contract being interpreted; that is, management tries to curtail the arbitrator's flexibility to change the contract or to rule outside of a strict interpretation of it. The pros and cons of these variations become evident as we examine arbitration in more detail. An interesting twist on arbitrator flexibility is presented in Box 19.1.

Formal arbitration is most commonly used as a dispute resolution mechanism in labor relations or in claims about violations of legal contracts. For example, in most states, "lemon laws"—legal protection given to consumers if they buy a product that does not work and cannot be effectively fixed, such as a car or major appliance—specify that most

In 2000, five law professors formed one of the first organizations to arbitrate disputes over ownership of Internet domain names (domain names, such as yahoo.com, serve as addresses on the Internet for World Wide Web and e-mail accounts). Disputes are commonly over ownership of a specific address or whether the choice of an address infringes on a company's name or trademark.

The law professors arbitrate the disputes entirely online. Operating as Disputes.org, they have the authority to stop the use of a domain name or transfer the name to its rightful owner.

"This new arbitration body will make a useful contribution to the world of the Internet," said Professor Ethan Katsch, a professor of undergraduate legal studies at the University of Massachusetts at Amherst and one of the organization's founders. "Resolving domain-name disputes on-line will be quicker and far less expensive than going to court."

Source: W. R. Leibowitz, "Law Professors Create Group to Arbitrate Disputes over Domain Names," *Chronicle of Higher Education,* January 28, 2000, p. A45.

---

claims will be resolved through arbitration. Arbitration is also being used in several new areas—for example see Box 19.2 on the use of arbitration to resolve problems on the Internet.[4] New contracts, typically in the public sector, that cannot be achieved through negotiation are frequently submitted for consideration to an arbitrator. When a new contract is submitted to arbitration this process is called *interest arbitration.* On the other hand, *grievance arbitration* refers to decisions about the interpretation of existing contracts. For instance, a union may grieve management's decision to discipline an employee if they believe that management did not follow the negotiated discipline policy (e.g., did management act in a fair and consistent manner?). While interest and grievance arbitration have many similarities, the fundamental difference between them concerns the types of decisions that they process.

Arbitration initially appears to have two distinct advantages as a resolution procedure: it imposes a clear-cut resolution to the problem in dispute, and it helps the parties avoid the costs of prolonged, unresolved disputes. Arbitration has come under increasing scrutiny and criticism as a dispute resolution mechanism, even in the labor relations area,[5] and it appears to have several negative consequences, five of which we describe here.

The Chilling Effect   When the parties in negotiation anticipate that their own failure to agree will lead to binding arbitration they may stop working seriously for a negotiated settlement. This *chilling effect* occurs as "the parties avoid making compromises they might be otherwise willing to make, because they fear that the fact finder or arbitrator will split the difference between their stated positions" (Kochan, 1980, p. 291). If negotiators anticipate that the arbitrator will split the difference, then it is in their best interest to maintain an extreme, hard-line position because the hard-liner will be favored (Kritikos, 2006). Research suggests that negotiators expecting a split-the-difference rule in the case of impasse may be chilled, and final-offer arbitration is an alternative to reduce the chilling effect.[6] In *final-offer arbitration,* the arbitrator must choose either one party's position or the other's—nothing in between, no splitting the difference. Given this constraint, negotiators should be more motivated to settle, or to close the gap that will be arbitrated as much as possible, in order to increase the likelihood that the arbitrator will choose their final offer. If both parties act this way it also minimizes the loss that will occur if the arbitrator picks the other party's submission as the basis for the arbitration award. It also appears that if at least one party is risk averse, then there will be a strong likelihood that agreement will be reached before invoking final-offer arbitration (Hanamy, Kilgour, and Gerchak, 2007).

Research suggests that splitting the difference may not be common practice in professional business arbitration. Keer and Naimark (2001) examined a sample of arbitration cases and found that two-thirds of arbitrators ruled either 100 percent for the claimants or 0 percent for the claimants, while only one-third of the cases involved some form of splitting. A related study cited by these authors showed that 72 percent of a large sample of commercial arbitration awards gave less than 20 percent or greater than 80 percent of the award to the claimant. These findings suggest that the tendency for the arbitrator to split the difference may not be common in commercial contexts, perhaps due to the fundamental characteristics of the issues in dispute or due to the fact that these arbitrators are highly experienced and know an extreme demand when they see it.

The Narcotic Effect   When arbitration is anticipated as a result of the failure of parties to agree, negotiators may lose interest in the process of negotiating. Bargaining takes time and effort, especially in complex situations, and there is no guarantee that agreement will be reached. Negotiator passivity, loss of initiative, and dependence on the third party are common results of recurring dispute arbitration and collectively are known as the *narcotic effect* of arbitration. The narcotic effect is even more likely when negotiators are accountable to constituencies because negotiators can take tough, unyielding stands on issues and blame compromise settlements on the arbitrator rather than on their own concessions.

The Half-Life Effect   Parents are quite aware that as the demand for arbitration between siblings increases, both the sheer number of decisions required and the likelihood that those decisions will not please one or both sides increase as well. This is known as the *half-life effect.* For example, as one of the authors worked at home on a Sunday afternoon, he was frequently subject to his children's demands to arbitrate disputes over sharing a videogame. After a series of decisions involving both his own children and half of the surrounding neighborhood, he was informed by one of his children that his decisions were generally viewed as outrageous, unfair, and without appropriate compassion for his own children, and that his services were no longer desired. As the frequency of arbitration increases, disenchantment with the adequacy and fairness of the process develops (Anderson and Kochan, 1977), and the parties may resort to other means to resolve their disputes.

The Biasing Effect   Arbitrators must be careful that their decisions do not systematically favor one side or the other and that they maintain an image of fairness and impartiality, or they may be perceived as subject to a *biasing effect* (see Conlon and Ross, 1993). Even if each separate decision appears to be a fair settlement of the current situation, perceived patterns of partiality toward one side may jeopardize the arbitrator's acceptability in future disputes. Negotiators anticipating labor arbitration typically review different arbitrators' decisions in an effort to secure one who is likely to favor their own side or to avoid one who may make awards more consistently supportive of the other side. While arbitrators deny that they are subject to a biasing effect, negotiators continue to look for any clue that may help them in arbitration.

The Decision-Acceptance Effect   Arbitrated disputes may also engender less commitment to the settlement than alternative forms of dispute resolution, and this is known as the *decision-acceptance effect*. Research on the dynamics of group decision making has demonstrated that commitment to a given solution and willingness to implement it are significantly greater when group members participate in developing that solution than when it is imposed by a single member (Vroom, 1973). Lasting dispute resolution requires timely and effective implementation, and "one of the most powerful drivers of effective implementation is the commitment to [a] decision that derives from prior participation in making it" (Leavitt and Bahrami, 1988, p. 173). For this reason, arbitration is likely to lead to situations in which disputants are less than fully committed to following through, especially if they feel dissatisfied with the arbitrator's decision.

Section Summary

Arbitration remains an important mechanism for resolving disputes when negotiators cannot reach an agreement on their own. It has many advantages as a dispute resolution mechanism, but also several disadvantages. The largest disadvantage is removal of decision control from the negotiators themselves; this can have very negative consequences when they must implement and live with the decision after the arbitrator has gone home. We now turn to a discussion of mediation, a process that leaves decision control with the negotiators.

Mediation

In contrast to arbitration, mediation has developed considerable support and it has been studied with increasing frequency and intensity.[7] Brett, Barsness, and Goldberg (1996) found that mediation was less costly and time-consuming, and it produced greater disputant satisfaction than arbitration. Although the ultimate objective of mediation is the same as arbitration—to resolve the dispute—the major difference is that mediation seeks to achieve the objective by having the parties themselves develop and endorse the agreement. In fact, mediation has been called a form of "assisted negotiation" (Susskind and Cruikshank, 1987, p. 136), "an extension and elaboration of the negotiation process" (Moore, 1996, p. 8), and "an informal accompanist of negotiation" (Wall and Blum, 1991, p. 284). Mediation can help reduce or remove barriers to settlements, adding value to the negotiation process because it tends to produce or enhance much of what parties desire and value in negotiation itself (Bush, 1996; Esser and Marriott, 1995a). Mediators may also help resolve the root causes of an ongoing conflict rather than simply solving the dispute (Brown, 1999), an almost impossible outcome for arbitration to achieve. Finally, mediation has the potential to profoundly change relationships. A growing focus on *transformative mediation* has sparked debate in mediation about the extent to which mediation should focus on the issues at hand versus focusing on two tranformative dimensions: *empowering* the negotiators to express themselves, and increasing the capacity of negotiators to *recognize* the other's perspective (Bush and Folger, 1994, 2005; Folger and Bush, 1996; Kuttorer, 2006). Ten hallmarks of transformative mediation are presented in Box 19.3.

As with arbitration, mediation's modern roots are in the field of labor relations, sometimes as a preliminary step to arbitration in grievance and contractual negotiations. Mediation has also been described, however, as "the second oldest profession," having been around as long as conflict itself (Kolb, 1983a), and it has become a very popular alternative to the courts—particularly when the parties want low-cost solutions that they can largely

BOX 19.3 Ten Hallmarks of Transformative Mediation

1. Describe the mediator's role and objectives in terms based on empowerment and recognition.

2. Leave responsibility for outcomes with the parties.

3. Consciously refuse to be judgmental about the parties views and decisions.

4. Take an optimistic view of parties' competence and motives.

5. Allow and be responsive to parties' expression of emotions.

6. Allow and explore parties' uncertainty.

7. Remain focused on the here and now of the conflict interaction.

8. Be responsive to parties' statements about past events.

9. View an intervention as one point in a larger sequence of conflict interaction.

10. Feel a sense of success when empowerment and recognition occur, even in small degrees.

Source: J. P. Folger and R. A. Baruch Bush, "Transformative mediation and third-party intervention: Ten hallmarks of a transformative approach to practice." *Mediation Quarterly, 13,* (4), (2004), pp. 263–278.

shape them selves (see Lovenheim, 1989). Singer (1994) has noted the many different contexts in which mediation and alternatives dispute resolution (ADR—see the section later in this chapter) have been used: malpractice suits, tort cases, liability claims, pretrial diversions of alcohol and drug cases to treatment centers rather than criminal proceedings, business disputes, consumer complaints, and community and government disputes, to name a few. Mediation has become an extremely popular alternative in divorce proceedings because the parties must be willing to abide by the terms of the settlement and therefore have the most influence in shaping its terms (Donohue, 1991; Kressel, 1985). Mediation has also become a more common form of resolution for civil and community disputes (D'Alo, 2003; Duffy, Grosch, and Olczak, 1991; Kessler, 1978). Community mediation centers, staffed by trained volunteers, have opened across the United States (Duffy, Grosch, and Olczak, 1991; Lovenheim, 1989; Singer, 1994). Mediation is also used increasingly to avoid costly litigation in business settings (Coulson, 1987) and to resolve business–government disputes, particularly in the area of environmental regulation.[8] Finally, mediation is being suggested more frequently as a mechanism for the resolution of international disputes (Bebchick, 2002; Butler, 2007; Chayes, 2007). Rubin (1981) documented Henry Kissinger's success as an extremely skilled international mediator, and Jandt and Pedersen (1996) show how mediation is used around the world to resolve both local and cross-border disputes.

It is important to note that formal or contractual mediation is based on established and accepted rules and procedures. When examining informal interventions later in this chapter, we discuss emergent mediation, which is less well defined (Pruitt and Carnevale, 1993). Mediators have no formal power over outcomes, and they cannot resolve the dispute on their own or impose a solution. Instead, their effectiveness comes from their ability to meet with the parties individually, secure an understanding of the issues in dispute, identify areas of potential compromise in the positions of each side, and encourage the parties to make concessions toward agreement.

Mediators come in all shapes and sizes and use several different skills and tactics (Mareschal, 2005). It appears that the most critical skill for successful mediators is their ability to develop rapport with the disputants (Goldberg, 2005; Goldberg and Shaw, 2007). Stephen Goldberg defines rapport as developing "an empathic, trusting relationship with the parties," and this appears to be more important to successful mediation than particular mediation tactics (2005, p. 372).

It is important to recognize that mediators are not powerless. Mediators with access to resources that negotiators want, such as preferred trade status with the mediator's home country in an international dispute, or preferred work assignments in a workplace disagreement, can have considerable power in the mediation process. In addition, mediators can give disputants "face," a very powerful force in a dispute (van Ginkel, 2004).

When to Use Mediation   Two elements of the mediation process are integral to its success: timing and mediator acceptability. Mediation is far more successful if it occurs when the parties are open to receiving help; this phenomenon is known as *ripeness*.[9] Ripeness refers to a negotiation where an intractable situation is just on the verge of being addressable (Coleman, 1997). There has been considerable research on ripeness, and it appears that the odds of the successful resolution of an intractable negotiation are best if there has been enough pain to inspire motivation to settle but not too much pain to cause lasting animosity.[10]

Mediation is frequently a voluntary process—the parties are not forced to enter into mediation—and it cannot be effective if the parties choose not to cooperate. If they believe that they have more to gain by delaying or protracting the dispute, then mediation cannot work. Many parties in disputes do not seek mediation because they don't really understand the process. They may also get caught up in the momentum of conflict, becoming involved in a *metadispute* (a dispute about the dispute), or they may fear a loss of leverage or advantage at the hands of a third party (McEwen and Milburn, 1993). Mediators who identify that negotiators are not ready for their intervention frequently say, "Call me when you're ready," and leave until the parties have achieved a greater willingness to participate in the process. Formal mediation in some settings (e.g., divorce, international hostilities, or certain types of organized labor strikes) may be imposed if doing so might prevent a situation from escalating or deteriorating beyond any hope of reclamation. This imposition is usually a judgment call by an experienced mediator who is empowered by an external agency or authority to intervene (Bercovitch, 1989; Donohue, 1991). Research suggests that even when parties are pressured or required to enter mediation, they generally come away finding it to be a fair and satisfactory process (Brett, Barsness, and Goldberg, 1996; McEwen and Milburn, 1993).

The second element that influences the success of mediation is the mediator's acceptability to all the parties to the dispute. It is important to note that while mediators may use common language to describe disputes and their interventions, style and behavior vary widely across different mediators (Picard, 2002). The mediator is traditionally viewed as a neutral individual whom the parties recognize as impartial, experienced, and potentially helpful. Some would argue, however, that a completely neutral mediator is virtually impossible to find because any active intervention by a mediator may influence the process and outcome of a negotiation in a way that unintentionally favors one of the parties (see Gibson, Thompson, and Bazerman, 1996). Mediators may be certified by an organization of third parties (such as the Federal Mediation and Conciliation Service of the U.S. Department of Labor) or a local mediation service or dispute settlement center, adding to their credibility. In addition, a variety of qualities such as skill, trustworthiness, integrity, impartiality, and experience in comparable disputes may be required for both sides to view a potential mediator as acceptable. At times, however, the most appropriate or only mediator available is

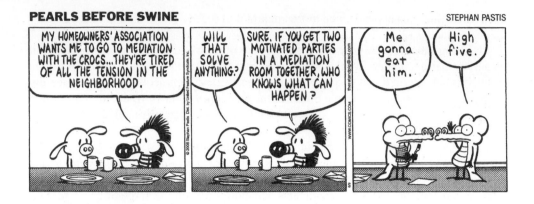

not without some bias. Although mediator bias has usually been thought to be incompatible with mediation effectiveness (Young, 1972), recent research has produced a more complex view of this issue.[11] Carnevale and Conlon (1990) suggest that mediator bias has two forms: general alignment or affiliation with parties prior to mediation, or the greater support of one side during mediation. Negotiators may overlook affiliation bias if they are convinced that the mediator mediates evenhandedly and treats both sides fairly during the mediation (Conlon and Ross, 1993; Wall and Stark, 1996).

Mediator Models, Choices, and Behaviors   The idea of a neutral individual mediating a dispute between two parties seems simple enough, but the process actually involves a large number of facets.[12] Mediators may choose any of a variety of levels and approaches to accomplish what they think needs to be done. Esser and Marriott (1995b) tested three types of mediator interventions: *content mediation* (helping the parties manage trade-offs), *issue identification* (enabling the parties to prioritize the issues), and *positive framing of the issues* (focusing on desired, positively stated outcomes). While content mediation proved to be the most effective intervention in the study, all three approaches were found to be more satisfying to disputants than no mediation at all. As Rubin (1980) noted, mediators primarily "facilitate concession-making without loss of face by the parties, and thereby promote more rapid and effective conflict resolution than would otherwise occur" (p. 380).

A powerful way to conceptualize the mediation process is to understand the key stages or phases of a mediation. Several stage models of mediation have been proposed, most often as important tools for training mediators.[13] Figure 19.3 presents a model described by Moore (1996). Stages in the mediation process can be roughly grouped into four categories: premediation preparation (Stages 1–5); beginning stages of the mediation (Stages 6 and 7); middle stages of the mediation (Stages 8, 9, and 10); and ending stages of the mediation (Stages 11 and 12). In the premediation stages, the mediator attempts to get to know the parties, help them understand the process that will be followed, and gain their confidence. The mediator is most concerned with understanding the nature of the dispute and with securing acceptance by the parties. Mediator strategies may include separating the parties, questioning them about the issues, and actively listening to each side. The mediator must

FIGURE 19.3 | Twelve Stages of Mediator Moves

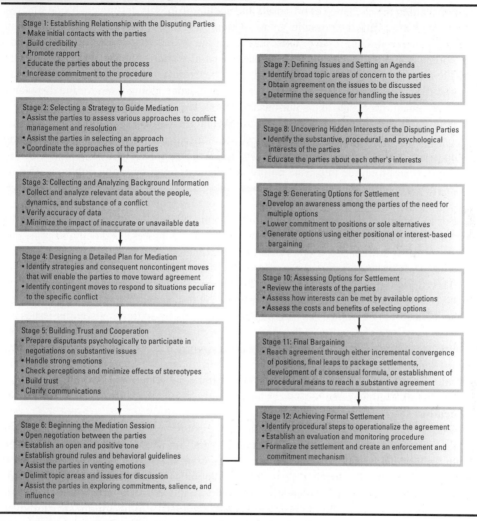

Stage 1: Establishing Relationship with the Disputing Parties
• Make initial contacts with the parties
• Build credibility
• Promote rapport
• Educate the parties about the process
• Increase commitment to the procedure

Stage 2: Selecting a Strategy to Guide Mediation
• Assist the parties to assess various approaches to conflict management and resolution
• Assist the parties in selecting an approach
• Coordinate the approaches of the parties

Stage 3: Collecting and Analyzing Background Information
• Collect and analyze relevant data about the people, dynamics, and substance of a conflict
• Verify accuracy of data
• Minimize the impact of inaccurate or unavailable data

Stage 4: Designing a Detailed Plan for Mediation
• Identify strategies and consequent noncontingent moves that will enable the parties to move toward agreement
• Identify contingent moves to respond to situations peculiar to the specific conflict

Stage 5: Building Trust and Cooperation
• Prepare disputants psychologically to participate in negotiations on substantive issues
• Handle strong emotions
• Check perceptions and minimize effects of stereotypes
• Build trust
• Clarify communications

Stage 6: Beginning the Mediation Session
• Open negotiation between the parties
• Establish an open and positive tone
• Establish ground rules and behavioral guidelines
• Assist the parties in venting emotions
• Delimit topic areas and issues for discussion
• Assist the parties in exploring commitments, salience, and influence

Stage 7: Defining Issues and Setting an Agenda
• Identify broad topic areas of concern to the parties
• Obtain agreement on the issues to be discussed
• Determine the sequence for handling the issues

Stage 8: Uncovering Hidden Interests of the Disputing Parties
• Identify the substantive, procedural, and psychological interests of the parties
• Educate the parties about each other's interests

Stage 9: Generating Options for Settlement
• Develop an awareness among the parties of the need for multiple options
• Lower commitment to positions or sole alternatives
• Generate options using either positional or interest-based bargaining

Stage 10: Assessing Options for Settlement
• Review the interests of the parties
• Assess how interests can be met by available options
• Assess the costs and benefits of selecting options

Stage 11: Final Bargaining
• Reach agreement through either incremental convergence of positions, final leaps to package settlements, development of a consensual formula, or establishment of procedural means to reach a substantive agreement

Stage 12: Achieving Formal Settlement
• Identify procedural steps to operationalize the agreement
• Establish an evaluation and monitoring procedure
• Formalize the settlement and create an enforcement and commitment mechanism

Source: C. Moore, *The Mediation Process: Practical Strategies for Resolving Conflict*, 2nd ed. (San Francisco, CA: Jossey-Bass, 1996), pp. 66–67.

be able to separate rhetoric from true interest in order to identify each side's priorities, and often they keep the negotiators separate during the prenegotiation stage.

Inspiring parties at impasse to begin to speak to each other and to engage in discussions is an important activity of mediators early in the process. Poitras, Bowen, and Byrne (2003) propose a two-phase strategy to motivate parties to negotiate.[14] The first stage works to improve the relationship between the parties and concentrates on building trust through conflict analysis workshops. The second stage concentrates on understanding the benefits of entering discussions and works to bridge those benefits with the relationship between the parties.

Once the parties have moved beyond the prenegotiation stage, the mediator may then begin managing the exchange of proposals and counterproposals, testing each side for areas where concessions may be possible. As mediation progresses, mediators often become increasingly active and aggressive. They may bring the parties together for face-to-face deliberations, or they may continue to keep them separate. They may press one or both sides to make concessions that the mediator judges to be essential. At this stage, mediators use many of the tactics we described in Chapter 17—in essence, doing them for the disputants. They may invent proposals and solutions they think will be acceptable, testing them with each side or even announcing them publicly. Mediators may also use electronic decision support systems to organize the needs and positions of the disputing parties (Ehtamo, Kettunen, and Hamalainen, 2001; Mumpower and Rohrbaugh, 1996). The mediator will try to get the parties to agree in private before announcing anything to the public, so that the parties may consult with their constituencies if necessary. If the mediation effort has been successful, the mediator will ultimately bring the parties together to endorse a final agreement or to announce their settlement publicly. Cobb (1993) suggests that effective mediators empower bargainers by balancing power, controlling the process, and being neutral—and that their ability to repackage otherwise thorny exchanges into less confrontational verbiage helps create "descriptions of responsibility without blame" (p. 256).

The appropriate sequence of issues to be discussed in the negotiation is another strategic choice that mediators need to consider. Weiss (2003) suggests that there are three general sequences: (1) *gradualism,* where the mediator starts by addressing simpler issues and moves to more complex issues as the discussion progresses; (2) *boulder-in-the-road,* where the mediator begins with the most complex issues in order to identify if the conflict is ripe for resolution; and (3) the *committee strategy,* where parties are divided into subgroups to deal with different issues. Weiss examined intractable communal conflicts and found that mediators used all three sequences successfully, although gradualism was used most frequently.

The influence of *mediator style* has been studied extensively (e.g., Bowling and Hoffman, 2001). In the field of divorce and child custody mediation, Kressel and his associates identified two distinct mediator orientations: a *settlement orientation,* marked by strict neutrality and a narrow focus on arriving at a specific resolution; and a *problem-solving orientation,* marked by attempts to deal with underlying problems and including departures from strict neutrality. Participants found the problem-solving orientation to be a more structured, active approach to resolving conflict, and one that leads to more frequent and desirable outcomes. It also seemed to produce more positive attitudes toward mediation (Kressel, Frontera, Forlenza, Butler, and Fish, 1994; also see Alberts, Heisterkamp, and McPhee, 2005). As mediators involve the parties in more joint problem solving, disputant hostility—especially with regard to intangible issues such as fairness, face-saving, and pride—seems to decrease (Zubek, Pruitt, Pierce, McGillicuddy, and Syna, 1992).

Kolb's (1983a) study of mediator styles identified two main types of mediators: *deal makers,* whose style was marked by a high degree of issue management, issue packaging, and coordination of exchanges between the parties, and *orchestrators,* whose style was less issue-specific but more oriented toward sequencing conversations between the parties. Research that has tested and extended Kolb's model suggests that the two mediator styles vary as a function of the degree of third-party control exercised over (1) the process, (2) the outcome, or (3) the motivation of the parties to continue deliberations. Field studies revealed four types of mediator approaches: parties who controlled all three, those who controlled only outcome and motivation, those who controlled only process and outcome, and—interestingly enough—those who controlled none of these (Baker and Ross, 1992). Research on mediator style reveals that mediators vary tremendously in terms of the degree of process and outcome control, with all types and variations depending on the individual and the context in which he or she is mediating (Kolb and Associates, 1994). Botes and Mitchell (1995) suggest that mediator flexibility is a prerequisite for effective mediators, just as it is for negotiators. In this case, mediator flexibility is defined as decreased constraints, increased freedom of action, increased autonomy, and increased ability to entertain imaginative ideas (see Botes and Mitchell, 1995; Druckman and Mitchell, 1995; also see Balachandra, Barrett, Bellman, Fisher and Susskind, 2005).

Recognizing that mediators deal with a variety of situations and choose their behaviors based on what a given situation warrants, Carnevale (1986) developed a *strategic choice model* of mediator behavior. Carnevale proposes that the mixture of high or low levels of two variables—concern for the disputing parties' aspirations and perception of parties' common ground (i.e., areas of agreement)—will produce four basic mediation strategies: problem solving, compensation, pressure, or inaction (see Figure 19.4). *Problem solving* (high concern for parties' aspirations, high perception of common ground) takes the form of assisting the parties to engage in integrative negotiation and search for solutions with integrative potential (see Chapter 3). *Compensation* (high concern for aspirations, low perception of common ground) involves mediator application of rewards and inducements to entice the parties into making concessions and agreements. *Pressure* (low concern for aspirations, low perception of common ground) involves trying to force the parties to reduce their levels of aspiration in the absence of perceived potential for an integrative (win–win) resolution. Finally, *inaction* (low concern for aspirations, high perception of common ground) involves standing back from the dispute, leaving the parties to work things out on their own. Subsequent research has provided support and additional

FIGURE 19.4 | Carnevale's Strategic Choice Model of Mediator Behavior

	Mediator's Perception of "Common Ground"	
	Low	**High**
High	Compensation	Problem solving
Low	Pressure	Inaction

Mediator's Concern for Parties' Aspirations

evidence for the model.[15] Carnevale's (1986) model may not be complete, however, because it does not take into account power imbalances between parties or the mediator's aspirations (Carnevale, 1992; van de Vliert, 1992). Possible effects of mediator aspirations and preferences on negotiators' perceptions and behaviors raise interesting questions about the nature of mediator bias and flexibility (see Botes and Mitchell, 1995). The results of one study suggested that disputants distrusted even favorable recommendations from mediators whom they saw as biased, while a perceived favorable bias was sufficient to offset unfavorable recommendations (Wittmer, Carnevale, and Walker, 1991). On the other hand, mediators who have high levels of insight are perceived as more credible, and perceptions of mediator credibility were related to more positive perceptions of the mediator (Arnold, 2000).

Mediator-applied pressure seems to interact with the type of situation being mediated. Parties who are in disputes marked by high intensity (e.g., major conflicts involving many issues and disagreement over major priorities) and high levels of interparty hostility tend to respond well to forceful, proactive mediation behaviors. In contrast, disputants in low-hostility situations tend to respond better to a less active, more facilitative mediator approach.[16] When high hostility was accompanied by high levels of problem-solving behavior by the negotiators, mediators assisted best by posing problems, challenging negotiators to solve them, and suggesting new ideas and soliciting negotiator responses to them (Zubek, Pruitt, Pierce, McGillicuddy, and Syna, 1992). This suggests that mediators may get in the way when negotiators are capable of solving their own problems; although a mediator's forceful intervention and a proactive style may be appropriate when hostility is high, these same qualities may be counterproductive when hostility is low, or even when high hostility is accompanied by high negotiator problem-solving skill (see Hiltrop and Rubin, 1982). In such situations, process consultation (which we discuss later) may be a better intervention choice.

When Is Mediation Effective?   Kressel and Pruitt (1989) report that mediation was effective in about 60 percent of the cases studied, ranging from 20 to 80 percent across a variety of settings. Wall, Stark, and Standifer (2001) found similar support for mediation effectiveness, and they also reported numerous benefits to disputant satisfaction and improved relationships between negotiators. Carnevale and Pruitt (1992) suggest

NON SEQUITUR   BY WILEY

TABLE 19.2 | Aspects of Effective Mediation

Mediator–parties relationship
Improve acceptance of mediation by the parties.
Increase parties' trust in the mediator.

Relationship between the parties
Control communication between the parties.
Have separate meetings with the parties to influence them.

The issues
Uncover the underlying interests and concerns.
Set agendas.
Package, sequence, and prioritize agenda items.
Interpret and shape proposals.
Make suggestions for possible settlements.

The parties
Help parties save face when making concessions.
Help parties resolve internal disagreements.
Help parties deal with constituents.
Apply positive incentives for agreement or concession making.

Source: Adapted from P. J. D. Carnevale and Dean G. Pruitt, "Negotiation and Mediation," *Annual Review of Psychology* 43 (1992), pp. 531–42.

that mediation effectiveness can be viewed from a variety of perspectives, including the mediator–parties relationship, the relationship between the parties, the issues, and the parties themselves (see Table 19.2). Mediation appears to be more effective in situations marked by moderate levels of conflict (see Glasl, 1982; Hiltrop and Rubin, 1982). By *moderate conflict,* we mean situations in which tension is apparent and tempers are beginning to fray, but negotiations have not deteriorated to the point of physical violence or irrevocably damaging threats and actions. Disputes beyond the moderate stage are often characterized by drastic actions and reactions, through which the parties harm the relationship beyond repair. Other research suggests that mediation is more effective when negotiators experience a *hurting stalemate* (Touval and Zartman, 1985). Several other studies have shown that mediation is effective only in certain kinds of disputes (see Carnevale and Pruitt, 1992; and Posthuma, Dworkin, and Swift, 2002). Kochan and Jick (1978), for example, in their review of mediation in the public sector, report that mediation was most successful in conflicts that involved a breakdown in negotiations due to bargainers' inexperience or over commitment to their positions. In contrast, mediation was less effective when one or both of the negotiating parties had internal conflict; for example, when major differences existed between the demands of a union's rank-and-file and their chief negotiator's belief about what was attainable at the negotiating table. Mediation was also less effective as a strategy when the parties differed on important economic issues or had major differences in their expectations for a settlement.

When the resistance points of the two sides don't overlap, mediators may have to exert greater direct and indirect pressure on the negotiators to create a positive bargaining zone (see Chapter 2). Direct pressure occurs when the mediator uses tactics to encourage the parties to soften their positions; indirect pressure typically comes through wearing the parties down over time and increasing the cost of holding out. Some mediators achieve results by being aggressive and applying pressure on the negotiators to settle or to consider options (Johnson, 1993; Kolb, 1983a, 1983b). It appears that mediation is not always effective in highly intense conflicts, such as those in which many issues are at stake or the parties disagree on major priorities (Rubin, 1980). Under such conditions, mediation tactics may not be sufficient to move the parties toward mutual agreement.

Zubek, Pruitt, Pierce, McGillicuddy, and Syna (1992) examined the process and outcome of 73 hearings at two community dispute resolution centers. They found that some mediator behaviors were perceived as positively related to mediation success, some as negatively related, and others as unrelated. For instance, mediator behaviors positively related to successful mediation included demonstrating empathy; structuring discussions by creating and controlling the agenda; helping the parties establish priorities; and maintaining calm, friendly, but firm control over the mediation process. On the other hand, mediator behaviors negatively related to mediation success included displaying expertise, criticizing, and asking embarrassing questions. Finally, mediator behaviors unrelated to mediation success included providing reassurance, order keeping, and mediator experience.

Gibson, Thompson, and Bazerman (1996) took a different approach to examining mediator effectiveness by analyzing common cognitive errors made by mediators. The results of their analysis led them to advise mediators to:

- Push for agreement only when a positive bargaining zone exists (see Chapter 2).
- Search for "fully efficient" agreements (i.e., "there exists no other outcome or set of outcomes that at least one party prefers and toward which the other party would at least be indifferent," p. 74).
- Help the parties think through the issue(s) of fairness.
- Avoid reaching an agreement for "agreement's sake" (the agreement-is-good bias).
- Avoid accepting the first agreement discovered (the first acceptable agreement may not be the best agreement).
- Avoid the 50–50 split if it doesn't treat both parties equally.

More recently, researchers have surveyed mediators in order to understand their perspectives of successful mediation (Goldberg, 2005; Goldberg and Shaw, 2007; Mareschal, 2005). This research shows that mediators believe that their skill base, ability to create rapport, and a collaborative orientation are critical aspects of mediating successfully, while mediator tactics were not related to mediation success.

Section Summary

A great deal of theory and research has examined mediation in the past 20 years and provided considerable evidence for its effectiveness in resolving disputes. Mediation has its disadvantages as well, however, in that it can take a large investment of time and resources, and it is not always effective. In a sense, the advantages and disadvantages of mediation and arbitration are complementary, so it is not surprising that they have also been linked together as hybrid procedures. In the next section, we examine the third major type of third-party intervention, process consultation, and then in the following section we examine mediation-arbitration hybrid procedures.

Process Consultation

The third formal approach to the resolution of disputes is *process consultation* (Walton, 1987), which has been defined as "a set of activities on the part of the consultant that helps the client to perceive, understand, and act upon the process events which occur in the client's environment" (Schein, 1987, p. 34). The objective of process consultation is to defuse the emotional aspect of conflict and improve communication between the parties, leaving them with renewed or enhanced ability to manage future disputes.

The difference between mediation and process consultation is that mediators are at least somewhat concerned with addressing the substantive issues in the dispute, whereas process consultants focus only on improving communication and conflict management procedures (see Cross and Rosenthal, 1999). Process consultants work under the assumption that teaching the parties how to manage conflict more productively and effectively will lead them to produce better outcomes. The purpose of third-party interventions is to create the foundation for productive dialogue over substantive issues and to teach the parties how to prevent conflicts from escalating destructively in the future.

Process Consultation Behaviors   Process consultants employ a variety of tactics. Their first step is usually to separate the parties and interview them to determine each side's view of the other party, positions, and history of the relationship. The consultant uses the information gathered in this diagnostic phase to structure a series of dialogues or confrontations between the parties (Walton, 1987). These meetings are designed to address the causes of past conflicts and each side's perceptions of the other. Meetings are held in a neutral area, and the issues to be discussed and who is attending the meetings are planned ahead of time. The purpose of the third party is to encourage the negotiators to confront their differences and the reasons for them. The process consultant is the referee, timekeeper, and gatekeeper of the process, working to keep the parties on track while also ensuring that the conflict does not escalate. The process consultant also directs all sides toward problem solving and integration, assuming that by confronting and airing their differences the parties can create a method for working on their substantive differences in the future and can pursue this approach without unproductive escalation recurring. The process consultant works to change the climate for conflict management, promote constructive dialogue around differences of opinion, and create the capacity for people in the relationship to act as their own third parties.

Process consultants should possess many of the same attributes that we have outlined for other third parties. First, they should be perceived as experts in the technique, knowledgeable about conflict and its dynamics, able to be emotionally supportive while confronting the parties, and skilled in diagnosing the dispute. Second, they should be perceived as clearly neutral, without bias toward one side or the other. Third, they should be authoritative—that is, able to establish power over the process that the conflicting parties are pursuing, so they may intervene in and control it. Although they do not attempt to impose a particular solution or outcome, process consultants must be able to shape how the parties interact, separating them or bringing them together, and to control the agenda that they follow when interaction occurs (the shadow negotiation; see Chapter 18). Without such control, the parties will resort to their earlier pattern of destructive hostility.

The primary focus of process consultation is to teach the parties how to resolve substantive differences themselves, not to resolve their differences for them. Process consultation puts the issues under dispute into the hands of the disputing parties. To make process consultation work, however, the parties must be able to manage their own potentially destructive conflict processes in order to be able to work through their substantive differences—something that is frequently very hard for them to do.

Process consultation has been most frequently used to improve longstanding relationships that the parties want to continue. Marital and family therapy are forms of process consultation, as are organizational development and team building among work groups. Process consultation has also been tried in labor–management relationships and in international conflict among ethnic, political, and cultural groups such as Protestants and Catholics in Northern Ireland and Palestinians and Israelis in the Middle East (Kelman, 1996). Many of the early efforts at process consultation in these environments were not completely successful.[17] Research studies have contributed to a better understanding of process consultation in the following ways:

1. *Process consultation is less likely to work as an intervention when the parties are deeply locked in a dispute over one or more major unresolved issue(s).* Because process consultation seeks to change the nature of the working relationship between the parties, it may only work before the parties are in open conflict or between major outbreaks of hostility (Walton, 1987).

2. *Process consultation may be an ineffective technique when dealing with short-term relationships.* There is little need to teach parties to resolve disputes effectively when they will not be working together in the future.

3. *Process consultation may be ineffective when the substantive issues in the dispute are distributive, or zero-sum.* The objectives of process consultation are to improve both the relationship and the skills for integrative negotiation. If the nature of the dispute or constituency pressures on the negotiators do not encourage and support the integrative process, then process consultation is not likely to be effective. Divisive issues or constituency pressures to maintain a hard-line stance will undermine efforts at process consultation.

4. *Process consultation may be ineffective when the level of conflict is so high that the parties are more intent on revenge or retribution than reconciliation.* Process consultation may only work when sustained conflict has worn the parties out, making them want resolution more than continued fighting, or when the parties sincerely want to coexist but do not know how to act. If the parties do not have sufficient incentive to work together, they will undermine efforts at process consultation. One side will exploit trust, cooperation, and honesty, and the dispute will quickly escalate.

Several leading practitioners have detailed procedures for using facilitation to structure dialogue between parties, move them toward problem solving, and transform their relationship. Kelman (1996) conducted a large number of interactive problem-solving workshops between Israelis and Palestinians and describes how these experiences not only improved the relationship between the parties but also improved the basis for larger negotiations between the two groups. Mitchell and Banks (1996) provide a useful road map for how the workshop model can be used and offer several exercises and activities that can bring very adversarial groups together. Finally, Bunker and Alban (1997) reviewed different large group interventions, in which the objective is to bring together many diverse groups, stakeholders, or constituencies in order to coordinate and facilitate systemwide planning and change. Bunker and Alban show how facilitation and process consultation can be applied to organizational development in order to enhance the ability of large groups and systems to coordinate change efforts in a single planning initiative.

Combining Formal Intervention Methods

It is clear that mediation and arbitration have their advantages and disadvantages. Some work has been done to try to ameliorate the disadvantages of each. The disadvantages of arbitration include:

- Negative consequences for negotiators when they anticipate a third-party intervention (e.g., chilling and narcotic effects).
- Removal of outcome control from negotiators.
- Possible lack of commitment to implementing the imposed outcome.

The disadvantages of mediation include:

- Lack of impetus or initiative to adhere to any particular settlement or to settle at all.
- Possible perpetuation of the dispute, perhaps indefinitely.
- Possible escalation of the dispute into more damaging, more costly forms.

Several researchers have proposed that combining mediation and arbitration into a two-stage dispute resolution model may minimize the disadvantages of each.[18]

Mediation-Arbitration (med-arb)   Starke and Notz (1981) proposed that mediation as a preliminary step to arbitration, known as *mediation-arbitration* or *med-arb* for short, should have a complementary and facilitating effect on dispute resolution, but only for final-offer arbitration. This is because in conventional arbitration the parties expect a compromise ruling by the arbitrator; because mediation also promises a compromise, the parties may choose to wait for the arbitration ruling rather than make concessions during mediation. In contrast, when expecting final-offer arbitration, mediation provides the parties with an incentive to evaluate the reasonableness of their current positions. As a result, they may be more willing to modify their positions prior to arbitration in order to improve their chances that the arbitrator will rule in favor of their side. In a laboratory study of arbitration and negotiation, Grigsby and Bigoness (1982; also see Grigsby, 1981) found that anticipated mediation reduced the chilling effect in negotiators expecting final-offer-by-issue arbitration, but negotiators expecting conventional arbitration, final-offer-by-package arbitration, or no arbitration were more subject to the chilling effect when they were anticipating mediation as an intervening step.

Arbitration-Mediation (arb-med)   Another hybrid approach is *arbitration-mediation* (*arb-med*), and it has three stages. First, the arbitrator holds a hearing and reaches a decision "which is placed in a sealed envelope and is not revealed to the parties" (Conlon, Moon and Ng, 2002, p. 979). Mediation occurs at stage 2. If an agreement is not reached, in stage 3 the arbitration ruling is revealed and is binding on both parties. In a simulation study examining the effectiveness of arb-med, Conlon et. al (2002) found that arb-med led to a higher resolution rate and higher joint outcomes compared to med-arb (also see Ross and Conlon, 2000).

Informal Intervention Methods

In this chapter we have reviewed the three major formal approaches third parties use to resolve disputes: arbitration, mediation, and process consultation. Other third-party approaches are possible, and managers, parents, counselors, and others who become involved in other people's disputes, use many of them informally. Sheppard (1984) proposed a generic classification of third-party intervention procedures. Rather than prescribing how managers should intervene in conflicts, Sheppard's model describes how they actually intervene. The model is an extension of Thibaut and Walker's (1975) work on procedural justice systems. As noted earlier in this chapter, Thibaut and Walker conceived of dispute resolution as involving two stages: a procedural or process stage, in which evidence and arguments are gathered and presented, and an outcome or decision stage, in which the evidence is evaluated to determine which party it favors. They distinguished among conflict intervention styles based on the amount of process control, decision control, or both used by the third party. These two approaches to control may be thought of as independent dimensions of conflict intervention, and a third party may exert varying amounts of each in handling a dispute. We shall refer to situations where a third party exerts high or low amounts of process or decision control and represent the possibilities in matrix form (refer back to Figure 19.2). Sheppard (1983) asked practicing managers to describe the last time they intervened in a dispute between their subordinates and then coded their responses according to the amount of process and decision control the third party used. He concluded that managers use one of three dominant styles when they intervene in a subordinate conflict (see Figure 19.5).

1. **Inquisitorial intervention.** This was the most common style. A manager using an inquisitorial intervention exerts high control over both the process and the decision. She tells both sides to present their cases, asks several questions to probe each side's position, and frequently controls who is allowed to speak and what topics they may discuss. She then invents a solution that she thinks will resolve the dispute and imposes that solution on both parties. Inquisitorial intervention is a judicial style of handling conflicts that is found most commonly in European courtrooms.

2. **Adversarial intervention.** Managers who use adversarial intervention exert high control over the decision but not the process. The manager does not ask questions, try to get the whole story, or control the destructive aspects of the conflict between the parties. Instead, he passively listens to what each side chooses to tell him and then tells the parties how to solve the conflict based on their presentations. This style is most similar to arbitration and to the style used by most American courtroom judges.

3. **Providing impetus.** Managers who provide impetus typically do not exert control over the decision, and they exert only a small amount of control over the process. The

FIGURE 19.5 | Managerial Third-Party Intervention Styles

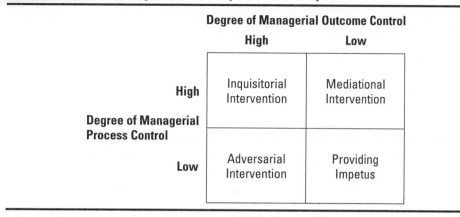

Source: Adapted from B. H. Sheppard, "Managers as Inquisitors: Some Lessons from the Law," in M. Bazerman and R. J. Lewicki, Eds., *Negotiating in Organizations* (Beverly Hills, CA: Sage Publications, 1983).

manager typically tries to make a quick diagnosis of what the conflict is about and then tells the parties that if they don't find a solution, she will impose one on them. In short, the manager first asks, "What's going on here?" When she finds out what's going on, she says, "You'd better solve this problem, or else I'll solve it for you, and neither of you will like the solution!"

Which Approach Is More Effective?

Sheppard's research indicates that managers spontaneously act like an inquisitorial judge or an arbitrator, or they threaten to settle the dispute for the parties in an undesirable way if they can't settle it themselves. Note that the remaining cell in Figure 19.5, which we have labeled "mediational intervention," is the same as formal mediation, but it is not a style commonly observed among managers. While subsequent research examining how managers behave has shown that they claim to prefer mediation as a third-party style, it is not clear that managers actually use mediation unless they are specifically trained in the process (Lewicki and Sheppard, 1985). When managing a conflict, managers seem to assume that because the parties cannot resolve the dispute on their own, the manager must primarily deal with deciding the outcome (see Sheppard, Blumenfeld-Jones, Minton, and Hyder, 1994). Managers appear to think they mediate, but when observed in actual situations they typically exert far more control over the outcome than mediators; their actual behavior is more like an inquisitor than a mediator.

Sheppard's work has generated a growing body of research on informal managerial dispute intervention. Elangovan (1995a; 1998) has developed a prescriptive model to guide managers in choosing intervention strategies (see Figure 19.6).[19] The model provides a decision tree in which potential third parties ask a series of diagnostic questions about the dispute (see the questions at the top of Figure 19.6). Based on whether the dispute is judged to be high or low on each of these questions, the potential third party arrives at an end point on the decision tree that suggests a particular style. These styles—described as means-control,

FIGURE 19.6 | A Prescriptive Model for Managerial Dispute Intervention

DI	How important is this dispute to the effective functioning of the organization?
TP	How important is it to resolve the dispute as quickly as possible?
ND	Does the dispute concern the interpretation of existing rules, procedures, and arrangements or the changing of existing rules, procedures, and arrangements?
NR	What is the expected frequency of future work-related interactions between the disputants?
CP	If you were to impose a settlement on your subordinates (disputants), what is the probability that they would be committed to it?
DO	What is the orientation of the disputants? That is, if you were to let your subordinates (disputants) settle the dispute, what is the probability that they would come to an organizationally compatible settlement?

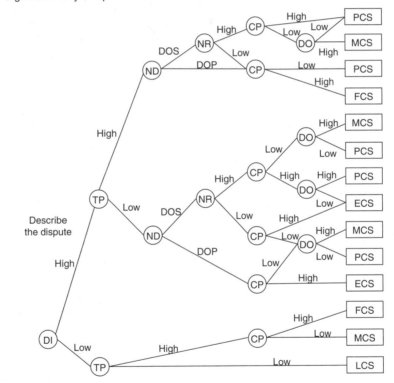

Legend:
MCS = Means-control strategy
ECS = Ends-control strategy
LCS = Low-control strategy
FCS = Full-control strategy
PCS = Part-control strategy

Source: Reprinted with permission of Academy of Management, P. O. Box 3020, Briarcliff Manor, NY 10510-8020. From A. R. Elangovan, "Managerial Third-Party Dispute Intervention: A Prescriptive Model of Strategy Selection," *Academy of Management Review* 20, no. 4 (1995), p. 820. Reproduced by permission of the publisher via Copyright Clearance Center.

TABLE 19.3 | Managerial Dispute Intervention Strategies

Means-control strategy (MCS)	Manager intervenes in the dispute by influencing the process of resolution (i.e., facilitates interaction, assists in communication, explains one disputant's views to another, clarifies issues, lays down rules for dealing with the dispute, maintains order during talks) but does not attempt to dictate or impose a resolution (thought he or she might suggest solutions); the final decision is left to the disputants; high on process control but low on outcome control (e.g., mediation, conciliation).
Ends-control strategy (ECS)	Manager intervenes in the dispute by influencing the outcome (i.e., takes full control of the final resolution, decides what the final decision will be, imposes the resolution on the disputants) but does not attempt to influence the process; the disputants have control over what information is presented and how it is presented; high on outcome control but low on process control (e.g., arbitration, adjudication, adversarial intervention).
Low-control strategy (LCS)	Manager does not intervene actively in resolving the dispute; he or she either urges the parties to settle the dispute on their own or merely stays away from the dispute; low on both process and outcome control (e.g., encouraging or telling the parties to negotiate or settle the dispute by themselves, providing impetus).
Full-control strategy (FCS)	Manager intervenes in the dispute by influencing the process and outcome (i.e., decides what information is to be presented and how it should be presented and also decides on the final resolution); he or she asks the disputants specific questions about the dispute to obtain information and imposes a resolution; manager has full control of the resolution of the dispute; high on both process and outcome control (e.g., inquisitorial intervention, autocratic intervention).
Part-control strategy (PCS)	Manager intervenes in the dispute by sharing control over the process and outcome with the disputants (i.e., manager and disputants jointly agree on the process of resolution as well as strive for a consensus on the settlement decision); he or she works with the disputants to help them arrive at a solution by facilitating interaction, assisting in communication, discussing the issues, and so on. In addition, he or she takes an active role in evaluating options, recommending solutions, persuading the disputants to accept solutions, pushing for a settlement; moderate on managerial process and outcome control (e.g., group problem solving, mediation-arbitration).

ends-control, full-control, part-control, and low-control—are similar to the styles described in Figures 19.2 and 19.5, except Elangovan explicitly chooses not to use the more common terms *mediation* and *arbitration* to describe these styles (see Table 19.3 for his description of the styles). Elangovan prefers to describe the degree of outcome and process control, which provides more precision about what the third party should do, while avoiding value-laden terms like *mediation* and *arbitration,* which may be confusing because of their numerous variations and forms. Extending his thinking to the global environment, Elangovan (1995b) has also done preliminary work on the role that culture plays in third-party intervention processes. His studies show that preferences for third-party intervention vary as a function of cultural differences, as one might predict from Hofstede's categories of cross-cultural differences (see Chapter 16).

Pinkley and her colleagues have also examined the key factors that motivate a third party to assume a particular style (Pinkley, Brittain, Neale, and Northcraft, 1995). They found evidence that judgments along five key dimensions could account for a manager's choice of intervention:

1. The amount of attention the manager gives to the parties' statements of the issues in dispute rather than to underlying problems.

2. The degree of voluntary (versus mandated) acceptance of the solution proposed by the third party.

3. Third-party versus disputant control over shaping the outcomes.

4. The third party's personal approach to conflict.

5. Whether the dispute is to be handled publicly or privately.

It is clear that managers and others in authority usually have the right to intervene in disputes. Not only are they interested in workplace disputes and their resolutions, but they usually have the power to involve themselves. Research by Conlon, Carnevale, and Murnighan (1994) found that managers-as-third-parties chose to impose outcomes about two-thirds of the time, and even more often when they perceived the disputants as being uncooperative. This is consistent with other empirical findings related to managerial dispute intervention (Sheppard et al., 1994), and Watkins and Winters (1997) have extended the model to illustrate some of the dilemmas associated with each intervention style.

There is good evidence that mediation should be used more often as an informal third-party intervention style. Karambayya and Brett (1989), studying classroom simulations, found that managers assume different roles depending on how they diagnose the situation. They found general support for Sheppard's (1983, 1984) model and reported that mediation in particular led to fairer outcomes than other forms of dispute resolution. Mediation was also perceived to be a fairer process by disputants, lending support to Brett and Rognes's (1986) advice that managers should act as mediators when acting as third parties. Karambayya, Brett, and Lytle (1992), again using a classroom simulation, found that managers were most likely to intervene in autocratic or mediational styles, but that relative authority and experience had distinct effects. Experience aside, third parties in authority over the disputants were more likely to be autocratic than those who were not in authority, and peer interveners were no more likely to act like mediators. Autocratic interventions tended to produce one-sided outcomes and impasses, whereas mediational interventions tended to produce compromises. It is likely that managers' failure to use mediation more extensively is due to beliefs about the managerial role, in that managers have a tendency to frame conflicts as hands-on opportunities, which this may cause them to decide not to mediate (Sheppard et al., 1994). Interveners with greater managerial experience, though, were significantly less likely to be autocratic than those with less experience, and third parties with both authority and more experience tended to exhibit the most mediational behavior in the study group.

Finally, research by Conlon and Fasolo (1990) suggests that while mediational interventions may be preferable to autocratic ones, timing appears to be critical. The timing of the mediator's intervention (i.e., earlier versus later in the dispute) was found to influence disputant perceptions of procedural fairness. Quick interventions tended to produce disputant feelings of lack of control and loss of voice—that is, the negotiators felt they had lost their ability to have a say and present their case to their satisfaction. Disputants also expressed lower satisfaction with third-party interventions that they perceived were inappropriate due to violations of due process; that is, negotiators were not satisfied when they perceived that they were denied access to normal procedural steps and safeguards.

The most extensive treatment of the role that third parties can play in informal dispute resolution and conflict management can be found in William Ury's (2000) book *The Third Side*. Ury suggests that third parties can influence conflict at three general stages: they can (1) *prevent conflicts,* where interventions inhibit latent conflict from emerging; (2) *resolve conflict,* where conflicts that have emerged are managed; and (3) *contain conflict,* where ongoing conflicts that have been a challenge to resolve are contained (see Table 19.4). Ury describes 10 roles that third parties can play to help others resolve their disputes. Each of these stages and potential third-party roles is discussed in more detail herein.

Conflict may escalate at the "prevent" stage for three reasons: (1) frustrated needs, (2) poor skills, and (3) weak relationships (see Table 19.4). Humans have several fundamental needs (e.g., security, love, recognition), and the blocking of these needs can lead to conflict. The role of the Provider is to enable others to fulfill their needs. For instance, good manager should ensure that her staff receives positive recognition for their work with regular

TABLE 19.4 | Ten Roles Third Parties Play

Why Conflict Escalates	Ways to Transform Conflict
Prevent	
Frustrated needs	The Provider
Poor skills	The Teacher
Weak relationships	The Bridge-Builder
Resolve	
Conflicting interests	The Mediator
Disputed rights	The Arbiter
Unequal power	The Equalizer
Injured relationships	The Healer
Contain	
No attention	The Witness
No limitation	The Referee
No protection	The Peacekeeper

Source: From William Ury, *The Third Side* (New York: Penguin, 2000), p. 190.

merit increments or promotions so that staff members do not become disgruntled and create conflict at work. Conflicts also result from poor conflict management skills and intolerance of differences of opinion. The role of the Teacher is to educate people in the skills of managing differences and conflict. Weak relationships are another source of conflict that third parties may help to prevent from escalating. The role of the Bridge-Builder is to find ways to bring parties together to improve relationships in order to avoid conflict escalation. For instance, a manager may assign members of two office factions to the same project team in order to create ties across the office.

Conflict may escalate at the "resolve" stage for four reasons: (1) conflicting interests, (2) disputed rights, (3) unequal power, and (4) injured relationships (see Table 19.4). The role of the Mediator is to help parties reconcile their differences of opinion by opening channels of communication between parties and helping them search for their own solution. The role of the Arbiter is to choose from opposing positions when disputing parties are unable to decide for themselves. For instance, a manager may choose which of two marketing plans the organization will adopt when her subordinates are divided on which to support. The role of the Equalizer is to ensure that the voices of weaker parties are heard when resolving conflicts. For instance, the influence of quiet members of a project team may be minimized unless the Equalizer takes action to ensure that they are heard. The role of the Healer is to ensure that the emotional aftermath of a conflict is managed so that it does not become the source of a future conflict. For instance, after an angry dispute between two co-workers has been settled, the Healer may still need to listen to both parties and help them deal with residual hurt feelings that could lead to further conflict.

Conflict may escalate at the "contain" stage for three reasons: (1) lack of attention, (2) lack of limitation, and (3) lack of protection (see Table 19.4). The role of the Witness is to contain escalating conflict by watching and remembering the events that occur in his or her presence. The mere presence of a neutral witness can act to contain conflict because people are often less willing to escalate a conflict when witnesses are present. The role of the Referee is to place limits on the extent to which behaviors are tolerated. For instance, the Referee may endorse harsh, pointed words but not sanction physical violence in an argument. The role of the Peacekeeper is to intervene in a dispute to prevent violence or to stop it once it occurs. The United Nations plays this role between warring states, but it is also a role that people may play between hostile individuals.

Taken as a whole, Ury's model is a very creative way of looking at formal and informal third-party interventions in any kind of conflict. This is not a stage model in the sense that third parties should act in a prescribed order when dealing with conflict. Rather, Ury notes that different disputes will require different interventions, and that third parties will find themselves using different interventions in different sequences depending on the challenges they face. Ury does offer one clear piece of advice that is appropriate for all third parties, however: "Contain if necessary, resolve if possible, best of all prevent" (2000, p. 113).

Although research findings suggest that negotiators should increase their use of mediation as an informal third-party intervention, further research is necessary. More attention needs to be focused on determining how managers can better identify mediational opportunities, how they can learn to mediate more effectively, and whether the managerial findings of recent research are true for third parties in other conflict situations (e.g., among peers or friends). For instance, a recent study by Shestowsky (2004) found that disputants in civil disputes prefer neutral third parties who facilitate the disputants reaching their own solution over third parties who assume control of the process, outcome, or decision rule. More research is needed to identify which type of informal third parties are preferred and effective in both legal and nonlegal situations and to identify what situational factors drive those outcomes.

Alternative Dispute Resolution Systems

From an organizational standpoint conflict seems inevitable, and a certain type and level of conflict is healthy and advisable. We strongly believe that conflict resolution is best left to the disputants. This chapter has addressed a variety of situations, though, that call for a departure from that standard—such as when disputants are incapable of self-resolution or when the consequences of ongoing, unresolved conflict become damaging. A similar concern exists with many different organizations including businesses, courts, and not-for-profits. Conflict costs for organizations include:

- Wasted time and money, emotional damage, drained energy, and lost opportunities.
- Low levels of disputant satisfaction.
- Damage to necessary relationships.
- The likelihood of conflict spreading and/or recurring (Brett, Goldberg, and Ury, 1990).

The inspiration for alternative dispute resolution (ADR) systems may be traced to a speech by Frank Sander in 1976 (Moffitt, 2006). Addressing legal professionals at the Pound Conference, Sander noted that litigation was only effective for certain types of disputes and mused about the creation of other mechanisms to manage a wide variety of disputes (Moffitt, 2006).

Beginning in the 1980s, many large American organizations introduced ADR systems, and their popularity has increased consistently (Bingham, 1999). Since then, ADR has spread to other countries (see Jackson and Caligari, 2007) and to online dispute resolution (Miller-Moore and Jennings, 2007). We present an interesting example in Box. 19.4. ADR has also been defined by the United States court system as "any process or procedure, other than an adjudication by a presiding judge" (28 U.S.C. 651, 1998) to resolve a dispute. We limit our discussion of ADR systems in this section to the *formal ADR procedures* that organizations adopt to manage their disputes. These procedures have been found to provide several benefits to organizations and individual disputants, including faster and more economical resolution of disputes.[20]

Costantino and Merchant (1996) suggest six broad categories of ADR systems (see Figure 19.7):

1. *Preventive ADR systems* are those that companies adopt to prevent disputes. For example, companies can build clauses into contracts so that any dispute automatically goes to ADR; the company can also specify ways for parties to meet and problem-solve if disputes occur.

BOX 19.4   Peers Decide Co-worker's Fate

A waitress in a Red Lobster restaurant was accused of stealing a guest comment card from the comment card box at the restaurant where she worked. The comment card complained that the prime rib was "rare" and their waitress had been "uncooperative." Ms. Hatton, a 19-year veteran of the restaurant, said she intended to show the comment card to her boss, not to steal it. But because the boss discovered the card missing when the customers verbally complained as well, she fired Ms. Hatton. In Ms. Hatton's words, being fired felt like "a knife going through me."

Normally, workers who feel that they have been unjustly treated will take legal action and sue the restaurant. But Red Lobster is one of a growing number of employers who permit fired or disciplined workers to appeal to a peer review panel of co-workers, who can hear testimony, overturn management decisions, and even award damages. So a general manager, an assistant manager, a server, a hostess, and a bartender, all of whom worked for other Red Lobster restaurants, met to decide Ms. Hatton's fate. And Ms. Hatton enthusiastically chose the peer review procedure because she said it was a lot cheaper and she felt better being judged by people who knew how things work in a small restaurant. The panel interviewed the general manager, Ms. Hatton, and the hostess, reconstructing the events that occurred and what the parties had said and done that day. After an hour and a half of deliberation, they unanimously restored Ms. Hatton's job. They said she had done all she could in trying to placate the unhappy customers and that the unofficial policy against reading the contents of a comment card box had not been enforced at the restaurant. But because the policy had been violated, they decided to punish Ms. Hatton by not granting her the three weeks of lost wages she also sought. The waitress was happy with the decision, the restaurant counsel said that the panel had made the right choice, and the restaurant manager was cooperative and helpful when Ms. Hatton returned to her job.

Darden Industries, the company that owns the Red Lobster chain, adopted peer reviews in 1994. In four years, the company estimates that it saved $1 million in legal fees set aside for handling employee disputes. They said about 100 cases per year went to peer review. The program has also been credited with reducing racial tension between workers and customers.

Source: Adapted from Margaret A. Jacobs, "Red Lobster Tale: Peers Decide Fired Waitress's Fate," *The Wall Street Journal,* January 20, 1998, pp. B1, B6.

2. *Negotiated ADR systems* are mechanisms that allow the parties to resolve their own disputes without the help of any third party, using the negotiation processes we discussed earlier in this book.

3. *Facilitated ADR systems* provide a third-party neutral (an ombudsperson) who assists the parties in negotiating a resolution. An ombudsperson is like a mediator but frequently takes a strong advocacy position on behalf of weaker parties to ensure they are heard.

4. *Fact-finding ADR systems* use the technical expertise of third parties to determine the facts in a specific situation and how the facts should be interpreted. The parties usually agree in advance about whether they are going to abide by the information or conclusion provided by the fact-finder.

5. *Advisory ADR systems* use the expertise of a third party to determine what the resolution would likely be if the dispute went to arbitration, court, and so on. In this approach, each party can get a realistic idea of how strong the other's case is and what

FIGURE 19.7 | Dynamics of ADR Techniques

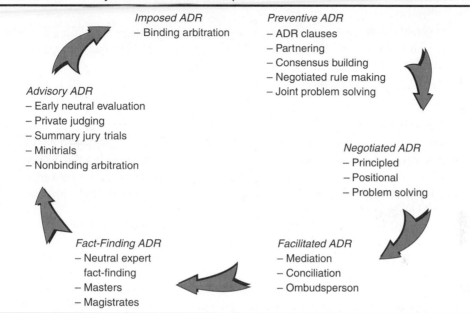

Imposed ADR
 – Binding arbitration

Preventive ADR
 – ADR clauses
 – Partnering
 – Consensus building
 – Negotiated rule making
 – Joint problem solving

Advisory ADR
 – Early neutral evaluation
 – Private judging
 – Summary jury trials
 – Minitrials
 – Nonbinding arbitration

Negotiated ADR
 – Principled
 – Positional
 – Problem solving

Fact-Finding ADR
 – Neutral expert
   fact-finding
 – Masters
 – Magistrates

Facilitated ADR
 – Mediation
 – Conciliation
 – Ombudsperson

Source: From C. A. Costantino and C. S. Merchant, *Designing Conflict Management Systems* (San Francisco: Jossey-Bass, 1996), p. 38.

the arbitrator or judge might do, without having to pay the full cost of that process or actually live with the outcome.

6. *Imposed ADR systems* are those in which the third party makes a binding decision that the parties must live with. Binding arbitration is the most common form of imposed ADR.

The growth of alternative dispute resolution systems over the past 30 years has been remarkable. The good news is that many companies have learned to use ADR effectively and that they are reaping the benefits of the process: an immense savings of time and money and relationships that are not destroyed and may in fact be improved by the process (e.g., see Bourdeaux, O'Leary, and Thorburgh, 2001). What makes ADR effective is the commitment of the company to make it work as an alternative to litigation with employees, customers, suppliers, regulators, and so on. The bad news is that many systems that start out as well-intended efforts to handle employee conflict are poorly designed and poorly operated, often mutating "into a private judicial system that looks and costs like the litigation it's supposed to prevent" (p. 120).

In addition, some professionals have expressed concerns about unequal access to ADR, the lack of diversity of ADR professionals, and the uneven ability of ADR professionals (Hoffman, 2006). It is also clear that there are numerous types of ADR systems, and the design of the overall system is a critical aspect of its effectiveness (Bendersky, 2003, 2007).

Carver and Vondra (1994) identify the following factors that can undermine ADR systems:

- The belief that winning is the only thing that matters, rather than settling disputes (or, conversely, some people use ADR only when they believe that they cannot win in court).
- The perception of ADR as an alternative to litigation, rather than the preferred alternative.
- The perception that ADR is nothing more than litigation in disguise.

There are several key factors that should drive the design of an effective dispute resolution system.[21] One is to ensure that the parties understand their choices before they begin using a particular procedure, that disputants understand the chosen procedure well, and that they try low-cost options first. Second, it appears that users may need to be involved in the design of alternative dispute resolution systems in order for them to be effective (Carter, 1999). A third factor in ADR success is to appoint, train, and support people (e.g., ombudsmen) to advise and assist disputants in dispute resolution (Gadlin, 2000; Stieber, 2000). An ombudsman is typically charged with being "a confidential and informed information resource, communications channel, complaint-handler, and a person who helps an organization work for change" (Rowe, 1995, p. 103). Ombudsmen traditionally are generators of options, working in strict confidentiality to assist disputants by serving as "mediators, counselors, and third-party interveners" (Rowe, 1995, p. 105). Finally, McEwen (1999) suggests that the way to improve alternative dispute resolution systems is through systematic research and suggests several directions that this research should take.

Should the organization decide to take a more expansive approach, Brett, Goldberg, and Ury (1990) suggest following key principles in designing and operating such a system:

1. Consult before disputing, and give feedback after (i.e., attempt to air issues and decisions that are potential conflict creators and make sure that the lessons learned in handling the dispute are recorded and reported).
2. Keep the focus on interests, not positions or personalities (per Fisher, Ury, and Patton, 1991).
3. Build in "loop-backs" to disputants (i.e., make sure the disputing process is informed by the lessons learned through system operations).
4. Develop and use cost-efficient mechanisms for protection of rights and for restoring power imbalances.
5. Arrange and pursue remedies in a cost-efficient manner by using and exhausting low-cost remedies before trying higher-cost approaches.
6. Provide disputants with the necessary skills, resources, and motivation to use the system easily and constructively.
7. Work with all concerned parties to make the system design viable and valuable.

Lynch (2001) suggests that ADR systems need to be evaluated differently than conflict managed on a case-by-case basis. According to Lynch, healthy ADR systems share five features across organizations: (1) they are *all-encompassing,* so they are available for use by all people and for all types of problems; (2) there is a *conflict competent culture,* with a positive atmosphere where conflict can be surfaced and managed safely; (3) there are *multiple access points* to the system with knowledgeable people to support it; (4) there are *options and choices* that allow disputants access to coaches and mediators if they choose to involve them; and (5) *support structures* such as support from top management and educational programs that institutionalize the ADR system as well as provide safeguards.

Chapter Summary

When negotiators are unable to reach an agreement or resolve a conflict, a third-party intervention may help. In this chapter, we reviewed three formal types of third-party intervention: arbitration, mediation, and process consultation. Each of these types has its strengths and weaknesses as an intervention and approach to dispute resolution. The styles differ in the degree to which the disputants surrender control to the third party over the negotiation process and/or the outcome. Arbitration involves a structured process in which disputing parties have relatively free rein to present their stories, while the arbitrators decide the outcome, often imposing a resolution on the disputants. Mediators exert a great deal of control over how the parties interact, both in terms of their physical presence and their communication; although mediators may point the parties toward possible resolutions through suggestions and guidance, they typically do not choose the resolution for the disputants. Finally, process consultants are less involved in the disputed issues than arbitrators or mediators, but they are heavily involved in helping to establish or enhance communication and dispute resolution skills that the parties can then apply to the immediate dispute and future communication.

Other third-party roles and types, including informal versions of the three formal approaches we addressed, are increasingly being studied systematically to determine their application and impact. Organizational support for alternative dispute resolution procedures promises great dividends for organizations willing to invest the necessary resources in system design and operations. A great deal remains to be done to determine the mastery and propriety of particular informal third-party styles and techniques for various types of conflict and to achieve a better understanding of how third parties—individually and organizationally—can effectively assist in resolving disputes.

Finally, we briefly reviewed some of the emerging work on alternative dispute resolution (ADR). ADR encompasses a variety of techniques that employers adopt to handle workplace disputes and avoid litigation with employees and with others outside the organization. ADR can include not only mediation and arbitration but also several hybrid methods that use neutral third parties to hear employees' concerns. The purpose of ADR is to find dispute resolution processes that reduce costs, minimize lawsuits and court cases, and allow organizations to handle employee conflicts efficiently and effectively.

Endnotes

[1] For a broad treatment of these and related issues, see Lewicki, Weiss, and Lewin (1992); Mayer (2000); Singer (1990, 1994); and Ury (2000).

[2] See Bingham, Chesmore, Moon, and Napoli (2000); Carnevale and Pruitt (1992); Moore (1996); Nabatchi and Bingham (2001); Sulzner (2003); and Ury, Brett, and Goldberg (1988).

[3] We have described the three most frequent third-party roles, but several authors have suggested numerous other formal roles (for instance, see Diehl, Druckman, and Wall, 1998; and Ury, 2000). Interested readers should consult the references cited throughout this chapter to explore the research and practice on third parties in greater detail.

[4] Further discussion of dispute resolution and the Internet may be found in Clark (2003), Hagewood (2001), and Katsh and Rifkin (2001).

[5] For instance, see Brett and Goldberg (1983), Devinatz and Budd (1997), Kanowitz (1985), and Kochan (1980).

[6] See Grigsby and Bigoness (1982), Kritikos (2006), Long and Feuille (1974), Neale and Bazerman (1983), and Starke and Notz (1981).

[7] See Bush (1996); Carnevale and Pruitt (1992); Kochan (1980); Kochan and Jick (1978); Lewicki, Weiss, and Lewin (1992); Wall and Lynn (1993), and Wall, Stark, and Standifer (2001).

[8] See Drayton (1981), Reich (1981), and Susskind and Cruikshank (1987).

[9] See Kriesberg (1991), Rubin (1981), and Zartman (1989).

[10] Further discussion of ripeness can be found in Coleman (2000a), Eliasson (2002), and Greig (2001).

[11] See Carnevale and Conlon (1990), Conlon and Ross (1993), Kaufman and Duncan (1992), Smith (1985), Touval and Zartman (1985), and van de Vliert (1992).

[12] A complete framework for understanding mediation must take into consideration a very large number of factors, and a complete understanding of the role and impact of these factors is beyond the scope of this book. For more detail, see Barrett (1999); Herrman, Hollett, Gale, and Foster (2001); and Wall and Lynn (1993).

[13] See Folberg and Taylor (1984), Holaday (2002), Kochan (1980), Kressel (1972), Lovenheim (1989), Moore (1996), Poitras and Bowen (2002), Saunders (2003), and Wall (1981).

[14] Poitras, Bowen, and Byrne's (2002) model applies to negotiations that have reached impasse or that have yet to start; "prenegotiation" is similar to the early stages of mediation in Moore's model.

[15] See Carnevale and Conlon (1988), Chaudrhy and Ross (1989), and Harris and Carnevale (1990).

[16] See Donohue (1989), Hiltrop (1989), and Lim and Carnevale (1990).

[17] See Benjamin and Levi (1979); Boehringer, Zeruolis, Bayley and Boehringer (1974); Brown (1977); Cohen, Kelman, Miller, and Smith (1977); Hill (1982); and Lewicki and Alderfer (1973).

[18] See Grigsby (1981), Grigsby and Bigoness (1982), Ross and Conlon (2000), and Starke and Notz (1981).

[19] Elangovan's model is based on a model of managerial decision making developed by Vroom and Yetton (1973).

[20] For discussion of the benefits of ADR systems see Bingham (1999), Bingham and Napoli (2001), Loomis (2001), and Lynch (2001). For discussion about ADR design issues see Bordwin (1999) and Levy (1999).

[21] For further discussion see Brett, Goldberg, and Ury (1990); Costantino and Merchant (1996); Lynch (2001); Sheppard, Lewicki, and Minton (1992); and Ury, Brett, and Goldberg (1988).

CHAPTER 20

Best Practices in Negotiations

Objectives

1. Appreciate the extent to which negotiation is both an art and science.
2. Explore the 10 Best Practices that all negotiators can follow to achieve a successful negotiation.

Negotiation is an integral part of daily life and the opportunities to negotiate surround us. While some people may look like born negotiators, negotiation is fundamentally a skill involving analysis and communication that everyone can learn. The purpose of this book is to provide students of negotiation with an overview of the field of negotiation, perspective on the breadth and depth of the subprocesses of negotiation, and an appreciation for the art and science of negotiation. In this final chapter we reflect on negotiation at a broad level by providing 10 best practices for negotiators who wish to continue to improve their negotiation skills (see Table 20.1).

1. Be Prepared

We cannot overemphasize the importance of preparation, and we strongly encourage all negotiators to prepare properly for their negotiations (see Chapter 4). Preparation does not have to be a time-consuming or arduous activity, but it should be right at the top of the best practices list of every negotiator. Negotiators who are better prepared have numerous

TABLE 20.1 | Ten Best Practices for Negotiators

1.	Be prepared.
2.	Diagnose the fundamental structure of the negotiation.
3.	Work the BATNA.
4.	Be willing to walk away.
5.	Master paradoxes.
6.	Remember the intangibles.
7.	Actively manage coalitions.
8.	Savor and protect your reputation.
9.	Remember that rationality and fairness are relative.
10.	Continue to learn from the experience.

advantages, including the ability to analyze the other party's offers more effectively and efficiently, to understand the nuances of the concession-making process, and to achieve their negotiation goals. Preparation should occur *before* the negotiation begins so that the time spent negotiating is more productive. Good preparation means understanding one's own goals and interests as well as possible and being able to articulate them to the other party skillfully. It also includes being ready to understand the other party's communication in order to find an agreement that meets the needs of both parties. Few negotiations are going to conclude successfully without both parties achieving at least some of their goals, and solid work up front to identify your needs and to understand the needs of the other party is a critical step to increasing the odds of success.

Good preparation also means setting aspirations for negotiation outcomes that are high but achievable. Negotiators who set their sights too low are virtually guaranteed to reach an agreement that is suboptimal, while those who set them too high are more likely to stalemate and end the negotiation in frustration. Negotiators also need to plan their opening statements and positions carefully so they are especially well prepared at the start of negotiations. It is important to avoid preplanning the complete negotiation sequence, however, because while negotiations do follow broad stages, they also ebb and flow at irregular rates. Overplanning the tactics for each negotiation stage in advance of the negotiation is not a good use of preparation time. It is far better that negotiators prepare by understanding their own strengths and weaknesses, their needs and interests, the situation, and the other party as well as possible so that they can adjust promptly and effectively as the negotiation proceeds.

Finally, it is important to recognize and prepare for the effects of the broader context of the negotiation, such as the nature of existing relationships, the presence of audiences, opportunities for forming coalitions, and negotiation within or between teams (see Part 3 of this book) as well as for the effects of cross-cultural differences (see Chapter 16). Negotiators need to consider how these broad contextual factors will influence the negotiation.

2.   Diagnose the Fundamental Structure of the Negotiation

Negotiators should make a conscious decision about whether they are facing a fundamentally distributive negotiation, an integrative negotiation, or a blend of the two, and choose their strategies and tactics accordingly. Using strategies and tactics that are mismatched will lead to suboptimal negotiation outcomes. For instance, using overly distributive tactics in a fundamentally integrative situation will likely result in reaching agreements that leave integrative potential untapped because negotiators tend not to readily share the information needed to succeed in integrative negotiations when confronted with distributive tactics. In these situations, money and opportunity are often left on the table.

Similarly, using integrative tactics in a distributive situation may not lead to optimal outcomes either. For instance, one of the authors of this book was recently shopping for a new car and the salesman spent a great deal of time and effort asking questions about the author's family and assuring him that he was working hard to get the highest possible value for his trade-in. Unfortunately, the salesman met the author's requests for clarification about the list price of the car and information about recently advertised manufacturer incentives with silence or by changing the topic of conversation. This was a purely distributive situation for the author, who was not fooled by the salesman's attempt to bargain "integratively." The author bought a car from a different dealer who was able to provide the requested information in a straightforward manner—and whose price was $1,500 lower than the first dealer for the same car!

Negotiators also need to remember that many negotiations will consist of a blend of integrative and distributive elements and that there will be distributive and integrative phases to these negotiations. It is especially important to be careful when transitioning between these phases within the broader negotiation because missteps in these transitions can confuse the other party and lead to impasse.

Finally, there are also times when accommodation, avoidance, and compromise may be appropriate strategies (see Chapter 1). Strong negotiators will identify these situations and adopt appropriate strategies and tactics.

3. Identify and Work the BATNA

One of the most important sources of power in a negotiation is the alternatives available to a negotiator if an agreement is not reached. One alternative, the best alternative to a negotiated agreement (BATNA), is especially important because this is the option that likely will be chosen should an agreement not be reached. Negotiators need to be vigilant about their BATNA. They need to know what their BATNA is relative to a possible agreement and consciously work to improve the BATNA so as to improve the deal. Negotiators without a strong BATNA may find it difficult to achieve a good agreement because the other party may try to push them aggressively, and hence they may be forced to accept a settlement that is later seen as unsatisfying.

For instance, purchasers who need to buy items from sole suppliers are acutely aware of how the lack of a positive BATNA makes it difficult to achieve positive negotiation outcomes. Even in this situation, however, negotiators can work to improve their BATNA in the long term. For instance, organizations in a sole-supplier relationship have often vertically integrated their production and started to build comparable components inside the company, or they have redesigned their products so they are less vulnerable to the sole supplier. These are clearly long-term options and would not be available in a current negotiation. However, it may be possible to refer to these plans when negotiating with a sole supplier in order to remind them that you will not be dependent forever.

Negotiators also need to be aware of the other negotiator's BATNA and to identify how it compares to what you are offering. Negotiators have more power in a negotiation when their potential terms of agreement are significantly better than what the other negotiator can obtain with his or her BATNA. On the other hand, when the difference between your terms and the other negotiator's BATNA is small, then negotiators have less room to maneuver. There are three things negotiators should do with respect to the other negotiator's BATNA: (1) monitor it carefully in order to understand and retain your competitive advantage over the other negotiator's alternatives; (2) remind the other negotiator of the advantages your offer has relative to her BATNA; and (3) in a subtle way, suggest that the other negotiator's BATNA may not be as strong as he or she thinks it is (this can be done in a positive way by stressing your strengths or in a negative way by highlighting competitors' weaknesses).

4.   Be Willing to Walk Away

The goal of most negotiations is achieving a valued outcome, not reaching an agreement *per se.* Strong negotiators remember this and are willing to walk away from a negotiation when no agreement is better than a poor agreement or when the process is so offensive that the deal isn't worth the work. While this advice sounds easy enough to take in principle, in practice, negotiators can become so focused on reaching an agreement that they lose sight of the real goal, which is to reach a good outcome (and not necessarily an agreement). Negotiators can ensure that they don't take their eyes off the goal by making regular comparisons with the targets they set during the planning stage and by comparing their progress during their negotiation against their walkaway and BATNA. While negotiators are often optimistic about goal achievement at the outset, they may need to reevaluate these goals during the negotiation. It is important to continue to compare progress in the current negotiation with the target, walkaway, and BATNA and to be willing to walk away from the current negotiation if their walkaway or BATNA becomes the truly better choice.

Even in the absence of a good BATNA, negotiators should have a clear walkaway point in mind where they will halt negotiations. Sometimes it is helpful if the walkaway is written down or communicated to others so that negotiators can be reminded during difficult negotiations. When in team negotiations, it is important to have a team member monitor the walkaway point and be responsible for stopping the negotiation if it appears that a final settlement is close to this point.

5.   Master the Key Paradoxes of Negotiation

Excellent negotiators understand that negotiation embodies a set of paradoxes—seemingly contradictory elements that actually occur together. We discuss five common paradoxes that negotiators face. The challenge for negotiators in handling these paradoxes is to strive for *balance* in these situations. There is a natural tension in choosing between one or the other alternative in the paradox, but the best way to manage paradox is to achieve a balance between the opposing forces. Strong negotiators know how to manage this tension.

Claiming Value versus Creating Value

All negotiations have a value-*claiming* stage, where parties decide who gets how much of what, but many negotiations also have a value-*creation* stage, where parties work together to expand the resources under negotiation. The skills and strategies appropriate to each stage are quite different; in general terms, distributive skills are called for in the value-claiming stage and integrative skills are useful in value creation. Typically, the value-creation stage will precede the value-claiming stage, and a challenge for negotiators is to balance the emphasis on the two stages and the transition from creating to claiming value. There is no signpost to mark this transition, however, and negotiators need to manage it tactfully to avoid undermining the open brainstorming and option-inventing relationship that has developed during value creation. One approach to manage this transition is to publicly label it. For instance, negotiators could say something like, "It looks like we have a good foundation of ideas and alternatives to work from. How can we move on to decide what is a fair distribution of the expected outcomes?" In addition, research shows that most negotiators are overly biased toward thinking that a negotiation is more about claiming value rather than creating value, so managing this paradox will likely require an overemphasis on discussing the creating value dynamics.

Sticking by Your Principles versus Being Resilient to the Flow

The pace and flow of negotiations can move from an intense haggle over financial issues to an equally intense debate over deeply held principles about what is right or fair or just. These transitions often create a second paradox for negotiators. On the one hand, effective negotiation requires flexible thinking and an understanding that an assessment of a situation may need to be adjusted as new information comes to light; achieving any deal will probably require both parties to make concessions. On the other hand, core principles are not something to back away from easily in the service of doing a deal. Effective negotiators are thoughtful about the distinction between issues of principle, where firmness is essential, and other issues where compromise or accommodation are the best route to a mutually acceptable outcome. A complex negotiation may well involve both kinds of issues in the same encounter. And it is not enough for the negotiator to know in his or her own mind that an unwavering commitment on issue X is grounded in a deep personal value or principle; good negotiators know that it is critical to convey that principle to the other party so that he or she will not misread firmness based on principle as hostility or intransigence.

Sticking with the Strategy versus Opportunistic Pursuit of New Options

New information will frequently come to light during a negotiation, and negotiators need to manage the paradox between sticking with their prepared strategy and pursuing a new opportunity that arises during the process. This is a challenging paradox for negotiators to manage because new "opportunities" may in fact be Trojan horses harboring unpleasant surprises. On the other hand, circumstances do change and legitimate one-time, seize-the-moment deals do occur. The challenge for negotiators is to distinguish phantom opportunities from real ones; developing the capacity to recognize the distinction is another hallmark of the experienced negotiator.

Strong preparation is critical to being able to manage the "strategy versus opportunism" paradox. Negotiators who have prepared well for the negotiation and who understand the circumstances are well positioned to make this judgment. We also suggest that negotiators pay close attention to their intuition. If a deal doesn't feel right, if it seems too good to be true, then it probably *is* too good to be true and is not a viable opportunity. If negotiators feel uneasy about the direction the negotiation is taking, then it is best to take a break and consult with others about the circumstances. Often explaining the "opportunity" to a colleague, friend, or constituent will help distinguish real opportunities from Trojan horses.

We are not suggesting that negotiators become overly cautious, however. Frequently, there are genuinely good opportunities that occur during a negotiation, legitimately caused by changes in business strategy, market opportunities, excess inventory, or a short-term cash flow challenge. Negotiators who have prepared well will be able to take full advantage of real opportunities when they arise and reduce the risk presented by Trojan horses.

Honest and Open versus Closed and Opaque

Negotiators face the *dilemma of honesty:* how open and honest should I be with the other party? Negotiators who are completely open and tell the other party everything expose themselves to the risk that the other party will take advantage of them. In fact, research suggests that too much knowledge about the other party's needs can actually lead to suboptimal negotiation outcomes. On the other hand, being completely closed will not only have a negative effect on your reputation (discussed later), but it is also an ineffective negotiation strategy because you don't disclose enough information to create the groundwork for agreement. The challenge of this paradox is deciding how much information to reveal and how much to conceal—both for pragmatic and ethical reasons.

Strong negotiators have considered this paradox and understand their comfort zone, which will likely vary depending on the other party. We suggest that negotiators should remember that negotiation is an ongoing process. As the negotiators make positive progress, they should be building trust and hopefully feeling more comfortable about revealing more information to the other party. That said, there is some information that should probably not be revealed (e.g., the bottom line in a distributive negotiation) regardless of how well the negotiation is progressing.

Trust versus Distrust

As a mirror image of the dilemma of honesty, negotiators also face the *dilemma of trust*: how much to trust what the other party tells them. Negotiators who believe everything the other party tells them make themselves vulnerable to being taken advantage of by the other party. On the other hand, negotiators who do not believe anything the other party tells them will have a very difficult time reaching an agreement. As with the dilemma of honesty, we suggest that negotiators remember that negotiation is a process that evolves over time. First, as we noted, trust can be built by being honest and sharing information with the other side, which hopefully will lead to reciprocal trust and credible disclosure by the other side. Moreover, there will be individual differences in trust. Some negotiators will start off by being more trusting, but become less trusting if information comes to light showing that the other party is not trustworthy. Other negotiators will be more comfortable having the other party earn their trust and will be more skeptical early in negotiations. There is no right or wrong approach to managing this dilemma. Strong negotiators are aware of this dilemma, however, and consciously monitor how they are managing this challenge.

6. Remember the Intangibles

It is important that negotiators remember the intangible factors while negotiating and remain aware of their potential effects. Intangibles frequently affect negotiation in a negative way, and they often operate out of the negotiator's awareness. As noted in Chapter 1, intangibles are deep psychological factors that motivate negotiators and they include winning, avoiding loss, looking tough or strong to others, not looking weak, being fair, and so on. For instance, if the other party is vying with his archrival at the next desk for a promotion, he may be especially difficult when negotiating with you in front of his boss in order to look tough and impress his boss. It is unlikely that the other negotiator will tell you this is what he is doing, and in fact he may not even be aware of it himself. The best way to identify the existence of intangible factors is to try to see what is not there. In other words, if your careful preparation and analysis of the situation reveals no tangible explanation for the other negotiator's behavior—adamant advocacy of a certain point, refusal to yield another one, or behavior that just doesn't make sense—then it is time to start looking for the intangibles driving his behavior.

For example, several years ago one of the authors of this book was helping a friend buy a new car, and the price offered from the dealer was $2,000 less than any other dealer in town. The only catch was that the car had to be sold that day. On the surface this looked like a trick (see "Strategy versus Opportunism"), but there was no obvious tangible factor that explained this special price. The friend had never purchased from the dealer before, the car was new and fully covered by a good warranty, and the friend had price shopped at several dealers and knew this price was substantially lower. As they continued to discuss the potential deal, the salesman became more and more agitated. Sweat was literally falling from his brow. The friend decided to purchase the car, and as soon as he signed, the salesman was simultaneously relieved and excited. He asked for a moment to telephone his wife to share with her some good news. It turned out that the salesman had just won a complicated incentive package offered by the dealer which included a two-week all expenses paid Caribbean vacation for his family of four. The incentive package required that a total of 10 vehicles, one from each category of vehicle at the dealership, be sold in a month. The salesman, who specialized in selling trucks, felt immense pressure when the friend hesitated because he had given the friend a huge discount on a sports car to close the deal.

The intangible factor of trying to win the vacation package explained the salesman's agitated behavior in the preceding example. The buyer learned of this only when the salesman could no longer contain his excitement and shared the good news with his family. Often, negotiators do not learn what intangible factors are influencing the other negotiator unless the other chooses to disclose them. Negotiators can see evidence of their existence, however, by looking for changes in the other negotiator's behavior from one negotiation to another, as well as by gathering information about the other party before negotiation begins. For instance, if you find out that the other party has a new boss that she doesn't like and she is subsequently more difficult to deal with in the negotiation, the intangible of the new boss may be to blame.

There are at least two more ways to discover intangibles that might be affecting the other. One way to surface the other party's intangibles is to ask questions. These questions should try to get the other party to reveal why he or she is sticking so strongly to a given point. It is important to remember that strong emotions and/or values are the root of many intangibles, so surfacing intangibles may result in the discussion of various fears and anxieties. The question-asking process should also be gentle and informal; if the questioning is aggressive, it may only make the other defensive, adding another intangible to the mix and stifling effective negotiations! A second way is to take an observer or listener with you to the negotiation. Listeners may be able to read the other's emotional tone or nonverbal behavior, focus on roadblock issues, or try to take the other's perspective and put themselves in the other's shoes (role reversal). A caucus with this listener may then help refocus the discussion so as to surface the intangibles and develop a new line of questions or offers.

Negotiators also need to remember that intangible factors influence their own behavior (and that it is not uncommon for us to not recognize what is making us angry, defensive, or zealously committed to some idea). Are you being particularly difficult with the other party because he does not respect you, are you trying to teach a subordinate a lesson, or do you want to win this negotiation to look better than another manager? Without passing judgment on the legitimacy of these goals, we strongly urge negotiators to be aware of the effect of intangible factors on their own aspirations and behavior. Often talking to another person—a sympathetic listener—can help the negotiator figure these out. Strong negotiators are aware of how both tangible and intangible factors influence negotiation, and they weigh both factors when evaluating a negotiation outcome.

7.   Actively Manage Coalitions

Coalitions can have very significant effects on the negotiation process and outcome. Negotiators should recognize three types of coalitions and their potential effects: (1) coalitions against you; (2) coalitions that support you; and (3) loose, undefined coalitions that may materialize either for or against you. Strong negotiators assess the presence and strength of coalitions and work to capture the strength of the coalition for their benefit. If this is not possible, negotiators need to work to prevent the other party from capturing a loose coalition for their purposes. When negotiators are part of a coalition, communicating with the coalition is critical to ensuring that the power of the coalition is aligned with their goals. Similarly, negotiators who are agents or representatives of a coalition must take special care to manage this process (see Chapter 11).

Successfully concluding negotiations when a coalition is aligned against a negotiator is an extremely challenging task. It is important to recognize when coalitions are aligned against you and to work consciously to counter their influence. Frequently this will involve a divide-and-conquer strategy, where negotiators try to increase dissent within the coalition by searching for ways to breed instability.

Coalitions occur in many formal negotiations, such as environmental assessments and reaching policy decisions in an industry association. Coalitions may also have a strong influence in less formal settings, such as work teams and families, where different subgroups of people may not have the same interests. Managing coalitions is especially important when negotiators need to rely on other people to implement an agreement. It may be possible for negotiators to forge an agreement when the majority of people influenced are not in favor, but implementing the outcomes of that agreement will be very challenging. Strong negotiators need to monitor and manage coalitions proactively, and while this may take considerable time throughout the negotiation process, it will likely lead to large payoffs at the implementation stage.

8.   Savor and Protect Your Reputation

Reputations are like eggs—fragile, important to build, easy to break, and very hard to rebuild once broken. Reputations travel fast, and people often know more about you than you think that they do. Starting negotiations with a positive reputation is essential, and negotiators should be vigilant in protecting their reputations. Negotiators who have a reputation for breaking their word and not negotiating honestly will have a much more difficult time negotiating in the future than those who have a reputation for being honest and fair. Consider the following contrasting reputations: "tough but fair" versus "tough and underhanded." Negotiators prepare differently for others with these contrasting reputations. Negotiating with a tough but fair negotiator means preparing for potentially difficult negotiations while being aware that the other party will push hard for her perspective but will also be rational and fair in her behavior. Negotiating with a tough but underhanded other party means that negotiators will need to verify what the other says, be vigilant for dirty tricks, and be more guarded about sharing information.

How are you perceived as a negotiator? What is your reputation with others at this point? What reputation would you like to have? Think about the negotiators you respect the most and their reputation. What is it about their behavior that you admire? Also think about the negotiators who have a bad reputation. What would it take for them to change your image of them?

Rather than leaving reputation to chance, negotiators can work to shape and enhance their reputation by acting in a consistent and fair manner. Consistency provides the other party with a clear set of predictable expectations about how you will behave, which leads to a stable reputation. Fairness sends the message that you are principled and reasonable. Strong negotiators also periodically seek feedback from others about the way they are perceived and use that information to strengthen their credibility and trustworthiness in the marketplace.

9. Remember That Rationality and Fairness Are Relative

Research on negotiator perception and cognition is quite clear (Chapter 5): people tend to view the world in a self-serving manner and define the rational thing to do or a fair outcome or process in a way that benefits themselves. First, negotiators need to be aware of this tendency in both themselves and the other party. Negotiators can do three things to manage these perceptions proactively. First, they can question their own perceptions of fairness and ground them in clear principles. Second, they can find external benchmarks and examples that suggest fair outcomes. Finally, negotiators can illuminate definitions of fairness held by the other party and engage in a dialogue to reach consensus on which standards of fairness apply in a given situation.

Moreover, negotiators are often in the position to collectively define what is right or fair as a part of the negotiation process. In most situations, neither side holds the keys to what is absolutely right, rational, or fair. Reasonable people can disagree, and often the most important outcome that negotiators can achieve is a common, agreed-upon perspective, definition of the facts, agreement on the right way to see a problem, or standard for determining what is a fair outcome or process. Be prepared to negotiate these principles as strongly as you prepare for a discussion of the issues.

10. Continue to Learn from Your Experience

Negotiation epitomizes lifelong learning. The best negotiators continue to learn from the experience—they know there are so many different variables and nuances when negotiating that no two negotiations are identical. These differences mean that for negotiators to remain sharp, they need to continue to practice the art and science of negotiation regularly. In addition, the best negotiators take a moment to analyze each negotiation after it has concluded, to review what happened and what they learned. We recommend a three-step process:

- Plan a personal reflection time after each negotiation.
- Periodically take a lesson from a trainer or coach.
- Keep a personal diary on strengths and weaknesses and develop a plan to work on weaknesses.

This analysis does not have to be extensive or time consuming. It should happen after every important negotiation, however, and it should focus on *what* and *why* questions: what happened during this negotiation, why did it occur, and what can I learn? Negotiators who take the time to pause and reflect on their negotiations will find that they continue to refine their skills and that they remain sharp and focused for their future negotiations.

Moreover, even the best athletes—in almost any sport—have one or more coaches on their staff and stop to take a lesson, when necessary. Negotiators have access to seminars to enhance their skills, books to read, and coaches who can help refine their skills. This book should be seen as one step along the way to sharpening and refining your negotiation skills, and we encourage you to continue to learn about the art and science of negotiation. We wish you the best of luck in all of your future negotiations!

Aaronson, K. (1989). *Selling on the fast track.* New York: Putnam.

Abu-Nimer, M. (1996). Conflict resolution approaches: Western and Middle Eastern lessons and possibilities. *American Journal of Economics and Sociology, 55,* 35–52.

Acuff, F. L. (1993). *How to negotiate anything with anyone anywhere around the world.* New York: AMACOM.

Adachi, Y. (1998). The effects of semantic difference on cross-cultural business negotiation: A Japanese and American case study. *Journal of Language for International Business, 9,* 43–52.

Adair, W. (2002). *Reciprocal information sharing and negotiation outcomes in East/West negotiations.* Working paper, Dispute Resolution Research Center, Northwestern University, Evanston, IL.

Adair, W. (2003). Integrative sequences and outcome in same- and mixed-culture negotiations. *International Journal of Conflict Management, 14* (314), 273–96.

Adair, W., Brett, J., Lempereur, A., Okumura, T., Shikhirev, P., Tinsley, C., et al. (2004). Culture and negotiation strategy. *Negotiation Journal, 20,* 87–110.

Adair, W., Kopelman, S., Gillespie, J., Brett, J. M., & Okumura, T. (1998). *Cultural compatibility in the U.S./Israeli negotiations: Implications for joint gains.* DRRC working paper. Evanston, IL: Northwestern University.

Adair, W. L., & Brett, J. M. (2005). The negotiation dance: Time, culture, and behavioral sequences in negotiation. *Organization Science, 16* (1), 33–51.

Adair, W. L., Okumura, T., & Brett, J. M. (2001). Negotiation behavior when cultures collide: The United States and Japan. *Journal of Applied Psychology, 86,* 371–85.

Adair, W. L., Weingart, L., & Brett, J. (2007). The timing and function of offers in U.S. and Japanese negotiations. *Journal of Applied Psychology, 92,* 1056–68.

Adler, N. J. (2002). *International dimensions of organizational behavior* (4th ed.). Cincinnati, OH: South-Western.

Adler, N. J., Brahm, R., & Graham, J. L. (1992). Strategy implementation: A comparison of face-to-face negotiations in the People's Republic of China and the United States. *Strategic Management Journal, 13,* 449–66.

Adler, N. J., & Graham, J. L. (1987). Business negotiations: Canadians are not just like Americans. *Canadian Journal of Administrative Sciences, 4,* 211–38.

Adler, N. J., & Graham, J. L. (1989). Cross-cultural interaction: The international comparison fallacy? *Journal of International Business Studies, 20,* 515–37.

Adler, N. J., Graham, J. L., & Schwarz, T. (1987). Business negotiations in Canada, Mexico, and the United States. *Journal of Business Research, 15,* 411–29.

Adler, R., Rosen, B., & Silverstein, E. (1996). Thrust and parry: The art of tough negotiating. *Training and Development, 50,* 42–48.

Adler, R. S. (2007). Negotiating with liars. *MIT Sloan Management Review, 48* (4), 69–74.

Adler, R. S., Rosen, B., & Silverstein, E. M. (1998). Emotions in negotiation: How to manage fear and anger. *Negotiation Journal, 14,* 161–79.

Adorno, T. W., Frenkl-Brunswick, E., Levinson, D. J., & Sanford, R. N. (1950). *The Authoritarian Personality.* New York: HarperCollins.

Agha, H., & Malley, R. (2002). The last negotiation: How to end the Middle East peace process. *Foreign Affairs, 81,* 10–18.

Agnvall, E. (2007). Women and negotiation. *HRMagazine, 52* (12), 69–73.

Alberts, J. K., Heisterkamp, B. L., & McPhee, R. M. (2005). Disputant perceptions of and satisfaction with a community mediation program. *The International Journal of Conflict Management, 16* (3), 218–44.

Albin, C. (1993). The role of fairness in negotiation. *Negotiation Journal, 9,* 223–43.

Alderfer, C. P. (1977). Group and intergroup relations. In J. R. Hackman & J. L. Suttle (Eds.), *Improving life at work: Behavioral science approaches to organizational change* (pp. 227–96). Santa Monica, CA: Goodyear.

Alexander, J. F., Schul, P. L., & Babakus, E. (1991). Analyzing interpersonal communications in industrial marketing negotiations. *Journal of the Academy of Marketing Science, 19,* 129–39.

Alexander, J. F., Schul, P. L., & McCorkle, D. E. (1994). An assessment of selected relationships in a model of the industrial marketing negotiation process. *Journal of Personal Selling & Sales Management, 14* (3), 25–41.

Al-Khatib, J. A., Vollmers, S. M., & Liu, Y. (2007). Business-to-business negotiating in China: The role of morality. *Journal of Business & Industrial Marketing, 22* (2), 84–96.

565

Allhoff, F. (2003). Business bluffing reconsidered. *Journal of Business Ethics, 45,* 283–89.

Allred, K. G. (1999). Anger-driven retaliation: Toward an understanding of impassioned conflict in organizations. In R. J. Bies, R. J. Lewicki, & B. H. Sheppard (Eds.), *Research on negotiation in organizations* (Vol. 7, pp. 27–58), Stanford, CT: JAI Press.

Allred, K. G., Mallozzi, J. S., Matsui, F., & Raia, C. P. (1997). The influence of anger and compassion on negotiation performance. *Organizational Behavior and Human Decision Processes, 70,* 175–87.

Alon, I., & Brett, J. M. (2007). Perceptions of time and their impact on negotiations in the Arabic-speaking Islamic world. *Negotiation Journal, 23,* 55–73.

Amabile, T. M., Hadley, C. N., & Kramer, S. J. (2002). Creativity under the gun. *Harvard Business Review,* August, 52–61.

Ambrose, M. L., & Arnaud, A. (2005). Are procedural justice and distributive justice conceptually distinct? In J. Greenberg & J. Colquitt (Eds.), *Handbook of organizational justice* (pp. 59–85). Mahwah, NJ: Lawrence Erlbaum Associates.

Ancona, D., & Caldwell, D. F. (1988). Beyond task and maintenance: External roles in groups. *Group and Organizational Studies, 13,* 468–91.

Anderson, C., & Thompson, L. L. (2004). Affect from the top down: How powerful individuals' positive affect shapes negotiations. *Organizational Behavior and Human Decision Processes, 95,* 125–39.

Anderson, J. C., & Kochan, T. (1977). Impasse procedures in the Canadian Federal Service. *Industrial & Labor Relations Review, 30,* 283–301.

Anton, R. J. (1990). Drawing the line: An exploratory test of ethical behavior in negotiations. *International Journal of Conflict Management, 1,* 265–80.

Antonioni, D. (1994). The effects of feedback accountability on upward appraisal ratings. *Personnel Psychology, 47,* 249–56.

Aquino, K. (1998). The effects of ethical climate and the availability of alternatives on the use of deception during negotiations. *International Journal of Conflict Management, 9* (3), 195–217.

Aquino, K., & Becker, T. E. (2005). Lying in negotiation: How individual and situational factors influence the use of neutralization strategies. *Journal of Organizational Behavior, 26,* 661–79.

Argyris, C., & Schön, D. (1996). *Organizational learning II: Theory, method, and practice.* Reading, MA: Addison-Wesley Longman.

Arino, A., Abramov, M., Rykounina, I., & Vila, J. (1997). Partner selection and trust building in west European–Russian joint ventures. *International Studies of Management and Organization, 27,* 19–37.

Armilla, J. (2001). *Negotiate with feng shui.* St. Paul, MN: Llewellyn Publications.

Arnold, J., & Carnevale, P. (1997). Preferences for dispute resolution procedures as a function of intentionality, consequences, expected future interaction, and power. *Journal of Applied Psychology, 27,* 371–98.

Arnold, J. A. (2000). Mediator insight: Disputants' perceptions of third parties' knowledge and its effect on mediated negotiation. *International Journal of Conflict Management, 11,* 318–36.

Arnold, J. A., & O'Connor, K. M. (1999). Ombudspersons or peers? The effect of third-party expertise and recommendations on negotiation. *Journal of Applied Psychology, 84,* 776–85.

Arnold, J. A., & O'Connor, K. M. (2006). How negotiator self-efficacy drives decisions to pursue mediation. *Journal of Applied Social Psychology, 36,* 2649–69.

Arunachalam, V., & Dilla, W. N. (1995). Judgment accuracy and outcomes in negotiation: A causal modeling analysis of decision-aiding effects. *Organizational Behavior and Human Decision Processes, 61,* 289–304.

Arunachalam, V., Wall, J. A., Jr., & Chan, C. (1998). Hong Kong versus U.S. negotiations: Effects of culture, alternatives, outcome scales, and mediation. *Journal of Applied Social Psychology, 28,* 1219–44.

Asherman, I. G., & Asherman, S. V. (1990). *The negotiation sourcebook.* Amherst, MA: Human Resource Development Press.

Ashkanasy, N. M., & Daus, C. S. (2005). Rumors of the death of emotional intelligence in organizational behavior are vastly exaggerated. *Journal of Organizational Behavior, 26,* 441–52.

Athos, A. G., & Gabarro, J. J. (1978). *Interpersonal behavior: Communication and understanding in relationships.* Englewood Cliffs, NJ: Prentice Hall.

Avruch, K. (2000). Culture and negotiation pedagogy. *Negotiation Journal, 16,* 339–46.

Axtell, R. E. (1990). *Do's and taboos of hosting international visitors.* New York: John Wiley and Sons.

Axtell, R. E. (1991). *Gestures: The do's and taboos of body language around the world.* New York: John Wiley and Sons.

Axtell, R. E. (1993). *Do's and taboos around the world* (3rd ed.). New York: John Wiley and Sons.

Ayres, I. (1991). Fair driving: Gender and race discrimination in retail car negotiations. *Harvard Law Review, 104,* 817–72.

Ayres, I., & Siegelman, P. (1995). Race and gender discrimination in bargaining for a new car. *American Economic Review, 85,* 304–21.

Babcock, L., Gelfand, M., Small, D., & Stayn, H. (2006). Gender differences in the propensity to initiate negotiations. In D. De Cremer, M. Zeelenberg, & J. K. Murnighan (Eds.), *Social psychology and economics* (pp. 239–62). Mahwah, NJ: Erlbaum.

Babcock, L., & Laschever, S. (2003). *Women don't ask.* Princeton, NJ: Princeton University Press.

Babcock, L., & Loewenstein, G. (1997). Explaining bargaining impasse: The role of self-serving biases. *Journal of Economic Perspectives, 11* (1), 109–26.

Babcock, L., Wang, X., & Loewenstein, G. (1996). Choosing the wrong pond: Social comparisons in negotiations that reflect a self-serving bias. *Quarterly Journal of Economics, 111,* 1–19.

Bacon, N., & Blyton, P. (2007). Conflict for mutual gains? *Journal of Management Studies, 44* (5), 814–34.

Bahn, C., & Louden, R. J. (1999). Hostage negotiation as a team enterprise. *Group, 23* (2), 77–85.

Baker, C., & Ross, W. (1992). Mediation control techniques: A test of Kolb's "orchestrators" vs. "deal-makers" model. *International Journal of Conflict Management, 3,* 319–41.

Balachandra, L., Barrett, F., Bellman, H., Fisher, C., & Susskind, L. (2005). Improvisation and mediation: Balancing acts. *Negotiation Journal, 21* (4), 425–34.

Ball, S. B., Bazerman, M. H., & Carroll, J. S. (1991). An evaluation of learning in the bilateral winner's curse. *Organizational Behavior and Human Decision Processes, 48,* 1–22.

Bar-Hillel, M. (1980). The base-rate fallacy in probability judgments. *Acta Psychologica, 44,* 211–13.

Barada, P. W. (2008). Power relationships and negotiation. http://www.career-advice.monster.com/salary-negotiation/Power-Relationships-and-Negotiation/home.asp

Baranowski, T. A., & Summers, D. A. (1972). Perceptions of response alternatives in a prisoner's dilemma game. *Journal of Personality and Social Psychology, 21,* 35–40.

Barki, H., & Hartwick, J. (2004). Conceptualizing the construct of interpersonal conflict. *The International Journal of Conflict Management, 15* (3), 216–44.

Barnard, C. (1938). *The functions of the executive.* Cambridge, MA: Harvard University Press.

Baron, R. A. (1990). Environmentally induced positive affect: Its impact on self efficacy and task performance, negotiation and conflict. *Journal of Applied Social Psychology, 20,* 368–84.

Barrett, J. T. (1999). In search of the Rosetta Stone of the mediation profession. *Negotiation Journal, 15,* 219–27.

Barrick, M. R., & Mount, M. K. (1991). The Big Five personality dimensions and job performance: A meta-analysis. *Personnel Psychology, 44,* 1–26.

Barron, L. A. (2003). Gender differences in negotiator's beliefs. *Human Relations, 56,* 635–62.

Barry, B. (1999). The tactical use of emotion in negotiation. In R. Bies, R. J. Lewicki, & B. H. Sheppard (Eds.), *Research on negotiation in organizations* (Vol. 7, pp. 93–121). Stamford, CT: JAI Press.

Barry, B. (2001). Influence tactics in organizations from a social expectancy perspective. In A. Y. Lee-Chai & J. A. Bargh (Eds.), *The use and abuse of power.* Philadelphia, PA: Psychology Press.

Barry, B. (2008). Negotiator affect: The state of the art (and the science). *Group Decision and Negotiation, 17,* 97–105.

Barry, B., & Friedman, R. (1998). Bargainer characteristics in distributive and integrative negotiation. *Journal of Personality and Social Psychology, 74,* 345–59.

Barry, B., & Fulmer, I. S. (2004). The medium and the message: The adaptive use of communication media in dyadic influence. *Academy of Management Review, 2,* 272–92.

Barry, B., Fulmer, I. S., & Goates, N. (2006). Bargaining with feeling: Emotionality in and around negotiation. In L. Thompson (Ed.), *Negotiation Theory and Research* (pp. 99–127). New York: Psychology Press.

Barry, B., Fulmer, I. S., & Long, A. (2000). Ethically marginal bargaining tactics: Sanction, efficacy, and performance. Presented at the annual meeting of the Academy of Management, Toronto.

Barry, B., Fulmer, I. S., & Van Kleef, G. A. (2004). I laughed, I cried, I settled: The role of emotion in negotiation. In M. Gelfand and J. Brett (Eds.), *Culture and negotiation: Integrative approaches to theory and research.* Stanford, CA: Stanford University Press.

Barry, B., & Oliver, R. L. (1996). Affect in dyadic negotiation: A model and propositions. *Organizational Behavior and Human Decision Processes, 67,* 127–43.

Bateson, B. (1972). *Steps to an ecology of mind.* New York: Ballantine Books.

Batson, C. D., & Thompson, E. R. (2001). Why don't moral people act morally? Motivational considerations. *Current Directions in Psychological Science, 10* (2), 54–57.

Bazerman, M. (1998). *Judgment in managerial decision making* (4th ed.). New York: John Wiley and Sons.

Bazerman, M. H., & Carroll, J. S. (1987). Negotiator cognition. In B. M. Staw & L. L. Cummings (Eds.)., *Research in organizational behavior* (Vol. 9, pp. 247–88). Greenwich, CT: JAI Press.

Bazerman, M. H., Curhan, J. R., Moore, D. A., & Valley, K. L. (2000). Negotiation. *Annual Review of Psychology, 51,* 279–314.

Bazerman, M. H., & Gillespie, J. J. (1999, September/October). Betting on the future: The virtues of contingent contracts. *Harvard Business Review,* 155–60.

Bazerman, M. H., Magliozzi, T., & Neale, M. A. (1985). Integrative bargaining in a competitive market. *Organizational Behavior and Human Decision Processes, 35,* 294–313.

Bazerman, M. H., Mannix, E. A., & Thompson, L. L. (1988). Groups as mixed motive negotiations. In E. J. Lawler & B. Markovsky (Eds.), *Advances in group processes* (Vol. 5, pp. 195–216). Greenwich, CT: JAI Press.

Bazerman, M. H., Moore, D. A., & Gillespie, J. J. (1999). The human mind as a barrier to wiser environmental agreements. *American Behavioral Scientist, 42,* 1277–1300.

Bazerman, M. H., & Neale, M. A. (1983). Heuristics in negotiation: Limitations to effective dispute resolution. In M. H. Bazerman & R. J. Lewicki (Eds.), *Negotiating in organizations.* Beverly Hills, CA: Sage.

Bazerman, M. H., & Neale, M. A. (1992). *Negotiating rationally.* New York: Free Press.

Bazerman, M. H., Neale, M. A., Valley, L., Zajac, E. J., & Min Kim, J. (1992). The effect of agents and mediators on negotiation outcomes. *Organizational Behavior and Human Decision Processes, 53,* 55–73.

Bazerman, M. H., & Samuelson, W. F. (1983). I won the auction but don't want the prize. *Journal of Conflict Resolution, 27,* 618–34.

Bazerman, M. H., Tenebrunsel, A. E., & Wade-Benzoni, K. (1998). Negotiating with yourself and losing: Making decisions with competing internal preferences. *Academy of Management Review, 23* (2), 225–41.

Bebchick, B. (2002). The philosophy and methodology of Ambassador Dennis Ross as an international mediator. *International Negotiation, 7,* 115–31.

Beckhard, R. (1978, July–September). The dependency dilemma. *Consultants' Communique, 6,* 1–3.

Beckman, N. (1977). *Negotiations.* Lexington, MA: Lexington Books.

Beebe, S. A. (1980). Effects of eye contact, posture, and vocal inflection upon credibility and comprehension. *Australian SCAN: Journal of Human Communication, 7–8,* 57–70.

Beechey, J. (2000). International commercial arbitration. *Dispute Resolution Journal, 55* (3), 32–34.

Beisecker, T., Walker, G., & Bart, J. (1989). Knowledge versus ignorance in bargaining strategies: The impact of knowledge about other's information level. *Social Science Journal, 26,* 161–72.

Bem, D. (1972). Self-perception theory. In L. Berkowitz (Ed.), *Advances in experimental social psychology* (Vol. 6, pp. 1–62). New York: Academic Press.

Bendersky, C. (2003). Organizational dispute resolution systems: A complementaries model. *Academy of Management Review, 28* (4), 643–56.

Bendersky, C. (2007). Complementaries in organizational dispute resolution systems: How system characteristics affect individuals' conflict experiences. *Industrial & Labor Relations Review, 60* (2), 204–24.

Benfar, K., Peterson, R. S., Mannix, E. A., & Trochin, M. K. (2008). The critical role of conflict resolution in teams: A close look at the links between conflict type, conflict management strategies and team outcomes. *Journal of Applied Psychology, 93* (1), 170–88.

Benjamin, A. J., & Levi, A. M. (1979). Process minefields in intergroup conflict resolution: The Sdot Yam workshop. *Journal of Applied Behavioral Science, 15,* 507–19.

Benne, K. D., & Sheates, P. (1948). Functional roles of group members. *Journal of Social Issues, 4,* 41–49.

Bentham, J. (1987). *An introduction to the principles of morals and legislation.* Oxford: Oxford Press.

Benton, A. A. (1972). Accountability and negotiations between representatives. *Proceedings,* 80th annual convention, American Psychological Association, Hawaii, 227–28.

Benton, A. A., & Druckman, D. (1974). Constituent's bargaining orientation and intergroup negotiations. *Journal of Applied Social Psychology, 4,* 141–50.

Ben-Yoav, O., & Pruitt, D. G. (1984a). Accountability to constituents: A two-edged sword. *Organizational Behavior and Human Performance, 34,* 283–95.

Ben-Yoav, O., & Pruitt, D. G. (1984b). Resistance to yielding and the expectation of cooperative future interaction in negotiation. *Journal of Experimental Social Psychology, 34,* 323–35.

Bercovitch, J. (1989). Mediation in international disputes. In K. Kressel & D. Pruitt (Eds.), *Mediation research* (pp. 284–99). San Francisco: Jossey-Bass.

Berkowitz, L. (1989). The frustration-aggression hypothesis: An examination and reformulation. *Psychological Bulletin, 106,* 59–73.

Berlo, D. K., Lemert, J., & Mertz, R. (1966). *Dimensions for evaluating the acceptability of message sources.* East Lansing, MI: Michigan State University.

Bernstein, J., & Rosen, S. (1989). *Dinosaur brains: Dealing with all those impossible people at work.* New York: John Wiley and Sons.

Bettinghaus, E. P. (1966). *Message preparation: The nature of proof.* Indianapolis: Bobbs-Merrill.

Bettinghaus, E. P. (1980). *Persuasive communication* (2nd ed.). New York: Holt, Rinehart & Winston.

Bies, R., & Moag, J. (1986). Interactional justice: Communication criteria of fairness. In R. J. Lewicki, B. H. Sheppard, & M. H. Bazerman (Eds.), *Research on negotiation in organizations* (Vol. 1, pp. 43–55). Greenwich, CT: JAI Press.

Bies, R., & Shapiro, D. (1987). Interactional fairness judgments: The influence of causal accounts. *Social Justice Research, 1,* 199–218.

Bies, R., & Tripp, T. (1998). Revenge in organizations: The good, the bad and the ugly. In R. W. Griffin, A. O'Leary-Kelly, & J. Collins (Eds.), *Dysfunctional behavior in organizations,* Vol. 1: *Violent behavior in organizations* (pp. 49–68). Greenwich, CT: JAI Press.

Bies, R. J., Lewicki, R. J., & Sheppard, B. H. (1995). Preface. In R. J. Bies, R. J. Lewicki, & B. H. Sheppard (Eds.), *Research on negotiation in organizations* (Vol. 5, p. ix). Greenwich, CT: JAI Press.

Bingham, L. B. (1999). *Alternative dispute resolution in the workplace.* Bloomington, IN: Research paper, Indiana Conflict Resolution Institute.

Bingham, L. B., Chesmore, G., Moon, Y., & Napoli, L. M. (2000). *Review of Public Personnel Administration, 20* (1), 5–19.

Bingham, L. B., & Napoli, L. (2001). Employment dispute resolution and workplace culture: The REDRESS program at the United States Postal Service. In M. Breger & J. Schatz (Eds.), *The Federal Dispute Resolution Deskbook* (Chapter 22, pp. 507–26). New York: American Bar Association.

Binnendijk, H. (1987). *National negotiating styles.* Washington, DC: Foreign Service Institute, Department of State.

Blake, R. R., & Mouton, J. S. (1961a). *Group dynamics: Key to decision making.* Houston, TX: Gulf Publications.

Blake, R. R., & Mouton, J. S. (1961b). Comprehension of own and outgroup positions under intergroup competition. *Journal of Conflict Resolution, 5,* 304–10.

Blake, R. R., & Mouton, J. S. (1961c). Loyalty of representatives to ingroup positions during intergroup competition. *Sociometry, 24,* 177–83.

Blau, P. (1964). *Exchange and power in social life.* New York: John Wiley and Sons.

Bless, H., Bohner, G., Schwarz, N., & Strack, F. (1988). Happy and mindless: Moods and the processing of persuasive communication. Unpublished manuscript, Mannheim, GR.

Blessing, L. (1988). *A walk in the woods.* New York: New American Library, Dutton.

Block, P. (1987). *The empowered manager: Positive political skills at work.* San Francisco: Jossey-Bass.

Blumenstein, R. (1997, December 30). Haggling in cyberspace transforms car sales. *The Wall Street Journal,* pp. B1, B6.

Boatright, J. R. (2000). *Ethics and the conduct of business* (3rd ed.). Upper Saddle River, NJ: Prentice Hall.

Boehringer, G. H., Zeruolis, V., Bayley, J., & Boehringer, K. (1974). Stirling: The destructive application of group techniques to a conflict. *Journal of Conflict Resolution, 18,* 257–75.

Bok, S. (1978). *Lying: Moral choice in public and private life.* New York: Pantheon.

Boles, T. L., Croson, R. T. A., & Murnighan, J. K. (2000). Deception and retribution in repeated ultimatum bargaining. *Organizational Behavior and Human Decision Processes, 83,* 235–59.

Bone, D. (1988). *The business of listening.* Los Altos, CA: Crisp Publications.

Bordwin, M. (1999). Do-it-yourself justice. *Management Review,* January, 56–58.

Boster, F. J., & Mongeau, P. (1984). Fear-arousing persuasive messages. In R. N. Bostrom (Ed.), *Communication Yearbook* (Vol. 8, pp. 330–75). Beverly Hills, CA: Sage.

Bostrom, R. N. (1990). *Listening behavior: Measurement and application.* New York: Guilford.

Botes, J., & Mitchell, C. (1995). Constraints on third-party flexibility. *Annals of the American Academy of Political and Social Science, 542,* 168–84.

Bottom, W. P. (1998). Negotiator risk: Sources of uncertainty and the impact of reference points on negotiated agreements. *Organizational Behavior and Human Decision Processes, 76,* 89–112.

Bottom, W. P., Gibson, K., Daniels, S., & Murnighan, J. K. (2002). When talk is not cheap: Substantive penance and expressions of intent in the reestablishment of cooperation. *Organization Science, 13,* 497–513.

Bottom, W. P., Holloway, J., Miller, G. J., Mislin, A., & Whitford, A. (2006). Building a pathway to cooperation: Negotiation and social exchange between principal and agent. *Administrative Science Quarterly,* 51, 29–58.

Bottom, W. P., & Paese, P. W. (1999). Judgment accuracy and the asymmetric cost of errors in distributive bargaining. *Group Decision and Negotiation, 8,* 349–64.

Bottom, W. P., & Studt, A. (1993). Framing effects and the distributive aspect of integrative bargaining. *Organizational Behavior and Human Decision Processes, 56,* 459–74.

Bourdeaux, C., O'Leary, R., & Thorburgh, R. (2001). Control, communication, and power: A study of the use of alternative dispute resolution of enforcement actions at the U.S. Environmental Protection Agency. *Negotiation Journal, 17,* 175–91.

Bowers, J. W. (1964). Some correlates of language intensity. *Quarterly Journal of Speech, 50,* 415–20.

Bowers, J. W., & Osborn, M. M. (1966). Attitudinal effects of selected types of concluding metaphors in persuasive speeches. *Speech Monographs, 33,* 147–55.

Bowie, N. (1993). Does it pay to bluff in business? In T. L. Beauchamp & N. E. Bowie (Eds.), *Ethical theory and business* (pp. 449–54). Englewood Cliffs, NJ: Prentice Hall.

Bowie, N., & Freeman, R. E. (1992). *Ethics and agency theory.* New York: Oxford University Press.

Bowles, H. R., Babcock, L., & Lai, L. (2007). Social incentives for gender differences in the propensity to initiate negotiations: Sometimes it doesn't hurt to ask. *Organizational Behavior and Human Decision Processes, 103,* 84–103.

Bowles, H. R., Babcock, L., & McGinn, K. L. (2005). Constraints and triggers: Situational mechanics of gender in negotiation. *Journal of Personality and Social Psychology, 89,* 951–65.

Bowling, D., & Hoffman, D. (2001). Bringing peace into the room: The personal qualities of the mediator and their impact on the mediation. *Negotiation Journal, 16,* 5–28.

Braganti, N. L., & Devine, E. (1992). *European customs and manners: How to make friends and do business in Europe* (rev. ed.). New York: Meadowbrook Press.

Braginsky, D. D. (1970). Machiavellianism and manipulative interpersonal behavior in children. *Journal of Experimental Social Psychology, 6,* 77–99.

Brams, S. J., & Doherty, A. E. (1993). Intransigence in negotiations: The dynamics of disagreement. *Journal of Conflict Resolution, 37,* 692–708.

Bramson, R. (1981). *Coping with difficult people.* New York: Anchor Books.

Bramson, R. (1992). *Coping with difficult bosses.* New York: Carol Publishing Group.

Brass, D. J. (1984). Being in the right place: A structural analysis of individual influence in an organization. *Administrative Science Quarterly, 29,* 518–39.

Breaugh, J. A., & Klimoski, R. J. (1977). The choice of group spokesman in bargaining member or outsider. *Organizational Behavior and Human Performance, 19* (2), 325–36.

Brehm, J. W. (1976). Responses to loss of freedom: A theory of psychological reactance. In J. W. Thibaut, J. T. Spence, & R. C. Carson (Eds.), *Contemporary topics in social psychology* (pp. 53–78). Morristown, NJ: General Learning Press.

Brett, J. (1991). Negotiating group decisions. *Negotiation Journal, 7,* 291–310.

Brett, J., Adair, W., Lempereur, A., Okumura, T., Shikhirev, P., Tinsley, C., et al. (1998). Culture and joint gains in negotiation. *Negotiation Journal, 14* (1), 61–86.

Brett, J., Barsness, Z., & Goldberg, S. (1996). The effectiveness of mediation: An independent analysis of cases handled by four major service providers. *Negotiation Journal, 12,* 259–69.

Brett, J., & Gelfand, M. (2004). *A cultural analysis of the underlying assumptions of negotiation theory.* Unpublished paper, Dispute Resolution Research Center, Northwestern University, Evanston, IL.

Brett, J., Goldberg, S., & Ury, W. (1990). Designing systems for resolving disputes in organizations. *American Psychologist, 45,* 162–70.

Brett, J. F., Pinkley, R. L., & Jacofsky, E. F. (1996). Alternatives to having BATNA in dyadic negotiation: The influence of goals, self-efficacy, and alternatives on negotiated outcomes. *International Journal of Conflict Management, 7,* 121–38.

Brett, J. M. (2001). *Negotiating globally.* San Francisco: Jossey-Bass.

Brett, J. M., & Goldberg, S. B. (1983). Grievance mediation in the coal industry: A field experiment. *Industrial & Labor Relations Review, 37,* 3–17.

Brett, J. M., & Okumura, T. (1998). Inter- and intracultural negotiation: U.S. and Japanese negotiators. *Academy of Management Journal, 41,* 495–510.

Brett, J. M., & Rognes, J. (1986). Intergroup relations in organizations: A negotiations perspective. In P. Goodman (Ed.),

Designing effective work groups (pp. 202–36). San Francisco: Jossey-Bass.

Brett, J. M., Shapiro, D. L., & Lytle, A. L. (1998). Breaking the bonds of reciprocity in negotiation. *Academy of Management Journal, 41,* 410–24.

Brief, A. (1992). *Sanctioned corruption in the corporate world.* Unpublished manuscript.

Brock, T. C. (1963). Effects of prior dishonesty on post-decision dissonance. *Journal of Abnormal and Social Psychology, 66,* 325–31.

Brockner, J. (1992). The escalation of commitment to a failing course of action: Toward theoretical progress. *Academy of Management Review, 17,* 39–61.

Brockner, J., & Weisenfeld, B. (2005). How, when and why does outcome favorability interact with procedural fairness? In J. Greenberg and J. Colquitt (Eds.), *Handbook of organizational justice* (pp. 525–55). Mahwah, NJ: Lawrence Erlbaum Associates.

Brodt, S. E. (1994). "Inside information" and negotiator decision behavior. *Organizational Behavior and Human Decision Processes, 58,* 172–202.

Brodt, S. E., & Tuchinsky, M. (2000). Working together but in opposition: An examination of the "good-cop/bad-cop" negotiating team tactic. *Organizational Behavior and Human Decision Processes, 81* (2), 155–77.

Brooks, E., & Odiorne, G. S. (1984). *Managing by negotiations.* New York: Van Nostrand.

Brouthers, K. D., & Bamossy, G. J. (1997). The role of key stakeholders in international joint venture negotiations: Case studies from Eastern Europe. *Journal of International Business Studies, 28,* 285–308.

Brown, B. L. (1999). Contextual mediation. *Meditation Quarterly, 16,* 349–56.

Brown, B. R. (1968). The effects of need to maintain face on interpersonal bargaining. *Journal of Experimental Social Psychology, 4,* 107–22.

Brown, L. D. (1977). Can "haves" and "have-nots" cooperate? Two efforts to bridge a social gap. *Journal of Applied Behavioral Science, 13,* 211–24.

Brown, L. D. (1983). *Managing conflict at organizational interfaces.* Reading, MA: Addison-Wesley.

Bruner, J. S., & Tagiuri, R. (1954). The perception of people. In G. Lindzey (Ed.), *The handbook of social psychology* (Vol. 2, pp. 634–54). Reading, MA: Addison-Wesley.

Buber, M. (1958). *I and thou.* New York: Charles Scribners & Sons.

Buber, M. (1963). *Pointing the way.* New York: Harper & Row.

Buechler, S. M. (2000). *Social movements in advanced capitalism.* New York, Oxford University Press.

Buelens, M., & Van Poucke, D. (2004). Determinants of a negotiator's initial opening offer. *Journal of Business and Psychology, 19,* 23–35.

Bunker, B. B., & Alban, Billie T. (1997). *Large group interventions: Engaging the whole system for rapid change.* San Francisco: Jossey-Bass.

Burgess, G., & Burgess, H. (1995). Constructive confrontation: A transformative approach to intractable conflicts. *Mediation Quarterly, 13,* 305–22.

Burgoon, J. K., Coker, D. A., & Coker, R. A. (1986). Communication of gaze behavior: A test of two contrasting explanations. *Human Communication Research, 12,* 495–524.

Burgoon, M., & King, L. B. (1974). The mediation of resistance to persuasion strategies by language variables and active-passive participation. *Human Communication Research, 1,* 30–41.

Burgoon, M., & Stewart, D. (1975). Empirical investigations of language: The effects of sex of source, receiver, and language intensity on attitude change. *Human Communication Research, 1,* 244–48.

Burnstein, D. (1995). *Negotiator pro.* Beacon Expert Systems, 35 Gardner Road, Brookline, MA.

Burris, E. R. (2005). Negotiators' bargaining histories and their effects on future negotiation performance. *Journal of Applied Psychology, 90* (2), 350–62.

Burton, J. (1984). *Global conflict.* Center for International Development, University of Maryland, College Park, MD.

Bush, R. A. B. (2003). Realizing the potential of international conflict work: Connections between practice and theory. *Negotiation Journal, 19* (1), 97–103.

Bush, R. B. (1996). What do we need a mediator for? Mediation's "value-added" for negotiators. *American Psychologist, 45,* 162–70.

Butler, J. K., Jr. (1991). Toward understanding and measuring conditions of trust: Evolution of a conditions of trust inventory. *Journal of Management, 17,* 643–63.

Butler, J. K., Jr. (1994). Conflict styles and outcomes in negotiation with fully-integrative potential. *International Journal of Conflict Management, 5,* 309–25.

Butler, J. K., Jr. (1995). Behaviors, trust and goal achievement in a win-win negotiation role play. *Group & Organization Management, 20,* 486–501.

Butler, J. K., Jr. (1996). Two integrative win-win negotiating strategies. *Simulation and Gaming, 27,* 387–92.

Butler, J. K., Jr. (1999). Trust expectations, information sharing, climate of trust, and negotiation effectiveness and efficiency. *Group and Organization Management, 24* (2), 217–38.

Butler, M. J. (2007). Crisis bargaining and third-party mediation: Bridging the gap. *International Negotiation, 12,* 249–74.

Byrne, D. (1971). *The attraction paradigm.* Academic Press: New York.

Cacioppo, J. T., & Petty, R. E. (1985). Central and peripheral routes to persuasion: The role of message repetition. In L. F. Alwitt & A. A. Mitchell (Eds.), *Psychological processes and advertising effects: Theory, research, and application* (pp. 91–111). Hillsdale, NJ: Lawrence Erlbaum.

Cai, D. A. (1998). Culture, plans, and the pursuit of negotiation goals. *Journal of Asian Pacific Communication, 8,* 103–23.

Camerer, C. F., & Loewenstein, G. (1993). Information, fairness, and efficiency in bargaining. In *Psychological perspectives on justice. Theory and applications* (pp. 155–79). Cambridge: Cambridge University Press.

Cantrell, R. S., & Butler, J. K., Jr. (1997). Male negotiators: Chivalry or machismo or both? *Psychological Reports, 80,* 1315–23.

Carlisle, J. A., & Parker, R. C. (1989). *Beyond negotiation: Redeeming customer-supplier relations.* New York: John Wiley.

Carnevale, P. J. (2006). Creativity in the outcomes of conflict. In M. Deutsh et al. (Eds.), *The handbook of conflict resolution: Theory and practice* (2nd ed., pp. 414–35). San Francisco: Jossey-Bass.

Carnevale, P. J., & Isen, A. M. (1986). The influence of positive affect and visual access on the discovery of integrative solutions in bilateral negotiation. *Organizational Behavior and Human Decision Processes, 37,* 1–13.

Carnevale, P. J. D. (1986). Strategic choice in negotiation. *Negotiation Journal, 2,* 41–56.

Carnevale, P. J. D. (1992). The usefulness of mediation theory. *Negotiation Journal, 8,* 387–90.

Carnevale, P. J. D., & Conlon, D. E. (1988). Time pressure and strategic choice in mediation. *Organizational Behavior and Human Decision Processes, 42,* 111–33.

Carnevale, P. J. D., & Conlon, D. E. (1990, June). Effects of two forms of bias in mediation of disputes. Paper presented at the third International Conference of the International Association of Conflict Management, Vancouver, B. C., Canada.

Carnevale, P. J. D., & Keenan, P. A. (1990). Decision frame and social goals in integrative bargaining: The likelihood of agreement versus the quality. Paper presented at the annual meeting of the International Association of Conflict Management, Vancouver, B. C., Canada.

Carnevale, P. J. D., & Lawler, E. J. (1987). Time pressure and the development of integrative agreements in bilateral negotiations. *Journal of Conflict Resolution, 30,* 636–59.

Carnevale, P. J. D., & Pruitt, D. G. (1992). Negotiation and mediation. In M. Rosenberg & L. Porter (Eds.), *Annual Review of Psychology* (Vol. 43, pp. 531–82). Palo Alto, CA: Annual Reviews, Inc.

Carnevale, P. J. D., Pruitt, D. G., & Britton, S. D. (1979). Looking tough: The negotiator under constituent surveillance. *Personality and Social Psychology Bulletin, 5,* 118–21.

Carnevale, P. J. D., Pruitt, D. G., & Seilheimer, S. D. (1981). Looking and competing: Accountability and visual access in integrative bargaining. *Journal of Personality and Social Psychology, 40,* 111–20.

Caro, R. A. (2006, April). Lessons in Power: Lyndon Johnson revealed. *Harvard Business Review, 47–52.*

Carr, A. Z. (1968, January–February). Is business bluffing ethical? *Harvard Business Review, 46,* 143–53.

Carroll, J., Bazerman, M., & Maury, R. (1988). Negotiator cognitions: A descriptive approach to negotiators' understanding of their opponents. *Organizational Behavior and Human Decision Processes, 41,* 352–70.

Carroll, J., Delquie, P., Halpern, J., & Bazerman, M. (1990). *Improving negotiators' cognitive processes.* Working paper, Massachusetts Institute of Technology, Cambridge, MA.

Carter, S. (1999). The importance of party buy-in in designing organizational conflict management systems. *Mediation Quarterly, 17,* 61–66.

Carver, C. S., & Scheir, M. E. (1990). Origins and foundations of positive and negative affect: A control process view. *Psychological Review, 97,* 19–35.

Carver, T., & Vondra, A. (1994 May/June). Alternative dispute resolution: Why it doesn't work and why it does. *Harvard Business Review, 72,* 120–30.

Caton, J. (2001, June). Big league agents. *Columbus Monthly,* 54–60.

Cellich, C. (1997). Closing your business negotiations. *International Trade Forum, 1,* 14–17.

Chaiken, S. (1986). Physical appearance and social influence. In C. P. Herman, M. P. Zanna, & E. T. Higgins (Eds.), *Physical appearance, stigma, and social behavior: The Ontario symposium* (Vol. 3, pp. 143–77). Hillsdale, NJ: Lawrence Erlbaum.

Chaiken, S. (1987). The heuristic model of persuasion. In M. Zanna, J. Olson, & C. Herman (Eds.), *Social influence: The Ontario symposium* (Vol. 5, pp. 3–39). Hillsdale, NJ: Lawrence Erlbaum.

Chaiken, S., & Maheswaran, D. (1994). Heuristic processing can bias systematic processing: Effects of source credibility, argument ambiguity, and task importance on attitude judgment. *Journal of Personality and Social Psychology, 66,* 460–73.

Chan, C. W. (1998). Transfer pricing negotiation outcomes and the impact of negotiator mixed-motives and culture: Empirical evidence from the U.S. and Australia. *Management Accounting Research, 9,* 139–61.

Charan, R. (1991, September/October). How networks reshape organizations—for results. *Harvard Business Review, 69* (5), 104–15.

Chatman, J., Putnam, L., & Sondak, H. (1991). Integrating communication and negotiation research. In M. H. Bazerman, R. J. Lewicki, & B. H. Sheppard (Eds.), *Research on negotiation in organizations* (Vol. 3, pp. 139–64). Greenwich, CT: JAI Press.

Chaudhuri, A., Khan, S. A., Lakshmiratan, A., Py, A., & Shah, L. (2003). Trust and trustworthiness in a sequential bargaining game. *Journal of Behavioral Decision Making, 16,* 331–40.

Chaudrhy, S. S., & Ross, W. R. (1989). Relevance trees and mediation. *Negotiation Journal, 5,* 63–73.

Chayes, A.H. (2007). Sleeves rolled up on peacemaking: Lessons from international mediators. *Negotiation Journal, 23,* 185–192.

Chen, C. C., Chen, X., & Meindl, J. R. (1998). How can cooperation be fostered? The cultural effects of individualism-collectivism. *Academy of Management Review, 23,* 285–304.

Chen, F. F., & Kenrick, D. T. (2002). Repulsion or attraction? Group membership and assumed attitude similarity. *Journal of Personality and Social Psychology, 83,* 111–25.

Chertkoff, J. M., & Conley, M. (1967). Opening offer and frequency of concessions as bargaining strategies. *Journal of Personality and Social Psychology, 7,* 181–85.

Christie, R., & Geis, F. L. (Eds.), (1970). *Studies in Machiavellianism.* New York: Academic Press.

Cialdini, R. B. (2001). *Influence: Science and practice* (4th ed.). Boston: Allyn and Bacon.

Cialdini, R. B., & Goldstein, N. J. (2004). Social influence: Compliance and conformity. *Annual Review of Psychology, 55,* 591–621.

Clark, E., Cho, G., & Hoyle, A. (2003). Online dispute resolution: Present realities, pressing problems and future prospects. *International Review of Law, Computers and Technology, 17,* 7–25.

Clark, M. S., & Mills, J. (1979). Interpersonal attraction in exchange and communal relationships. *Journal of Personality and Social Psychology, 37* (1), 12–24.

Clark, R. A. (1984). *Persuasive messages.* New York: Harper & Row.

Cloke, K., & Goldsmith, J. (2005). *Resolving Conflicts at Work.* Second Edition. San Francisco: Jossey-Bass.

Clyman, D. R., & Tripp, T. M. (2000). Discrepant values and measures of negotiator performance. *Group Decision and Negotiation, 9,* 251–74.

Cobb, A. (1986). Coalition identification in organizational research. In R. J. Lewicki, B. H. Sheppard, & M. H. Bazerman (Eds.), *Research on negotiation in organizations* (Vol. 1, pp. 139–54). Greenwich, CT: JAI Press.

Cobb, S. (1993). Empowerment and mediation: A narrative perspective. *Negotiation Journal, 9,* 245–59.

Cohen, A. R., & Bradford, D. L. (1989). Influence without authority: The use of alliances, reciprocity, and exchange to accomplish work. *Organizational Dynamics, 17* (3), 5–17.

Cohen, G. L., Sherman, D. K., Bastardi, A., Hsu, L., McGoey, M., & Ross, L. (2007). Bridging the partisan divide: Self-affirmation reduces ideological closed-mindedness and inflexibility in negotiation. *Journal of Personality and Social Psychology, 93,* 415–30.

Cohen, H. (1980). *You can negotiate anything.* Secaucus, NJ: Lyle Stuart.

Cohen, H. (2003). *Negotiate this!* New York: Warner Books.

Cohen, S. P., Kelman, H. C., Miller, F. D., & Smith, B. L. (1977). Evolving intergroup techniques for conflict resolution: An Israeli–Palestinian pilot workshop. *Journal of Social Issues, 33,* 165–89.

Cohen, W. H. (2003). The importance of expectations on negotiation results. *European Business Review, 15* (2), 87–93.

Coleman, P. (1997). Refining ripeness: A social-psychological perspective. *Peace and Conflict: Journal of Peace Psychology, 3,* 81–103.

Coleman, P. (2000a). Fostering ripeness in seemingly intractable conflict: An experimental study. *International Journal of Conflict Management, 11,* 300–17.

Coleman, P. (2000b). Power and conflict. In M. Deutsch & P. Coleman (Eds.), *Handbook of conflict resolution.* San Francisco: Jossey-Bass.

Coleman, P., & Lim, Y. Y. J. (2001, October). A systematic approach to evaluating the effects of collaborative negotiation training on individuals and groups. *Negotiation Journal,* 364–92.

Coleman, P. T. (1997). "Psychological Resistance to and Facilitation of Power-Sharing in Organizations. *Dissertation Abstracts.*

Conger, J. A. (1998). The necessary art of persuasion. *Harvard Business Review, 76* (3), 84–95.

Conlon, D., Carnevale, P. J. D., & Murnighan, K. (1994). Intravention: Third-party intervention with clout. *Organizational Behavior and Human Decision Processes, 57,* 387–410.

Conlon, D. E., & Fasolo, P. M. (1990). Influence of speed of third-party intervention and outcome on negotiator and constituent fairness judgments. *Academy of Management Journal, 33,* 833–46.

Conlon, D. E., & Hunt, C. S. (2002). Dealing with feeling: The Influence of outcome representations on negotiation. *International Journal of Conflict Management, 13,* 38–58.

Conlon, D. E., Moon, H., & Ng, K. Y. (2002). Putting the cart before the horse: The benefits of arbitrating before mediating. *Journal of Applied Psychology, 87,* 978–84.

Conlon, D. E., & Ross, W. H. (1993). The effects of partisan third parties on negotiator behavior and outcome perceptions. *Journal of Applied Psychology, 78,* 280–90.

Conte, J. M. (2005). A review and critique of emotional intelligence measures. *Journal of Organizational Behavior, 26,* 433–40.

Cooper, W. (1981). Ubiquitous halo. *Psychological Bulletin, 90,* 218–44.

Corley, R. N., Black, R. L., & Reed, O. L. (1977). *The legal environment of business* (4th ed.). New York: McGraw-Hill.

Corwin, R. G. (1969). Patterns of organizational conflict. *Administrative Science Quarterly, 14,* 504–20.

Coser, L. (1956). *The functions of social conflict.* New York: Free Press.

Costantino, C. A. (1994). How to set up an ADR program. *Government Executive, 26,* 44.

Costantino, C. A., & Merchant, C. S. (1996). *Designing conflict management systems.* San Francisco: Jossey-Bass.

Coulson, R. (1987). *Business mediation: What you need to know.* New York: American Arbitration Association.

Count, D. (2007, December). Making relationships work: A conversation with psychologist John Gottman, *Harvard Business Review,* 45–50.

Crano, W. D., & Prislin, R. (2006). Attitudes and persuasion. *Annual Review of Psychology, 57,* 345–74.

Cronkhite, G., & Liska, J. (1976). A critique of factor analytic approaches to the study of credibility. *Communication Monographs, 32,* 91–107.

Cronkhite, G., & Liska, J. (1980). The judgment of communicant acceptability. In M. E. Roloff & G. R. Miller (Eds.), *Persuasion: New directions in theory and research* (pp. 101–39). Beverly Hills, CA: Sage.

Cropanzano, R., & Folger, R. (1991). Procedural justice and worker motivation. In R. M. Steers & L. W. Porter (Eds.), *Motivation and work behavior* (2nd ed., pp. 131–43). New York: McGraw-Hill.

Croson, R. T. A. (1999). Look at me when you say that: An electronic negotiation simulation. *Simulation & Gaming, 30,* 23–37.

Cross, S., & Rosenthal, R. (1999). Three models of conflict resolution: Effects on intergroup experiences and attitudes. *Journal of Social Issues, 55* (3), 561–80.

Crott, H., Kayser, E., & Lamm, H. (1980). The effects of information exchange and communication in an asymmetrical negotiation situation. *European Journal of Social Psychology, 10,* 149–63.

Curhan, J. R., Neale, M. A., & Ross, L. (2004). Dynamic valuation: Preference changes in the context of face-to-face negotiation. *Journal of Experimental Social Psychology, 40,* 142–51.

Curhan, J. R., & Pentland, A. (2007). Thin slides of negotiation: Predicting outcomes from conversational dynamics within the first 5 minutes. *Journal of Applied Psychology, 92,* 802–11.

Cutcher-Gershenfeld, J., & Watkins, M. (1999). Toward a theory of representation in negotiation. In R. H. Mnookin and L. E. Susskind (Eds.), *Negotiating on behalf of others* (pp. 23–51). Thousand Oaks, CA: Sage.

Dahl, R. A. (1957). The concept of power. *Behavioral Science, 2,* 201–15.

Dallinger, J. M., & Hample, D. (1995). Personalizing and managing conflict. *International Journal of Conflict Management, 6,* 273–89.

D'Alo, G. E. (2003). Justice, understanding, and mediation. When talk works, should we ask for more? *Negotiation Journal, 19,* 215–27.

Daly, J. (1991). The effects of anger on negotiations over mergers and acquisitions. *Negotiation Journal, 7,* 31–39.

Dant, R. P., & Schul, P. L. (1992). Conflict resolution processes in contractual channels of distribution. *Journal of Marketing, 56,* 38–54.

Davidson, M. N., & Greenhalgh, L. (1999). The role of emotion in negotiation: The impact of anger and race. In R. J. Bies, R. J. Lewicki, & B. H. Sheppard (Eds.), *Research on negotiation in organizations* (Vol. 7, pp. 3–26). Stamford, CT: JAI Press.

Davis-Blake, A., & Pfeffer, J. (1989). Just a mirage: The search for dispositional effects in organizational research. *Academy of Management Review, 14,* 385–400.

Dawson, R. (1997). Ethical differences between men and women in the sales profession. *Journal of Business Ethics, 16,* 1143–52.

Deal, J. J. (2000). Gender differences in the intentional use of information in competitive negotiations. *Small Group Research, 31,* 702–23.

Deaux, K. (1985). Sex and gender. *Annual Review of Psychology, 36,* 49–81.

De Bono, E. (1990). *Lateral thinking: Creativity step-by-step* (Reissue ed.). New York: HarperCollins.

De Cremer, D. (2002). Respect and cooperation in social dilemmas: The importance of feeling included. *Personality and Social Psychology Bulletin, 28,* 1335–41.

de Dreu, C. K. W. (1995). Coercive power and concession making in bilateral negotiation. *Journal of Conflict Resolution, 39,* 646–70.

de Dreu, C. K. W. (2003). Time pressure and closing of the mind in negotiation. *Organizational Behavior and Human Decision Processes, 91,* 280–95.

de Dreu, C. K. W., Carnevale, P. J. D., Emans, B. J. M., & van de Vliert, E. (1994). Effects of gain-loss frames in negotiation: Loss aversion, mismatching, and frame adoption. *Organizational Behavior and Human Decision Processes, 60,* 90–107.

de Dreu, C. K. W., Giebels, E., & van de Vliert, E. (1998). Social motives and trust in integrative negotiation: The disruptive effects of punitive capability. *Journal of Applied Psychology, 83,* 408–22.

de Dreu, C. K. W., Koole, S. L., & Steinel, W. (2000). Unfixing the fixed pie: A motivated information processing approach to integrative negotiation. *Journal of Personality and Social Psychology, 79,* 975 87.

de Dreu, C. K. W., Nauta, A., & van de Vliert, E. (1995). Self-serving evaluations of conflict behavior and escalation of the dispute. *Journal of Applied Social Psychology, 25,* 2049–66.

de Dreu, C. K. W., & Van Kleef, G. A. (2004). The influence of power on the information search, impression formation and demands in negotiation. *Journal of Experimental Social Psychology, 40,* 303–19.

de Dreu, C. K. W., & van Lange, P. A. M. (1995). The impact of social value orientation on negotiator cognition and behavior. *Personality and Social Psychology Bulletin, 21,* 1178–88.

de Dreu, C. K. W., Weingart, L. R., & Kwon, S. (2000). Influence of social motives on integrative negotiation: A meta-analytic review and test of two theories. *Journal of Personality and Social Psychology, 78,* 889–905.

Deep, S., & Sussman, L. (1993). *What to ask when you don't know what to say: 555 powerful questions to use for getting your way at work.* Englewood Cliffs, NJ: Prentice Hall.

De George, R. T. (2006). *Business ethics* (6th ed.). Upper Saddle River, NJ: Pearson Prentice Hall.

Demick, B. (1998). Saddam, United States play high stakes chicken. *Knight-Ridder Newspapers:* Tribune Media Service, pp. 1A, 2A.

Dennis, A. R., & Reinicke, B. A. (2004). Beta versus VHS and the acceptance of electronic brainstorming technology. *MIS Quarterly, 28,* 1–20.

Derong, C., & Faure, G. O. (1995). When Chinese companies negotiate with their government. *Organization Studies, 16,* 27–54.

DeSteno, D., Petty, R. E., Rucker, D. D., Wegener, D. T., & Braverman, J. (2004). Discrete emotions and persuasion: The role of emotion-induced expectancies. *Journal of Personality and Social Psychology, 86,* 43–56.

Deutsch, M. (1949). A theory of cooperation and competition. *Human Relations, 2,* 129–51.

Deutsch, M. (1958). Trust and suspicion. *Journal of Conflict Resolution, 2,* 265–79.

Deutsch, M. (1962). Cooperation and trust: Some theoretical notes. In M. R. Jones (Ed.), *Nebraska symposium on motivation* (pp. 275–318). Lincoln, NE: University of Nebraska Press.

Deutsch, M. (1973). *The resolution of conflict.* New Haven, CT: Yale University Press.

Deutsch, M. (1985). *Distributive justice: A social-psychological perspective.* New Haven, CT: Yale University Press.

Deutsch, M., & Coleman, P. (2000). *The handbook of conflict resolution.* San Francisco: Jossey-Bass.

Devinatz, V. G., & Budd, J. W. (1997). Third-party dispute resolution. Interest disputes. In D. Lewin, D. J. R. Mitchell, & M. A. Zaida (Eds.), *The human resource management handbook* (Vol. 1, pp. 95–135). Greenwich, CT: JAI Press.

Dialdin, D., Kopelman, S., Adair, W., Brett, J. M., Okumura, T., & Lytle, A. (1999). *The distributive outcomes of cross-cultural negotiations.* DRRC working paper. Evanston, IL: Northwestern University.

Dickerson, C. A., Thibodeau, R., Aronson, E., & Miller, D. (1992). Using cognitive dissonance to encourage water conservation. *Journal of Applied Social Psychology, 22,* 841–54.

Diehl, P. F., Druckman, D., & Wall, J. (1998). International peacekeeping and conflict resolution: A taxonomic analysis with implications. *Journal of Conflict Resolution, 42* (1), 33–55.

Diekmann, K. A., Tenbrunsel, A. E., Shah, P. P., Schroth, H. A., & Bazerman, M. H. (1996). The descriptive and prescriptive use of previous purchase price in negotiations. *Organizational Behavior and Human Decision Processes, 66,* 179–91.

Dingwall, R. (2002). What makes conflict resolution possible? *Negotiation Journal, 18* (4), 321–26.

Docherty, J. S., & Campbell, M. C. (2005). Teaching negotiators to analyze conflict structure and anticipate the consequences of principal-agent relationships. *Marquette Law Review, 87,* 655–64.

Dolinski, D., Nawrat, M., & Rudak, I. (2001). Dialogue involvement as a social influence technique. *Personality and Social Psychology Bulletin, 27,* 1395–1406.

Donaldson, T., & Werhane, P. (2008). *Ethical issues in business: A philosophical approach* (8th ed.). Upper Saddle River, NJ: Prentice Hall.

Donohue, W., & Taylor, P. (2007, July). Role effects in negotiation: The one-down phenomenon. *Negotiation Journal.*

Donohue, W. A. (1981). Analyzing negotiation tactics: Development of a negotiation interact system. *Human Communication Research, 7,* 273–87.

Donohue, W. A. (1989). Communicative competence in mediators. In K. Kressel & D. Pruitt (Eds.), *Mediation research* (pp. 322–43). San Francisco: Jossey-Bass.

Donohue, W. A. (1991). *Communication, marital dispute and divorce mediation.* Hillsdale, NJ: Lawrence Erlbaum.

Donohue, W. A., & Kolt, R. (1992). *Managing interpersonal conflict.* Newbury Park, CA: Sage.

Donohue, W. A., & Roberto, A. J. (1996). An empirical examination of three models of integrative and distributive bargaining. *International Journal of Conflict Management, 7,* 209–99.

Douglas, A. (1962). *Industrial peacemaking.* New York: Columbia University Press.

Drake, L. E. (1995). Negotiation styles in intercultural communication. *International Journal of Conflict Management, 6,* 72–90.

Drayton, W. (1981, July–August). Getting smarter about regulation. *Harvard Business Review, 59,* 38–52.

Dreher, G. F., Dougherty, T. W., & Whitely, W. (1989). Influence tactics and salary attainment: A gender specific analysis. *Sex Roles, 20,* 535–50.

Drolet, A. L., & Morris, M. W. (2000). Rapport in conflict resolution: Accounting for how face-to-face contact fosters mutual cooperation in mixed-motive conflicts. *Journal of Experimental Social Psychology, 36,* 26–50.

Drory, A., & Ritov, I. (1997). Effect of work experience and opponent's power on conflict management style. *International Journal of Conflict Management, 8,* 148–61.

Druckman, D. (1994). Determinants of compromising behavior in negotiation: A meta-analysis. *Journal of Conflict Resolution, 38* (3), 507–57.

Druckman, D. (1996). Is there a U.S. negotiating style? *International Negotiation, 1,* 327–34.

Druckman, D. (2001). Turning points in international negotiation. A comparative analysis. *Journal of Conflict Resolution, 45,* 519–44.

Druckman, D., & Broome, B. (1991). Value difference and conflict resolution: Familiarity or liking? *Journal of Conflict Resolution, 35* (4), 571–93.

Druckman, D., & Druckman, J. N. (1996). Visibility and negotiation flexibility. *Journal of Social Psychology, 136* (1), pp. 117–20.

Druckman, D., & Mitchell, C. (1995). Flexibility in negotiation and mediation. *Annals of the American Academy, 542,* 10–23.

Dudley, B. S., Johnson, D. W., & Johnson, R. T. (1996). Conflict-resolution training and middle school students' integrative negotiation behavior. *Journal of Applied Social Psychology, 26,* 2038–52.

Duffy, K., Grosch, J., & Olczak, P. (1991). *Community mediation: A handbook for practitioners and researchers.* New York: Guilford.

Dukes, E. F., Piscolish, M. A., & Stephens, J. B. (2000). *Reaching for higher ground in conflict resolution.* San Francisco: Jossey-Bass.

Eagly, A. H., & Chaiken, S. (1975). An attribution analysis of the effect of communicator characteristics on opinion change: The case of communicator attractiveness. *Journal of Personality and Social Psychology, 32,* 136–44.

Ehtamo, H., Kettunen, E., & Hamalainen, R. P. (2001). Searching for joint gains in multi-party negotiations. *European Journal of Operational Research, 130,* 54–69.

Elahee, M., & Brooks, C. M. (2004). Trust and negotiation tactics: Perceptions about business-to-business negotiations in Mexico. *The Journal of Business & Industrial Marketing, 19* (6), 397–404.

Elahee, M. N., Kirby, S. L., & Nasif, E. (2002). National culture, trust, and perceptions about ethical behavior in intra- and cross-cultural negotiations: An analysis of NAFTA countries. *Thunderbird International Business Review, 44,* 799–818.

Elangovan, A. R. (1995a). Managerial third-party dispute intervention: A prescriptive model of strategy selection. *Academy of Management Review, 20,* 800–30.

Elangovan, A. R. (1995b). Managerial conflict intervention in organizations: Traversing the cultural mosaic. *International Journal of Conflict Management, 6,* 124–46.

Elangovan, A. R. (1998). Managerial interventions in organizational disputes: Testing a prescriptive model of strategy selection. *International Journal of Conflict Management, 9,* 301–35.

Elfenbein, H. A., Foo, M. D., White, J., Tan, H. H., & Aik, V. C. (2007). Reading your counterpart: The benefit of emotion recognition accuracy for effectiveness in negotiation. *Journal of Nonverbal Behavior, 31,* 205–23.

Elkouri, F., & Elkouri, E. (1985). *How arbitration works* (4th ed.). Washington, DC: BNA, Inc.

Elliott, M., Gray, B., & Lewicki, R. J. (2003). Lessons learned about the framing and reframing of intractable environmental conflicts. In R. J. Lewicki, B. Gray, & M. Elliott (Eds.), *Making sense of intractable environmental disputes.* Washington, DC: Island Press.

Ellis, A. P. J., West, B. J., Ryan, A. M., and DeShon, R. P. (2002). The use of impression management tactics in structured interviews: A function of question type? *Journal of Applied Psychology, 87,* 1200–08.

Elms, D. (2006). How bargaining alters outcomes: Bilateral trade negotiations and bargaining strategies. *International Negotiation, 11,* 399–429.

Epley, N., Caruso, E. M., & Bazerman, M. H. (2006). When perspective taking increases taking: Reactive egoism in social interaction. *Journal of Personality and Social Psychology, 91,* 872–89.

Esser, J., & Marriott, R. (1995a). Mediation tactics: A comparison of field and laboratory research. *Journal of Applied Social Psychology, 25,* 1530–46.

Esser, J., & Marriott, R. (1995b). A comparison of the effectiveness of substantive and contextual mediation tactics. *Journal of Applied Social Psychology, 25,* 1340–59.

Exline, R., Thibaut J., Hickey, C., & Gumpert, P. (1970). Visual interaction in relation to Machiavellianism and an unethical act. In R. Christie & F. Geis (Eds.), *Studies in Machiavellianism* (pp. 53–75). New York: Academic Press.

Eyuboglu, N., & Buja, A. (1993). Dynamics of channel negotiations: Contention and reciprocity. *Psychology & Marketing, 10,* 47–65.

Fan, Y. (2002). Guanxi's consequences. *Journal of Business Ethics, 38,* 371–80.

Fang, T. (2006). Negotiation: The Chinese style. *The Journal of Business & Industrial Marketing, 21* (1), 50–60.

Fassina, N. E. (2004). Constraining a principal's choice: Outcome vs. behavior contingent agency contracts in representative negotiations. *Negotiation Journal,* July, 435–59.

Faure, G. O. (1999). The cultural dimension of negotiation: The Chinese case. *Group Decision and Negotiation, 8,* 187–215.

Fayerweather, J., & Kapoor, A. (1976). *Strategy and negotiation for the international corporation.* Cambridge, MA: Ballinger.

Feigenbaum, C. (1975). Final-offer arbitration: Better theory than practice. *Industrial Relations, 14,* 311–17.

Feingold, P. C., & Knapp, M. L. (1977). Anti-drug abuse commercials. *Journal of Communication, 27,* 20–28.

Felstiner, W. L. F., Abel, R. L., & Sarat, A. (1980–81). The emergence and transformation of disputes: Naming, blaming, and claiming. *Law and Society Review, 15,* 631–54.

Fern, E. F., Monroe, K. B., & Avila, R. A. (1986). Effectiveness of multiple request strategies: A synthesis of research results. *Journal of Marketing Research, 23,* 144–52.

Ferris, G. R., Blas, F. R., Douglas, C., Kolodinsky, R. W., & Treadway, D. C. (2005). Personal reputation in organizations. In J. Greenberg (Ed.), *Organizational Behavior: The State of the Science.* Mahwah, NJ: Lawrence Erlbaum.

Festinger, L. (1957). *A theory of cognitive dissonance.* Stanford, CA: Stanford University Press.

Festinger, L. A., & Maccoby, N. (1964). On resistance to persuasive communication. *Journal of Abnormal and Social Psychology, 68,* 359–66.

Filley, A. C. (1975). *Interpersonal conflict resolution.* Glenview, IL: Scott Foresman.

Fishbein, M., & Azjen, I. (1975). *Belief, attitude, intention, behavior.* Reading, MA: Addison-Wesley.

Fisher, R. (1964). Fractionating conflict. In R. Fisher (Ed.), *International conflict and behavioral science: The Craigville papers.* New York: Basic Books.

Fisher, R. (1969). *International conflict for beginners.* New York: Harper & Row.

Fisher, R. (1997). *Interactive conflict resolution.* Syracuse, NY: Syracuse University Press.

Fisher, R., & Davis. W. (1999). Authority of an agent: When less is better. In R. H. Mnookin and L. E. Susskind (Eds.), *Negotiating on behalf of others* (pp. 59–80). Thousand Oaks, CA: Sage.

Fisher, R., & Ertel, D. (1995). *Getting ready to negotiate: The getting to yes workbook.* New York: Penguin.

Fisher, R., Schneider, A. K., Borgwardt, E., & Ganson, B. (1997). *Coping with international conflict.* Upper Saddle River, NJ: Prentice Hall.

Fisher, R., Ury, W., & Patton, B. (1991). *Getting to yes: Negotiating agreement without giving in* (2nd ed.). New York: Penguin.

Fiske, A. P. (1991). *Structures of social life.* New York: The Free Press.

Fiske, S. T., & Taylor, S. W. E. (1991). *Social cognition.* Reading, MA: Addison-Wesley.

Folberg, J., & Taylor, A. (1984). *Mediation: A comprehensive guide to resolving conflicts without litigation.* San Francisco: Jossey-Bass.

Folger, J. P., & Bush, R. A. B. (1996). Transformative mediation and third-party intervention: Ten hallmarks of a transformative approach to practice. *Mediation Quarterly, 13* (4), 263–78.

Folger, J. P., Poole, M. S., & Stutman, R. K. (1993). *Working through conflict: Strategies for relationships, groups and organizations* (2nd ed.). New York: HarperCollins.

Follett, M. P. (1940). *Dynamic administration: The collected papers of Mary Parker Follett.* H. C. Metcalf & L. Urwick (Eds.). New York: Harper & Brothers.

Follett, M. P. (1942). Constructive conflict. In H. C. Metcalf & L. Urwick (Eds.), *Dynamic administration: The collected papers of Mary Parker Follett* (pp. 30–49). New York: Harper & Brothers.

Foo, M. D., Elfenbein, H. A., Tan, H. H., & Aik, V. C. (2004). Emotional intelligence and negotiation: The tension between creating and claiming value. *International Journal of Conflict Management, 15,* 411–29.

Ford, D. L., Jr. (1983). Effects of personal control beliefs: An explanatory analysis of bargaining outcomes in intergroup negotiation. *Group and Organization Studies, 8,* 113–25.

Foreman, P., & Murnighan, J. K. (1996). Learning to avoid the winner's curse. *Organizational Behavior and Human Decision Processes, 67,* 170–80.

Forgas, J. P. (1992). Affect in social judgments and decisions: A multiprocess model. *Advances in Experimental Social Psychology, 25,* 227–75.

Forgas, J. P., & Fiedler, K. (1996). Us and them: Mood effects on intergroup discrimination. *Journal of Personality and Social Psychology, 70,* 28–40.

Fortgang, R. S., Lax, D. A., & Sebenius, J. K. (2003, February). Negotiating the spirit of the deal. *Harvard Business Review,* 66–75.

Fortune, A., & Brodt, S. E. (2000). Face-to-face or virtually, for the second time around: The influence of task, past experience and media on trust and deception in negotiation. Paper presented at the annual meeting of the Academy of Management, Toronto, Canada.

Foster, D. A. (1992). *Bargaining across borders: How to negotiate business successfully anywhere in the world.* New York: McGraw-Hill.

Foulger, D. (2004, February). Models of the communication process. Unpublished paper, available at http://foulger.info/davis/researc/unifiedModelOfCommunicaittion.htm.

Fox, C. (2006, June/July). International negotiator. *The British Journal of Administrative Management,* 20–27.

Fragale, A. R., & Heath, C. (2004). Evolving informational credentials: The (mis)attribution of believable facts to credible sources. *Personality and Social Psychology Bulletin, 30,* 225–36.

Francis, J. N. P. (1991). When in Rome? The effects of cultural adaptation on intercultural business negotiations. *Journal of International Business Studies, 22,* 403–28.

Freedman, J. L., & Fraser, S. C. (1966). Compliance without pressure: The foot in the door technique. *Journal of Personality and Social Psychology, 4,* 195–202.

Friedman, R. (1994). *Front stage, backstage:* The dramatic structure of labor negotiations. Cambridge, MA: MIT Press.

Friedman, R., Anderson, C., Brett, J., Olekalns, M., Goates, N., & Lisco, C. C. (2004). The positive and negative effects of anger on dispute resolution: Evidence from electronically mediated disputes. *Journal of Applied Psychology, 89,* 369–76.

Friedman, R. A., & Currall, S. C. (2003). Conflict escalation: Dispute exacerbating elements of e-mail communication. *Human Relations, 56,* 1325–47.

French, J. R. P., & Raven, B. (1959). The bases of social power. In D. Cartwright (Ed.), *Studies in social power.* Ann Arbor, MI: Institute for Social Research.

Freund, J. C. (1994, Winter). Being a smart negotiator. *Board and Directors, 2* (18), 33–36.

Froman, L. A., & Cohen, M. D. (1970). Compromise and logrolling: Comparing the efficiency of two bargaining processes. *Behavioral Sciences, 15,* 180–83.

Frost, P. (1987). Power, politics and influence. In F. M. Jablin (Ed.), *Handbook of Organizational Communication* (pp. 403–548). Newbury Park, CA: Sage.

Fry, W. R. (1985). The effect of dyad Machiavellianism and visual access on integrative bargaining outcomes. *Personality and Social Psychology Bulletin, 11,* 51–62.

Fry, W. R., Firestone, I. J., & Williams, D. (1979, April). Bargaining process in mixed-singles dyads: Loving and losing. Paper presented at the annual meeting of the Eastern Psychological Association, Philadelphia, PA.

Fry, W. R., Firestone, I. J., & Williams, D. L. (1983). Negotiation process and outcome of stranger dyads and dating couples: Do lovers lose? *Basic and Applied Social Psychology, 4,* 1–16.

Fuller, R. G. C., & Sheehy-Skeffington, A. (1974). Effects of group laughter on responses to humorous materials: A replication and extension. *Psychological Reports, 35,* 531–34.

Fulmer, I. S., & Barry, B. (2004). The smart negotiator: Cognitive ability and emotional intelligence in negotiation. *International Journal of Conflict Management, 15,* 245–72.

Funder, D. C. (2001). Personality. *Annual Review of Psychology, 52,* 197–221.

Gadlin, H. (2000). The ombudsman: What's in a name? *Negotiation Journal, 16,* 37–48.

Galinsky, A. D., Gruenfeld, D. H., & Magee, J. C. (2003). From power to action. *Journal of Personality and Social Psychology, 85,* 453–66.

Galinsky, A. D., Maddux, W. M., Gilin, D., & White, J. B. (2008). Why it pays to get inside the head of your opponent: The differential effects of perspective taking and empathy in negotiations. *Psychological Science, 19,* 378–84.

Galinsky, A. D., Magee, J. C., Inesi, M. N., & Gruenfeld, D. H. (2006). Power and perspectives not taken. *Psychological Science, 17,* 1068–74.

Galinsky, A. D., & Mussweiler, T. (2001). First offers as anchors: The role of perspective-taking and negotiator focus. *Journal of Personality and Social Psychology, 81* (4), 657–69.

Galinsky, A. D., Mussweiler, T., & Medvec, V. H. (2002). Disconnecting outcomes and evaluations: The role of negotiator focus. *Journal of Personality and Social Psychology, 83* (5), 1131–40.

Galinsky, A. D., Seiden, V. L., Kim, P. H., & Medvec, V. H. (2002). The dissatisfaction of having your first offer accepted: The role of counterfactual thinking in negotiations. *Personality and Social Psychology Bulletin, 28* (2), 271–83.

Gallupe, R. B., & Cooper, W. H. (1993). Brainstorming electronically. *Sloan Management Review, 35* (1), 27–36.

Gamson, W. A. (1961). A theory of coalition formation. *American Sociological Review, 26,* 565–73.

Ganesan, S. (1993). Negotiation strategies and the nature of channel relationships. *Journal of Marketing Research, 30,* 183–203.

Garcia, S. M., Darley, J. M., & Robinson, R. J. (2001). Morally questionable tactics: Negotiations between district attorneys and public defenders. *Personality and Social Psychology Bulletin, 27* (6), 731–43.

Geis, F. L., & Moon, T. H. (1981). Machiavellianism and deception. *Journal of Personality and Social Psychology, 41,* 766–75.

Gelfand, M., & McCusker, C. (2002). Metaphor and the cultural construction of negotiation: A paradigm for theory and practice. In M. Gannon & K. L. Newman (Eds.), *Handbook of cross-cultural management.* New York: Blackwell.

Gelfand, M. J., & Christakopoulou, S. (1999). Culture and negotiator cognition: Judgment accuracy and negotiation processes in individualistic and collectivistic cultures. *Organizational Behavior and Human Decision Processes, 79,* 248–69.

Gelfand, M. J., & Dyer, N. (2000). A cultural perspective on negotiation: Progress, pitfalls, and prospects. *Applied Psychology: An International Review, 49,* 62–99.

Gelfand, M. J., Higgins, M., Nishii, L. H., Raver, J. L., Dominguez, A., Murakami, F. et al. (2002). Culture and egocentric perceptions of fairness in conflict and negotiation. *Journal of Applied Psychology, 87* (5), 833–45.

Gelfand, M. J., Nishii, L. H., Holcombe, K. M., Dyer, N., Ohbuchi, K., & Fukuno, M. (2001). Cultural influences on cognitive representations of conflict: Interpretations of conflict episodes in the United States and Japan. *Journal of Applied Psychology, 86,* 1059–74.

Gelfand, M. J., & Realo, A. (1999). Individualism-collectivism and accountability in intergroup negotiations. *Journal of Applied Psychology, 84,* 721–36.

Gentner, J., Loewenstein, J., & Thompson, L. (2003). Learning and transfer: A general role for analogical encoding. *Journal of Educational Psychology, 95,* 393–408.

George, A. L. (1993). *Bridging the gap: Coercive diplomacy as an alternative to war.* Washington, DC: U.S. Institute of Peace Press.

George, J. M., Jones, G. R., & Gonzalez, J. A. (1998). The role of affect in cross-cultural negotiations. *Journal of International Business Studies, 29,* 749–72.

Gerhart, B., & Rynes, S. (1991). Determinants and consequences of salary negotiations by male and female MBA graduates. *Journal of Applied Psychology, 76,* 256–62.

Gersick, C. J. G. (1988). Time and transition in work teams: Toward a new model of group development. *Academy of Management Journal, 31,* 9–41.

Gersick, C. J. G. (1989). Making time: Predictable transitions in task groups. *Academy of Management Journal, 32,* 274–309.

Geyelin, M. (1997, July 7). Mississippi becomes first state to settle suit against big tobacco companies. *The Wall Street Journal,* p. B1.

Ghauri, P., & Fang, T. (2001). Negotiating with the Chinese: A socio-cultural analysis. *Journal of World Business, 36,* 303–25.

Ghosh, D. (1996). Nonstrategic delay in bargaining: An experimental investigation. *Organizational Behavior and Human Decision Processes, 67,* 312–25.

Ghosh, D., & Boldt, M. N. (2006). The effect of framing and compensation structure on seller's negotiated transfer price. *Journal of Managerial Issues, 18,* 453–67.

Gibb, J. (1961). Defensive communication. *Journal of Communication, 3,* 141–48.

Gibbons, P., Bradac, J. J., & Busch, J. D. (1992). The role of language in negotiations: Threats and promises. In L. Putnam & M. Roloff (Eds.), *Communication and negotiation* (pp. 156–75). Newbury Park, CA: Sage.

Gibson, K., Thompson, L., & Bazerman, M. (1996). Shortcomings of neutrality in mediation: Solutions based on rationality. *Negotiation Journal, 12,* 69–80.

Giebels, E., de Dreu, C. K. W., & van de Vliert, E. (2003). No way out or swallow the bait of two-sided exit options in negotiation: The influence of social motives and interpersonal trust. *Group Processes and Intergroup Relations, 6,* 369–86.

Gillespie, J. J., & Bazerman, M. H. (1997). Parasitic integration: Win-win agreements containing losers. *Negotiation Journal, 13,* 271–82.

Gillespie, J. J., & Bazerman, M. H. (1998, April). Pre-settlement settlement (PreSS): A simple technique for initiating complex negotiations. *Negotiation Journal, 14,* 149–59.

Gillespie, J. J., Brett, J. M., & Weingart, L. R. (2000). Interdependence, social motives, and outcome satisfaction in multiparty negotiation. *European Journal of Social Psychology, 30,* 779–97.

Gilligan, C. (1982). *In a different voice.* Cambridge, MA: Harvard University Press.

Gilovich, T., Vallone, R., & Tversky, A. (1985). The hot hand in basketball: On misperception of random sequences. *Cognitive Psychology, 17,* 295–314.

Gilson, R. J., & Mnookin, R. H. (1994). Disputing through agents: Cooperation and conflict between lawyers in litigation. *Columbia Law Review, 94* (2), 509–66.

Girard, J. (1989). *How to close every sale.* New York: Warner Books.

Gire, J. T. (1997). The varying effect of individualism-collectivism on preference for methods of conflict resolution. *Canadian Journal of Behavioural Science, 29,* 38–43.

Gist, M. E., Stevens, C. K., & Bavetta, A. G. (1991). Effects of self-efficacy and post-training intervention on the acquisition and maintenance of complex interpersonal skills. *Personnel Psychology, 44,* 837–61.

Glasl, F. (1982). The process of conflict escalation and roles of third parties. In G. B. J. Bomers & R. B. Peterson (Eds.), *Conflict management and industrial relations* (pp. 119–41). Boston: Kluwer.

Glasman, L. R., & Albarracín, D. (2006). Forming attitudes that predict future behavior: A meta-analysis of the attitude-behavior relation. *Psychological Bulletin, 132,* 778–822.

Glick, S., & Croson, R. (2001). Reputations in negotiation. In S. Hock & H. Kunreuther (Eds.), *Wharton on decision making* (Ch. 10, pp. 177–86). New York: John Wiley & Sons.

Glover, S. H., Bumpus, M. A., Logan, J. E., & Ciesla, J. R. (1997). Re-examining the influence of individual values on ethical decision making. *Journal of Business Ethics, 16,* 1319–29.

Goates, N. (2008, August). Reputation as a basis for trust: Social information, emotional state and trusting behavior. Paper presented to the Academy of Management Annual Meetings.

Goffman, E. (1969). *Strategic interaction.* Philadelphia: University of Philadelphia Press.

Goffman, E. (1974). *Frame analysis.* New York: Harper & Row.

Goldberg, L. R. (1993). The structure of phenotypic personality traits. *American Psychologist, 48,* 26–34.

Goldberg, S. B. (2005). The secrets of successful mediators. *Negotiation Journal, 21* (3), 365–76.

Goldberg, S. B., & Shaw, M. L. (2007). The secrets of successful (and unsuccessful) mediators continued: Studies two and three. *Negotiation Journal, 23,* 393–418.

Goleman, D. (1995). *Emotional intelligence.* New York: Bantam Books.

Gonzalez, R. M., Lerner, J. S., Moore, D. A., & Babcock, L. C. (2004). Mad, mean, and mistaken: The effects of anger on strategic social perception and behavior. Paper presented at the annual meeting of the International Association for Conflict Management, Pittsburgh.

Goodstadt, B. E., & Hjelle, L. A. (1973). Power to the powerless: Locus of control and the use of power. *Journal of Personality and Social Psychology, 27,* 191–96.

Gordon, R. A. (1996). Impact of ingratiation on judgments and evaluations: A meta-analytic investigation. *Journal of Personality and Social Psychology, 71,* 54–70.

Gordon, T. (1977). *Leader effectiveness training.* New York: Wyden Books.

Gottfredson, L. (1997). Mainstream science on intelligence: An editorial with 52 signatories, history and bibliography. *Intelligence, 24,* 13–23.

Gottman, J. M. (2007, December). The seven principles for making marriage work. *Harvard Business Review,* 45–50.

Gottman, J. M. (2007, December). Making relationships work: A conversation with psychologist John Gottman. *Harvard Business Review,* 45–50.

Gouldner, A. W. (1960). The norm of reciprocity: A preliminary statement. *American Sociological Review, 25,* 161–78.

Graham, J. L. (1983). Brazilian, Japanese, and American business negotiations. *Journal of International Business Studies, 14,* 47–61.

Graham, J. L. (1984). A comparison of Japanese and American business negotiations. *International Journal of Research in Marketing, 1,* 50–68.

Graham, J. L. (1993). The Japanese negotiation style: Characteristics of a distinct approach. *Negotiation Journal, 9,* 123–40.

Graham, J. L., Evenko, L. L., & Rajan, M. N. (1992). An empirical comparison of Soviet and American business negotiations. *Journal of International Business Studies, 23,* 387–418.

Graham, J. L., & Mintu-Wimsat, A. (1997). Culture's influence on business negotiations in four countries. *Group Decision and Negotiation, 6,* 483–502.

Graham, J. L., & Sano, Y. (1989). *Smart bargaining.* New York: Harper Business.

Granovetter, M. (1973). The strength of weak ties. *American Journal of Sociology, 78,* 1360–80.

Gray, B. (1991). The framing of disputes: Partners, processes and outcomes in different contexts. Paper presented at the annual conference of the International Association of Conflict Management, Den Dolder, The Netherlands.

Gray, B. (1994). The gender-based foundation of negotiation theory. In B. H. Sheppard, R. J. Lewicki, & R. J. Bies (Eds.), *Research in negotiation in organizations* (Vol. 4, pp. 3–36). Greenwich, CT: JAI Press.

Gray, B. (1997). Framing and reframing of intractable environmental disputes. In R. J. Lewicki, R. J. Bies, & B. Sheppard (Eds.), *Research on negotiation in organizations* (Vol. 6, pp. 163–88). Greenwich, CT: JAI Press.

Gray, B. (2003a). Framing of environmental disputes. In R. J. Lewicki, B. Gray, & M. Elliott, *Making sense of intractable environmental disputes.* Washington, DC: Island Press.

Gray, B. (2003b). Negotiating with your nemesis. *Negotiation Journal, 19* (4), 299–310.

Gray, B., & Donnellon, A. (1989). *An interactive theory of reframing in negotiation.* Unpublished manuscript.

Gray, B., Younglove-Webb, B., & Purdy, J. M. (1997). Frame repertoires, conflict styles and negotiation outcomes. Paper read at the International Association of Conflict Management, Bonn, Germany.

Green, G. M., & Wheeler, M. (2004). Awareness and action in critical moments. *Negotiation Journal, 20* (2), 349–64.

Green, R. M. (1994). *The ethical manager: A new method for business ethics.* Upper Saddle River, NJ: Prentice Hall.

Greenberg, B. S., & Miller, G. R. (1966). The effects of low-credible sources on message acceptance. *Speech Monographs, 33,* 135–36.

Greenberg, J. (1990). Organizational justice: Yesterday, today, tomorrow. *Journal of Management, 16,* 299–432.

Greenberg, J., & Colquitt, J. (2005). *Handbook of organizational justice.* Mahwah, NJ: Lawrence Erlbaum Associates.

Greenhalgh, L. (1986). Managing conflict. *Sloan Management Review, 27,* 45–51.

Greenhalgh, L. (2001). *Managing strategic relationships.* New York: Free Press.

Greenhalgh, L., & Chapman, D. (1996). Relationships between disputants: Analysis of their characteristics and impact. In S. Gleason (Ed.), *Frontiers in dispute resolution and human resources* (pp. 203–28). East Lansing, MI: Michigan State University Press.

Greenhalgh, L., & Chapman, D. (1998). Negotiator relationships, construct measurement, and demonstration of their impact on the process and outcomes of negotiation. *Group Decision and Negotiation, 7,* 465–89.

Greenhalgh, L., & Gilkey, R. W. (1993). The effect of relationship orientation on negotiators cognitions and tactics. *Group Decision and Negotiation, 2,* 167–86.

Greenhalgh, L., & Kramer, R. M. (1990). Strategic choice in conflicts: The importance of relationships. In K. Zald (Ed.), *Organizations and nation states: New perspectives on conflict and cooperation* (pp. 181–220). San Francisco: Jossey-Bass.

Greenhalgh, L., & Neslin, S. A. (1983). Determining outcomes of negotiations. In M. H. Bazerman & R. J. Lewicki (Eds.), *Negotiating in organizations* (pp. 114–34). Beverly Hills, CA: Sage.

Greig, J. M. (2001). Recognizing conditions of ripeness for international mediation between enduring rivals. *Journal of Conflict Resolution, 45,* 691–718.

Grigsby, D. W. (1981, November). The effects of an intermediate mediation step on bargaining behavior under various forms of compulsory arbitration. Paper presented to the Annual Meeting of the American Institute for Decision Sciences, Boston, MA.

Grigsby, D. W., & Bigoness, W. J. (1982). Effects of mediation and alternative forms of arbitration on bargaining behavior: A laboratory study. *Journal of Applied Psychology, 67,* 549–54.

Gross, M. A., & Guerrero, L. K. (2000). Managing conflict appropriately and effectively: An application of the competence model to Rahim's organizational conflict styles. *International Journal of Conflict Management, 11,* 200–26.

Gruder, C. L. (1971). Relationships with opponent and partner in bargaining. *Journal of Conflict Resolution, 15,* 403–16.

Gruder, C. L., & Rosen, N. (1971). Effects of intragroup relations on intergroup bargaining. *International Journal of Group Tension, 1,* 301–17.

Guadagnoa, R. E., & Cialdini, R. B. (2007). Persuade him by email, but see her in person: Online persuasion revisited. *Computers in Human Behavior, 23,* 999–1015.

Gulliver, P. (1979). *Disputes and negotiations: A cross-cultural perspective.* New York: Academic Press.

Guo, X., & Lim, J. (2007). Negotiation support systems and team negotiations: The coalition formation perspective. *Information and Software Technology, 49,* 1121–27.

Guth, W., Schmittberger, R., & Schwarze, B. (1982). An experimental analysis of ultimatum bargaining. *Journal of Economic Behavior and Organization, 3,* 367–88.

Guth, W., & Tietz, R. (1990). Ultimatum bargaining behavior: A survey and comparison of experimental results. *Journal of Economic Psychology, 11,* 417–49.

Habeeb, W. M. (1988). *Power and tactics in international negotiation.* Baltimore, MD: Johns Hopkins University Press.

Haccoun, R. R., & Klimoski, R. J. (1975). Negotiator status and source: A study of negotiation behavior. *Organizational Behavior and Human Performance, 14,* 342–59.

Haddock, G., Maio, G. R., Arnold, K., & Huskinson, T. (2008). Should persuasion be affective or cognitive? The moderating effects of need for affect and need for cognition. *Personality and Social Psychology Bulletin, 34,* 769–78.

Hagewood, K. (2001, April 26–28). *Online solution for online problems.* Paper presented at Collaboration in the Capital: The power of ADR, The American Bar Association meeting.

Hall, E. T. (1959). *The silent language.* New York: Anchor Press.

Hall, E. T. (1960, May–June). The silent language of overseas business. *Harvard Business Review, 38,* 87–96.

Hall, E. T. (1976). *Beyond culture.* New York: Anchor Press.

Hall, E. T., & Hall, M. R. (1990). *Understanding cultural differences.* Yarmouth, ME: Intercultural Press.

Hall, J. (1969). *Conflict management survey: A survey of one's characteristic reaction to and handling conflict between himself and others.* Conroe, TX: Teleometrics International.

Halpern, J. J., & Parks, J. M. (1996). Vive la difference: Differences between males and females in process and outcomes in a low-conflict negotiation. *International Journal of Conflict Management, 7,* 45–70.

Hamilton, J. B., & Strutton, D. (1994). Two practical guidelines for resolving truth telling problems in business transactions. *Journal of Business Ethics, 13,* 899–912.

Hammond, J. S., Keeney, R. L., & Raiffa, H. (1998). The hidden traps in decision making. *Harvard Business Review, 76* (5), 47–58.

Hamner, W. C. (1980). The influence of structural, individual, and strategic differences. In D. L. Harnett & L. L. Cummings (Eds.), *Bargaining behavior* (pp. 21–80). Houston, TX: Dame Publications.

Hanany, E., Kilgour, D. M., & Gerchak, Y. (2007). Final-offer arbitration and risk aversion in bargaining. *Management Science, 53* (11), 1785–92.

Hardin, R. G. (1968). The tragedy of the commons. *Science, 162,* 1243–48.

Harding, S. (1986). *The science question in feminism.* Ithaca, NY: Cornell University Press.

Harinck, F., de Dreu, C. K. W., & Van Vienen, A. E. M. (2000). The impact of conflict issues on fixed-pie perceptions, problem solving, and integrative outcomes in negotiation. *Organizational Behavior and Human Decision Processes, 81,* 329–58.

Harris, K. L., & Carnevale, P. J. D. (1990). Chilling and hastening: The influence of third-party power and interests on negotiation. *Organizational Behavior and Human Decision Processes, 47,* 138–60.

Hartzell, C. A. (1999). Explaining the stability of negotiated settlements to intrastate wars. *Journal of Conflict Resolution, 43,* 3–22.

Harvey, O. J. (1953). An experimental approach to the study status relations in informal groups. *Sociometry, 18,* 357–67.

Hassett, J. (1981, June). Is it right? An inquiry into everyday ethics. *Psychology Today,* 49–53.

Hassett, J. (1981, November). But that would be wrong . . . *Psychology Today,* 34–53.

Hassett, J. (1982, August). Correlates of moral values and behavior. Paper presented at the annual meeting of the Academy of Management, New York.

Hatsumi, R. (1993, April 15). A single "hai" won't do. *The New York Times.*

Hegarty, W., & Sims, H. P. (1978). Some determinants of unethical decision behavior: An experiment. *Journal of Applied Psychology, 63,* 451–57.

Hegtved, K. A., & Killian, C. (1999). Fairness and emotions: Reactions to the process and outcomes of negotiations. *Social Forces, 78,* 269–303.

Heider, F. (1958). *The psychology of interpersonal relations.* New York: John Wiley and Sons.

Henderson, B. (1973). *The nonlogical strategy.* Boston: Boston Consulting Group.

Henderson, M. D., Trope, Y., & Carnevale, P. J. (2006). Negotiation from a near and distant time perspective. *Journal of Personality and Social Psychology 91,* 712–29.

Hendon, D. W., & Hendon, R. A. (1990). *World-class negotiating: Dealmaking in the global marketplace.* New York: John Wiley and Sons.

Hendon, D. W., Roy, M. H., & Ahmed, Z. U. (2003). Negotiation concession patterns: A multi-country, multiperiod study. *American Business Review, 21,* 75–83.

Henkoff, R. (1997, December 8). Are you (more than) ready for a pay raise? *Fortune,* 233–38.

Hermann, M. G., & Kogan, N. (1977). Effects of negotiators' personalities on negotiating behavior. In D. Druckman (Ed.), *Negotiations: Social-psychological perspectives* (pp. 247–74). Beverly Hills, CA: Sage.

Herrman, M. S., Hollett, N., Gale, J., & Foster, M. (2001). Defining mediator knowledge and skills. *Negotiation Journal, 17,* 139–54.

Higgins, E. T. (1987). Self discrepancy theory: A theory relating self and affect. *Psychological Review, 94,* 319–40.

Hill, B. J. (1982). An analysis of conflict resolution techniques: From problem-solving workshops to theory. *Journal of Conflict Resolution, 26,* 109–38.

Hill, L. A. (1997). Building effective one-on-one relationships. Harvard Business School note 9-497-028.

Hiltrop, J. (1989). Factors associated with successful labor mediation. In K. Kressel & D. Pruitt (Eds.), *Mediation research* (pp. 241–62). San Francisco: Jossey-Bass.

Hiltrop, J. M., & Rubin, J. Z. (1982). Effects of intervention mode and conflict of interest on dispute resolution. *Journal of Personality and Social Psychology, 42,* 665–72.

Hilty, J. A., & Carnevale, P. J. (1993). Black-hat/white-hat strategy in bilateral negotiation. *Organizational Behavior and Human Decision Processes, 55,* 444–69.

Hinton, B. L., Hamner, W. C., & Pohlan, N. F. (1974). Influence and award of magnitude, opening bid and concession rate on profit earned in a managerial negotiating game. *Behavioral Science, 19,* 197–203.

Hirokawa, R. Y. (1981). Improving intra-organizational communication: A lesson from Japanese management. *Communication Quarterly, 30,* 35–40.

Hitt, W. (1990). *Ethics and leadership: Putting theory into practice.* Columbus, OH: Battelle Press.

Hoare, C. H. (1994). Psychological identity development in United States society: Its role in fostering exclusion of other cultures. In E. P. Salett & D. R. Koslow (Eds.) *Race, ethnicity and self: Identity in multicultural perspective* (pp. 24–41). Washington, DC: National Multicultural Institute.

Hochberg, A. M., & Kressel, K. (1996). Determinations of successful and unsuccessful divorce negotiations. *Journal of Divorce and Remarriage, 25,* 1–21.

Hocker, J. L., & Wilmot, W. W. (1985). *Interpersonal conflict* (2nd ed.). Dubuque, IA: Wm. C. Brown.

Hoffman, D. A. (2006). The future of ADR practice: Three hopes, three fears, and three predictions. *Negotiation Journal, 22* (4), 467–73.

Hofstede, G. (1980a). Motivation, leadership, and organization: Do American theories apply abroad? *Organizational Dynamics, 9,* 42–63.

Hofstede, G. (1980b). *Culture's consequences: International differences in work related values.* Beverly Hills, CA: Sage.

Hofstede, G. (1989). Cultural predictors of national negotiation styles. In. F. Mautner-Markhof (Ed.), *Processes of international negotiations* (pp. 193–201). Boulder, CO: Westview Press.

Hofstede, G. (1991). *Culture and organizations: Software of the mind.* London, UK: McGraw-Hill.

Hofstede, G., & Bond, M. H. (1988). Confucius and economic growth: New trends in culture's consequences. *Organizational Dynamics, 16,* 4–21.

Hogg, M. A., Terry, D. J., & White, K. M. (1995). A tale of two theories: A critical comparison of identity theory with social identity theory. *Social Psychology Quarterly, 58,* 255–69.

Holaday, L. C. (2002). Stage development theory: A natural framework for understanding the mediation process. *Negotiation Journal,* 191–210.

Hollingshead, A. B., & Carnevale, P. J. (1990, August). Positive affect and decision frame in integrative bargaining: A reversal of the frame effect. Paper presented at the 50th Annual Meeting of the Academy of Management, San Francisco.

Holmes, J. G., & Murray, S. I. (1996). Conflict in close relationships. In E. T. Higgins & A. W. Kruglanski (Eds.), *Social psychology: Handbook of basic principles* (pp. 579–621). New York: Guilford.

Holmes, M. (1992). Phase structures in negotiation. In L. Putnam & M. Roloff (Eds.), *Communication and negotiation* (pp. 83–105). Newbury Park, CA: Sage.

Holmes, M., & Poole, M. S. (1991). Longitudinal analysis of interaction. In S. Duck & B. Montgomery (Eds.), *Studying interpersonal interaction* (pp. 286–302). New York: Guilford.

Homans, G. C. (1961). *Social behavior: Its elementary forms.* New York: Harcourt, Brace & World Co.

Hopmann, P. T. (1995). Two paradigms of negotiation: Bargaining and problem solving. *Annals of the American Academy, 542,* 24–47.

Hornstein, H. (1965). Effects of different magnitudes of threat upon interpersonal bargaining. *Journal of Experimental Social Psychology, 1,* 282–93.

Hosmer, L. T. (2003). *The ethics of management* (4th ed.). Boston: McGraw-Hill/Irwin.

House, R. J., Shane, S. A., & Herold, D. M. (1996). Rumors of the death of dispositional research are vastly exaggerated. *Academy of Management Review, 21,* 203–24.

Hovland, C. I., & Mandell, W. (1952). An experimental comparison of conclusion drawing by the communicator and by the audience. *Journal of Abnormal and Social Psychology, 47,* 581–88.

Howard, D. J. (1990). The influence of verbal responses to common greetings on compliance behavior: The foot-in-the-mouth effect. *Journal of Applied Social Psychology, 20,* 1185–96.

Huang, X., & van de Vliert, E. (2004). A multilevel approach to investigating cross-national differences in negotiation processes. *International Negotiation, 9,* 471–84.

Hullett, C. R. (2005). The impact of mood on persuasion: A meta-analysis. *Communication Research, 32,* 423–42.

Hunt, C. S., & Kernan, M. C. (2005). Framing negotiations in affective terms: Methodological and preliminary theoretical findings. *International Journal of Conflict Management, 16,* 128–56.

Hurn, B. J. (2007). The influence of culture on international business negotiations. *Industrial and Commercial Training, 39* (7), 354–60.

Husted, B. W. (1996). Mexican small business negotiations with U.S. companies: Challenges and opportunities. *International Small Business Journal, 14,* 45–54.

Ibarra, H., & Andrews, S. (1993). Power, social influence and sense making: Effects of network centrality and proximity on employee perceptions. *Administrative Science Quarterly, 38,* 277–303.

Ikle, F. C. (1964). *How nations negotiate.* New York: Harper & Row.

Isajiw, W. W. (2000). Approaches to ethnic conflict resolution: paradigms and principles. *International Journal of Intercultural Relations, 24,* 105–24.

Isen, A. M., & Baron, R. A. (1991). Positive affect as a factor in organizational behavior. In B. M. Staw & L. L. Cummings (Eds.), *Research in organizational behavior* (Vol. 13, pp. 1–53). Greenwich, CT: JAI Press.

Ivey, A. E., & Simek-Downing, L. (1980). *Counseling and psychotherapy.* Englewood Cliffs, NJ: Prentice Hall.

Jackall, R. (1988). *Moral mazes.* New York: Oxford University Press.

Jackman, R. (1996, April). Back room politics solve today's problem—but create tomorrow's? *Consensus,* 1, 2.

Jackson, C., and King, D. (1983). The effects of representatives' power within their own organization on the outcome of a negotiation. *Academy of Management Journal, 26,* 1, 178–85.

Jackson, R., & Caligari, R. (2007, November 22–25). Mediation and intervention. *Credit Management.*

Jackson, S., & Allen, M. (1987). Meta-analysis of the effectiveness of one-sided and two-sided argumentation. Paper presented at the annual meeting of the International Communication Association, Montreal, Quebec, Canada.

Jacobs, A. T. (1951). Some significant factors influencing the range of indeterminateness in collective bargaining negotiations. Unpublished doctoral dissertation, University of Michigan, Ann Arbor, MI.

Jacobs, Margaret, A. (1998, January 20). Red Lobster tale: Peers decide fired waitress's fate. *The Wall Street Journal,* B1, B6.

Jandt, F., & Pedersen, P. B. (Eds.). (1996). *Constructive conflict management: Asia-Pacific cases.* Thousand Oaks, CA: Sage.

Janis, I. (1982). *Groupthink: Psychological studies of policy decisions and fiascoes.* Boston: Houghton Mifflin.

Janis, I. (1989). *Crucial decisions: Leadership in policymaking and crisis management.* New York: Free Press.

Janis, I., & Mann, L. (1977). *Decision making.* New York: Free Press.

Janosik, R. J. (1987). Rethinking the culture-negotiation link. *Negotiation Journal, 3,* 385–95.

Jehn, E., & Mannix, E. (2001). The dynamic nature of conflict: a longitudinal study of intragroup conflict and group performance. *Academy of Management Journal, 44* (2), 238–51.

Jensen, L. (1995). Issue flexibility in negotiating internal war. *Annals of the American Academy of Political and Social Science, 542,* 116–30.

Johns, G. (1989). Substantive and methodological constraints on behavior and attitudes in organizational research. *Organizational Behavior and Human Decision Processes, 49,* 80–104.

Johnson, B. T., & Eagly, A. H. (1989). Effects of involvement on persuasion: A meta-analysis. *Psychological Bulletin, 106,* 290–314.

Johnson, B. T., & Eagly, A. H. (1990). Involvement and persuasion: Types, traditions, and the evidence. *Psychological Bulletin, 107,* 375–84.

Johnson, D. W. (1971). Role reversal: A summary and review of the research. *International Journal of Group Tensions, 1,* 318–34.

Johnson, D. W., & Dustin, R. (1970). The initiation of cooperation through role reversal. *Journal of Social Psychology, 82,* 193–203.

Johnson, D. W., & Lewicki, R. J. (1969). The initiation of superordinate goals. *Journal of Applied Behavioral Science, 5,* 9–24.

Johnson, R. (1993). *Negotiation basics: Concepts, skills, and exercises.* Newbury Park, CA: Sage.

Johnston, R. W. (1982, March–April). Negotiation strategies: Different strokes for different folks. *Personnel, 59,* 36–45.

Jones, E. E. (1964). *Ingratiation.* New York: Appleton-Century-Crofts.

Jones, E. E., & Nisbett, R. E. (1976). The actor and the observer: Divergent perceptions of causality. In J. W. Thibaut, J. T. Spence, & R. C. Carson (Eds.), *Contemporary topics in social psychology* (pp. 37–52). Morristown, NJ: General Learning Press.

Jones, M., & Worchel, S. (1992). Representatives in negotiation: "Internal" variables that affect "external" negotiations. *Basic and Applied Social Psychology, 13* (3), 323–36.

Jones, S. B., & Burgoon, M. (1975). Empirical investigations of language intensity: 2. The effects of irrelevant fear and language intensity on attitude change. *Human Communication Research, 1,* 248–51.

Jones, T. S., & Bodtker, A. (2001). Mediating with heart in mind: Addressing emotion in mediation practice. *Negotiation Journal, 17,* 217–44.

Jones, T. S., & Remland, M. S. (1993). Nonverbal communication and conflict escalation: An attribution-based model. *International Journal of Conflict Management, 4,* 119–37.

Jordan, J. M., & Roloff, M. E. (1997). Planning skills and negotiator goal accomplishment. *Communication Research, 24,* 31–63.

Joseph, M. L., & Willis, R. H. (1963). An experimental analog to two-party bargaining. *Behavioral Science, 8,* 1117–27.

Kabanoff, B. (1987). Predictive validity of the MODE conflict instrument. *Journal of Applied Psychology, 72,* 160–63.

Kadushin, C. (1968). Power, influence and social circles: A new methodology for studying opinion makers. *American Sociological Review, 33,* 685–99.

Kahneman, D., Knetsch, J. L., & Thaler, R. H. (1990). Experimental tests of the endowment effect and the Coase Theorem. *Journal of Political Economy, 98,* 1325–48.

Kahneman, D., & Miller, D. T. (1986). Norm Theory— Comparing Reality to Its Alternatives. *Psychological Review, 93,* 136–53.

Kahneman, D., & Tversky, A. (1979). Prospect theory: An analysis of decisions under risk. *Econometrica, 47,* 263–91.

Kalbfleisch, P. J. (1994). The language of detecting deceit. *Journal of Language and Social Psychology, 13* (4), 469–96.

Kale, S. H., & Barnes, J. W. (1992). Understanding the domain of cross-national buyer-seller interactions. *Journal of International Business Studies, 23,* 101–32.

Kamen, V. S., & Hartel, C. E. (1994). Gender differences in anticipated pay negotiation strategies and outcomes. *Journal of Business and Psychology, 9,* 183–97.

Kanowitz, L. (1985). *Alternative dispute resolution.* St. Paul, MN: West.

Kant, I. (1963). *Lectures on ethics.* New York: Harper & Row.

Kant, I. (1964). *Groundwork of the metaphysic of morals.* New York: Harper & Row.

Kanter, R. (1979). Power failures in management circles. *Harvard Business Review, 57,* 65–75.

Kaplan, Robert. (1984, Spring). Trade routes: The manager's network of relationships. *Organizational Dynamics, 12,* 37–52.

Karambayya, R., & Brett, J. M. (1989). Managers handling disputes: Third-party roles and perceptions of fairness. *Academy of Management Journal, 32,* 263–91.

Karambayya, R., Brett, J. M., & Lytle, A. (1992). Effects of formal authority and experience on third-party roles,

outcomes, and perceptions of fairness. *Academy of Management Journal, 35,* 426–38.

Karrass, C. L. (1974). *Give and take.* New York: Thomas Y. Crowell.

Karrass, C. L. (1999, May 6). The art of win-win negotiations. *Purchasing,* 28.

Karrass, G. (1985). *Negotiate to close: How to make more successful deals.* New York: Simon & Schuster.

Katsh, E., & Rifkin, J. (2001). *Introduction to online dispute resolution.* San Francisco: Jossey-Bass.

Kaufman, S., & Duncan, G. (1992). A formal framework for mediator mechanisms and motivations. *Journal of Conflict Resolution, 36,* 688–707.

Keer, S., & Naimark, R. W. (2001). Arbitrators do not "split the baby": Empirical evidence from international business arbitration. *Journal of International Arbitration, 18* (5), 573–78.

Keiser, T. (1988). Negotiating with a customer you can't afford to lose. *Harvard Business Review, 66* (6), 30–37.

Kellerman, J. L., Lewis, J., & Laird, J. D. (1989). Looking and loving: The effects of mutual gaze on feelings of romantic love. *Journal of Research in Personality, 23,* 145–61.

Kelley, H. H. (1966). A classroom study of the dilemmas in interpersonal negotiation. In K. Archibald (Ed.), *Strategic interaction and conflict: Original papers and discussion* (pp. 49–73). Berkeley, CA: Institute of International Studies.

Kelley, H. H., Berscheid, E., Christensen, A., Harvey, J., Houston, T. L., Levinger, G., et al. (1983). Analyzing close relationships. In H. H. Kelley et al. (Eds.), *Close relationships* (pp. 20–67). San Francisco: Freeman.

Kelley, H. H., & Schenitzki, D. P. (1972). Bargaining. In C. G. McClintock (Ed.), *Experimental social psychology* (pp. 298–337). New York: Holt, Rinehart & Winston.

Kelley, H. H., & Stahelski, A. J. (1970). Social interaction basis of cooperators' and competitors' beliefs about others. *Journal of Personality and Social Psychology, 16,* 66–91.

Kelley, H. H., & Thibaut, J. (1969). *Group problem solving.* In G. Lindzey & E. Aronson (Eds.), *Handbook of social psychology* (2nd ed., Vol. 4, pp. 1–101). Reading, MA: Addison-Wesley.

Kelman, H. C. (1996). Negotiation as interactive problem solving. *International Negotiation, 1,* 99–123.

Kelman, H. C., & Hamilton, V. L. (1989). *Crimes of obedience.* New Haven, CT: Yale University Press.

Keltner, D., & Robinson, R. J. (1993). Imagined ideological differences in conflict escalation and resolution. *International Journal of Conflict Management, 4,* 249–62.

Kemp, K. E., & Smith, W. P. (1994). Information exchange, toughness, and integrative bargaining: The roles of explicit cues and perspective-taking. *International Journal of Conflict Management, 5,* 5–21.

Kennedy, G. (1985). *Doing business abroad.* New York: Simon & Schuster.

Kessler, S. (1978). *Creative conflict resolution: Mediation.* Atlanta, GA: NIPT.

Kilmann, R. H., & Thomas, K. W. (1977). Developing a forced-choice measure of conflict-handling behavior: The MODE instrument. *Educational and Psychological Measurement, 37,* 309–25.

Kim, M. S., & Kitani, K. (1998). Conflict management styles of Asian- and Caucasian-Americans in romantic relationships in Hawaii. *Journal of Asian Pacific Communication, 8,* 51–68.

Kim, P. H. (1997). Strategic timing in group negotiations: The implications of forced entry and forced exit for negotiators with unequal power. *Organizational Behavior and Human Decision Processes, 71,* 263–86.

Kim, P. H., Dirks, K. T., Cooper, C. D., & Ferrin, D. L. (2006). When more blame is better than less: The implications of internal vs. external attributions for the repair of trust after a competence- vs. integrity-based trust violation. *Organizational Behavior and Human Decision Processes, 99,* 49–65.

Kim, P. H., Pinkley, R. L., & Fragale, A. R. (2005). Power dynamics in negotiation. *Academy of Management Review, 30* (4), 799–822.

Kim, S. H., & Smith, R. H. (1993). Revenge and conflict escalation. *Negotiation Journal, 9,* 37–43.

Kim, S. H., Smith, R. H., & Brigham, N. L. (1998). Effects of power imbalance and the presence of third parties on reactions to harm: Upward and downward revenge. *Personality and Social Psychology Bulletin, 24,* 353–61.

Kimmel, M. J., Pruitt, D. G., Magenau, J. M., Konar-Goldband, E., & Carnevale, P. J. D. (1980). Effects of trust aspiration and gender on negotiation tactics. *Journal of Personality and Social Psychology, 38,* 9–23.

King, D. C., & Zeckhauer, R. (1999). Legislators as negotiators. In R. H. Mnookin and L. E. Susskind, *Negotiating on behalf of others* (pp. 203–25). Thousand Oaks, CA: Sage.

Kinsman, M. (1992, November 30). Résumé lies seem to be on increase. *Upper Arlington* (Ohio) *This Week,* 26.

Kipnis, D. (1976). *The powerholders.* Chicago: University of Chicago Press.

Kirby, S. L., & Davis, M. A. (1998). A study of escalating commitment in principal-agent relationships: Effects of monitoring and personal responsibility. *Journal of Applied Psychology, 83* (2), 206–17.

Kleinke, C. L. (1986). Gaze and eye contact: A research review. *Psychological Bulletin, 100,* 78–100.

Klimoski, R. J. (1972). The effects of intragroup forces on intergroup conflict resolution. *Organizational Behavior and Human Performance, 8,* 363–83.

Klimoski, R. J., & Ash, R. A. (1974). Accountability and negotiator behavior. *Organizational Behavior and Human Performance, 11,* 409–25.

Kochan, T. A. (1980). *Collective bargaining and industrial relations.* Homewood, IL: Richard D. Irwin.

Kochan, T. A., & Jick, T. (1978). The public sector mediation process: A theory and empirical examination. *Journal of Conflict Resolution, 22,* 209–40.

Koehler, J. J., & Conley, C. A. (2003). The "hot hand" myth in professional basketball. *Journal of Sport and Exercise Psychology, 25,* 253–59.

Koehn, D. (1997). Business and game playing: The false analogy. *Journal of Business Ethics, 16,* 1447–52.

Koeszegi, S. (2004). Trust building strategies in inter-organizational negotiations. *Journal of Managerial Psychology, 19* (6), 640–60.

Kogan, N., Lamm, H., & Trommsdorf, G. (1972). Negotiation constraints in the risk taking domain: Effects of being observed by partners of higher or lower status. *Journal of Personality and Social Psychology, 23,* 143–56.

Koh, T. T. B. (1996). American strengths and weaknesses. *Negotiation Journal, 12,* 313–17.

Kohlberg, L. (1969). Stage and sequence: The cognitive development approach to socialization. In D. Goslin (Ed.), *Handbook of socialization theory and research* (pp. 347–80). Chicago: Rand McNally.

Kolb, D. (1983a). *The mediators.* Cambridge, MA: MIT Press.

Kolb, D. (1983b). Strategy and the tactics of mediation. *Human Relations, 36* (3), 247–68.

Kolb, D. (1985). *The mediators.* Cambridge, MA: MIT Press.

Kolb, D. (1992, August). Is it her voice or her place that makes a difference? A consideration of gender issues in negotiation. Paper presented at the annual meeting of the Academy of Management, Las Vegas, Nevada.

Kolb, D. (1995). The love for three oranges, or: What did we miss about Ms. Follett in the library? *Negotiation Journal, 11,* 339–48.

Kolb, D., & Coolidge, G. G. (1991). Her place at the table: A consideration of gender issues in negotiation. In J. Z. Rubin and J. W. Breslin (Eds.), *Negotiation theory and practice* (pp. 261–77). Cambridge, MA: Harvard Program on Negotiation.

Kolb, D. M., & Associates. (1994). *When talk works: Profiles of mediators.* San Francisco: Jossey-Bass.

Kolb, D. M., & Putnam, L. L. (1997). Through the looking glass: Negotiation theory refracted through the lens of gender. In S. Gleason (Ed.), *Frontiers in dispute resolution in labor relations and human resources* (pp. 231–57). East Lansing, MI: Michigan State University Press.

Kolb, D. M., & Williams, J. (2001). Breakthrough bargaining. *Harvard Business Review, 79* (2), 89–97.

Kolb, D. M., & Williams, J. (2001). *The shadow negotiation: How women can master the hidden agendas that determine bargaining success.* New York: Simon & Schuster.

Komorita, S. S., & Brenner, A. R. (1968). Bargaining and concessions under bilateral monopoly. *Journal of Personality and Social Psychology, 9,* 15–20.

Kopelman, S., Rosette, A. S., & Thompson, L. (2006). The three faces of eve: An examination of strategic positive, negative, and neutral emotion in negotiations. *Organizational Behavior and Human Decision Processes, 99,* 81–101.

Koslowsky, M., Schwarzwald, J., & Ashuri, S. (2001). On the relationship between subordinates' compliance to power sources and organizational attitudes. *Applied Psychology: An International Review, 50,* 455–76.

Kotter, J. (1977, July–August). Power, dependence and effective management. *Harvard Business Review, 55,* 125–36.

Kotter, J. (1979). *Power in management.* New York: AMACOM.

Kozan, M. K. (1997). Culture and conflict management: A theoretical framework. *International Journal of Conflict Management, 8* (4), 338–60.

Kozan, M. K., & Ergin, C. (1999). The influence of intra-cultural value differences on conflict management processes. *International Journal of Conflict Management, 10,* 249–67.

Krackhardt, D., & Hanson, J. R. (1993, July–August). Informal networks: The company behind the chart. *Harvard Business Review, 71,* 104–11.

Kramer, R. (1994). The sinister attribution error: Paranoid cognition and collective distrust in organizations. *Motivation and Emotion, 18,* 199–203.

Kramer, R. (2004). The dark side of social context. In M. Gelfand and J. M. Brett (Eds.), *The handbook of negotiation and culture* (pp. 219–37). Stanford, CA: Stanford Business Books.

Kramer, R. M. (1991). The more the merrier? Social psychological aspects of multiparty negotiations in organizations. In M. H. Bazerman, R. J. Lewicki, & B. H. Sheppard (Eds.), *Research on negotiation in organizations* (Vol. 3, pp. 307–32). Greenwich, CT: JAI Press.

Kramer, R. M. (1995). Power, paranoia and distrust in organizations: The distorted view from the top. In R. J. Bies, R. J. Lewicki, & B. H. Sheppard (Eds.), *Research on negotiation in organizations* (Vol. 5, pp. 119–54). Greenwich, CT: JAI Press.

Kramer, R. M., Newton, E., & Pommerenke, P. L. (1993). Self-enhancement biases and negotiator judgment: Effects of self-esteem and mood. *Organizational Behavior and Human Decision Processes, 56,* 110–33.

Kramer, R. M., Pommerenke, P., & Newton, B. (1993). The social context of negotiation: Effects of trust, aspiration and gender on negotiation tactics. *Journal of Personality and Social Psychology, 38* (1), 9–22.

Kramer, R. M., Shah, P. P., & Woerner, S. L. (1995). Why ultimatums fail: Social identity and moralistic aggression in coercive bargaining. In R. M. Kramer & D. M. Messick (Eds.), *Negotiation as social process* (pp. 285–308). Thousand Oaks, CA: Sage.

Kray, L., & Babcock, L. (2006). Gender in negotiations: A motivated social and cognitive analysis. In L. Thompson (Ed.), *Negotiation theory and research.* Madison, CT: Psychosocial Press.

Kray, L., Galinsky, A. D., & Markman, K. (2007). Adding versus subtracting what might have been: The impact of counterfactual activation on integrative negotiations. Presented at the annual meeting of the International Association of Conflict Management.

Kray, L. J., Galinsky, A. D., & Thompson, L. (2002). Reversing the gender gap in negotiations: An exploration of stereotype regeneration. *Organizational Behavior and Human Decision Processes, 87,* 386–409.

Kray, L. J., & Haselhuhn, M. P. (2007). Implicit negotiation beliefs and performance: Experimental and longitudinal evidence. *Journal of Personality and Social Psychology, 93,* 49–64.

Kray, L. J., Reb, J., Galinsky, A. D., & Thompson, L. (2004). Stereotype reactance at the bargaining table: The effect of stereotype activation and power on claiming and creating value. *Personality and Social Psychology Bulletin, 30,* 399–411.

Kray, L. J., Thompson, L., & Galinsky, A. D. (2001). Battle of the sexes: Gender stereotype confirmation and reactance in negotiation. *Journal of Personality and Social Psychology, 80,* 942–58.

Kremenyuk, V. A. (Ed.). (1991). *International negotiation: Analysis, approaches, issues.* San Francisco: Jossey-Bass.

Kressel, K. (1972). *Labor mediation: An exploratory survey.* Albany, NY: Association of Labor Mediation Agencies.

Kressel, K. (1985). *The process of divorce.* New York: Basic Books.

Kressel, K., Frontera, E., Forlenza, S., Butler, F., & Fish, L. (1994). The settlement-orientation vs. the problem-solving style in custody mediation. *Journal of Social Issues, 50,* 67–84.

Kressel, K., & Pruitt, D. (Eds.). (1989). *Mediation research.* San Francisco: Jossey-Bass.

Kristensen, H. (2000). Does fairness matter in corporate takeovers? *Journal of Economic Psychology, 21* (1), 43–56.

Kristensen, H., & Garling, T. (1997). The effects of anchor points and reference points on negotiation process and outcome. *Organizational Behavior and Human Decision Processes, 71,* 85–94.

Kristensen, H., & Garling, T. (2000). Anchor points, reference points, and counteroffers in negotiations. *Group Decision and Negotiation, 9,* 493–505.

Kritikos, A. S. (2006). The impact of compulsory arbitration on bargaining behaviour: an experimental study. *Economics of Governance, 7,* 293–315.

Ku, G. (2008). Learning to de-escalate: The effects of regret in escalation of commitment. *Organizational Behavior and Human Decision Processes, 105,* 221–32.

Kumar, R. (1997). The role of affect in negotiations: An integrative overview. *Journal of Applied Behavioral Science, 3* (1), 84–100.

Kumar, R. (2004). Brahmanical idealism, anarchical individualism, and the dynamics of Indian negotiating behavior. *International Journal of Cross Cultural Management, 4,* 39–58.

Kumar, R., & Worm, V. (2003). Social capital and the dynamics of business negotiations between the northern Europeans and the Chinese. *International Marketing Review, 20,* 262–85.

Kumar, R., & Worm, V. (2004). Institutional dynamics and the negotiation process: comparing India and China. *International Journal of Conflict Management, 15* (3), 304–34.

Kurtz, H. (1998). *Spin cycle.* New York: Free Press.

Kurtzberg, T., Moore, D., Valley, K., & Bazerman, M. H. (1999). Agents in negotiations: Toward testable propositions. In R. H. Mnookin and L. E. Susskind, *Negotiating on behalf of others* (pp. 283–98). Thousand Oaks, CA: Sage Publications.

Kurtzberg, T. R. (1998). Creative thinking, cognitive aptitude, and integrative joint gain: A study of negotiator creativity. *Creativity Research Journal, 11,* 283–93.

Kurtzberg, T. R., Dunn-Jensen, L. M., & Matsibekker, C. L. Z. (2005). Multi-party e-negotiations: Agents, alliances, and negotiation success. *International Journal of Conflict Management, 16,* 245–64.

Kuttner, R. (2006). Striving to fulfill the promise: *The purple house conversations* and the practice of transformative mediation. *Negotiation Journal, 22* (3), 331–49.

LaFasto, F., & Larson, C. (2001) *When teams work best.* Thousand Oaks, CA: Sage.

Landon, E. L., Jr. (1997). For the most fitting deal, tailor negotiating strategy to each borrower. *Commercial Lending Review, 12,* 5–14.

Landy, F. J. (2005). Some historical and scientific issues related to research on emotional intelligence. *Journal of Organizational Behavior, 26,* 411–24.

Lane, H. W., DiStefano, J. J., & Maznevski, M. L. (1997). *International Management Behavior* (3rd ed.). Cambridge, MA: Blackwell.

Langner, C. A., & Winter, D. G. (2001). The motivational basis of concessions and compromise: Archival and laboratory studies. *Journal of Personality and Social Psychology, 81,* 711–27.

Larrick, R. P., & Boles, T. L. (1995). Avoiding regret in decisions with feedback: A negotiation example. *Organizational Behavior and Human Decision Processes, 63,* 87–97.

Latz, M. (2004). Gain the edge! Negotiating to get what you want. In C. Fazzi (Ed.), *The five golden rules of negotiations. Dispute Resolution Journal, 59* (4), 88–89.

Laubach, C. (1997, January–February). Negotiating a gain-gain agreement. *Healthcare Executive,* 14.

Lax, D., & Sebenius, J. (1986). *The manager as negotiator: Bargaining for cooperation and competitive gain.* New York: Free Press.

Lax, D., & Sebenius, J. (2006). *3-D negotiation.* Boston: Harvard Business School Publishing.

Lax, D. A., & Sebenius, J. K. (2002). Dealcrafting: The substance of three-dimensional negotiations. *Negotiation Journal, 18,* 5–28.

Lax, D. A., & Sebenius, J. K. (2003, November). 3-D negotiation. *Harvard Business Review,* 65–74.

Lazarus, R. S. (1991). *Emotion and adaptation.* New York: Oxford University Press.

Leavitt, H. J., & Bahrami, H. (1988). *Managerial psychology: Managing behavior in organizations* (5th ed.). Chicago, IL: University of Chicago Press.

Lee, K. H., Yang, G., & Graham, J. L. (2006). Tension and trust in international business negotiations: American executives negotiating with Chinese executives. *Journal of International Business Studies, 37,* 623–41.

Lefcourt, H. M. (1982). *Locus of control: Current trends in theory and research* (2nd ed.). Hillsdale, NJ: Lawrence Erlbaum.

Lepine, J. A., Colquitt, J. A., & Erez, A. (2000). Adaptability to changing task contexts: Effects of general cognitive ability, conscientiousness, and openness to experience. *Personnel Psychology, 53,* 563–93.

Le Poole, S. (1989). Negotiating with Clint Eastwood in Brussels. *Management Review, 78,* 58–60.

Leung, K., Tong, K., & Ho, S. S. (2004). Effects of interactional justice on egocentric bias in resource allocation decisions. *Journal of Applied Psychology, 89* (3), 405–15.

Leung, T., & Yeung, L. L. (1995). Negotiation in the People's Republic of China: Results of a survey of small businesses in Hong Kong. *Journal of Small Business Management, 33,* 70–77.

Levinson, J. C., Smith, M. S. A., & Wilson, O. R. (1999). *Guerilla negotiating.* New York: John Wiley.

Levy, T. I. (1999, November). Designing a program for arbitration. *Management Review, 88* (10), 46–48.

Lévy-Leboyer, C. (2005). The handbook of negotiation and culture. *Personnel Psychology, 58* (2), 561–64.

Lewicki, R., & Hiam, A. (2006). *The master negotiator.* San Francisco: Jossey-Bass.

Lewicki, R., Wiethoff, C., & Tomlinson, E. (2005). What is the role of trust in organizational justice? In J. Greenberg and J. Colquitt (Eds.), *Handbook of organizational justice* (pp. 247–72). Mahwah, NJ: Lawrence Erlbaum.

Lewicki, R. J. (1983). Lying and deception: A behavioral model. In M. H. Bazerman & R. J. Lewicki (Eds.), *Negotiating in organizations* (pp. 68–90). Beverly Hills, CA: Sage.

Lewicki, R. J. (1992). Negotiating strategically. In A. Cohen (Ed.), *The portable MBA in management* (pp. 147–89). New York: John Wiley and Sons.

Lewicki, R. (2006). Trust, trust development and trust repair. In M. Deutsch, P. Coleman, and E. Marcus (Eds.), *The handbook of conflict resolution.* (2nd ed.). San Francisco: Jossey-Bass.

Lewicki, R. J., & Alderfer, C. P. (1973). The tensions between research and intervention in intergroup conflict. *Journal of Applied Behavioral Science, 9,* 424–68.

Lewicki, R. J., & Bunker, B. B. (1995). Trust in relationships: A model of trust development and decline. In B. B. Bunker & J. Z. Rubin (Eds.), *Conflict, cooperation and justice* (pp. 133–74). San Francisco: Jossey-Bass.

Lewicki, R. J., & Bunker, B. B. (1996). A model of trust development and decline. In R. Kramer & T. Tyler (Eds.), *Trust in organizations* (pp. 114–39). Newbury Park, CA: Sage.

Lewicki, R. J., & Dineen, B. R. (2002). Negotiating in virtual organizations. In R. Heneman & D. Greenberger (Eds.), *Human resource management in virtual organizations.* New York: John Wiley and Sons.

Lewicki, R. J., Gray, B., & Elliott, M. (2003). *Making sense of intractable environmental disputes.* Washington, DC: Island Press.

Lewicki, R. J., & Hiam, A. (1999). *The fast forward MBA in negotiation and dealmaking.* New York: John Wiley and Sons.

Lewicki, R. J., Hiam, A., & Olander, K. (1996). *Think before you speak: The complete guide to strategic negotiation.* New York: John Wiley and Sons.

Lewicki, R. J., McAllister, D., & Bies, R. H. (1998). Trust and distrust: New relationships and realities. *Academy of Management Review. 23* (3), 438–58.

Lewicki, R. J., & Robinson, R. (1998). A factor-analytic study of negotiator ethics. *Journal of Business Ethics, 18,* 211–28.

Lewicki, R. J., & Sheppard, B. H. (1985). Choosing how to intervene: Factors affecting the use of process and outcome control in third party dispute resolution. *Journal of Occupational Behavior, 6,* 49–64.

Lewicki, R. J., & Spencer, G. (1990, June). Lies and dirty tricks. Paper presented at the annual meeting of the International Association for Conflict Management, Vancouver, B. C., Canada.

Lewicki, R. J., & Spencer, G. (1991, August). Ethical relativism and negotiating tactics: Factors affecting their perceived ethicality. Paper presented at the annual meeting of the Academy of Management, Miami, FL.

Lewicki, R. J., & Stark, N. (1995). What's ethically appropriate in negotiations: An empirical examination of bargaining tactics. *Social Justice Research, 9,* 69–95.

Lewicki, R. J., & Stevenson, M. (1998). Trust development in negotiation: Proposed actions and a research agenda. *Journal of Business and Professional Ethics, 16* (1–3), 99–132.

Lewicki, R. J., & Wiethoff, C. (2000). Trust, trust development and trust repair. In M. Deutch & P. Coleman (Eds.), *Theory and practice of conflict resolution.* San Francisco: Jossey-Bass.

Lewicki, R. J., Weiss, S., & Lewin, D. (1992). Models of conflict, negotiation and third-party intervention: A review and synthesis. *Journal of Organizational Behavior, 13,* 209–52.

Lewis, M. (1990). *Liar's poker.* New York: Penguin Books.

Lewis, M. H., & Reinsch, N. L. (1988). Listening in organizational environments. *Journal of Business Communication, 25,* 49–67.

Liebert, R. M., Smith, W. P., & Hill, J. H. (1968). The effects of information and magnitude of initial offer on interpersonal negotiation. *Journal of Experimental Social Psychology, 4,* 431–41.

Liebowitz, W. R. (2000, January 28). Law professors create group to arbitrate disputes over domain names. *Chronicle of Higher Education,* A45.

Liebschutz, M. (1997, June 8). Negotiating the best deal requires a poker strategy. *The Wall Street Journal,* B1.

Lim, R. G. (1997). Overconfidence in negotiation revisited. *International Journal of Conflict Management, 8,* 52–70.

Lim, R. G., & Carnevale, P. J. D. (1990). Contingencies in the mediation of disputes. *Journal of Personality and Social Psychology, 58,* 259–72.

Lim, R. G., & Murnighan, J. K. (1994). Phases, deadlines, and the bargaining process. *Organizational Behavior and Human Decision Processes, 58,* 153–71.

Lin, X., & Miller, S. J. (2003). Negotiation approaches: Direct and indirect effects of national culture. *International Marketing Review, 20,* 286–303.

Lindskold, S., Bentz, B., & Walters, P. D. (1986). Trust development, the GRIT proposal and the effects of conciliatory acts on conflict and cooperation. *Psychological Bulletin, 85,* 772–93.

Lipin, S. (1996, August 22). In many merger deals, ego and pride play big roles in which way talks go. *The Wall Street Journal,* C1, C6.

Lituchy, T. R. (1997). Negotiations between Japanese and Americans: The effects of collectivism on integrative outcomes. *Canadian Journal of Administrative Sciences, 14,* 386–95.

Liu, L. A., Friedman, R. A., & Chi, S. C. (2005). 'Ren Qinq' versus the 'Big Five': The role of culturally sensitive measures of individual difference in distributive negotiations. *Management and Organization Review, 1,* 225–47.

Locke, E. A. (2005). Why emotional intelligence is an invalid concept. *Journal of Organizational Behavior, 26,* 425–31.

Locke, E., & Latham, G. (1984). *Goal setting: A motivational technique that works!* Englewood Cliffs, NJ: Prentice Hall.

Loewenstein, G. F., Thompson, L., & Bazerman, M. H. (1989). Social utility and decision making in interpersonal contexts. *Journal of Personality and Social Psychology, 57* (3), 426–41.

Loewenstein, J., Morris, M. W., Chakravarti, A., Thompson, L., & Kopelman, S. (2005). At a loss for words: Dominating the conversation and the outcome in negotiation as a function of intricate arguments and communication media. *Organizational Behavior and Human Decision Processes, 98,* 28–38.

Loewenstein, J., & Thompson, L. (2000). The challenge of learning. *Negotiation Journal, 16,* 399–408.

Loewenstein, J., Thompson, L., & Gentner, D. (1999). Analogical encoding facilitates knowledge transfer in organizations. *Psychonomic Bulletin and Review, 6,* 586–97.

Loewenstein, J., Thompson, L., & Gentner, D. (2002). Analogical learning in negotiation teams: Comparing cases promotes learning and transfer. *Academy of Management Learning and Education, 2,* 119–27.

Long, G., & Feuille, P. (1974). Final offer arbitration: Sudden death in Eugene. *Industrial and Labor Relations Review, 27,* 186–203.

Loomis, T. (2001, June 21). Mediation. An effect way to settle disputes catches on. *New York Law Journal,* 5.

Lovenheim, P. (1989). *Mediate, don't litigate: How to resolve disputes quickly, privately, and inexpensively without going to court.* New York: McGraw-Hill.

Lowe, T. (1986, January). Eight ways to ruin a performance appraisal. *Personnel Journal, 65,* 60–62.

Luce, R. D., & Raiffa, H. (1957). *Games and decisions: Introduction and critical survey.* New York: John Wiley and Sons.

Lukov, V. (1985). International negotiations of the 1980s: Features, problems and prospects. *Negotiation Journal, 1,* 139–48.

Lynch, J. E. (2001). Beyond ADR: A systems approach to conflict management. *Negotiation Journal, 17,* 207–16.

Lytle, A. L., Brett, J. M., & Shapiro, D. L. (1999). The strategic use of interests, rights, and power to resolve disputes. *Negotiation Journal, 15* (1), 31–51.

Ma, Z. (2006). Negotiating into China: the impact of individual perception on Chinese negotiation styles. *International Journal of Emerging Markets, 1* (1), 64–83.

Ma, Z. (2007). Chinese conflict management styles and negotiation behaviours: An empirical test. *International Journal of Cross Cultural Management, 7* (1), 101–19.

Ma, Z., & Jaeger, A. (2005). Getting to yes in China: Exploring personality effects in Chinese negotiation styles. *Group Decision and Negotiation, 14,* 415–37.

Macduff, I. (2006). Your pace or mine? Culture, time, and negotiation. *Negotiation Journal, 22* (1), 31–45.

Machinov, E., & Monteil, J. (2002). The similarity–attraction relationship revisited: Divergence between the affective and behavioral facets of attraction. *European Journal of Social Psychology, 32,* 485–500.

Macneil, I. R. (1980). *The new social contract.* New Haven, CT: Yale University Press.

Magee, J. C., Galinsky, A. D., & Gruenfeld, D. (2007). Power, propensity to negotiate, and moving first in competitive interactions. *Personality and Social Psychology Bulletin, 33* (2), 200–12.

Maier, N. R. F. (1952). *Principles of human relations.* New York: John Wiley and Sons.

Maier, N. R. F., & Hoffman, L. R. (1960). Quality of first and second solution in group problem solving. *Journal of Applied Psychology, 44,* 278–83.

Maier, R. A., & Lavrakas, P. J. (1976). Lying behavior and the evaluation of lies. *Perceptual and Motor Skills, 42,* 575–81.

Major, B., & Konar, E. (1984). An investigation of sex differences in pay expectations and their possible causes. *Academy of Management Journal, 27,* 777–92.

Malhotra, D. K. (2003). Reciprocity in the context of trust: The differing perspective of trustors and trusted parties. *Dissertation Abstracts, 63,* 11–18.

Malhotra, D. K. (2004). Trust and reciprocity decisions: The differing perspectives of trustors and trusted parties. *Organizational Behavior and Human Decision Processes, 94* (2), 61–73.

Malhotra, D., & Bazerman, M. H. (2007). Investigative negotiation. *Harvard Business Review, 85,* 72–78.

Malhotra, D., & Bazerman, M. H. (2008). Psychological influence in negotiation: An introduction long overdue. *Journal of Management, 34,* 509–31.

Malhotra, D., Ku, G., & Murnighan, J. K. (2008, May). When winning is everything. *Harvard Business Review,* 78–86.

Mannix, E. A., Tinsley, C. H., & Bazerman, M. (1995). Negotiating over time: Impediments to integrative solutions. *Organizational Behavior and Human Decision Processes, 62,* 241–51.

Manz, C. C., Neck, C. P., Mancuso, J., & Manz, K. P. (1997). *For team members only.* New York: AMACOM.

March, J. (1962). The business firm as a political coalition. *Journal of Politics, 24,* 662–78.

Marcus, A. D. (1996, September 30). In Mideast politics, controlling the past is a key to the present. *The Wall Street Journal,* A1, A13.

Mareschal, P. M. (2005). What makes mediation work? Mediators' perspectives on resolving disputes. *Industrial Relations, 44* (3), 509–17.

Martin, J. (1996, May 27). How to negotiate with really tough guys. *Fortune,* 173–74.

Martinez, J., & Susskind, L. (2001). Parallel informal negotiation: An alternative to second track diplomacy. *International Negotiation, 5,* 569–86.

Mason, E. S., & Mudrack, P. E. (1997). Do complex moral reasoners experience greater ethical work conflict? *Journal of Business Ethics, 16,* 1311–18.

Matsumoto, D., & Yoo, S. H. (2006). Toward a new generation of cross-cultural research. *Perspectives on Psychological Science, 1* (3), 234–50.

Mautner-Markhof, F. (Ed.). (1989). *Processes of international negotiations.* Boulder, CO: Westview Press.

Maxwell, S., Nye, P., & Maxwell, N. (1999). Less pain, some gain: The effects of priming fairness in price negotiations. *Psychology and Marketing, 16* (7), 545–62.

Maxwell, S., Nye, P., & Maxwell, N. (2003). The wrath of the fairness-primed negotiator when the reciprocity is violated. *Journal of Business Research, 56* (5), 399–409.

Mayer, B. (2000). *The dynamics of conflict resolution.* San Francisco: Jossey-Bass.

Mayer, J. D., & Salovey, P. (1997). What is emotional intelligence? In P. Salovey & D. J. Sluyter (Eds.), *Emotional development and emotional intelligence: Educational implications* (pp. 3–31). New York: BasicBooks.

Mayer, J. D., Salovey, P., & Caruso, D. (2000). Emotional intelligence. In R. Sternberg (Ed.), *Handbook of intelligence* (pp. 396–420). Cambridge: Cambridge University Press.

Mayer, F. W. (1992). Managing domestic differences in international negotiations: The strategic use of internal side-payments. *International Organization, 46,* 793–818.

Mayfield, M., Mayfield, J., Martin, D., & Herbig, P. (1997). Time perspectives of the cross-cultural negotiations process. *American Business Review, 15,* 78–85.

McAllister, D. J. (1995). Affect- and cognition-based trust as foundations for interpersonal cooperation in organizations. *Academy of Management Journal, 38,* 24–59.

McAndrew, I. (2003). Final-offer arbitration: A New Zealand example. *Industrial Relations, 42,* 736–44.

McCallum, D. M., Harring, K., Gilmore, R., Drenan, S., Chase, J. P., Insko, C., et al. (1985). Competition and cooperation between groups and between individuals. *Journal of Experimental Social Psychology, 21,* 301–20.

McClelland, D. C. (1975). *Power: The inner experience.* New York: Irvington.

McClelland, D. C., & Burnham, D. H. (1976). Power is the great motivator. *Harvard Business Review, 43* (2), 100–10.

McClintock, C. G., & Liebrand, W. B. (1988). Role of interdependence structure, individual value orientation, and another's strategy in social decision making: A transformation analysis. *Journal of Personality and Social Psychology, 55,* 396–409.

McCornack, S. A., & Levine, T. R. (1990). When lies are uncovered: Emotional and relational outcomes of discovered deception. *Communication Monographs, 57,* 119–38.

McDonald, J. (1963). *Strategy in poker, business & war.* New York: William Norton.

McDonald, J. W. (1996). An American's view of a U.S. negotiating style. *International Negotiation, 1,* 323–26.

McEwen, C. A. (1999). Toward a program-based ADR research agenda. *Negotiation Journal, 15,* 325–38.

McEwen, C., & Milburn, T. (1993). Explaining a paradox of mediation. *Negotiation Journal, 9* (1), 23–36.

McGraw, D. (1997, October 20). Will he own the road? *U.S. News & World Report,* 45–54.

McGuire, W. J. (1964). Inducing resistance to persuasion: Some contemporary approaches. In L. Berkowitz (Ed.), Advances in experimental social psychology (Vol. 1, pp. 191–229). New York: Academic Press.

McGuire, W. J. (1973). Persuasion, resistance and attitude change. In I. S. Poole, F. W. Frey, W. Schramm, N. Maccoby, & E. B. Parker (Eds.), *Handbook of communication* (pp. 216–52). Skokie, IL: Rand McNally.

McKersie, R. (1999). Agency in the context of labor relations. In R. H. Mnookin and L. E. Susskind, *Negotiating on behalf of others* (pp. 181–95). Thousand Oaks, CA: Sage.

Menkel Meadow, C. (2006). Why hasn't the world gotten to yes? An appreciation and some reflections. *Negotiation Journal, 22* (4), 485–503.

Metcalf, L., Bird, A., & Dewar, D. (2008). Mexico and the United States: Common border, common negotiating orientations. *Thunderbird International Business Review, 50* (1), 25–43.

Metcalf, L. E., Bird, A., Peterson, M. F., Shankarmahesh, M., & Lituchy, T. R. (2007). Cultural influences in negotiations: A four country comparative analysis. *International Journal of Cross Cultural Management, 7* (2), 147–68.

Metcalf, L. E., Bird, A., Shankarmahesh, M., Aycan, Z., Larimo, J., & Valdelamar, D. D. (2006). Cultural tendencies in negotiation: a comparison of Finland, India, Mexico, Turkey, and the United States. *Journal of World Business, 41,* 382–94.

Meyerson, D., Weick, K. E., & Kramer, R. M. (1996). Swift trust and temporary groups. In R. M. Kramer & T. R. Tyler (Eds.), *Trust in organizations: Frontiers of theory and research* (pp. 165–90). Thousand Oaks, CA: Sage.

Michener, S. K., & Suchner, R. W. (1971). The tactical use of social power. In J. T. Tedeschi (Ed.), *The social influence process* (pp. 235–86). Chicago: AVC.

Midgaard, K., & Underal, A. (1977). Multiparty conferences. In D. Druckman (Ed.), *Negotiations: Social psychological perspectives* (pp. 329–45). Beverly Hills, CA: Sage.

Milgram, S. (1974). *Obedience to authority: An experimental view.* New York: Harper & Row.

Mill, J. S. (1962). *Utilitarianism, on liberty, essay on Bentham.* New York: New American Library.

Miller, D. T., & Ross, M. (1975). Self-serving bias in the attribution of causality: Fact or fiction? *Psychological Bulletin, 82,* 213–25.

Miller, S. K., & Burgoon, M. (1979). The relationship between violations of expectations and the induction of the resistance to persuasion. *Human Communication Research, 5,* 301–13.

Mills, H., & Clark, M. S. (1994). Communal and exchange relationships: Controversies and research. In R. Erber & R. Gilmour (Eds.), *Theoretical frameworks for personal relationships* (pp. 29–42). Hillsdale, NJ: Lawrence Erlbaum.

Mintu-Wimsatt, A. (2002). Personality and negotiation style: The moderating effects of cultural context. *Thunderbird International Business Review, 44,* 729–48.

Mintu-Wimsatt, A., & Gassenheimer, J. B. (2000). The moderating effects of cultural context in buyer-seller negotiation. *Journal of Personal Selling and Sales Management, 1,* 1–9.

Mintzberg, H. (1973). *The nature of managerial work.* New York: Harper & Row.

Mintzberg, H., & Quinn, J. B. (1991). *The strategy process: Concepts, contexts, cases* (2nd ed.). Englewood Cliffs, NJ: Prentice Hall.

Mission, D. J., with J. Felice. (2004). *Negotiate and win.* New York: McGraw-Hill.

Missner, M. (1980). *Ethics of the business system.* Sherman Oaks, CA: Alfred Publishing.

Mitchell, C. P., & Banks, M. (1996). *Handbook of conflict resolution: The analytical problem solving approach.* London: Pinter.

Miyahara, A., Kim, M. S., Shin, H. C., & Yoon, K. (1998). Conflict resolution styles among "collectivist" cultures: A comparison between Japanese and Koreans. *International Journal of Intercultural Relations, 22,* 505–25.

Mizrahi, R., & Rosenthal, B. B. (2001). Complexities of coalition building: Leaders' successes, strategies, struggles, and solutions. *Social Work, 46,* 63–78.

Mnookin, R. H. (1993). Why negotiations fail: An exploration of barriers to the resolution of conflict. *Ohio State Journal on Dispute Resolution, 8,* 235–49.

Moberg, P. J. (1998). Predicting conflict strategy with personality traits: Incremental validity and the five factor model. *International Journal of Conflict Management, 9,* 258–85.

Moffitt, M. L. (2006). Before the big bang: The making of an ADR pioneer. *Negotiation Journal, 22* (4), 437–43.

Molm, L., Takahashi, N., & Peterson, G. (2003). In the eye of the beholder: Procedural justice in social exchange. *American Sociological Review, 68* (1), 128–52.

Moore, C. (1996). *The mediation process: Practical strategies for resolving conflict* (2nd ed.). San Francisco: Jossey-Bass.

Moore, D. A., Kurtzberg, T. R., Thompson, L. L., & Morris, M. W. (1999). Long and short routes to success in electronically mediated negotiations: Group affiliations and good vibrations. *Organizational Behavior and Human Decision Processes, 77,* 22–43.

Moran, R. T., & Stripp, W. G. (1991). *Dynamics of successful international business negotiations.* Houston, TX: Gulf Publishing.

Moran, S., & Ritov, I. (2002). Initial perceptions in negotiations: Evaluation and response to "logrolling" offers. *Journal of Behavioral Decision Making, 15,* 101–24.

Morris, M., Nadler, J., Kurtzberg, T., & Thompson, L. (2000). Schmooze or lose: Social friction and lubrication in e-mail negotiations. *Group Dynamics-Theory Research and Practice, 6,* 89–100.

Morris, M. W., & Gelfand, M. J. (2004). Cultural differences and cognitive dynamics: Expanding the cognitive perspective on negotiation. In M. J. Gelfand & J. M. Brett (Eds.), *The handbook of negotiation and culture: Theoretical advances and cultural perspectives* (pp. 45–70). Stanford, CA: Stanford University Press.

Morris, M. W., Larrick, R. P., & Su, S. K. (1999). Misperceiving negotiation counterparts: When situationally determined bargaining behaviors are attributed to personality traits. *Journal of Personality and Social Psychology, 77,* 52–67.

Mosterd, I., & Rutte, C. G. (2000). Effects of time pressure and accountability to constituents on negotiation. *International Journal of Conflict Management, 11* (3), 227–47.

Mouzas, S. (2006). Negotiating umbrella agreements. *Negotiation Journal, 22* (3), 279–301.

Movius, H., Matsuura, M., Yan, J., & Kim, D. K. (2006). Tailoring the mutual gains approach for negotiations with partners in Japan, China, and Korea. *Negotiation Journal, 22* (4), 389–435.

Mueller, J. S., & Curhan, J. R. (2006). Emotional intelligence and counterpart mood induction in a negotiation. *International Journal of Conflict Management, 17,* 110–28.

Mulvey, P. W., Veiga, J. F., & Elsass, P. M. (1996). When team members raise a white flag. *Academy of Management Executive, 10* (1), 40–49.

Mumpower, J. L., & Rohrbaugh, J. (1996). Negotiation and design: Supporting resource allocation decisions through analytical mediation. *Group Decision and Negotiation, 5,* 385–409.

Murnighan, J. K. (1978). Models of coalition behavior: Game theoretic, social psychological and political perspectives. *Psychological Bulletin, 85,* 1130–53.

Murnighan, J. K. (1982). Game theory and the structure of decision-making groups. In R. Guzzo (Ed.), *Improving group decision in organizations.* New York: Academic Press.

Murnighan, J. K. (1986). Organizational coalitions: Structural contingencies and the formation process. In R. J. Lewicki, B. H. Sheppard, & M. H. Bazerman (Eds.), *Research on negotiation in organizations* (Vol. 1, pp. 155–73). Greenwich, CT: JAI Press.

Murnighan, J. K. (1991). *The dynamics of bargaining games.* Englewood Cliffs, NJ: Prentice Hall.

Murnighan, J. K., & Brass, D. J. (1991). Intraorganizational coalitions. In M. H. Bazerman, R. J. Lewicki, & B. H. Sheppard (Eds.), *Research on negotiation in organizations: The handbook of negotiation research* (Vol. 3, pp. 283–306). Greenwich, CT: JAI Press.

Murnighan, J. K., & Conlon, D. E. (1991). The dynamics of intense work groups: A study of British string quartets. *Administrative Science Quarterly, 36,* 165–86.

Murnighan, J. K., & Pillutla, M. M. (1995). Fairness versus self-interest: Asymmetric model imperatives in ultimatum bargaining. In R. M. Kramer & D. M. Messick (Eds.), *Negotiation as a social process* (pp. 240–67). Thousand Oaks, CA: Sage.

Murnighan, J. K., & Volrath, D. A. (1984). Hierarchies, coalitions and organizations. In S. B. Bacharach & E. J. Lawler (eds.), *Research in the sociology of organizations* (Vol. 3, pp. 157–87). Greenwich, CT: JAI Press.

Murphy, K. (1992). *Honesty in the workplace.* Pacific Grove, CA: Brooks-Cole.

Nabatchi, T., & Bingham, L. B. (2001). Transformative mediation in the USPS Redress Program: Observations of ADR specialists. *Hofstra Labor & Employment Journal, 18* (2), 399–427.

Nadler, J., Thompson, L., & Van Boven, L. (2003). Learning negotiation skills: Four models of knowledge creation and transfer. *Management Science, 49,* 529–40.

Naquin, C. E. (2002). The agony of opportunity in negotiation: Number of negotiable issues, counterfactual thinking, and feelings of satisfaction. *Organizational Behavior and Human Decision Processes, 91,* 97–107.

Naquin, C. E., & Paulson, G. D (2003). *Journal of Applied Psychology, 88* (1), 113–20.

Nash, J. F. (1950). The bargaining problem. *Econometrica, 18,* 155–62.

Natlandsmyr, J. H., & Rognes, J. (1995). Culture, behavior, and negotiation outcomes: A comparative and cross-cultural study of Mexican and Norwegian negotiators. *International Journal of Conflict Management, 6,* 5–29.

Neale, M., & Bazerman, M. H. (1983). The role of perspective-taking ability in negotiating under different forms of arbitration. *Industrial and Labor Relations Review, 36,* 378–88.

Neale, M., & Bazerman, M. H. (1985). The effects of framing and negotiator overconfidence on bargaining behaviors and outcomes. *Academy of Management Journal, 28,* 34–49.

Neale, M., & Bazerman, M. H. (1991). *Cognition and rationality in negotiation.* New York: Free Press.

Neale, M., & Bazerman, M. H. (1992a). Negotiating rationally: The power and impact of the negotiator's frame. *Academy of Management Executive, 6* (3), 42–51.

Neale, M., Huber, V., & Northcraft, G. (1987). The framing of negotiations: Contextual vs. task frames. *Organizational Behavior and Human Decision Processes, 39,* 228–41.

Neale, M. A. (1984). The effect of negotiation and arbitration cost salience on bargainer behavior: The role of arbitrator and constituency in negotiator judgment. *Organizational Behavior and Human Performance, 34,* 97–111.

Neale, M. A., & Bazerman, M. H. (1992b). Negotiator cognition and rationality: A behavioral decision theory perspective. *Organizational Behavior and Human Decision Processes, 51,* 157–75.

Neale, M. A., & Northcraft, G. B. (1986). Experts, amateurs, and refrigerators: Comparing expert and amateur negotiators in a novel task. *Organizational Behavior and Human Decision Processes, 38,* 305–17.

Neale, M. A., & Northcraft, G. B. (1991). Behavioral negotiation theory: A framework for conceptualizing dyadic bargaining. In L. L. Cummings & B. M. Staw (Eds.), *Research in organizational behavior* (Vol. 13, pp. 147–90). Greenwich, CT: JAI Press.

Nelson, D., & Wheeler, M. (2004). Rocks and hard places: Managing two tensions in negotiation. *Negotiation Journal, 20,* 113–25.

Nemeth, C. J. (1986). Differential contributions to majority and minority influence. *Psychological Review, 93,* 23–32.

Nemeth, C. J. (1989). The stimulating properties of dissent. Paper presented at the first annual Conference on Group Process and Productivity, Texas A&M University, College Station, TX.

Neslin, S. A., & Greenhalgh, L. (1983). Nash's theory of cooperative games as a predictor of the outcomes of buyer-seller negotiations: An experiment in media purchasing. *Journal of Marketing Research, 20,* 368–79.

Neu, J., Graham, J. L., & Gilly, M. C. (1988). The influence of gender on behaviors and outcomes in a retail buyer-seller negotiation simulation. *Journal of Retailing, 64,* 427–51.

Nierenberg, G. (1976). *The complete negotiator.* New York: Nierenberg & Zeif.

Nierenberg, G., & Calero, H. (1971). *How to read a person like a book.* New York: Simon & Schuster.

NLRA Sections 8(a)(5) and 8(b)(3). United States National Labor Relations Act, Washington, D. C.

Northcraft, G. B., & Neale, M. A. (1987). Experts, amateurs, and real estate: An anchoring and adjustment perspective on property pricing decisions. *Organizational Behavior and Human Decision Processes, 39,* 228–41.

Northrup, H. R. (1964). *Boulwarism.* Ann Arbor, MI: Bureau of Industrial Relations, University of Michigan.

Northrup, T. A. (1995). The uneasy partnership between conflict theory and feminist theory. Syracuse University, unpublished paper.

Novemsky, N., & Schweitzer, M. E. (2004). What makes negotiators happy? The differential effects of internal and external social comparisons on negotiator satisfaction. *Organization Behavior and Human Decision Processes, 95,* 186–97.

O'Connor, K. M. (1997a). Motives and cognitions in negotiation: A theoretical integration and an empirical test. *International Journal of Conflict Management, 8,* 114–31.

O'Connor, K. M. (1997b). Groups and solos in context: The effects of accountability on team negotiation. *Organizational Behavior and Human Decision Processes, 72,* 384–407.

O'Connor, K. M., & Arnold, J. A. (2001). Distributive spirals: Negotiation impasses and the moderating role of disputant self-efficacy. *Organizational Behavior and Human Decision Processes, 84,* 148–76.

O'Connor, K. M., Arnold, J. A., & Burris, E. R. (2005). Negotiators' bargaining histories and their effects on future negotiation performance. *Journal of Applied Psychology, 90,* 350–62.

O'Connor, K. M., & Carnevale, P. J. (1997). A nasty but effective negotiation strategy: Misrepresentation of a common-value issue. *Personality and Social Psychology Bulletin, 23,* 504–15.

O'Connor, K. M., & Tinsley, C. H. (2004). Looking for an edge in negotiation? Cultivate an integrative reputation. Unpublished manuscript.

Oetzel, J. G., & Ting-Toomey, S. (2003). Face concerns in interpersonal conflict. *Communication Research, 30,* 599–624.

Ogawa, N. (1999). The concept of facework: Its function in the Hawaii model of mediation. *Mediation Quarterly, 17,* 5–20.

Ogilvie, J. R., & Carsky, M. L. (2002). Building emotional intelligence in negotiations. *International Journal of Conflict Management, 13,* 381–400.

Ohanyan, A. (1999). Negotiation culture in a post-Soviet context: An interdisciplinary perspective. *Mediation Quarterly, 17,* 83–104.

Ohbuchi, K., & Fukushima, O. (1997). Personality and interpersonal conflict: Aggressiveness, self-monitoring, and situational variables. *International Journal of Conflict Management, 8,* 99–113.

Ohbuchi, K., & Takahashi, Y. (1994). Cultural styles of conflict management in Japanese and Americans: Passivity, covertness, and effectiveness of strategies. *Journal of Applied Social Psychology, 24,* 1345–66.

O'Keefe, D. J. (1990). *Persuasion: Theory and research.* Newbury Park, CA: Sage.

Okhuysen, G. A., Galinsky, A. D., & Uptigrove, T. A. (2003). Saving the worst for last: The effect of time horizon on the efficiency of negotiating benefits and burdens. *Organizational Behavior and Human Decision Processes, 91,* 269–79.

Oldmeadow, J. A., Platow, M. J., Foddy, M., & Anderson, D. (2003). Self-categorization, status, and social influence. *Social Psychology Quarterly, 66,* 138–44.

Olekans, M. (2002). Negotiation as social interaction. *Australian Journal of Management, 27,* 39–46.

Olekalns, M., Lau, F., & Smith, P. (2002). The dynamics of trust in negotiation. Paper presented at the International Association of Conflict Management, Park City, Utah. Melbourne Business School Working Paper 2002–09.

Olekalns, M., Lau, F., & Smith, P. L. (2007). Resolving the empty core: Trust as a determinant of outcomes in three-party negotiation. *Group Decision and Negotiation, 16,* 527–38.

Olekalns, M., Robert, C., Probst, T., Smith, P. L., & Carnevale, P. (2005). The impact of message frame on negotiators' impressions, emotions, and behaviors. *International Journal of Conflict Management, 16,* 379–402.

Olekalns, M., & Smith, P. (2001). Metacognition in negotiation: The identification of critical events and their role in shaping trust and outcomes. Melbourne Business School Working Paper 2001–15.

Olekalns, M., & Smith, P. (2005). Moments in time: Metacognitions, trust and outcomes in dyadic negotiations. *Personality and Social Psychology Bulletin, 31* (12), 1696–1707.

Olekalns, M., & Smith, P. L. (1999). Social value orientations and strategy choices in competitive negotiations. *Personality and Social Psychology Bulletin, 25,* 657–68.

Olekalns, M., & Smith, P. L. (2003). Social motives in negotiation: The relationships between dyad composition, negotiation processes and outcomes. *International Journal of Conflict Management, 14,* 233–54.

Olekalns, M., & Smith, P. L. (2007). Loose with the truth: Predicting deception in negotiation. *Journal of Business Ethics, 76,* 225–38.

Olekalns, M., Smith, P. L., & Kibby, R. (1996). Social value orientations, negotiator strategies and outcomes. *European Journal of Social Psychology, 26,* 299–313.

Olekalns, M., Smith, P. L., & Walsh, T. (1996). The process of negotiating: Strategy and timing as predictors of outcomes. *Organizational Behavior and Human Decision Processes, 68,* 68–77.

Oliver, R. L., Balakrishnan, P. V., & Barry, B. (1994). Outcome satisfaction in negotiation: A test of expectancy disconfirmation. *Organizational Behavior and Human Decision Processes, 60,* 252–75.

Orbell, J. M., Van de Kragt, A. J., & Dawes, R. M. (1988). Explaining discussion-induced cooperation. *Journal of Personality and Social Psychology, 54,* 811–19.

Osgood, C. E. (1962). *An alternative to war or surrender.* Urbana, IL: University of Illinois Press.

Parrott, W. (1994). Beyond hedonism: Motives for inhibiting good moods and for maintaining bad moods. In D. M. Wegner & J. W. Pennebaker (Eds.), *Handbook of mental control* (pp. 278–305). Englewood Cliffs, NJ: Prentice Hall.

Palich, L. E., Carini, G. R., & Livingstone, L. P. (2002). Comparing American and Chinese negotiating styles: The influence of logic paradigms. *Thunderbird International Business Review, 44,* 777–98.

Parrott, W. G. (2001). Emotions in social psychology: Volume overview. In W. G. Parrott (Ed.), *Emotions in social psychology* (pp. 1–19). Philadelphia: Psychology Press.

Patterson, J., & Kim, P. (1991). *The day America told the truth.* New York: Prentice Hall.

Pearce, J. L., Stevenson, W. B., & Porter, L. W. (1986). Coalitions in the organizational context. In R. J. Lewicki, B. H. Sheppard, & M. H. Bazerman (Eds.), *Research on negotiation in organizations* (Vol. 1, pp. 97–115). Greenwich, CT: JAI Press.

Pearson, V. S., & Stephan, W. G. (1998). Preferences for styles of negotiation: A comparison of Brazil and the U.S. *International Journal of Intercultural Relations, 22,* 67–83.

Pecorino, P., & Van Boening, M. (2001). Bargaining and information: Empirical analysis of a multistage arbitration game. *Journal of Labor Economics, 19,* 922–48.

Pendergast, W. R. (1990). Managing the agenda. *Negotiation Journal,* 135–45.

Perry, G. M., & Nixon, C. J. (2005). The influence of role models on negotiation ethics of college students. *Journal of Business Ethics, 62,* 25–40.

Peterson, E., & Thompson, L. (1997). Negotiation teamwork: The impact of information distribution and accountability on performance depends on the relationship among team members. *Organizational Behavior and Human Decision Processes, 72,* 364–83.

Petty, R. E., & Briñol, P. (2008). Psychological processes underlying persuasion: A social psychological approach. *Diogenes, 55,* 52–67.

Petty, R. E., Briñol, P., & Tormala, Z. L. (2002). Thought confidence as a determinant of persuasion: The self-validation hypothesis. *Journal of Personality and Social Psychology, 82,* 722–41.

Petty, R. E., & Brock, T. C. (1981). Thought disruption and persuasion: Assessing the validity of attitude change experiments. In R. E. Petty, T. M. Ostrom, & T. C. Brock (Eds.), *Cognitive responses in persuasion* (pp. 55–79). Hillsdale, NJ: Lawrence Erlbaum.

Petty, R. E., & Cacioppo, J. T. (1986a). *Communication and persuasion: Central and peripheral routes to attitude change.* New York: Springer Verlag.

Petty, R. E., & Cacioppo, J. T. (1986b). The elaboration likelihood model of persuasion. In L. Berkowitz (Ed.), *Advances in experimental social psychology* (Vol. 19, pp. 123–205). New York: Academic Press.

Petty, R. E., & Cacioppo, J. T. (1990). Involvement and persuasion: Tradition versus integration. *Psychological Bulletin, 107,* 367–74.

Petty, R. E., Cacioppo, J. T., Strathman, A., & Priester, J. R. (1994). To think or not to think: Exploring two routes to persuasion. In S. Shavitt & T. Brock (Eds.), *Persuasion: Psychological insights and perspectives.* Needham Heights, MA: Allyn & Bacon.

Petty, R. E., Cacioppo, J. T., Strathman, A. J., & Priester, J. R. (in press). To think or not to think: Exploring two routes to persuasion. In T. Brock & S. Shavitt (Eds.), *Psychology of persuasion.* San Francisco, CA: Freeman.

Petty, R. E., Haugtvedt, C., & Smith, S. M. (1995). Elaboration as a determinant of attitude strength: Creating attitudes that are persistent, resistant, and predictive of behavior. In R. E. Petty and J. A. Krosnick (Eds.), *Attitude strength: Antecedents and consequences* (pp. 93–130). Mahwah, NJ: Erlbaum.

Petty, R. E., Wells, G., & Brock, T. (1976). Distraction can enhance or reduce yielding to propaganda: Thought disruption versus effort justification. *Journal of Personality and Social Psychology, 34,* 874–84.

Pfau, M., Szabo, E. A., Anderson, J., Morrill, J., Zubric, J., & Wan, H. (2001). The role and impact of affect in the process of resistance to persuasion. *Human Communication Research, 27,* 216–52.

Pfeffer, J. (1992). *Managing with power.* Boston: Harvard Business School Press.

Pfeffer, J., & Salancik, G. R. (1974). Organizational decision making as a political process: The case of a university budget. *Administrative Science Quarterly, 19,* 135–51.

Pfouts, R. W. (1994). Buying a pig when both buyer and seller are in a poke. *Atlantic Economic Journal, 22,* 80–85.

Phatak, A. V., & Habib, M. H. (1996). The dynamics of international business negotiations. *Business Horizons, 39,* 30–38.

Picard, C. (2002). Common language, different meaning: What mediators mean when they talk about their work. *Negotiation Journal, 18* (3), 251–69.

Pillutla, M. M., & Murnighan, J. K. (1996). Unfairness, anger and spite: Emotional rejections of ultimatum offers. *Organizational Behavior and Human Decision Processes, 68* (3), 208–24.

Pines, A. M., Gat, H, & Tal, Y. (2002). Gender differences and content and style of argument between couples during divorce mediation. *Conflict Resolution Quarterly, 20* (1), 23–50.

Pinkley, R. L. (1990). Dimensions of conflict frame: Disputant interpretations of conflict. *Journal of Applied Psychology, 75,* 117–26.

Pinkley, R. L. (1992). Dimensions of conflict frame: Relation to disputant perceptions and expectations. *International Journal of Conflict Management, 3,* 95–113.

Pinkley, R. L. (1995). Impact of knowledge regarding alternatives to settlement in dyadic negotiations: Whose knowledge counts? *Journal of Applied Psychology, 80,* 403–17.

Pinkley, R. L., Brittain, J., Neale, M., & Northcraft, G. (1995). Managerial third-party dispute intervention: An inductive analysis of intervenor strategy selection. *Journal of Applied Psychology, 80,* 386–402.

Pinkley, R. L., Griffith, T. L., & Northcraft, G. B. (1995). "Fixed pie" a la mode: Information availability, information processing, and the negotiation of suboptimal agreements. *Organizational Behavior and Human Decision Processes, 62,* 101–12.

Pinkley, R. L., Neale, M. A., & Bennett, R. J. (1994). The impact of alternatives to settlement in dyadic negotiation. *Organizational Behavior and Human Decision Processes, 57,* 97–116.

Pinkley, R. L., & Northcraft, G. B. (1994). Cognitive interpretations of conflict: Implications for dispute processes and outcomes. *Academy of Management Journal, 37,* 193–205.

Poitras, J., & Bowen, R. E. (2002). A framework for understanding consensus-building initiation. *Negotiation Journal, 18,* 211–32.

Poitras, J., Bowen, R. E., & Byrne, S. (2003). Bringing horses to water? Overcoming bad relationships in the pre-negotiating stage of consensus building. *Negotiation Journal, 19* (3), 251–63.

Polzer, J. T. (1996). Intergroup negotiations: The effects of negotiating teams. *Journal of Conflict Resolution, 40,* 678–98.

Polzer, J. T., Mannix, E. A., & Neale, M. A. (1995). Multiparty negotiations in a social context. In R. Kramer & D. Messick (Eds.), *Negotiation as a social process* (pp. 123–42). Thousand Oaks, CA: Sage.

Polzer, J. T., Mannix, E. A., & Neale, M. A. (1998). Interest alignment and coalitions in multiparty negotiation. *Academy of Management Journal, 41* (1), 42–54.

Poole, M., & Doelger, J. (1986). Developmental processes in group decision-making. In R. Hirokawa & M. Poole (Eds.), *Communication in group decision-making* (pp. 35–62). Beverly Hills, CA: Sage.

Pornpitakpan, C. (2004). The persuasiveness of source credibility: A critical review of five decades' evidence. *Journal of Applied Social Psychology, 34,* 243–281.

Post, F. R., & Bennett, R. J. (1994). Use of collaborative collective bargaining processes in labor negotiations. *International Journal of Conflict Management, 5* (1), 34–61.

Posthuma, R. A., & Dworkin, J. B. (2000). A behavioral theory of arbitrator acceptability. *International Journal of Conflict Management, 11,* 249–66.

Posthuma, R. A., Dworkin, J. B., & Swift, M. S. (2002). Mediator tactics and sources of conflict: Facilitating and inhibiting effects. *Industrial Relations, 41,* 94–109.

Prasow, P., & Peters, E. (1983). Arbitration and collective bargaining: Conflict resolution in labor relations (2nd ed.). New York: McGraw-Hill.

Prestwich, R. (2007). Cross-cultural negotiating: A Japanese-American case study from higher education. *International Negotiation, 12,* 29–55.

Provis, C. (1996). Interests vs. positions: A critique of the distinction. *Negotiation Journal, 12,* 305–23.

Pruitt, D. G. (1981). *Negotiation behavior.* New York: Academic Press.

Pruitt, D. G. (1983). Strategic choice in negotiation. *American Behavioral Scientist, 27,* 167–94.

Pruitt, D. G. (1994). Negotiation between organizations: A branching chain model. *Negotiation Journal, 10,* 217–30.

Pruitt, D. G. (1995). Networks and collective scripts: Paying attention to structure in bargaining theory. In R. Kramer & D. Messick (Eds.), *Negotiation as a social process* (pp. 37–47). Thousand Oaks, CA: Sage.

Pruitt, D. G., & Carnevale, P. J. D. (1993). *Negotiation in social conflict.* Pacific Grove, CA: Brooks-Cole.

Pruitt, D. G., Carnevale, P. J. D., Ben-Yoav, O., Nochajski, T. H., & Van Slyck, M. (1983). Incentives for cooperation in integrative bargaining. In L. Tietz (Ed.), *Aspiration levels in bargaining and economic decision making* (pp. 22–34). Berlin: Springer.

Pruitt, D. G., Carnevale, P. J. D., Forcey, B., & Van Slyck, M. (1986). Gender effects in negotiation: Constituent surveillance and contentious behavior. *Journal of Experimental Social Psychology, 22,* 264–75.

Pruitt, D. G., & Lewis, S. A. (1975). Development of integrative solutions in bilateral negotiation. *Journal of Personality and Social Psychology, 31,* 621–33.

Pruitt, D. G., Parker, J. C., & Mikolic, J. M. (1997). Escalation as a reaction to persistent annoyance. *International Journal of Conflict Management, 8,* 252–70.

Pruitt, D. G., & Rubin, J. Z. (1986). *Social conflict: Escalation, stalemate and settlement.* New York: Random House.

Pruitt, D. G., & Syna, H. (1985). Mismatching the opponent's offers in negotiation. *Journal of Experimental Social Psychology, 21,* 103–13.

Puccinelli, N. M., Tickle-Degnen, L., & Rosenthal, R. (2003). Effect of dyadic context on judgments of rapport: Dyad task and partner presence. *Journal of Nonverbal Behavior 27,* 211–36.

Putnam, L. L. (1994). Productive conflict: Negotiation as implicit coordination. *International Journal of Conflict Management, 5,* 284–98.

Putnam, L. L., & Geist, P. (1985). Argument in bargaining: An analysis of the reasoning process. *Southern Speech Communication Journal, 50,* 225–45.

Putnam, L. L., & Holmer, M. (1992). Framing, reframing, and issue development. In L. Putnam & M. Roloff (Eds.), *Communication and negotiation* (pp. 128–55). Newbury Park, CA: Sage.

Putnam, L. L., & Jones, T. S. (1982). Reciprocity in negotiations: An analysis of bargaining interaction. *Communication Monographs, 49,* 171–91.

Putnam, L. L., & Poole, M. (1987). Conflict and negotiation. In F. Jablin, L. Putnam, K. Roberts, & L. Porter (Eds.), *Handbook of organizational communication: An interdisciplinary perspective* (pp. 549–99). Newbury Park, CA: Sage.

Putnam, L. L., & Wilson, S. R. (1989). Argumentation and bargaining strategies as discriminators of integrative outcomes. In M. A. Rahim (Ed.), *Managing conflict: An interdisciplinary approach* (pp. 121–31). New York: Praeger.

Putnam, L., Wilson, S., & Turner, D. (1990). The evolution of policy arguments in teachers' negotiations. *Argumentation, 4,* 129–52.

Putnam, L., & Wondolleck, J. (2003). Intractability: Definitions, dimensions and distinctions. In R. J. Lewicki, B. Gray, & M. Elliott (Eds.), *Making sense of intractable environmental disputes.* Washington, DC: Island Press.

Pye, L. W. (1992). *Chinese negotiating style.* New York: Quorum Books.

Quinn, J. B. (1991). Strategies for change. In H. Mintzberg & J. B. Quinn (Eds.), *The strategy process: Concepts, contexts, cases* (2nd ed., pp. 4–12). Englewood Cliffs, NJ: Prentice Hall.

Rachels, J. (2003). *The elements of moral philosophy* (4th ed.). Boston: McGraw-Hill.

Rackham, N. (1980). The behavior of successful negotiators. Huthwaite Research Group. Reprinted in R. J. Lewicki, D. M. Saunders, & J. W. Minton (Eds.), *Negotiation: Readings, exercises and cases* (1999, 3rd ed.). Chicago: McGraw-Hill.

Rackham, N. (1980). *The behavior of successful negotiators.* London: Huthwaite Research Group Limited.

Rahim, M. A. (1983). A measure of styles of handling interpersonal conflict. *Academy of Management Journal, 26,* 368–76.

Rahim, M. A. (1990). *Rahim organizational conflict inventory: Professional manual.* Palo Alto, CA: Consulting Psychologists Press.

Rahim, M. A. (1992). *Managing conflict in organizations* (2nd ed.). Westport, CT: Praeger.

Raider, E. B., Coleman, S., & Gerson, J. (2000). Teaching conflict resolution skills in a workshop. In M. Deutsch & P. Coleman (Eds.), *Handbook of conflict resolution.* San Francisco: Jossey-Bass.

Raiffa, H. (1982). *The art and science of negotiation.* Cambridge, MA: Belknap Press of Harvard University Press.

Rammal, H. G. (2005). International business negotiations: The case of Pakistan. *International Journal of Commerce & Management, 15* (2), 129–40.

Rapoport, A. (1964). *Strategy and conscience.* New York: Harper & Row.

Rapoport, A., Erev, I., & Zwick, R. (1995). An experimental study of buyer-seller negotiation with one-sided incomplete information and time discounting. *Management Science, 41,* 377–94.

Rau, B. L., & Feinauer, D. (2006). The role of internal agents in starting salary negotiations. *Human Resource Management Review, 16,* 47–56.

Raven, B. (1993). The bases of power: Origins and recent developments. *Journal of Social Issues, 49* (4), 227–51.

Raven, B. (1999). Reflections on interpersonal influence and social power in experimental social psychology. In A. Rodrigues and R. Levine (Eds.), *Reflections on 100 years of experimental social psychology* (pp. 114–34). New York: Basic Books.

Raven, B., Schwartzwald, J., & Koslowski, M. (1998). Conceptualizing and measuring a power/interaction model of interpersonal influence. *Journal of Applied Social Psychology, 28* (4), 297–332.

Raven, B. H., & Rubin, J. Z. (1976). *Social psychology: People in groups.* New York: John Wiley and Sons.

Rayner, S. (1996). *Team traps.* New York: John Wiley and Sons.

Reardon, K. K. (1981). *Persuasion theory and context.* Beverly Hills, CA: Sage.

Ree, M. J., & Earles, J. A. (1991). Predicting training success: Not much more than g. *Personnel Psychology, 44,* 321–32.

Reich, R. B. (1981, May–June). Regulation by confrontation or negotiation. *Harvard Business Review, 59,* 82–93.

Reis, H. T., & Patrick, B. C. (1996). Attachment and intimacy: Component processes. In E. T. Higgins & A. W. Kruglanski (Eds.), *Social psychology: Handbook of basic principles* (pp. 523–63). New York: Guilford.

Reynolds, N., Simintiras, A., & Vlachou, E. (2003). International business negotiations. Present knowledge and directions for future research. *International Marketing Review, 20,* 236–61.

Richardson, R. C. (1977). *Collective bargaining by objectives.* Englewood Cliffs, NJ: Prentice Hall.

Right Management Consultants (2007). The cost of losing employee trust. Philadelphia: Author.

Ring, P. S., & Van de Ven, A. H. (1994). Developmental processes of cooperative interorganizational relationships. *Academy of Management Review, 19,* 90–118.

Rion, M. (1999). *The responsible manager: Practical strategies for ethical decision making.* West Hartford, CT: Resources for Ethics and Management.

Ritov, I. (1996). Anchoring in simulated competitive market negotiation. *Organizational Behavior and Human Decision Processes, 67,* 16–25.

Rivers, C., & Lytle, A. L. (2007). Lying, cheating foreigners!! Negotiation ethics across cultures. *International Negotiation, 12,* 1–28.

Robinson, R. J. (1995). Defusing the exploding offer: The far-point gambit. *Negotiation Journal, 11,* 389–404.

Robinson, R., Lewicki, R. J., & Donahue, E. (2000). Extending and testing a five factor model of ethical and unethical bargaining tactics: The SINS scale. *Journal of Organizational Behavior, 21,* 649–64.

Roch, S. G., & Samuelson, C. D. (1997). Effects of environmental uncertainty and social value orientation in resource dilemmas. *Organizational Behavior and Human Decision Processes, 70,* 221–35.

Rogers, C. R. (1957). *Active listening.* Chicago: University of Chicago Press.

Rogers, C. R. (1961). *On becoming a person: A therapist's view of psychotherapy.* Boston: Houghton Mifflin.

Rogers, C. R., & Roethlisberger, F. J. (1991). Barriers and gateways to communication. *Harvard Business Review, 69,* 105–11.

Rosenbaum, M. E. (1986). The repulsion hypothesis: On the nondevelopment of relationships. *Journal of Personality and Social Psychology, 51,* 1156–66.

Rosette, A., Brett, J. M., Barsness, Z., & Lytle, A. L. (2004). *When cultures clash electronically: The impact of e-mail and culture on negotiation behavior.* DRRC working paper. Evanston, IL: Northwestern University.

Roskos-Ewoldsen, D. R., Bichsel, J., & Hoffman, K. (2002). The influence of accessibility of source likeability on persuasion. *Journal of Experimental Social Psychology, 38,* 137–43.

Rosnow, R. L., & Robinson, E. J. (1967). *Experiments in persuasion.* New York: Academic Press.

Ross, L. (1997). The intuitive psychologist and his shortcomings: Distortions in the attribution process. In L. Berkowitz (Ed.), *Advances in Experimental Social Psychology* (Vol. 10, pp. 173–220). Orlando, FL: Academic Press.

Ross, L., Green, D., & House, P. (1977). The false consensus phenomenon: An attributional bias in self-perception and social-perception processes. *Journal of Experimental Social Psychology, 13,* 279–301.

Ross, L., & Stillinger, C. (1991). Barriers to conflict resolution. *Negotiation Journal, 7,* 389–404.

Ross, M. H. (2000). "Good-enough" isn't so bad: Thinking about success and failure in ethnic conflict management. *Peace and Conflict: Journal of Peace Psychology, 6,* 21–27.

Ross, W., & Conlon, D. E. (2000). Hybrid forms of third-party dispute resolution: The theoretical implications of combining mediation and arbitration. *Academy of Management Review, 25* (2), 416–27.

Ross, W., & LaCroix, J. (1996). Multiple meanings of trust in negotiation theory and research: A literature review and integrative model. *International Journal of Conflict Management, 7,* 314–60.

Ross, W. T., & Robertson, D. C. (2000). Lying: The impact of decision context. *Business Ethics Quarterly, 10,* 409–40.

Roth, A., & Malouf, M. (1979). Game-theoretic models and the role of information in bargaining. *Psychological Review, 86,* 574–94.

Roth, A. E., Murnighan, J. K., & Schoumaker, F. (1988). The deadline effect in bargaining: Some empirical evidence. *American Economic Review, 78,* 806–23.

Roth, J., & Sheppard, B. H. (1995). Opening the black box of framing research: The relationship between frames, communication, and outcomes. *Academy of Management Proceedings.*

Rothman, J. (1997). *Resolving identity-based conflict in nations, organizations and communities.* San Francisco: Jossey-Bass.

Rotter, J. B. (1966). Generalized expectancies for internal versus external control of reinforcement. *Psychological Monographs, 80* (1).

Rotter, J. B. (1967). A new scale for the measurement of interpersonal trust. *Journal of Personality, 35,* 651–65.

Rotter, J. B. (1971). Generalized expectancies for interpersonal trust. *American Psychologist, 26,* 443–52.

Rotter, J. B. (1980). Interpersonal trust, trustworthiness, and gullibility. *American Psychologist, 35,* 1–7.

Rousseau, D. (2001). The idiosyncratic deal: Flexibility vs. fairness? *Organizational Dynamics, 29* (4), 260–73.

Rousseau, J. J. (1947). *The social contract.* New York: Hafner Publishing Commune.

Rowe, M. (1995). Options, functions, and skills: What an organizational ombudsman might want to know. *Negotiation Journal, 11,* 103–14.

Rubin, J., & Sander, F. (1988). When should we use agents? Direct vs. representative negotiation. *Negotiation Journal, X* (4), 395–401.

Rubin, J., Pruitt, D., & Kim, S. H. (1994). *Social conflict: Escalation, stalemate and settlement* (2nd ed.). New York: McGraw-Hill.

Rubin, J. Z. (1980). Experimental research on third party intervention in conflict: Toward some generalizations. *Psychological Bulletin, 87,* 379–91.

Rubin, J. Z. (Ed.). (1981). *Dynamics of third party intervention: Kissinger in the Middle East.* New York: Praeger.

Rubin, J. Z., & Sander, F. E. A. (1991). Culture, negotiation, and the eye of the beholder. *Negotiation Journal, 7* (3), 249–54.

Rubinstein, R. A. (2003). Cross cultural considerations in complex peace operations. *Negotiation Journal, 19* (1), 29–49.

Ruble, T. L., & Thomas, K. W. (1976). Support for a two-dimensional model of conflict behavior. *Organizational Behavior and Human Performance, 16,* 143–55.

Rudman, L. A. (1998). Self-promotion as a risk factor for women: The cost and benefits of counter stereotypical impression management. *Journal of Personality and Social Psychology, 74,* 629–45.

Rudman, L. A., & Glick, P. (1999). Feminized management and backlash towards agentic women: The hidden costs to women of a kinder, gentler image of middle managers. *Journal of Personality and Social Psychology, 77,* 1004–10.

Rusbult, C., & Van Lange, P. A. M. (1996). Interdependence processes. In E. T. Higgins & A. W. Kruglanski (Eds.), *Social psychology: Handbook of basic principles* (pp. 564–96). New York: Guilford.

Rusk, T., with Miller, D. P. (1993). *The power of ethical persuasion.* New York: Penguin.

Russo, J. E., & Schoemaker, P. J. H. (1989). *Decision traps: The ten barriers to brilliant decision making and how to overcome them.* New York: Simon & Schuster.

Salacuse, J. (1998). So, what's the deal anyway? Contracts and relationships as negotiating goals. *Negotiation Journal, 14* (1), 5–12.

Salacuse, J. (1999). Law and power in agency negotiations. In R. H. Mnookin and L. E. Susskind (Eds.), *Negotiating on behalf of others* (pp. 157–75). Thousand Oaks, CA: Sage.

Salacuse, J. (2001). Renegotiating existing agreements: How to deal with "life struggling against form." *Negotiation Journal, 17* (4), 311–32.

Salacuse, J. W. (1988). Making deals in strange places: A beginner's guide to international business negotiations. *Negotiation Journal, 4,* 5–13.

Salacuse, J. W. (1995). The art of advising negotiators. *Negotiation Journal, 11,* 391–401.

Salancik, G. R., & Pfeffer, J. (1977). Who gets power and how they hold on to it: A strategic-contingency model of power. *Organizational Dynamics, 5,* 3–21.

Sander, F. E. A., & Bordone, R. C. (2006). All in the family: Managing business disputes with relatives. *Negotiation, a newsletter from Harvard Business School Publishing and the Program on Negotiation at Harvard Law School.*

Salter, C. (2007, May). Lessons from the tarmac. *Fast Company,* 31–32.

Santos, M. D., Leve, C., & Pratkanis, A. R. (1994). Hey buddy, can you spare seventeen cents? Mindful persuasion and the pique technique. *Journal of Applied Social Psychology, 24,* 755–64.

Saorin-Iborra, M. C. (2006). A review of negotiation outcome: A proposal on delimitation and subsequent assessment in joint venture negotiation. *Canadian Journal of Administrative Sciences, 23* (3), 237–52.

Sauer, P., Dvorak, A., Lisa, A., & Fiala, P. (2003). A procedure for negotiating pollution reduction under information asymmetry. *Environment and Resource Economics, 24,* 103–19.

Saunders, Harold H. (2003). Sustained dialogue in managing intractable conflict. *Negotiation Journal, 19* (1), 85–95.

Savage, G. T., Blair, J. D., & Sorenson, R. L. (1989). Consider both relationships and substance when negotiating strategically. *Academy of Management Executive, 3* (1), 37–48.

Schatzski, M. (1981). *Negotiation: The art of getting what you want.* New York: Signet Books.

Schein, E. (1987). *Process consultation Volume II: Lessons for managers and consultants.* Reading, MA: Addison-Wesley.

Schein, E. (1988). *Organizational Culture and Leadership.* San Francisco: Jossey-Bass.

Schelling, T. C. (1960). *The strategy of conflict.* Cambridge, MA: Harvard University Press.

Schelling, T. C. (1978). *Micromotives and macrobehavior.* New York: Norton.

Schlenker, B. R., Helm, B., & Tedeschi, J. T. (1973). The effects of personality and situational variables on behavioral trust. *Journal of Personality and Social Psychology, 25* (3), 419–27.

Schlenker, B. R., & Riess, M. (1979). Self-presentation of attitudes following commitment to proattitudinal behavior. *Journal of Human Communication Research, 5,* 325–34.

Schmidt, F. L., & Hunter, J. E. (1998). The validity and utility of selection methods in personnel psychology: Practical and theoretical implications of 85 years of research findings. *Psychological Bulletin, 124,* 262–74.

Schminke, M., Ambrose, M. L., & Miles, J. A. (2003). The impact of gender and settings on perceptions of others' ethics. *Sex Roles, 48,* 361–75.

Schneider, A. K. (1994). Effective responses to offensive comments. *Negotiation Journal, 10,* 107–15.

Schneider, A. K. (2002). Shattering negotiation myths: Empirical evidence on the effectiveness of negotiation style. *Harvard Law Review, 7,* 143–233.

Schön, D. A., & Rein, M. (1994). *Frame reflection: Toward the resolution of intractable policy controversies.* New York: Basic Books.

Schoppa, L. J. (1993). Two-level games and bargaining outcomes: Why gaiatsu succeeds in Japan in some cases but not in others. *International Organization, 47,* 353–86.

Schotter, A., Zheng, W., & Snyder, B. (2000). Bargaining through agents: An experimental study of delegation and commitment. *Games and Economic Behavior, 30,* 248–92.

Schreisheim, C., & Hinkin, T. R. (1990). Influence strategies used by subordinates: A theoretical and empirical analysis and refinement of the Kipnis, Schmidt, and Wilkinson subscales. *Journal of Applied Psychology, 75,* 246–57.

Schroth, H. A., Bain-Chekal, J., & Caldwell, D. F. (2005). Sticks and stones may break bones and words can hurt me: Words and phrases that trigger emotions in negotiations and their effects. *International Journal of Conflict Management, 16,* 102–27.

Schurr, P. H. (1987). Effects of gain and loss decision frames on risky purchase negotiations. *Journal of Applied Psychology, 72,* 351–58.

Schwartz, S. H. (1992). Universals in the content and structure of values: Theoretical advances and empirical tests in 20 countries. In M. Zanna (Ed.), *Advances in experimental social psychology* (Vol. 25, pp. 1–65). Orlando, FL: Academic Press.

Schwartz, S. H. (1994). Beyond individualism and collectivism: New cultural dimensions of values. In U. Kim, H. C. Triandis, C. Kagitcibasi, S-C. Choi, & G. Yoom (Eds.), *Individualism and collectivism: Theory, method and application* (pp. 85–122). Thousand Oaks, CA: Sage.

Schwartz, S. H., & Bilsky, W. (1990). Toward a theory of universal content and structure of values: Extensions and cross-cultural replications. *Journal of Personality and Social Psychology, 58,* 878–91.

Schweitzer, M. (2004). Promises and lies: Restoring violated trust. Unpublished manuscript. Wharton School of Business Administration.

Schweitzer, M., Ordonez, L., & Douma, B. (2004). Goal setting as a motivator of unethical behavior. *Academy of Management Journal, 47,* 422–32.

Schweitzer, M. E. (1997). *Omission, friendship and fraud: Lies about material facts in negotiation.* Unpublished manuscript.

Schweitzer, M. E., Brodt, S. E., & Croson, R. T. A. (2002). Seeing and believing: Visual access and the strategic use of deception. *International Journal of Conflict Management, 13,* 258–75.

Schweitzer, M. E., & Croson, R. (2001). Curtailing deception: The impact of direct questions on lies and omissions. *International Journal of Conflict Management, 10* (3), 225–48.

Schweitzer, M. E., Hershey, J. C., & Bradlow, E. T. (2006). Promises and lies: Restoring violated trust. *Organizational Behavior and Human Decision Processes, 101,* 1–19.

Schweitzer, M. E., & Kerr, J. L. (2000). Bargaining under the influence: The role of alcohol in negotiations. *Academy of Management Executive, 14,* 47–57.

Sebenius, J. K. (1983). Negotiation arithmetic: Adding and subtracting issues and parties. *International Organization, 37,* 1–34.

Sebenius, J. K. (1992). Negotiation analysis: A characterization and review. *Management Science, 38,* 18–38.

Sebenius, J. K. (2001, April). Six habits of merely effective negotiators. *Harvard Business Review,* 87–95.

Sebenius, J. K. (2002a, March). The hidden challenge of cross-border negotiations. *Harvard Business Review, 80,* 76–85.

Sebenius, J. K. (2002b). Caveats for cross-border negotiations. *Negotiation Journal, 18* (2), 121–33.

Selekman, B. M., Fuller, S. H., Kennedy, T., & Baitsel, J. M. (1964). *Problems in labor relations.* New York: McGraw-Hill.

Selekman, B. M., Selekman, S. K., & Fuller, S. H. (1958). *Problems in labor relations.* New York: McGraw-Hill.

Seligman, C., Bush, M., & Kirsch, K. (1976). Relationship between compliance in the foot in the door paradigm and size of first request. *Journal of Personality and Social Psychology, 33,* 517–20.

Sen, A. K. (1970). *Collective choice and individual values.* San Francisco: Holden-Day.

Senge, P. (1990). *The Fifth Discipline: The Art and Practice of the Learning Organization,* New York: Doubleday Currency.

Seudfeld, P., & Bluck, S. (1988). Changes in integrative complexity prior to surprise attacks. *Journal of Conflict Resolution, 32,* 626–35.

Shah, P. P., & Jehn, K. A. (1993). Do friends perform better than acquaintances? The interaction of friendship, conflict and task. *Group Decision and Negotiation, 2,* 149–65.

Shannon, E., & Weaver, W. (1948). *The mathematical theory of communication.* Urbana, IL: University of Illinois Press.

Shapiro, D. L. (1991). The effects of explanations on negative reactions to deceit. *Administrative Science Quarterly, 36,* 614–30.

Shapiro, D. L. (2006). Teaching students how to use emotions as they negotiate. *Negotiation Journal, 22,* 105–09.

Shapiro, D. L., & Bies, R. J. (1994). Threats, bluffs and disclaimers in negotiation. *Organizational Behavior and Human Decision Processes, 60,* 14–35.

Shapiro, D. L., Sheppard, B. H., & Cheraskin, L. (1992). Business on a handshake. *Negotiation Journal, 8,* 365–77.

Shapiro, D. L., & Von Glinow, M. A. (1999). Negotiation in multicultural teams: New world, old theories? In R. Bies, R. J. Lewicki, & B. H. Sheppard (Eds.), *Research on negotiation in organizations* (Vol. 7, pp. 231–62). Stamford, CT: JAI Press.

Shea, G. F. (1983). *Creative negotiating.* Boston, MA: CBI Publishing Co.

Sheehy, B., & Palanovics, N. (2006). E-negotiations: Rapport building, anonymity and attribution. *Australasian Dispute Resolution Journal, 17,* 221–32.

Sheldon, A., & Johnson, D. (1994). Preschool negotiators: Linguistic differences in how girls and boys regulate the expression of dissent in same-sex groups. In B. H. Sheppard, R. J. Lewicki, & R. Bies (Eds.), *Research on negotiation in organizations* (Vol. 4, pp. 37–67). Greenwich, CT: JAI Press.

Shell, G. R. (1991). When is it legal to lie in negotiations? *Sloan Management Review, 32* (3), 93–101.

Shell, G. R. (1999). *Bargaining for advantage.* New York: Viking Books.

Sheppard, B. H. (1983). Managers as inquisitors: Some lessons from the law. In M. H. Bazerman & R. J. Lewicki (Eds.), *Negotiating in organizations* (pp. 193–213). Beverly Hills, CA: Sage.

Sheppard, B. H. (1984). Third-party conflict intervention: A procedural framework. In B. M. Staw & L. L. Cummings (Eds.), *Research in organizational behavior* (Vol. 6, pp. 141–90). Greenwich, CT: JAI Press.

Sheppard, B. H. (1995). Negotiating in long term mutually interdependent relationships among relative equals. In R. J. Bies, R. J. Lewicki, & B. H. Sheppard (Eds.), *Research on negotiation in organizations* (Vol. 5, pp. 3–44). Greenwich, CT: JAI Press.

Sheppard, B. H., Blumenfeld-Jones, K., Minton, J. W., & Hyder, E. (1994). Informal conflict intervention: Advice and dissent. *Employee Rights and Responsibilities Journal, 7,* 53–72.

Sheppard, B. H., Lewicki, R. J., & Minton, J. W. (1992). *Organizational justice: The search for fairness in the workplace.* New York: Lexington Books.

Sheppard, B. H., & Sherman, D. M. (1998). The grammars of trust: A model and general implications. *Academy of Management Review, 23* (3), 422–37.

Sheppard, B. H., & Tuchinsky, M. (1996a). Micro-OB and the network organization. In R. Kramer & T. Tyler (Eds.), *Trust in organizations* (pp. 140–65). Thousand Oaks, CA: Sage.

Sheppard, B. H., & Tuchinsky, M. (1996b). Interfirm relations: A grammar of pairs. In B. M. Staw & L. L. Cummings (Eds.), *Research on organizational behavior* (Vol. 18, pp. 331–73). Greenwich, CT: JAI Press.

Sherif, M., Harvey, L., White, B., Hood, W., & Sherif, C. (1988). *The Robbers' Cave experiment: Intergroup conflict and cooperation.* Middletown, CT: Wesleyan University Press. (Original work published 1961.)

Shestowsky, D. (2004). Procedural preferences in alternative dispute resolution: A closer, modern look at an old idea. *Psychology, Public Policy & Law, 10* (3), 211–49.

Shi, X., & Wright, P. C. (2001). Developing and validating an international business negotiator's profile. The China context. *Journal of Managerial Psychology, 16,* 364–89.

Short, J., Williams, E., & Christie, B. (1976). *The social psychology of telecommunications.* London: John Wiley and Sons.

Siegel, S. R., & Fouraker, L. E. (1960). *Bargaining and group decision making: Experiments in bilateral monopoly.* New York: McGraw-Hill.

Sims, R. L. (2002). Support for the use of deception within the work environment: A comparison of Israeli and United States employee attitudes. *Journal of Business Ethics, 35,* 27–34.

Simons, T. (1993). Speech patterns and the concept of utility in cognitive maps: The case of integrative bargaining. *Academy of Management Journal, 36,* 139–56.

Sinaceur, M., & Neale, M. A. (2005). Not all threats are created equal: How implicitness and timing affect the effectiveness of threats. *Group Decision and Negotiation, 14,* 63–85.

Sinaceur, M., & Tiedens, L. Z. (2006). Get mad and get more than even: When and why anger expression is effective in negotiations. *Journal of Experimental Social Psychology, 42,* 314–22.

Singer, L. R. (1990). *Settling disputes: Conflict resolution in business, families, and the legal system.* Boulder, CO: Westview Press.

Singer, L. R. (1994). *Settling disputes: Conflict resolution in business, families, and the legal system* (2nd ed.). Boulder, CO: Westview Press.

Sitkin, S. B., & Bies, R. J. (1993). Social accounts in conflict situations: Using explanations to manage conflict. *Human Relations, 46,* 349–70.

Skarlicki, D. P., & Folger, R. (1997). Retaliation in the workplace: The roles of distributive, procedural and interactive justice. *Journal of Applied Psychology, 82* (3), 434–43.

Skinner, B. F. (1953). *Science and human behavior.* New York: Macmillan.

Slutsky, J., & Slutsky, M. (1998, February 23). Learning others' goals is important to successful negotiations. *The Columbus* (Ohio) *Dispatch,* 9.

Small, D. A., Gelfand, M., Babcock, L., & Gettman, H. (2007). Who goes to the bargaining table? The influence of gender and framing on the initiation of negotiation. *Journal of Personality and Social Psychology, 93,* 600–13.

Smith, P., & Schwartz, S. H. (1997). Values. In J. W. Berry, M. H. Segall., & C. Kagitcibashi (Eds.), *Handbook of cross-cultural psychology* (Vol. 3, pp. 77–118). Needham Heights, MA: Allyn & Bacon.

Smith, P. B., Dugan, S., Peterson, M. F., & Leung, K. (1998). Individualism/collectivism and the handling of disagreement: A 23 country study. *International Journal of Intercultural Relations, 22,* 351–67.

Smith, T. H. (2005). Metaphors for navigating negotiations. *Negotiation Journal, 21,* 343–64.

Smith, W. P. (1985). Effectiveness of the biased mediator. *Negotiation Journal, 1,* 363–72.

Smyth, L. F. (1994). Intractable conflicts and the role of identity. *Negotiation Journal, 10,* 311–21.

Snyder, M. (1974). Self-monitoring of expressive behavior. *Journal of Personality and Social Psychology, 30,* 526–37.

Snyder, M. (1987). *Public appearances/private realities.* New York: Freeman.

Solnick, S. J. (2001). Gender differences in the ultimatum game. *Economic Inquiry, 39,* 189–200.

Solomon, M. (1990). *Working with difficult people.* Englewood Cliffs, NJ: Prentice Hall.

Solomon, R. H. (1987). China: Friendship and obligation in Chinese negotiating style. In H. Binnendijk (Ed.), *National negotiating styles* (pp. 1–16). Washington, DC: Foreign Service Institute.

Sondak, H., Neale, M. A., & Pinkley, R. (1995). The negotiated allocation of benefits and burdens: The impact of outcome valence, contribution and relationship. *Organizational Behavior and Human Decision Processes, 64* (3), 249–60.

Sondak, H., & Tyler, T. R. (2001). What shouldn't money buy? The psychology of preferences for market solutions to allocation problems. As quoted in T. Tyler and S. R. Blader, Justice and Negotiation, in M. Gelfand, and J. Brett (Eds.), (2004). *The handbook of negotiation and culture* (pp. 295–312). Stanford, CA: Stanford University Press.

Song, F. (2004). Trust and reciprocity: The differing norms of individuals and group representatives. Unpublished paper.

Song, Y. J., Hale, C. L., & Rao, N. (2004). Success and failure of business negotiations for South Koreans. *Journal of International and Area Studies, 11* (2), 45–65.

Song, Y. J., Hale, C. L., & Rao, N. (2005). The South Korean chief negotiator: Balancing traditional values and contemporary business practices. *International Journal of Cross Cultural Management, 5* (3), 313–27.

Spector, B. I. (1995). Creativity heuristics for impasse resolution: Reframing intractable negotiations. *Annals of the American Academy of Political and Social Science, 542,* 81–99.

Spector, B. I. (1998). Deciding to negotiate with villains. *Negotiation Journal, 14,* 43–59.

Spector, B. I. (2006). Resiliency in negotiation: Bouncing back from impasse. *International Negotiation, 11,* 273–86.

Spitzberg, B. H., & Cupach, W. R. (1984). *Interpersonal communication competence.* Beverly Hills, CA: Sage.

Sproull, L., & Kiesler, S. (1986). Reducing social context cues: Electronic mail in organizational communication. *Management Science, 32,* 1492–1512.

Stacks, D. W., & Burgoon, J. K. (1981). The role of non-verbal behaviors as distractors in resistance to persuasion in interpersonal contexts. *Central States Speech Journal, 32,* 61–80.

Stark, A., Fam, K. S., Waller, D. S., & Tian, Z. (2005). Chinese negotiation practice: A perspective from New Zealand exporters. *Cross Cultural Management, 12* (3), 85–102.

Starke, F. A., & Notz, W. W. (1981). Pre- and postintervention effects of conventional vs. final-offer arbitration. *Academy of Management Journal, 24,* 832–50.

Staw, B. M. (1981). The escalation of commitment to a course of action. *Academy of Management Review, 6,* 577–87.

Steele, C. M. (1997). A threat in the air: How stereotypes shape intellectual identity and performance. *American Psychologist, 52,* 613–29.

Steers, R. M. (1984). *Introduction to organizational behavior* (2nd ed.). Glenview, IL: Scott Foresman.

Stein, J. (1996). The art of real estate negotiations. *Real Estate Review, 25,* 48–53.

Stein, J. G. (1999). Problem solving as metaphor: Negotiation and identity conflict. *Peace and Conflict: Journal of Peace Psychology, 5,* 225–35.

Steinberg, L. (1998). *Winning with integrity.* New York: Random House.

Steinel, W., & de Dreu, C. K. W. (2004). Social motives and strategic misrepresentation in social decision making. *Journal of Personality and Social Psychology, 86,* 419–34.

Stieber, C. (2000). 57 varieties: Has the ombudsman concept become diluted? *Negotiation Journal, 16,* 49–57.

Sternberg, R. (Ed.). (1988). *The nature of creativity.* New York: Cambridge University Press.

Stevens, C. K., Bavetta, A. G., & Gist, M. E. (1993). Gender differences in the acquisition of salary negotiation skills: The role of goals, self-efficacy, and perceived control. *Journal of Applied Psychology, 78,* 723–35.

Stevens, C. K., & Gist, M. E. (1997). Effects of self-efficacy and goal-orientation training on negotiation skill maintenance: What are the mechanisms? *Personnel Psychology, 50,* 959–78.

Stevens, C. M. (1963). *Strategy and collective bargaining negotiations.* New York: McGraw-Hill.

Stewart, J. B. (1992). *Den of thieves.* New York: Touchstone Books.

Stillenger, C., Epelbaum, M., Keltner, D., & Ross, L. (1990). The "reactive devaluation" barrier to conflict resolution. Working paper, Stanford University, Palo Alto, CA.

Stolte, J. F. (1983). Self-efficacy: Sources and consequences in negotiation networks. *Journal of Social Psychology, 119,* 69–75.

Stone, D., Patton, B., & Heen, S. (1999). *Difficult conversations: How to discuss what matters most.* New York: Penguin Books.

Straus, M. A. (2004). Cross-cultural reliability and validity of the revised conflict tactics scales: A study of university student dating couples in 17 nations. *Cross-Cultural Research, 38* (4), 407–32.

Street, M. D., Robertson, C., & Geiger, S. W. (1997). Ethical decision making: The effects of escalating commitment. *Journal of Business Ethics, 16,* 1153–61.

Stuhlmacher, A. F., Citera, M., & Willis, T. (2007). Gender differences in virtual negotiation: Theory and research. *Sex Roles, 57,* 329–39.

Stuhlmacher, A. F., Gillespie, T. L., & Champagne, M. V. (1998). The impact of time pressure in negotiation: A meta-analysis. *International Journal of Conflict Management, 9* (2), 97–116.

Stuhlmacher, A. F., & Walters, A. E. (1999). Gender differences in negotiation outcomes: A meta-analysis. *Personnel Psychology, 52,* 653–77.

Subramanian, G. (2006). Contracts 101: What every negotiator should know about contract and agency law. *Negotiation: A Newsletter.* Harvard Business School Publishing and The Program on Negotiation at Harvard Law School, Article Reprint N0602D.

Sullivan, B. A., O'Connor, K. M., & Burris, E. R. (2006). Negotiator confidence: The impact of self-efficacy on tactics and outcomes. *Journal of Experimental Social Psychology, 42,* 567–81.

Sulzner, G. T. (2003). Adjudicators (arbitrators) acting as mediators: An experiment in dispute resolution at the Public Service Staff Relations Board in Canada. *Journal of Collective Negotiations in the Public Sector, 30,* 59–75.

Susskind, L., & Cruikshank, J. (1987). *Breaking the impasse: Consensual approaches to resolving public disputes.* New York: Basic Books.

Susskind, L., McKearnan, S., & Thomas-Larmer, J. (1999). *The consensus building handbook.* Thousand Oaks, CA: Sage.

Sutton, S. R. (1982). Fear-arousing communications: A critical examination of theory and research. In J. R. Eiser (Ed.), *Social psychology and behavioral medicine* (pp. 303–37). New York: John Wiley and Sons.

Swaab, R., Postmes, T., van Beest, I., & Spears, R. (2007). Shared cognition as a product of, and precursor to, shared identity in negotiations. *Personality and Social Psychology Bulletin, 33,* 187–99.

Swaab, R. I., Kern, M. C., Diermeier, D., & Medvec, V. (in press). Who says what to whom? The impact of communication on social exclusion. *Social Cognition.*

Swaab, R. I., Phillips, K. W., Diermeier, D., & Medvec, V. H. (2008). The pros and cons of dyadic side conversations in small groups. *Small Group Research.*

Swaab, R. I., Postmes, R., & Spears, R. (2008). Identity formation in multiparty negotiations. *British Journal of Social Psychology, 47,* 167–87.

Swacker, F. W., Redden, K. R., & Wenger, L. B. (2000). The World Trade Organization and dispute resolution. *Dispute Resolution Journal, 55* (3), pp. 35–39.

Swenson, R. A., Nash, D. L., & Roos, D. C. (1984). Source credibility and perceived expertness of testimony in a simulated child-custody case. *Professional Psychology, 15,* 891–98.

Tajima, M., & Fraser, N. M. (2001). Logrolling procedure for multi-issue negotiation. *Group Decision and Negotiation, 10,* 217–35.

Tannen, D. (1990). *You just don't understand: Women and men in conversation.* New York: Ballantine Books.

Tannen, D. (1998, March 3). How to turn debate into dialogue. *USA Weekend,* 4–5.

Taylor, P. J., & Donald, I. (2003). Foundations and evidence for an interaction based approach to conflict negotiation. *International Journal of Conflict Management, 14,* 213–32.

Taylor, S. E., & Brown, J. D. (1988). Illusion and well-being: A social-psychological perspective on mental health. *Psychological Bulletin, 103,* 193–210.

Tedeschi, J. T., Heister, D. S., & Gahagan, J. P. (1969). Trust and the prisoner's dilemma game. *Journal of Social Psychology, 79,* 43–50.

Tedeschi, J. T., Schlenker, B. R., & Bonoma, T. V. (1973). *Conflict, power and games: The experimental study of interpersonal relations.* Chicago: AVC.

Teger, A. (1980). *Too much invested to quit.* New York: Pergamon Press.

Tenbrunsel, A. E. (1998). Misrepresentation and expectations of misrepresentation in an ethical dilemma: The role of incentives and temptation. *Academy of Management Journal, 4* (3), 330–39.

Tenbrunsel, A. E. (1999). Trust as an obstacle in environmental-economic disputes. *American Behavioral Scientist, 42,* 1350–67.

Terhune, K. W. (1970). The effects of personality in cooperation and conflict. In P. Swingle (Ed.), *The structure of conflict* (pp. 193–234). New York: Academic Press.

Thibaut, J., & Walker, L. (1975). *Procedural justice: A psychological analysis.* Hillsdale, NJ: Lawrence Erlbaum.

Thomas, K. W. (1976). Conflict and conflict management. In M. D. Dunnette (Ed.), *Handbook of industrial & organizational psychology* (pp. 889–935). Chicago: Rand McNally.

Thomas, K. W. (1977). Toward multidimensional values in teaching: The example of conflict behavior. *Academy of Management Review, 2,* 484–90.

Thomas, K. W. (1992). Conflict and negotiation processes in organizations. In M. D. Dunnette and L. H. Hough, *Handbook of industrial & organizational psychology* (2nd ed., Vol. 3, pp. 651–718). Palo Alto, CA: Consulting Psychologists Press.

Thomas, K. W., & Kilmann, R. H. (1974). *Thomas-Kilmann conflict mode survey.* Tuxedo, NY: Xicom.

Thompson, J. D. (1967). *Organizations in action.* New York: McGraw-Hill.

Thompson, L. (1990a). An examination of naïve and experienced negotiators. *Journal of Personality and Social Psychology, 59,* 82–90.

Thompson, L. (1990b). Negotiation behavior and outcomes: Empirical evidence and theoretical issues. *Psychological Bulletin, 108,* 515–32.

Thompson, L. (1991). Information exchange in negotiation. *Journal of Experimental Social Psychology, 27,* 161–79.

Thompson, L. (1995). They saw a negotiation: Partnership and involvement. *Journal of Personality and Social Psychology, 68,* 839–53.

Thompson, L. (1998). *The mind and heart of the negotiator.* Upper Saddle River, NJ: Prentice Hall.

Thompson, L. (2000). *Making the team: A guide for managers.* Englewood Cliffs, NJ: Prentice Hall.

Thompson, L., & DeHarpport, T. (1994). Social judgment, feedback, and interpersonal learning in negotiation. *Organizational Behavior and Human Decision Processes, 58,* 327–45.

Thompson, L., Gentner, J. & Loewenstein, J. (2000). Avoiding missed opportunities in managerial life: Analogical training more powerful than individual case training.

Organizational Behavior and Human Decision Processes, 82, 60–75.

Thompson, L., & Hastie, R. (1990a). Social perception in negotiation. *Organizational Behavior and Human Decision Processes, 47,* 98–123.

Thompson, L., & Hastie, R. (1990b). Judgment tasks and biases in negotiation. In B. H. Sheppard, M. H. Bazerman, & R. J. Lewicki (Eds.), *Research on negotiation in organizations* (Vol. 2, pp. 31–54). Greenwich, CT: JAI Press.

Thompson, L., & Hrebec, D. (1996). Lose-lose agreements in interdependent decision making. *Psychological Bulletin, 120,* 396–409.

Thompson, L., & Loewenstein, G. (1992). Egocentric interpretations of fairness and interpersonal conflict. *Organizational Behavior and Human Decision Processes, 51,* 176–97.

Thompson, L., & Nadler, J. (2002). Negotiating via information technology: Theory and application. *Journal of Social Issues, 58,* 109–24.

Thompson, L., Peterson, E., & Brodt, S. E. (1996). Team negotiations: An examination of integrative and distributive bargaining. *Journal of Personality and Social Psychology, 70,* 66–78.

Thompson, L., Peterson, E., & Kray, L. (1995). Social context in negotiation: An information processing perspective. In R. Kramer & D. Messick (Eds.), *Negotiation as a social process* (pp. 5–36). Beverly Hills, CA: Sage.

Thompson, L., Valley, K. L., & Kramer, R. M. (1995). The bittersweet feeling of success: An examination of social perception in negotiation. *Journal of Experimental Social Psychology, 31,* 467–92.

Thompson, L. L., & Kim, P. H. (2000, March). How the quality of third parties' settlement solutions is affected by the relationship between the negotiators. *Journal of Experimental Psychology: Applied, 6* (1), 3–14.

Thompson, L. L., Nadler, J., & Kim, P. H. (1999). Some like it hot: The case for the emotional negotiator. In L. L. Thompson, J. M. Levine, & D. M. Messick (Eds.), *Shared cognition in organizations: The management of knowledge* (pp. 139–61). Mahwah, NJ: Erlbaum.

Tibon, S. (2000). Personality traits and peace negotiations: Integrative complexity and attitudes toward the middle east peace process. *Group Decision and Negotiation, 9,* 1–15.

Ting-Toomey, S., & Kurogi, A. (1998). Facework competence in intercultural conflict: An updated face-negotiation theory. *International Journal of Intercultural Relations, 22,* 187–225.

Tinsley, C. H. (1996, June). Understanding conflict in other cultural contexts: The Chinese example. Paper presented at the International Association of Conflict Management, Ithaca, New York.

Tinsley, C. H. (1997). Understanding conflict in a Chinese cultural context. In R. J. Bies, R. J. Lewicki, & B. H. Sheppard (Eds.), *Research on negotiation in organizations* (Vol. 6, pp. 209–25). Greenwich, CT: JAI Press.

Tinsley, C. H. (1998). Models of conflict resolution in Japanese, German, and American cultures. *Journal of Applied Psychology, 83,* 316–23.

Tinsley, C. H. (2001). How negotiators get to yes: Predicting the constellation of strategies used across cultures to negotiate conflict. *Journal of Applied Psychology, 86,* 583–93.

Tinsley, C. H., Brett, J. M., Shapiro, S. L., & Okumura, T. (2004). When do cultural values explain cross-cultural phenomena? An introduction and test of cultural complexity theory. Unpublished paper, Dispute Resolution Research Center, Northwestern University, Evanston, IL.

Tinsley, C. H., O'Connor, K. M., & Sullivan, B. A. (2002). Tough guys finish last: The perils of a distributive reputation. *Organizational Behavior and Human Decision Processes, 88,* 621–42.

Tjosvold, D. (1977). The effects of the constituent's affirmation and the opposing negotiator's self-presentation in bargaining between unequal status groups. *Organizational Behavior and Human Decision Processes, 18,* 1, 146–57.

Tjosvold, D. (1988). *Getting things done in organizations.* Lexington, MA: Lexington Books.

Tjosvold, D. (1997). The leadership relationship in Hong Kong: Power, interdependence and controversy. In K. Leung, U. Kim, S. Yamaguchi, & Y. Kashima (Eds.), *Progress in Asian social psychology* (Vol. 1). New York: John Wiley.

Tjosvold, D., & Sun, H. F. (2001). Effects of influence tactics and social contexts in conflict: An experiment on relationships in China. *International Journal of Conflict Management, 12,* 239–58.

Tomlinson, E., Dineen, B., & Lewicki, R. (2004). The road to reconciliation: Antecedents of victim willingness to reconcile following a broken promise. *Journal of Management, 30,* 165–87.

Tompkins, P. K. (1993). *Organizational communication imperatives: Lessons of the space program.* Los Angeles: Roxbury Publishing Company.

Touval, S. (1988). Multilateral negotiation: An analytical approach. *Negotiation Journal, 5* (2), 159–73.

Touval, S., & Zartman, I. (1985). *International mediation in theory and practice.* Boulder, CO: Westview Press.

Trenholm, S. (1989). *Persuasion and social influence.* Englewood Cliffs, NJ: Prentice Hall.

Trevino, L. K. (1986). Ethical decision making in organizations: A person-situation interactionist model. *Academy of Management Review, 11,* 601–17.

Trevino, L. K., & Youngblood, S. (1990). Bad apples in bad barrels: A causal analysis of ethical decision-making behavior. *Journal of Applied Psychology, 75,* 378–85.

Triandis, H. C. (1982). Review of culture's consequences: International differences in work values. *Human Organization, 41,* 86–90.

Tripp, T. M., Sondak, H., & Bies, R. J. (1995). Justice as rationality: A relational perspective on fairness in negotiations. In R. J. Lewicki, B. H. Sheppard, & R. J. Bies (Ed.), *Research on negotiation in organizations* (Vol. 5, pp. 45–64). Greenwich, CT: JAI Press.

Tse, D. K., Francis, J., & Walls, J. (1994). Cultural differences in conducting intra- and inter-cultural negotiations: A Sino-Canadian comparison. *Journal of International Business Studies, 25,* 537–55.

Tuchinsky, M. (1998). Negotiation approaches in close relationships. Duke University. Unpublished doctoral dissertation.

Tuchinsky, M. B., Edson Escalas, J., Moore, M. B., & Sheppard, B. H. (1994). Beyond name, rank and function: Construals of relationships in business. In D. P. Moore (Ed.), *Proceedings of the Academy of Management,* 79–83.

Tung, R. L. (1991, Winter). Handshakes across the sea: Cross-cultural negotiating for business success. *Organizational Dynamics, 19,* 30–40.

Turner, M. E., & Pratkanis, A. R. (1994). Social identity maintenance prescriptions for preventing groupthink: Reducing identity protection and enhancing intellectual conflict. *International Journal of Conflict Management, 5,* 254–70.

Tutzauer, F. (1991). Bargaining outcome, bargaining process, and the role of communication. *Progress in Communication Science, 10,* 257–300.

Tutzauer, F. (1992). The communication of offers in dyadic bargaining. In L. Putnam, & M. Roloff (Eds.), *Communication and negotiation* (pp. 67–82). Newbury Park, CA: Sage.

Tversky, A., & Kahneman, D. (1971). Belief in the law of small numbers. *Psychological Bulletin, 76,* 105–10.

Tversky, A., & Kahneman, D. (1981). The framing of decisions and the psychology of choice. *Science, 211,* 453–58.

Tversky, A., & Kahneman, D. (1982). Judgment under uncertainty: Heuristics and biases. In D. Kahneman, P. Slovic, & A. Tversky (Eds.), *Judgment under uncertainty: Heuristics and biases* (pp. 3–22). Cambridge: Cambridge University Press.

Tye, L. (1998, April 19). They're not in it for the long haul. *The Columbus* (Ohio) *Dispatch,* 10E.

Tyler, T., & Hastie, R. (1991). The social consequences of cognitive illusions. In M. H. Bazerman, R. J. Lewicki, and B. H. Sheppard (Eds.), *Research on negotiation in organizations* (Vol. 3, pp. 69–98). Greenwich, CT: JAI Press.

Tyler, T., & Blader, S. R. (2004). Justice and negotiation. In M. Gelfand, and J. Brett (Eds.), *The handbook of negotiation and culture* (pp. 295–312). Stanford, CA: Stanford University Press.

Tzu, Sun (1983). *The art of war.* New York: Dellacorte Press.

Ulman, N. (1996, May 20). Unlikely allies: Pact for river's use unites conservationists and a power company. *The Wall Street Journal,* A6, A9.

Ury, W. (1991). *Getting past no: Negotiating with difficult people.* New York: Bantam Books.

Ury, W. (2000). *The third side.* New York: Penguin.

Ury, W. L., Brett, J. M., & Goldberg, S. B. (1988). *Getting disputes resolved.* San Francisco: Jossey-Bass.

Ury, W. L., Brett, J. M., & Goldberg, S. B. (1993). *Getting disputes resolved.* (2nd ed.). San Francisco: Jossey-Bass.

Valenzuela, A., Srivastava, J., & Lee, S. (2005). The role of cultural orientation in bargaining under incomplete information: Differences in casual attributions. *Organizational Behavior and Human Decision Processes, 96,* 72–88.

Valley, K., & Longo, E. L. *Power and influence: Achieving your objectives.* Boston: Harvard Business School Publishing, Note 9-801-425.

Valley, K. L., Moag, J., & Bazerman, M. H. (1998). A matter of trust: Effects of communication on the efficiency and distribution of outcomes. *Journal of Economic Behavior and Organization, 34,* 211–38.

van Beest, I., Wilke, J., & van Dijk, E. (2003). The excluded player in coalition formation. *Personality and Social Psychology Bulletin, 29,* 237–47.

Van Boven, L., Gilovich, T., & Medvec, V. H. (2003). The illusion of transparency in negotiations. *Negotiation Journal, 19,* 117–31.

van de Vliert, E. (1985). Escalative intervention in small group conflicts. *Journal of Applied Behavioral Science, 21,* 19–36.

van de Vliert, E. (1992). Questions about the strategic choice model of mediation. *International Journal of Conflict Management, 8,* 379–86.

van de Vliert, E., & Kabanoff, B. (1988). Toward theory-based measures of conflict management. Paper presented at the annual meeting of the Academy of Management, Anaheim, CA.

van de Vliert, E., & Prein, H. C. M. (1989). The difference in the meaning of forcing in the conflict management of actors and observers. In M. Rahim (Ed.), *Managing conflict: An interdisciplinary approach* (pp. 51–63). New York: Praeger.

van Dijk, E., Van Kleef, G., Steinel, W., & van Beest, I. (2008). A social functional approach to emotions in bargaining: When communicating anger pays and when it backfires. *Journal of Personality and Social Psychology 94,* 600–14.

Van Dyke, N. (2003). Crossing movement boundaries: Factors that facilitate coalition protest by American college students, 1930–1990. *Social Problems, 50,* 226–50.

Van Es, R., French, W., & Stellmaszek, F. (2004). Resolving conflicts over ethical issues: Face-to-face versus internet negotiations. *Journal of Business Ethics, 53,* 165–72.

van Ginkel, E. (2004). The mediator as face-giver. *Negotiation Journal, 20* (4), 475–87.

Van Kleef, G. A., & Côté, S. (2007). Expressing anger in conflicts: When it helps and when it hurts. *Journal of Applied Psychology, 92,* 1557–69.

Van Kleef, G. A., de Dreu, C. K. W., & Manstead, A. S. R. (2004). The interpersonal effects of anger and happiness in negotiations. *Journal of Personality and Social Psychology, 86,* 57–76.

Van Kleef, G. A., de Dreu, C. K. W., & Manstead, A. S. R. (2006). Supplication and appeasement in conflict and negotiation: The interpersonal effects of disappointment, worry, guilt, and regret. *Journal of Personality and Social Psychology 91,* 124–42.

Van Pouke, D., & Buelens, M. (2002). Predicting the outcome of a two-party price negotiation: Contribution of reservation price, aspiration price, and opening offer. *Journal of Economic Psychology, 23,* 67–76.

Van Rooy, D. L., & Viswesvaran, C. (2004). Emotional intelligence: A meta-analytic investigation of predictive validity and nomological net. *Journal of Vocational Behavior, 65,* 71–95.

Van Zandt, H. F. (1970, November–December). How to negotiate in Japan. *Harvard Business Review, 48* (6), 45–56.

Veitch, R., & Griffith, W. (1976). Good news–bad news: Affective and interpersonal affects. *Journal of Applied Social Psychology, 6,* 69–75.

Vergin, R. C. (2000). Winning streaks in sports and the misperception of momentum. *Journal of Sport Behavior, 23,* 181–97.

Victor, B., & Cullen, J. (1988). The organizational bases of ethical work climates. *Administrative Science Quarterly, 33,* 1010–25.

Vitz, P. C., & Kite, W. A. R. (1970). Factors affecting conflict and negotiation within an alliance. *Journal of Experimental Social Psychology, 5,* 233–47.

Volkema, R. (1997). Perceptual differences in appropriateness and likelihood of use of negotiation behaviors: A cross-cultural analysis. *The International Executive, 39* (3), 335–50.

Volkema, R. (1998). A comparison of perceptions of ethical negotiation behavior in Mexico and the United States. *International Journal of Conflict Management, 9* (3), 218–33.

Volkema, R. (1999). Ethicality in negotiations: An analysis of perceptual similarities and differences between Brazil and the United States. *Journal of Business Research, 45,* 49–67.

Volkema, R. (2001). Predicting unethical negotiating behavior: An empirical examination of the incidents in negotiation questionnaire. Paper presented at the annual meeting of the Academy of Management, Washington, DC.

Volkema, R. J., & Fleury, M. T. L. (2002). Alternative negotiating conditions and the choice of negotiation tactics: A cross-cultural comparison. *Journal of Business Ethics, 36,* 381–98.

von Neumann, J., & Morgenstern, O. (1944). *Theory of games and economic behavior.* Princeton, NJ: Princeton University Press.

Von Oech, R. (1990). *A whack on the side of the head: How you can be more creative* (rev. ed.). New York: Warner Books.

Vonk, R. (2002). Self-serving interpretations of flattery: Why ingratiation works. *Journal of Personality and Social Psychology, 82,* 515–26.

Vroom, V. H. (1973). A new look at managerial decision making. *Organizational Dynamics, 4,* 66–80.

Wade, J. H. (2004). Dueling experts in mediation and negotiation: How to respond when eager expensive entrenched expert egos escalate enmity. *Conflict Resolution Quarterly, 21* (4), 419–36.

Wade-Benzoni, K., Hoffman, A., Thompson, L., Moore, D., Gillespie, J., & Bazerman, M. (2002). Barriers to resolution in ideologically based negotiations: The role of values and institutions. *Academy of Management Review, 27* (1), 41–57.

Wade-Benzoni, K. A., Okumura, T., Brett, J. M., Moore, D. A., Tenbrunsel, A. E., & Bazerman, M. H. (2002). Cognitions and behavior in asymmetric social dilemmas. A comparison of two cultures. *Journal of Applied Social Psychology, 87,* 87–95.

Walcott, C., & Hopmann, P. (1975). Interaction analysis and bargaining behavior. *Experimental Study of Politics, 4,* 1–19.

Walcott, C., Hopmann, P. T., & King, T. D. (1977). The role of debate in negotiation. In D. Druckman (Ed.), *Negotiations: Social-psychological perspectives* (pp. 193–211). Beverly Hills, CA: Sage.

Walker, S. G., & Watson, F. L. (1994). Integrative complexity and British decisions during the Munich and Polish crises. *Journal of Conflict Resolution, 38,* 3–23.

Wall, J. A. (1981). Mediation: An analysis, review and proposed research. *Journal of Conflict Resolution, 25,* 157–80.

Wall, J. A., & Blum, M. (1991). Negotiations. *Journal of Management, 17,* 273–303.

Wall, J. A., & Lynn, A. (1993). Mediation: A current review. *Journal of Conflict Resolution, 37,* 160–94.

Wall, J. A., & Stark, J. B. (1996). Techniques and sequences in mediation strategies: A proposed model for research. *Negotiation Journal, 12,* 231–39.

Wall, J. A., Stalk, J. B., & Standifer, R. L. (2001). Mediation. A current review and theory development. *Journal of Conflict Resolution, 45,* 370–91.

Wallace, M. D., Suedfeld, P., & Thachuk, K. (1993). Political rhetoric of leaders under stress in the gulf crisis. *Journal of Conflict Resolution, 37,* 94–107.

Wallihan, J. (2003, July). Reverse bargaining: Some oddities that illustrate the rules. *Negotiation Journal,* 207–14.

Walters, A. E., Stuhlmacher, A. F., & Meyer, L. L. (1998). Gender and negotiator competitiveness: A meta-analysis. *Organizational Behavior and Human Decision Processes, 76,* 1–29.

Walton, R. (1987). *Managing conflict: Interpersonal dialogue and third-party roles* (2nd ed.). Reading, MA: Addison-Wesley.

Walton, R. E., & McKersie, R. B. (1965). *A behavioral theory of labor negotiations: An analysis of a social interaction system.* New York: McGraw-Hill.

Wang, G., Jing, R., & Klossek, A. (2007). Antecedents and management of conflict: Resolution styles of Chinese top managers in multiple rounds of cognitive and affective conflict. *International Journal of Conflict Management, 18* (1), 74–97.

Wanis-St. John, A. (2006). Back-channel negotiation: International bargaining in the shadows. *Negotiation Journal, 22* (2), 119–44.

Wanis-St. John, A. C. (2002, March). Back-channel diplomacy: The strategic use of multiple channels of negotiation in Middle East peacemaking. *Dissertation Abstracts International, Section A: Humanities & Social Sciences, 62,* 8-A.

Warren, R. P. (1946). *All the king's men.* New York: Harcourt, Brace and Company.

Watkins, M. (2001). Principles of Persuasion. *Negotiation Journal, 17,* 115–37.

Watkins, M. (2002). *Breakthrough business negotiations.* San Francisco: Jossey-Bass.

Watkins, M. (2006). *Shaping the game: The new leaders guide to effective negotiating.* Boston: Harvard Business School Press.

Watkins, M., & Winters, L. (1997). Intervenors with interests and power. *Negotiation Journal, 13,* 119–42.

Watson, C. (1994a). Gender differences in negotiating outcomes: Fact or artifact? In A. Taylor & J. Beinstein-Miller (Eds.), *Conflict and gender* (pp. 191–210). Cresskill, NJ: Hampton Press.

Watson, C. (1994b). Gender versus power as a predictor of negotiation behavior and outcomes. *Negotiation Journal, 10,* 117–27.

Watson, C., & Hoffman, L. R. (1996). Managers as negotiators: A test of power versus gender as predictors of feelings, behavior, and outcomes. *Leadership Quarterly, 7,* 63–85.

Watson, C., & Kasten, B. (1988). *Separate strengths? How men and women negotiate.* Newark, NJ: Center for Negotiation and Conflict Resolution, Rutgers University.

Weeks, H. (2001, July–August). Taking the stress out of stressful conversations. *Harvard Business Review,* 112–19.

Weingart, L. R., Bennett, R. J., & Brett, J. M. (1993). The impact of consideration of issues and motivational orientation group negotiation process and outcome. *Journal of Applied Psychology, 78* (3), 504–17.

Weingart, L. R., Hyder, E. B., & Prietula, M. J. (1996). Knowledge matters: The effect of tactical descriptions on negotiation behavior and outcome. *Journal of Personality and Social Psychology, 70,* 1205–17.

Weingart, L. R., Prietula, M. J., Heider, E. B., & Genovese, C. R. (1999). Knowledge and the sequential processes of negotiation: A Markov chain analysis of response-in-kind. *Journal of Experimental Social Psychology, 35,* 366–93.

Weingart, L. R., Thompson, L. L., Bazerman, M. H., & Carroll, J. S. (1990). Tactical behaviors and negotiation outcomes. *International Journal of Conflict Management, 1,* 7–31.

Weiss, J. (2003). Trajectories toward peace: Mediator sequencing strategies in intractable communal disputes. *Negotiation Journal,* 109–15.

Weiss, S. E. (1994). Negotiating with "Romans": A range of culturally-responsive strategies. *Sloan Management Review, 35* (1), 51–61; (2), 1–16.

Weiss, S. E. (1996). International negotiations: Bricks, mortar, and prospects. In B. J. Punnett & O. Shenkar (Eds.), *Handbook for international management research* (pp. 209–65). Cambridge, MA: Blackwell.

Weiss, S. E. (1997). Explaining outcomes of negotiation: Toward a grounded model for negotiations between organizations. In R. J. Lewicki, R. J. Bies, & B. H. Sheppard (Eds.), *Research on negotiation in organizations* (Vol. 6, pp. 247–333). Greenwich, CT: JAI Press.

Weiss, S. E. (2003). Teaching the cultural aspects of negotiation: A range of experiential techniques. *Journal of Management Education, 27,* 96–121.

Weiss, S. E. (2004). International business negotiations research: Revisiting "Bricks, mortar and prospects." In B. J. Punnett & O. Shenkar (Eds.), *Handbook for international management research* (pp. 415–76). Ann Arbor, MI: University of Michigan Press.

Weiss, S. E. (2006). International business negotiation in a globalizing world: Reflections on the contributions and future of a (sub) field. *International Negotiation, 11,* 287–316.

Weiss, S. E., & Stripp, W. (1985). Negotiating with foreign business persons: An introduction for Americans with propositions on six cultures. New York: New York University Graduate School of Business Administration, Working Paper 85–6.

Weitzman, E. B., & Weitzman, P. F. (2000). Problem solving and decision making in conflict resolution. In M. Deutsch, & P. Coleman (Eds.), *Handbook of conflict resolution.* San Francisco: Jossey-Bass.

Weldon, E., & Jehn, K. A. (1995). Examining cross-cultural differences in conflict management behavior: A strategy for future research. *The International Journal of Conflict Management, 6,* 387–403.

Werth, L. F., & Flannery, J. (1986). A phenomenological approach to human deception. In R. W. Mitchell, & N. S. Thompson (Eds.), *Deception: Perspectives on human and nonhuman deceit* (pp. 293–311). Albany, NY: State University of New York Press.

Wheeler, M. (1999). First, let's kill all the agents! In R. H. Mnookin and L. E. Susskind, *Negotiating on behalf of others* (pp. 235–62). Thousand Oaks, CA: Sage.

Wheeler, M. (2000). *Negotiation analysis: An introduction.* Harvard Case 9-801-156. Cambridge, MA: Harvard Business School Publishing.

Wheeler, M. (2004). Anxious moments: Openings in negotiation. *Negotiation Journal, 20,* 153–69.

White, J. B., Tynan, R., Galinsky, A. D., & Thompson, L. (2004). Face threat sensitivity in negotiation: Roadblock to agreement and joint gain. *Organizational Behavior and Human Decision Processes, 94,* 101–24.

Whiting, C. S. (1958). *Creative thinking.* New York: Reinhold.

Whittemore, M. (1996). Hard-ball negotiation. *Success, 43,* 14.

Whyte, G., & Sebenius, J. K. (1997). The effect of multiple anchors on anchoring in individual and group judgment. *Organizational Behavior and Human Decision Processes, 69,* 75–85.

Wilson, S. R., & Putnam, L. L. (1990). Interaction goals in negotiation. In J. Anderson (Ed.), *Communication Yearbook* (Vol. 13, pp. 374–406). Newbury Park, CA: Sage.

Wittmer, J., Carnevale, P., & Walker, M. (1991). General alignment and overt support in biased mediation. *Journal of Conflict Resolution, 35,* 594–610.

Wolfe, R. J., & McGinn, K. L. (2005). Perceived relative power and its influence on negotiations. *Group Decision Process and Negotiation, 14,* 3–20.

Wolff, F. I., Marsnik, N. C., Tacey, W. S., & Nichols, R. G. (1983). *Perceptive listening.* New York: Holt, Rinehart & Winston.

Wolvin, A. D., & Coakley, C. G. (1988). *Listening* (3rd ed.). Dubuque, IA: Wm. C. Brown.

Wolvin, A. D., & Coakley, C. G. (1991). A survey of the status of listening training in some Fortune 500 corporations. *Communication Education, 40,* 152–64.

Wood, R., & Bandura, A. (1989). Social cognitive theory of organizational management. *Academy of Management Review, 14,* 361–84.

Xing, F. (1995). The Chinese cultural system: Implications for cross-cultural management. *SAM Advanced Management Journal, 60,* 14–20.

Yama, E. (2004). Buying hardball, playing price. *Business Horizons, 47* (5), 62–66.

Yan, A., & Gray, B. (1994). Bargaining power, management control, and performance in United States-China joint ventures: A comparative case study. *Academy of Management Journal, 37,* 1478–1517.

Yankelovich, D. (1982, August). Lying well is the best revenge. *Psychology Today, 71,* 5–6, 71.

Yook, E. L., & Albert, R. D. (1998). Perceptions of the appropriateness of negotiation in educational settings: A cross-cultural comparison among Koreans and Americans. *Communication Education, 47,* 18–29.

Yoshino, M. Y., & Rangan, U.S. (1995). *Strategic alliances.* Boston: Harvard University Press.

Young, O. (1972). Intermediaries: Additional thoughts on third parties. *Journal of Conflict Resolution, 16,* 51–65.

Yukl, G. (1974). Effects of the opponent's initial offer, concession magnitude, and concession frequency on bargaining behavior. *Journal of Personality and Social Psychology, 30,* 323–35.

Yukl, G., & Tracey, J. A. B. (1992). Consequences of influence tactics used with subordinates, peers and the boss. *Journal of Applied Psychology, 77,* 525–35.

Zand, D. (1972). Trust and managerial problem solving. *Administrative Science Quarterly, 17,* 229–39.

Zand, D. (1997). *The leadership triad: Knowledge, trust and power.* New York: Oxford University Press.

Zarkada-Fraser, A., & Fraser, C. (2001). Moral decision making in international sales negotiations. *Journal of Business and Industrial Marketing, 16,* 274–93.

Zartman, I. W. (1977). Negotiation as a joint decision making process. In I. Zartman (Ed.), *The negotiation process: Theories and applications* (pp. 67–86). Beverly Hills, CA: Sage.

Zartman, I. W. (1997). Conflict and order: Justice in negotiation. *International Political Science Review, 18,* 121–38.

Zartman, I. W., & Berman, M. (1982). *The practical negotiator.* New Haven, CT: Yale University Press.

Zebrowitz, L. A., Voinescu, L., & Collins, M. A. (1996). "Wide-eyed" and "crooked-faced": Determinants of perceived and real honesty across the life span. *Personality and Social Psychology Bulletin, 22,* 1258–69.

Zhou, L., Burgoon, J. K., Nunamaker, J. F., & Twitchell, D. (2004). Automating linguistics-based cues for detecting deception in text-based asynchronous computer-mediated communication. *Group Decision and Negotiation, 13,* 81–106.

Zhu, Y., McKenna, B., & Sun, Z. (2007). Negotiating with Chinese: Success of initial meetings is the key. *Cross Cultural Management: An International Journal, 14* (4), 354–64.

Zimbardo, P. G., Ebbesen, E. B., & Maslach, C. (1977). *Influencing attitudes and changing behavior.* Reading, MA: Addison-Wesley.

Zubek, J., Pruitt, D., Pierce, R., McGillicuddy, N., & Syna, H. (1992). Disputant and mediator behaviors affecting short-term success in mediation. *Journal of Conflict Resolution, 36,* 546–72.

Name Index

Subject Index

A

Abilities, 431–435
Abundance mentality, 72
Acceptability of solutions, 92
Accommodating strategy
  as basic negotiating approach, 112, 113–115
  in conflict management, 23, 422, 423
  in relationship negotiations, 301
Accountability, 152, 335–336, 401, 464
Achieving closure, 195–196
Acknowledgment, 192
Action plans, 398
Action-reaction spirals, 511
Active-engagement strategies, 113–115
Active listening, 192–194, 488
Active participation, encouraging, 227
Actor-observer effect, 158
Adapting negotiating styles, 467–471
Additional team members as audience, 325–326
ADRs, 549–553
Adversarial intervention, 542
Adversaries, coalition, 374
Advisory ADR systems, 550–551
Advocacy, balancing with inquiry, 305
Affiliation motives, 177
Age, ethical conduct and, 281
Agency relationships, 28, 323; *see also* Agents
Agendas, 135, 387, 388–390; *see also* Planning; Preparation
Agents; *see also* Negotiators
  audience communications with, 342–349
  audience effects on, 331–336
  audience visibility, managing, 338–342
  building relationships with, 349–351
  clarifying expectations for, 337–338
  cross-cultural, 470
  defined, 28, 324
  effects of status on ethical conduct, 288
  gender differences in views of role, 406
  limiting information given to, 44–45
  managing, 353
  for professional athletes, 11, 333, 334
  when to use, 351, 352
Aggressive behavior, 68–69; *see also* Difficult negotiations; Difficult people
Aggressive tactics, 68–69, 413; *see also* Hardball tactics
Agitation-related emotions, 164–165
Agreeableness, 429, 430
Agreement Circumplex, 84–88
Agreement in principle, 224
Agreement stage in multiparty negotiations, 398–400
Agreements; *see also* Outcomes
  analyzing after conclusion, 564
  closing, 60–61, 118, 195–196
  culture's role in, 459–462
  evaluating and choosing, 78–79
  generating alternatives, 83–90
  satisfaction with, 424
Air traffic controllers, 340
All the King's Men, 229
Allies
  in coalitions, 372, 374
  outsiders as, 48, 57
  use in power moves, 505
Altered information, 292
Alternative coalition partners, 370

Alternative dispute resolution systems (ADRs), 549–553
Alternative settlements
  evaluating and choosing in integrative negotiations, 91–95
  generating in integrative negotiations, 83–90
  suggesting in distributive situations, 60
Alternatives to negotiated agreements; *see also* BATNAs
  communicating, 178
  impact on negotiations, 10–12, 113
  of other parties, discovering, 131–132
  planning for, 125
  role in distributive bargaining, 36–37
  shaping perceptions of, 246
  understanding costs, 386–387
Ambassadors, group members as, 391
Analogical learning, 101
Analogical reasoning, 499
Analogies, 227–228, 499
Anchoring and adjustment bias, 153, 162, 430
Anger; *see also* Emotions
  as hardball tactic, 67
  impact on perceptions of negotiation, 166, 167, 168
  influence on persuasion, 238
  as information gathering tactic, 44
  leading to impasse, 480
  managing, 516
  in response to being deceived, 275
Anonymity in coalitions, 368
AOL, 9
Apologies, 315
Appearances
  influence on persuasion, 233–234, 235
  maintaining, 181
Appreciative moves, 505, 506
Arbiter role, 548
Arbitration, 522, 526–529
Arbitration-mediation, 541–542
Argument culture, 490
Arguments; *see* Conflict; Counterarguments
Asking prices, 34, 125–127
Aspiration frames, 143, 145
Aspirations, 34
Assertiveness dimension, 22, 422
Associates, influence on persuasion, 235
Assuming the close, 60–61
Assumptions, 133–134, 383, 411
Athletes, 11, 333, 334
Attainability of goals, 109
Attending behaviors, 184–185
Attention, signaling, 184–185
Attorneys, 9
Attractiveness of offers, 223
Attractiveness of others, 235–239
Auctions, 244
Audience effects, 325
Audiences; *see also* Constituents
  building relationships with, 349–351
  common characteristics, 328–331
  defined, 324
  impact of gender on negotiations, 410
  influence on negotiators, 9, 331–336, 381
  managing visibility to, 338–342
  negotiator communications with, 342–349
  types, 325–328
Auditing decision processes, 161

Authoritarian personality, 206–207
Authority; *see also* Influence; Power
  of agents, 338, 339–340, 353
  influence on persuasion, 239–240
  of other parties, discovering, 132–133
Authority-ranking relationships, 302, 303
Auto-Line program, 526
Automobiles; *see* Car-buying negotiations
Availability bias, 154–155
Avoidance of conflict, 480
Avoiding strategy
  as basic negotiating approach, 112, 113
  in conflict management, 23, 25, 422, 423

B

Back-channel diplomacy, 345
Bad faith, 7
Bait-and-switch technique, 241–242
Balanced negotiations, 181
Bargaining, negotiation versus, 3
Bargaining mix
  defining in planning process, 123–124
  discovering other parties', 131
  in distributive situations, 38
Bargaining range, 13, 35–36
Base rate fallacy, 159
BATNAs; *see also* Alternatives to negotiated agreements
  best-practice advice for, 557, 558
  communicating, 178
  concept described, 12
  cultivating, 509–510
  influence on opening offers, 49
  leveraging agreements with, 515
  neglecting, 483
  power and influence of, 37, 215–216, 248–249
Bedfellows, 373, 374
Befriending other parties, 63
Behavior contingent contracts, 336, 337
Behavioral commitments, 249
Behavioral resolution of impasses, 485
Behavioral studies of negotiator success, 436–438
Belligerence, 50
Benefits of conflict, 20
Best Alternative to a Negotiated Agreement; *see* BATNAs
Best practices, 555–564
Best solutions, 398
Better Business Bureaus, 526
Bias
  common cognitive errors, 150–160
  common perceptual distortions, 16, 19, 102, 139–142
  in e-mail negotiations, 188–189
  effects of conflict on, 19–20
  effects of culture on, 465
  effects of trust on, 313
  efforts to manage, 160–164
  of mediators, 532, 536
  in multiparty negotiations, 387
  in perceptions of fairness, 317–318, 563
  reframing in response to, 162
  relation to negative emotions, 166
Biasing effect of arbitration, 528
Bidding, 118
Big Five personality factors, 429–430